CW01390866

To THE INSPIRED TEAM.

IT IS MY PLEASURE TO FEATURE
THE INSPIRED VILLAGES' BRAND
IN THIS BOOK! THE WORK YOU
ALL DO FOR EACH OTHER, THE RESIDENTS
AND WIDER COMMUNITY IS IMPACTFUL
& HAS REAL MEANING!

HOPE YOU ENJOY!

THANKS
TOM (FUZE)

Terry Smith, Tom Williams
Brand Fusion

—

Purpose-driven brand strategy

DE GRUYTER

ISBN 978-3-11-071834-8
E-ISBN (PDF) 978-3-11-071863-8
E-ISBN (EPUB) 978-3-11-071873-7

Library of Congress Control Number: 2021952030

Bibliographic information published by the Deutsche Nationalbibliothek
The Deutsche Nationalbibliothek lists this publication in the Deutsche Nationalbibliografie;
detailed bibliographic data are available on the Internet at http://dnb.dnb.de.

MIX
Papier aus verantwor-
tungsvollen Quellen
FSC
www.fsc.org   FSC® C083411

Contents

Section 3: **The development of strategy**

Section 4: **The application and purpose of practice**

Preface

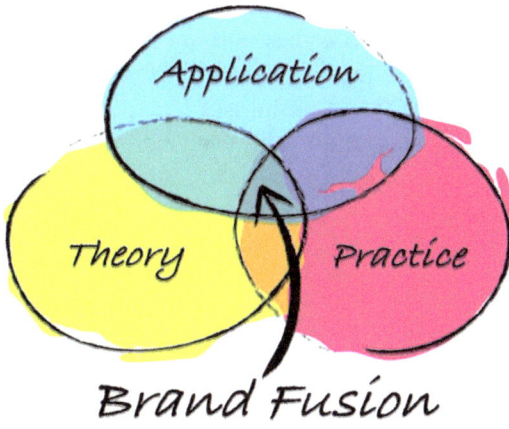

https://doi.org/10.1515/9783110718638-001

Even with all the excitement and energy surrounding the ever-evolving big data analytics, the transformative effects of digital technology, the interactivity of user experience (UX), and the importance of customer experience (CX) – all extensively covered in this text – research amongst 400 top Chief Marketing Officers (CMOs) and 432 other key marketing leaders identified *brand strategy* as "the most vital marketing capability in 2020".[1] As businesses now position themselves in a post-COVID-19 world, brand strategy is arguably even more important than ever.

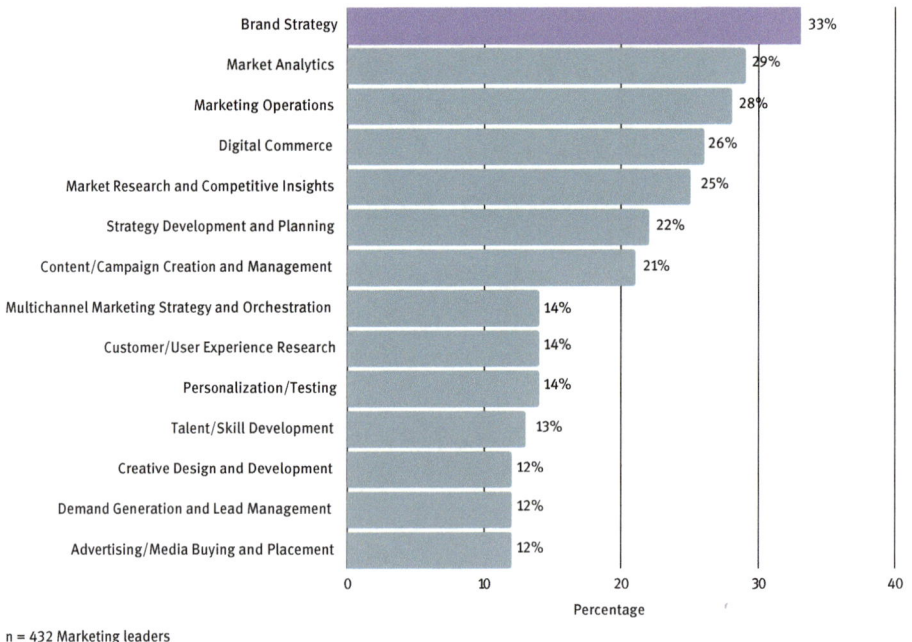

Capability	Percentage
Brand Strategy	33%
Market Analytics	29%
Marketing Operations	28%
Digital Commerce	26%
Market Research and Competitive Insights	25%
Strategy Development and Planning	22%
Content/Campaign Creation and Management	21%
Multichannel Marketing Strategy and Orchestration	14%
Customer/User Experience Research	14%
Personalization/Testing	14%
Talent/Skill Development	13%
Creative Design and Development	12%
Demand Generation and Lead Management	12%
Advertising/Media Buying and Placement	12%

n = 432 Marketing leaders

Figure 0.1: Importance of Brand Strategy.
Source: Gartner Research & Advisory, CMO Survey 2020

Brand strategy which is *purpose-driven* – customer-company, stakeholder-organisation mutuality which transcends profit-only goals – is espoused by the likes of the *CMI, CIM, Harvard Business School, Deloitte, Forbes*, the *Regenerate Trust, Mars Catalyst, B Corps, Oxford University, Säid Business School*, as well as the guru of effectiveness Peter Field, to name but a few from a rapidly expanding list, and is gaining some traction in academic research, and, most importantly, is increasingly being put into practice by some of the world's most successful and influential companies. Mayer (2018) sums this new focus up well, claiming that the aim of today's companies is "To

---

1 Gartner Research & Advisory, CMO Survey 2020.

produce profitable solutions to the problems of people and planet, and not to profit from producing problems for people or planet".

This book is a document of, and testament to, the theory, practice, and application of purpose-driven brand strategy. As authors, our role in conceiving, researching, and writing this book has been both as curators and creators: collecting and examining a wide range of theory and practice which underpins the discipline and dynamics of strategic brand management; as well as presenting to you some exciting philosophical and practical ideas on the *meaning, mechanics and magic* of purpose-driven brand strategy in its broader organisational and societal contexts.

It is apparent that there isn't a 'one-size-fits-all' brand strategy: it should be unique and contextualised to its macro and micro environments. However, one consistent anchor of all the organisations we have worked with, consulted for, or analysed, is that for brand strategy to be purposeful, then its meaning must be mapped out, evaluated, and refined.

Brand Fusion, as a core strategic brand management proposition, is a central driver to organisational strategy development and execution, with the customer and key stakeholder held at the centre of the brand's mind-set. It is not a bifurcation; there should not be friction, only *fusion*. It is the synthesis of theory and practice.

Like all innovations and paradigm shifts, extolling the virtues of **brand purpose** is not without criticism. For some companies, distracted by the survival instinct instilled by post-COVID-19 disruption, looking to the long-term may seem unrealistic or even inappropriate. For others, communications aimed at projecting 'purpose' may not be immediately effective. Byron Sharp, Director at the *Ehrenberg-Bass Institute*, speaking at last year's *Festival of Marketing*,[2] argues that differentiation through purpose could eventually lead to lack of differentiation. Short-term tactics can be proven, but long-term impacts may be more difficult to evaluate. Targets may not just be existing customers but those on the periphery of categories. Purpose is often the balance between idea and ideal.

Yet this textbook is absolutely crammed with examples of successful organisations and brands which have purpose as not merely a temporary tool but a permanent part of strategy. According to Cone, "Authentic purpose equals thoughtful, real, and sustained actions that impact the business internally and externally, while having a positive impact on society. And the organisations with the most authentic purpose have it baked into their cultures, mandated and modelled by CEOs who understand their leadership role".[3] Effectiveness expert Peter Field, a stalwart of purpose-driven brand strategy, points to research showing that when purpose campaigns are well-executed and have a "commitment by a commercial brand or its

---

2 Michaela Jefferson, "Purpose could be 'the death of brands' warns Byron Sharp, *Marketing Week*, 18th October 2021.
3 Carol Cone, "What Will Be Your Organisation's Authentic Purpose in 2021?", *Sustainable Brands*, April 2021.

parent company to goals other than improved profits or products, involving contribution towards one or more positive social impacts"[4] meeting growing pressure from government, investors, and regulators on ESG matters such as environmental sustainability, equality, and inclusivity, can also deliver positive effects on differentiating from the competitive and enhancing customer-company relationships. Success is in the execution. *Sustainable Brands*, an organisation who describe themselves as "a global community of brand leaders who are tapping into environmental and social challenges to drive innovation, business, and value" claim that brands are uniquely positioned "to align business and society on the path to a flourishing future . . . and discover the next economy".[5]

As Field warns, "If you are seen to be non-credible, or even hypocritical, and if your brand in no way connects with the business of your brand, it isn't going to stick". It's how you do it, but, more importantly, it's increasingly about *why* you do it. It's in the authenticity of values which emanate from, and resonate with, customers. It's in the credibility of co-created symbiotic symbolic meaning. It's in the connection, the relevance, and the focused application of purpose-*driven* brand strategy.

This textbook **Brand Fusion: Purpose-driven brand strategy** takes a cross-functional, omni-subject, cross-discipline approach: a practitioner-business perspective which acknowledges that all aspects of marketing – service marketing, relationship marketing, branding, research, data analysis, and marketing communications – are *integrated* and part of the value creation process of *integrated brand strategy*. Whilst it traces the development of strategy from exchange logic to service logic, its axis is *socially*-dominant, giving a broader conceptual framework and a natural progression from product, service, customer, and consumer-dominant perspectives which have attempted to blend factors affecting and affected by intangible resources, value-in-context, customer-centricity and, most importantly, social meaning. This text offers a holistic branding approach, setting out the intellectual perspectives and practical insights which makes this such a compelling current issue.

It is an in-depth analysis of the *philosophy* and *practice* of purpose-driven brand strategy.

The content is packed with contemporary case studies from companies like *Patagonia, Gillette, Absolut Vodka, Ava, Amazon, Danone, Netflix, Chilitz Socios, Chester Zoo, Marks & Spencer, The Coop, WW (Weight Watchers), The English Premier League, and the London Science Museum,* to SMEs and micro-brands like *Tirtyl, Causeway Rescue, Dubbed Campers, Pact, Raiys, and Dyslexic Advantage.* You'll find lots of other examples of companies starting to recognise that 'purpose' is becoming an effective way to differentiate their value propositions, and, in some cases, re-position their brands and organisations. (These are listed in Table 0.1).

---

4 "Criticism of brand purpose is 'naïve and unjustified claims Peter Field". Michaela Jefferson in an interview with Peter Field, *Marketing Week*, 12th October 2021.
5 *Sustainable Brands* website, 2021.

Topics covered in these cases range from: circularity in brand strategy, the application of purpose mutuality, inclusive capitalism, feminism in the media, customer insights from data, customer experience and engagement, social meaning, sustainability, the 'marketisation' of aged care services, the positioning of dyslexia, LGBQT+ inclusivity, male emasculation, the digitalisation of the customer journey, culturally-constituted social meaning, brand engagement through fan token crypro-currency, 'marketisation' in the Higher Education sector, the development of brand equity, informing SME micro-brand strategies, finding a brand identity franchising formula, and a whole range of other topical issues in between.

A unique feature of this book, which brings an urgency and relevance to its content, is the chapter-long extended 'living cases' documenting the work of *FUZE*, Tom's data-driven insight-tech-learning agency which specialises in using technology to evaluate customer-culture-employee experiences against organisation's branding strategy, and empower individuals, teams and organisations to learn and develop. *Section 4 The Application & Purpose of Practice* evidences featured cases and detailed examples of real-world application, a unique blend of targeted 'empirical case data', cutting-edge methodologies, and academic application demonstrating how clients have been helped to build insight-driven system solutions.

FUZE's customer-driven methodology – specialising in deep analysis of segmentation, customer experiences, employee experience, and the development of brand strategy – consistently achieves commercially-focused outcomes with all types of project, clients and contexts. The live cases include a variety of sectors and perspectives and are balanced between primary/empirical data and secondary data/public sources. The primary data-driven cases represent clients who have a commercial relationship with and have commissioned *FUZE*. These organisations have kindly agreed to support the goal of this book – learning *through* practice *in* practice. The value of this inside/applied view was fundamental in developing the concept of *brand fusion*, providing a robust, authentic, and credible foundation in terms of qualitative and quantitative data/evidence. We are grateful to the contributors and senior decision-makers in supporting this unique perspective. These include: *Inspired Villages, Freedome, Chester Zoo, Festival of Thrift, University of Cumbria, Everton Football Club, Be the Business*, and *Tirtyl* as well as a range of SMEs and enterprising microbrands.

The secondary data 'featured' cases are based on public facing materials and are an interpretation of brand strategy via the brand fusion lens. These brands include *Dell Technologies, Headspace, and Legal & General*. Whilst the cases present a detailed review, they do not represent the view, opinions and/or an endorsement of these organisations.

***Brand Fusion:* Purpose-driven brand strategy** is both an academically essential text and a practically useful guide discussing:
– How purpose has moved from a peripheral consideration to a central driver of brand strategy.

- What impact the notion of 'values' has had on value co-creation.
- Why the shift from the organisational-dominant brand paradigm to one of a socially-dominant force is becoming the more effective strategic approach.
- How the disruption of digital communications has empowered the consumer and why brand communities are vital customer-company conduits in the process.
- How knowledge from data-driven insights both informs and directs brand strategy.
- Why the development of strategy in terms of business purpose, market orientation, competitive positioning must be aligned to be effective.
- How purpose and profit are inextricably linked and why a good purpose always generates more profit, sustains brand equity, co-creates value, shapes appropriate company culture, builds engaging, mutually beneficial brand narratives. All of which are key brand drivers.

We are at the threshold of a world transformed. At the heart of the post-COVID-19, digitally-transformed age of interactivity and mutuality has been a sea change which has shifted company orientation from transactional to transformative, from product management to customer management, from a focus on competitive advantage to a broader perspective rooted in social and environmental conscience. COVID-19 "elevates the social impact of every business and throws a spotlight on the nature of our companies, our character, and our brand(s)".[6] Focusing on meaning as well as money, purpose beyond profit, and putting values alongside value are vital hallmarks of the successful modern-day organisation.

Brand Fusion: **Purpose-driven brand strategy** is in the vanguard of documenting the essential shift to purpose-driven organisations. The aim of the book is an inquiry into the theoretical and practical dynamics of strategic brand management, providing practising managers with effective analytical tools, dynamic discussion, and evidence of contemporary applied practice to help improve the maintenance of brand profitability. With an impressive academic grounding, but very accessible practice-orientated content, this text will be well received by the Graduate, Post-Graduate, and post-experience Executive Education market, as well as having significant 'practitioner traction'.

We offer you our 5 'Es' – Expertise, Experience, Empirical Evidence, and, most importantly of all Enthusiasm.

In this text, we document how companies are managing: the creation of meaning; the balancing of value with values; the alignment of purpose, proposition and positioning; the strategic application of segmentation; the digitisation

---

6 "A brand. New. Purpose. Navigating the human and business impacts of COVID-19", *Accenture*, April 2020.

of the customer journey service processes; the effectiveness of customer-company fusion; the conversation between all stakeholders; and, most importantly, the development of brand equity.

Brand Fusion: **Purpose-driven brand strategy** will show you how to create and develop meaning, relevance, and purpose for the biggest strategic asset your organisation has – **YOUR BRAND**.

Table 0.1: Mini Cases, Principles in Practice boxes, and Full Chapter Cases.

Opening and Closing Chapter Cases and Principle in Practice Boxes

	Chapter Opening Case	Chapter Closing Case	Principles in Practice Box	Subject matter
Chapter 2	*M&S* ABC of Strategy: C Suite joins B Corps with Plan A.	Analogue strategy in a digital world. Trying for just one more *Kodak* moment.	1 Consumer adoption and company adaption accelerate changes in strategy. 2 Consumers are brand champions of the ESG ecosystem. 3 Is there life after profit on *Mars*?	Development of strategy. Inclusive Capitalism.
Chapter 3	You've Come A Long Way Baby. Because You're Worth It. Period.	"Us Not Me". Social salience and brand science.	1 *Absolut's* contradictory campaign to start 'consent' conversation. 2 Social media influence and stakeholder capitalism. 3 Building future markets through social innovation.	Social Meaning.
Chapter 4	*Tirtyl:* Refill not landfill. Conscious consumption goes mainstream.	*Patagonia* walks the talk with purpose.	1 Co-op's focus on values proposition reinforces positioning. 2 What is Purpose? 3 Pact putting purpose into their packs.	Purpose and positioning.

Table 0.1 (continued)

Opening and Closing Chapter Cases and Principle in Practice Boxes			
	Chapter Opening Case	Chapter Closing Case	Principles in Practice Box	Subject matter
Chapter 5	*Absolut* LGBTQ+ engagement or Rainbow Washing?	Exemplar Engagement from Enterprising *Everton*.	1 *Amazon's* 'fresh' approach to retail. 2 *Socios'* social sports scheme. Coining it in with genuine or token engagement? 3 *McDonald's* creates new 'customer experience' team.	Customer engagement. Customer-company fusion.
Chapter 6	*Ava* bridges gender data gap producing insights into reproduction.	*Causeway Rescue:* From rescue and tragedy to micro-brand strategy.	1 New ways to connect for brands through Connected TV. 2 Steve Jobs: Market research myth busting. 3 Brand Advantage: Reframing neurodiversity via 'brand' *Dyslexic Advantage*.	Customer insights from data.
Chapter 7	*Premier League Fantasy*: Tribal boundaries cast aside for points.	*Raiys*: Repositioning wellness to help wellbeing.	1 Predicting digital trends in 2021. 2 The *Netflix* customer journey that revolutionised TV viewing. 3 *Danone*: staying relevant by staying attentive.	Customer journey.

Table 0.1 (continued)

	Chapter Opening Case	Chapter Closing Case	Principles in Practice Box	Subject matter
	Opening and Closing Chapter Cases and Principle in Practice Boxes			
Chapter 8	*Gillette*: Managing A Man's Conversation.	*Dubbed Campers*: Big lessons on the road to building a micro-brand through camper conversations.	1 Like brands only cheaper. Every *Lidl* helps with #lidlsurprises. 2 The Autocomplete Truth: *Google Search* sparks a discrimination conversation. 3 Conversation, community, and cookies. Oreo flies the LGBTQ+ PFLAG flag.	Integrated Marketing Communications.
Chapter 9	ESG problems for *Ben & Jerry's* brand purpose, politics, and equity.	*Chester Zoo*: The Not So Secret Life of Building Brand Equity.	1 Did the Science Museum kill irony (and their own reputation)? 2 *Weight Watchers'* rebranding takes the eye off the ball. 3 Negative brand image results in negative brand equity.	Brand equity
FUZE Chapter Cases				
Chapter 10	*Legal & General*: inclusive capitalism, change, sustainability, and purpose.			Inclusive capitalism, corporate brand purpose, change, credibility and sustainability.
Chapter 11	*Inspired Villages*: purpose, values & alignment.			Purpose, values, & alignment.
Chapter 12	Small is beautiful: big ambitions for SMEs.			SME brand strategies, brand orientation.

Table 0.1 (continued)

Opening and Closing Chapter Cases and Principle in Practice Boxes				
	Chapter Opening Case	**Chapter Closing Case**	**Principles in Practice Box**	**Subject matter**
Chapter 13	*Festival of Thrift*: sustainability through brand community.			Brand equity building through community conscience.
Chapter 14	*Headspace*: Immersive digital meditation & mindfulness			Higher purpose brand building.
Chapter 15	*Freedome*: building franchise brand equity.			Building franchise brand equity.
Chapter 16	*University of Cumbria*: brand anchor, pledge, and persona.			Branding, IMC, Segmentation.
Chapter 17	*Dell Technologies*: Person to person in B2B.			Industrial marketing, B2B.

Section 1: **Introduction to themes and conceptual frameworks**

Section 1 is a broad overview of the book's structure and content, outlining the parameters of discussion within which the key themes and narrative threads are presented, helping us to understand the complexities and dynamics involved in creating and sustaining brand longevity through strategic brand management. The andragogic logic of the book is established to help guide you through the menu of concepts and contexts, together with a layout diagram showing a comprehensive stage-by-stage account of adopting a blended approach which integrates branding, data analysis, consumer behaviour, service marketing, marketing communications, and a whole range of other relevant subject matter.

https://doi.org/10.1515/9783110718638-002

1 Overview

1.1 Outline of chapter

The intention of this introductory chapter is: to present a broad overview of the book's structure; to establish its scope and content; to introduce the key themes and narrative threads; to outline the main discussion points which will help us understand the dynamics involved in creating and sustaining brand longevity through strategic brand management; and to explain the andragogic logic of the book to guide you through the menu of concepts and contexts and help with understanding the content and complexities of the book.

Learning outcomes

After reading this chapter, you'll be able to:
- Understand how the book is organised and what the contents of each chapter cover.
- Identify and apply the many forms and formulations within which 'fusion' is featured throughout the book.
- Explore the many themes, conceptual frameworks, and discussion points throughout the book.
- Understand the 'andragogic logic' or teaching methodology of each chapter to help with your teaching and learning of the subject matter.
- Justify the importance of a purpose-driven brand strategy from theoretical, practical, strategic, and operational perspectives.

1.2 Brief introduction

Any introductory chapter has the 'promise of the premise' as its starting point: what the point of the book is, what the key discussion points are, what unique proposition is being proposed, and how we intend to go about delivering it. One principle that we uphold – as authors with extensive expertise and experience in the broad conceptual, practical, and andragogical aspects of marketing as students, managers, authors, academics, consultants, and teachers at every level of UG, PG and Post-Experience – is that the approach should be 'bilingual' (in the sense that it speaks both the language of the academic and also the practitioner) in its approach, and have an integrated logic in its delivery. That is, it has a *solid academic foundation fused with comprehensive practice-based experience.* The intention is to synthesise cutting-edge brand theory and well-proven practice, demonstrating how this has been, and is being, successfully applied by real organisations in real contexts.

The panorama is *broad and complex,* but our focus is *narrow.* Although the discussions are set in a contemporary marketing landscape, the focus is brand strategy.

https://doi.org/10.1515/9783110718638-003

However, the complexity in business need not be complicated. The difference is context: something which is complicated can be difficult, convoluted, full of contradictory or conflicting components; something which is complex comprises many parts, a composite picture of multiple concepts and ideas. Complexity may have interrelated theories and dynamics which may benefit from more than just formulaic reductionism of platforms and processes. That's what this textbook is about. Managers tend to default to *complicated* thinking instead of "consciously managing complexity" (Nason, 2017). He encourages managers to develop a complexity mindset, and we ask you, the reader, to do the same. Managers locked in everyday commercial reality need to embrace the latest theoretical developments in brand strategy. Academics, teachers, and students need to infuse andragogy with the imperative of practice.

Think *omni-subject*. Think *integration*. Think *purpose-driven brand strategy*.

This holistic and bi-lingual perspective is how we have thought about, written, practised, and taught marketing, and it's how good purpose-driven brand strategy is practised too. Our intention is to take simplicity from the complexity, fusion from the confusion.

Our approach is to present a wide canvas of concepts and contexts and show how there is *simplicity in synergy* – in fusion. We believe that to understand the part, we must understand the whole: to find workable 'best-fit' strategic solutions, a comprehensive understanding of contextual dynamics, and a broad appreciation of integrated marketing must be part of any meaningful understanding of what is involved in managing brands.

Indeed, an aspect of the book's logic is *simplifying the complex*, looking for those 'unrecognised simplicities',[7] panning for gold in the many disparate streams of knowledge and experience but by appreciating context and broader understanding. It is a sort of holistic hermeneutic perspective where individual conceptual information is collected and synthesised with aggregated understanding, an approach which acknowledges that executives and students should have a comprehensive understanding of marketing theory even if in practice their focus is on only a limited part of it.

Although the book is split into four distinct sections, a cohesive thread of integration – fusion – runs throughout, pulling together subjects which are often siloed and separated as parts of the overall value creation process.

So, to the main point – *the promise of the premise*.

Brand Fusion is a theory-based, practice-informed, holistic perspective with a unique integrative logic showcasing ideas from marketing, brand strategy, service marketing, data analysis, management praxis, leadership tutelage, and a broad

---

7 Charlie Munger, Berkshire Hathaway from 'Poor Charlie's Almanack: The Wit and Wisdom of Charles T. Munger', Peter Kaufman, 1996.

cultural canvas of anthropological, socio-psychological, and philosophical theory and practice. As the title suggests, our goal is to put forward a distinctive perspective on *purpose-driven brand strategy* by analysing the complementarity between a number of 'fusions' across different subject areas, providing comprehensive width and depth of explication, expertise, and experience.

Throughout this book, 'fusion' is featured in many forms and formulations:

- Author *point of view* is from a 'bilingual' perspective, *fusing* our 'insider' experience as proven academics and successful practitioners, echoing the contemporary encouragement of 'ambidexterity' in scholars who do not *produce* practice-relevant research or practitioners who are not *using* contemporary relevant theory.
- A broad range of marketing concepts, developed often in isolation with different approaches, are given a sort of Gestalt grouping in *fusion*. Subject areas which are apparently disparate – such as experiential branding, service marketing, digital technology, relationship marketing, dialogical communications, societal marketing amongst others – are seen to have similar isomorphic 'social' roots and are interrelated parts of a holistic synthesis or brand fusion.
- Orientation is purposeful praxis, a *fusion* of both empirically grounded marketing theory and managerially relevant marketing practice.
- Style and content have an engaging, blended *fusion* of description and prescription.
- Convergence of customer-company roles in value co-creation is a magpie *fusion* of disparate business and marketing phenomena, collaborative service production and consumption. In *Chapter 2 Developing strategy: roots, resources, relationships,* we see how a blend of service philosophy, customer experience management, symmetrical B2C/C2B communications, symbolic symbiosis of meaning, organisational culture and collaboration, are all essential aspects of the focus on a single goal: *customer centricity.*
- In *Chapter 3 Managing meaning: social dominant logic,* key social and psychological components of branding are linked, demonstrating how value creation is forged in an interactive ecosystem of complexity and connectedness. This *social synthesis* covers: culturally constituted meaning; the principles of service marketing; the universal language of branding; the social mechanics of digital technology; the crucial impact of societal marketing; the imperative of constructing brand narratives and the phenomenon of brand communities; and the dynamic of exchange relationships and dialogical communications, all developed and discussed within a *socially*-dominant context.
- *Chapter 4 Managing the alignment of strategy: purpose, proposition and positioning* describes why purpose is not just a strategic 'add-on' but a fundamental bonding agent between company assets and customer aspirations, corporate mission, the motivational drives of consumption, consumer empowerment, and company transformation. It demonstrates how 'purpose' can be an integrative

fusion with scope to be a catalyst for change: *from transaction to transformation to transcendental.*

– *Chapter 5 Managing customer-company fusion: customer experience management* discusses the potential of the customer-company interface as a facilitating hub, bringing together a community of customers, suppliers, and intermediaries as complementary partners in mutually beneficial relationships and customer experience.

– *Chapter 6 Managing strategic segmentation: customer insights from data* demonstrates how customer insight can be produced from a mixture of traditional segmentation techniques and state-of-the-art digital analytics.

– *Chapter 7 Managing the customer journey: strategic service approaches to the consumption experience* examines how service marketing principles are *fused* with digital dynamics and customer behaviour to look closely at the consumption experience in the setting of a customer journey process.

– At the heart of current Marketing Communications is connectivity, integration, and managing a cohesive, consistent conversation. *Chapter 8 Managing the conversation: integrated marketing communications* demonstrates that a communication *fusion* of systematically integrated multiple messages across multi-media channels can achieve maximum effectiveness and efficiency.

– The subject matter of *Chapter 9 Managing brand equity: tangible results from intangible assets*, describes how a combination of brand, customer, and employee equity can build authentic, relevant, sustainable brands. The elements which affect brand strategy – *Purpose-Driven Brand Vision, Company Brand Culture,* and *Customer Brand Image* – are synthesised in a 'brand *fusion*' showing how they intersect and are aligned with organisational values and customer expectations.

– Customers' views of relationships are holistic – cumulative singular experiences project an organised whole perceived as more than the sum of its parts. The core of relationship marketing is the *interaction* process where the solution is often the relationship itself, the *fusion* of process not outcome.

– Each chapter has its own *fusion* comprising often disparate subjects which have been blended to show how brand theory and brand practice work together harmoniously in synthesis. Table 1.1 illustrates this.

Brand Fusion is the point where theory-based, practice-informed knowledge and experience blend to offer a strategic holistic perspective. It is purposeful praxis – applied theory and established practice. It is the point where the bottom-line imperative, functionality, and aesthetics of the brand intersect and coalesce.

The premise of this book is to examine the isomorphic roots of separate marketing subjects and show how they have a powerful grouping in integrative *fusion*.

Now that is a premise we promise to deliver on!

Table 1.1: Individual chapter 'fusion' components.

	Circle component 1	Circle component 2	Circle component 3	Outside circle text
Chapter 2	Resources	Roots	Relationships	Strategy
Chapter 3	Culture	Marketing	Consumption	Meaning
Chapter 4	Purpose	Positioning	Strategy	Alignment
Chapter 5	Company	Brand Experience	Service	Customer-Company Fusion
Chapter 6	Analysis	Data	Insight	Segmentation Integration
Chapter 7	Digital	Service Marketing	Buyer Behaviour	The Customer Journey
Chapter 8	Owned Media	Paid For Media	Earned Media	Converged Communications
Chapter 9	Culture	Image	Vision	Brand Fusion
Chapter 10	Corporate Brand Identity	Corporate Identity	Brand Credibility	Purposeful Gaze
Chapter 11	Lifestyle	Community	Meaning	Hybrid Orientated Purpose
Chapter 12	Brand Building	Brand Identity Prism	SME Dynamics	Brand Strategy Foundations
Chapter 13	Relationship Marketing	Brand Community	Sustainable Living	Social Purpose
Chapter 14	Digital Innovation	Market Orientation	Purpose	Immersive Experience
Chapter 15	Brand Image	Franchises	Brand Identity	Franchise Brand Equity
Chapter 16	Segmentation	Embedded Branding	Customer Personas	Integrated Marketing Communications
Chapter 17	Digital Transformation	B2B Buyer Behaviour	Personal Relationships	B2B Brand Strategy

1.3 How this book is organised

Brand Fusion: **Purpose-driven brand strategy** is organised in sequential chapters for your practical use: as a developing, conceptual framework where ideas are described in the context of practical application and as cumulative knowledge building, each chapter examining specific, individual subject matter for ease of referencing.

To help navigation of the text, there is a layout diagram showing the chapter structure and content both in the context of the relevant section and as part of the overall schematic (see Figure 1.1). It is essentially a break-down of cumulative brand building (as well as an illustration of progressive learning), and will act as a backdrop blueprint of the nature of adopting a blended approach which integrates key elements such as branding, data analysis, consumer behaviour, service marketing, marketing communications, and a wide range other relevant subject matter.

The book is structured into four parts providing a holistic perspective of strategic brand management:

Firstly, we present in *Section 1* **Introduction to Themes and Conceptual Frameworks** the scaffolding of theory, ideas, and perspectives together with an introductory discussion on the overriding contemporary organisational focus: *purpose.*

Next, *Section 2* **The Foundations of Theory and Practice** advances a necessary in-depth discussion of the socio-psychological foundation of understanding of how meaning is created through the culture of consumption, cultural narratives, and the social language of brands. Here, mutual understanding and symbiotic symbolic loyalty bonds are forged between company and customer.

To evaluate the *mechanics* of marketing – in this case how branding strategy, tactics and techniques are deployed to achieve marketing goals – a review of the full range of traditional and contemporary strategic branding methods and techniques is required. This is covered in great depth in *Section 3* **The Development of Strategy** which analyses how organisations build value, purpose and positioning between client, company, and competition by evaluating key brand strategy drivers, building brand narratives, achieving holistic, strategic marketing.

When *meaning* and *mechanics* are totally understood and implemented, the insight from data-driven, customer-specific marketing research can reveal the '*magic*' of how creativity and applied analysis achieve real commercial goals. Extensive in-depth discussions of how this is applied to actual organisations in actual contexts is covered in *Section 4* **The Application and Purpose of Practice** which features the empirical evidence – both retrospective and 'living' organic extended cases – demonstrating, often in real-time, how organisations have used deep analysis of data to produce commercial results from insight and with foresight.

If you follow Figure 1.1 *Chapter structure* as a guide of how to use this book, you'll see that each section is full of stand-alone discussions covering foundational, strategic, and applied evidence and practice. However, they are also interrelated, working as cumulative knowledge, building towards a fully integrated, comprehensive examination of brand strategy.

So, let's take a look at the contents of each chapter as detailed in Figure 1.1.

Introduction to Themes and Conceptual Frameworks	The Foundations of Theory and Practice	The Development of Strategy	The Application and Purpose of Practice
Chapter 1 Overview	*Chapter 2* Developing brand strategy: Roots, roles, & relationships	*Chapter 4* Managing the Alignment of Strategy: Purpose, proposition, and positioning	*Chapter 10* Legal & General: Inclusive capitalism, change, sustainability, and purpose
	Chapter 3 Managing Meaning: Creating shared value in marketing	*Chapter 5* Managing Customer-Company Fusion: Customer experience management	*Chapter 11* Inspired Villages: Purpose, values, & alignment
		Chapter 6 Managing Strategic Segmentation: Customer insights from data	*Chapter 12* Festival of Thrift: Sustainability through brand community
		Chapter 7 Managing the Customer Journey: The digital consumption experience	*Chapter 13* Small is beautiful: Big ambitions for SMEs
		Chapter 8 Managing the Conversation: Integrated marketing communications	*Chapter 14* Headspace: Immersive digital meditation and mindfulness
		Chapter 9 Managing Brand Equity: Tangible results from intangible assets	*Chapter 15* Freedome: Building franchise brand equity
			Chapter 16 University of Cumbria: Brand anchor, pledge, and persona
			Chapter 17 Dell Technologies: Person-to-person in B2B

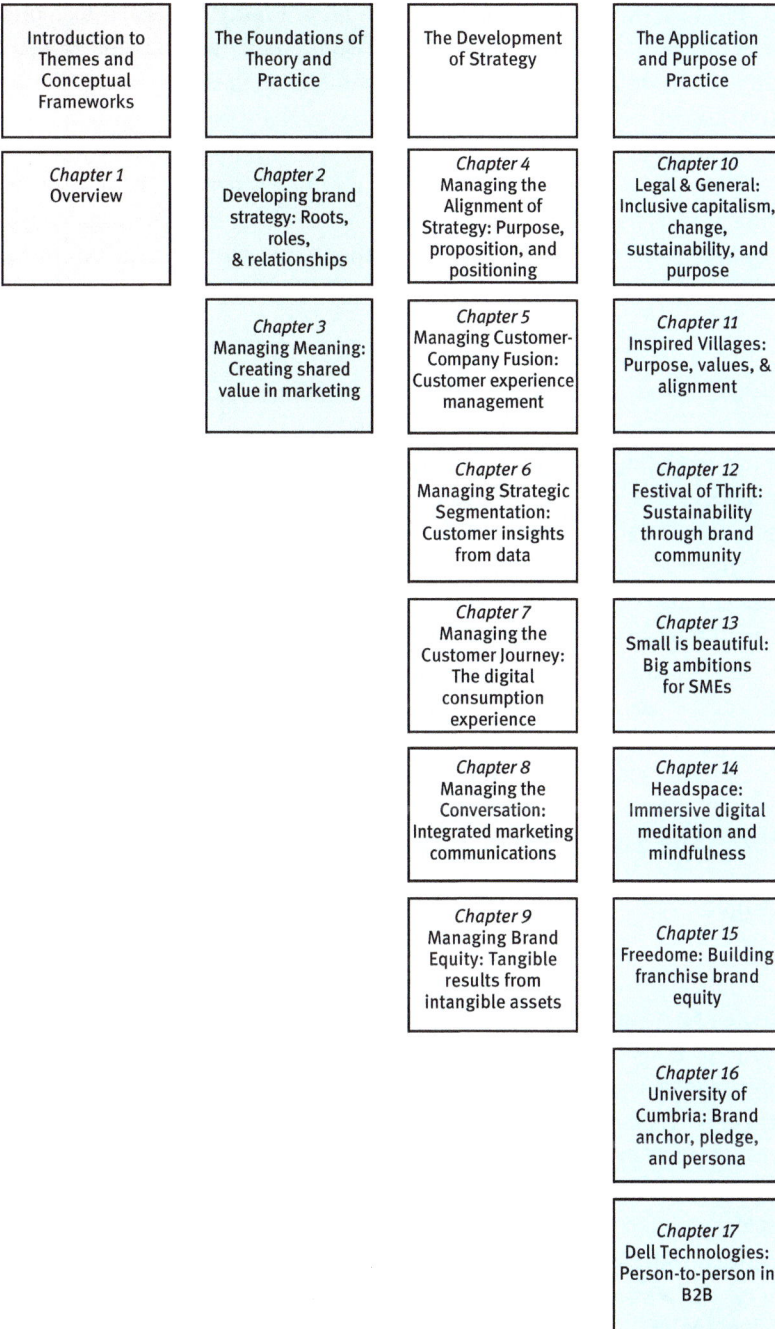

Figure 1.1: Chapter Structure.

Section One: **Introduction to Themes and Conceptual Frameworks** acts as a prefatory part, outlining the main arguments, discussion points, and 'golden threads' which are woven into the narrative of the book, and how the andragogic logic is implemented throughout.

Section Two: **The Foundations of Theory and Practice** provides a solid theoretical and empirical evidence base for the two sections covering the development and application of brand strategy, introducing the reader to received wisdom in terms of current practice and extant knowledge.

Chapter 2 Developing strategy: Roots, resources, relationships

This chapter examines the isomorphic roots of the well-established but often disparate elements of marketing strategy; how synthesis rather than silo underpins cohesive brand strategy; and how digitisation has changed service processes in practice but not in principle. It discusses the roles of the key players in value creation, what relationships are forged in the process; and how the key elements of marketing strategy originate in the marketplace as well as in the dynamic application of other business disciplines. We discuss how the roots and discourses that shape strategy – the role and impact of operations, marketing, and HRM – have impacted on perspectives of 'linkage' between operational performance to business drivers, the re-engineering of service and service technology, and the design of internal networks and managing service capacity. We look at how the network and relationship essence of industrial marketing (B2B), with its emphasis as much on the intangible 'service' elements of people, networks, and relationships as much as the tangible product of manufacturing, predates the so-called transition from goods to service-orientation.

Chapter 3 Managing meaning: Social-dominant logic

This chapter provides a detailed discussion of *'meaning in marketing'* with a socio-psychological exposition of the importance of understanding how it is created, and the importance it plays in strategic brand management. Topics covered include: the culture of consumption in terms of the sociological, psychological, and anthropological aspects; symbolic, conspicuous, and conscience consumption; cultural connectivity; the social language of brands; and the marketing of meaning.

In addition, a new conceptual framework – 'The *Social*-Dominant Logic' – offers a comprehensive analysis of socially-oriented phenomena such as: social *value-in-use* (the service-oriented creation of value in marketing); social *salience* (culturally-constituted experiential marketing); social *semiotics* (the social language of branding); socialised *media* (digital technology); social *interaction* (brand communities and stakeholder impacts); social *conscience* (the new corporate socially responsible approach to strategy); social *stories* (the use of brand narratives to achieve brand longevity through loyalty), and social *partnerships*: exchange relationships and dialogical communications.

Section Three: **The Development of Strategy** analyses how organisations build value, purpose, and positioning between client, company, and competition through the evaluation of key brand strategy drivers and the building of brand narratives to achieve holistic, strategic branding. A common thread here is the emphasis on- 'managing', not solely in the practitioner sense, but focusing on the important *management* of the individual components of brand strategy: meaning, alignment of purpose with proposition positioning, segmentation, the customer journey, customer experience, integrated marketing communications, and brand equity.

Although there is a cohesive thread running through *Chapters 4* to *9*, they have been sequenced with logical 'couplings' of chapters which dovetail to help understanding of the complementary roles of individual strategy components:
– *Chapters 4 and 5* cover the internal strategic propositional and philosophical 'fit' of company resources to external customer requirements through the alignment of company purpose, culture and values.
– *Chapters 5 and 6* examine how the organisation is structured, organised, and how performance is mobilised in terms of strategic vision, leadership, and culture, and discusses what is required from data analytics to help the understanding of customer behaviour.
– *Chapters 6 and 7* examine how the principles of service processes and customer centricity are applied and controlled both online and offline – that is, the *customer journey* – and how the mechanics of service and buyer behaviour processes are informed through data insights from strategic segmentation.
– The management of the 'customer journey' is underpinned by the value framework of proposition, purpose, and organisational culture, informed by insights of customer 'persona' profiling and requirements from segmentation and other elements of data analyses. Therefore, there is also strategic synergy between *Chapters 5, 6 and 7*.
– *Chapters 8 and 9* discuss the company-customer image and identity interface and the development of brand equity by managing 'the conversation' through integrated marketing communications.

Chapter 4 Managing the alignment of strategy: Purpose, proposition, and positioning

The power of purpose complements shareholder primacy, reinforcing *shared* stakeholder value, meaning, and direction, giving companies a line of sight that connects to higher principles and a pathway to higher performance. Aligning purpose, values, and positioning, with a value system to support achieving organisational objectives, can provide a roadmap of organisational strategy, framing business decisions, integrating internal operations with external stakeholders, establishing mutually beneficial loyal relationships, and building brand longevity. Purpose is all-pervasive, affecting all aspects of the company, the environment, and customer needs and wants, value and values, and this is explored here.

This chapter describes how aligning brand strategy with how companies are perceived by customers and other stakeholders, how value propositions are judged against competitors, and how the *purpose* of the organisation affects its markets and environments is the key to sustainable success for organisations competing in today's dramatically changing and often fragile economic and social landscape.

Chapter 5 Managing customer-company fusion: Customer experience management

Chapter 5 recognises the transition from an 'inside-out' company-orientation of service processes to an 'outside-in' one of customer-dominant multi-contextual value creation processes. Managing customer experience in the interface between company and customer is a crucial crucible where value is co-created. Corporate identity and organisational culture, as well as the attitude towards innovation and continuous improvement are examined in the context of creating and sustaining mutually beneficial relationships.

Chapter 6 Managing strategic segmentation: Customer insights from data

Knowledge is vital in finding, converting, satisfying, building, and maintaining long-term relationships, customer lifetime value (CLV), loyalty, and brand advocacy. Understanding your customer is understanding your business. Therefore, any strategy that is customer-driven has to be *data*-driven. This chapter discusses the importance of customer centricity and the role that segmentation plays in helping to understand customer expectations, needs, perceptions, and experiences of their buying 'journey'.

Strategically, segmentation allows better assessment and selection of market attractiveness, deeper analysis of customer-company congruity, and more mutually beneficial value proposition creation, helping to develop successful customer engagement and communication. The fundamental pillar of segmentation – *classifying heterogenous customers into homogenous groups* – is converting customer data into meaningful, actionable strategy. This chapter discusses how segmentation can reveal deep, actionable customer insights, can enhance retention and customer development, monitor for indications of unwanted customer churn and lost patronage, examine potential for leveraging loyalty or re-motivating lapsed users, and continuously innovate customer-centric brands.

Chapter 7 **Managing the customer journey: Strategic service approaches to the consumption experience**

This chapter analyses how customer experience (CX) is a key arena of strategy development for organisations and is crucial in creating value and understanding individual and often complex buyer behaviour. An essential part of the value proposition, therefore, is dependent upon how the customer experiences a brand through consumption encounters with the company via service processes. Taking a process view in order to model interactions, touchpoints, pain points, customer decision points, and idiosyncratic consumption behaviour, is really mapping the process of customer experience against expectations, a method of trying to systemise the value creation process. That is, the *customer journey*

Managing the customer journey is a service instrument for detailing individual customer decision process cycles and analysing what organisations need to understand to compete in the increasingly digital world of service, how it affects consumption, and how AI-powered platforms enable automation of the customer experience (ACX), effectively and efficiently providing an omni-channel, differentiated, pro-active, seamless customer engagement experience which integrates traditional and digital channels.

Chapter 8 **Managing the conversation: Integrated marketing communications**

This chapter examines the role that marketing communications plays in creating and protecting brand identity and sustaining brand equity. It argues that it is the vocal and visual representation of the brand proposition, and that the strategic imperative for integration stems from the convergence and connectivity inherent in communication strategy. Integrated Marketing Communications (IMC) is fundamentally about looking at the whole marketing process from the viewpoint of the customer, and therefore the essence of IMC is *customer-centricity*.

IMC has moved towards a more holistic view of communication – a synthesis of messages and media (owned, shared, and earned) – where co-creation, mutually beneficial relationships, and interactive dialogue is vitally important to "managing the conversation". Given the heightened urgency in the context of the new globalised highly competitive economy infused with the dynamics of digitalisation, omni-channel connectivity, and the gravitation towards customer power, this chapter discusses why the vigilance with which customer engagement and experience must be managed presents organisations with considerable challenge and opportunity.

Chapter 9 Managing brand equity: Tangible results from intangible assets

Market-based assets are principally of two related types: external *relational* assets (customers, channels, strategic partners, providers of complementary goods and services, outsourcing agreements, networks and eco-system relationships), and internal *intellectual* assets (explicit and tacit knowledge, process-based capabilities, experience, and knowledge, cross-disciplinary, intraorganisational know-how and relationships). The intangible assets of an organisation's brands are the primary source of value in a company.

This chapter – in some ways a summative chapter, pulling together the threads of purpose-driven brand strategy – analyses how brand management is strategic and visionary as opposed to tactical and reactive. It analyses the role strong brands play as the most significant part of an organisation's value creation process, how they consistently outperform their markets, and are the driving force of marketing communications strategy. It argues that managing brands is not just a managerial imperative or a product-oriented output of an organisation, but represents *the management of meaning*. The discussion describes how brand identity and brand image are linked but separate elements in building brand equity, and how tangible results can be leveraged from the most intangible of assets. It also acknowledges and examines the apparent conflict of balancing short-term 'activation' of sales with long-term development of the brand.

Section Four: **The Application and Purpose of Practice** features the empirical evidence – cases both featured from secondary sources as well as 'living' organic extended cases – from *FUZE* (Tom's data-driven insight-tech-learning agency), demonstrating how organisations have used deep analysis of both secondary and primary data to produce commercial results with insight and foresight.

This section illustrates how *FUZE*'s hybrid academic rigour/practiced-based commercial know-how and data analysis are a fully integrated, organic part of the creation, development, and management of strategy. This is a unique differentiator of this text, evidencing a holistic approach through the documentation of 'living' cases which describe, diagnose, and deliver 'primary data-insight, empirically driven' exemplar analyses. Each real-world case has different applications of theory, and each have a consistent structure. All cases have a global appeal and are (either and/or empirical/primary and featured secondary public sources) data gathered from across the world.

Chapter 10 Legal & General: Inclusive capitalism, change, sustainability, and purpose

Based on secondary evidence and public-facing materials, this chapter is a *featured* case study highlighting the importance of a purpose-driven corporate brand strategy as an area of responsible business and investment, and illustrates how reframing capitalism as a catalyst for social good and long-term change has been applied in practice. The organisation under focus – *Legal & General Group Plc* – *(Legal & General)* are tackling this challenge head on, delivering what they believe is a key strategic catalyst for delivering meaningful and sustainable change for employees, investors, customers, communities and wider society. That is, *their* 'inclusive capitalism' agenda.

Chapter 11 Inspired Villages: Purpose, values, and alignment

Chapter 11 is an empirically-evidenced case study detailing the exploration into one of the UK's leading operators in retirement communities, *Inspired Villages*, demonstrating how they have been able to deliver *meaning in their shared brand purpose* by positioning themselves as a community-driven, lifestyle brand that delivers overall health and well-being for their customers. Working in partnership with *FUZE*, applying years of continuous proactive and reactive market orientation (or a hybrid approach) diagnosis has been applied in order to convert 'customer' intelligence into value across their business model. This exemplifies the core proposition of this book: cultivating an ever-evolving, dynamic marketing/branding capability by capturing and exploiting mutually beneficial value that is grounded in delivering brand purpose and meaning-making.

Chapter 12 Small is beautiful: Big ambitions for SMEs

Chapter 12 is devoted entirely to the dynamics of SMEs, focusing on how effective brand management for SMEs can unlock growth and help strengthen the sustainability of these types of organisations, and how effective brand orientation The binary choice of reductive versus sophisticated approaches to branding with SMEs are too restrictive. The chapter features *FUZE* primary data and highlights the growing evidence that SMEs are adopting an embedded and sophisticated approach albeit at different stages. *Be the Business* features prominently, supporting the notion that the concept of brand fusion in this context has a crucial role to play in SMEs helping tackle the UK's productivity puzzle.

Chapter 13 Festival of Thrift

Chapter 13 looks at brand community sustainability by examining the formation and purpose of *Festival of Thrift* a community interest company (CIC) whose mission is to "benefit the community and advance public awareness of sustainable living".

The case explores how *Festival of Thrift's* 'The Shift to Thrift' company ethos demonstrates how galvanising the values of a group of like-minded individuals can build a company with purpose from a collective conscience.

Chapter 14 Headspace: Immersive digital meditation and mindfulness

This chapter is a *featured* case study, based on secondary evidence/research and public facing materials, focused on the global meditation and mindfulness content app *Headspace,* and is an example of the *social*-dominant logic in action, one that embodies the fusing of deep existential imperatives, health and well-being outcomes, and digital innovation. Here, a purpose-driven brand strategy follows an effective market orientation evaluation, an aligned and clear raison d'etre, and a deep understanding of user's needs, wants and preferences, resulting in the effective delivery of a tailored and powerful immersive digital experience.

Chapter 15 Freedome: Building franchise brand equity

The brand relationships between franchisors and franchisees, and the subsequent brand equity created, is the subject of this chapter, where *Freedome,* a global trampoline park specialist who are part of the *Freedome Parks (Freedome) Group,* are examined as part of a mutually dependent relationship of brand identity, image, and equity. *FUZE* have worked with *Freedome* since 2017, with a clear brief to contributing to the understanding of the practical realities of executing brand strategy on a *local* basis whilst also enhancing the overall *global* brand equity of the original franchise model.

Chapter 16 University of Cumbria: Brand anchor, pledge, and persona

The case featured in *Chapter 16* discusses how *The University of Cumbria (UoC)* worked with *FUZE* to implement a University-wide strategic segmentation project that combined dual-perspectives per persona groups, relevant to the new 'student as consumer' marketisation of the Higher Education sector. A 'deep dive analysis' of University course selection, involving decision pathways across all digital and traditonal touch-points, as well as mapping the full customer and learning journey from the perspective of 1st year entrants, helped the university to focus on improving conversion rates and income as part of the implementation of a university 'Action Plan'.

Chapter 17 **Dell Technologies: Person-to-person in B2B**

Chapter 17, a case study based on secondary evidence, public facing materials, and data obtained from a global technology company, *Dell Technologies,* examines how developing brand value and innovative digital transformation through in a Business-to-Business (B2B) customer journey 'model' required an investment of trust in a 'personal' brand. It discusses the ambiguity of individual subjectivity and corporate personality in decision-making, developing brand value, and strengthening brand relationships in the rational context of Business-to-Business B2B marketing. The case demonstrates how customer expectations rely on underpinning brand relationships both at a macro-level (corporate identity) and through cultivating relationships at a micro-level (importance of personal aspects of the brand).

1.4 Themes and discussions

As a quick guide to the overall themes used throughout the book, Table 1.2 details the section references to help you easily locate specific discussion points. It acts like an index of intellectual inquiry – how *values* have balanced our perceptions of *value*; how social 'relevance' and brand 'authenticity' inform brand strategy; and how branding objectives have become mixed with politics and environmental issues. It also discusses how conceptual frameworks of brand identity, image, equity, purpose, customer-company relationships, and indeed brand fusion, are part of a cohesive thread running throughout the narrative of this textbook.

Table 1.2: Themes and conceptual frameworks.

Themes	Content
Brand equity	1.2, 1.3, 1.5, 2.1, 2.4, 2.8, 3.1, 3.6, 3.12, 4.15, 5.2, 5.9, 6.5, 7.4, 8.1, 8.3, 8.5, 9.1, 9.2, 9.4–9.10, 10.1, 10.4, 10.5, 10.7, 11.3, 11.7, 11.10, 12.2, 12.4, 12.6, 12.7, 13.4, 14.2, 14.3, 14.6, 15.1–15.8, 16.4, 17.2, 17.5
Brand identity	1.5, 3.10, 3.12, 4.7, 4.12,5.2, 5.8, 7.4, 8.1, 8.5, 9.1–9.4, 9.6, 9.8, 9.10, 10.5, 10.7, 12.2, 12.4–12.6, 12.7, 14.3, 14.5, 15.4–15.8, 16.3, 16.8, 17.1
Brand image	2.5, 2.11, 3.2, 3.10, 3.12, 4.15, 5.5, 5.6, 5.8, 5.9, 6.9, 7.4, 8.3, 9.1, 9.3, 9.4, 9.7, 9.8, 11.5, 12.4, 12.5, 12.8, 15.5, 15.6, 12.8
Brand strategy	2.1–2.4, 2.6, 2.8, 3.1–3 3, 3.7 3.9, 3.11–3.13, 3.15–3.17, 4.1, 4.2, 4.7, 4.9, 4.10, 4.15, 4.16, 5.1, 5.2, 5.4, 5.5, 5.7, 6.1, 6.2, 6.5, 6.6, 7.2, 7.4, 7.6, 8.2, 8.4, 8.6, 8.8, 8.10, 9.2–9.4, 9.6, 9.8–9.10, 10.1, 10.2, 10.4, 10.6–10.8, 11.1, 11.6, 11.7, 11.8, 11.10, 12.1, 12.3–12.8, 13.2, 13.3, 14.2, 15.1, 25.4–15.6, 15.8, 16.1, 16.5, 16.11, 17.1, 17.3–17.5

Table 1.2 (continued)

Themes	Content
Buyer/consumer behaviour & decision-making	2.2, 2.8, 2.9, 3.6, 3.12, 5.6, 7.1–7.4, 7.7, 8.4, 8.5, 9.4, 9.5, 9.10, 17.3
Corporate identity	2.2, 5.1, 5.8, 9.1–9.4, 9.6, 10.2, 10.6, 10.7, 16.1, 17.1, 17.3, 17.6
Customer centricity	1.2, 1.3, 2.2, 3.5, 5.2, 6.1, 6.3, 6.5, 7.5, 17.1
Customer Experience	2.4, 2.9, 4.7, 5.1–5.3, 5.5, 5.6, 5.8, 6.2, 6.3, 7.1–7.7, 9.2–9.5, 9.8, 9.10, 11.7–11.10, 12.2, 13.2–13.5, 14.2, 15.6, 16.6, 17.1, 17.3, 17.5, 17.6
Customer-company fusion/interface	2.2–2.5, 2.8–2.10, 3.1, 3.2, 3.5–3.8, 3.11, 4.1, 4.5, 4.14, 5.1, 5.3, 5.4, 5.6–5.8, 6.2,6.3, 6.5, 7.1–7.7, 8.3–8.5, 9.1, 9.2, 9.4, 9.6, 9.8, 9.10, 12.3, 12.6, 12.7, 12.8, 16.5, 16.6, 16.8, 17.3–17.6
Data	1.2–1.4, 2.4, 2.7, 2.10, 2.4, 2.7, 2.10, 3.5, 3.11, 3.13, 4.2, 4.7, 4.15, 5.2, 5.5–5.7, 5.10, 6.1–6.5, 6.7–6.9, 7.1–7.6, 8.4,16.3, 16.5, 16.6, 17.1, 17.4
Digital	1.2, 1.3, 2.2, 2.3, 2.4, 2.7, 2.9, 2.10, 3.1, 3.2, 3.6, 3.11, 3.14, 3.16, 4.4, 5.1, 5.2, 5.3, 5.5, 5.6, 6.2–6.6, 6.8, 7.1–7.4, 7.6–7.8, 8.1–8.6, 8.8, 9.1, 9.4, 9.7, 9.9, 10.3, 13.5, 14.2, 14.4, 14.5, 16.2, 16.3, 17.1, 17.4–17.6
Ecosystems	2.4, 3.5, 3.11, 5.2–5.4, 7.6, 7.11, 8.2, 12.9
Encounters	2.6, 5.1, 5.2, 5.7, 6.1, 6.2, 6.5, 7.1–7.4, 7.6, 8.3–8.5,9.2, 9.4, 17.3
Engagement	2.2, 2.4, 2.8, 2.11, 3.2, 3.6, 3.8, 3.11, 3.12, 4.7, 4.12, 5.1–5.6, 5.9, 5.10, 6.1–6.3, 6.5, 7.1–7.7, 8.1–8.4, 8.6, 8.8, 9.2, 9.4–9.6, 9.8, 9.9, 11.2,11.12, 12.7, 12.8, 13.2, 16.6
Ethics	2.2–2.4, 2.8, 2.10, 4.2–4.5, 5.14,5.8, 9.4, 9.8, 10.8, 14.4
Fusion	1.2–1.5, 2.2, 3.1, 3.2, 3.4, 3.5, 3.7, 3.9, 3.11, 3.12, 3.16, 4.2, 4.4, 4.6, 4.9, 4.13, 4.16, 5.1–5.4, 5.7, 5.8, 6.1, 7.6, 7.7, 8.1, 8.2, 16.5, 16.6, 17.4–17.6
Inclusive and conscious capitalism	2.7, 5.8, 10.1–10.4, 10.6–10.8, 12.3
Integrated Marketing Communications	5.8, 7.4, 8.1, 8.4, 8.5, 8.7, 8.10, 9.1, 9.2, 9.6, 9.10, 16.6, 16.8
Integration	2.4, 5.7, 3.2, 3.10, 4.2, 4.4, 5.2, 5.6, 5.8, 6.3, 7.4, 7.7, 8.1, 8.2, 8.4, 8.7, 8.8, 9.1–9.3
Marketing (macro and micro) environment	1.1, 2.5, 3.3, 3.7, 4.3, 4.4, 5.4, 6.5, 7.3, 8.3, 8.4, 9.5, 9.15, 10.1, 11.5, 11.6, 11.8, 12.7, 14.4, 17.1, 17.3

Table 1.2 (continued)

Themes	Content
Orientation (multiple forms)	1.3, 2.1, 2.3, 2.5, 2.6, 2.9, 2.10, 2.11, 3.1, 3.2, 3.7, 3.8, 3.12, 3.13, 4.2, 4.5, 4.7, 4.8, 4.14, 4.15, 4.16, 4.17, 4.18, 5.2, 5.7, 5.8, 6.3, 7.4, 8.7, 9.2, 9.5, 9.10, 9.11, 9.15, 10.2, 10.7, 10.8, 11.1, 10.6, 10.7, 11.8, 11.9, 11.10, 11.1, 11.3, 12.2, 12.3, 12.6, 12.7, 12.10, 14.2, 14.4, 14.6, 15.2, 16.2, 16.6, 16.11, 17.4
Philosophy of Business	1.22, 1.4, 2.1, 2.2, 2.4, 2.8, 2.11, 3.6, 3.7, 3.15, 4.1, 4.2, 4.4, 5.2, 5.7, 5.8, 6.3, 8.7, 9.4, 9.7, 9.8, 9.9, 9.10
Positioning	1.2, 1.3, 2.4, 2.7, 2.8, 2.10, 3.2, 3.4, 3.5, 3.8, 3.9, 3.10, 3.14, 4.1, 4.3, 4.4, 4.7, 4.12–4.15, 5.8, 6.1, 6.2, 6.5, 7.3, 7.4, 8.2, 8.4, 8.5, 8.7, 8.10, 9.2–9.5, 9.8, 10.2, 10.7, 10.8, 11.5, 11.7, 11.10, 11.11, 12.1, 12.4, 12.5, 13.1, 14.4, 15.1, 15.5, 15.7, 16.1, 16.2, 16.4, 16.10, 17.5
Purpose	1.1–1.6, 2.1–2.11, 3.1, 3.2, 3.6, 3.10, 3.12, 3.14, 3.17, 6.2, 6.3, 6.5, 8.2, 8.5, 8.7, 8.11, 11.1, 11.2, 11.6, 11.7, 12.3,12.5, 12.7,12.8, 15.6, 17.2–17.6
Relationships	1.2–1.5, 2.2–2.5, 2.7–2.10, 3.2, 3.6, 3.8, 3.9, 2.12, 3.14, 3,15, 4.1, 4.2, 4.4, 4.6, 4.9, 4.10, 4.12, 4.13, 4.16, 5.1–5.7, 5.9, 6.1, 6.2, 6.6, 6.8, 6.9, 7.1, 7.3, 7.4, 7.6, 8.1–8.5, 8.7, 8.8, 9.1–9.10, 10.1, 10.7, 11.6, 11.10, 11.12, 12.7, 13.1, 15.1, 16.6, 17.1, 17.3–17.6
Reputation	2.4, 2.5, 2.5, 2.8, 2.10, 3.5, 4.16, 5.6, 5.8, 5.9, 6.4, 8.4, 8.5, 9.3–9.5, 9.8, 10.4, 11.6, 12.7, 15.6, 16.0, 16.16
Segmentation	1.2, 1.3, 1.5, 3.3, 3.13, 6.1–6.6, 8.5, 8.10, 9.5 9.7, 9.9, 11.4, 12.1, 12.5, 15.1, 15.7, 16.1, 16.2, 16.3, 16.5, 16.6, 16.8, 16.10, 17.1, 17.5
Service processes	2.2, 2.4, 5.1, 5.3, 5.5, 7.1, 2.4, 9.2, 9.5, 9.9, 9.10
Social conscience	2.3, 2.7, 3.4, 3.5, 3.13, 3.14, 3.17. 4.4, 5.4, 5.8, 8.5, 9,4
Social construction	3.5, 3.5, 3.7, 3.12, 5.8, 9.4, 9.8
Social meaning	3.4, 3.6, 3.7, 3.12, 3.16, 3.17, 4.4, 6.4, 9.5, 9.10, 14.5
Social value	2.3–2.5, 2.7, 2.8, 3.8, 3.9, 3.13, 4.4, 5.9, 7.4
Stakeholders	2.1–2.5, 2.7–2.10, 3.1, 3.2, 3.6, 3.8, 4.1–4.10, 4.14–4.16, 5.2, 5.6, 5.8, 5.9, 6.1, 6.2, 7.6, 8.1–8.5, 8.7, 8.8, 9.3, 9.4, 9.6, 10.1, 10.1, 10.4–10.8, 11.6, 11.7, 12.3, 12.5, 13.5, 15.1, 15.6, 15.8, 16.3, 16.6, 16.8, 17.1, 17.4
Value creation	2.2, 2.4–2.7, 2.9, 3.2, 3.6, 3.7, 3.8, 3.12, 4.2, 4.4, 5.3–5.7, 5.9, 6.5, 7.7, 8.4, 9.2, 9.5, 9.6, 9.11
Value proposition	2.2, 2.8, 2.10, 3.9, 3.10,3.11, 3.12,3.13,4.4, 4.5, 4.7, 4.8, 4.11–4.14, 5.2–5.8, 6.2, 6.3, 6.5, 7.3, 7.5, 7.6, 8.5, 8.10, 9.2–9.4, 9.6–9.8, 9.10, 11.3, 11.9–11.11, 15.5, 16.6

Table 1.2 (continued)

Themes	Content
Values	2.2–2.4, 2.6–2.10, 3.1–3.5, 3.8, 3.9, 3.14, 4.4, 4.5, 4.7, 4.9, 4.13, 4.16, 4.19, 5.7–5.10, 6.2, 6.9, 8.2, 8.4–8.8, 9.2–9.4, 9.6–9.8, 9.10, 10.5, 10.7, 11.6, 11.7, 11.12, 12.3, 12.6, 12.7, 13.1, 13.4, 14.2, 14.4, 14.5, 15.5, 15.6, 15, 8, 16.3, 16.5, 17.2, 17.4, 17.6

1.5 Andragogic logic

Aimed at instructors and students, as well as being a strategic instructional manual of applied empirical marketing research, the teaching methodology (or 'Andragogic logic' as we refer to it) below describes how the fusion of marketing theory and marketing practice will be addressed in the textbook, how it can be delivered in the classroom, and how it is practiced in context.

Each chapter comprises the following teaching techniques which follow this format:

- *Golden thread*: An integrative, on-going narrative of theory to practice/practice to theory is present throughout each chapter, illustrating how practice is reified in theory and theory is verified in practice.
- *'4Es' lecture, seminar and workshop plan*: Each chapter has an implicit '4Es' lecture plan which is consistent with good teaching practice – Exposition, Explanation, Example, Exercise.
- *'Learning outcomes' and 'Chapter takeaways' boxes*: The 'learning outcomes' approach is a standard teaching method, an objective expectation of learning for each chapter. 'Chapter takeaways' are both chapter summaries and 'learning prompts' for conceptual frameworks and discussion points.
- *'Opening' and 'Closing' mini cases:* These four page 'stories' are designed to illustrate key conceptual and contextual examples within the context of each chapter evidenced in good practice enacted by a wide selection of global organisations and SMEs.
- *'Principles in Practice' boxes:* These short contemporary examples of 'branding strategy in action' provide a useful punctuation and supplement to the chapter text and illustrate concepts in context.
- *Extended 'theory-practice symbiosis' case analyses*: A whole portion of the book – Chapters 10–14 in *Section 4 The Application and Purpose of Practice* – is devoted to demonstrating how a functioning consultancy integrates theory, practice and praxis based on data-driven, customer-specific marketing research through in-depth living case analyses. There is a set 'structure' to allow the reader to have

consistent learning points as the concept/topic rationale is set, analysed, and learning is brought to life.

– *Conceptual frameworks*: A range of traditional, contemporary, and innovative author practical models offer visual explanation of marketing and brand theory used in practice, a useful feature for workshop, lecture or seminar teaching and learning.

– *Fusion 'logo' (as part of the brand identity)*: The trusted old 'Venn Diagram', a perennial stalwart of teaching, management training, and many a session on creative thinking, appears throughout the book as a kind of learning *leitmotif*, highlighting each chapter's content and key focus, emphasising the synthesis of subjects and the main thread of the book. As a graphical illustrator of the fusion of elements in conceptual frameworks such as meaning construction, brand, service, and buyer behaviour, IMC, brand equity components, relationships between types of 'persona' in segmentation analysis, PR profile strategy, Kapferer's (2012) 'Product/ Brand Halo Effect' model, and even as a simple representation of 'brand fusion' itself, it's repetition focuses the reader on the essential hybridity in our thinking which is a hallmark of this book.

Chapter takeaways

– A broad overview of the book's structure was presented.
– The authors' intended scope and selected content was established.
– Key themes and narrative threads used throughout the book were sign-posted.
– An outline of the main discussion points was given to help understanding of the dynamics involved in creating and sustaining brand longevity through strategic brand management.
– The *Foundations of Theory and Practice* section provided a solid theoretical and empirical evidence base for the two sections covering the development and application of brand strategy.
– The *Development of Strategy* section analysed how organisations build value, purpose, and positioning between client, company, and competition through the evaluation of key brand strategy drivers and building brand narratives to achieve holistic, strategic branding.
– The 'promise of the premise' was developed: **Brand Fusion**, a theory-based, practice-informed, integrative, holistic perspective.
– The andragogic logic of the book was introduced to act as a guide through the menu of concepts and contexts and help with understanding of the content and complexities of the book.
– A distinctive perspective on *purpose-driven brand strategy* was discussed analysing the complementarity between a number of 'fusions' across different subject areas.

Section 2: **The foundations of theory and practice**

Section 2 is a detailed analysis of the academic underpinnings and empirical evidence which provide us with the structure, content, and dynamics of what constitutes the theoretical thought and practical application of the extant knowledge and current received wisdom on strategic brand management. *Chapter 2* examines the roots of marketing discourses and business philosophy, development of current thought on strategy, and how value is a product of eco-systems of mutually beneficial co-creation. A discussion on the impact of critical marketing perspectives on what constitutes marketing strategy introduces the emerging imperative of 'purpose' as a key element in company missions. There has been many proposed paradigm shifts on the orientation of strategy, and in *Chapter 3* a parallax perspective – the *social-dominant logic* of meaning – is offered for discussion.

https://doi.org/10.1515/9783110718638-004

2 Developing brand strategy: Roots, resources, relationships

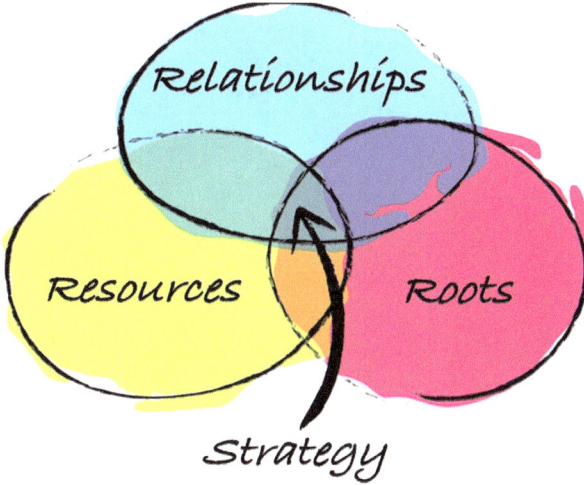

https://doi.org/10.1515/9783110718638-005

Opening case

© Gajus - stock.adobe.com.

M&S ABC of Strategy:
C Suite joins B Corps with Plan A

For over 30 years, *Baird Textile Holdings*, a textile manufacturer based in the UK, had been supplying clothing materials under instruction to *Marks & Spencer plc (M&S)*, a British food, clothing, and household product retailer. Suddenly, in 1999, they found their contract to supply had been terminated without notice, a hammer blow for a company that had a big percentage of their turnover dramatically affected and with no time to react. To make matters worse, there had been no on-going legal written contract governing the long-term relationship between the parties. *Baird* sued *M&S* for loss of profit on two grounds: there was an on-going implied contract that required reasonable notice of termination; *M&S* were 'estopped'[8] from terminating the contract without reasonable notice. *M&S* countered that there was no contract, arguing the arrangement was based on individual short-term orders. In those days, this asymmetrical strategy was standard business practice for *M&S*, whose enormous power and buying orientation dominated suppliers and dictated relationships. The Judge ruled for *M&S* and this was upheld in The Court of Appeal, but the negative PR for its out-dated supply chain strategy, and the harm done to brand equity, was much more damaging. The *M&S* 'C Suite'[9] needed a Plan B. Or Plan A as it turned out.

With over 1,000 stores world-wide, 85% of which are based in the UK, *M&S* sells product under their own brand name, made almost entirely from a supply chain of over 368 direct suppliers,

---

8 A judicial device which may be used to prevent or 'estop' a person from making assertions or going back on his word.

9 Executive level managers such as Chief Executive Officer (CEO), Chief Operating Officer (COO), Chief Marketing Officer (CMO), Chief Financial Officer (CFO), and Chief Information Officer (CIO) constitute the 'C Suite'.

employing 119,000 people employed in 302 food factories and 38 drink factories. Furthermore, the supply chain has spread much wider than its UK roots. Consequently, over 90% of social and environmental impacts occur *within* its supply chain. In response to growing customer pressure and competitive sustainability strategies, it was clear that an asymmetrical strategy was no longer appropriate; leadership in minimising environmental impact and fostering sustainability throughout its supply chain was required.

Developing deeper relationships and building closer collaboration with its suppliers is now the central instrument of *M&S's* 'Supplier Collaboration Programme' strategy with benefits such as: sustainability-based innovations in packaging design, load-sharing transportation, environmental and social risk reduction, and better sourced materials. To secure its long-term future and sustain its operating ecosystem, changes began to be made to *M&S* strategy with the implementation of their 'Plan A' £200m, 100 Point pioneering 'eco plan' in 2007 which focused on corporate responsibility, and the introduction of a 'Sustainability Scorecard' system[10] in 2010 which allows tracking of sustainability progress amongst its suppliers. Criteria based on 'environment' (eg: energy and water use, waste, and carbon outputs), 'human resources and ethical trade' (eg: employee representation, workforce cohesion, external accreditation), and 'lean manufacturing' (eg: value-stream mapping, standardised problem-solving tools, manufacturing process analyses), mark out *M&S's* eco aims. Encouragement to share the *M&S* online 'knowledge platform' which highlights business benefits, advice, and help through skill share, training and development programmes, and also financial and no-financial incentives, helps cement a new partnership ethos, and an acknowledgement that the old 'buyer power' asymmetrical strategy is being progressively changed from compliance to cooperation. Some initiatives (eg: the *Sedex* Supplier Ethical Data Exchange) have been partly successful but constrained by supplier defensiveness.

By the time of its 10th anniversary in 2017, Plan A was updated with extended targets for packaging to be widely recyclable by 2022, food waste to be halved and operational emissions reduced by 80% by 2025, with the aim of net-zero across its operations by 2035. Over 296 eco and ethical commitments were achieved – cutting supply chain emissions by 13.3m tonnes, carbon neutrality, improving energy efficiency of UK and Ireland-located facilities by 39%, 27 million items of clothing "shwopped"[11] since 2008, 100% RSPO certification showing palm oil compliance, with 99% wood and 27% leather derived from sustainable sources.

This was further updated in 2021, accelerated by the climate crisis. This key focus of strategy became the "centre of the company's customer story". On his appointment as Chairman, Archie Norman reinforced the company's purpose and sense of responsibility declaring *M&S:*

> *a pioneer in creating an industry-leading, fully-integrated sustainability plan under the 'Plan A' banner, reflecting values that have been core to M&S's culture since its inception. The organisation's inherent and enduring community spirit has been borne out in its response to the pandemic, and in many areas -particularly on sourcing and supply chain standards – we continue to lead the market.*

---

10 Sustainability Scorecard: Capacity Building Initiatives', corporate.marksandspencer.com, https://cor porate.marksandspencer.com/plan-a/our-approach/food-and-household/capacity-buildinginitiatives/ sustainability-scorecard
11 "Shwopping" partnership with *Oxfam* since 2008, reselling, reusing, or recycling donated by customers.

Acknowledgement has also come in the form of *'B Corps'* recognition – those companies transforming the global economy to benefit people, communities, and planet, proving their status as one of the best in the world and best *for* the world. *B Lab,*[12] a non-profit organisation founded in 2006, issues a B Impact Assessment (BIA) (analogous to *Fairtrade* for products) for top-performing organisations evaluated in 5 'impact' areas: community, customers, environment, governance, and employees. Other *B Corp* recipients include *Danone, Unilever* with 5 core B Corp brands including *Ben & Jerry's*. UK brands like *Brewdog, Mulberry,* and *Leon* – supplying, respectively, hand sanitiser, *NHS* gowns, and food during the pandemic – also feature. *B Corp* recognition can have a material impact on brand equity and overall appeal to key stakeholders.[13] Appropriately, the creation of a new ESG Board Sub-Committee, coinciding with the re-launch of Plan A in December 2020, was created to provide focus and oversight.

With the after-effects of COVID-19 dramatically impacting on customer expectations, *M&S's* transformation has also involved re-appraisal of the retail estate (including store closures, format re-assessment, and shopping experience evaluation) in the context of the overall omni-channel retail experience.

All of this has resulted in supply risks being minimised, reputational damage being restored, and brand equity being boosted. It has delivered savings of over £700 million since 2007. The *M&S* 'C Suite' of executives may have changed in recent years, but consistency sticking to Plan A has secured their place as a *B Corp* company for some time to come.

Questions
1. How has past strategy informed current *M&S* strategy?
2. Why is supply chain management an important element of brand strategy?
3. How significant is *'B Corps'* recognition as acknowledgement of an organisation's strategic credentials?

Note: The photo(s) used in this case study is/are not connected and/or does not represent any brand(s) mentioned. It/they is/are used to make a visual discussion point by the authors.

2.1 Outline of chapter

Branding strategy is about company strategic direction, long-term vision, a mutuality of meaning, and unifying purpose: *it drives the business more than any other aspect of marketing strategy*. Its roots, like so many aspects of marketing, are in marketplace performance more than academic contemplation. Theories of branding are in abundance now, but up until recently they were scarce. As Franzen & Moriarty (2008, p. 10) suggest, "brand management is an old practice but a very young science".

Iconic companies such as *Coca Cola* (origins in 1886), *Colgate* (1873), the *Ford Motor Company* (1903), and even *LEGO* (1932), were pioneers in building businesses

---

12 'B' stands for 'beneficial' and indicates an awardee has met stringent ESG standards of transparency, accountability, sustainability, and performance and creates value for society.
13 Neil Sutton, Global Deals Leader, *Price Waterhouse Cooper* Consumer Markets, 2021, pwc.com.

through their brands, but things really changed in the 1990s, the moment organisations recognised that brands were perhaps the most valuable assets they owned. In terms of an organisation's competitiveness, branding strategy might not be an impenetrable force, but it is its most defensible asset.

Branding was still very much a *practical* phenomenon at this time, but the vacuum of scientific thought was suddenly replaced by a plethora of concepts and strategic frameworks. Now, branding strategy is discussed and applied in every organisation in all parts of the world, and 'purposeful' concepts such as 'creating shared value' (CSV), corporate social responsibility (CSR), stakeholder theory, and ecosystem orchestration are the footprints of a new direction for brand strategy.

For a long time branding was seen as just another element considered in the 'promotional mix', but has recently progressed to being 'brand-*based* strategy', an all-pervasive integrating force, a reference point for 'strategic fit' between company resources and customer aspirations. It has become so integral to a company's philosophy and operations that it's importance has matured into a unifying organisational nucleus which has become the locus and the focus of all activities.

Haque (2011, p. 3) describes those early brand renegades as being an essential part of an age of new enlightenment: "At the root, it's about cornerstones: how, as the anchors of companies, countries, and economies, they are the foundations of plenitude – or of penury. Today's economic enlightenment is culminating in new cornerstones for production, consumption, and exchange, like *value cycles, value conversations*, and *betters*".[14]

This chapter looks at the strategic role of branding and its impact on both marketing and society, investigating its source, history, and development. Theory often merely reflects practice, and here we look at how those practical roots have shaped strategy. The essence of branding (and indeed its extended concept *brand equity*) lies in its *intangible* quality. This notion finds resonance with: the concept of actual and *perceived* quality in Total Quality Management (TQM) and service marketing; the essence of *trust* in the network and relationship logic of industrial marketing (B2B), and latterly relationship marketing (RM); the strategic transition from manufactured goods to service-orientation; and, most importantly, the co-creation of immaterial value between customer and company. It is the synergy in its isomorphic roots where we will find insight into what brand strategy is and where it comes from.

---

14 Haque uses the word 'betters' in the context of constructive capitalism making 'better' or enhanced bundles of products and services making a difference to people and environment. He illustrates this with *Nike* emphasising making customers better runners as opposed to simply selling them cooler shoes.

Learning outcomes

After reading this chapter, you'll be able to:
- Comprehend the fundamental principles or philosophy of organisations: the purpose, mission, goals, objectives, and the methods by which these are achieved.
- Understand how customers and stakeholders affect how an organisation's view of brand strategy is rapidly changing.
- Examine the concept of a stakeholder ecosystem.
- Analyse the role of resources and assets in the creation of value.
- Assess the alternative perspectives of capitalism and how inclusivity, consciousness, and ethics is changing how brands are perceived.
- Identify the new dynamics of a 'balanced scorecard' and how this impacts on customer-company trust, purpose, and the internal/external dynamic in the branding the branding of the organisation.

2.2 Introduction

Kozinets, De Valck & Wojnicki warn: "as markets change, marketing theories must change" (2010, p. 71). The pressure to accommodate a rapidly expanding ecosystem of stakeholders, often understandably concentrating on the most demanding, may actually result in a focus on narrow goals with a lack of customer-centricity. Kay (2010, p. 8) advocates 'obliquity' of brand strategy – indirect direction. Indeed, brand strategy formation may happen intentionally or unintentionally (Vallaster & Lindgreen, 2011). There is "an inherent tension between the rational logic of clear, focused, narrow strategic alignment . . . and broader oblique approaches implemented on the basis of values" (Robson, 2013, p. 215). Companies must be agile, willing and able to change, and so too must marketing strategy be organic, adaptable, and respond proactively to the dynamics of changing customer needs, market conditions, and ever-changing environmental challenges of the Volatile, Uncertain, Chaotic, Ambiguous (VUCA) world we live in.

Understanding how branding strategy has developed, from all the iterations of the marketing concept through to its role as the dynamo of the organisation, necessitates an examination of its roots, its progression to primacy in the hierarchy of company resources, and an appreciation of how it affects and is affected by its relationships with other components of corporate strategy. To separate brand strategy from marketing strategy is to confuse branding as a mere communications tool not an engine, as a tactic not a strategy. Everything in marketing strategy and everything in the marketing mix is about branding. Branding isn't a corollary of marketing, it is the heartbeat, not just marketing strategy, but the whole organisation. It is not only a key differentiator but an essential driver. Its symbiotic relationship with marketing strategy sees branding as strategy mediator, conduit, and energy. Brand strategy effectively *is* marketing strategy.

Let's firstly take a closer look at how marketing strategy and then (in parallel) how branding strategy has evolved.

Strategy describes a company's distinctive approach to its environments and market competitive conditions, and, in matching its capabilities to that dynamic, the unique value it creates with its customer. It is fundamentally about how internal organisational purpose, promise, and principles reflect external customer values.

The focus of *brand* strategy is, therefore, simply to make a difference: transforming the product category; creating and sustaining a long-term vision; facilitating a holistic approach to managing a company's assets by integrating brand strategy with business strategy; fusing customer expectation with company capability, having a stakeholder not just shareholder perspective. Brand strategy therefore needs a sustainable interconnected and interdependent business system involving brand equities and identities, brand architecture and relational structures, a meaning-making mechanism designed to create value *and* values.

A graphical representation of the isomorphic roots of marketing illustrating how there is an overlap in silo subject development and market application is included for reference (See Figure 2.1). It shows how there is a synergy (a fusion) of purpose in the various developments of strategy: value creation, customer centricity, market relevance, values, responsibility, relationships, sustainability, customer engagement, experience and satisfaction. Whilst these goals are manifest in all the various strands of customer-oriented disciplines such as selling, B2B account development, service marketing, digital relations, and so on, marketing strategy, and indeed brand strategy, can be seen as an eclectic, cross-disciplinary synthesis of subjects and concepts which have separate origins but similar foci: *reciprocal customer-company value co-created through integrating complementary resources.*

Branding strategy is about merging diverse elements – business philosophy, cultural interaction, service processes – and the managerial imperative of encouraging and cultivating voluntary mutually beneficial relationships. In this fusion, the constant driving force has been, and remains, *the centrality and satisfaction of the customer and the co-creation of mutually beneficial value.*

The need to analyse value-creating processes is a perennial constant in marketing strategy. From Porter's '5 Forces' and 'value chain' frameworks – both activity-based views of value creation with roots in operations analysis – to the market-based, Network Theory roots of relationship marketing – built on the existing industrial partnership paradigm of complementarity and complicity – the concept of value creation has been a magpie amalgam of disparate business and marketing phenomena, the fusion of disciplines, and the iteration of value-creating innovations. The 'relationship' metaphor in marketing is often traced back to Fournier's (2002) model based on marriage and social models with intimacy, commitment, trust, partner quality, attachment, interdependence and, strangely, love being the six factors which are vital to create meaning for consumers.

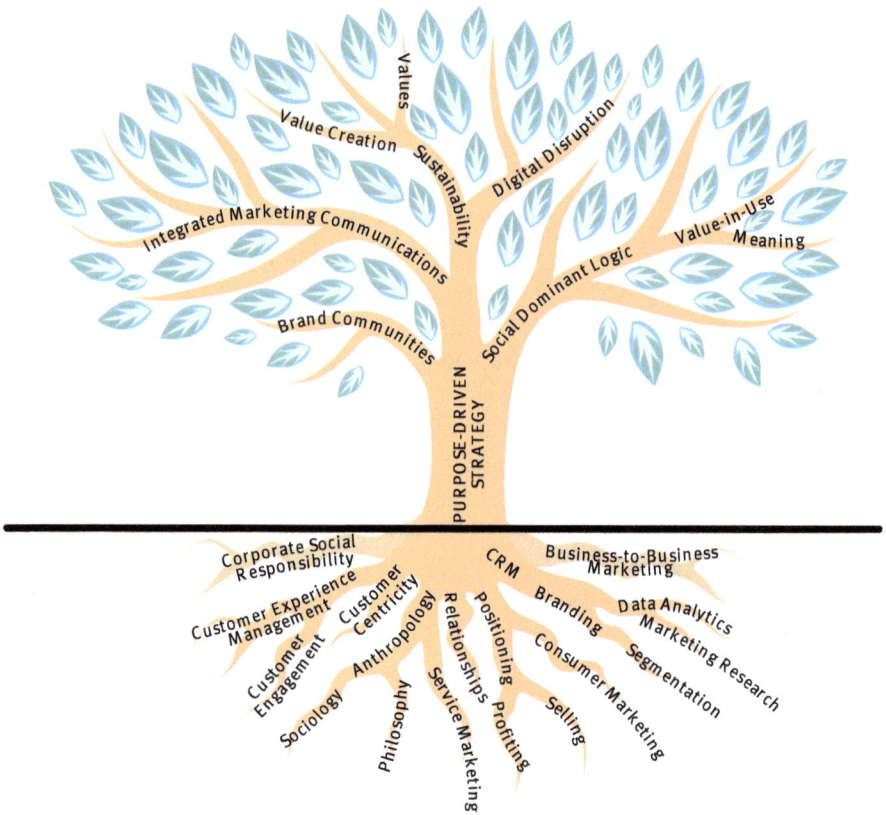

Figure 2.1: The Isomorphic Roots of Marketing.
Source: Authors' representation (2022)

We prefer *fusion* as a broader term to describe a melding, a co-existence. The impact (and relevance) of constituencies and institutions and their intermediary function as company-customer conduits is a recurring foundation.

One of the original frameworks for analysing the creation of value – the original 'value chain' (Porter, 1985) – has proved a reliable framework for disaggregating components of product or service and viewing activities as *assets* not just costs. However, criticism of its linearity, its focus on "one end point and one desired outcome for one stakeholder, the shareholder" (Freeman, Philips, & Sisodia, 2018, p. 5) is reflected in the call for adopting an integrated systems approach involving all stakeholders. It's strength is in its theoretical use as a *diagnostic tool*.

However, in reality, its silo, compartmentalised framework does not fully reflect actual organisational process nor customer requirement. It demonstrates a misunderstanding about the integrating role of a service/brand logic which is not merely the add-on after-sales service mentality. Normann & Ramirez (1993) took issue not just with the metaphor but also its root. The metaphor of "constellation" is a more embracing framework than a chain, an industrial-based model far too restrictive: "Successful companies increasingly do not just add value, they *reinvent* it. The key strategic task is to reconfigure roles and relationships among a constellation of actors – suppliers, partners, customers – in order to mobilise the creation of value by new combinations of players" (1993, p. 65).

This new "logic of value" paved the way for those that espoused a unifying service logic by identifying the need to break down the product/service dichotomy and dynamically combining them into activity-based offerings from which customer can create value for themselves. A shared value approach presents a different integrated perspective, with a social dimension essential to the value proposition creating new opportunities for a wider franchise in the value-creating process.

But where does brand strategy come from? Where are its roots?

In New York, 1922, the power of radio was used for the first time to advertise a brand. By 1930, almost 90% of radio stations across the United States were taking branding to an unprecedented level of exposure. Evidence of the new consumer culture was everywhere in Post-World War 2 America, with brands on every billboard, subway, and all types of product packaging. *Bulova Watches* were the first to use TV in 1941 and then, in 1953, came the bright technicolour lights of colour TV and a fuse was lit: branding, culture, and social meaning were inextricably linked.

In the face of saturated, uniform competition, with an abundance of identical product offerings, companies started to develop what we now know as 'brand management'. Creating unique identities for brands from emotive and perceptual imagery became the norm and the socio-psychological axis of branding started to take root. Technological advances in media carrying brand messages continue to drive branding, as we can see from the connected, digitised world of today's brandscapes.

Companies must evolve as customers evolve.

Heding, Knudtzen, & Bjerre (2020, p. 6) provide a useful framework to consider the different approaches that have been used since 1985 onwards:

- *Economic approach:* Based on the exchange logic from microeconomic theory, the principles of embryonic fast-moving consumer goods marketing – targeting audiences with the 'appropriate' marketing mix produces optimal sales – this approach to brand strategy was largely theoretical.
- *Identity approach:* A corporate identity practitioner orientation based on consistent 'sender-to-receiver' B2C communications projecting visual and behavioural identity.
- *Consumer-based approach:* The notion that the brand "resides in the mind of the consumer" embraces externalised strategy formation, and has more of an 'outside-in' perspective than the other two approaches. The decision-making constructs of cognitive psychology, where company stimuli provokes consumer action, has 'processing' as a central element of consumption.

- *Personality approach:* Matching purchasers with brand 'personalities' also reflected a social constructive approach, with strategy being informed by the 'emotional' social science strands of human psychology, sociology, and consumer behaviour. This was a more interactive company-customer proposition, infused with social symbolic value.
- *Relational approach*: The 'lived experience' approach, grounded in the existentialist qualitative constructionist research tradition of phenomenology, implied "a major paradigmatic shift in brand management and can be identified as the one approach leading brand management into the twenty first century" according to Heding, Knudtzen, & Bjerre (2020). It's logic, based on "a brand-consumer exchange as a dyadic and cyclical process", is a human relationship metaphor.
- *Community approach:* Neo-tribes, group affiliation, socially-mediated, culturally-constituted meaning underpins this approach with subculture consumption and the autonomy of brand communities the main premise.
- *Cultural approach:* Here, the brand is subject to macro-level social and cultural change more than the intended organisation's controlled planning, with brand strategy filtered through a cultural lens.
- *Sensory approach:* Set against the rationality of the information processing conceptual framework, this approach infuses the 'experiential' perspective of branding, where the product is an artifact and customers build allegiance through brand experience.

The key takeaway here is that the "implied shift from information to meaning is the underlying premise of brand management" Heding, Knudtzen, & Bjerre (2020, p. 12).

2.3 Philosophy of business

The blueprint of strategy, the underlying fundamental principles – the purpose, mission, goals, objectives, and methods of achieving these – can be described as the organisation's *philosophy*. How organisations view strategy and how their stakeholders affect that view is rapidly changing. The prevailing model of *shareholder primacy*, with its emphasis on profit, is being questioned. Former *Unilever* CEO and now co-founder of *Imagine*, (a collective of "courageous alumni CEOs") Paul Polman, describes it as "a failed doctrine that has shown to destroy natural resources and social cohesion",[15] and calls for a longer-term, *multi-stakeholder* model which moves "from corporate social responsibility to responsible social corporations".

---

15 Vivian Hunt, Paul Polman, and Diane Brady, "Stakeholder capitalism: A conversation with Vivian Hunt and Paul Polman", May 6, 2021, | *McKinsey* Podcast.

Despite the obvious advantages of capitalism in a free market economy, there is distrust of its motives and this is reflected in polls such as the reputable *Edelman Trust Barometer*, whose recent survey of over 34,000 indicated 56% believed that "Capitalism was doing more harm than good globally, with majorities in 22 of 28 markets surveyed".[16] Critics will point to the 'hypernormalisation'[17] of capitalism, accepted as the natural state. But that orthodoxy is being challenged on many fronts: the static is contested by the dynamic. Even those companies on the periphery, or those ignoring the trends, risk being competitively disadvantaged and are being drawn into dealing with issues dear to their customers, employees, and wider, evolving stakeholder ecosystem.

This hints at a re-examination of the role of strategy both inside the company and outside in the social environment. The organisation's philosophy is a touchstone for focusing on a company's shared values, relationships, and raison d'etre, as well as helping to formulate how and what is communicated. A fairly constant tenet of corporate strategy philosophy has been the marketing concept aimed at promoting shareholder primacy, but, as we have seen, the application of Freidman's single-focus on owners and investors has been challenged as not being inclusive, too limited in stakeholder scope, responsible for the global recession, even considered immoral, with some accusing executives of an abnegation of responsibility.

There is a contradiction, a tension between what strategy should be. "The illusion of conflict has occurred because many managers have confused maximising shareholder value and maximising *profitability*. The two are completely different. Maximising profitability is short-term and invariably erodes a company's long-term market competitiveness. Strategies aimed at maximising shareholder value are different . . . they punish short-term strategies " (Doyle, 2000, p. 26).

Alternative perspectives which embrace a social framework, compassionate capitalism (Bejou, 2011), greater stakeholder inclusivity, and a broader sense of social and environmental responsibility, are being offered as a better philosophical approach to deploying business strategy. Some (Beschorner, 2013) advocate a "reinventing of capitalism", going further than that outlined by Porter & Kramer (2011, p. 13), claiming the "re-localisation and re-embedding of businesses in society requires companies to engage in a broader spectrum of societal governance" and global cooperation. The language reflected *in situ* should extend beyond the dominant economic discourse of unrestrained consumption (or "mismanagement of desire" as Buddhist opprobrium states), and relentless growth, and develop certain capabilities like asceticism, moral imagination, communication, and sustainable practices (Hartman & Werhane, 2013).

---

16 *Edelman Trust Barometer*, Daniel J. Edelman Holdings, January 19, 2020, *Edelman.com*.
17 The origins of this phrase by Alexei Yurchak, in his book *Everything Was Forever, Until It Was No More: The Last Soviet Generation (2006)* describes the acceptance of the 'norm' and the assumed inability of not being able to change it. It is used in a consumer not political context here.

Instilling a purpose-orientation into a company's raison d'etre should be seen not just as a method of revitalising brands but a way of resetting the strategic compass. The tendency to be drawn to immediate sales not long-term brand building is understandable, but the pressure to realign strategy with lasting purpose is not just coming from the micro environment of customers, stakeholders, and competitors, but the social, ecological, and political macro forces of government, regulation, and investment. Peter Field, drawing from the *IPA Effectiveness Awards Databank*, compared 47 companies who systematically and holistically applied brand purpose principles to 333 companies who didn't.[18] 57% of brand purpose cases were deemed to have performed strongly in terms of key metrics of acquisition of new customers, driving large market growth share, exceptionally strong brand effects such as building distinctiveness, awareness, and differentiation, as well as enhancing brand appeal and reinforcing trust and commitment. He claims its impact can also be seen in "quite powerful B2B and collateral benefits" of supplier, distributor, and investor relationships, elements which, by their very nature, are long-term and long-lasting. Supply chain and employee commitment are essential ingredients. The impact on employee 'buy-in' and satisfaction was reported as being as high as 59%. Physical availability, bespoke in-store presence like retailers who repackage to highlight their support for causes like LGBTQ+, partnerships like *Waitrose*'s farmer initiative, companies promoting target market customer educational programmes, all contribute to solidifying purpose into strategy.

Some academics advocate taking the position of "advocating a service-strategy-based understanding of business models for all of marketing strategy" (Wieland, Hartmann, & Vargo, 2017, p. 925). As the *quality* of business decisions is becoming increasingly critical, it is essential to view decisions in the round, in multiple contexts. One developing phenomenon in strategic decision-making is the application of Tibetan Buddhist principles to business. 'Buddhist Economics',[19] a proposed hybrid business strategy – fusing the best aspects of the competing economic models of capitalism and socialism. The 'Middle Path' – originally suggested by Inoue (1997) – is a 'sustainable' perspective which supports conventional capitalist free market competivity but balanced with support of nature and societal awareness. This balanced view supports the conventional forces of a free market and competition without destroying either nature or human society. His alternate vision of sustainable economics is meant to be more just and more ecologically sound.

This application of Buddhist principles espouses the concept of freedom. However, the Western orientation of upholding the rights of the individual contrasts

---

18 "Criticism of brand purpose is 'naïve and unjustified claims Peter Field". Michaela Jefferson in an interview with Peter Field, *Marketing Week*, 12th October 2021.

19 This phrase originally coined by E. F. Schumacher's in 'Small is Beautiful: Economics as if People Mattered' in 1973.

with the Buddhist freedom from personal desires or attachments. Because it is involved with ethics and global concerns and takes a rational, logical perspective on major issues, Buddhism has been applied to solving strategic business problems. "If we view Buddhist teachings in terms of secular ethics and fundamental human values, then perhaps they too have something to contribute to the business world" (HRH the Dalai Lama & van den Muyzenberg, 2011, p. 4). Set against the World view post-2008, is the notion of an organisation seeing itself as an individual entity *set against* rather than with other organisations: as a competitor not a collaborator. This is referred to in Buddhist belief as "the realisation of interdependence". Another which resonates with a theme of the book is that of hermeneutics: understanding the specific by understanding the general. One more is the principle of 'Right View and Right Conduct'.

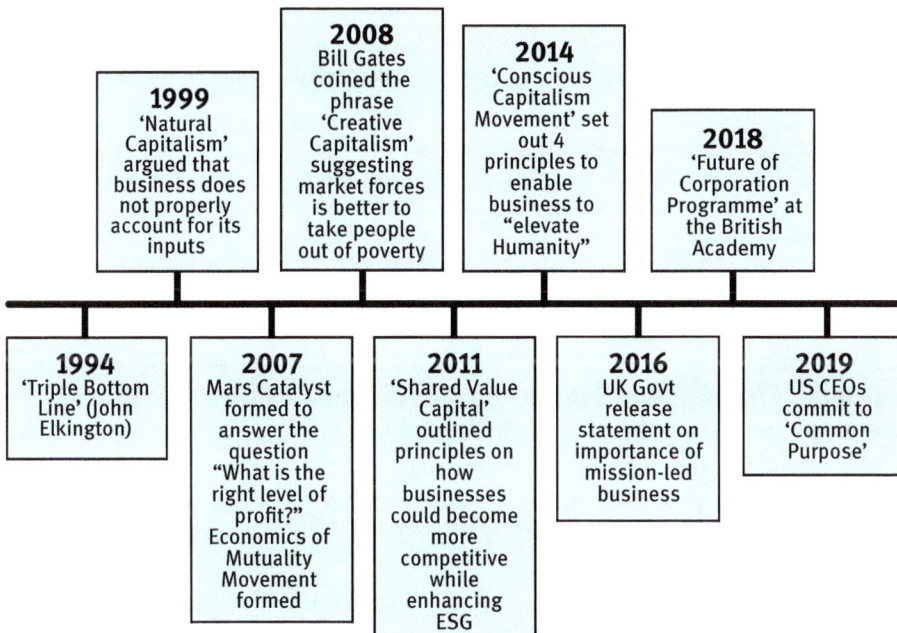

Figure 2.2: Timeline of Business Philosophy.
Source: Regenerate Trust, 2020[20]

In Figure 2.2 we can trace the timeline developments in philosophy of strategy from the start of corporate conscience with CSR to the latest manifestations of purpose-driven strategy and the sources which have driven those iterations of strategic thinking outlined in the companying Table 2.1.

Product purchase is now not just a rational, economic decision-making process, but just as much about what a brand says, what it does, and what it stands for. According to *Edelman's Brand Share Report (2015)*, 87% of consumers around the

Table 2.1: Purpose timeline detail.

1999	P. Hawken, A. Lavins, L. Hunter-Lovins, *Natural Capitalism*
2007	Economics of Mutuality, *Mars Catalyst* (accessed via eom.org/mars-catalyst)
2008	N. Koehn, The Time is Right for Creative Capitalism, *Harvard Business School*, 2008 (accessed via hbswk.hbs.edu/item/the-time-is-right-for-creative-capitalism)
2011	M. Porter & M. Kramer, "Creating Share Value", *Harvard Business Review*, 2011 (accessed via hbr.org/2011/01/the-big-idea-creating-shared-value)
2014	*'consciouscapitalism.com'*, (accessed via www.consciouscapitalism.org)
2016	'On a Mission in the UK Economy', Independent Review for the Department for Digtal, Culture, Media, & Sport, 2016 (accessed via assets.publishing.service.gov.uk/government/ uploads/system/attachment data/file/574694/Advisory Panel Report – Mission-led Business.pdf)
2018	Professor, C. Meyer, "The Future of the Corporation, *The British Academy*, 2018 (accessed via www.thebritishacademy.ac.uk/sites/default/files/Reforming-Business-for-21st-Century-British-Academy.pdf)
2019	Business Roundtable Redefines the Purpose of a Corporation to Promote 'An Economy That Serves All Americans', August 2019 (accessed via www.businessroundtable.org/business-roundtable-redefines-the-purpose-of-a-corporation-to-promote-an-economy-that-serves-all-americans)

Source: *Regenerate Trust* 2020

world want a meaningful relationship with brands, and only 23% believe they have one (Freeman, Spenner, & Bird, 2012). Strategy is moving closer on the *customer-company continuum* and companies have to assess their strategic raison d'etre, why they exist, and how organisational values align with their customers' beliefs.

This we refer to as *purpose*, and it can be a core competitive differentiator, a unifier of company and stakeholders, and provide an organisation with meaning and direction.

A clear purpose is everything to an organisation: it is a platform to build upon and a mirror to reflect its existence to the world; it is an organisation's soul and identity. Added value and authentic values can give companies a competitive advantage. Whilst Drucker's 1954 (p. 39) definition of business purpose as being "to create a customer . . . any business enterprise has two – and only two – basic functions: marketing and innovation" still holds true some 60+ years later, today it has a much broader resonance. The distinction he drew between the prevailing 'selling organisation' paradigm and a market-driven orientation is now extended to embrace organisations which are purpose-driven.

---

20 'What is a Purpose-Driven Business', *Regenerate Trust,* June 2020.

Corporate preoccupation with 'purpose' has outstripped strategic interest in hot button topics such as 'disruption' and 'innovation'. 'Doing well by doing good' may be the new Zeitgeist idea. This chapter relates very much to *Chapter 3 Managing Meaning: Creating Shared Values in Marketing* which discusses how shared social values between company and customer can create a sort of symbolic symbiosis, a mutually negotiated vision and direction. As Stengel says, "A good business is a community with a purpose, and a community is not something to be owned." (2011, p. 10). Purpose describes what a company does to create value and reinforce values. The confluence of value-creation and value-orientation – the new crucible for strategy – reveals an apposite antimetabole: *the purpose of brand management is the management of brand purpose.*

Principles in practice

Consumer adoption and company adaption accelerate changes in strategy

Strategy is contingent on the relevant application of organisational resources to the dynamics of the environment within which a company operates. Anticipating, sensing, responding, and adapting to the complexities of economic, social, and technological disruption determines strategic relevance and conditions company competitiveness. Resilience, agility in volatility, and alignment of strategy present urgent challenges and exciting opportunities for all businesses. Changes to value propositions and new entrants into value chains is the order of the day.

Global disruption has reached epic proportions: the rise of China and India, emerging economies, the proliferation of digital technologies, dramatically changing consumer needs, the Covid-19 pandemic, remote working and customer interaction, the withdrawal from the European Union (EU) by the UK, as well as a plethora of explosive social and political trends, have all had a disruptive and transformative impact on the complexities of most industry sectors across the globe. Adoption rates of new technology have been unprecedented. A global survey of C-Suite executives shows companies have accelerated the rate of digitisation of customer-company interactions, supply chain logistics, and internal operations by three to four years, and the share of digitally-enabled products by up to a staggering seven years.[21]

Digital impact has been varied – sectors with physical products such as manufacturing has been slower; healthcare, pharma, and companies with service-orientation have been most affected – but there is clear evidence that all these factors have caused a tipping point: corporate strategy and digital strategy are becoming one and the same.

One sector perhaps most affected by disruption and transformation has been retail. For the online 'click', offline traditional 'brick', or even the omni-channel 'click and brick' retailers, the effects have been devastating. Brands with in-store reliance have undergone serious losses and, in some cases, closure. Many have desperately turned to approaches based on deploying new online-to-offline (O2O) technologies to try and push traffic flow into store (ie: "click and collect"), but only a few have succeeded. For example, *Boots*, the UK's leading pharmacy-led health and beauty retailer, have compensated for poor high street footfall with enhanced online sales (up 85% from March 2020 to March 2021). An exclusive partnership with international

---

21 *McKinsey* Global Online Survey of 955 C-Suite executives in July 2020.

online food delivery service *Deliveroo* delivering health and beauty products direct to consumer's doors[22] looks likely to be a more permanent strategy.

With lock downs forcing social isolation measures, commercial activity has been driven online – risen by 28% in the US and 25% in the EU year-on-year 2020 – in what has been described as the "new normal". In the UK grocery sector, for example, more than 60% of consumers have shopped online with sales up 11.1% year-on-year in June 2020. According to some, this trend is now "irreversible".[23] In the US, 79% of shoppers went online in 2021.

Contrast how two organisations competing in the UK fast fashion sector have fared: *Boohoo*, an online-only brand founded in 2006 specialising in its own brand clothing range, has benefitted from the trend for online shopping experiences and seen sales rise by 40% during the pandemic; in contrast, *Primark*, a company who has steadfastly refused to change its High Street strategy and sell online, is expected to lose more than £1 billion during the first half of its financial year 2021.

Would *Primark* have achieved better results if it had embraced online retailing? Well *Debenhams* and *Arcadia's Topshop* tried and they failed. *Boohoo* currently sell the old *Debenhams'* brand but will eventually limit their value proposition to their own brand. *ASOS*, already strategically and operationally placed to take advantage of the digitisation of the high street, have absorbed *Topshop, Miss Selfridge*, and *River Island* stores. With their unique 'One-off £10 annual distribution fee/ free return system', they operate similarly to *Boohoo*. *GAP* and *NEXT* have been forced to close UK stores and operate via online and 'click and collect' only. Sustainable success in this sector is partly attributable to the medium-term focus on a specific value proposition, but, according to *Econsultancy's* Parry Malm, companies like *Boohoo* and *ASOS* will have an increasingly negative effect on mid-market 'jack-of-all-trades' retailers because they understand better than most of the changing dynamics of the digitised customer journey.[24]

This is true in other sectors where remote and often automated service provision is changing the nature of the customer-service interface and therefore strategy. Banks and financial institutions have transitioned to remote sales and service teams; education is becoming more 'blended' in philosophy and delivery; telemedicine and remote consultation have supplemented the consultative dynamics of doctors surgeries; and, as we have seen above, online ordering and delivery has become the primary focus of grocery stores. Indirect remote relationships are becoming a hybrid benefit of company efficiency and customer preference.

Engaging with customers online has become the 'new norm' for business, and fused brand experience and service provision much more cohesively and consistently. The rate at which companies have adapted to change and consumers have adopted those changes has fundamentally transformed the nature of brand strategy forever.

22 Emily Hawkins, "*Boots* launches *Deliveroo* partnership from today", City AM News, 24th August 2021.

23 "Impact of COVID-19 pandemic on grocery shopping behaviours", Kantar FMCG for Public Health England, June 2020.

24 Parry Malm, 'Ecommerce Trends in 2021', *Econsultancy*, January 2021.

2.4 Marketing philosophies

The discourses of marketing are *context-specific phenomena*, affected and structured by the social ecosystem of the relationships between embedded empirical practice and theory, expressed through dialogues of extant power and knowledge relations (Foucault, 1980). Normative perspectives are predominantly signified textually in a micro-context presented and represented *horizontally* – knowledge developed through practice – and *vertically* – knowledge developed through hierarchical structures of academic knowledge – (Bernstein, 1999, p. 157).

Often, theory informs practice through discourse. Academics, such as Hackley (2003) and Brown (2005), have criticised the lack of practitioner 'voice', echoing the earlier work of such as Whittington (1996) who urged that academics take seriously not just the *work* but the *talk* of marketing practitioners. There is often fusion of these separate perspectives – the discipline-knowledge from the discipline-control – as it "simultaneously describes and constructs its subject matter . . . . . . and arises in and through unified discourse" (Cochoy, 1998, p. 196). Hackley claims that part of the 'practice-into-theory' challenge, is determining what it is to be "an expert at marketing management and strategic levels of decision making, and how might theory in marketing conceptualise this expertise in such a way as to promote its acquisition" (2001, p. 735).

At the heart of transferring knowledge from context to text to context is the debate about *research-informed practice* and *practice-informed theory*.

"Theory is just the distillation of previous work in a particular field; it enables us to learn from experience" (Hastings, 2008, p. 19). In any examination of the performative nature of marketing – whether marketing theory shapes practice or is merely reflective of it – it is important to take a reflexive, non-partisan perspective. Empirical evidence taken from the marketplace is often reified in theory and then the resulting theory verified in practice. Contextualising the evidence of marketing thought – how the marketing discipline is embedded in the practice of marketing constituencies – and connecting context with explanation enrichens data captured by documenting the personal 'lived-in' experience of practitioners.

Denzin and Lincoln's (2005) claim that " . . . there are no objective observations, only observations socially situated . . . between observer and the observed . . . individuals are seldom able to give full explanations . . . all they can offer are accounts, or stories, about what they did and why . . . " (p. 6) gets to the essence of empirical evidence.

Highlighting the serious dislocation between theory and practice and between academia and practitioner logics, Smith *et al* (2015, p. 1072) refer to the transfer of knowledge from "context to text to context". Practitioners and academics "approach different goals and strive for different metrics" (Piercy, 2015), the different perspectives of "production and consumption of marketing theories are subject to two different technologies and processes that are not always mutually compatible" (Ardley & Quinn, 2014, p. 97).

According to Smith, (2013, p. 1) marketing as examined by academics has sometimes presented a "nomethetic, reductionist, introspective view of the discipline, characterised by a fixation with formula not form, an insider game of abstraction not application". The polarities inherent in the 'theory-practice conundrum' are evidenced in those that claim research can offer managerially useful insights (Elliott & Jankel-Elliott, 2003), and those, like Holbrook (2005) and Cayla and Eckhardt (2008), who claim the principle of research is not primarily directed at practical application.

And yet, as theory often has explicit knowledge not related to the experience of the practitioner, practice often has tacit knowledge which is not expressed as theory. Sometimes. However, marketing is the product of the dynamics of the marketplace as well as the conceptual observations of theory. It is also sometimes a hybrid of the two: a "synthetic and magpie approach" (Sim, van Loom, & Appignanessi, 2004). The "all-consuming clamour for reliance and relevance of theory to practice dictates that the form, function and philosophy of marketing must be co-created in the practical pragmatism of praxis. Praxis is "practice informed by theory and theory informed by practice, a cyclical process of experiential, contextual learning" (Smith, Williams, Lowe, Rod, & Hwang, 2015, p. 1027).

Brand planning often exposes a tactical bias over strategy, of practice over philosophy. Whilst this book pivots on the performative axis of praxis, there is also a strong thread of reflection: thinking about *how* we do branding and *why* we do it. This book attempts to interweave theoretical and practice-based knowledge into the overall narrative of 'fusion', acknowledging their separate perspectives and recognising the synthesis.

2.5 Stakeholders, networks, and value-creating ecosystems

In 1963, at the Stanford Research Institute, the term 'stakeholder' was conceived as a direct counter to the concentrated emphasis on 'stockholder' concerns. It was asserted that strategy should have a broader perspective than what became known as 'shareholder primacy', acknowledging wider problems of complex change and challenge. For some time now there have been apparent tensions evident in the different narratives of strategic management, stakeholder theory, business in general, and ethics (Freeman, Philips, & Sisodia, 2018). For over 50 years, both academics and practitioners have struggled with three interconnected business problems: the problem of understanding how value is created and traded; the problem of connecting ethics and capitalism; and the problem of helping managers think about management such that the first two problems are addressed (Parmar, Freeman, & Harrison, 2010).

Ever since Freeman's seminal work, which describes a view of the organisation in terms of "convergence and expectations that need to be considered and integrated into the firm's strategy" (1984, p. 15), Stakeholder Management (SM) has been the focus of building and developing constituent relationships. Central to the premise is that shareholders and stakeholders are not competing parties but there is equilibrium of objectives with profit maximisation not the sole objective. Engagement with all stakeholders – the various constituencies and interested parties who can help create or destroy an organisation's wealth and health – is a key pillar of strategy.

Stakeholder theory has been intimately connected to the idea of strategy from the earliest days (Freeman, Philips, & Sisodia, 2018, p. 2). Stakeholders are any external or internal groups or individuals who affect, and are affected by, an organisation's intended or actual plans, objectives, strategy, policies, ethics, and are an integral part of the businesses value-creating ecosystem. Branding complexity increases with the diversity of stakeholders' and target customers' needs (Hatch & Shulz, 2003) and their conflicting objectives (Trueman, Klemm, & Giroud, 2004).

There are two main perspectives: improving corporate performance; maximising social welfare and minimising the level of harm incurred in the exchange (Polonksy, Carlson, & Fry, 2003). Managing stakeholders requires a holistic perspective encompassing a *resource-based view (RBV)* (Barney, 1991) – how strategic resources can be exploited to achieve SCA – as well as a *market-based view (MBV)* – market positioning vis à vis its competitors. Stakeholder Theory is about how the value chain of these relationships works, it also focuses on values, how issues such as corporate social responsibility, morals ethics condition a company's mission.

Therefore, the *socio-political view* – the macro societal and political context – has become increasingly important to incorporate into an organisation's strategic purpose and direction. Payne, Ballantyne & Christopher (2005, p. 855) developed the 'Six Markets' model to outline a framework for analysing stakeholder relationships and planning stakeholder strategy – specifically industrial markets – consisting of four inter-related elements: stakeholder value propositions, value delivery design, stakeholder relationship marketing plans, and measurement. These markets are: Internal Market; Referral Markets; Influencer Markets; Recruitment Markets; Supplier and Alliance Markets; and centrally Customer Markets. Their findings suggest that research into the complexity of stakeholder relationships and networks generates valuable new stakeholder knowledge, leading to greater transparency between partners.

Although 'stakeholder theory' has had many iterations (Donaldson & Preston, 1995; Mitchell, Agle, & Wood, 1997; Harrison & Freeman, 1999), we can trace the importance of focusing attention on stakeholders as a key route to achieving objectives back to Edward Freeman's seminal text (2010). A 'stakeholder approach' – through innovativeness, risk management and reputation management – a vital component of overall strategy, is now a theoretical and empirical normative strategic approach. It is now established practice that ethical behaviours can lead to the creation of economic value (Ramakrishna Velamuri, Venkataraman, & Harvey, 2017); a deep understanding of the stakeholder dynamic is critical.

An essential truism (but one that is often not recognised) is that all stakeholders who affect the brand *own* the brand. Customers who consume, complain, influence, and advocate *own the brand*. Employees who create, shape, and maintain, *own the brand*. Intermediaries such as logistics and suppliers who stock, deliver, and service, *own the brand*. They are all essential parts of a brand ecosystem who own the brand and are integral to the value creation of the brand.

The proposition that this is all underpinned by a network of interdependent constituents and companies with shared interests is manifest in conceptual frameworks such as supply chain and customer relationship management, balanced scorecard analyses, and the leveraging of organisational resources such as intangible assets.

Freeman, Philips, & Sisodia get to the nub of the real issue: "It is not shareholder versus stakeholder, but a *narrow/reductionist versus broad/holistic perspective on business*. It is the difference between a value *chain* (linear and singularly focused on financial value) and a value *network* (which includes the importance of shared purpose and values)" (2018, p. 23). Porter & Kramer also recognise this limited strategic scope: "An out-dated approach to value creation has emerged over the last few decades . . . [where companies] continue to view value creation *narrowly*, optimising short-term financial performance in a bubble while missing the most customer needs and ignoring the broader influences that determine long-term success" (2011, p. 11). This chimes with *Harvard Business School's* 'Institute for Strategy & Competitiveness' whose views about strategy as being about how organisations must focus on competition is telling: "Many managers compete to be 'the best', but this is a dangerous mindset that leads to a destructive zero-sum competition that no one can win".[25]

The essence of this new approach to strategy is *engaging* with stakeholders as opposed to *managing* stakeholders.

This produces a *unique* strategy, a product of shared value with economic and societal objectives co-created rather than unilaterally implemented. This is where *purpose* is the new platform for strategy and is where an organisation forges its true identity. John Browne, former *BP* CEO echoes this: "Purpose is who we are and what makes us distinctive. It's what we as a company exist to achieve". Grant Reid, CEO at *Mars Inc.*, states their case forcefully: "For us, profit without purpose isn't meaningful. Equally, purpose without profit isn't possible. Our belief is that business can and should make the world a better place while delivering superior business performance" (Jakub, 2021).

Defining what it is we want to achieve, with clarity, is important. Strategy which is focused is unique, anchored with purpose, has systems of advantage,

---

25 *Institute for Strategy & Competitiveness* established by Michael Porter at *Harvard Business School*.

produce a difference that matters, and builds barriers to imitation. Lisa Hooker, Leader of Industry for Consumer Markets at *Price Waterhouse Cooper* (*PwC*) claims that "Consumer decisions may reinforce the need for change, and their response to specific issues, such as plastic waste, may shape the agenda. But the real, long-term change is being driven by growing pressure from investors, governments, employees, and the media holding organisations to account".

Integrating external relationships with internal resources for mutual benefit is the main method of ensuring continued relevance and demonstrating appropriate responsiveness to its stakeholders. Relevance, authenticity and transparency are strategy pre-requisites. In some companies, the product they sell and the purpose they have are becoming irreversibly interwoven, the two indistinguishable in the company's positioning in the marketplace where the wider stakeholder ecosystem is dictating direction. Phrases like "social justice" and "environmental justice" are starting to be included in a company's reason for existence. Such a company is *Ben & Jerry's*. CEO Matthew McCarthy puts his finger on the button: "You may not know it yet, but if you're not having a positive impact in the world around you, you're already in trouble. Businesses that don't deliberately try to do something good by addressing a specific social or environmental concern in their community, no matter how big or small, are going to find themselves irrelevant in the coming years".[26]

What is needed in developing sustainable *value* is what Jensen (2001) refers to as "enlightened value maximisation", inclusive of stakeholders whose presence in the value-creating process is essential. This 'Enlightened stakeholder theory' can be traced to his observation that "it is obvious that we cannot maximise the long-term value of an organisation if we ignore or mistreat any important constituency" (2001). An early reference to "relational phenomena" and the interrelated dynamic of complementary actors in an industrial context (Axelsson and Easton, 1992). Iacobucci (1996) defines three sociological constructs: competition (goal-oriented); conflict (opponent-centred); and cooperation (joint striving). Interaction is vital; remaining relevant and responsive are outcomes of interaction.

The traditional view of value, predicated on economic principles, is that it is created *by* companies *for* customers to receive through a supply chain of intermediaries for value to be *consumed* (Porter, 1985). However, this static, unidirectional perspective where customers are passive recipients in dyadic exchange has been challenged by those espousing value networks of "many-to-many interactions and relationships" (Gummesson, 2006, p. 339) within value-creating stakeholder networks. Value is created with, by, and for an organisation's stakeholders. Indeed, Parolini (1999) was one of the first to make the link between a network and value proposition.

---

26 Matthew McCarthy in an interview with Jeff Fromm quoted in "The Purpose Series: *Ben & Jerry's* Authentic Purpose", *Forbes Magazine*, 2021.

The customer-company relationship is vital here. Reciprocal value propositions (Ballantyne & Varey, 2006, p. 338) providing a solid basis for sustainability. Normann and Ramirez's (1993, p. 65) 'constellations' metaphor of value being created through "dynamic constellations of activities" involving customers in both production and delivery pointed the way to seeing markets as becoming places "where dialogue among the consumer and the firm, consumer communities and networks of firms can take place" (Prahalad & Ramaswamy, 2004, p. 5). Value is subjective, "phenomenologically determined by the beneficiary" (Vargo & Lusch, 2006, p. 19), very often conditioned by intangibility, and invariably requires a multidimensional value conceptualisation (Williams & Soutar, 2009). Prebensen presents four dimensions of value:

- *Functional value*: perceived quality and performance in relation to cost.
- *Emotional value*: relates to the capacity of the experience to generate well-being, excitement and happiness.
- *Social value*: derived from improved status in a social context and relates to how consumption enhances self-identity and image.
- *Epistemic value*: value from new knowledge that satisfy curiosity or adventure.

An important aspect of value demonstrated here is that it can be created outside service processes, without the input of organisational strategy, based on subjective narratives of individual imagination and the experiences of others (Helkkula, Kelleher, & Pihlström, 2012). As a consequence, subjective experiences can be justified as data and evidence of value in experience. The overall objective is for services-orientation to drive customer acquisition, retention, and loyalty not merely through operational efficiency but customer advocacy (Deloitte, 2013).

In this context, stakeholders can be seen as actors, resource integrators, interdependently but inextricably linked in adapting to and evolving in the dynamics of an ecosystem or 'network', "connected by shared institutional logics and mutual value creation through service exchange" (Vargo & Lusch, 2011, p. 15). Wieland *et al* (2012, p. 13) describe the difference between a system and a network as "in each instance of resource integration, service provision, and value creation, changes the nature of the system to some degree and thus the context for the next iteration and determination of value creation". Implicit in the relationships a firm has with its customers, supply chain, financiers, governmental bodies, household communities, internal managers, workforce, unions, media and so on, is the need to understand how these constituencies interrelate with one another and can help create sustainable competitive (SCA) and viable, mutually beneficial value. Within the networks which create value, there is a convergence of roles, a fusion of service production (and therefore value) as a shared phenomenon where customer and company are "*both* collaborators and competitors in co-creating value and competitors in extracting value" (Prahalad & Ramaswamy, 2004, p. 11).

Collaboration through synergistic brand partners helps develop new networks, protect against disruption, and build brand longevity. Indeed, Quinton queries the "well-established relational perspective of brand management" (Louro & Cunha, 2001, p. 849) that has served its audience well, and questions the lack of relevancy, suggesting that the "community paradigm offers an opportunity for brand managers to change their thinking about the process of managing brands in the digital era" (2013, p. 913). The advent of the Internet not only reorganised the way in which companies collect information, but also redefined stakeholder's expectations (Bonsón & Ratkai, 2013), with new features of innovation and transparency (Meijer & Thaens, 2010) necessitating stakeholders not just as customers but partners and co-creators (Chua, Goh, & Ang, 2012). In doing so, it redefines the stakeholder relationship – the user is no longer just a consumer of content but an active participant in communicating, collaborating, and sharing content – but also the company reputation online.

Consumers' expanded roles make them highly valuable stakeholders in an extended brand ecosystem. They insist on transparency at the corporate level, as well as about the products, services and promises they find meaningful. Even the word 'consumer' has been questioned as being an unsatisfactory description. 'User', 'customer', 'citizen', 'participant', 'community member', 'producer', and even the dreaded 'prosumer' are alternatives which describe the many interpretations of what a consumer is.

Competitive advantage traditionally comes from resource-based leveraging of assets, clever positioning, and high entry barriers. Much of marketing is relational with structured dyads and networks characteristic of market conditions. A new and substantive phenomenon is emerging: the 'new' approach is building ecosystems, value co-created through networks and relationships. Using the collaborative metaphor of 'network', the customer-company fusion has taken on a new dynamic, that of company hub facilitating a community of customers, suppliers, intermediaries, and complementary and collaborative producers. According to Reeves, "70% of the world's largest businesses are now built on digital platforms and involve the coordinated delivery of complex offerings by large numbers of enterprises" (2019). Digital services which are *primary gateways*. Just as the so-called 'GAFA' group (*Google, Apple, Facebook, and Amazon*) are building digital ecosystems consisting of networks of touchpoints, the customer interface mediates the service through multiple service layers.

Value can be lost in a brand as much as is gained. We can see this in Aaker's (1996, p. 7) estimation of brand equity being "a set of assets (and liabilities) linked to a brand's name and symbol that adds (or subtracts from) the value provided by a product or service to a firm and/or that firm's customers". There are some who call for interrogation into the value-*destructive* nature of brands; that is, whether "brands create value, provide value, or reduce value for customers" (Keller & Lehmann, 2006, p. 740). Bertilsson & Rennstam (2017, p. 4) posit a view of branding as "discursive closure and/or hypocrisy", marginalising some aspect of the overall product or presenting a false image of the organisation. Like a reverse-Gestalt projection, distillation of brand essence can be perceived as hiding other negative organisational components. Ashcraft *et al* (2012, p. 467) describe this as brands creating "a reflex rather than reflexive reaction".

Business ecosystems require dynamic and flexible internal structures, different than the traditional product-orientation where value extraction equates to value creation, stability gives way to dynamism, "biological rather than mechanical thinking . . . [with] skills of strategic empathy, collaborative leadership and communication" (Reeves, 2019). He claims that developments are likely to include new models of the 'internet of things' and 'industrial internet of things'; purpose-driven ecosystems aimed at solving major social challenges like elderly care are set to grow rapidly. (A comprehensive case study on the 'marketisation' of later living sector, with an emerging acceptance and demand for integrated retirement communities is presented in *Chapter 11*).

The changing strategic landscapes witnesses migration from competition-based business models to one immersed in ecosystems of connection with stakeholders. Stakeholder relationships are an inherently advantageous opportunity to leverage resources and capability in the attainment of strategic goals, from the outcomes rather than the structure itself. Organisations are tied to other organisations such as OEMs, trade associations, consortia, joint ventures, contractors and sub-contractors, intermediaries, supply chain partners, and so on. The relationships are institutionalised and interdependent parts of the value chain. This is referred to as Corporate Social Capital (CSC), the virtual or intangible resources from stakeholder or social relationships, the "aggregate of the actual or potential resources that are linked to possession of a durable network of more or less institutionalised relationships of mutual acquaintance and recognition" (Bourdieu, 1985, p. 249). When the structure obstructs organisations from achieving goals, that is referred to as 'corporate social liability'. Social Capital Theory (SCT) and Stakeholder Theory (ST) help to explain an organisation's position on CSR, sometimes influenced by other competitive forces more than an individual moral stance: competitive parity or advantage rather than altruism may be the primary motivator. CRM can be essential in sustaining competitive advantage and yet has been seen as a technical rather than marketing concern. Yet 'mutually satisfying exchange relationships' can be seen as leveraging internal resources.

2.6 The role of resources and assets in value creation

As we have seen, what constitutes value and how it can be generated and maintained is of primary importance to organisations. A "proper conception of the basis of the financial value of a company allows for the proper management of it" (2004, p. 22). The *market value* of a company – what people are prepared to pay for it – is not a reflection of investment, but the *consequence* of it. The fixed assets (eg: buildings, factories), those assets that feed the business (eg: raw materials, stock), and liquid assets (eg: investments, cash), all have, quite understandably, a financial orientation. However, it has become established practice to consider (and indeed nurture) other 'hidden' assets:

- The explicit *tradable* value of brands.
- The non-tangible assets of *exclusivity* implicit in trading arrangements and intellectual property.
- The value in customer-company *relationships*.
- The competitive advantage in the *people* element of customer service.

Principles in practice

Consumers are brand champions of the ESG ecosystem

Consider the by-products of manufacturing consumer products and the impact on the environment, and, in turn, on brand strategy. German consumers rejected *Pampers* disposable nappies until *Proctor & Gamble* reformulated production to make them biodegradable. In 2020, Elizabeth Clarke of the *World Wildlife Fund (WWF)* warned companies of the need to accept the devastating impact on forests, species, communities and the global climate caused by Palm Oil manufacture: "Companies need to accept their responsibility to support sustainable palm oil, including taking actions that are bigger, bolder and faster than ever before as part of a pro-environment agenda." The *WWF* has a 'Palm Oil Buyers Scorecard' which examines 173 major retailers, consumer goods manufacturers, and food service companies from the US, Canada, Europe, Australia, Singapore, Indonesia and Malaysia, and their Scorecard has reset the bar for companies with the expectation that they take commensurate, accelerated action in response to the planet's escalating environmental and climate challenges.

Companies on the list range from iconic brands such as *Carrefour, L'Oreal, McDonald's, Nestlé, Tesco,* and *Walmart* among others, but only ten (*Ferrero, Kaufland, L'Oréal, Marks & Spencer, dm-drogerie markt, The Co-operative Group UK, Rewe Group, Mars Inc., Friesland Campina* and *Nestlé*) have shown that they are leading on sustainable palm oil by scoring in the top 10%. *Unilever* have invested over $1bn in their *'Climate and Nature'* fund, recognising that sustainable living, alongside profit, is an acknowledged goal.

Consumers act as champions of brands they believe in, and foils to those they don't. Price, product quality, and customer experience are important (and expected) attributes that customers consider when making their purchase decisions. But they're now staple stakes: expected, but no bonus points awarded. The "creeping commoditisation of categories" (Ries, 2008, p. 11) is forcing companies to look to build their competitive agility in new ways to stand apart. Purpose provides the differentiation that many seek.

"What has changed is that the fastest growing and most successful companies like *Amazon, Google, Uber,* and *WeWork* are explicitly positioning themselves as ecosystem players" (Birkinshaw, 2021). *WeChat*, a Chinese version of the American *Facebook*, didn't follow the advertising model but grew by focusing on lifestyle experience features like 'Moments' and 'Red Packets'. *Alibaba*, a new third party e-commerce site like *Amazon's 'Marketplace'* site, is a company forsaking short-term profits for the long-term potential of building an ecosystem.

More recently, the culture of collaboration is engendered by fusion in the internal/external interface. As Kapferer claims, "There are very few strategic assets available to a company that can provide a long-lasting competitive advantage, and even then the time span of the advantage is getting shorter. Brands are one of them" (2012, p. 1).

The gravitation away from the marketplace to a focus on value-conscious consumers, from transactions to interactions, from exchanges to long-term relationships, has put the notion of value at the centre of strategy, and is therefore of central importance to organisations (Möller, 2006). Examining the complex nature of value-creation at the customer-company interface, has to be done by understanding how individually customers and companies perceive value, as well as looking at what kind of competences can constitute value. In this case, *market*-driven is not quite the same as *customer*-driven, and is not the only method of achieving market success. Organisations that are *value*-driven are customer-driven.

These days, any discussion of complex value-generation processes, has an increasingly prevalent *service logic* influence. Service-influenced marketing organises and creates a customer focus away from value proposition-only thinking and beyond conventional marketing. Or rather, it redefines what the value proposition is. Whilst certain academics have pushed a narrative of a product/service dichotomy, in the real world, practitioners have always deployed the underlying principles of 'service' marketing, and would argue that theory has merely *reified practitioner experience*.

This is reflected in a conceptual analysis by Grönroos & Ravaid (2011) who compare two differing approaches to understanding service perspectives in value creation which reveals direct and indirect marketing implications: Service Logic (SL) and Service-Dominant Logic (SDL). They contend that SDL is *firm*-driven, systemic, the organisation (service provider) driving value creation, and, as such, is not fully service perspective-based. In contrast, they suggest, SL is *customer*-driven, concentrating not on *company* processes but *customer* processes.

Grönroos (2015, p. 15) identifies the key characteristics of *service logic* as:
– The customer being the value *creator* (in value-in-use) in 'customer' and 'joint' spheres.
– The service provider being the value *facilitator* in the 'provider' sphere.
– Co-creation can then take place in a shared or 'joint' sphere.
– If interactions occur in the customer's ecosystem, *social value co-creation* takes place in the customer sphere.

In the early germination of service logic, the interaction of resources to create tangible and intangible value became an underlying principle. Adopting 'operant' and 'operand' terminology from mathematics – where 'operands' are seen as passive objects acted upon – a distinction is made between two types of asset: the hard, tangible, physical assets of *operand* resources; and the soft, intangible, dynamic, human, often cultural *operant* resources.[27] Oper*and* resources (eg: natural resources) are those that are *acted upon*; operand resources like coal, steel, petroleum, oil, or

---

27 The first reference was actually in Constantin, James A., and Robert F. Lusch 1994. 'Understanding Resource Management. Oxford', OH: The Planning Forum.

cotton, need other dynamic resources to bring them to life. The 'operand' emphasis (given a misleading 'goods' orientation) is often seen as profit being derived from the acquisition of resources, converted into the manufacture of 'goods', whose value is obtained from tangible resources, exchanged with the customer as an operand resource (ie: an entity to be targeted, segmented, promoted to etc.) for income. Oper*ant* resources are intangible (eg: human knowledge, skills, expertise, ingenuity), and act on operand (and sometimes other operant) resources to produce effects, transform natural resources, and create value. According to Vargo & Lusch (2008, p. 31), operand resources are those "resources which *require action* to create benefit": one is active; one is passive. Resources can be tacit, and need exposing and made explicit in order to be useful.

This internal perspective is resonant of the Resource Based View (RBV) of marketing strategy that emerged in the 1980s (Wernefelt, 1984) and 1990s (Prahalad & Hamel, 1990; Barney, 1991), and is perhaps the key foundation of marketing strategy – viewing the organisation as a collection of specific resources and core capabilities. Those who advocate this approach suggest that it is more feasible to exploit external opportunities by leveraging internal resources.

Like Service Marketing, resources are *tangible assets* (land, equipment, buildings, capital), and *intangible assets* (brand image, corporate reputation, intellectual property, trademarks). And also like Service Marketing, its essential principle is that there is *heterogeneity* of skills, capabilities, etc. which are unique to the firm, and there is *immobility* of assets which cannot be transferred. As each consumer has individual and therefore unique service demands, resources and capabilities are uniquely different and strategically applied in the customer's context.

It is, however, an 'inside-out' perspective positing that superior customer value and sustainable competitive advantage can be leveraged from the effective deployment of market-facing processes and value propositions aimed at target segments. The RBV view of the firm defines a 'strategic asset' as being valuable, rare, inimitable, and organised to capture value (the VRIO framework). Knowledge Management (KM) is a good example of an operant resource being used as a strategic asset which can be leveraged to create value and competitive advantage. Similarly, Akaka & Vargo argue that "technology can be conceptualised as an operant resource – one that is capable of acting on other resources to create value – and thus becomes a critical resource for value creation" (2013, p. 367).

Increasingly, businesses are seen as systems nested in ecosystems of other systems of supply chains, environment, and customer communities, rather than an aggregate of parts. Wieland, Hartmann, and Vargo (2017, p. 925) take the view that "a service-strategy based understanding of business models should be applied for all marketing strategy", advocating a 'fractal' model of value co-creation. This is a framework which incorporates external and internal constituencies to provide a better structure to improve performance and alignment. Analogously, it echoes a road roundabout (self-leadership and co-ordination with other actors, as opposed to a traffic lights metaphor of 'conform and comply'). Here, the actors are involved in resource integration and service exchange enabled by endogenously generated institutions and institutional arrangements, establishing nested and overlapping service ecosystems of market practices, business models, and technologies which create value.

2.7 Creating shared value and values

The notion of *value* and *values*, both in organisational and societal contexts, is a key focus of contemporary brand strategy. Economic value creation is linked but can often be separated from values: "desirable transitional goals, varying in importance, that serve as guiding principles in people's lives" (Schwartz, 1992, p. 1). Value is both an objective and subjective phenomenon; experience is a cognitive and affective interaction. As Duncan & Moriarty (1998, p. 1) state, "perception is more important than reality" in building brand value. It's a holistic or fragmented process, before, during, or after encounter with the service, and also with elements outside the direct control of the company. The sociological perspective views economic value as "the simulacrum of the meaning of value as intrinsic worth" (Baudrillard, 1994, p. 26), where brands are substituted as modes of meaning rather than individual worth. It is, more often than not, about representation of value, about experiencing subjective phenomena, making brands "economic contracts based on trust" (Salinas, 2009, p. 22)".

Branding helps create identity connectedness which adds a use-value of experience to the object. Generally speaking, brands are symbols which are expressed through rituals, reinforcing, and in some cases changing, cultural values. Some academics have accused Marketing of diluting the meaning of the notion of 'values'. According to Thompson, "it has moved away from the ethical concepts towards lifestyles and aspirational connotations with no tangible deliverables" (2002, p. 355). Smith claims that the "economics-oriented notion of the consumer 'value proposition' has to be supplemented with a more contextually and culturally reflective conceptualisation" (2007, p. 327). "The disembodied person is recast as consumer" (Gabriel & Lang, 2006, p. 20), life worth is replaced by lifetime customer value, and, to take advantage of this, organisations must conceive a strategy which resonates with individual's material, existential and spiritual needs (Jackson, 1999). Grönroos and Voima (2013) distinguish between two types of value co-creation: actual, interactional encounters, and a metaphorical process where consumers and businesses indirectly influence the value creation process. Ballantyne & Varey discuss user interaction with the organisation through processes made of people and technology, the customer being "the arbiter of whatever value is derived from their particular experience of both kinds of service interaction" (2006, p. 335). Resources interact with each other and with the customer aiming at supporting the customer's processes in a value generating way" (Grönroos, 2007, p. 65). It can be defined as the worth of a specific action or object relative to an individual's (or organisation's) needs at a particular point in time, less the costs involved in obtaining those benefits. Firms create value by offering the types of services that customers need, and, in return, receive value from their customers in the form of income streams, lifetime customer value and sustainability. Such transfers of value illustrate one of the most fundamental concepts in marketing: exchange. Sheth & Pavitar (1995, p. 412) describe the evolution of relationship marketing, with its pre-industrial roots, claiming that the hitherto prominent exchange paradigm was insufficient to explain the key element of customer collaboration in the production of value (See Figure 2.3).

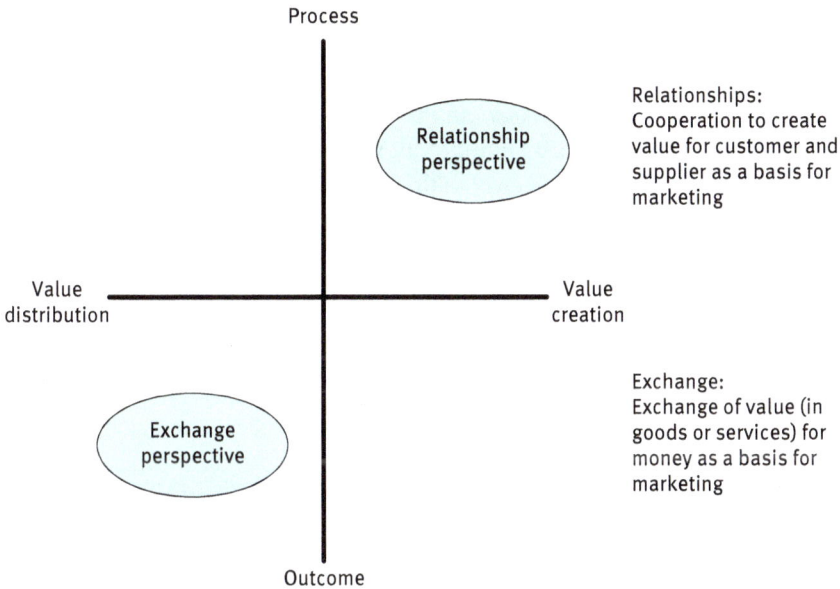

Figure 2.3: The exchange versus the relationship perspectives.
Source: Sheth & Pavitar, 1995, p. 412

It was more focused on the exchange of goods for money, more to do with value distribution than value creation. The premise of the alternative *relationship* paradigm is cooperation, creating mutually beneficial value, more focused on *process* than product, more concerned with *experience* than outcome.

2.8 Inclusive, conscious, and ethical capitalism

Capitalism remains the default operating system for business. It was conceived in the dynamics of 18th century industrialisation and had self-interest not humanity at its core. Haque (2011, p. 10) distils the cornerstones of industrial age capitalism down to: "*value chains* as the means of production; *value propositions* as the means of positioning; *strategy* as the means of competition; *protecting marketplaces* as the means of advantage; and, inertly, *goods* as the means of consumption". Neoliberal capitalism has engulfed all other forms of economy aimed not at sustainability but at creating surplus value; but Adam Smith's altruistic 'invisible hand of capitalism' has been eroded. Despite Mackey's (2014, p. 11) claim that "in the long arc of history, no human creation has had a greater positive impact on more people more rapidly than free-enterprise capitalism", today's businesses are under the microscope like never before. Blamed for society's economic, social, and environmental crises, trust in traditional forms of Capitalism is being eroded. In the midst of a global downturn and crippling pandemic, there is a need for a redefinition of the vision of free market economics and the relationships companies have with their customers. Corporate social responsibility must go beyond a tactical addendum and be an integral part of strategy. Following the financial disaster of 2008, the *Coalition for Inclusive Capitalism* – a US non-profit organisation engaging leaders across business, government, and civil society in their efforts to make capitalism more dynamic, sustainable, and inclusive – has been working towards creating a broad-based prosperity and restoring public trust in the prevailing economic system. Their message is that "firms should account for themselves not just the bottom line". Building shareholder value has been an unchallenged driving force in business for decades now.

However, as companies adjust to the dynamics of the 'Fourth Industrial Revolution', this single-focused objective is now being seriously questioned globally. Marc Benioff, CEO of *Salesforce* originally coined the phrase "inclusive capitalism" embracing human equality, diversity, and cherishing the ecology of the planet.

The "economics of mutuality" (Mayer & Roche, 2021), espoused by Oxford University and Säid Business School, describes how putting purpose into practice can empower organisations. Whilst this has contemporary importance it has resonance with early practice. The *Mars* food company's original objective in 1947 spoke of "promoting a mutuality of service and benefits among (sic) consumers, distributors, competitors, governmental bodies, direct suppliers, and all employees and shareholders" (Jakub, 2021).

Of course, this "inclusive capitalism" or "conscious capitalism" as Mackey & Sisodia (2014) refer to it, runs counter to the beliefs of the economist Milton Freidman and that of 'pure' Capitalism. This 'business with a social conscience' was anathema to one who believed that the social responsibility of business is to increase its profits. He excoriated business leaders without this single focus: "Businessman that take seriously their responsibilities for providing employment, eliminating discrimination, avoiding pollution . . . are preaching pure and unadulterated socialism". With the 'sustainability' agenda gaining more and more traction, the new emerging alternatives – "stakeholder capitalism", "regenerative capitalism", "responsible capitalism" amongst others – are in sync with a single goal of considering all stakeholder interests.

A sustainable brand should integrate issues of the environment, social aspect, and business governance (ESG) factors into strategy and business operations. Stakeholder capitalism means serving customers but it has a broader scope and must consider everyone its actions touch – employees, suppliers, activists, local communities, the environmental context – and is a long-term strategy serving not only shareholders.

Both the *World Economic Forum* (WEF) and The Conference Board have weighed in with their 'Davos Manifesto' and 'Purpose of a Corporation' treatises, with *The World Business Council for Sustainable Development* (WBCSD) focused on "reinventing Capitalism".[28] Speaking at that World economic Forum in Davos, Switzerland, Kofi Annan addressed hundreds of influential business leaders, planting the seeds for the ESG force for sustainability by imploring them to embed environmental, social, and governance values into their corporate strategies and practices: "I propose that you, the business leaders . . . and we the *United Nations* initiate a Global Impact of shared values and principles, which will give a human face to the global market". Today, his legacy as "The Father of the Corporate Sustainability Movement" is manifest in the UN Global Compact, the Principles for Responsible Investing (PRI) launched on the New York Stock Exchange in 2006, and the Sustainable Development Goals (SDGs) adopted in 2015.[29]

Perhaps most intriguing of all is the new *Council for Inclusive Capitalism* with the Vatican, which describes itself as "a movement of the world's business and public sector leaders who are working to build a more inclusive, sustainable and trusted economic system." The *Embankment Project for Inclusive Capital* (EPIC) is a market-led initiative working towards developing a standardised comparable set of metrics measuring long-term value and the effect of business activity on stakeholders including customers, employees, suppliers, communities, and shareholders.

Ignacio Galán, Chairman and CEO of *Iberdrola*, a Spanish multinational electric utility company with subsidiaries including *Scottish Power* and *Avangrid*, describes their strategy as 'Inclusive Capitalism', a more responsible form of capitalism which puts people at the heart of decision-making. Sir Nigel Wilson (2019), Group Chief Executive with financial services company *Legal & General*, echoes this, calling it "a form of capitalism that creatively puts in place what's to make more people beneficiaries of economic growth".

His 10 fundamental principles for making Capitalism more inclusive are:
- *Inclusive Capitalism is patient* and must not focus on short-term results but investment which is accretive and socially useful.
- *Inclusive Capitalism benefits a broad range of people* and must have social value.
- *Inclusive Capitalism creates new initiatives* leading to new assets and new jobs.

---

28 Joel Makower, "Can sustainability save capitalism?", Two Steps Forward, *Greenbiz*, March 30, 2021.
29 George Kell, "In Memory Of Kofi Annan: Father Of The Modern Corporate Sustainability Movement", *Forbes Magazine*, 19th August 2018.

- *Inclusive Capitalism helps solve market or policy failures* tackling social issues as well as profit.
- *Inclusive Capitalism should be politically agnostic* and collaborate without being divisive or populist.
- *Inclusive Capitalism supports environmental, social and governance measures* investing, for example, in initiatives like urban regeneration, affordable housing, clean energy, and the impact on the environment and market behaviours.
- *Inclusive Capitalism strives to use technology for broader benefits.*
- *Inclusive Capitalism requires that we break the cycle of combined educational, financial, and digital exclusion as well as intergenerational inequality.*
- *Inclusive Capitalism need not make a business less sustainable or financially successful* but should make an organisation more relevant to its customers.

Porter & Kramer (2011, p. 64) see an urgent need for Capitalism to "reinvent itself" around the concept of "shared value", convinced that a new approach of combining monetary and societal value creation is needed. Mackey too sees the importance in co-creation of value and meaning through capitalism: "It is unquestionably the greatest system for innovation and social cooperation that has ever existed. The system has afforded billions of us the opportunity to join in the great enterprise of earning our sustenance and finding meaning by creating value for each other" (2014, p. 11).

'Doing good' and 'the business of business' have become existential strategic questions. 'Doing well by doing good' may be the new Zeitgeist. As Kramer (2017) suggests, purpose and profit are intrinsically intertwined: "In the 21st century's societal context, a business cannot generate more revenue without a strong purpose, and in a business context, a good Purpose always generates profit". The adoption in 2016 of *The New Paradigm* by the *International Business Council of the World Economic Forum*, and again in 2020 of the *Davos Manifesto*, embracing the principles of sustainable ESG (environment, social and governance), has evolved into a more inclusive, environmentally responsible, sustainable vision of what a business's business should be. Measuring the effects of 'higher-order purpose' in marketing, brand, and corporate strategy, with ESG data valuing public sentiment about a company's sustainability performance, has seen some increase in valuation premium (Serafim, 2018).

But for those who cite the growing public opprobrium of Marketing – creating unwanted needs, encouraging hedonistic materialism, and failing to provide any moral compass in promoting the ideology of consumption – there are others like O'Shaughnessy and O'Shaughnessy who counter this by claiming that its influence has been "in the role more of facilitator than manufacturer" (2008, p. 207). Some are now arguing that a corporation is not property, corporate governance now stretches way beyond shareholder ownership and encompasses all stakeholder concerns, making an inclusive sustainable framework a fiduciary duty of the organisation.

Enlightened CEOs see themselves as committing to 'servant leadership', constantly living their organisation's purpose.[30]

The framework of *The New Paradigm* conceives of corporate governance as a collaboration among corporations, shareholders, and stakeholders. Over 75% of executives worldwide say they believe in sustainability but often embedding this in business practice is blocked by the lack of clear understanding of what it is. Some define it narrowly with regard to environmental performance: their version of greenhouse gas emissions, energy use, waste management etc. Interestingly, those that take it seriously typically have a more expansive and integrative perspective that links ESG responsibilities into an overall sustainability agenda (sometimes joined under the names of corporate responsibility, social responsibility, and corporate citizenship) (Mirvis, Googins, & Kinnicutt, 2010, p. 316). There are calls for 'circularity' in terms of recycling materials and by-product waste from production processes which leads to sustainability.

At the heart of the discussion is that, in order for an enterprise to be sustainable, it must balance moral purpose with performance, values with value, not to the detriment of profit, not by risking the bottom line, but with commitment to aligning strategy to the broader stakeholder community. Manifestations of this sea change can be seen in corporate mission statements like: "We wish to be an economic, intellectual and social asset in communities where we operate".[31]

In a *Business Roundtable* debate on corporate governance in August 2019 held in Washington, 181 top CEOs redefined the purpose of a corporation advocating a more inclusive economy. The age-old focus on shareholder primacy was to be replaced by a commitment to lead their companies for the benefit of all stakeholders – customers, employees, suppliers, communities, and shareholders. Since its inauguration in 1978, *The Business Roundtable* has periodically issued 'Principles of Corporate Governance' with each document issued since 1997 endorsing the principle of shareholder primacy (ie: that companies exist principally to serve shareholders). Bill McNabb, CEO of *Vanguard*, claimed that "By taking a broader, more complete view of corporate purpose, boards can focus on creating long-term value, better serving everyone – investors, employees, communities, suppliers, and customers". Tricia Griffith, President and CEO of *Progressive Corporation*, stated that "CEOs work to generate profits and return value to shareholders, but the best-run companies do more. They put the customer first and invest in their employees and communities. In the end, it's the most promising way to build long-term value". So too Alex Gorsky, Chairman of the Board and CEO of *Johnson & Johnson:* "This new statement reflects the way corporations can and should operate today . . . improving our society when CEOs are truly committed to meeting the needs of all stakeholders".

---

30 Carol Cone, "What will be your organisation's authentic purpose in 2021?", 2021.
31 *Starbucks.*

The phrase 'conscious capitalism', coined by *Whole Foods* CEO John Mackey, describes a call for a more humane form of sustainable capitalism in which the focus of business is social values not just financial value: "Leaders must re-think why their organisations exist and acknowledge their company's role in the interdependent marketplace" (Mackey & Sisodia, 2014). It has four pillars: spiritually-evolved, self-effacing servant leaders; a conscious culture; a stakeholder orientation; and a higher purpose beyond profit.

The notion that Capitalism is inherently unethical was challenged at the *Davos World Economic Forum* in 2014 (85% living in poverty 200 years ago, only 16% today; life expectancy doubled; individual freedom has bloomed). It is argued that it is not inherently Capitalism but the execution of it by capitalists which is at fault. As an economic model with a 'higher purpose', *Ethical Capitalism* has two essential tenets: creating long-term economic *and* social value; acknowledgement by business in its role as stewards to the full range of its stakeholders. Health Care Products and Services company *Henry Schein Inc.* (recognised twelve times as the 'World's Most Ethical Company') recently launched "Wearing Is Caring" public health campaign under their *'Henry Schein Cares'* platform designed to raise awareness of health care disparity in disadvantaged communities living by the code 'doing well by doing good'.

Being served by wealth not ruled by it is the essence of ethical capitalism. Conceptually, ethical 'capital', a stock to define and refine values that an economy possesses, involves *social investing*, a kind of social entrepreneurship, is an expansion of what the idea of 'capital' is. *Facebook's* problems with privacy can be traced to a lack of ethical capital; *Twitter* express a desire to be seen as "a force for good in the world". Looking at economic systems as a binary, one-dimensional choice between capitalism and socialism doesn't really help. Haque hints at a possible paradigm shift of "economic enlightenment" where a new generation of renegade companies like *Walmart, Nike, Google,* and *Unilever* are "thriving despite the tired orthodoxies of industrial age capitalism . . . radical innovators are vanguards, voyaging past the edge of the drab, lacklustre world of business as usual, exploring a *terra incognita* rich with possibility where peaks of prosperity, built on stronger, thicker, bedrock can be glimpsed".

The *World Economic Forum (WEF) Global Agenda Council on Values* is the "world's foremost multistakeholder and interdisciplinary knowledge network dedicated to promoting innovative thinking to shape a more resilient, inclusive, and sustainable future" has proposed what it calls a "new social covenant" based around human dignity, common good, and stewardship, advocating a more ethical brand of capitalism. This has roots in the 1980s *Brundtland Commission* who defined sustainability as an integration of economic, social, and environmental spheres.

2.9 Branding in context and contexts

This section briefly discusses the contexts not expanded on in depth in the rest of the book, but notice how the roots of purpose, inclusive capitalism, and the synthesis of traditional profit-orientation and social good begin to take influence in forming a newer approach to strategic branding.

According to Simeon (2006, p. 464), "A brand is a consistent group of characters, images, or emotions that consumers recall or experience when they think of a specific symbol, product, service, organisation or location". De Chernatony & McDonald's (2003, p. 25) definition of a brand as "an identifiable product, service, person, or place augmented in such a way that a buyer or user perceives relevant and unique added values which match their needs more closely", like Simeon's, suggests that branding does not only apply to consumer markets.

Some brands originate from domains other than mainstream marketing, such as *Place* branding (conceptualising a specific place as a brand); some apply commercial principles but for non-commercial purposes such as *Social Marketing* (affecting behavioural change to improve health, improve the environment, or contribute to communities).

Place branding

With its emphasis on *place promotion*, place branding has roots in urban policy, informed by geography, sociology, anthropology, and the work of regional economists. Some have argued that this has commodified places or queried whether consumer goods-oriented branding has been appropriately applied. In contrast, the likes of Ashworth & Kavardis (2010) argue that facets of place branding such as identities, image, promotion, or even sense of place, need to be analysed through the lens of branding. They do concede, however, "that the transfer of knowledge to the operational environment of cities has caused difficulties and misalignments which could be attributed to several reasons, all of which are related to the peculiar nature of places as marketable assets" (Ashworth & Kavaratzis, 2010, p. 2). Place branding can be defined as involving a network of interactions and complications – tourism operators and organisations – interrelated stakeholders embedded in a social network of community relationships.

To add to the complexity, variants include:
- *Place of origin branding*: Using the qualities, images, and stereotypes of people living in a place.
- *Nation Branding*: Often consultants to Governments are used to promote Tourism or encourage foreign investment. This is different to 'nation brand' which is an image not necessarily created by nation branding. For example, the publication in a Danish newspaper of cartoons depicting images of Muslim prophet

Mohamed triggered violence and anti-Danish sympathies amongst Muslims around the Globe. This affected attitudes to Denmark.
- *Destination Branding*: The most developed in theory and used in practice has been marketing tourist destinations. The branding of New York as the 'Big Apple' is an example of this.
- *Culture or Entertainment Branding*: Cultural, physical, economic, and social environment of a place.
- *Integrated Place Branding*: Using branding to integrate, guide, and focus place management.
- *Managing Place Reputation*
(Morgan, Pritchard & Pride, 2011).

Place branding is a powerful mediator of culture and communities and makes a country, region, area, or city more competitive and can create goodwill – that is, brand equity. The development of a brand strategy is a pre-requisite for *Destination Marketing Association International* accreditation. A destination brand is an intangible asset with unique attributes. By "tangibilising the intangible" such as experience, word of mouth and reinforcing the image can be achieved (Balakrishnan, 2009).

NFP, charity, and voluntary sector

The voluntary sector is a complex range of different organisations from local community groups to huge philanthropic charities, all affected by social, demographic, economic, technological and wider environmental changes.

As values-led organisations, with a philosophical and practical orientation and motivation, the adoption of branding by charities has gained increasing traction in academic and practitioner literature. With roots in altruism and concerns with the inadequacies of a private sector mentality, branding has become a mainstay of strategy in charities, by far the biggest category in the 'voluntary sector'. Understanding how values are conceptualised in branding is necessary in order to establish whether branding is an appropriate and effective tool in the charity context. In this case, it is the non-negotiability of charity values that differentiate them from commercial organisations (Stride, 2006). Charities fulfil public needs not met by the private sector – poverty relief; the expansion of the educational franchise; concern for the elderly – and focus on building 'social capital' within a civil society. Precursors to place branding are 'strategic image marketing', 'social marketing', and Not-for-profit (NFP) or non-profit marketing.

Not-for-Profit (NFP) or non-profit organisations – social or community groups – have goals which are behavioural rather than financial, emotional and often intangible. Appealing to the growing 'conscience consumption' phenomenon, NFP moves beyond the tangible elements of branding and provides consumers with a 'cause', an

3 Managing meaning: Social-dominant logic

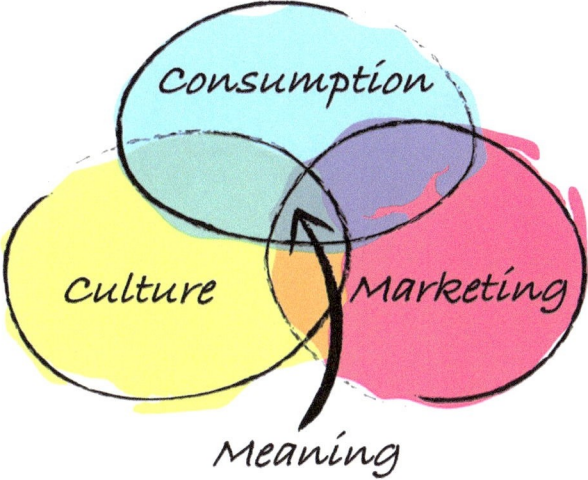

https://doi.org/10.1515/9783110718638-006

opportunity to express self-image and conscious consumption. The range of organisations is broad, all with specific targets and focus. Examples include *The British Heart Foundation, Oxfam, Save The Children, Amnesty International*, the *WWF (World Wildlife Fund for Nature)*, and *Mind* the mental health charity.

Chester Zoo, (one of the extensive case studies featured in this book), was registered as a non-profit making company in 1934 to be run as a charitable educational institution. Its strategic re-positioning as a centre for conservation and science, with its remit stretching into biodiversity, preventing wildlife extinction, and environmental responsibility, illustrates the commitment and scope of a non-profit organisation. The case study examines how the growth of the zoo as an operating charity and the parallel building of brand equity, and illustrates how NFPs are embracing strategic branding as a way of achieving not-for-profit goals and differentiating themselves.

Public sector

The Public Sector is the part of economic life, not in private ownership, that deals with the production, delivery, and allocation of public goods and services at global, national, regional, or local levels through direct administration, public corporations, and partial outsourcing (Serrat, 2010). Marketing as a language of discourse is being increasingly adopted, and corporate branding is an emergent concept deployed. There are four major forms which exist: marketing of products and services; social marketing; policy marketing; and demarketing.

However, when public organisations, such as hospitals, councils, and utilities, engage in corporate branding, a tension emerges between corporate branding's specific demand for uniqueness and differentiation on the one hand, and public institutions' general need for equal services and legitimacy on the other (Sataøen & Wæras, 2013). Nonetheless, marketing in the Public Sector and in public-private partnerships can lead to satisfied citizens and employees, and to a better perception of assumed risks of efficiency and responsiveness to public service (Grigorescu, 2006). Local councils and governmental QUANGOs develop marketing and branding campaigns in order to attract investors in the privatisation process, encourage energy conservation and environmental protection, combating smoking and heavy drinking, and traffic legislation compliance.

Social marketing

The traditional scope of marketing philosophy and conception, with its profit orientation of shareholder primacy, has been expanded beyond the limits of product and service value propositions to affect societal welfare and social value. Whilst there are differences in perspective between commercial, critical, and social marketing, there is a symbiotic relationship of purpose (Hastings & Saren, 2003) that is, affecting consumer behaviour. Governments across the globe have developed interventions through marketing for social and health challenges such as anti-smoking, crime, diseases like HIV, obesity, drug and alcohol abuse, climate change, and even engagement with the political process itself. Kotler and Saltzman's (1971) original founding definition is partly reflected in Kotler & Lee (2008) elaboration: "Social marketing is a process that applies marketing principles and techniques to create, communicate, and deliver value in order to influence target audience behaviours that benefit society as well as the target audiences".

Social marketing adapts commercial principles, recognising the applicability of exchange theory and relational-driven strategies, but also acknowleding the growing influence of environmental concerns and societal impacts, directing objectives towards influencing consumer behaviour for social good. Bridging the domains of commercial and social sectors gives social marketing a unique hybrid positioning. A sub-set of marketing thought which merges the critical marketing and social marketing paradigms is 'Critical Social Marketing'. Whilst there is definable, discrete theory, there is a cluster offering a framework for behaviour change (Stead & Gordon, 2009, p. 83). Defined as "research from a marketing perspective on the impact commercial marketing has upon society, to build the evidence base, inform upstream efforts such as advocacy, policy and regulation, and inform the development of downstream marketing interventions" (Gordon, 2011, p. 89), this approach is useful for analysis in a real-world context. This societal orientation has also greatly impacted on previously profit-only organisations. For companies created in the Industry 4.0 age, "societal impact has been woven throughout the fabric of their organisations from day one. But even more established organisations are starting to take their impact on wider society more seriously" (Deloitte, 2020, p. 1). Gordon refines this as also "critically analysing social marketing theories, concepts, discourses and practice, to generate critique, conflict and change that facilitates social good" (2018, p. 86), asserting that this approach adopts a more ethical, inclusive, reflexive, emancipatory social justice agenda.

Szablewska and Kubacki (2019) advocate a human rights orientation to achieving social good in social marketing. Indeed, a broader perspective – embracing gender politics, stigma, and gender equality (Gurrrieri, Cherrier, & Previte, 2013); non-Western representation (Badejo, Rundle-Thiele, & Kubacki, 2019); and power (Brace-Govan, 2015) – evidences a nascent marketing paradigm. Other threads in this area are ethics and morals, human rights, unintended consequences, divergences across social marketing paradigms, reflexivity, how behaviour and social change is shaped, and the use of interpretive and participatory methods. Ironically, this social ecology is a critical marketing orientation has received criticism for being neo-liberal, positivist, and lacking critical introspection,

The movement by organisations to transform their philosophy and practice to embrace a broader social purpose has its roots in the soul of social marketing, NFP, and the charity sector where goals of merely profiting the brand have been supplanted by a more holistic perspective of benefitting society as a whole.

Principles in practice

Is there life after profit on *Mars*?

Any shareholder questioning the *right* level of profit his company should make would ordinarily be accused of living on another planet. The goal of any business is surely to maximise profit? But when John Mars (son of Forrest), a family shareholder in *Mars Inc*, the global food and beverage company founded in 1911, posed the question "What should be the right level of profit for *Mars*?" to then *Mars* CEO Paul Michaels and CFO Olivier Goudet in late 2006, it didn't provoke ridicule but healthy debate.

John Mars had worries about the company value *and* values. Extracting too much profit from *Mars'* partners in the value chain (in order to ensure continued growth and satisfy shareholder dividends) would create a chain effect of squeezing margins and ultimately cause a dangerous disadvantage of disequilibrium. His comment to the *Mars* Science Advisory Council suggested a broader concern: "If you take care of the left [downstream] part of the value chain [growers, processors etc.], it will take care of the right [upstream] part of the value chain [manufacturers, distributors, consumers]."[32] This question was consistent with the company's 'mutuality principle', the remit of the internal 'think tank' *Catalyst* established to challenge orthodox business thinking.

Driven by the premise that 'businesses can only manage what they measure', *Catalyst* addressed the notion of "right level of profit", and, pointedly, what the value of a business was 'beyond just monetary profits'. The notion of a "mutual P&L" – non-monetised forms of capital for people (human and social capital) and planet (natural capital) is still an on-going goal of the organisation. Doing things the right way from a moralistic point of view is also good for business. As Jakub (2021) writes, these were the roots of the "mutuality of service and benefits for all stakeholders" which spawned the Economics of Mutuality (EoM) programme launched by *Catalyst* in 2007.

Although very much a secular organisation, the socially-oriented influence of a group of American and British family-owned confectionery firms (of which 7 were owned by practising Quakers), his time learning the chocolate business in the UK, as well as his exposure to the 'mutual' and cooperative' movement in the UK, imbued Forrest Mars with personal ethics and business values which have informed his organisation ever since. The best of these – *Cadbury's* and *Rowntree's* – had honesty, paternalism, and ethics as their core values, 'drinking' chocolate, for example, being originally developed as an alternative to alcohol (seen as one of the causes of poverty and deprivation). An obvious extension of this is manifest in The *Joseph Rowntree Charitable Trust* which supports peace and security, rights and justice, power and accountability, and sustainability.

Economics of Mutuality (EoM) morphed from a peripheral project into a central strategic programme. One of *Mars* External Peer Review panel described in 2013 its maturation into a powerful force for good:

"In electing the EoM Programme, *Mars* is positioning itself for leadership in the new scientific revolution focused on business and economics. The ground-breaking work started by the *Catalyst* organisation has the potential for creating an enduring legacy of corporate shared value nested within an environment of competitive advantage".[33]

---

32 John Mars comments in conversation about his 2006 'right level of profit' question with Frank Akers, chairman, *Mars Science Advisory Council*, 2012.
33 MarsEconomicsofMutuality/Principles-inActionMetricsExternalPeerReview Summary report, internal *Mars* document delivered by Frank Akers, July 2013.

2.10 The balanced scorecard

Before knowing what direction to take, businesses must constantly monitor and measure their position in terms of objectives, achievements, competition, and customer expectation. One of the essential truisms of strategy is that "What you measure is what you get" (Kaplan & Norton (1992). However, measurement cannot just be about assessing retrospectively but must also be about informing future strategy. As Nair (2004, p. 20) succinctly puts it: "The true fallacy of measurement is that it is not an end but a means to a *new beginning*. Measurement is the driver of the next direction, not just a document of today's position. From measurement comes the rudder of management, and from this rudder comes direction".

One such framework of measurement is the Balanced Scorecard (BSC), devised by Kaplan & Norton (1992) to identify and formalise the main financial and non-financial drivers – the most important KPIs of an organisation's strategy. Indeed, they claim that "A good balanced scorecard should tell the story of your strategy". It's strength is putting "strategy and vision, not control, at the centre" (1992, p. 79). Their work was originally intended as a "strategy map" with objectives categorised into the following:

– *Financial*: The shareholder's perception and interpretation of growth, profitability, and risk.
– *Customer:* The customer's perception and interpretation of value creation and differentiation.
– *Internal business processes*: The strategic priorities for business processes that create the above (ie: customer and shareholder satisfaction).
– *Learning and growth:* The priorities in creating the organisational climate that supports change, innovation, and growth.

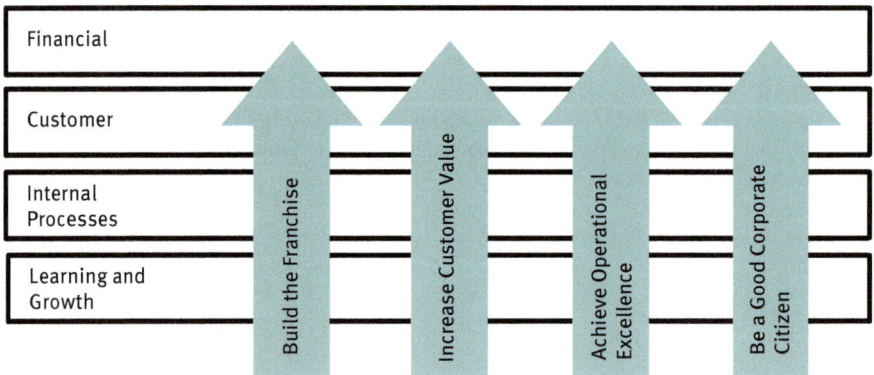

Figure 2.4: Balanced Scorecard: the architecture of strategy.
Source: Kaplan & Norton (2001)

As you can see in Figure 2.4 the four strategic themes provide a 'pillar' for the strategy structure which cross financial, customer, internal processes, learning and growth goals (the horizontal lines), represent those original four *measurement* categories which must be evaluated in parallel. In a later iteration, Kaplan & Norton (2001) describe how strategic themes provide a way to segment strategy into several categories of *objective action*:

- *Build the franchise*: the long wave of value creation – developing new products and services and penetrating new market segments.
- *Increase customer value*: expand, deepen, or re-define relatonships witht existing customers (eg: cross-sell, transform unprofitable customers).
- *Achieve operational excellence*: Productivity and supply chain management, the management of asset utilisation.
- *Be a good corporate citizen*: manage relationships with external stakeholders.

This is a useful strategic performance tool that integrates internal service systems and processes with customer needs and expectations. Its strength is in the vital customer-company interface because "it articulates the links between leading inputs (human and physical), processes, and lagging outcomes, and focuses on the importance of managing these components to achieve the organisation's strategic priorities" (Abernethy, Horne, Lillis, Malina, & Selto, 2005, p. 136).

This framework has been widely adopted and adapted in every sector, each based on the same premises of: objectives, targets, and initiatives being derived from measurement; a management system that creates focus, alignment, and leadership. These four perspectives are linked in a chain of cause and effect: measurements of process and learning are *drivers*; customer and financial measures are *outcomes*. It explains the circularity of strategy. It is not about strategy per se; it is about measurement and strategy execution – how strategy can be turned into action and the role intangible assets play in creating value-creating results. Financial measurements alone cannot capture the value-creating activities from an organisation's intangible assets such as skills, competencies, technologies, customer loyalty, relationships, and so on. It's about progression from monitoring to measurement, measurement to management, and from management to direction setting.

Critics have queried whether the use of BSC was a result of new and convincing theory or persuasive rhetoric, but there are some fairly well established reasons for its use:

- A comprehensive tool for understanding gaps in customer expectation and service delivery.
- Provides logic for focusing on intangible assets and intellectual capital which was more difficult under the traditional finance-oriented approach.
- Identify non-financial initiatives which affect business growth areas.
- Enables employees to understand and operationalise strategy.
- Facilitates continuous performance review.

The original framework was not meant to be fixed; adaptability reinforces its applicability. The impetus in digitalisation is still buyer behaviour; the support of fulfilling that demand is still brand-oriented services marketing. Efficiency metrics (eg: complaint reconciliation, average time per call, employee call rates), are important, but are these sufficient in measuring customer loyalty, end-to-end experience, relationship building, even individual agent's ability to make emotional connections? Accurate analyses of performance such as Net Promoter Score (NPS) and Customer Lifetime Value (CLV) must be part of the new Balanced Scorecard in order to balance company efficiencies with quality customer experience. Strategic objectives and performance measures such as financial, customer, learning and growth, internal processes, social responsibility, environmental concerns, and performance measures are derived from the organisation's purpose, vision, and strategy. Figure 2.5 sets the Balanced Scorecard in a wider strategic context where purpose, competencies, values, and mission frames measurement-orientation into a forward-facing strategic framework.

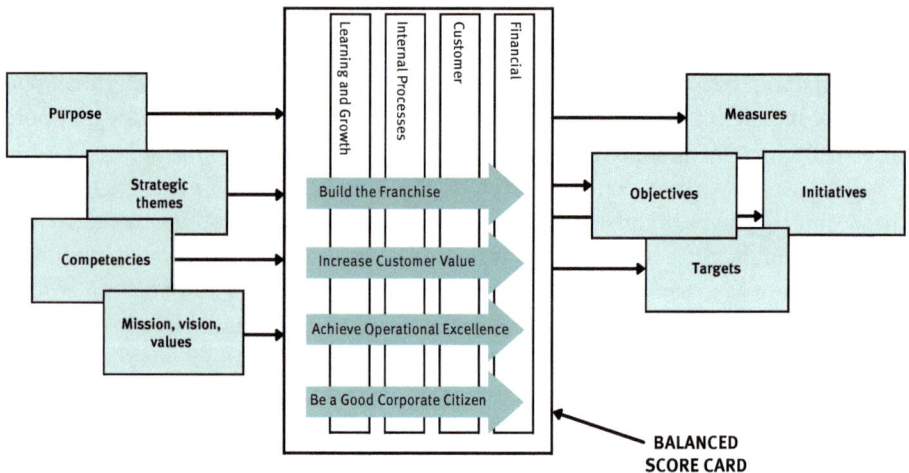

Figure 2.5: The Balanced Scorecard in a wider strategic context.
Source: Authors' representation (2022) Developed from Kaplan & Norton (2001)

Organisations who produce a 'balanced scorecard' of Triple Bottom Line (TBL) are taking into account the full cost of being involved in *doing business*. As the adage goes, "What you measure is what you get because what you measure is what you are likely to pay attention to". Purpose can reduce or eliminate waste within the brand communications ecosystem as well as operationally. Purpose-led brands co-create solutions in collaboration with their customers, and in relationships with other organisations of similar values.

2.11 Purpose, trust, and branding the organisation

Customer confidence in companies has been a pre-requisite for sustainable, profitable relationships. The need for companies to differentiate themselves is considered, both in theory and in practice, to be one of the main functions of corporate branding (Antorini & Schultz, 2005). In some respects, organisations are looking beyond strategy in its traditional sense to a paradigm that is evolving beyond profit. We are seeing growing importance placed by customers on aspects such as purpose, ethics, and a human-centric agenda. Balmer defines corporate identity as relating to "an entity's raison d'être, organisational type, ethos, activities, outputs in terms of products and services, quality standards, geographic scope and (2013, p. 723) so on". Consumers are increasingly aware of the relationship they have with brands: they are cause-conscious, demand better service, and create user-generated content to promote or attack an organisation's reputation.

Differentiation through trust, expressions of values, and ethical credentials are increasingly seen as essential ingredients of the customer-company relationship. Although trust in business is returning from its lowest point since the global financial crisis of 2007–2008 – considered by some economists as the most serious crisis since the Great Depression of the 1930s – business is still seen as "a *consumer* of trust rather than a *generator* of trust" (Hollensbe, Wookey, Hickey, George, & Nichols, 2014, p. 1227).

There is a balance in terms of leadership initiative and stakeholder complicity in strategy. Although the likes of Thorpe & Morgan (2007) – who compare three groups of strategy implementation types (change, collaborative, and cultural) – advocate a 'top-down' approach, a partnership strategy is essential. Companies, therefore, who show leadership and devise strategies which are as much about probity as profit, as much focused on values as on value, can benefit from increased loyalty, brand longevity, consistency, and relevance.

For example, the unprecedented economic and social impacts of the COVID-19 pandemic has put *trust* – the faith in organisations to collect, store, and use ever-expanding digitised information – to the top of the business agenda and one of today's key customer-company interaction currencies. Previously, trust and the bottom line did not have the same correlation, but digital transformation and the impacts of global environmental concerns is radically changing this perspective, with lack of trust beginning to have a quantifiable impact. Consumers with an expanded awareness of 'trust', have forced the scope to be augmented to cover not just security and privacy, but identity, fraud, risk mitigation, and data integrity. Companies that invest in building trust and establishing mutual purpose will have grounds to gain sustainable competitive advantage (SCA).

This has shifted the dial of how an organisation has to operate, the new corporate paradigm focusing on *purpose* which puts stakeholders at the centre of strategy. As Ellsworth puts it: "Infusing strategy and operational goals with a customer-focused purpose helps to align individual motivations and aspirations with the firm's strategic mission and objectives (2002, p. 45). Brands in the fashion sector have responded to high velocity churn of 'fast fashion' consumption by finding creative ways to reuse materials which would ordinarily end up in landfill. *Elvis & Kresse*, for example, use old fire hoses to make handbags. Similarly, Swedish retailer *H&M* recycles returned clothes by re-selling as second hand, converting into new clothes, or made into textile fibres for non-fashion products such as car insulation.

Brand *purpose* does not only originate from company strategy; in a metaphorical sense, it emerges from ongoing exchange between business and society, jointly shaping purposes, rights, and duties (Bhattacharya, Korschun, & Sen, 2009). In a new twist on traditional CSR, Biraghi and Gambetti refer to this as Societal Corporate Branding (SCB) which they define as "the humanistic tension of a company to use the corporate brand as an enabler of social discourses and actions through which the company carries out quasi-governmental interventions in favour of society" (2007, p. 208). Organisations assume the role of "socio-political citizens", engaged in the community, contributing to the common good (Aßländer & Curbach, 2014), embedding it in the brand value proposition and purpose (Biraghi & Gambetti, 2007).

How strategy is aligned with company purpose, value proposition, and competitive positioning is covered extensively later on in *Chapter 4*.

Chapter takeaways

- The focus of brand strategy is simply to make a difference that matters.
- The roots of branding was originally a practical phenomenon.
- Purposeful concepts such as 'creating shared value' (CSV), corporate social responsibility (CSR), stakeholder theory, and ecosystem orchestration are the footprints of a new direction for brand strategy.
- The exchange paradigm is more to do with value distribution than value creation. The premise of the alternative relationship paradigm is cooperation, creating mutually beneficial value, more focused on
- Purpose is as much about the 'know-why' of strategy as the 'know-how'.

- The Balanced Scorecard is a useful strategic performance tool that integrates internal service systems and processes with customer needs and expectations, its strength lying in the vital customer-company interface.
- Branding strategy is about merging diverse elements – business philosophy, cultural interaction, service processes.
- The implied shift from information to meaning is the underlying premise of brand management.
- Organisations are looking beyond strategy in its traditional sense to a paradigm that is evolving beyond profit.

Closing case

© Maksim Shmeljov - stock.adobe.com

Analogue strategy in a digital world.
Trying for just one more *Kodak* moment.

On January 19th, 2012, the mighty *Eastman Kodak Company* stood on the edge of bankruptcy, with an analogue strategy – both actually and metaphorically – in a digital world. At its peak, *Kodak* was one of the top five most valuable brands in the US with 90% of film and 85% of camera sales, with $16bn revenues in 1995 and $2.5bn profits in 1999. It's not that they didn't embrace the digital revolution – their digital camera prototype in 1975 was the first of its kind – but they were blinded by success and their reaction to the rise of disruptive developments like digital cameras and smartphones was myopic. Forced to sell off patents and exit legacy businesses, a much diminished giant re-emerged in 2013 with a different strategic approach to try and capture just one more "*Kodak* moment".

Strategy is often triggered by addressing that heat-seeking question of mission: "What business are we in?" In 1994, the then CEO George Fisher's definition of moving from the "photographic business" to "the picture business" had not worked. Even with investment in new technologies and products running into billions of dollars, the transformation from traditional photography-orientation to a new viable and sustainable digital imaging business had largely failed. Yet even on the day of bankruptcy, new CEO Antonio Perez was adamant: "*Kodak* is taking a significant step toward enabling our enterprise to complete its transformation . . . . We look forward to working with our stakeholders to emerge a lean, world-class imaging and materials science company".[34]

Strategy should be driven by the customer – the problem-solving value proposition to customers – not a focus on manufacturing or product strength. *Kodak's* strategy may have been more successful if, fundamentally, they had asked slightly different questions: "What business

---

34 "*Eastman Kodak Company* and its U.S. Subsidiaries Commence Voluntary Chapter 11 Business Reorganization," Press Release, January 19th, 2012.

are we in **TODAY?**" and "How can we turn our brand strengths into competitive advantage?" Although they actually did acknowledge the trend away from *printing* photographs to *sharing photographs online, Kodak* never made the natural transition from 'chemical film production' to 'imaging' to 'moment sharing'. Having had the foresight in 2001 to purchase *Ofoto* (a photo-sharing site), they missed a basic strategic open goal: instead of rebranding to take advantage of the brand equity in their '*Kodak Moments*' of the "Share Memories, Share Life" platform, they missed the opportunity. Its *EasyShare Gallery* photo sharing site was no match for the forced marriage of *Facebook* and *Instagram*. Their myopia was focusing on their strength in product not in its brand equity. Online sharing was seen as an opportunity to sell more existing printing product not transform from the existing business model. The venture into home printers is another example of this – product not brand-orientation.

Similarly, they demonstrated lack of agility by surrendering competitive advantage to rivals, and failure to adopt and adapt to the emerging disruptive business models. Compare this to *Fuji Photo Film* who emerged from the slipstream in 1980 to explore new product development for adjacent business opportunities (eg: magnetic tape optics, video tape, copiers and office automation in a joint venture with *Xerox*). Yet this was a digital strategy of sorts and had been in place for 22 years when Perez's bold remarks were made: *Photo CD* had been introduced in 1990; its first digital camera the following year; market leader in digital cameras from 2004–2010, third only behind *Canon* and *Sony*; technological leader in megapixel image sensors; global leader in innovative printing kiosks and digital minilabs. But they never recovered the ground lost.

Recently, *Kodak* have been faring better with a sort of 'back to the future' strategy based on leveraging the benefits of the *Kodak* name through a brand licensing business. As Chief Brand Officer (CBO) Dany Atkins says: "The ambition is for people to know and love the *Kodak* brand like they did in the past". While the business is currently 80% focused on commercial print technologies, "*Kodak* had almost forgotten that it was a massive consumer brand" she says. In both B2B and B2C sectors, creating new tech products, in-house digital start-ups, and licensing the brand with a strategy for those products very clearly positioned within the image economy. Acknowledging that the brand is (and has always been) the company's prime asset has finally been accepted.

One of the exciting new digital businesses is *Kodakit*, a wholly-owned separate start-up, a sort of photographer commission hub used by *Uber* and *Deliveroo*, with *Kodak* managing all processes as a sort of creative conduit. Launched in Singapore in 2016, it has had over 40,000 individual jobs with over 400,000 images shared across 35 countries.

The '*Kodak Moment*', almost lost in the past, might come ironically enough from a new generation's passion for analogue nostalgia. *Kodak* were able to leverage their assets and echo the past in a contemporary way. This has presented opportunities such as collaborations in the fashion industry with the likes of US clothing brand *Opening Ceremony*, whose sweatshirt and T-shirt range was inspired by *Kodak's Super 8* film camera a growing lucrative sector for *Kodak*. In addition, fast fashion retailer *Forever 21*, whose range of T-shirts, hoodies, and retro 90s 'bum bags' was inspired by *Kodak's* sponsorship of *Nascar* in the 1990s. 'Owned' and 'earned' media were integral components of the IMC campaign strategy, with 5 major photographic influencers given the range and instant print cameras to shoot the campaign. Independent media evaluation estimated that this was worth $5.8m in terms of 'reach' achieved. A tie-up with *Selfridges,* whose skate bowl event was used to launch its new menswear department, has helped forge connections with the skateboard community. Riders shot on *Super 8* film, wearing *Girl Skateboard Co* clothing, with fans getting engagement opportunities with the professional riders, was *Kodak's* most successful social content campaign so far. Extending inclusivity is the essence of the new strategy; expanding their *Instagram* followers by 350,000 in four years is phenomenal for a 130 year-old brand. Authenticity scores highly with this group and it is evidence of *Kodak* leading the conversation instead of following others and leveraging brand assets without being accused of irrelevant heritage associations. Other platforms such as *YouTube* are being targeted for deeper penetration to this sector. A video from London-based rock band Khartoum has been shot on *Super 8* film.

Could this new strategy of entrepreneurial initiatives, cool collaborations, and most importantly, leveraging the brand equity in the *Kodak* name provide the '*Kodak Moment*' the brand has been searching for? We'll have to see what develops!

Questions
1. If Kodak had such market dominance and a bank of brand equity, why wasn't this enough to secure their survival?
2. Do you think the new strategy of brand image and film imaging are compatible?
3. Has the new strategy emerged out of competitive pressure, the need to survive, or genuine creative thinking?

Note: The photo(s) used in this case study is/are not connected and/or does not represent any brand(s) mentioned. It/they is/are used to make a visual discussion point by the authors.

Opening case

© Uuganbayar - stock.adobe.com.

You've Come A Long Way Baby.
Because You're Worth It. Period.

Brands and consumers sometimes exist in symbolic symbiotic relationships. Mutual meaning-making can transcend mundane purchase decision-making. But how does cosmetics become a cause, make-up become a mission? Why does a catchy tagline about femininity morph into purpose statements about feminism and challenging patriarchal myths? "Because You're Worth It!" Period.

Using female bodies as a way to sell product is a contentious old cliché in advertising. Now, using female issues in campaigns as expressions of control and ownership, of emancipation and empowerment, is applauded. Or is 'femvertising'[35] (eg: social media 'hashtag feminism' using empowerment to connect with female audiences) just cynical surfing on the currents of social dynamic forces? Anti-sexist narratives are replacing 'selling sex' tropes, and the gender agenda in all its iterations is forcing companies to look at the way brands are positioned as well as empowering women to look at themselves as people not advertising images. The driving force for meaning, and therefore the thrust of brand strategy, is very much a *socially* constructed phenomenon.

Since its inception in 1971 by a female copywriter in an American ad agency, *L'Oréal*'s campaign strapline "Because You're Worth It" has not only positioned their brand as deserved hedonistic indulgence, but also as a unifying expression of self-worth and ambition for millions of women. The irony of *Unilever* originally selling 'beauty' in the form of soap bars emerging as a direct challenger to those stereotypical *L'Oréal* images of women in their ground-breaking purpose-led *Dove* "Campaign For Real Beauty" is not lost, but both portray the same hallmarks: *stand with your customers to stand out from your competitors*. Based on real conversations with

---

35 Nosheen Iqbal, "Femvertising: how brands are selling #empowerment to women", *The Guardian*, October 12, 2015.

real women, *Dove* urged the challenging of conventions of 'beauty', asking women to comment on media model images as being "Fat or Fab?", "Wrinkled or Wonderful?" This touched a nerve of deep-rooted insecurities and self-esteem issues amongst younger women and showed *Dove* to be empathetic and authentic. It gave the company a $4 billion boost in sales and women a rich, relevant omni-channel experience and a voice in reaffirming peer-to-peer (C2C) conversations. What *L'Oréal* achieved in speaking to culturally diverse women, *Dove* expanded upon such as their social media project #ShowUs featuring over 5,000 images of women in 39 countries which focused on under-represented groups such as Black, Asian, handicapped, pansexual, and elderly women. A partnership in 2022 with *UNICEF* helping 10 million Brazilian, Indian, and Indonesian women gain 'body confidence' and self-esteem is further evidence of this becoming an essential part of their purpose.

This sort of brand positioning which directly appeals to target audiences is a well-trodden path. *Eve*, a cigarette with feminine appeal and biblical connotions, followed in the footsteps of *Virginia Slims*, the progenitor gender brand which broke barriers in the early 60s. "You've Come A Long Way Baby", a powerful challenge to men's patriachal perception of women, a clarion call dressed up in brand usage. Connecting with women through authenticity and empathy is also part of *P&G's* global brand strategy. For over 35 years, their *Always* 'feminine care' brand has taken the dialogue into areas often considered taboo in conventional male-dominated advertising. In 2014, bringing "puberty and confidence education" to 18 million adolescent girls in the "#LIKEAGIRL" campaign[36] has turned a simple phrase into a powerful movement (90 million views and 12 billion impressions worldwide). Reappropriating the phrase "like a girl" from an insult to a compliment, *Always* expanded this under the theme of "Unstoppable", encouraging girls to "smash limitations" of gender misconceptions. *P&G* surveyed over 1400 16–24 year old girls in the UK and over 1800 in America as part of their "Always Confidence and Puberty". This socially-conscious purpose strategy has been taken to another level with *Always*-branded content hosted on the *TED-Ed* educational platform, changing the communications strategy from issue awareness to target audience education, and changing the image of the *Always* brand by imbuing it with a purpose.[37]

Another company breaking social taboos and building sustainable brand strategy is *Essity*, whose *Libresse* (*Body Form* in the UK) range has a very specific brand purpose: "Breaking taboos that hold women back". With their award-winning #BloodNormal campaign of 2017, their mission is to go beyond normalising periods and give exposure to broader women's health issues. In 2020, they tackled head on the social norm of discouraging women to talk openly about female personal health issues – the 'V-Zone unspoken' truths of women's physical experiences such as infertility, first periods, vulvas, wombs, the joy and pain of birth, menopause, and endometriosis – by focusing on these and other societal stigma in their "Womb Stories" campaign of 2020. Research showing 44% of women felt "staying silent" damaged their mental health informed the campaign which generated 1.1m views and 55k likes on *Instagram* and 3.4m likes on *Twitter*. This isn't just making a stand with your customers to stand out from your competitors, this can affect real social change.

Contrast this with *L'Oréal's* 2021 "Create the Beauty That Moves The World" campaign claims that beauty "stands for all people around the world, considers nature as its future, a force that moves us, tries to be as diverse, fights climate change, and gives people confidence in who they are and who they want to be". Social meaning is the driving force but it is presented with,

---

36 *Proctor & Gamble (P&G)*, "Like A Girl" Campaign, P&G website, 2020–2021.
37 Seb Joseph, "After redefining what it means to be #LikeAGirl, *P&G*'s Always shows how girls are 'unstoppable'", *The Drum*, 8th July 2015.

yet again, an over-glamourised version of 'beauty'. It might not get as many complaints as the *Libresse/Bodyform* #BloodNormal campaign, but "you break taboos without triggering visceral negativity. Otherwise, it wouldn't be a taboo."[38]

This fundamentally addresses the core of brand (and indeed company) purpose being socially driven. Testimony to this in the words of Jen Noon, the architect of the campaign:

> We are going through times where purpose is an important driver for purchase consideration. Amongst today's consumers 63% prefer to purchase from purpose-driven brands and 81% of millennials expect declarations of their corporate citizenship.[39]

Not only did the campaign receive acknowledgement in the form of a *Marketing Society Award* in 2018, the *Essity* marketing team managed to "galvanise their entire company to think and act more boldly than it could ever have imagined doing in order to bring to life its purpose and make a meaningful difference to its consumers: Women". Their brand platform, rooted in social salience and the values of its customers is "Live Fearless", surely an objective for all purpose-led brand strategies?

Questions
1. Is the driving force of the 'gender agenda' evidence of social forces reflected in branding strategies or are companies jumping on a feminist bandwagon selling young girls empowerment for short-term, tactical gain?
2. *Dove's* 'social purpose' success with challenging traditional stereotypes was seen as contradictory to the brand positioning of another of *Unilever's* products *Axe*, a range of male grooming products which used sexist images in its advertising. How were these two positions reconciled?
3. Are the cases quoted above examples of purpose-driven brands or the commercialisation of existing social phenomena?

Note: The photo(s) used in this case study is/are not connected and/or does not represent any brand(s) mentioned. It/they is/are used to make a visual discussion point by the authors.

3.1 Outline of chapter

Meaning in marketing has become increasingly a focal point for research, teaching, practice, and not least of all consumption. Strategically and sociologically, *the meaning of marketing is the marketing of meaning*. Economic exchange does not take place in a vacuum: it happens within a social context and other social structures are closely interwoven (Granovetter, 1985). Other values other than mere economic transactions are exchanged; there has been a shift in the way value is measured – from shareholder to social value. To reiterate one of our opening statements: there is no brand purpose if

---

38 https://www.bodyform.co.uk/our-world/our-purpose.
39 Jen Noon, "Libresse: Articulating Brand Purpose", 2020.

there is no brand meaning. The corollary to this is that *there is no meaning without value and values.*

The driving force for meaning, created through shared values, is very much a *socially* constructed phenomenon, acting as a communications conduit between company and customer, between customer and customer, and can bond organisations and stakeholders in symbolic symbiosis. This connecting mechanism has had, variously, branding, service marketing, experiential marketing, and relationship marketing as its energy, with iterations of customer-orientation, customer-focus, customer-centricity, as its goal. And increasingly, goals and energy are becoming more *socially*-driven.

As academics and practitioners, we are always trying to search for the latest paradigm to explain the ever-changing and dynamic phenomenon which we understand as marketing. And yet "marketing manuscripts are often palimpsests bearing the faint hallmark of existing insight and well-established praxis" (Smith, 2020). One such iteration – a parallax perspective rather than paradigm shift – is presented here as the *Social-Dominant Logic,* a natural progression from product, service, customer, and consumer-dominant conceptual perspectives which have attempted to synthesise factors affecting and affected by social meaning.

This chapter demonstrates how sometimes disparate subject areas – such as experiential branding, service marketing, digital technology, relationship marketing, social innovation, dialogical communications, societal marketing, together with the universal language of branding – have the same isomorphic 'social' roots, and are interrelated parts of a holistic synthesis or brand fusion. It identifies the changing role of brand management within the new community paradigm, and examines the increasing use of co-production and social production (Benkler, 2006) by organisations as sources of brand enhancement. The social nature of brand strategy and the importance of the co-creation of meaning and in particular "user generated branding" (Burmann, 2010) as part of a broad community ecosystem is what we will be discussing here.

Learning outcomes

After reading this chapter, you'll be able to:
- Understand how culture and consumption are joined together in creating social meaning and brand purpose.
- Discuss whether the meaning of marketing is the marketing of meaning.
- Evaluate the social and psychological function of branding.
- Analyse how service marketing dynamics underpin the mechanics of brand strategy.
- Critically apply the social-dominant logic of customer-company dynamics.
- Evaluate the role that negotiated meaning has in creating value and brand longevity for companies.

3.2 Introduction

There are periodic revolutions in business that fundamentally affect not just business but customers, employees, investors, economies, societies, and the environment at large (Mayer & Roche, 2021). The impact of the 'Fourth Industrial Revolution' is providing us with more dynamic means of communicating, consuming, socialising, thinking, and connecting people in ways that we couldn't have imagined just a few short years ago. Social forces are driving changes to how companies think about their customers, and this is impacting on brand strategies in every company in every sector. One CMO who claims that social forces are changing customer's attitudes to consumption values and societal considerations, and, in turn, have forced a transformation in her company's brand strategy, is Valérie Hernando-Presse of the Parisian[40] food corporation giant *Danone*: "Social progress is the most dominant trend. The public mood has shifted to more pressing and important social, ethical issues". Deep social listening by *Danone* (analysis of 225 million online conversations with over 33 million messages across all social media platforms) has revealed customer social concerns such as 'Food as medicine', 'planetary health', 'social progress', and 'caring for people in the supply chain' are all extensively expressed through social media. Re-positioning *Danone* as a "manifesto brand", in response to dramatic social changes, has been a tipping point moment, a phenomenon progressively reflected in so many organisations now. Hernando-Presse pinpoints the moment: "The pandemic has, of course, shaken our lives. It has also shaken up our relationship with food, and that led to a breakthrough in conversation from farm to fork to *fight*".[41]

Traditionally, theoretical perspectives of marketing have been viewed through the lens of the rational, market-oriented model, set within the disciplined dynamics of the market: resource maximisation and efficiency; a traditional approach to segmenting markets; and competitive positioning based on user product preference. In some cases, tactical success may actually produce strategic stasis. Maintaining the status quo is often complacent, reinforcing the received view whilst undermining the emergent. Prahalad & Bettis (1986, p. 485) coined the phrase "dominant logic" when linking the solid ground of performance with the uncertainty of diversity. The emerging world of co-creation, collaboration, and complexity presents a different strategic challenge. Changing from a "focus on mechanics to one of dynamics" (Vargo & Lusch, 2004, p. 15) describes a cumulative amalgam of TQM, CRM, CSR, and the overriding framework of service marketing principles. Theoretical marketing has been built on the rational structure of economic science: an American, product-oriented,

---

40 Founded in Barcelona.
41 Manny Pham, "From asking to listening: How Danone is using social insight to stay relevant", *Marketing Week*, July 20, 2021.

consumer goods model. But this has become a restrictive cage with little acknowledgement of the intangible, dialogic, relational, or co-productive nature of how marketing is enacted, and with service, environmental, non-profit, and *social* iterations challenging its basic premise and applicability.

However, an important part of managing brand strategy is managing the meaning created between company and customer. Consumers, companies, products, services, stakeholders, and brands, all exist in a social ecosystem, increasingly mediated through digital platforms, with meaning socially constructed. But whilst value creation involves shared *value* – service utility and experiential satisfaction for the customer; sustainable profits for the company – it is also concerned with the symbolic social meaning created through the shared *values* of identity and belonging. It is "creating economic value in a way that *also* creates value to society by addressing its needs and challenges" (Porter & Kramer, 2011, p. 63). Holt (1997, p. 343) claims that the symbolic-expressive characteristics of consumption have caused "the social patterning of consumption to become increasingly subtle and complexly intertwined". The 'consumer' is a social construct, and although there is an ethical issue concerning the "manufacture of consumers by marketers" (Zwick & Denegri Knott, 2009), where there is reciprocity between company and customer, *social production can add value to the brand* and therefore enhance an organisation's brand equity.

Customers now interact with firms through myriad touch points in an omnichannel experience which is social in nature (Lemon & Verhoef, 2016, p. 69). Miller (2015) claims that marketing has evolved from selling tangible product to become a relational, interactive, social process for the construction of social reality and the democratisation of the value creation concept. Indeed, as Edvardson, Tronvoll & Gruber (2011, p. 327) state in their criticism of the notion that all providers are service providers, "both service exchange and value co-creation are influenced by social forces". In other words, service is not the only axis of value creation; service is the processing of experience but it is not the driver. Key concepts from social construction theories (social structures, social systems, roles, positions, interactions, and reproduction of social structures) are hugely influential.

Famously, Gardner and Levy (1955) drew a distinction between a product and a brand claiming that "people buy things not only for what they can do, but also for what they *mean*". The 'classical economics approach', with its managerialist orientation, has been undermined by the "un-contestable hegemony of consumer capitalism" (Gabriel & Lang, 2006, p. 36). Marketing of products "took a cultural turn" (Hackley & Kitchen, 1998, p. 230), with meaning contingent within social construction, transferred through the consumption act via 'agents of influence' such as reference groups, celebrity endorsers, opinion leaders and the media.

Subjective perception of objects, imbued with personality, essence, ideas, beliefs, and associations projected through brand image, became the driving force of targeted marketing. The consumer exists in a social, symbolic arena of action and interaction, acknowledgement and recognition of self and group, internalised and on display, caught between the "discourses of capitalism, neo-liberalism and neo-classical economics on the one hand, with the search for a meaningful self through consumption on the other" (Shankar, Cherrier, & Canniford, 2005, p. 1020). As Holbrook suggests, the central focus of this act of consumption and social meaning-making – consumer value – "resides not in the product purchased, not in the object possessed, but rather in the consumption experiences derived" (2002, p. 95).

Consumption is a social, interactive phenomenon. The locus of interaction has gravitated away from purely economic exchange to one which is based on social relations.

Consumer capitalism has morphed "from a means to an end to be an end in its own right" (Gabriel & Lang, 2006, p. 7). Arvidsson (2005, p. 250) suggests that "the relationship between brands and consumption can be understood as exemplary of how capitalism has responded to the condition of modernity", and as Miller (2007, p. 1) suggests, "consumption rather than production is the vanguard of history". Cassidy (1997, p. 3) claims that the "influence of physical settings on behaviour is inextricably bound up with social aspects of the setting". The presence of other customers in the *servicescape* makes "the physical environment as much a social phenomenon as it is a physical one" (Proshanksy, Ittelson, & Rivlin, 1974, p. 5). The significant aspect of this user-to-user consumption interaction is referred to as *social capital*: the external linkages of different social actors within a social ecosystem or network, as well as the "internal linkages that constitute collective actors and which can give those actors cohesiveness and associated benefits" (Adler & Kwon, 2000, p. 89).

At the core of social capital is the idea of *mutuality*: a "combination of interpersonal links, shared beliefs, identities, and norms that together reduce the incidence of distrust in economic exchange" (Fafchamps, 2021). It can be created through group identity or cultivating individual behaviour norms, but what distinguishes the *mutuality* of social capital is the effort to invest by the interested parties. Consumers willing to invest time, money, resources, social effort, and endorsement of brands connect to a virtuous engagement circle of reciprocity and meaning making. Here, converting individual interests into shared community interests, mutual peer trust, source credibility, and reciprocity are key aspects. Social capital can be seen as a resource either developed and owned by individuals or by a social group. Either way, social capital is "the property of individuals but only by virtue of their membership in a group" (Szreter & Woolcock, 2004, p. 654). It takes a number of forms:

- *Bonding* social capital is the horizontal, face-to-face relationships in homogeneous social groups.
- *Bridging* social capital links members of distant groups through which external forces can be mobilised (Woolcock, 2001).
- *Linking* social capital refers to "linkages between people who are interacting across explicit, formal, or institutionalised power or authority gradients in society (Szreter & Woolcock, 2004, p. 655).

This social "linking value" (Cova, 1997, p. 398) is important in creating community expression, a fundamental shift from the *use* value of products or services to one of *social* use which reinforces peer-to-peer bonds. Cova and Cova (2012) later extended this notion to coin the phrase 'prosumption', a clumsy term adopted in service marketing discourse to describe the phenomenon of co-creation: part consumption; part production. This is emphasised by Prahalad & Ramaswamy (2004, p. 5): "The meaning of value and the process of value creation are rapidly shifting from a product- and firm-centric view to personalised consumer experiences, and active consumers are increasingly co-creating value with the firm". They are integrators of operant resources (physical, social, cultural knowledge skills) as they actively immerse themselves in an experiential service system. Spohrer *et al* define this as "value co-production configuration of people, technology, other internal and external service systems, and shared information" (2007, p. 71).

From a company's perspective, it is important to develop social capital within its ecosystem – the organisation's global network of customers and influencers – in order to affect the creation of value. Oh, Labianca & Chung (2006) discuss the concept of "group social capital" – that which is available through members' social relationships within the group social structure. The social dimension of sustainability is evidence of a company's positive affect on social capital. Shared information, encouragement of B2C and C2C dialogues, co-creation, and shared purpose are directly or indirectly roles of social capital and, in the context of value creation, are social resources.

Understanding how the resources of an organisation can be strategically leveraged to gain competitive advantage has occupied academics and practitioners for some time now. Indeed, as Campbell, O'Driscoll & Saren argue: "The need for a holistic conceptualisation of resources has moved beyond a strategic challenge for the firm to the most globally important issue facing humanity today" (2013, p. 306). The resource-based view (RBV), and then latterly the foundations of resource-based theory (RBT) established traction in this area. RBT contends that the possession of strategic resources provides an organisation with an opportunity to develop competitive advantage (Barney, 1991). Hart (1995, p. 986) argued that models of sustainable competitive advantage need to include constraints and challenges that the natural environment places on firms, and how resources rooted in interaction lead to competitive advantage.

The influence of the influencers in consumption is evident in social groups such as families, friendship groups, neo-tribes, brand communities, opinion leaders and opinion formers, media, vloggers, bloggers, and all sorts of influencers, who create operant resources related to consumption in the form of knowledge, purchase confidence and competence, product usage, brand preference and loyalty. The influential power of 'mavens' (ie: localised, learned, knowledgeable experts) is a good example of an operant *social* resource. Socialisation here is the driving force of imitative behaviour, group affiliation, and expressions of the self, translated into repeat purchase, customer-company relationships, brand loyalty, and sustainable business strategies. Therefore, social roles can be both operant and operand resources: they can act upon (influence) and be acted upon (be influenced) by value networks. They are subject to 'expectation' (eg: assuming the role of consumer of value produced in manufacturing) or 'enactment' (when an innovation creates a new customer or a new need).

Through the integration of roles as resources, customers and other stakeholders create value for themselves and for others (Akaka & Chandler, 2011, p. 252). The impact of *Influencer* Marketing, a by-product of the Information Age, evidences this. Interestingly, the concept of 'value-in-use' has been modified to value-in-*context*: "externally-based and dynamically determined in the context; that is, that cannot be owned or controlled by a single actor". This suggests a co-creative, collaborative, contextual, experiential way of creating value, one that is social. Orlikowski asserts that it is important to view resources not separately as tangible/intangible or operant/operand but in a social "web of inextricable entanglement" (2007, p. 1448).

Families, peer groups, brand influencers, companies, and even governments, are all resource integrators – not just of service systems but as influencers of socialisation and customer-company fusion. Organisations like *IBM, Microsoft, Dell Technologies, Google, eBay,* and *Facebook* are technology integrators, but the *social* application is the driver. Arguably these resources don't have *intrinsic* value, but the social linking value integrates them to the Internet and creates shared *social* value.

This social process of adoption implies that it is imperative for successful marketing communication to be grounded in social interaction (Varey, 2002), and this is instrumental in building brands as social constructions (Peñaloza & Venkatesh, 2006), and managing brand meanings "as community brands" (Brown, Kozinets, & Sherry, 2003, p. 31). Brand meaning is often constituted as "customer-centric communities" (Fournier, 1998, p. 343) with organisational omnipotence eroded by brands that have become citizen artists and cultural artefacts through which consumers assert themselves as individuals in society (Holt, 2002), through communities of other brand users. The brand becomes a facilitator and the centre of a relationship between those that share (McAlexander, Schouten, & Koenigg, 2002, p. 34). The brand manager, at best, is now less a 'guardian' more a 'host' (Christodoulides, 2009, p. 141); the consumer, no longer a passive recipient but "an active participant in a counterculture which has arisen against the dogmatic nature of brands" (Lim, 2009, p. 6).

Weidmann & Lang (2010) analyse the powerful word of mouth (WOM) phenomenon of social influencers on fashion adoption, evaluating those with the highest social influence potential and value – the fashion 'superspreaders', the narrative fashion experts, and helpful friends. From the contextually-relevant communication of *Facebook* to the online South Korean community of *Cyworld*, digitised social exchange interactions, fuelled by accelerated word of mouth, are essentially communal and instrumented, facilitating accurate connectivity to target markets for companies and other users for consumers. The accepted social roles of consumers, embedded in the value process (referred to as 'role congruence'), is evident in the co-production and social value co-created in assembling firm's offerings (eg: *Dell Technologies*, and *IKEA*) which goes beyond the traditional customer-company dyad.

These next sections look at the melting pot of culture, consumption, marketing, and meaning, examining how value creation and customer/company fusion are forged in an interactive ecosystem of complexity and connectedness, developed within a *social*-dominant context.

3.3 Culture and consumption

Consumption is a language, a facilitator of social relations, a form of expression, a social currency, a conduit for group affiliation and group expression, and behaviour-shaping activity. Consumer culture theory, therefore, is a "family of theoretical perspectives that address the dynamic relationship between consumer actions, the marketplace and cultural meanings" (Arnould & Thompson, 2005, p. 870). The culture/consumption connection provides a means of differentiation no longer described in mere socio-economic segmentation, but in experiential expression enabling individualism (Stearns, 2006). Projected through the social language of brands, the purchasing of commercial goods with high social significance (Miller, 2007) is a means of acquiring social status, cultural currency, and self-esteem. All pertinent human behaviour happens in a social context (Cova, 1997); consumption can be a way of differentiating classes and enabling individualism (Stearns, 2006).

With echoes of Maslow, Stearns's 'funnel model' plots the levels of influence on consumption:
- *Biological* (basic nutritional needs).
- *Individual* ('single actors' or subjects and individualised motivation and cognition).
- *Micro-social* ('concrete actors' subculture and tribe interaction and practices).
- *Macro-social* ('aggregated actors' of class, cultures, generations and lifestyles.

This is a key cornerstone of all successful brand strategies: meaning is generated by and with others; it is an atemporal phenomenon, a synthesis of organic evolution, and a culturally contingent experience. The 'economics' model of consumption has been undermined for some time now; latterly, demand is driven by diversity and choice. The rigid rationality doesn't allow for the variability of market forces or the fundamental exchange dynamics of consumption behaviour. Traditional methods of segmenting markets have "little appreciation of the presence of social connections and their influence upon consumption" (Mitchell & Imrie, 2011, p. 39). "Social connections" is critical here. Understanding consumer roles is a more fruitful method of leveraging customer resource in order to create sustainable brand longevity through customer loyalty based on the shared values of 'cultural capital' (Bourdieu & Passeron, 1990). The mechanics of brand strategy – awareness, identification, individual resonance, meaning, group belonging – essentially become supplementary if not substitutive of traditional methods of segmentation.

The post-modern 'marketplace' is characterised by diversity, choice, and difference with the deliberate promotion of status indicators aimed at particular market segments (Carruthers & Babb, 2000). Indeed, rather than attempting to create a homogenous segment from arbitrary characteristics, the development of self-formed groups or 'consumer tribes' that hold meaning and relevance for the individuals within them present an opportunity to connect with elusive postmodern consumers (Mitchell & Imrie, 2011, p. 42). To distort Rousseau: *man is born free but is everywhere in groups*. Webb, Shirato & Danaher identify the cultural connection to the psychological disposition of consumers: "Culture makes the invisible visible and brings into material form the unexpressed conditions of being" (2002, p. 15). The projection of self and belonging, the very essence of material social reality, is laced into the fabric of material goods. "Without consumer goods, certain acts of self-definition and collective definition in culture would not be possible" (McCracken, 1988, p. 12). Culture and consumption, therefore, are mutually constituted.

3.4 Social and psychological function of branding

From its origins in consumer marketing, there has been a diffusion of applications of the concept of branding. So much so that there is barely a space which has not been touched or influenced by this phenomenon. To some, branding represents "an exemplary embodiment of the prevailing logic of capitalism" (Lash, 2002, p. 142), a response to the condition of postmodernity, a mediatisation of socially constructed symbolic belonging and identity, even offering stability that the social environment no longer provides. Understanding brands implies an awareness of "basic cultural processes that affect contemporary brands, including historical context, concerns, consumer response and regulation" (Schroeder, 2015, p. 4). A brand is the sum of the great ideas used to build that brand – from product to experience to all sorts of cultural additions expressive of meaning and interconnected ideas – all with a consistent molecular structure, driven by singular cultural logic (Grant, 2006). A brand is a "cultural resource" (Holt, 2004) of emotions, linking values, attitudes, lifestyles, and associations, with enormous potential for creating meaning for consumers. As emotion is socially constructed, we learn the *feeling* rules through the socialisation process (Elliot & Percy, 2007, p. 22), associating 'feelings' to brands in a social context of meaning-making – coffee becomes associated with sex, clothes project self-identity and group affiliation, or advertise our conscience. As Aaker suggests though, "focusing on what is a tangible physicality rather than an emotional connotation or connection is a classic management error" (1996, p. 25).

Brands therefore have culturally symbolic meanings. Brands are templates of the self; culture is a crucible of identity where there is "no concept of self, outside a system of meaning" (Gergen, 1991, p. 78). The creation and management of brands, rather than the production of product, has developed as the predominant focus of organisations, "the core activity of many corporations is transformed from the production of *things* to the production of *images*" as Salzer-Morling & Strannegård, (2002, p. 224) suggest. Brands, therefore, become shorthand for proposition, positioning, and competitive parity, "in essence stories that project rhetorical symbolic metaphors" (Shankar, Elliott, & Goulding, 2001, p. 446).

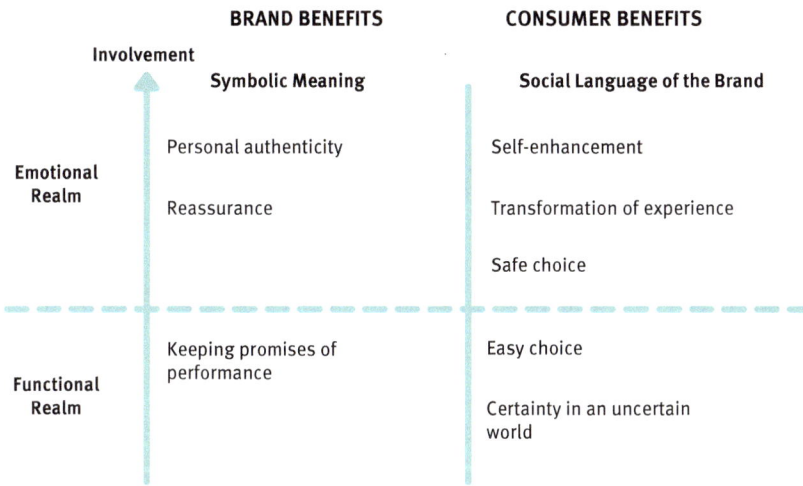

BRAND BENEFITS	CONSUMER BENEFITS
Involvement ↑	
Symbolic Meaning	Social Language of the Brand
Emotional Realm Personal authenticity	Self-enhancement
Reassurance	Transformation of experience
	Safe choice
- - - - - - - - - - - - - - - - -	- - - - - - - - - - - - - - - - -
Functional Realm Keeping promises of performance	Easy choice
	Certainty in an uncertain world

Figure 3.1: Socio-psychological aspects of branding.
Source: Elliott & Wattansuwan (1998, p.131)

In Figure 3.1, Elliott (1994) examines the social and psychological functions of the brand in a psychosocial (shown below in describing the emotional and functional 'realms' of the brand), as well as consumer and brand benefits framework.

The level of consumer 'involvement' is the key here. When a purchase decision is low-involvement, providing performance and quality promises are met, trust is an easy thing for an organisation to build and sustain. However, a brand which has the ability of projecting symbolic meaning – self-esteem, group affiliation, conspicuous consumption, conscience – must communicate some social meaning to the user through the language of brands. The driver is social and brands are carriers of social meaning, created in "the dialectical relationship between self-identity and social-identity, the domains of self-symbolism and social-symbolism, and the process of the mediated [brand] experience . . . lived experience of brand use" (Elliott & Wattanasuwan, 1998, p. 131).

From this we can see that a brand can be seen as all the emotional and tangible touchpoints surrounding a product. As Arvidsson (2005, p. 237) puts it, the brand is a "source of surplus value . . . a precondition for the self-valorisation of immaterial capital". As Mukherjee says, "A great brand today is a brand that people don't just buy, they buy into because they stand by the brand's values because it matches theirs".

3.5 Marketing and meaning

One of the binding elements of customer-company fusion is the creation of meaning and value. Kapferer captures this well: "Only brands that add value to the product and tell a story about its buyers, or situate their consumption in a ladder of immaterial values, can provide this meaning" (2008, p. 2). There is an increasing number of "phenomenological-oriented studies of consumer culture [which] reside in the use of brands in symbolic consumption" (Elliot & Davies, 2006, p. 140) and individual negotiated identity. McCracken (1988, p.6) claims that "culture and consumption are mutually constituted". The transfer of 'meaning' from brand to consumer – the "ideology of consumption" as (Baudrillard, 1968) refers to it – is inextricably woven into the concept of social salience and meaning, which Belk (1988, p. 184) describes as "brand consumption compensating for identity gaps".

It can be argued that marketing is the "proselytisation of this ideology" (O'Shaughnessy & O'Shaughnessy, 2008, p. 195). McCracken (1986) made the link between culture and consumption; his phrase "culturally-constituted meaning" has echoes in so many marketing strategies and so much individual consumption behaviour. Ever since he posed the question: "Are we searching for information or meaning?", the cultural meaning of consumer goods (and then progressively all goods and services) was established. Marketplace meaning, therefore, is a combination of competitive comparison, individual perception and culturally constituted group negotiated representation. Different perspectives describe this as: an anthroplogically-oriented culturally-derived phenomenon, or a cognitive psychologically view located in inner drives and internal schemas. An increasing amount of research in this area focuses on "phenomenological-oriented studies of consumer culture which reside in the use of brands in symbolic consumption" (Davies & Elliott, 2006, p. 1108), and where Social Constructionism provides a framework of 'interpretive' subjective realities.

The real commercial value of brands, therefore, is to be able to communicate cultural meaning and act as a linking social conduit: the "valuing of consumption as a social imperative" in identity construction as Ventkatesh (1999, p. 3) puts it. Smith (2007) analyses the three forces of meaning construction (represented in Figure 3.2) as:
- Represented group identity
- Targeted brand positioning
- Reconciled self-image

This is an illustration of the "existential meaning paradox" which describes an "underlying tension between mediated transmitted meaning, the brand's intended meaning and group/individual negotiated meaning which describes an existential paradox of expressiveness and connectedness" (2007, p. 327). This particularlism of consumption, where there is resonance between purchaser and product, is an "act of identity construction" (McCracken, 2005, p. 250), what Smith (2007, p. 330) refers to as "individual/brand congruity". Brand strategies using this notion create brands and propositions which are "metaphors and attach not only meanings to brands but brands to meanings" (Brierley, 2002, p. 144)".

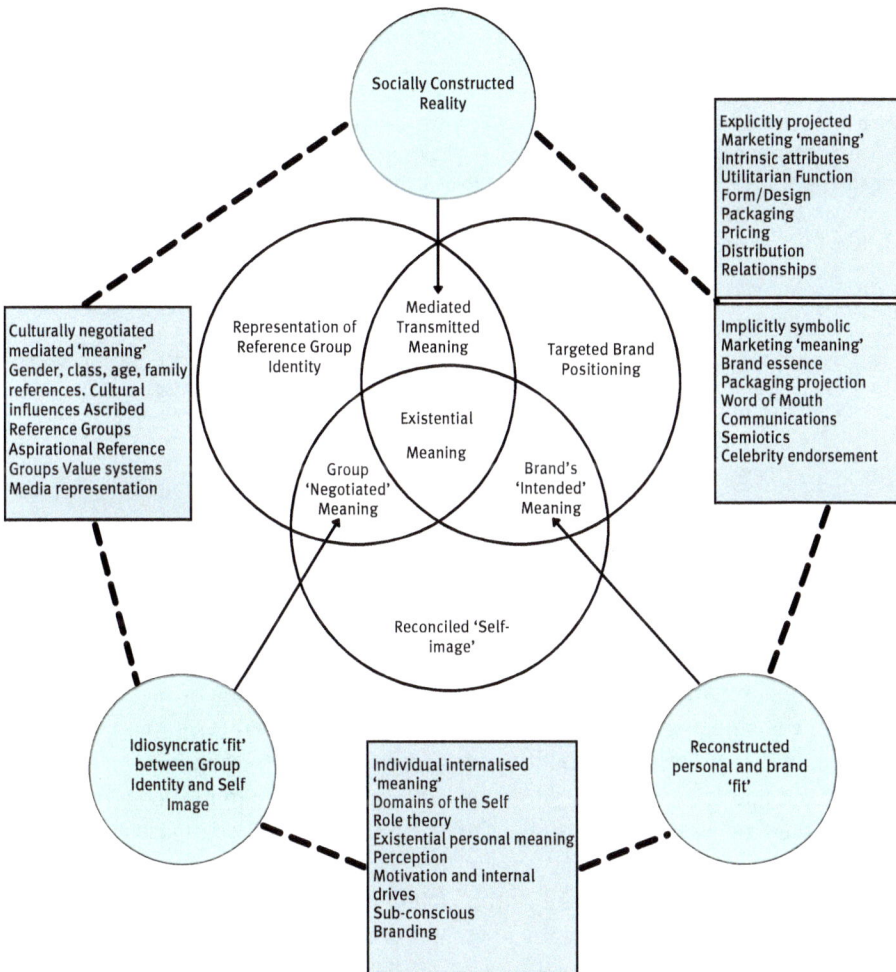

Figure 3.2: Components of Meaning Construction.
Source: Smith (2007)

Principles in practice

Absolut's contradictory campaign to start 'consent' conversation

When a drinks company wants to "start a dialogue on what it truly means to drink responsibly"[42] that's both an acknowledgement of their corporate social conscience and a reflection of changing consumer concerns. This would appear counterintuitive if not contradictory. Following the global reaction to high-profile incidents of sexual abuse precipitated by the Harvey Weinstein cases, the focus on 'consent' has become a big issue with young adults. The #metoo movement has put this social phenomenon centre stage.

Research conducted by *Absolut Vodka*, a global alcohol brand selling into a predominantly younger demographic, found that data from the focus groups interviewed yielded some alarming facts: 9 out of 10 21–30 year-olds discuss 'consent' with their family; 61% from that age bracket believed that companies should take the initiative in tackling this subject as a social conversation;[43] and 70% of all consumers want brands they purchase to address social issues.[44]

Absolut's 'Drink Responsibly, #SexResponsibly' campaign shines a direct spotlight on the relationship between alcohol and sexual activity. Messages such as "Only a Yes to Sex is a Yes", "Binge-Watch and Chill? Not a Yes", and "Buying Someone a Drink Doesn't Buy You a Yes" appear in ads alongside images of their iconic bottle logo and deals with perceived ambiguity over what 'consent' actually means. Ann Mukherjee, *Pernod Ricard* CEO, claims: "The conversation is, very simply, that everyone has the right to drink and have safe sex, but it starts with consent". Reinforcement of the company's commitment to this social cause is sponsorship of *RAINN*, the largest anti-sexual violence network in the States and reflects *Pernod Ricard's* efforts across all age groups and all brands in their portfolio. As a "provocateur brand" with a reputation for connecting to the social Zeitgeist, *Absolut* knows that conversation that connects with consumer conscience, even if apparently contradicting brand values, can resonate with audiences and reinforce purpose.

3.6 Service-oriented dynamics

From the late-70s, Shostack's seminal paper 'Breaking Free From Product Marketing' (1977, p. 75) questioned "myopic" marketing for "failing to create relevant paradigms" for what was then referred to as the 'service sector', laying the path for the perennial examination of what has been the various iterations of *the service perspective* in business strategy. Even before Shostack, Rathwell (1966) was querying the dominant logic of the product-service continuum with its 'purity' of *tangible* product and *intangible* services. Grönroos (2007, p. vii) refers to the consumption of services, the total service offering, as "value-creating support", and posits the imperative of adopting a 'service logic' or else "the firm's logic and the customer's logic will collide". This is really helpful as this notion is predicated on the lexicon of the early 80s. Normann, one of the early advocates of a 'service logic', described services

---

42 Ann Mukherjee, CEO of Pernod Ricard, USA.
43 KRC Research, 2021.
44 Certus Research, 2021.

as "activities (including the use of hard products) that make service marketing being essentially relational – a customer-focused approach to strategy which is centuries old". This was a concept Berry (1983) introduced to the "marketing of new relationships and new configurations of elements possible . . . viewing the economy as a web of activities and actors in co-productive value creation gives us a more creative view of the nature of 'offerings'. Offerings are artefacts designed to more effectively enable and organise value co-production" (2001, p. 40).

A progenitor to the B2B, quality, and service movement away from product-oriented marketing, (Kitson, 1922, p. 419), pre-empted this 'new' service logic paradigm by claiming that "Within recent years . . . service has come to be regarded not as an accessory but as a real part of the commodity, indeed the commodity itself". In B2B markets, the customer-company contact is often closer than in any other sector, its 'industrial marketing' tag a misnome in some respects. Whilst 'contract' markets may have a complicated buying decision process and exceptionally long lead times, the essence has always been the service logic of personal relationships, networks, and other non-product processes. One of Kitson's contemporaries, Sheldon (1929, p. 64), echoed Kitson's thoughts asserting that "no matter what you were doing, you are manufacturing service in some form".

This is so prescient: *manufacturing service in some form*. Some of the many metaphors subsequently used to illustrate similarity in form and function – like the 'service factory' (Chase & Erikson, 1988) – echoed this idea. A conceptual framework which rather plays on the idea of a product/service dichotomy[45] – the Service-Dominant Logic (SDL) – views brands in terms of collaborative, value co-creating activities of firms, and advocates placing the *service brand* as the most fundamental premise in the S-D logic. Brand value is discussed in terms of the stakeholders' collectively perceived *value-in-use*. Yet, whilst acknowledging that brands and brand equity are fundamental to value creation in service-oriented businesses (eg: Berry, 2000; de Chernatony, & McDonald 2003), there is "limited discussion of branding *per se* in Lusch and Vargo's (2004) work" (Brodie, Glynn, & Little, 2006, p. 363).

Furthermore, a *service*-dominant approach is essentially an inside-out orientation not a collaborative one. Indeed, in a further iteration, Merz, He & Vargo (2009) recognise this fact, suggesting that organisations should "invest resources in building strong brand relationships with all of their stakeholders and establishing a service-dominant firm philosophy built around brand value co-creation" (2009, p. 1), and view "all stakeholders as endogenous to the brand value-creation process" (2009, p. 3). And it is here that the recognition of brands as dynamic, socially constructed entities comes into play: "not only individual customers but also brand communities and all other stakeholders constitute operant resources" (2009, p. 10),

---

45 Some scholars have subsequently argued (eg: Brown, Tadajewski & Jones, O'Shaughnessy & O'Shaughnessy) that the original SDL research is actually predicated on a false dichotomy.

highlighting that the brand value co-creation process is continuous, social, highly dynamic, and interactive.

However, Merz *et al* recognise that "the more recent customer-based approaches to measuring brand value do not sufficiently account for the role of the brand communities, stakeholders, and dynamic and *social* interactions among the different actors in the brand value co-creation process" (2009, p. 13). Iansiti and Levien (2004) claim that brand value is not only co-created through isolated, dyadic relationships between firms and individual customers, but also co-created through social interactions amongst all the firm's stakeholders.

Tadajewski & Jones examine the framing of marketing thought offered by Vargo and Lusch, "problematising" their narrative of movement from goods-dominant to service-dominant logic by drawing attention to the multiple strands of service discourse already existing from the late 19th to mid-20th century – "the plurality of articulations of service marketing discourse" (2021, p. 113). They criticise the absence of acknowledgement of engagement with this and argue that there was more variety in thinking among earlier contributors, claiming that "the alleged transition from GDL to SDL is a myth" (2021, p. 114). O'Shaughnessy & O'Shaughnessy claim that SDL is "neither logically sound nor a perspective to displace others in marketing . . . . [accusing it of] focusing on marketing as a technology . . . with a single unitary perspective for marketing . . . [when] there is a need for multiple perspectives in marketing, together with the methodological pluralism that it implies" (2009, p. 786). Spohrer *et* al (2008, p. 104) describe an "abstraction that will be important to the service revolution of the 21st century" which puts "a foundation for an integrated science of service" where many systems (eg: families, companies, cities, etc.) can be viewed as service systems which combine in value-creation. This need for a holistic view of marketing strategy, embracing all aspects of branding, digital, services, relationship marketing, and experiential marketing, is why a *socially*-oriented perspective is more appropriate.

Recent gradual evolutions pinpoint a "customer-dominant" (Heinonen, et al., 2010) perspective (which implies a provider/user relationship) and a "consumer dominant" refinement (Anker, Sparks, Moutinho, & Grönroos, 2014) which can suggest that the act of consumption – value-in-use and in context – can occur separately from the provider. This consumer-dominant logic assumes consumer value is delivered through brand-mediated but provider-independent consumer behaviour. Anker *et al* (2014, p. 353) argue that product-dominant and service-dominant logic "are unable to explain three dimensions – value creation processes; the relational status between providers and consumers; the replication of product service qualities and properties" – claiming that "consumers engage in value creation practices that comprise ontological and semantic characteristics which [these perspectives] cannot explain". That ontology is *social*.

The thread which runs through all these approaches is the co-creation of value-in-use. Value-in-use is defined as "a customer's functional and/or hedonic outcome, purpose or objective that is directly served through product/service usage" (MacDonald, Wilson, Martinez, & Toosi, 2009). The real locus of logic here is the symbolic significance of brands in creating social meaning and facilitating communal consumption experiences (Csikszentmihalyi & Rochberg-Halton, 1981; Cooper, McLaughlin, & Keating, 2005). By shifting the way customer-company relationships are viewed – from dyadic to network with social roles as resources for change in co-production of meaning and value – the social role "is conceptualised as a particular set of practices that connects one actor to one or more actors . . . continually drawing on social roles and social positions as resources" (Akaka & Chandler, 2011, p. 243). *Social* roles and positions as resources are crucial to understanding the roots of meaning and the driving force of the brand.

3.7 Social-dominant logic

This next section puts forward the ontological basis and strategic arguments for a *Social-Dominant Logic* – a broader conceptual framework than, and a natural progression from, the product-, service-, customer-, and consumer-dominant perspectives which have attempted to synthesise factors affecting and affected by *social meaning*. As we have seen above with O'Shaughnessy & O'Shaughnessy's (2009) call for multiple perspectives in marketing, marketing can often be seen only from a managerialist perspective. Even with its separatist silos, differing theoretical and practitioner perspectives, and its partisan paradigmatic views, marketing, with its roots in economics, psychology, sociology, and anthropology, is still, and has always been, a synthetic discipline, and has always had an integrative, inter-disciplinary approach to business philosophy.

The ontological nucleus of branding as a socio-cultural phenomenon and managerial imperative is social transformation and value creation, charting an individual's socialisation through consumption and an organisation's development through relevance related to that consumption. The social essence of marketing is interaction and the fundamental interaction dynamic is *social*. Here, we examine the performative aspects of how marketing works, how the "strings of association" (Cooren & Fairhurst, 2009, p. 49) of the ontological instruments – service marketing, branding, relationship building, value creation etc. – constitute its *social-dominant logic*.

From 'satisfaction' to 'value', 'exchange' to relationship', from 'customer' to 'stakeholder', from Consumer Culture Theory to Service Science, and more recently Macro-marketing with its more inclusive, societal perspective, the range of orientations has swung between art and science, and the axis has moved from company to customer. There is now a "social-phenomenological gaze turned towards marketing work that will not approach marketing work as a pre-given object, but as a social phenomenon emerging in the everyday life of marketing practitioners" (Svensson, 2007, p. 275). Most schools of marketing have one central focus: *the customer-company relationship.*

Viewing branding (and indeed the broader marketing concept) as being driven by and rooted in social construction as opposed to service process is not intended

to be a paradigm shift; it is presented as a parallax perspective viewed through a polyphonic and multi-discipline lens with *fusion* at its heart. Implicit in its logic is:
- An emphasis on shared socially constituted meaning.
- The interrelated nature of the co-creation of value.
- The social subjectivity of agency in the consumption experience.
- The acknowledgement of symmetry in the customer-company relationship.
- The impact of social communal influence in forming loyalty.

It synthesises many customer-oriented marketing perspectives and brand strategy drivers to present an organic, culturally-sensitive, brand ecosystem of social dynamics reflective of contemporary macro and micro environmental influences. Figure 3.3 demonstrates the eight elements of the ecosystem which constitutes the *Social-Dominant Logic* framework.

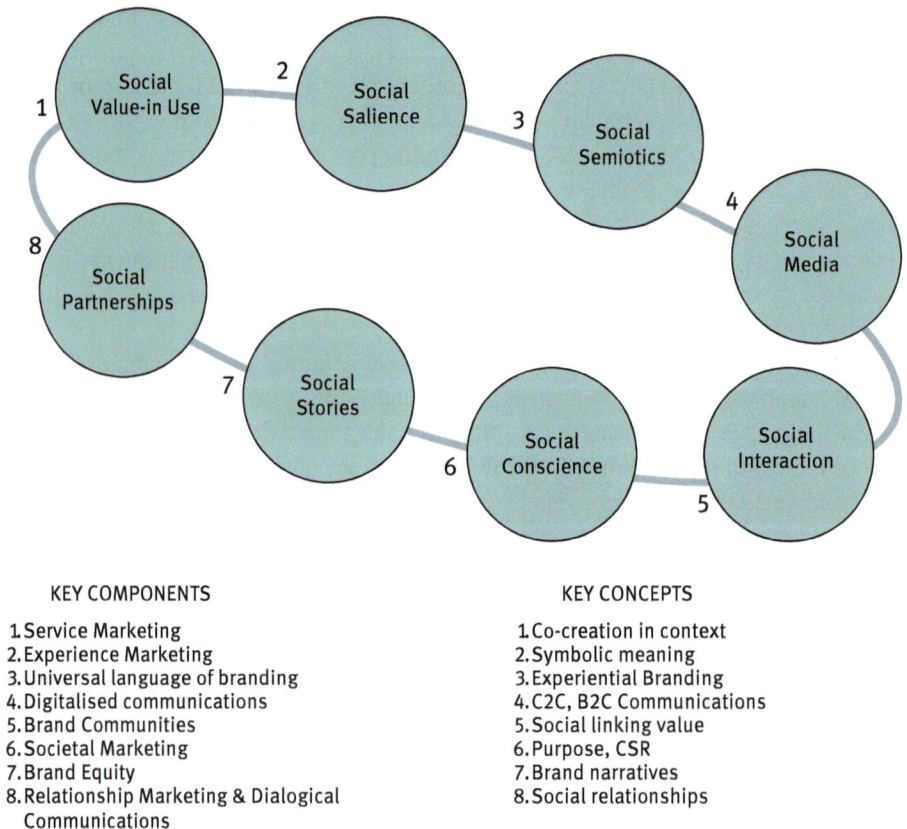

KEY COMPONENTS

1. Service Marketing
2. Experience Marketing
3. Universal language of branding
4. Digitalised communications
5. Brand Communities
6. Societal Marketing
7. Brand Equity
8. Relationship Marketing & Dialogical Communications

KEY CONCEPTS

1. Co-creation in context
2. Symbolic meaning
3. Experiential Branding
4. C2C, B2C Communications
5. Social linking value
6. Purpose, CSR
7. Brand narratives
8. Social relationships

Figure 3.3: Social-Dominant Logic Ecosystem.
Source: Authors' representation (2022)

3.8 Social value-in-use: The logic of service marketing

In the 1980s, when 'People', 'Physical Evidence' and 'Process' were added to an 'extended Marketing Mix', this was an acknowledgement that marketing services were similar but peculiarly different to the marketing of physical products. The transactional exchange view, with its product-orientation anchored in manufacturing, focused on 'utility' in the narrow economic sense. It minimised (if not excluded), the intangible, interactive, subjective, social element of people *interaction*. The subsequent augmented 'social' role of service, the interpersonal nature of the customer-company interface, acknowledged that "customers are service system entities; service system entities are both economic and social actors which integrate resources to co-create value" (Anderson, Pass, Ager, & Spohrer, 2008).

Implicitly, this identified and underpinned the *social* element. Furthermore, the increasing focus on the consumption experience in services (Shaw & Ivens, 2002), with experience not just limited to company actions *on* customers but the delivery in the presence of other customers, and the influence of other customers on that experience – the social context – added importance to this phenomenon. Arnould examines the motivating social and cultural contexts of retail patronage, applying a Consumer Culture Theory (CCT) perspective, declaring that "for consumers, retailers represent a field in which operant resources interact . . . firms compete for a role in the culturally constituted projects that consumers pursue by offering certain resource combinations" (2005, p. 89).

The value here is in use, in interaction, "rather than exchange being the fundamental construct in marketing" (Grönroos, 2008, p. 311), with the social role of the customer integral to value creation. Here, a customer-oriented social value-in-use perspective sees operant resources of both organisation and consumer converge "to co-create value through patterns of experiences and meanings embedded in the cultural life-worlds of consumers" (Arnould & Thompson, 2005, p. 868).

At the heart of this value-creation process is the fact that the essential phenomenological value is in the intangible value inherent in brands, particularly those services dominated by experiential attributes. In fairness, Vargo and Lusch (2004) do identify this, recognising that the value of brands is always "uniquely and phenomenologically determined by the beneficiary" (p. 14). This is heightened in services because of the lack of tangible, physical product. This absence is compensated for by the intangible elements in "the environment in which the service is being delivered and in which the firm and the customer interact, and any tangible commodities that facilitate performance or communication of the service" (Zeithaml & Bitner, 2003). One of the intangible elements not recognised in the original marketing 'mix' was *physical evidence* – spatial layout, signs, symbols, ambient conditions, artifacts, functionality – which act as environmental cues for customer expectations of service content and delivery.

Strategically, this can aid service facilitation, distinguish competitive differentiation, and frame socialisation of employees and customers in terms of roles and expected behaviours. This environment where interaction takes place is commonly referred to as the 'servicescape', a conceptual framework developed by Booms & Bitner (1981)[46] which pre-empts the customer journey [discussed at length in *Chapter 7*].

The servicescape is "the environment in which a service is assembled and in which the seller and customer interact, combined with tangible commodities that facilitate performance or communication of the service" (Bitner, 1992, p. 60). The *social* stimuli of the servicescape environment, according to Guerin (1993), are likely to receive more attention than non-social or physical stimuli. Indeed, Cassidy makes this very point: "The influence of physical settings on behaviour is inextricably bound up with the social aspects of the setting" (1997). The significance of non-verbal imitative behaviour in the presence of other customers in the servicescape is examined by Grove & Fisk (1997). Where there is a significant element of customer and company interaction, where the actions of employees are the actual service, where the employee's expertise and ability to build relationships becomes an indistinguishable and inseparable component of the service offering, this is critical in terms of customer evaluation. Tombs & McColl-Kennedy (2004) refer to this as the "*social*-servicescape" in their discussion of the importance of physical, social, and contextual elements of customer affect and repurchase decisions.

Brands with a significant service element have to be developed in a systems approach with the major focus on the culture of the organisation and the training and attitudes of its employees, with the need for "ruthless clarity about positioning and the corporation's genuinely felt shared values . . . [through which] there is a greater likelihood of commitment, internal loyalty, clearer brand understanding, and importantly, consistent brand delivery across all stakeholders" (de Chernatony & Segal-Horn, 2003, p. 1100).

The discussion on operand and operant resources focuses the functional and social role of the customer as integral to value creation. As Spohrer *et al* (2008) point out: "customers are service system entities; service system entities are both economic and social actors which integrate resources to co-create value" (p.11). The value is in use, in interaction, and, according to Grönroos (2008, p.311), "interaction rather than exchange is the fundamental construct in marketing". Interaction is focused on customers' value creation and value fulfilment, and at the heart of this value-creation process is the intangible value inherent in brands, a type of social currency that is difficult to assess in strictly financial terms.

The notion of value of course is a subjective one, interpreted by the individual's perception of use, and one reflecting the relationships of the actors. Consumers,

---

46 A concept developed in 1981 by Booms & Bitner to describe the physical and virtual environment within which customer and company interact and first impressions of service are formed.

through their "immaterial labour, add cultural and affective value to market offerings . . . at the primary level of *sociality* (interpersonal relationships) . . . companies capture this value when it enters the second level of sociality (the market)" (Cova & Dalli, 2009, p. 315). 'Immaterial labour' derives from Marks's 'living labour' in the sense that the consumers actively create 'their' meaning and is equivalent to an operant resource. Whilst customers may be value creators, "the supplier can become a co-creator with its customers (Grönroos, 2008, p. 298). This is really *value-in-context* (Chandler & Vargo, 2011), co-creation as a product of multiple social actions performed by multiple actors in a social context.

The value-creation process is one of mutuality and is socially-constituted. The value to consumers is in the intangible value of symbolic social experience in-use in the social context of other users. Companies who understand this will make it an essential ingredient of their brand strategy.

3.9 Social salience: Culturally constituted experiential marketing

Competitive differentiation is increasingly not achieved explicitly in the functional aspects of a brand but implicitly in the symbolic social or psychological attributes. Brands do not just fulfil utilitarian use but have "an emotional role that transcends historical category usage" (Morgan, 2009)". Brand loyalty which has permanency cannot merely be achieved by "transforming the product category" (Kapferer, 2004, p. 256), but by creating emotional engagement and social salience. In Social Psychology, social salience is described as the evaluation of a person or object (in our case, this is a brand) by an individual or group. It differs from cognitive salience (Rácz, 2013) by the fact that there is resonance of a *social* value.

The "emotionalisation of products" (Elliot & Percy, 2007) helps re-positioning, the brand itself becoming "a series of packaged consumer experiences based around emotive feelings" (Chatterton & Hollands, 2003, p. 56). Whilst purchase decisions are a combination of cognitive evaluation and emotional satisfaction (Gobé, 2001), the value of a brand to customers is based upon the extent to which a brand represents the customers' desired social image and self-identity (Kapferer, 2004). The symbolic-expressive characteristics of consumption have caused "the social patterning of consumption to become increasingly subtle and complexly intertwined" (Holt, 2003, p. 343).

Smith (2007, p. 326) asserts that "social salience lies in culturally-constituted, so-cially-mediated symbolic meaning within a group/self-identity framework". The company, customer, and reference group meaning of Smith's model (featured in Figure 3.2) echoes the three key elements of Palmer & Koenig-Lewis's (2009) experiential, social environment framework – the seller, the customer, and the community.

A key focus in consumption, and an essential ingredient in strategic brand management, is therefore, the phenomenological aspect of consumption: the experiential element. Culturally constituted brands are, after all, "first and foremost providers of experiences" (Schmitt, Experiential Marketing, 1999, p. 30), which is invariably a shared, indirect product consumption phenomenon, concerned with *perceptions* of experience. Brand narratives – the stories negotiated between producer and user – become a script (Carù & Cova, 2003); instead of experiencing the world, "we now experience the experience of it" (Eagleton, 2006). This is about the fabric of relationships where consumers define themselves in a 'brand community' through a social dialogue that occurs within the code structure of brands (Muñíz & O'Guinn, 2001). This brand-based behaviour is what Sherry refers to as "the principal form of secular ritual in contemporary life" (1986, p. 62). This is what social salience is: relevance in a culturally constituted setting, one where emotional and experiential bonds with brands can create brand loyalty through social linking. As Hill suggests (2008, p. 115), "If a brand delivers emotionally, its myth translates into reality for its tribe".

New technology products with social currency (eg: *Apple* products) may have had technological competitive advantage but whose sales were accelerated because of the social phenomenon of fashion, imitative behaviour, and neo-tribe group belonging. Technology must satisfy psycho-social needs in order for adoption and diffusion to occur. Smith postulates that "Postmodern brand engagement is manifest in: community involvement of causal marketing and social brand experiences; brands affecting and reflecting changing social values; the cultivation of brand authenticity and ethical integrity; and the new agenda of working through company/customer consensus in symbolic symbiosis" (2007, p. 324). For consumers, this engagement offers individual identification and group affiliation; for organisations, this lifestyle loyalty builds a bank of customer equity and competitive immunity.

For some consumers, the experience with some brands takes on a 'sacred' (as opposed to 'profane') aspect. The phenomenon of imbuing commodities with quasi-religious sacred meanings – turning products into cultural objects – is evident in many of the brands which create mythical narratives. Early identification of the "the secularization of religion and the sacralization of the secular" (Belk, Walldendorf, & Sherry Jr, 1989) produced insights into how objects contribute to our extended self on a social and emotional basis. The difference between the profane and sacred in symbolic consumption is rooted in social constructionism: the symbiotic, symbolic relationship *in consumption* between objects and consumers which has transcended purely functional utility to creating social salience in co-created psychological and social resonance. The transfer of meaning through celebrity endorsement, brand mythology played against the demise of the culturally-transfusive triad of family, religion and education, all contribute to this.

Social salience is the 'fit' between company value proposition and consumer individual and group need. Meaning which is projected through symbolic consumption and group identity imbues social significance on brands. Meaning construction is an important component of brand selection and should be a vital part of brand strategy.

3.10 Social semiotics: The universal language of branding

Brand management is frequently based on uniformist and integrationist assumptions (Gromark, 2020). Depending upon the extent of brand centrality and customer centrality, brand management paradigms may be classified as:
- *Product*: A planned strategy around product positioning in the market.
- *Projective*: An extension of the above but acknowledged the intangible assets as having value perceptual leverage in terms of competitive differentiation, although target markets were still viewed as segments of passive recipients.
- *Adaptive*: A significant development from the above, with the brand user as central and key co-creator of brand meaning, brand managers focused strategies on consumer image of the brand rather than the identity projected by the organisation.
- *Relational*: More consideration was given to consumer-company interaction, addressing longevity, the asymmetrical power nature of the organisation/customer, the acknowledgement of co-creation, and the increasing importance of brand communities. (Louro & Cunha, 2001)

Brands are social semiotic marketing systems which Conejo and Wooliscroft (2014, p. 287) describe as "multi-dimensional constructs with varying degrees of meaning, independence, co-creation, and scope". Brand culture – the cultural codes of brands such as myths, self identity, group affiliation, associations, images, narratives – influences brand meaning and what is considered as 'value'. Semiotics functions in a triad of interpretation between sign, meaning, and interpreter (Pierce, 2013). They have a transnational ability to communicate social norms, identity, and group affiliation through the social semiotics of symbolic meaning.

Tonks (2002) describes semiotics as "marketing rhetoric shaping consumption and existence". Brands are the language of consumption, and "a cluster of strategic cultural ideas" (Grant, 2007, p. 27). Schroeder (2009, p. 124) described this brand culture as "the cultural codes of brands that influence brand meaning and value in the marketplace". Brand culture in conjunction with traditional research areas of brand identity, brand image, and brand culture provides the necessary cultural, historical, and political grounding to understand brands in context.

The brand culture concept occupies the theoretical space between strategic concepts of brand identity and consumer interpretations of brand image, shedding light on the gap often seen between managerial intention and market response, in other words between strategic goals and consumer perceptions (eg: Schroeder and Salzer-Mörling, 2006). How do brands interact with culture? From a cultural perspective, brands can be understood as communicative objects that the brand manager wants consumers to buy into – a symbolic universe as defined by, in part, the brand identity (cf. Faurholt Csaba and Bengtsson, 2006). In theory, brand management is about communicating messages, which are received in line with the brand owner's intention (Kapferer, 2004). But this perspective fails to take into account consumers' active negotiation of brand meaning, contextual effects, such as time, space, and personal history, and cultural processes, including 'anti-branding' phenomena.

Brands are vessels of meaning, able to communicate social norms, identity, and group affiliation through the social semiotics of symbolic meaning. They are quintessentially the language of consumption and as such are an effective channel from company to customer to articulate purpose, value proposition, and positioning,

3.11 Socialised media: Digital technology

Whilst there are pre-digital antecedents (Tupperware 'parties' involved a key social ingredient of peer group pressure in the adoption process), digital technology has driven the recent trend for ecosystems which combine high complexity, low cost, broad reach, and social interaction. Le Guin (2021) re-defines technology as a cultural carrier bag rather than a weapon of domination. This image chimes with the notion of consumption as "bricolage" (Lévi-Strauss, 1962) or 'DIY consumption' (Tadajewski & Wagner-Tsukamoto, 2006, p. 10), identifying utilitarian and symbolic consumption and the acquisition of implicit and explicit meaning through the influence of *socialised* media.[47]

Digital technology facilitates one-voice multi-media exposure and interactivity. The digital conversations of socialised media allow levels of customer-to-company (C2B) and consumer-to-consumer (C2C) communications unprecedented in marketing. The mainstream adoption of digital technology "heralds the single most disruptive development in the history of marketing" (Ryan & Jones, 2008, p. 5). According to Solis (2011, p. 1), it has:
- Rewired the processes by which consumers share experiences, expertise, and opinions.
- Broadened the channels available to consumers who seek information.
- Changed how companies approach markets.
- Altered how companies develop products.
- Remodelled the processes by which companies connect with and show appreciation for their customers.

---

47 This is a sort of portmanteau, an amalgam of the community aspect of 'social media' and the 'socialisation' effect of individuals learning to behave in both the contexts of social norms and brand usage.

- Transformed the method of influence, augmenting the ranks of traditional market experts and thought leaders with enthusiasts and innovators who self-create content-publishing platforms for their views.
- Facilitated customers' direct engagement in the conversations that were previously taking place without their participation.

The importance of social network media lies in the combination of 'paid-for' and 'earned' communications,[48] the interaction between consumers and the community, and in the facilitation of "asynchronous, immediate, interactive, low-cost communications" (Miller, Fabian, & Lin, 2009, p. 305). The COVID-19 pandemic has had many vectors – economic, technology, work conceptualisation, health, social justice – all with different impacts and directions, with a cumulative effect but all requiring individual transformative strategies. The impacts have forced us to think about how our conceptions of the way we live, our attitudes to work, and the very notion of socialisation in its broadest sense. There is greater connectedness and increased reliance on digital technology. Artificial Intelligence (AI) is used increasingly to simulate customer-to-customer communication. Wilson-Nash, Good & Currie (Wilson-Nash, Goode, & Currie, 2020)describe the 'social-bot' mechanism on *Facebook Messenger* as "a valued customer service agent to young adult" with some favouring this over conventional telephone and email communications.

Data analysis, particularly through computer-assisted, collection, analysis, and dissemination, IoT-enables infrastructure and sense-capable physical objects like tags, smart meters, smart phones, drones, consumer electronic devices, health sensors, wearable lifestyle indicators, as well as in healthcare, offices, smart cities, factories and so on. According to *statistica.com*, 10 billion devices will exist by 2022. *Ericson* estimate that there will be an installed base of 75.44 billion IoT connected devices.

What this digital disruption has done to the diffusion and adoption of brands is to more closely integrate the socialised aspect of the customer-company relationship. The digital landscape of user democracy and symmetrical dialogue has seen the customer as being the medium through which digital conversations are spread and meaning negotiated, an essential part of contemporary brand strategy.

3.12 Social interaction: Brand communities and stakeholder impacts

The 'Information Age', mainly facilitated by personal computing and the ubiquitous power of the Internet, shifted the tectonic plates from a broadcast B2C model to a

---

48 Covered extensively in *Chapter 8.*

social world of C2C peer-to-peer communications. As Solis (2011, p. 13) observes, "Marketers are embracing a new recipe that injects a proactive, social approach to outbound communications and engagement". Whilst the concept of 'influence' is a vital tick box on most brand strategies, it is not new: it reflects us as consumers, as people, as *social* animals.

This is a sociological perspective and is rooted in social relationships, mutuality, dependency, social bonding, *social interaction*. It is social identity, reinforced by social group membership which is the driving force here. However, this is an essential part of brand strategy with brand orientation expressed through group affiliation and self-projection, being a social construction built through complex networks of stakeholder interactions, and may be with a shared social interest or with affiliation to a specific brand (eg: riding bikes or, specifically, riding *Harley Davidson* bikes).

The concept of a 'brand community' is an important strategic brand management tool for facilitating customer/company fusion (Koh, Kim, Butler, Bock, & Woo, 2007), which for group membership can give self-enhancement, self-efficacy, purposive value (Dholakia, Bagozzi, & Pearo, 2004), and positively affect buyer behaviour. Muniz & O'Guinn (2001, p. 412), were first to identify the social aspect of these brand communities, describing them as "a specialised, non-geographically bound community, based on a structured set of social relationships". Postmodern consumers seek out brand experiences both at the individual and community levels (Cova & Pace, 2006, p. 316). According to Stratton and Northcote, "the veneration of brands as part of *brand communities* reflects the expansion of consumerism in advanced capitalism" (2016, p. 493).

Although communities may act and interact either on- or offline, communication via social media networks and online brand communities is most common now. Whilst consumers in social exchange build identities in virtual communities, companies can gain some influence by sponsoring or co-opting communities: a 'market community' develops. Communities may be self-funded and governed or facilitated by the company. *Unilever* had the good sense to fund an online conversation about 'being a woman' which featured use of their *Dove* brand, facilitating the *Dove Real Beauty Campaign* to "free woman from today's beauty stereotypes and to help embrace their own beauty"[49] based on research claiming that women preferred the 'natural look' as opposed to "unrealistic body perfection they are confronted with on a regular basis".[50] It spawned a counter narrative to competitors *L'Oreal's* 'You're Worth It' campaign and focused on the community social concerns of 'age', 'femininity', 'beauty', 'being a woman'. The product was the facilitator of the community.

---

49 *Dove Self Esteem Fund* website.
50 *BBC* Website.

This is not just good competitive brand strategy, it is also a good example of how a social force, a 'market community', has *in-context* social brand experience, and how meaning as the linking value is instilled into the brand by brand owners and negotiated by brand users. Similarly, *Innocent Drinks*, a brand created *from social meaning*, relaunched a new brand platform reinforcing its health and sustainability credentials to resonate with a new target audience of younger drinkers. These examples shows cultural exchange where cultural *production* is exchanged by consumers, and culturally relevant products are offered by companies. *Cadbury* launched its first *Google+* community – 'Cakes & Baking: The *Cadbury* Kitchen' – a recipe-sharing online community with 2,500 recipes posted from over 20,000 members which drives brand engagement with authentic user-generated content. These content creators, flourishing in an influencer ecosystem of multi-channel networks (MCN), deliver credible, relevant content (websites, text, video, blogs, photography, YouTube user community knowledge, news, consumer reviews, information, advice, experiential reference and so on) are conduits for brand creation and consumer socialisation.

Communities collectively generate and curate brand culture in various ways: through construction of self, emotional relationships, storytelling, and ritualistic practices (Schembri & Latimer, 2016, p. 628). Amongst the popular social network sites (SNSs) *Twitter* is the preferred site for creating and enhancing group affiliation and individual user uniqueness within the community (López, Sicilia, & Moyeda-Carabaza, 2017).

Against a back-drop of the increasingly expensive acquisition of customers, retention through reinforcing relationships through the inherent trust of peers provides a strong platform for brand building online. The phenomenon of online community platforms serve as an opportunity for both company and consumer to create additional value that stretches beyond existing brand identity and value proposition (Schau, Muñíz, & Arnould, 2009, p. 31). Empowered, Internet-enabled, passionate consumers, collectively as brand communities, are coercing brand management to re-examine the basic tenets on which brand management has been based for decades (Kucuk & Krishnamurthy, 2007).

Brand communities differ from other types of communities in that they have a secondary, rather than primary, effect of brand community association (through subcultures and hobby groups), with the brand as symbol (even brands with iconic or mythic significance) preceding the emergence of the community. They are part of a social continuum; the relationships between consumers and between consumers and the provider *is* the brand experience: the value is from the interaction. It is the "shared consciousness", the "rituals and traditions", and a sense of "shared community morality" (Muñiz & O'Guinn, 2001) which marks out the social nature of brand communities. A good example of this is cited by O'Sullivan, Richardson & Collins (2011) who describe the pseudo-sacred brand rituals – conversion ceremonies, transcendent experience, and sacralisation maintenance – amongst a community of users of the niche beer brand *Beamish* in Cork City, Ireland.

The transition of consumers from passive recipients of B2C communications into hyper-active information creating social actors (Prahalad & Ramaswamy 2004) is a characteristic of integrated marketing communications (IMC) in general but particularly with embedded brand communities (EBC) and social networking sites (SNSs) such as *Facebook, Twitter, and LinkedIn* where consumers engage in social connections that shape attitudes. They become the medium with word-of-mouth (WOM) influencers becoming C2C communication diffusers. Brand communities are evidence of connectedness between user and brand – but not necessarily customer and company – and comprise relatively homogenous clusters of people organised around commonality of lifestyle, shared social activities, and the ethos of the brand personified in its purpose.

Whilst these groups may not be ideally segmented in the traditional sense, they represent brand loyalty, recommendation influence, greater sales, more cost-efficient marketing, and a great source of value creation. As C2C conduits for pre-purchase information gathering and shared brand experience, they can be an essential form of trust and counter the bias of corporate websites. Interestingly, netnographic research (participant observation) found that "brand communities are effective tools for influencing sales "regardless of whether these communities reside on company-owned or independently-owned websites . . . [and] the positive information shared by community members has a stronger moderating influence on purchase . . . and are effective customer retention tools for retaining both experienced and novice customers" (Adjei, Noble, & Noble, 2010, p. 634).

Witz *et al* (2013, p. 223) offer a framework for better understanding the engagement of online brand communities (OBCs) identifying brand orientation, internet use, funding, and governance as key dimensions, with function, brand-related activities, and relational motivations as antecedents. They identify three characteristics of a brand community: brand orientation, internet use, and funding and governance.

Brands, therefore, are now seen as *social constructs* (Peñaloza & Venkatesh, 2006), which need to be managed "as community brands" in an environment where brand meanings are animated by social and cultural forces (Brown *et al*, 2003, p. 31). According to Muñíz & O'Guinn (2001), a brand community from a customer-experiential perspective is a fabric of relationships in which the customer is situated and can define themselves through the social dialogue that occurs within the code structure of brands. Support discussions are interlinked with social conversations (Dholakia, Bagozzi, & Pearo, 2004). There is a sharp distinction between "purposeful, strategic company communications – the projection of brand *image* to achieve marketing objectives – and cultural experience – brand innovation occurring 'naturally' in the social setting of brand community" (Grant, 2007, p. 4).

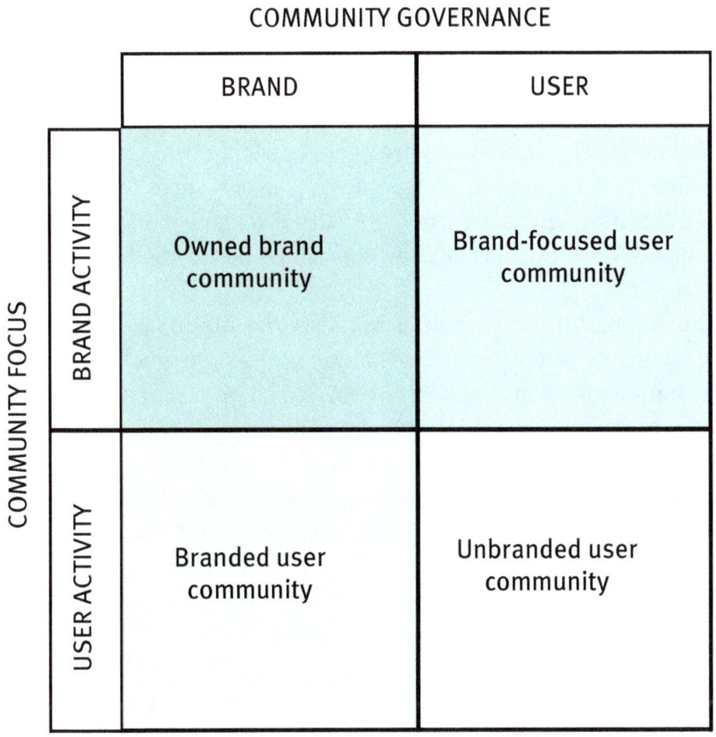

COMMUNITY GOVERNANCE

	BRAND	USER
BRAND ACTIVITY	Owned brand community	Brand-focused user community
USER ACTIVITY	Branded user community	Unbranded user community

COMMUNITY FOCUS

Figure 3.4: Brand Community Matrix.
Source: Adapted from Breitsohl, Dowell, & Kunz, (2013)

Brand strategy needs to acknowledge the interlinked dynamic and recursive nature of the brand community covering:
- Providing a B2C communication conduit fusing corporate brand identity and community partnership meanings.
- Facilitating interaction and nurturing brand loyalty through shared community passion.
- Facilitating activities related to community relationship building.
- Facilitating activities related to community relationship building.

Figure 3.4 describes the dynamic between customer-company *brand* interaction and C2C *social* interaction. on two axes of 'community focus' and 'community governance'. Irrespective of whether the community is 'owned' by company or customer, or whether brands are the focus, the key driving force of how brands grow and provide brand equity to organisations is in the development and nurturing of social relationships, mutuality, dependency, and social bonding. Successful brand strategy is encouraging and leveraging social interaction. Communal experience and social group membership, sometimes self-created, sometimes company-sponsored, can provide a solid social framework on which to build successful brand strategy. For companies with a 'community strategy' at the centre of their brand strategy, Fournier & Lee,[51] however, offer some myth-busting cautionary advice:

- A brand community should not be seen just as part of a marketing strategy but integrated as a high-level business-wide strategy.
- A brand community exists to serve the people in it not to serve the business. Camping and enthusiasts enthusiast use the Austrian website *outdoorseiten.net* and brands originate from the specialised social links that come from using a brand in a community.
- Engineering the community (rather than building the brand) will make the brand stronger. There are three types of community affiliation: 'pools' (membership based on shared values and goals); 'webs' (based on strong C2C, one-to-one connections like social networking sites for example) and 'hubs' (members are united by affection for an individual which may attract different types of members to the group). Effective community strategies combine all three.
- Brand communities can be based on negative energy. The *Dove* campaign started as a reaction to *L'Oreal's* projection of what constitutes 'beauty'. *Apple* users hate *Microsoft* users and define themselves by what they are *not*; the famous "I am a *Mac*" and "I am a PC" campaigns evidence that.
- Focus on opinion leaders may be short-term tactic (good for creating 'buzz'), whereas enabling everyone to be involved is a better long-term strategy, members staying involved and adding lasting value.
- Online social networks may serve valuable community functions but anonymity emboldens antisocial behaviour and my weaken social bonds.
- Communities often defy managerial control.

3.13 Social conscience: Social marketing

Social Marketing is focused on creating social good through the creation of social value for individuals, communities, and whole societies (iSMA, 2021). Promoting or facilitating behaviour change or 'interventions' can be u*pstream* (involving policy change such as limiting fast food portions or supplying healthy alternatives), *midstream* (working with partners or groups in co-creative relationship initiatives in the user's community), or *downstream* (through individual behavioural change). The core is all about behaviour, seen here in the National Social Marketing Centre's (2006, p. 1) definition as being "the systematic application of marketing concepts and techniques to achieve specific *behavioural* goals, for a social or public good".

---

51 Susan Fournier & Lara Lee, "Getting Brand Communities Right", *Harvard Business Review*, April 2009.

The International Social Marketing Association (iSMA) definition is:

Social Marketing seeks to develop and integrate marketing concepts with other approaches to influence behaviours that benefit individuals and communities for the greater social good. Social Marketing practice is guided by ethical principles. It seeks to integrate research, best practice, theory, audience and partnership insight, to inform the delivery of competition-sensitive and segmented social change programmes that are effective, efficient, equitable, and sustainable.

(iSMA, 2021)

The six core Social Marketing concepts are:
- *Setting of explicit social goals*: An essential feature of setting explicit social goals is that they are accompanied by equally explicit metrics that facilitate the ongoing measurement and evaluation of interventions. Often expressed as strategic goals and more specific behavioural objectives.
- *Citizen orientation and focus*: Built around a commitment to understand and engage communities and beneficiaries of social programmes. This means that rather than experts alone deciding what needs to be done and how it should be done, citizens should be engaged in identifying problems, developing solutions, and implementing them. Citizen orientation is concerned with ensuring that the people who are the focus of the Social Marketing interventions are engaged in the selection, development, delivery and evaluation of programmes designed to assist or enable them.
- *Value propositions delivery via the Social Marketing Intervention Mix*: Social Marketing value propositions are developed based on the target audience insight, evidence and data gathered, and the means through which social good is delivered. Value propositions are developed through a process of critical reflexive thinking. Social Marketing nearly always uses a mix of interventions to create social good. Value propositions create value for citizens by helping them achieve what they want to, solve problems and make life easier and better. Value propositions come in many forms including: service provision, social products, policy, systems, environments, economic incentives and socially approved sanctions, recommended behaviours and actions.
- *Theory, insight, data and evidence informed audience segmentation*: Gathering of understanding by audience segmentation is the process of clustering people together who share similar beliefs, attitudes, behaviours and social pressures. Segmentation enables a more customised development of support programmes for individuals and groups.
- *Competition, barrier and asset analysis*: Within Social Marketing it is not enough to seek to influence policy, individuals and group behaviour, it is often also necessary to influence the 'competition' who are trying to influence target groups in a negative way. Influences on social behaviour include personal significant others, the media, environmental factors, cultural factors, economic factors and social norms. All of these factors can act as barriers to adopting or sustaining

positive social behaviour. For example, if you want to encourage people to recycle their waste, use a bed net or use less energy. It is also necessary to understand who or what might be encouraging people to not do these things. Once identified, strategies to reduce the influence of competing factors, actors, and barriers can be developed as part of the Social Marketing strategy. Social Marketing involves developing implementation coalitions with other organizations, sectors, professionals, and communities to address identified social challenges and competition. Scoping what assets exist in the wider community of interest and encouraging them to make a contribution to solving social challenges is a marker of good Social Marketing practice.

– *Critical thinking, reflexivity, and ethical practice*: The Social Marketing process is both systematic and systemic. It involves comprehensive research, analysis, planning, management and evaluation of programmes. In addition to logical planning and evaluation Social Marketing also involves the use of theory, critical reflexivity and an adaptive approach to analysis and development. This reflexive approach includes a commitment to ensuring that Social Marketing programmes are both culturally acceptable and relevant. Social Marketers continuously assess multiple environmental, social, and economic factors that are having or may have an impact on the social goals they are promoting. Social Marketing practice is also informed by ethical considerations including acceptability, transparency, and the balancing of potential benefits and costs associated with programme intervention.

Social forces such as norms, influences, obedience, compliance, conformity, self-image, and peer group affiliation, are vitally important to explaining the nature and efficacy of social marketing. Role models and influencers can help ideas diffuse (eg: the anti-racism *Black Lives Matter* movement) and reach a 'tipping point' (Gladwell, 2000) of acceptance and adoption. The impact of opinion leaders and other consumers can be very influential in terms of the adoption or resistance to social ideas, practices, or changes in behaviour. For example, during the restrictions and vaccinations implemented during the recent COVID-19 pandemic, the roll-out of this was hampered by an aggressive 'Anti-Vaxer' contingent.

Around the world governments of different kinds and their people use a variety of approaches to agree what behaviours and beliefs are socially valuable and how they should be brought about or sustained. Another example, the peer pressure to drive is being undermined by the popularity of cycling, fuelled by peer practice and accelerated by initiatives such as Government *'Bike2Work'* tax-free cycle scheme. The recognition that commercial marketing can have negative or malignant consumption effects (eg: tobacco smoking) has led to some referring to the counter consumption reduction goals (ie: campaigns to *stop* tobacco consumption) as 'anti-marketing'. As Hastings & Saren (2003, p. 305) suggest, this is best described as a "symbiotic relationship between social, commercial, and critical marketing thought" working together to provide insights for combatting anti-social and personally harmful behaviour.

Creating social good through the creation of social value for individuals, communities, and whole societies is fast becoming a new paradigm in brand strategy. Encouraging behaviour change, working with partners or groups in co-creative relationship initiatives in the user's community, or through individual behavioural change social or public good will become more prominent in brand strategy.

3.14 Social stories: Brand narratives

An emerging theme in academic research and practitioner communications campaigns is the imperative of brand narratives – "interlocking story arcs which help to change the emotional, symbolic and social connections between company and customer, buyer and brand" (Smith, 2011, p. 32). According to Holt (2004, p. 56), "creating mythical brand narratives can be through real consumer affiliation with an imaginary world based on emotional connections through the brand". Brand narratives are not always initiated by strategic stimuli but may emanate from cultural resonance within target audiences – some Zeitgeist spirit of the moment – and are sometimes post hoc. As we have seen in the Opening Case, *Unilever*'s famous *Dove 'Campaign For Real Beauty'* recognised and facilitated an online C2C debate on the aging process and the use of cosmetics and won many hearts, minds, and market share, and *Libresse* had a very specific brand purpose of breaking female taboos.

Principles in practice

Social media influence and stakeholder capitalism

The digital revolution, with its implicit democratic orientation and shift of power away from companies, has encouraged consumers to begin or end relationships with companies based on organisational stance on social issues. The social power of groups has given the ability to make a difference, and this has changed the customer-company dynamic.

"The recent embrace of stakeholder capitalism is, at least in part, an illustration of the influence that Millennials and Gen Zs have already had. Businesses are increasingly being held accountable for their impact on society" says Michele Parmelee, *Deloitte* Global Deputy CEO. The other half of her title – Chief People and Purpose Officer – clearly focuses on a key role in the customer-company relationship: driving organisational purpose-led meaningful change as articulated by the changing social conscience of its customers.

Research reveals that younger consumers have an enhanced need for pushing for social change – racial injustice, inequality, and care for the environment – and believe the world has reached a social tipping point. Following the murder of American black man George Floyd, the *Black Lives Matter Movement*, fuelled by social media, made racial justice a key millennial issue and solidarity a key motivator. Organisations, reluctantly or otherwise, had no choice but to align with their customers' social causes. It was seen as a significant moment: people and organisations joined in united purpose. Consumers were soon realising that the power to change things was in their hands; companies acknowledged their role in standing alongside their customers in making a stand.

Following the enforced reduction of carbon emissions during the various Covid-19 lockdowns, a new imagined eco-friendly world has led to societal pressures to rethink product effects on the environment, with packaging recycling, use of public transport, changing eating habits, and making fewer fast-fashion clothes amongst many societal trends to emerge. In contrast, 65% of business leaders stated that environmental sustainability initiatives needed to be curtailed due to the pandemic. "Driving societal change is not just the right thing for leaders to do, but it's also good for business" Parmalee says, adding that "Those who are purpose-led and share and support these younger generation's vision for a brighter future will come out on top".

Source: "Deloitte Global Millennial and Gen Z Survey" Deloitte, July 2021.

Brown's (2005, p. 215) perceptive reflection that "Marketing isn't something applied to culture, culture is a component of the marketing-industrial complex that holds the entire developed world in its thrall" captures the essence of what Marketing affects and is affected by. McAlexander, Schouten, & Koenig (2002, p. 48) identify the connection between brand community and brand loyalty claiming that the more relationships are "internalised as part of the consumer's life experience, the more the customer is integrated into the brand community, and the more loyal the customer is consuming the brand". Community lifestyle can lead to lifetime customer value.

As Cayla & Arnould (2008, p. 86) suggest, "To talk of brands as cultural forms is to acknowledge that branding is a specific form of communication which tells stories". The strategic act of storytelling has become essential to modern branding (Herskovitz & Crystal, 2010), adding symbolic value to products and using emotional components to differentiate from competitors (Lundqvist, Liljander, Gummerus, & Van, 2013). Branding has been elevated to a commercial and personal prose of storytelling whence we gain most of our shared knowledge about ourselves (Twitchell, 2004), and often interpret experiences with brands in a narrative process (Abbott, 2002). Here, brands become more meaningful the more closely they are linked to a consumer's self-concept (Escalas, 2004), and the imperative of customer/company co-created, socially-situated brand story arcs manifest in every brand encounter and iteration of culture, positioning, and perception (Dahlén, Lange, & Smith, 2010).

Gus Griffin, Global Director for *Jack Daniel's*, points to two elements of the *Jack Daniel's* narrative: the projection of authenticity and integrity from formal marketing communications, and the popular culture negotiated meaning in-use of independence and masculinity values of the brand. Co-authorship is also evident in the realignment of the *Adidas* brand. Once Hip-Hop act *Run DMC* adopted use of the three stripes and their fans followed suit, the transition from a sports-orientated brand to one with sub-culture vitality and street cred was underway. When they actually sang about the social use of the brand (not a homage to the brand itself) – 'My Adidas' – and encouraged the audience to wave their *Adidas* shoes, a new narrative was created not by the company but by the users.

A totally different story built around shoes is *Toms Shoes*. After witnessing the hardship of children growing up without shoes, founder Blake Mycoskie turned a mission into a strategy into a narrative with *Toms Shoes*, matching every purchase with a new pair for a child in need. 50 million free pairs later, the narrative has been extended to help restoring sight to over 500,000 people, safe water to over 400,000 people, and launched its 'Bag Collection' in 2015 providing safe birth for a mother and child in need.

3.15 Social partnerships: Exchange relationships and dialogue

For quite a considerable time now, the Relationship Marketing (RM) paradigm "has become embedded in the rhetoric and lexicon of marketing discourses" (Fitchett & McDonagh, 2000, p. 209), driving the meta-narrative away from a managerialist, prescriptive formula, and providing an alternative perspective from which to view marketing philosophy and, indeed, marketing practice. It is the contribution to discourse which is of primary significance, encouraging the transition from:
– Product 'marketing-as-exchange' to 'exchange relations'.
– Economic transactions to social relationships.
– Customer satisfaction to customer retention.
– Need satisfaction to promise fulfilment and creating ongoing positive customer relations.
– Customer complaint to customer loyalty.
– Changing the way, we look at customers not just as passive participants to active agents.

Its fundamental premise is that the acknowledgement of creating and maintaining a stable customer base is a primary business asset, and at the centre of this is the notion of loyalty. Relationship Marketing offered "the potential of an evolutionary praxis . . . of business practice and social development" (Fitchett & McDonagh, 2000, p. 213). Indeed, customer-oriented relationships now must be triadic *social partnerships* between the company, the customer, and the community to which the customer belongs (Palmer and Koenig-Lewis, 2009). From a business perspective, the value is in maintaining mutually beneficial bonded relationships; from the customer's point of view, this notion of proper 'social partnerships' is taking the concept of 'service provision' to 'service of others' and is extending the meaning of what is being exchanged in the relationship.

Iacobucci (1996) describes these sociological network constructs as:
- *Competition*: Behaviour that is goal or object-centred, based on scarcity, indirect, and impersonal, in which a third party controls the goal or object.
- *Conflict*: Behaviour that is opponent-centred, very direct, and highly personal, in which the goal or object is controlled by the opponent.
- *Cooperation*: Behaviour that involves joint striving for a goal or object, is direct or indirect, and personal, in which the goal or object that is controlled by a third party can only be secured if the focal parties coalesce.

Customers are increasingly aware of the relationships they have with brands; equally, they are conscious of what brands they want to have relationships with. Relationship marketing, often developed within a service context, is an essential part of brand strategy.

3.16 Social innovation and value

Social innovation is becoming one of the critical business challenges. Social and environmental concerns are now integrated into standard business performance metrics. Lars Rebien Sørensen of *Novo Nordisk* identifies this shift in business measurement as a crucial element of taking an integrated approach to strategy alignment: "In the long term, social and environmental issues become financial issues".[52] Companies are not new to non-profit goals as essential tandem strategic objectives. The deployment of methods and tactics to demonstrate citizenship, corporate governance, philanthropy, and social responsibility demonstrate this. However, the notion (and more importantly the practice), of social innovation is becoming an increasingly relevant component of business strategy.

Recent consumption practices which are forged in collaboration, 'crowd-sourcing', and 'user-led innovation' have triggered the externalising of the research and development function. For example, a detailed Global CEO study (*IBM*, 2006).[53] found that "customers and business partners have, for many companies, by far surpassed the internal R & D Department in importance as a source of innovation".[54] Where products or services are 'innovative' in terms of new markets or new applications, the 'diffusion of innovation' (Rogers, 1962) – the process by which innovation is communicated and spread across members of a social system – is the driving force for adoption and is fundamentally *social*, relying heavily on the social 'risk' (often for intangible psychosocial reasons) being mitigated through social influencing power of human capital.

---

52 "No 1 top 100 performing CEOs in the world", *Harvard Business Review*, 2015.
53 Global CEO study, (*IBM*, 2006).
54 CEO Study, *IBM*, 2006.

Rogers' diffusion theory is a synthesis of anthropology and sociology and pinpoints memetic social behaviour as the key to new ideas or products being adopted. Resistance to innovation through perceived influencers with source credibility. The significance is found not in the

Principles in practice

Building future markets through social innovation

As growth slows in developed markets, the "next 4 billion" consumers in emerging economies represent a growth opportunity for local and multinational companies alike. In the short term, the relatively low purchasing power of these consumers makes it harder to achieve profit margins, yet forward-looking companies view their market-building and business development efforts in this segment as a form of "long tail" investment. In doing so, they can gain insights on the unique needs and preferences of these customers, drive awareness and behavioural change, and innovate to make product lines more affordable and relevant.

Companies that successfully pursue social innovation as an opportunity for developing new markets typically innovate in three specific ways. First, they design products and services that respond to the unique needs and behaviours of low-income customers. This can include developing new products and services or adapting existing product lines for their needs (eg: food brands fortifying existing products with micronutrients to address malnutrition). Second, the products and services must offer strong value for money despite (or because of) low purchasing power, necessitating the design of cost-effective products.

Third, products must be made accessible across large geographies with poor infrastructure, which requires thinking creatively about distribution channels. As demonstrated by *Nova Nordisk's* experience, in addition to enhancing the quality of life of low-income customers, such innovations can also present opportunities to promote micro-entrepreneurship and enhance incomes.

Source: 2020 *World Economic Forum*

transfer of ownership of output but in the transfer of *meaning*, the market exchange of co-created value experienced by the consumer in the act of consumption in the unique context of his or her own life (Grönroos, 2006). It is in the *interaction*. The customer and company are operant resources, collaborative partners who co-create value.

The driving force behind the "diffusion of innovation" (Rogers, 1962) is not just technological but social; it is based on the impact of social agents in the creation of social meaning. This well-established theory is concerned with how and why new technological disruption or new ideas spread within a social system. Here, adoption is by aspiration and imitation and can be "trickle up" or "trickle down" driving diffusion. Besides the peer group pressure of imitative behaviour and the need for group belonging, the effect of endorsement from celebrities and 'influencers' accelerates adoption. Meaning is transferred from the influencer onto the brand and it is imbued with associations of the third party's credibility and persuasive power, valorised with social significance.

This is the essence of Malcolm Galdwell's "tipping point" premise. He refers to this phenomenon as "social epidemics", the social changes instigated by powerful and persuasive influencers spreading WOM about a brand or a cause like an infectious disease or virus. Hence the label 'viral marketing', a socially-engineered brand strategy using established social networks as a medium for message dissemination. In fact the term "tipping point" has roots in the distribution analysis basis of epidemiology, and Gladwell acknowledges this: "If we understand the way in which social epidemics, such as crime waves and fashion fads reach critical mass – what epidemiologists call the *tipping point* – we can shape history" (2002, p. 2).

A brand strategy which uses the principle of difussion – to spread word of mouth communications about a new product or brand to gain attention, start a conversation, create awareness, build an audience, drive traffic, and convert into sales – deploys a 'viral' approach. Although the objectives may well be those of brand strategy, the driving force is social. Distribution of message is more often than not digital through electonic word of mouth (eWOM), making the impact immediate and the diffusion accelerated.

Those brands which have social *visibility* have better adoption rates and are more readily diffused. Adoption criteria – relative advantage (superior to competition); is compatible with user's existing consumption patterns and usage habits; is less or no more complex to use than existing offering; can be trialled in advance of purchase, and can be observed amongst fellow brand users – can be subjective, open to individual interpretation and perception, but these criteria must be met before adoption is considered. Perceived risk can be a barrier to adoption. Functional, physical, financial, and time risks are sometimes secondary to the psychosocial concerns of damaging ego or social embarrassment of not choosing a product/brand within peer group or celebrity endorsement.

The difussion effect of imitative social behaviour is like a *social contagion*. This can be an effective element of spreading product knowledge by WOM, encouraging adoption by brand socialisation, rewarding social influence, and is a fundamental element of brand strategy.

Chapter takeaways

- One of the binding elements of customer-company fusion is the creation of meaning and value, and the driving force for meaning, created through shared values, is a *socially constructed phenomenon.*
- A brand is a cultural resource of emotions, linking values, attitudes, lifestyles, and associations, with enormous potential for creating meaning for consumers.
- Service is not the only axis of value creation; service is the processing of experience but it is not the driver.
- Where there is reciprocity between company and customer, *social production can add value to the brand* and therefore enhance an organisation's brand equity.
- Social salience is relevance in a culturally constituted setting, one where emotional and experiential bonds with brands can create brand loyalty through social linking.
- Brands are not just vehicles to carry fixed meanings, but increasingly they are the meaning itself.
- The concept of a 'brand community' is an important strategic brand management tool for which group membership can give self-enhancement, self-efficacy, purposive value and positively affect buyer behaviour.
- Creating social good through the creation of social value for individuals, communities, and whole societies is fast becoming a new paradigm in brand strategy.
- Creating mythical brand narratives can be through real consumer affiliation with an imaginary world based on emotional connections through the brand,
- The driving force behind the diffusion of innovation is not just technological but social; it is based on the impact of social agents in the creation of social meaning.

Closing case

© solidcolours from Getty Images Signature via canva.com

"Us Not Me". Social salience and brand science

For the modern day consumer, brand loyalty lies somewhere between "the discourse of capital, neo-liberalism, and neo-classical economics on the one hand, with the search for a *meaningful* self through consumption on the other" (Shankar, Elliott, & Goulding, 2001, p. 430). For companies, brand loyalty is created by infusing "meaning into products and transforming commodities into concepts and lifestyles" (Salzer-Morling & Strannegård, 2002, p. 224). However, culturally constituted meaning is not imposed but *negotiated* between customer and company. Now, a socially-driven approach to building brand longevity – linking consumption and culture, marketing and meaning – is fast becoming an essential element of brand strategy. The brand equity which resides in culturally constituted meaning is borne out of a new socially-dominant logic. Brands that resonate with how we live – anything from the nature of being a woman to protecting the environment – succeed by adding values to value. Social salience is the linking value of brands that have relevancy and authenticity, where meaning is fused in co-created social brand dialogues of belief and belonging. But can a cause always be credible? When does topical alignment become embedded social purpose?

Take sportswear. *Reebok*, not normally a brand to weave politics into their brand communications, reacted instinctively with "Nevertheless, She Persisted" T-Shirts when Elizabeth Warren was silenced on the floor of the US Senate. This triggered a 'social spike' in sales but it was short-lived. However, when they made gender inclusiveness a cause by telling the story of *Reebok Freestyle*, the first athletic shoe made specifically for women in 1982, this became a salient narrative of how "women got a foot in the door". In a series of podcasts entitled "Flipping the Game", the story of the creation of the brand is used as a vehicle for exposing deep inequalities that still exist for women, not just in the sports industry but in society in general.

Similarly, competitor *Nike* have encouraged the participation of young girls in sport since 1995, a message which resonated with a key target market (at the time representing only 10% of *Nike's* revenues), reinforcing associations of courage and competition. With women's apparel now 23% and the fastest growing segment, this social connection has proved successful in terms of sales *and* social goals. This social salience has been extended into their social sponsorships of grassroots football, making access and community the focus of its "The Architects of New Football" and "The Land of New Football" campaigns. *Nike* are investing in the future of football by creating grassroots sports community programmes for unrepresented kids, specifically from Black and Asian communities. Players such as Manchester United's Marcus Rashford, whose football skills have almost become of secondary importance to his work on homelessness, child hunger, and youth literacy, is used as the perfect role model "to inspire the next generation through on-field excellence and civic responsibility". This is part of *Nike's* 'corporate social credit score' (the Environmental, Social, and Corporate Governance (ESG) intangible asset value metrics) which measure sustainability and societal impact. *Nike* have invested heavily in reducing environmental waste in manufacturing and taking the initiative in 2010 when they launched their 'Environmental Apparel Design' software tool, an open-source application allowing any garment manufacturers to gauge environmental impact, and again in 2012 with its waste-reducing 'flyknit' technology.

This illustrates that brand meaning is a socially constituted, negotiated phenomenon. Its essence is socio-anthropological, a brand being "a cluster of strategic cultural ideas" (Grant, 2007, p. 27), linking people's personal experience and social and cultural events, "driven by a narrative view of the brand that braids the filaments of everyday empirical truth into a common strand" (Sherry Jr., 2005, p. 41). Of course the cataclysmic events of COVID-19 in 2020 has put truth and authenticity of purpose centre stage. Consumers are more value-vigilant; brands which tactically position – topical alignment rather than embedded social purpose – can alienate consumers,[55] with Millennials and Generation Z having the highest expectation of brand authenticity. In 2017, *Pepsi* fell foul of their customer base and were accused of cultural appropriation when ill-advisedly associating a white supermodel Kendall Jenner with the Black Lives Matter protest movement. Silence isn't an option for a brand now, as *Netflix* demonstrated when they *tweeted* "To be silent is to be complicit". Not for the first time, *Nike* struck the right note, firstly in 2018 with a campaign supporting NFL player Colin Kaepernick (from whom 'taking the knee' originated), and then in 2020 following the murder of George Floyd with a *Twitter* plea for unity in the fight against racism with a spin on their famous motto "For Once, Just Don't Do It". This caused rivals *Adidas* to retweet the sentiment and *Nike* themselves to be forced to look at their support of black communities and their own workforce.

Riding on this wave of diversity and social cohesion, and conscious of the damage to creative industries because of the COVID-19 pandemic, *Tommy Hilfiger* has re-oriented its fashion clothing positioning to encourage unity and inspiration with their "Moving Forward Together" campaign, extolling the virtues of recyclability with "Together We Create", and supporting grassroots tailoring with "Together With Local Heroes". So too *Stella Artois*, who had repositioned from a male-dominant user image to one appealing to female consumers, extended this narrative into activism with their "Buy a Lady a Drink" campaign in 2017, promoting awareness of the global water crisis in partnership with *Water.org*. Sales of limited-addition packs of lager resulted in a month of clean water being supplied to families in developing countries.

As with so many purpose-led brands today, the value proposition which resonates with a group sense of social and environmental conscience, which encourages consumers to use brands that make a stand, stands a chance of surviving and growing.

---

55 "2021 media trends and predictions", Kantar, *BizCommunity*, November 18, 2020.

Questions

1. Companies are moving towards purpose-driven models of brand strategy, aligning with cultural and social values. Why is social salience and cause-consciousness so important?
2. Do you agree that purpose-led brands can encourage brand loyalty?
3. Is the "Buy a Lady a Drink" campaign by *Stella Artois* a short-term tactic or long-term commitment?

Note: The photo(s) used in this case study is/are not connected and/or does not represent any brand(s) mentioned. It/they is/are used to make a visual discussion point by the authors.

Section 3: **The development of strategy**

Building brand equity by co-creating long-lasting symbolic symbiosis between customer and company is the *sine qua non* of marketing and indeed organisational strategy. Mutually beneficial worth represents social value to customers and profitable sustainable income streams to companies. *Section 3* covers the detail and dynamics of how that value creation is achieved. The essence of what the brand stands for, the memories and experiences engendered by its use, and how it is hopefully perceived and positioned against the competition in the minds of the consumer, requires a strategy built on customer insights derived from customer segmentation, aligned with purpose, proposition and positioning, forged in the experience management of customer-company fusion, and with a carefully engineered customer journey built into service provision and process.

Section 3 puts the conceptualisation of managing brand strategy into contemporary context: the impact of traditional segmentation and current data analysis techniques on customer centricity; how and why it is vital for purpose, value proposition, and positioning to be aligned; how the customer-company interface represents the crucible of customer experience; the mechanics and dynamics of how digitally-infused, service-oriented customer journeys; the connectivity and convergence of marketing communications; and how the equity in the brand, customer, and employee can produce tangible results from intangible assets.

https://doi.org/10.1515/9783110718638-007

4 Managing the alignment of strategy: Purpose, proposition, and positioning

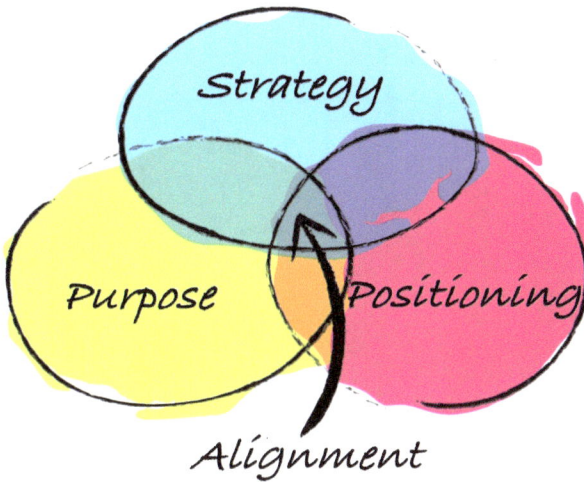

https://doi.org/10.1515/9783110718638-008

Opening case

Tirtyl: **Refill not Landfill.**
Conscious consumption goes mainstream.

The recent academic discussion centred around *conscious consumption* reflects the social, cultural, environmental, and historical contextualisation of consumption and the focus on purpose as a central thrust of contemporary strategy. This case study discusses how this 'efficiency-focused rationalisation' discourse affects company value propositions and how this now resonates with consumers buying into the notion of sustainable consumption.

For some years now, motivation for consumption has been analysed from a range of social, psychological, and anthropological perspectives. The term 'societal marketing' emerged in the early 80s where the disconnect between short-term consumer needs and long-term social and environmental concerns caused marketers to rethink. Offering consumers value which protected the environment seemed to be a mutually beneficial way to approach strategy.

As a research topic, the term 'sustainable consumption' emerged in the early 2000s (Cohen & Murphy, 2003). The indirect effects of high consumption lifestyles have negative impacts on the environment and other people (Lorek & Vergragt, 2016). Building a better world through *'conscious consumption'* – consumer's social responsibility and attitude towards adopting environmentally-conscious behaviour – affects attitudes to products, brands, and companies. Conscious consumption is an alternative to "foment big changes in an impetuous future that threatens humanity's survival" (Avallone & Giraldi, 2012, p. 122). But will this prove to be more than a fad? That's certainly not the view of one forward-thinking company founded by Australians Lachlan and May – *Tirtyl*, an ethical company with a mission to "create amazing products that unwaste" and to make *conscious consumption mainstream*. May's view is that:

> Conscious consumption and sustainability are widespread, becoming front of mind for the consumer of today, in particular Millennials and Gen Z. As these demographics further increase in purchasing influence, the trends are likely to only continue, and more pressure will be placed on companies and brands to adopt a "social good" purpose or strategy.
>
> Majority of consumers are not ready to sacrifice a significant degree of convenience or cost in order to "do the right thing", so in order for conscience consumption to continue to spread,

companies will have to innovate and develop better, smarter products. Government policy will also have a significant influence.

Efforts to develop alternative materials that are less aggressive to the environment have been valorised by organisations with conscience. Research shows that 'material green' consumers are "buying into a particular image in their consumption practices very much connected to the meanings of their consumption that are derived from the communication value they attach to commodities" (Connolly & Prothero, 2003, p. 275).

The average person consumes over 100lbs of single-use plastic annually and yet only 9% of all plastics are recycled, with over 8 million tonnes of waste pouring into our oceans each year. Marine life are dying as a consequence, and toxic micro plastics are ending up in our food supply chains. *Tirtyl* developed household cleaning and personal care products that eliminate plastic waste, starting with a hand soap. The range of 'smart soap kits' include recyclable refillable dispensers and foaming *Hand Soap* tablets that dissolve in household tap water to form a full bottle of soap. This eliminates the need to buy a plastic bottle every time you need to replenish your hand soap. It also means customers don't pay for water or plastic packaging. Their 'impact philosophy' is based on a simple customer-centric mantra of "Doing the right thing", such as their give-back programme *Tirtyl Tip*, donating a percentage of sales to social causes, as well as working with partnerships to remove plastic waste, marine-life conservation, clean-water initiatives, and lobbying for plastic policy reform.

One such social partnership is with *Plastic Bank*, the world's leading ocean-bound plastic clean-up organisation with collection infrastructure in developing communities world-wide. Here, ocean-bound plastic waste is harvested and upcycled as "Social Plastic" which is sold back into the Private Sector as new consumer goods. For every tablet sold, the equivalent of a plastic bottle of ocean-bound plastic is collected from *Tirtyl's* contributions. That's a bottle prevented and collected with each tablet sold. In the first 6 months since launching in Jan 2021, over 250,000 equivalent plastic bottles have been collected.

Lachlan describes this venture as a "real win-win" as contributions made to *Plastic Bank* are used to pay wages to locals in Indonesia, Brazil, and Haiti, who harvest the ocean-bound plastic waste. Another partnership is *Greenfleet* who help address *Tirtyl's* carbon footprint by reforesting parts of Australian habitat.

Interestingly, May describes the cost to offset carbon emissions to be quite affordable, and is surprised that most companies do not proactively aim to factor this into their profit models or unit economics as a foregone expense. It is also helpful that *Tirtyl's* products are concentrated to prevent shipping water, and hence consume less energy and emissions to transport. Whether the economic environment will restrict purchase of conscience consumption products may limit their adoption. May's comments do strike a note of caution:

> *Economic factors will always impact the adoption of conscious consumption. In many cases this is due to the simple fact that there is a higher cost associated to "doing the right thing", and often only the more affluent are willing to pay extra for ethical goods/services.*

> *Additionally, government policy also plays an important role. An example of which is the recent bans to categories of single-use plastics across many states and territories in the Western world. Such policy forces the hand and leaves no choice to the consumer.*

> *Whilst product innovation and policy will continue to lift the overall rate of conscious consumption, economic factors will always likely have an influence.*

Better supply chains are built through life-cycle assessment (LCA) analysis and ethical sourcing, and this is a hallmark of *Tirtyl's* mantra: "conscious consumption meets conscious production".

Questions
1. What factors will prevent 'conscience consumption' from becoming just a fad?
2. Do you think that that the general application of 'conscience consumption' will be hampered by economic factors?
3. Distinguish between mission statements and purpose statements.

Source: Tirtyl website and sources as referenced

4.1 Outline of chapter

For organisations competing in today's dramatically changing and often fragile economic and social landscape, aligning brand strategy with how companies are perceived by customers and other stakeholders, how value propositions are judged against competitors, and how the purpose of the organisation affects its markets and environments, is the key to sustainable success. A company that has an authentic, relevant, and consistent philosophy, a strong point of view of what the company stands for and why it does it what it does, has a solid strategic platform for creating and sustaining, in its holistic totality, *purpose-driven brand strategy*.

With the emphasis on values as much as value, the relationship the company has with the customer, and by extension the environment, has dramatically changed. Purpose is sometimes referred to as "the new differentiation" but its permanency is the rock of strategy. Purpose-led brands have a sense of responsibility and accountability imbued in their raison d'être and are aware of how their activities affect their customers, employees, other stakeholders, society, and the environment as a whole as much as how they relate to its customers' direct needs and wants. Coherence and constancy reifies and reinforces organisational philosophy, and this will help positioning in the long-term.

Positioning is a company's attempt, both actual and perceptual, to match the promise of its value proposition with the value expectation of its target market. Because it reflects and sometimes affects the values of its target audiences, it has to be a fluid concept. Whereas positioning is a strategic device which links organisation to marketplace, purpose is all-pervasive affecting all aspects of the company. Now more than ever, an organisation that stands for something has a better chance of remaining standing. "What you do" and "How you do it", are fundamental strategic and positional statements. Now, "Why you do it" and looking beyond to "So what?", determine an organisation's purpose. Purpose drives everything and positioning everything through the lens of purpose makes decision-making easier: *if it is the right thing to do given your purpose or cause, then do it.*

Of course, purpose erroneously does get used as a short-term promotional tactic rather than a fundamental part of long-term strategy. A common misconception of what sceptics of purpose think is that "because it is about prioritising societal benefit, its pursuit automatically requires an organisation to sacrifice its profits" (Ebert, Hurth, & Prabhu, 2018, p. 9). In reality, proper alignment of purpose is beneficial for long-term financial performance. Purpose-led brand strategy is a powerful way to drive not only the brand but overall business strategy by providing a backbone for innovation and transformation. In the Post-COVID-19 era, resilience is key. Evidence is growing that having purpose beyond profit is becoming central to that.[56] Aligning purpose, values and positioning, with a value system to support achieving organisational objectives, can provide a roadmap of organisational strategy, framing business decisions, integrating internal operations with external stakeholders, establishing mutually beneficial loyal relationships, and building brand longevity.

This chapter examines how the power of purpose complements shareholder primacy, as well as reinforcing *shared* stakeholder value, meaning, and direction. It explores how it can give companies a line of sight that connects to higher principles and a pathway to higher performance, demonstrating how clear articulation of purpose can ignite the life of the external perception of the brand reflecting the strength and authenticity of the internal company culture, foster visionary innovation, as well as impacting on company competitiveness, stakeholders, and the environment.

---

56 Nell Debevoise, "Why Purpose-Driven Businesses Are Faring Better in COVID-19, 12th May 2020 (accessed via www,forbes,com/sitesnelldebevoise/2020/05/12/why-purpose-driven-businesses-are-faring-better-in-covid-19)

Learning outcomes

After reading this chapter, you'll be able to:
- Distinguish the arguments regarding shareholder primacy and stakeholder democracy.
- Analyse the concept of the 'value proposition' and discuss its importance in building brands.
- Understand the concept of 'purpose', what are its characteristics and how this is fundamentally changing the customer-company relationship.
- Differentiate between purpose, vision, mission, and value statements.
- Demonstrate how value alignment and environmental adaptability is at the heart of purpose-driven brand strategy.
- Define and apply what is meant by 'strategic positioning' and how this links to purpose and value positioning.

4.2 Introduction

There are strategic, managerial, and moral dimensions to the debate about why and how there should be a shift from corporate purpose locked onto shareholder requirements to one with a clearer and more relevant customer-orientation as its focus. The notion of being 'purpose-driven' is actually an age-old phenomenon: "The first corporations, since the Industrial Revolution, existed amidst a cultural expectation and understanding that they existed to fulfil a public purpose that went beyond returning profit to owners".[57] Ironically, it was a cultural shift in the 1950s *away from* this perspective to one of *profit*-driven orientation – instigated primarily by the Chicago School of Business and Milton Freidman – which for a considerable period of time achieved hegemony in business philosophy.

However, the world has changed dramatically in this last decade and customer expectation is evolving in parallel. In a little over 20 years, organisational purpose has grown from an elite company USP (Hollensbe *et al*, 2004) and an extension of CSR, to a method of ranking companies,[58] and as a serious challenge to the orthodox normative strategic paradigm. It is argued that "today's main actors of globalisation are no longer nation states but a growing body of multinational corporations and large international non-governmental organisations (NGOs)" (Mayer & Roche, 2021, p. 6) who have gained power and influence over shaping the global agenda through the power and influence of their brands.

According to Ellsworth (2002), leaders must assume responsibility for the process of developing and guiding individuals to challenge the orthodox ideology and accepted assumptions inherent in conventional corporate wisdom. "In an era of

---

[57] "What is a purpose-driven business?", *Regenerate Trust*, 17th June 2020, (accessed via regenerate.org)

[58] The *MSL Group* has created the *PurPle Index* designed to rank the *Fortune Top 100* companies on the basis of the level of participation in those companies' purpose-based initiatives.

radical visibility, technology and media have given individuals the power to stand up for their opinions and beliefs on a grand scale. This power, reflected in everything from the #*MeToo* movement to the growing intolerance for 'fake news', is infiltrating every aspect of people's lives, including their purchasing decisions".[59] As Kramer suggests, a carefully calibrated and brand-aligned purpose can "bridge functions, markets, and socio-demographics . . . . . . and build the connective tissue that aligns all stakeholders beyond financial returns" (2017, p. 2). Or to put it more succinctly: "People don't buy what you do. They buy why you do it" (Sinek, 2009). His simple analysis – "All organisations know WHAT they do. Some organisations know HOW they do it. Very few organisations know WHY they do what they do". – perfectly describes the location of this debate of purpose.

Purpose is becoming a key focal point of creating deeper connections and reciprocal relationships with consumers, do more for the communities within which they work, attract and retain talent, and in the process achieve greater results and impacts. Purpose is not about making better things; it is about making things better.

According to *Deloitte*'s Global CEO Purrit Renjin, "Brands that authentically lead with purpose are changing the nature of business today . . . . . . leaders ranked societal impact as the No 1 way to measure annual performance – more than financial performance or customer and employee satisfaction".[60] It has become a hot-button issue in terms of strategic alignment. Extensive research by *Mars Catalyst*, the internal think tank of food and beverage giant *Mars Incorporated*, (in conjunction with *Säid Business School* at *Oxford University*), has been conducting extensive research for some 9 years now, providing profound insights on purpose, value creation, and reciprocal environmental projects.

Brands that have emotional and ethical connectivity that transcends product functionality have a solid base for building brand longevity. "Without a sense of purpose, no company, either public or private, can achieve its full potential" (Fink, 2017, p. 6). Extensive research by *Deloitte*[61] indicates that "focusing on *purpose* rather than *profit* builds business confidence and drives investment. This is a critical finding and underscores the significant impact a "culture of purpose" can play in fostering a thriving business community".

Purpose is the essence of brand relevance and the bedrock of every experience co-created between company and customer. In 1909, *Chanel* marketed suits for women at a time when this was strictly a male dominion. Market potential and

59 "To Affinity and Beyond: From me to we: The rise of the purpose-led brand", *Accenture* Strategy Research Report, 2018.
60 "Success personified in the Fourth Industrial Revolution: Four leadership personas for an era of change" *Deloitte*, 2020.
61 "Culture of Purpose – Building business confidence; driving growth. Core Beliefs & Culture Survey", *Deloitte*, 2014.

competitive advantage may have been the primary objective, but it may have inadvertently planted a seed for inclusivity and relevance. According to the *EY Institute*, purpose can "act as a guiding light through uncertainty" for companies seeking to navigate disruption. It has moved the concerns and aims of Corporate Social Responsibility from the periphery of strategy and now situates it as a key management platform at the centre of dynamic decision-making and business leadership.

Companies that lead with purpose and build around it "can achieve continued loyalty, consistency, and relevance in the lives of its consumers. Those that fail to identify and articulate their purpose may survive in the short-term, but, over time, people are likely to demand more" (O'Brien, Main, Kounkel, & Stephan, 2019, p. 5). For example, everything *BMW* designs and manufactures must adhere to the brand purpose of 'enabling people to experience the joy of driving'. Companies who are purpose-driven experience higher market share, grow three times faster than their competitors, and achieve higher customer satisfaction. *P&G*'s belief that *Pampers* were more than just diapers that prevent baby wetness led to a transformation from product principles to brand purpose. A complete reorientation from being in the 'dryness business' into the 'baby development business' resulted in, for example, a vaccination partnership with *UNICEF* in over 40 countries and *Pampers* becoming *P&G*'s first ever $8 billion brand.

When Jim Stengel, former *P&G* Marketing Director, and Benoit Garbe, *Millward Brown Optimor VP*, analysed 10 years' worth of data across 50,000 brands (the 'Stengel 50'), they wanted to uncover the common principle between the brands that grew the most in terms of "customer bonding" and "shareholder value". Their extensive study found that there was a direct relationship between a brand's ability to serve a higher purpose and its financial performance.[62] Table 4.1 shows the list of top brands involved in the study:

Table 4.1: The 'Stengel 50'.

Accenture, management and enterprise consulting services	*L'Occitane*, personal care
Airtel, mobile communications	*Louis Vuitton*, luxury apparel and leather goods
Amazon.com, e-commerce	*MasterCard*, electronic payments
Apple, personal computing technology and mobile devices	*Mercedes-Benz*, automobiles

62 Jim Stengel & *Millward Brown*, "*Millward Brown*, in Partnership with Jim Stengel, Reveals the 50 Fastest-Growing Brands in the World and Uncovers the Source of Their Success", *Business Wire*, 2012.

Table 4.1 (continued)

Aquarel, bottled water	*Method*, household cleaners and personal care
BlackBerry, mobile communications	*Moët & Chandon*, champagne
Calvin Klein, luxury apparel and accessories	*Natura*, personal care
Chipotle, fast food	*Pampers*, baby care
Diesel, youth- targeted fashion apparel and accessories	*Rakuten Ichiba*, e-commerce
Discovery Communications, media	*Red Bull*, energy drinks
Dove, personal care	*Royal Canin*, pet food
Emirates, air travel	*Samsung*, electronics
FedEx, delivery services	*Sedmoy Kontinent ("Seventh Continent")*, retail grocery
Google, Internet information	*Sensodyne*, oral care
Heineken, beer	*Seventh Generation*, household cleaners and personal care
Hennessy, spirits	*Snow*, beer
Hermès, luxury apparel and leather goods	*Starbucks*, coffee and fast food retailer
HP, information technology products and services	*Stonyfield Farm*, organic dairy products
Hugo Boss, luxury apparel and accessories	*Tsingtao*, beer
IBM, information technology products and services	*Vente-Privee.com*, e-commerce
Innocent, food and beverages	*Visa*, electronic payments
Jack Daniel's, spirits	*Wegmans*, retail grocery
Johnnie Walker, spirits	*Zappos*, e-commerce
Lindt, chocolate	*Zara*, affordable apparel

Source: *Regenerate Trust* (2000).

In the book which builds on this discovery, Stengel states that "companies with ideals of improving people's lives at the centre of all they do outperform the market by a huge margin" (2011, p. 1). In fact, businesses with high ideals grew three times faster than their competitors according to the research conducted for this study.[63]

---

63 Bryon Sharp offers some criticism of what he refers to as "confirmation bias" in the selection of this group of established successful companies in "The flawed Stengel Study of Business Growth",

Companies are building deeper customer bonds through emotional connectivity as well as economic activity. Examples of purpose being practiced evidences a new fusion of commerce and cause, characteristic of companies seeing altruism and competitive advantage as a more relevant and therefore stronger strategic approach:

– Organisations like *P&G* are becoming "a force for good and a force for growth" with their diversity, equality, and 'unconscious bias' campaigns 'The Look' and 'Wash Away Labels'. It is significant that the organisation says that it "has a responsibility to highlight racial bias and to create a constructive conversation on the issue". 'The Talk', one of the films in the recent *P&G* campaign which addressed the conversation that African Americans have with their children about racism and implicit stereotyping (or unconscious bias) has been extensively praised throughout social media and awarded with an Emmy.

– In the cosmetics sector, *The Body Shop,* founded on Anita Roddick's 'environmental sustainability' principles in 1976, is to a large extent a progenitor of the movement of putting 'good' into everything that a company produces and stands for. Their brand purpose, rooted in ethics, fair trade, and equality, is manifest in everything they do – such as 100% traceable natural ingredients protecting 10,000 hectares of forest and other habitat or building bio-bridges to regenerate 75 million square meters of habitat. Recently, they have transformed their stores into activist hubs in support of gender equality. The notion of business being a force for good, driving positive change by pursuing purpose not just profit, is still indelibly stamped into *The Body Shop's* motto which became a manifesto: "Enrich Not Exploit".

– Similarly, *Unilever* facilitated an online conversation about "age" and 'being a woman' as well as self-esteem for younger girls in their *Dove Real Beauty Campaign* to "free woman from today's beauty stereotypes and to help embrace their own beauty". Their website *#speakbeautiful* fights negativity about appearance. Of course, *Unilever* makes money put it makes a point too.

– This is similar to what Japanese cosmetics brand *SK-11* did to inspire women to set their own rules, campaigning on gender and age issues across Asia.

– Food sector brands have emphasised values such as kindness and generosity in their marketing communications campaigns: *Cadbury's* with their 'Fence' campaign which highlights the issue of loneliness amongst the elderly, have linked the cause to *Age UK* and encouraged people to "donate their words" by talking to the elderly; *McVities'* 'Sweeter Together' explores social isolation; and *Mr Kiplings* 'Little Thief' shows care between siblings.

---

in *Marketing Science*, 30th December 2011 which was subsequently countered by Jim Stengel and this does not detract from purpose being a significant contributory factor of success.

- In September 2017, UK retailer *John Lewis*, responding to the 'gender neutral' movement, decided to make a stand against 'gender stereotyping' by moving away from 'Boys' and 'Girls' clothing categorisation.[64]
- Swedish furniture manufacturer *IKEA*, a world leader in environmental sustainability, has extended its corporate purpose goal of employing 200,000 disadvantaged people around the world by committing to employ refugees at production centres in Jordan.[65]

Organisations that lead with a purpose-driven strategy can establish a brand name for trust and authenticity. The *Chartered Management Institute* (*CMI*) define organisational purpose as "An organisation's meaningful and enduring reason to exist that aligns with long-term financial performance, provides a clear context for daily decision-making and unifies and motivates relevant stakeholders". Indeed, according to Ann Francke (2018, p. 6), CEO of the *CMI*, "The idea that organisational purpose is key to creating better businesses and reporting the fractured relationship between business and society has grown dramatically in recent years".[66] The challenge of managing stakeholder balance can be helped by establishing and maintaining a unifying sense of shared meaning, raised awareness, and enhanced vision.

In terms of brand strategy, two pivotal tenets are inextricably linked but separate: being a value-creating enterprise focused on generating and building stakeholder financial outcomes, and, in parallel, being a value-based organisation. The former used to be the sole purpose of an enterprise; the latter is an organisation based on a culture of sharing core values, internally amongst employees, and externally with the changing environment.

Most contemporary organisations who successfully achieve shareholder and stakeholder goals are purpose-driven, human-centric, technology-led, and data-driven. And, as with most successful enterprises, at the heart of contemporary marketing is *integration*: of the interface between internal marketing capabilities and external customer requirements; of the seamless customer journey of marketing communications and the service experience; and of the creation of shared value and values.

---

64 Olivia Rudgard, "*John Lewis* removes 'boys' and 'girls' labels from children's clothes". *The Telegraph*, September 2, 2017.
65 Marcus Fairs, "*IKEA* aims to take 200,000 people out of poverty in massive social sustainability drive", Dezeen, April 2018.
66 Anne Franke, "The What, The Why and How of Purpose: A Guide for Leaders", *Chartered Management Institute*, 2018.

4.3 Shareholder primacy and stakeholder democracy

Value is social utility, organisational profitability, and contingent on the "preferential judgement" (Holbrook, 1994, p. 23) of consumers; 'values' are the guiding principles by which that judgement is made. Whilst the role of any business is to create value, this has been distorted by the emphasis on value not *values*.

Corporate Governance which prioritises the maximising of creating value for shareholders before considering the interests of all other stakeholders – society, local community, customers, and employees – is sometimes referred to as 'shareholder primacy'. It is a business irony that the greatest damage done to shareholder value is shareholder primacy. It can be like looking upside down through a telescope: tightly focused but myopic in its vision. One of the reasons proffered for a distrust of Capitalism's orientation – economic governance – and the perceived incompatibility with non-financial objectives, has been "the canonisation of shareholder value maximisation as the sole legitimate expression of corporate purpose" (Salter, 2019, p. 1). Set against a complex and changeable competitive and macro environment, the focus on organisational purpose has taken centre stage.

In the eyes of an increasingly vocal business community, not enough consideration is given to environmental impact and economic sustainability, as well as undermining the moral integrity needed to build mutual trust. Until fairly recently, shareholder primacy and maximising profit has been the unchallenged ideology of business. As Salter claims, "shareholder value maximisation remains the *de facto* expression of the institutional purpose that guides the decision making of many managers" (2019, p. 2). Philosophically and ethically, that paradigm is shifting.

The battle for hegemony presents both shareholder and stakeholder theories as *normative* corporate strategy and business ethics, jostling for strategic positioning of determining what is the 'right' way to do business, particularly in the context of corporate social responsibility. The two theories are mainly viewed as binary opposites: Freidman's assertion that "There is one and only one social responsibility of business – to use its resources and engage in activities designed to increase its profits" (1962, p. 133) contrasts with normative 'stakeholder' theory which prescribes *how* managers should behave, *descriptive* versions which advocate actual behaviour, and *instrumental* versions which predict outcomes such as profit for example (Jones & Wicks, 1999, p. 210). Freidman's mantra was reinforced when Jensen and Meckling (1976) declared there to be an inherent conflict ('principal/agent problem') between the principals of the company (shareholders) and its agents (the company executives). Today, critics view shareholder primacy as myopic, dangerously insular, with shareholder value seen as an outcome not an objective, a result not a strategy (Welch, 1999). As Handy (1990) suggests, "It is up to each individual business to work out its own purpose and that optimising shareholder value over the medium to long-term should be the consequence, not the purpose, of a well-run business".

Of the many academics expressing doubt about the sustainability of shareholder primacy, Bernabou and Tyrol are characteristically to the point: "Society's demands for individual and corporate social responsibility as an alternative response to market and distributive failures are becoming increasingly prominent" (2010, p. 3). The key priority for today's leaders is the formulation and defence of corporate purpose, to enhance competitiveness by having a value and values proposition embedded into the company culture and organisational structure which resonates with stakeholder moral codes.

The organisation's ultimate value lies in the definition of its character and direction, providing an ethical touchstone, a framework for stability and change, and, therefore, its purpose. Ellsworth, challenging conventional corporate wisdom, claims that "Purpose expresses the company's fundamental value – the raison d'etre or over-riding reason for existing. It is the end to which the strategy is directed" (2002, p. 64). Geoff McDonald, a former Global President of Human Resources at *Unilever* described purpose as bringing a sense of meaning to the organisation: "It's around creating meaning, and answering the question 'Why do you do what you do?'". Salter takes the definition of corporate purpose a stage further advancing the principle of "*ethical reciprocity* – an exemplary kind of social cooperation in a transactional setting" (2019, p. 2). Here, he says, ethical self-interest "resonates mutuality and reflects practicality".

Freidman's 'free market manifesto' (launched over 50 years ago), extolling the virtues of libertarian economics, became the unassailable putative blueprint for organisations. Its "The business of business is business" logic adopted by CEOs, academics, Presidents, Prime Ministers, Economists, Managers, and virtually everybody else in the world of business. This view proffers that social issues are peripheral to the challenges of corporate management: "The sole legitimate purpose of business is to create shareholder value" (Davis, 2005). Its platform of "the social responsibility of business is to increase its profits" spawned a fixation with the 'Greed is Good' mantra of the market which was ascendant in the 1980s. However, the financial crash of 2008 was a milestone wake-up call which caused a lot of businesses to think about pressing the reset button. It was seen as myopic, characterised by short-termism, where the relentless pursuit of profit maximisation, juxtaposed with widening equalities, public distrust, and environmental degradation, fuelled by the post-COVID-19 evolution of work, resulted in a shift in the business paradigm from shareholder primacy to 'stakeholder capitalism'.

Short-term value generation, with its shareholder primacy orientation, often seen as being at the expense of other stakeholders, is now set in a completely different context than originally envisaged. Indeed, according to Porter and Kramer (2011, p. 75), "Not all profit is equal – an idea that has been lost in the narrow, short-term focus of financial markets and in much management thinking. Profits involving a social purpose represent a higher form of capitalism".

There is little argument that profit is the central reason for an organisation to exist, but, as Drucker (1967, p. 23) reminds us, "Profit for a company is like oxygen for a person: if you don't have enough of it, you're out of the game, but if you think your life is about breathing, you're really missing something". This is an apposite analogy: profit, like oxygen, is a facilitator, not a raison d'etre; it identifies how organisations survive but not why they exist – why they do what they do. Customers look beyond the economic exchange for value. Profit gives life to an organisation, but purpose gives meaning. Therefore, a meaningful brand driven by higher purpose drives profits (Kouly, 2018).

The debate about corporate priorities has fluctuated between the stances of stakeholder primacy espoused by free market economists and the broader perspective of stakeholder theorists – in some Anglo-American systems shareholder primacy is still the regnant theory in corporation law – but it is the pursuit of purpose which is getting increasing traction.

4.4 The value proposition

Although the concept of the 'value proposition' has ubiquitous use and often narrow application, it is the epicentre of brand, and indeed corporate, strategy. It focuses on the essential reason for an organisation's existence: *the creation of value.* Whilst this has to be customer-centric, often 'customer value models' have a 'cost benefit' monetary fixation, a data-driven company-orientated calculation of what products and services are 'worth'. The only meaningful assessment of value is what the customer believes value to be. This isn't a new idea; Levitt's (1975) marketing manifesto led the way by arguing for companies to define themselves not by what they made but what their customers needed. Therefore, value isn't what *goes into* the value proposition by the company, it is what is *taken out* by the customer, in the "customer's space rather than in the producer's space" (Vandermerwe, 1996, p. 80). Therefore, a company's value proposition is what customers see of value, the aggregate of functional and emotional benefits users may get from the company and the company's brand. These may be *functional* benefits – product features, quality of materials, price, shape, size etc. – and *emotional* benefits – protection from risk, feelings experienced during use of the brand alone or with others. It is fundamentally rooted in customer expectation and experience, the "events most critical to a business [which] happen *outside* the firm" (Lanning, 1998, p. 20). Therefore, it must have a broader definition beyond an economic transactional perspective, encompassing competitive, social, and ethical dimensions. In the final analysis, the 'value proposition' is the *value experience* as perceived by the customer, and as integrated, implemented, and delivered by the company.

When we begin to look at the underlying forces of *customer-company fusion* in developing a meaningful, profitable value proposition, the use of metaphors draws out some insightful concepts: reciprocity, resource commitment, inter-dependency of service ecosystem perspective, co-creation of value, value-in-use, value-in-context, interactive actors, dynamic knowledge sharing, and, critically, dialogue. Mutually beneficial value co-creation – reciprocity – is a central element of relationship development between organisations and consumers (Tadajewski & Saren, 2009). Resource production and consumption is the locus of the 'value proposition', described as "a dynamic and adjusting mechanism for negotiating how resources are shared within a service ecosystem" (Frow, et al., 2014, p. 327).

Here, confusion might possibly be in the use of the word 'proposition'. As a proposal where value is presented *by* the company *to* the customer, it implies a one-way, outward-looking plan of action, but as a statement of negotiated co-creation it is an expression of mutuality. Here the emphasis is on *interaction* not *transaction*: value isn't embedded in exchange but created in relationships. It is a blended construct of financial and non-financial expectation. Values describe the desired culture and principles, a behavioural compass and direction for the organisation and its employees.

Every company across all sectors needs some sort of *value proposition* to help focus on the most essential element of successfully achieving strategic objectives: how a company creates a value experience for its customers and how it communicates and delivers it. Bower and Garda (1985) first hinted at the conceptualisation of this phenomenon, but the man credited with coining the phrase (Michael Lanning) claimed: "Contrary to how things may seem, customers don't really care about your product. They care about their lives and businesses. They care about what they may or may not get out of using your products or services" (Lanning, 2019, p. 239). Hilton *et al* (2012) assert that value propositions arise from the value potential inherent in the resources possessed by actors: functional benefits, emotional benefits, and self-expressive benefits.

What matters, therefore, is at the heart of the value proposition customers' experiences of your brand must warrant them continuing to use it over some other competitive option. Companies need to know what the specific, measurable experiences are which differentiate. The value proposition should be seen as an iterative process of re-evaluation, a best fit of company goals and customer desires. It is corporate commitment to strategic direction. It encapsulates relationship values like trust, reliability, and commitment. It demonstrates how it can resolve customers' problems or is a better choice than competitor offerings. It is a company's promise to its customers.

When we look at the crux of the value proposition – value *creation* – there are different perspectives. A *system* view differs from a *network* view in that "each instance of resource integration, service provision, and value creation changes the nature of a system to some degree and thus the context for the next iteration and determination of value creation" (Weiland, Polese, Vargo, & Lusch, 2012, p. 10). Gummesson (2008) criticises the 'value chain paradigm' as being based on the premise that there is a distance between company and customer, suggesting a gap between value proposition and value realisation. Normann & Ramírez (1993, p. 65) criticise the linear nature of the value chain claiming that "Successful companies increasingly do not just add value, they *reinvent* it" and advocate reconfiguring roles and relationships among a constellation of actors (suppliers, partners, customers) in order to mobilise the creation of value and in particular value-in-use.

Woodruff & Gardial (1996) were one of the earliest to observe practice and espouse 'value-in-use' as opposed to 'value-in-exchange'. Value-in-use is the enactment of the value proposition, and value propositions are mutually created, quid pro quo (Ballantyne, 2003, p. 1243). This is an important distinction from Vargo & Lusch's (2004) view that it is the customer alone who determines value. Value propositions are *reciprocal* promises of value, operating *to and from* suppliers and customers seeking an equitable exchange (Ballantyne & Varey, 2006, p. 344). Strategic imperative or not, it is of critical importance that value propositions of any merit must have customer input. Value-focused organisations therefore take an 'outside-in' view of value creation, adopting the customer's perspective, not just because of the growing orientation towards customer primacy, but because value has to be sustainable.

Assessments of value depend on the context within which value is created. The migration in organisational philosophy away from marketing products or services to perceiving value propositions as customer *solutions* is mostly established in complex, high value sectors like computer systems, aerospace, medical services, and telecommunications, and in organisations like *GE*, *IBM*, and *Ericsson* who provide vertical customer solutions and have achieved substantial growth from "service-intensive solutions" (Krishnan, Balsaubramanian, & Sawhney, 2004). For example, Amit and Zott's (2001, p. 496) criteria for E-commerce value creation – efficiency, complementarities, lock-in, and novelty – are exemplified by *eBay's* value proposition of low transaction costs, wide merchandise selection, the hook of transaction repetition, and the easy-to-use novel environment of technological empowerment. This resonates with general social media usage: new value can be created by the ways in which transactional exchanges are enabled. *Complementarity* is a key ingredient here; it is the non-product elements such as service and meaning which enhances users' perception of value. And, of course, 'value' is a loaded word, meaning different things to different people, so it is a subjective assessment. These days, it is also a much broader concept, embracing more than its original economic assessment of value: ethics, morals, ecological considerations, social meaning for example.

Principles in practice

Co-op's focus on social values proposition reinforces positioning

The highly competitive Retail Sector, perhaps exposed more than most to the restrictions of Covid-19, has made the *Co-op* focus even harder on assessing their value proposition and positioning, especially as their spend is far less than their supermarket rivals. As one of the few companies who have always put 'purpose before profit', in some ways they've been ahead of the game. But, as Chief Membership Officer Matt Atkinson has pointed out:

Our challenge is choosing which parts of the business to talk about at any given time, as the Co-op Group spans not only food, funeral care, insurance, and legal services, but also a variety of community initiatives and support of the Fairtrade movement. The main issue for us is that we're so propositionally rich. We have so many things we're doing and not enough money to bring them to life, so the main problem we have is – what do we talk about the most? Do we shine a light on Co-op Academies? Do we shine a light on the fact we're the largest Fairtrade producer? Do we shine a light on Co-operate, which is our community platform? Our main problem is choosing what to really talk about.

To help make sense of all the different aspects of the group, rather than "trading off" different parts of the organisation, the *Co-operate community* initiative and wider 'It's what we do' tagline was used as an overarching, inclusive message. Atkinson claims that "Focusing on a message of cooperating for a fairer world helps create distinctiveness for the brand and helps refine who it is the company wants to appeal to. He is clear the brand's values are not for everyone and trying to convert every potential shopper to the *Co-op* mindset would be a waste of time and resources".

In addition, they decided to pull its Easter 2020 campaign to fit the mood of the time, donating £3.4m worth of ad spend to food poverty charity *FareShare*.

For the *Co-op*, focusing on their values proposition has helped to reinforce their positioning in the market.

Source: *Co-operative Society*

Value delivery and value exchange, interaction between supplier and customer, is the essence of what we mean by the value proposition. However, value proposition is often used as a synonym for positioning statement. Where these concepts overlap, and indeed align, is their respective impact on customer-company fusion and in shaping value perceptions. Both can help customers understand the value being created and focus the organisation's efforts in creating it. Developing dynamic, organic value propositions are a good facilitating mechanism for evaluation and resource allocation of relationships in a service ecosystem and therefore a critical strategic imperative. Drawing on the dramaturgical metaphor of service marketing, Frow *et al* (2014, p. 19) identify seven more that help throw light on the dynamics and characteristics of value propositions and the relational fusion between actors in this value exchange:

– *'Promise' and 'proposal'*: A promise of in-use value that is offered to an actor (Grönroos, 2011) whereas a proposal implies the reciprocity between active actors (Ballantyne & Varey, 2006). Here, at the *micro* level, value-in-context is seen as operating to and from actors (providers and users).

– *'Invitation to play' and 'bridge connecting our worlds'*: Operating at the *meso* level, the emphasis with the former is on the reciprocity of resource sharing and collaboration, the latter being on building propositions that meet in the middle. Both imply reciprocal value sharing. The notion of 'invitation to play' is a fundamental principle of interactivity.

– *Wild card' and 'Journeys to a destination'*: Analysis at the *macro* level, involving gaining awareness of the potential of disruptive, disintermediating opportunities and threats that may affect stakeholders. Journeys are similar to 'road maps' in terms of envisioning the future

Table 4.2 lists some examples of value propositions.

Table 4.2: Value Proposition examples.

Company	Value Propositions
Uber	One tap and a car comes directly to you ("Your ride, On demand")
	Seamlessly connects drivers with riders through apps
	Your driver knows exactly where to go
	Payment is completely cashless
	No phone calls
	Rebellious taxi alternative redefined transportation
Apple iPhone	Unique experience
	Sleek, elegant product design
	Ease of use
	Aspirational qualities that an iPhone supposedly offers the user ("should be more than a collection of features").
	Focus on Internet security
Pinterest	Visually-based social media image platform
	Evernote-type method of curating, saving, and organising web items
	User-generated content (recipes, home décor, hobbies, body modifications etc.)
	Aspirational appeal across demographics
	Gold standard for trends in food, home, family
	Initial audience female; evolved into including male audience
Airbnb	Trusted community marketplace for consumers
	Non-traditional boutique offer
	Independent rental arrangement
	Leisure and Business travellers
	'Local' culture experience-oriented
	VP not economy-based
	Non-traditional vacation concept
GoFundMe	Premier crowdfunding platform
	User-friendly method to raise money
	USP is ability to associate fundraising with human emotions
ASOS	Accessibility
	Customisation
	Price
	Cost reduction
	Convenience
	Brand Status
Spotify	Call-up song facility transformed how we consume music and invented a category.

Source: Authors' representation (2022)

The digitally-disrupted post-COVID-19 landscape has affected the very nature of value propositions. There is an increasing element of remote, simulation-based consumption which may prove to be either supplementary or substitutive to the real settings of the original produce and service offers.

4.5 Vision and mission statements

If the values espoused by the company emotionally resonate and passionately motivate target audiences, the congruence of the values between what an organisation and its constituencies stand for can transform purchase and production into aspiration and behaviour and realise higher purpose and meaning. How that value is expressed to stakeholders is a key strategic imperative. A unified expression of values can be a highly effective way of achieving customer-company cohesion and complicity, and yet achieving the coalescence of a wide heterogeneous range of customers, staff, employees, and other stakeholders can be difficult. Two effective management tools – the *vision statement* and *mission statement* – are used to achieve this and are powerful organisational heuristics which can help visualise organisational goals. Vision and mission are potent statements of internalised intent and external influence.

A vision articulates a desired future for the company. It provides an intellectual framework for company strategy, a definition of strategic direction, and presents a conceptual map of how a company moves from its current reality to a desired future state (Mirvis, Googins, & Kinnicutt, 2010). It is the BHAG (big hairy audacious goal) which top companies use to make their vision tangible and emotionally energising. A timeless envisioning of the organisation's future, the vision is an articulation of destination, a guide for the action of strategy, and a touchstone by which everyone can measure their progress in the joint operation of moving the organisation forward. It indicates broad direction and distinguishes the company's value proposition from its competitors.

Vision might indicate what and to whom strategy is aimed at, even to non-users, but it must always be measured. An example of this is Swedish communications company *Ericsson* who defines its vision as "The prime driver in an all-communicating world". *IKEA*'s succinct "Our vision is to create a better everyday life for many people" is aspirational. So too is *Oxfam's* "A world without poverty". But are these too broad to be meaningful? Can they realistically be achieved? Is this unattainable quality contradictory or is it actually the perfect, timeless mission that galvanises a company and its stakeholders in a unified vision?

Notice that 'vision' and 'mission' appeared to be used as synonyms above. Often, wrongly or rightly, 'vision statement' and 'mission statement' are used interchangeably. Sometimes they are combined into a single statement even though they are separate things. *LinkedIn's* vision "To create economic opportunity for every member of the global workforce" and its mission "To connect the world's professionals to make them more productive and successful" points to what they do (which is to *connect*) and to whom they aim to do it (the "world's professionals"). *Google* does a similar thing with "organise" and "access" (to the world's information) clearly being what they do and aspire to. When the lines between these separate strategic vehicles of value are blurred, this can distort their meaning.

A mission statement, on the other hand, highlights core values and focuses on competitive differentiation; it describes and defines the market space within which strategy is created. So whilst a vision statement is an aspirational roadmap pointing the way to customers and employees, mission focuses on the present and the immediate future, is on-going and atemporal. Mission focuses on describing and defining the direction and destination that can be imagined; vision imagines the distant future. The language used is important as it both signals and influences the priorities of the organisation. It can project utilitarian ethics (eg: chocolate manufacturer *Green & Black's* fair trade supplier provenance) or suggest a challenger brand service promise mantra (*Avis's* "We Try Harder").

Mission statements can give insight into how the organisation sees its core values, direction, and focus. Breznik & Law's (2019) analysis of UK HEIs revealed four core dimensions: "Education Philosophies", "Strategic Orientation", "Social Responsibility", and "Value to Shareholders". Some of the mission statements examined were service-oriented (ie: aimed towards the students as customers); some were socially-oriented (ie: aimed towards stakeholders and society in general). A mission statement is what the organisation is doing *right now*; a vision statement is hope for the future: where you are in contrast to where you are going. Both are vital in determining organisational goal direction, but whereas a vision statement is tomorrow's aspiration, a mission statement focuses on how that is achieved today. A vision gives direction; a mission gives focus.

Tesla, an American electric automotive vehicle and clean energy company, states that their vision is "To create the most compelling car company of the 21st Century by driving the world's transition to electric vehicles", and its mission as "To accelerate the world's transition to sustainable energy". Implicit in the words "driving force" and "accelerate" is an expression of action to achieve. Contrast this lofty vision to *Amazon's* more down-to-earth aims: "We strive to offer our customers the lowest possible prices, the best selection, and the utmost convenience" (Mission), as well as "To be Earth's most customer-centric company, where customers can find and discover anything they might want to buy online" (Vision). The word "anything" in the vision statement takes a fairly straight forward goal much further. Even sharper is *TED* (derived from a Technology, Entertainment, Design conference in 1984), a "non-profit, non-partisan" organisation devoted to spreading ideas. In fact, their vision "We believe passionately in the power of ideas to change attitudes, lives, and, ultimately, the world" is condensed into the simple but powerful mission to "Spread ideas".

Similarly, *Airbnb*'s "Belong anywhere" is both a basic, universal human desire and a strategic focus. However, contrast these succinct statements to *GoDaddy's* (website and domain name builder) esoteric and cheeky use of "kick ass" in their lengthy mission statement: "We are here to help our customers kick ass. We do that by living our strategy and ruthlessly prioritising our work to create simple, elegant technology that delights our customers – all while delivering service that is second to none. Every single day, we join forces across teams and groups to break down barriers, build new markets, and stare down the impossible until the impossible blinks".

Vision and mission are both reflective of an organisation's changing operating environment and a re-orientation of customers' expectations. For example, the dramatic changes in the structure and ethos of the UK Higher Educational (HE) sector has witnessed a neo-liberal marketisation ethos as well as the governmentality of institutions, together with a transformation of recipients from 'students of knowledge' to 'service customers' where quality has become objectively assessed in league tables of compliance and standardisation. This re-orientation of education has radically altered the basis upon which UK HE andragogy was originally predicated.

Vision and mission statements are important parts of strategy in all types of public or private, multinational or SME, profit or non-profit to help project marketplace differentiation and customer-company meaning, but are they different to *purpose*?

4.6 Purpose, vision, and mission statements

As with the blurring of lines between mission and vision statements, so too they are often confused with an organisation's *purpose statement*. Mission and vision statements clarify *what* an organisation does and what stakeholders it serves; purpose addresses *why* a company does what it does. Purpose is, in some ways, a balance between having a long-term vision and managing the key decisions which are implicit in achieving this. As Kramer (2017, p. 1) argues: "For a brand to navigate towards a future where it thrives rather than merely survives, finding, articulating and applying a higher purpose is a sine qua non". It is a desirable but essential heartbeat of contemporary business strategy.

In order to begin to examine the role of purpose and the relationships it has to and with other components of strategy, we must firstly establish that purpose is not a *vision* (ie: a time-bound destination envisioning the future of the organisation, where it should be heading); nor is it a *mission statement* (ie: an integral part of the strategic plan which clarify actions like 'What business we are in?', 'What customers do we serve?', and 'How do we solve their problems?'). Often there is confusion. Put simply, mission statements – in which clarifying actions and how stakeholders are served – describe *what* a company does, and purpose statements describe *why* it does it what it does. Australians Lachlan and May who founded *Tirtyl*, an ethical company with a mission to "create amazing products that unwaste", describes their purpose as "To *conscious consumption mainstream*".

Purpose is an enduring ambition, a state of mind, expressed with meaning, authenticity, and inclusiveness, resonating throughout the company's social ecosystem (including, customers, employees, stakeholders, and the wider reach of society), because it expresses what impact the business has on people's lives and therefore *why a company exists*. A purpose statement is therefore vital as it gives meaning to where the organisation is heading. It is a goal, but it is also a guide. "If vision is where you are going, the brand an expression of where you are, and strategy how you get there, purpose is *why* you do what you do" (Kramer & Husein-zadeh, 2017).

Nonetheless, a purpose statement can only be truly meaningful if it is set and viewed in context, the scope of which is to provide wide-ranging philosophical guidance and direction to address strategic challenges. And yet, "high-level direction and individual freedom of interpretation gives organisational purpose the sense of being like a doctrine" (Ebert, Hurth, & Prabhu, 2018, p. 10). Doctrines, or sets of beliefs, are "particularly useful for organisations and groups that span multiple countries and diverse contexts" (Challagalla, Murtha, & Jaworski, 2014, p. 4). Salim (2016) cites *Vodaphone's* collaboration with its direct competitors to tackle the challenge of societal impacts of its strategy. *Unilever* is working closely with The Department for International Development (DFID) to fund a global programme to urgently tackle the spread of Coronavirus, reaching over a billion people worldwide, raising awareness and changing hygiene behaviour. This reinforces *Unilever's* citizen credentials. Similarly, when its employees became its owners, *Harley-Davidson* redefined its motorcycle manufacturing business when they re-aligned its purpose to "fulfilling dreams of personal freedom", a clear case of bringing customers, dealers, suppliers, and employees into a brand community with shared purpose.

The *United Nations International Children's Emergency Fund* (UNICEF), a social welfare agency providing humanitarian and development aid to children around the world, have a purpose of "working with others to overcome the obstacles that poverty, violence, disease, and discrimination put in a child's path". *Apple's* overarching purpose statement is 'Humanising Technology'. *3M*, a diversified technology company, and *GE*, an American multinational conglomerate, are dedicated to turning imaginative ideas into leading products. *Google* and *Wikipedia* express purpose in similar fashion: one to organise the World's information and make it universally accessible; the to facilitate free world-wide information system, encouraging open content.

Making sense of an organisation's purpose – not just for enhanced performance but strategic alignment – is a key platform of business analyses which take a *cultural* approach. Certain critiques of organisational culture and workplace spirituality focus on individual and collective congruity value alignment in providing some sort of sensemaking framework by which organisational 'meaning' can either be a negotiated, constructed arrangement (Long & Helms-Mills, 2010), or a form of pastoral power managerial control whether explicitly or implicitly expressed. These practices "foster transcendence" (Pratt & Ashforth, 2003, p. 309) – communicating how employee activity and organisational purpose contribute to the greater good.

Table 4.3 is a comparison between purpose and mission statements.

Table 4.3: Examples of purpose and mission statements.

	Examples of purpose statements	Examples of mission statements
UNICEF		"To work with others to overcome the obstacles that poverty, violence, disease and discrimination place in a child's path".
UBER		"Evolving the way the world moves. By seamlessly connecting riders to drivers through our apps, we make cities more accessible, opening up more possibilities for riders and more business for drivers".
Twitter		"To give people the power to share and make the world more open and connected".
Paypal		"To build the Web's most convenient, secure, cost-effective payment solution".
Microsoft		"To enable people and businesses throughout the world to realise their full potential".
BBC		"To enrich people's lives with programmes and services that inform, educate, and entertain".
Spotify	"To unlock the potential of human creativity by giving a million creative artists the opportunity to live their art and billions of fans the opportunity to be inspired".	
Facebook	"Giving people the power to build community and bring the world together".	
Apple	"Think Different".	
P&G	"Touching lives and improving lives".	
Southwest Airlines	"To give people the freedom to fly".	

Table 4.3 (continued)

	Examples of purpose statements	Examples of mission statements
Johnson & Johnson	"To alleviate pain and suffering".	
Barclays Bank	"Our common purpose is to help people achieve their ambitions".	
Disney	"To use our imaginations to bring happiness to millions".	
Google	"To organise the world's information, and make it universally accessible and useful".	
Coca Cola	"To refresh the world. To inspire moments of optimism and happiness. To create value and make a difference".	
LEGO	"Our ultimate purpose is to inspire and develop children to think creatively, reason systematically, and release their potential to shape their own future – experiencing the endless human possibility".	
Sanofi (French Pharma company)	"To understand and solve healthcare needs of people across the world".	
Harley Davidson	"We fulfil dreams of personal freedom – it's our purpose, and we take it seriously. And while freedom means different things to different people, it's a bond that brings Harley-Davidson customers, employees, dealers, suppliers and enthusiasts together".	
BMW	'To enable people to experience the joy of driving'.	
Mace Construction	"Our purpose is to redefine the boundaries of ambition".	
Anglian Water (UK)	"Our Purpose is to bring environmental and social prosperity to the region we serve through our commitment to Love Every Drop".	

Source: Authors' representation (2022)

4.7 Defining purpose

Defining purpose is an abstract exercise which has practical consequences: it can be described as 'high ideals with bottom line benefits'. Is purpose the same as 'mission'? The *Nissan Motor Corporation* has the following as its mission statement: "To provide unique and innovative automotive products and services that deliver superior measurable values to all stakeholders in alliance with *Renault*". Its focus is on the production of profitable product; it is not a purpose statement.

So what exactly is purpose? According to the *Association of National Advertisers (ANA)*, purpose is defined as "a long-term business strategy tied to a societal benefit that guides every decision and action, from product development and customer/employee engagement to marketing and hiring" (2018, p. 2). Or, as *EY (Ernst & Young)* put it[67] put it, "To build a better working world, is an inspirational reason for being that is grounded in humanity and inspires a call to action".

An early iteration of purpose describes it (along with values) as being part of "the core ideology which provides the glue that holds an organisation together through time . . . defines what we stand for and why we exist" (Collins & Porras, 1996). It is impossible to *fulfill* purpose. It's not like achieving goals or accomplishments; they're part of driving *towards* purpose. Purpose doesn't change but it can be inspirational and be a catalyst *for* change. The *CMI* define purpose as being "a transcendent, meaningful reason for an organisation to exist; an enduring attribute of the organisational identity; aligned with long-term financial performance, a clear context for daily decision making, and as unifying and motivating for stakeholders".[68] Ellsworth (2002) gives us some guidelines for defining a common purpose:

– Develop alternative constructs (of purpose) to elicit individual assessments of *why the company exists* and *what the primary purpose for being is.*
– Differentiate between the 'current reality' and the 'desired normative'.
– Delineate 'purposes' into sequential categories based on stakeholder perceptions.
– State priorities in terms of vision, mission, strategy, objectives.

Purpose has had many iterations to date: In the 1980s, marketing was strategically linked with philanthropy; then there came Customer Relationship Marketing with customer-orientation and brand longevity as its focus; this became structured by 1999 in terms of 'Cause Marketing' where companies' identities were built on affiliation with a cause; the 'Triple Bottom Line of profit, people, planet' approach (Elkington, 1994) of doing well, doing good, and being sustainable morphed into Corporate Social Responsibility (CSR). They all helped set the agenda and the

---

67 http://www.ey.com/Publication/vwLUAssets/ey-the-state-of-the-debate-on-purpose-in-business /$FILE/ey-the-state-of-the-debate-on-purpose-in-business.pdf
68 Jermaine Haughton, "How to Define Your Business Purpose", *CMI* Report, 11th April 2019.

targets for organisational financial, social, and environmental sustainability. Supply convenance became a growing concern in the customer buying process. Societal engagement at the ethical level took a more defined turn. Employee and community environmental matters were seen as strategic necessities. Suddenly, sustainability was centre stage in synchronising strategy. Embedding purpose in every action drove strategy towards what is valued and what values can be created. Circularity, mutuality, and sustainability became the new mantras.

Ebert, Hurth & Prabhu (2020) suggest that there are two approaches to defining purpose: *retrospective* – looking back to where the organisation has come from – and *prospective* – analysing what is unique about past strategy and previous accomplishments and projecting where that can lead. They define purpose as "an organisation's meaningful and enduring reason to exist that aligns with long-term financial performance, provides a clear context for daily decision making, and unifies and motivates relevant stakeholders".[69] As Stengel suggests "Maximum growth and high ideals are not incompatible. They're inseparable" (2011, p. 6). Purpose is a North Star metaphor and metric framework for organisational direction and decision-making, focusing on vision, beliefs, values, strategic assets, and creating meaningful, authentic customer experiences. It is the company's driving, transformative force from which true brand identity is expressed.

Although some claim that purpose is the new positioning, it is crucial to examine how purpose, value proposition, and positioning are separate but vital components of sustainable brand strategy. Here, "more important than the quest for certainty is the quest for clarity" (Gautier, 2008). Purpose is the core beliefs and values that drive and align strategy. A value proposition describes the overarching promise of a product, service, or company. Positioning statements are a subtype of value propositions, but they are not the same thing. They are targeted to specific data or market segments and buyer personas (ie: customer archetypes). Positioning connects the value proposition to key customers, as well as to the broader stakeholder ecosystem, with competitive relevance in the moment, but purpose is the permanent corporate core which drives the business. It charts the evolution of strategy, underpinning the company-customer bonds of value and values. It is the organisation's essential reason for existing, defining and aligning corporate belief, direction, and long-term breadth of vision.[70]

According to another study, a key element of taking an integrated approach to strategy alignment: "In the long term, social and environmental issues become financial issues".[71] An integrated strategy – aligned with an organisation's business innovation agenda, and leveraging assets such as human capital, value chains,

69 Charlie Ebert, Victoria Hurth, & Jaideep Prabhu, "The What, The Why and the How of Purpose: A Guide for Leaders", *CMI*, 2008.
70 CEO Study, *IBM*, 2006.
71 "No 1 top 100 performing CEOs in the world", *Harvard Business Review*, 2015.

technology, and supply chain logistics, as well as addressing societal challenges – can also yield tangible business benefits: brand longevity; sustainable competitiveness; market expansion; strengthened supply chains; employee complicity.

Principles in practice

What is Brand Purpose?

Carol Cone, founder of '*Carol Cone On Purpose*', a US-based consultancy, is a great advocate of organisations leveraging 'purpose' by creating stronger businesses with lasting societal impact – by standing for something beyond the bottom line.

Working with organisations such as *Microsoft, Unilever, South West Airlines*, and the *Bezos Family Foundation*, she describes purpose as the aspirational reason for going beyond profits. Cone identifies a pivotal moment: "In 1999, we created the term 'Cause Branding' to describe companies like *Avon* who had built a cause into its brand identity. (In 2007, PR Week called her "arguably the most powerful and visible figure in the world of Cause Branding"). She continues:

> *I always say don't get stuck on the name. Understand the journey – goals, objectives, and rationale. Then engage with sincerity and a long-term commitment. Brand Purpose matters because of its power to galvanise an organisation and its constituencies around a higher-order goal and mission, while benefitting people and society. Purpose makes an organisation or brand vital to people's lives. Purpose-driven brands win people's hearts and minds. They generate more loyalty, trust, love, and respect than any other kind of brand. In its most powerful form, Purpose is the North Star for an organisation.*

Source: "Carol Cone on Purpose", Sarah Martzloff, *CharityComms.com*, 2021

4.8 Characteristics of purpose

Purpose can "help companies *redefine the playing field*, allow them to *reshape the value proposition*, and, in turn, enable them to overcome the challenges of slowing growth and declining profitability" (Malnight, Buche, & Dhanaraj, 2019). 'Redefining the playing field' involves using existing stakeholders' interests to expand into a wider social and environmental ecosystem, and is guided by the principles of purpose. An example might be an oil company extending into renewable energy, or a pet food company broadening their appeal to 'pet health', both achieving transformation in re-orientation. Purpose can allow companies to broaden their mission, creating a holistic value proposition by responding to trends, building on trust, and focusing on pain points. Putting purpose as the organisation's soul but also as its driving force can make organisations more coherent and unified, can produce more motivated stakeholders, and have a positive impact on society and the environment. Table 4.4 illustrates some characteristics.

Table 4.4: Characteristics of purpose.

A meaningful reason to exist.	More than just selling a product or service, the executive interviews revealed that managers expect their companies to have a meaningful and higher objective. This typically ties in with motivating employees, customers, and investors by contributing – directly or indirectly – to defeating societal, economic, and environmental challenges in the UK and abroad.	The *Body Shop's* success selling all-natural personal care products is underpinned by their higher purpose – help worldwide, find sustainable employment, and protect 10,000 hectares of forest and woodlands.
Purpose forms organisational identity	Purpose is connected to a company's aims, needs, desires, and helps mould the perception of the business to everyone it interacts with – from marketing to customer service. It's the essence of who you are. Purpose is the fundamental essence of an organisation.	Embodying its identity as a fresh and healthy organisation, fruit juice manufacturer *Innocent Drinks* has incorporated its sustainability purpose into its core business strategy. For example, all its cartons are made from 100% *Forest Stewardship Council (FSC)* certified card, and the company has incorporated at least 25% recycled content in bottles since 2003.
Purpose needs profits (and vice versa)	One of the clearest findings showed most executives strongly believe that purpose and profitability go hand-in-hand.	"I think it's really, really important that without profit the achievements of purpose are completely flawed" said Brandan McCafferty, CEO *Flood Re*. Similarly, Laura Turkington, Senior Manager of Global Innovation and Business Development at *Vodaphone* stated: "We can only create the social impact if it does make profit".
A clear context for daily decision-making	Purpose provides a clear guideline on business values and objectives to all stakeholders, while allowing creative freedom for individuals to determine the best course of action in specific scenarios.	"There is a link between and autonomy if you know where you are going, it's much easier to be able to be autonomous. I think purpose creates some real clarity and therefore real agility" explained John Rosling (CEO, *Contexis*).
Unifying and challenging stakeholders	There have been instances where purpose-driven organisations have made decisions that upset certain stakeholders to protect their purpose.	*Unilever*, adhering to its purpose, ended quarterly reporting to the City and actively managed away its hedge fund investors, whilst *Barclays* used its purpose to justify ending its tax reduction department, which may have upset some stakeholders.

Source: *CMI* 2019; *EY Institute* 'The Business Case for Purpose', *Harvard Business Review*, 2020; *McKinsey* Organizational Purpose Survey, 2020.

4.9 Advantages of purpose

Purpose-driven organisations do not just have a well-defined idea of what purpose is, they can also demonstrate one which delivers measurable value, integrates decision-making, coherent communication, and co-creation of value across the organisation and all stakeholders. Purpose isn't just a strategic 'add-on' but an integrative fusion which can be far greater in scope: can effect a sea change from transaction to transformative to transcendental, embracing compassion as well as competitiveness, community as well commerciality, seeking something beyond the status quo, a new normative model, to shape a vision and actuality which shakes the prevailing paradigm.

Brand strategy alignment presents opportunities for an organisation to demonstrate competitive agility in creating and sustaining meaningful, authentic profitable customer relationships anchored in brand affinity, mutual purpose, and company/customer congruity. Purpose-driven organisations can act like a beacon for all organisational decision-making and create core differentiation (30% higher levels of innovation 40% higher employee retention). Aligning values with corporate vision and mission is the driver of purpose-driven organisations: they project the image of personalised qualities in the mind of the public; they become an inherent part of the company culture "common language" (Holden, 2002) that socialises a workforce to a common purpose. The role of leadership in focusing the organisation on purpose scope in aligning mission and values is crucial.

Purpose-driven organisations have the following advantages:
- Consumers are more likely to demonstrate loyalty and commitment to brands, pay a premium, and also advocate use of brands that 'do good'.
- Consumers are more likely to switch from competitor brands to trial from a brand they trust. The *Cone/Porter Novelli Survey* found that 66% of consumers would change their loyalty to an existing brand to one from a purpose-driven organisation. When Millennials were polled, this percentage rose to 91%.

For companies, the tangible value of making purpose a core driver of growth and differentiation can reinforce product portfolio strength and brand heritage. For example, nearly half of *Unilever's* top 40 brands focus on sustainability. These "Sustainable Living" brands, including *Knorr, Dove*, and *Lipton*, are good for society, but they are also good for *Unilever* – growing 50 percent faster than the company's other brands and delivering more than 60 percent of the company's growth (*Unilever*, 2017).

4.10 Value alignment and environmental adaptability

External stakeholders provide both a challenge and an opportunity for organisations. "Companies that succeed in building a profitable relationship with the external world define themselves through what they contribute . . . generating long-term value for shareholders by delivering value to society as well" (McKinsey, 2020). Aligning purpose beyond profit and shareholder primacy is essential, as Cone (2019) suggests: "We live in a world of radical transparency and instant communications, rich in content yet poor in attention, with increasingly savvy citizens, employees and millennials demanding more, and sustainability moving from the fringe to daily life. People expect brands and organisations to stand for something meaningful and want to know more about how our products are sourced and made, what businesses do to minimise their impact, and how they make a positive difference in the world".

Most successful enterprises are purpose-driven, aligning leadership and strategy with organisational mission and values. But what is 'purpose'? It's about group belief. The *CMI* list 5 'purpose-driven' strategic criteria:
– To maintain and increase legitimacy in business.
– To attract, motivate, and retain talent.
– To drive strong customer and stakeholder relationships.
– To increase employee psychological wellbeing.
– To increase business performance.

Attuned to a moral compass, aligned to external and customer values and societal concerns, purpose is the driving force which resonates with societal needs; it's not CSR but an integrated not intermittent force.

According to *Deloitte*, aligning purpose with strategy can amplify an organisation's relevance to its stakeholders, build deeper relationships with its customers, improve market share, and grow three times faster than the competition, and have real impact through creating core differentiation such as 30% higher levels of innovation and 40% higher employee retention. Purpose-driven organisations – leveraging brand purpose by standing for something above and beyond 'bottom line' profitability – can act like a beacon for all organisational decision-making. Brand purpose and value alignment are now essential components of integrated brand strategy. Aligning purpose with doing good can amplify company relevance to its customers and stakeholders.

4.11 Aligning purpose, value, and values

The uncertainty caused by the impacts of the financial crisis, economic downturn, and the devastating effects of the COVID-19 pandemic, have emphasised the importance of adaptability to changing environments, and the need for readjusted business models and value propositions. Exploiting organisational assets and resources for competitive advantage is what defines the agility of a company. In other words, aligning strategy is having "a clear sense of how value is being created and how activities should be coordinated and streamlined to deliver that value" (Birkinshaw & Gibson, 2004, p. 47). The key to surviving and thriving for a company is to be 'ambidextrous', being able to succeed in both adapting and aligning strategy. Birkinshaw & Gibson advocate viewing "contextual ambidexterity" and "structural ambidexterity" (alignment- and adaptability-oriented) as complementary. Separation, without "sufficient connective tissue with the core business can be damaging on both counts" (2004, p. 60).

4.12 Strategic positioning

Whilst user expectations and anticipated benefits are transmitted via the value proposition, a clear indication of competitive position – through product or service leadership, operational excellence or superlative customer engagement or relationships – is projected explicitly or implicitly through the *positioning statement*. Where values inherent in the value proposition are projected into the marketplace and into the minds of consumers, that's *strategic positioning*.

Brand positioning is about "establishing a core promise within the marketplace and relevant to a target constituency which enables a brand to function on both a rational and emotional level" (Keller, 2013, p. 30). It articulates the consumer's goal achievement and the company's competitive advantages. Tybout & Sternthal (2005, p. 26) suggest that: "Perhaps the most important contribution of a sound brand positioning is to offer guidelines for the execution of marketing strategy". Positioning is both *strategic* – the two long-term key points of reference of customer and competitor selection, how they are targeted and communicated with – and *tactical* – the short-term expediency of fending off competition, enhancing immediate sales, preparing for long-term strategy. The consumer sees positional tactics (essentially the marketing mix) – symbols, packaging, advertising, pricing, point of sale materials (POS), brand name, logotypes and typefaces – but doesn't see the strategy: marketing strategy, positioning strategy, marketing communications strategy, branding strategy, production, sales, supply chain, quality processes.

Porter asserts that strategy should reflect a "distinctive value chain that configures all key business processes and operations in a unique way that is difficult for competitors to imitate" (2001, p. 50). This superior contemporaneous alignment of value proposition (more often than not by cost leadership or differentiation) and demand expectation is the function of positioning. Any element of brand strategy originates from the assumptions behind positioning; only well-defined brand identity will determine brand positioning.

The relative position of a company within an industry, sector or segment, juxtaposed to its competitors, affects how successful a strategy is. And whilst marketing communications is the main point of reference, positioning has a much wider strategic impact. Indeed, as part of the traditional triad of 'Segmentation, Targeting, and Positioning (STP)', it is a main pillar of strategy, reflecting the selection and presentation of a company's value and purpose propositions. Positioning is a key element of strategy for bringing together the company value proposition and the customer's expectation, and acts as a *brand preference heuristic.*

A positioning 'statement' should include target group, frame of reference, point of difference, and reason to believe (Tybout & Sternthal, 2005, p. 12). They cite *Black & Decker's De Walt* professional power tools as an example, and quote their formal positioning statement:

> *To the tradesman who uses his power tools to make a living and cannot afford downtime on the job* **(target)**, *DeWalt professional power tools* **(frame of reference)** *are more dependable than other brands of professional power tools* **(point of difference)** *because they are engineered to the brand's historic high-quality standards and are backed by Black & Decker's extensive service network and guarantee to repair or replace any tool within 48 hours* **(reasons to believe)**.

Therefore, establishing points of difference is a key task in brand positioning (Dinnie, 2008). Achieving a perceived competitive advantage through what Aaker (1996, p. 176) refers to as "creating favourably evaluated associations that function as a point of differentiation and are unique to the brand and imply superiority over other competing brands" is the chief purpose of positioning. To succeed in amongst all the noise of competition, and in a society where omni-channel exposure brings an overbearing amount of communications that needs processing, a company must "create a position in the prospect's mind, a position that takes into consideration not only a company's own strengths and weaknesses, but those of its competitors as well" (Ries & Trout, 2000).

Successful positioning is achieved by owning specific set of associations against the competition and is "one of the key concepts conditioning a brand's competitive market position" (Guidry, 2011). Positioning, therefore, is both *in the market* and *in the mind.* It is at once an organisation's competitive location in the market and also a consumer's subjective, perceived frame of reference of the suitability and worth of the value proposition. As Ries and Trout (2000) famously claimed: "Positioning is not what you do to the product. Positioning is what you do to the mind of the prospect". Or as Keller (2013, p. 10) puts it: "the act of designing the company's offer and image so that it occupies a distinct and valued place in the target customer's mind".

From a consumer's perspective, brands (and by association, organisations) are chosen which will fulfil their need for meaningful connections, self-esteem, status, group affiliation, balance, and simplicity. Although strategy and positioning are not (obviously!) explicitly stated to users, they are aware of positioning being either: value-based, features-based, lifestyle-based, experience-oriented, solution-based, or parent brand driven. From a company's point of view, the benefits of strategic positioning are: market differentiation, value confirmation, simplifying purchase decisions, and magnifying IMC messaging. Positioning has an *internal* application (guidance and verification of creation and fulfilment of value; as an instrument of employee brand; as a monitoring and control tool), as well as an *external* function (premise for building brand architecture; as an indicator of IMC strategy). Figure 4.1 illustrates the strategic positioning options explained in Table 4.5.

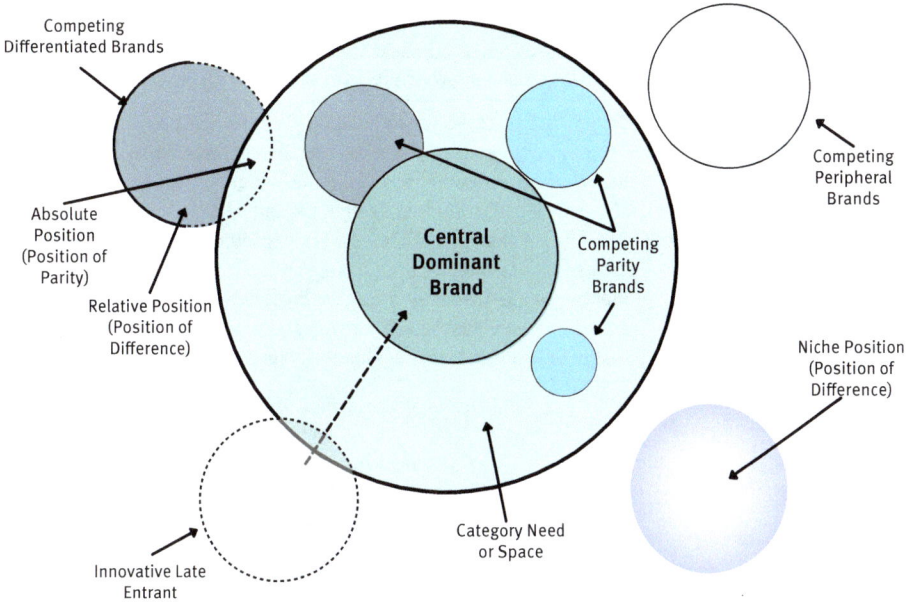

Competing
Differentiated Brands

Absolute
Position
(Position of
Parity)

Relative Position
(Position of
Difference)

Innovative Late
Entrant

Central
Dominant
Brand

Competing
Parity
Brands

Competing
Peripheral
Brands

Niche Position
(Position of
Difference)

Category Need
or Space

Figure 4.1: Strategic positioning options.
Source: Dahlen, Lange, & Smith (2010)

Table 4.5: Strategic positioning options.

Position	Description and approach to market
Category need or space	Total segment for a particular category need.
Central dominant position	Actual or perceived image as 'first in', 'best in class', or radically different to how the market is served, a pioneer or an innovative late entrant has the leading position in a category.
Competing parity brands achieving similarity with other brands	Same category fulfilment with similar attributes that copy the market leader's position. Similarity describes brand-to-brand comparisons (ie: how similar two brands are). *Dell Technologies*, *Compaq*, *Fujitsu*, *Toshiba*, *Samsung* and *Apple* have a similarity when alternative brands are being evaluated for the 'laptop' category. Every time a new design of car is launched, there soon appears similar generic shapes (eg:, *Ford Focus*, *Vauxhall Astra*).

Table 4.5 (continued)

Position	Description and approach to market
Competing differentiated brands achieving 'absolute position' by being associated with the category but differentiated by having competitive advantage.	Several brands have specialised on a certain attribute. Absolute position requires conformity to common characteristics and associations with other brands in the category. Semiotics of elements such as product design, packaging design, pricing, and distribution channels, dictates a brand protocol in which all elements of competing brands are similar. However, a brand's identity can be lost in amongst the competition. It may not be sufficient to be 'associated' with a category; differentiation from the rest of the category propositions may be essential.
Competing peripheral brands achieving 'typicality' whilst not directly challenging.	Brands sharing some aspect of main brand's value proposition. Diluted 'me too' positioning. Typicality is the degree to which a brand is characteristic of its product category; some brands are seen as more typical than others. Some are so typical that they are more or less synonymous with (or seen as the prototype brand for) the product category. *Kellogg's* and *Gillette* have the heritage, image and equity in their specific categories. *Hoover* was seen as such a closely associated name with vacuum cleaners that the word 'hoover' became generic for 'vacuuming'. *Google* is synonymous with 'search'. Some brands in effect create a category: *Nokia* had an early focus on design and became a prototype brand in the mobile phone category. *Coca-Cola* is the proto-typical cola brand; *Red Bull* is the proto-typical energy drink brand and has created a new category. Other brands may be less typical in their respective category, and this may provide competitive advantage. *Egg* provided the market with financial services in a less typical way than the way the market was being served. Similarity is about how alike two brands are, whereas typicality relates to the strength of the link between the individual brand and the product category.
Innovative late entrant achieving 'relative position' but differentiation distinguishes the brand in a significant way.	Late entrants to a mature market appealing to central positioning value propositions but have radically different approaches to how the market is served. A brand's relative position gives the brand a unique and special label in the category giving the target audience explicit and/or implicit reasons to differentiate from the competition. It may become an exemplar for the category, and it may be more difficult for competitors to position themselves against identical attributes or benefits.
Niche	Brands that have created a sub-category of their own based on a distinctive attribute but still serve a very similar category need. Radically approach to how the market is served (eg: luxury, environment)

Source: Dahlen, Lange, & Smith (2010)

Table 4.6: Purpose, vision, mission, and values matrix.

Purpose	Why an organisation exists beyond financial goals. An expression of credible and achievable meaning.
Vision	Is time-bound and the result of purpose in terms of customer value and impact in the wider social and environmental context. It imagines where the organisation is heading.
Mission	The organisation's purpose translated into achievable goals. This never changes and defines the business and its most important objectives and goals. It describes what a company does, how it is done, who it is done for, and what value is created in doing so.
Value and Values	Closely linked with the organisation's mission, values are the mutual principles which bond customer and company. The DNA of the company which conditions strategic priorities and influences strategic direction.

Source: Authors' representation (2022)

"Companies need to determine what position their products already occupy in the consumers mind and relative to other products; only then they can act to reinforce or change that position." (Ries & Ries, 1998, p. 7).

4.13 Purpose, value proposition, and strategic positioning

Anderson *et al* (2006) advocated three approaches to presenting or positioning value to its consumers: identify all benefits that a company can offer; identify relevant points of difference to those delivered by key competitors; or resonating focus by offering those benefits highly valued by a selection of customers. In presenting what the elements and benefits of strategy are to its various audiences, the dialogue between company and customer tries to make the intangible tangible. Mission, vision, positioning statements, value propositions, and now expressions of purpose, can often be presented and received as competing rather complementary strategic instruments. There is overlap or confusion of meaning. This is exacerbated because of the need to address a multiplicity of products and services, target audiences, heterogeneous customer personas, multiple need states, and different customer journey experiences.

To fully understand the role that 'purpose' plays in all this, we need to distinguish between the various strategic components and determine what they focus on and what they convey to target audiences. These next sections examine these distinctly different elements and the relationships between them.

4.14 Purpose and value positioning

An organisation's value proposition is a product, service, brand, or organisational promise to its customer and stakeholders. It is the rationale of competitive advantage and an articulation of why prospective customers should connect with a business and the particular value offered. Dependent upon the multiple targets and buyer personas, there may be different variations. Keeping that promise can legitimise strategy, underpin governance ethics, and establish credentials in the customer-company relationship. Brand *positioning*, a subtype of the value proposition, is that promise strategically placed in the landscape of the marketplace.

Value positioning differentiates these companies who resonate with consumers who identify with authenticity. Authenticity is a quintessential brand quality: it is fundamentally intangible and yet like a delivered brand promise. According to Deloitte (2013), "Organisations with a strong sense of purpose are buoyed by factors that are non-financial and more intangible, with a longer horizon for positive returns. Other organisations are often driven by short-term financial gain -which hinders overall confidence". Companies that try and make an emotional connection through group identification, conscience, or cause can personalise organisational stance and give another narrative layer of perceived value to their brand. Consumer brand awareness can be as a result of company social awareness.

Strategic focus on brand purpose evolved from the societal principles of CSR and is evident today, with consumers looking for brands who affect or discuss societal issues. Edelman (2017), in the '*Edelman* Earned Brand Study', found that 50% of consumers worldwide are driven by 'belief' and 67% bought a brand because they agreed or connected with its position on controversial topic.

A company which manages people and resources without purpose merely manages, but if purpose is a key driver mobilises people and resources. Companies with a social purpose as a strategic positioning are transformed in terms of growth potential, and a broader culturally relevant social and environmental orientation. *Nestlé* evolved from a 'Food & Beverage Company' to one which embraces nutrition, health and wellness company. *Nike* recognised that being a footwear and apparel company was restrictive, but a transition to a purpose-based strategic positioning of a 'health and fitness' company would offer a more relevant, sustainable proposition.

4.15 Repositioning and rebranding

As we have seen, life in the Fourth Industrial Revolution (Industry 4.0) is causing companies to rethink and reboot brand strategy. Not all organisations are 'facing the right way' in terms of moral purpose. Brand repositioning can offer a new path forward (and upward) when growth has stalled, competitors are taking the lead, or customers aren't connecting with your company like they used to. A *brand repositioning* strategy is not a complete remake of a company's identity – it's a calculated adjustment. Companies reposition to keep up with evolving customer needs, update brand status, associations, personality, or core message while retaining a continuous, recognizable identity.

The decision to rebrand, to redefine an organisation's or a brand's identity, may be as a result of scandal or crises, a change in organisational strategy or orientation, structural change through a merger or acquisition, bankruptcy, parent company brand portfolio rationalisation, underperformance, overall brand image deterioration, or even the inability to differentiate from competitors.[72] Rebranding may involve a drastic change of business model, presentation of value proposition, name or logo. Cost of resources and damage to brand equity may determine the scope of rebranding. Rebranding has been described as " the practice of building anew a name, representative of a differentiated position in the mind frame of stakeholders and a distinctive identity with competitors" (Muzellec, Doogan, & Lambkin, 2003, p. 32).

Rebranding can fail and be costly. In 1985, *Coca Cola*'s now infamous '*New Coke*' slid into brand oblivion when consumer perception was disastrously under-estimated. Changing to '*Consignia*' cost the UK's *Royal Mail* in 2002 cost £1.5 million to change and £1 million to change back, contributing to 17,000 jobs being lost and revenue losses of £1.1 billion. American clothes brand *Gap* rebranded and branded back within 6 weeks in 2010. Even the mighty *Facebook* failed with a logo change when trying to differentiate the company from the app in 2019. However, rebranding can produce positive results and long-term benefits: refocusing operations within an organisation or the internal perception of service; shared common goals are solidified; increase morale or motivation; it may even improve awareness and relevance and therefore increase competitiveness.

The decision to re-position could be different reasons. *Starbucks* famously created a social "third place" between home and work which succeeded, and a socio-political community appeal with #*RaceTogether* which, not unlike the UK #*TakingTheKnee* campaign in support of anti-racism at EPL football matches, alienated part of its core customer base and failed. In contrast, *Airbnb* appeared to deliberately alienate to reinforce their targeted customer base by taking advantage of a forced reinvention of the Hospitality Sector and deploying a community purpose of 'belong anywhere'.

In 2010, following the success of *Axe* in disrupting the Men's Body Wash sector, the well-established masculine brand *Old Spice* was suddenly exposed and vulnerable. It took a full year of convincing a new generation to "Smell Like A Man", but *Old Spice* gained a new identity and the brand had been restored to category leadership.

---

72 Taylor, Aaron. "Rebranding: The Essential Guide for Professional Services Firms." *Hinge Marketing*. Web. 4 May 2013.

Veolia, a B2B environmental service company, used repositioning to redefine its brand – from 'waste management' to 'social responsibility'. Even the rational, logic-centric B2B sector still responded to the environmental realignment. As we have seen above with *Netflix* being forced by environmental factors to reposition its value proposition, *Spotify* transitioned from a 'free music with advertising' music aggregator to 'content creator and tastemaker' in response to consumer usage data and changing music consumption trends. *Spotify*'s business model is advertising revenue-dependent and this was severely affected by the 'new normal' post-COVID-19. Curated playlists and enhanced *Spotify*® Originals content like podcasts helped differentiate and reposition.

4.16 Purpose-driven brand strategy

As we have discussed above, profit isn't a purpose, it is a result. Purpose is a fundamental bonding agent between company assets and customer aspirations, the fusion of corporate mission and the motivational drives of consumption. Putting purpose at the heart of strategy can provide guidance and relevance. Purpose-driven brand strategy is about consumer empowerment and company transformation. "By acting on their purpose, companies can create more value for their shareholders and society over the long term than by pursuing purely financial goals or a narrowly defined self-interest".[73]

Organisations are progressively integrating 'purpose' into strategy for three main reasons:

- Purpose can be a core competitive differentiator, having greater productivity and better growth rates, satisfied work force, higher levels of innovation, and closer customer relationships. EY's research shows that exhibiting greater citizenship with applied social responsibility such as "*Unilever's* sustainable living brands like *Dove*, *Vaseline*, and *Lipton* helps market penetration, growth and brand longevity through resonating with user perceptions of values and relevance". Promoting sustainability and supply convenance can secure value proposition differentiation by embodying the company's purpose. Indeed, brands only really achieve credibility through the unwritten 'contract' of their brand promise: the permanency and reiteration of their unique value proposition.
- Purpose can be a unifier of company, customers, and stakeholders as it can create and communicate a shared meaning personified in mutual value and values. Meaningful connectivity through authentic relationships allows greater ownership of the brand amongst its producers and users. For example, 53% of South

---

73 "The state of the debate on purpose in business", *EY Beacon Institute*, 2021.

African 'millennial' consumers have reported a changed relationship with businesses who have a positive environmental impact.

– Purpose can communicate what an organisation stands for, embedding purpose in strategy, processes, actions, communications, and any service encounter in the interface between customer and company. This is drives operations towards outcomes that are valued by its customers.

Purpose here is truly meaningful because "it taps into universal values about what is good and our fundamental drive as human beings to serve the wellbeing of others" (Frankl, 1985). It is like a philosophical pulse or heartbeat which drives organisational orientation and guides the behavioural compass of values. The *EY Beacon Institute* – who see their role as supporting and A advising businesses on how to place purpose at the heart of their strategy – define purpose as "an organisation's aspirational, human-first reason for being", serving many stakeholders.

Companies like *LEGO* recognise the polyphony of patrons in the form of 'promises' for each key stakeholder group: shareholders, owners, employees, customers, and suppliers, as well as societal and environmental pressure groups. Purpose is "the most important thing in terms of what we are, and it's a foundation of everything we do" (Marjorie Lao, *LEGO* CFO). Based on extensive research with top CEOs, the *EY Institute* listed the following suggestions for organisations attempting to transform purpose-driven orientation:

– Make leadership buy-in a starting point not a finish line. Purpose must be real with vision constantly reinforced, leadership buy-in cascading and employee commitment present at every level. Use purpose as a decision-making filter. Accept or reject decisions based on delivery of financial goals as well as value judgements. However, financials should follow on from making the right decisions as an outcome but not an end goal.

– Drive purpose beyond culture into long-term sustainable strategy, explicitly linking purpose with financial performance and other KPI success.

– Measure purpose but don't over-measure it, focusing on the most important elements of sustainable living purpose and the bigger picture and not obsess over micro-management of measures. It is really about doing the right thing. Don't confuse purpose with CSR. Social purpose should not be siloed into a single department but an integrated, scalable core element of creating added value within business strategy.

– Position purpose as a North Star not a to-do list. The 'means' of the business – the day-to-day operational activities which aggregate up to the achievement of objectives – may evolve, but the overall 'end' remains con constant purpose, therefore, must align with core competencies as well as directing company culture.

Principles in practice

Pact **putting purpose into their packs**

At 9.5 tonnes roasted per week, and 21 million cups drank, *Pact*, founded in 2012 by Stephen Rapoport, are starting to make an impact on the UK coffee market. However, 54% of that production was by farmers living on small, rural farms in Brazil, Rwanda, Columbia, Honduras, Ethiopia, El Salvador, Kenya, Guatemala, and Peru. With 2 billion cups drank every day world-wide (British Coffee Association), their mission to "transform the coffee industry one cup at a time" may be a long-term goal, but by trying to "make life better for farmers at source and to make speciality coffee accessible to everyone", *Pact* are certainly putting purpose into their packs.

Fairtrade has been seen as a ceiling not the floor, and with a traditional 3 year growing cycle and complicated supply chain, the difficult journey from seed to cup has been exacerbated by the coffee price crisis, small farm vulnerability to climate change, and the Covid-19 pandemic. *Pact's* solution is to: put the power into the hands of the farmers by going straight to source; achieve more security for farmers by building long-term relationships; invest in the next generation through education; invest in equipment; champion gender equality in production (35% are female-led farms); and help change farming practices. Some of those Rwandan farmers were even bought cows through the 'Girinka Project'.

The brand reputation, built through both direct-to-consumer and B2B supply models, is traceability and tracking. As one of the UK's largest independent roasteries, *Pact* is making "coffee a force for good to drive positive, sustainable change" in 124 farms across 9 regions, and spreading its purpose "beyond the bean".

Source: "*Pact Coffee* 2020 Transparency Report: Transforming the coffee industry one cup at a time", *pactcoffee.com*

– Bring purpose to life with stories. The human experience is an essential communication conduit, conveying through historical narratives, heritage, personal achievement, ways in which lives have been enhanced, allowing the company to plot progress.
– Lean on purpose during good times too.
– Accept that purpose is not always a win-win.

Purpose-driven brand strategy involves four stages: the definition of brand purpose; the creation of the brand (or value) proposition; the presentation of that proposition to target markets and stakeholders; and the articulation of the brand persona. Figure 4.2 and Table 4.7 illustrate the components of this strategy: vocation, vision, value, values, visualisation, and voice.

4.17 Measuring purpose, value, and values

The purpose of Purpose is to act as a management tool, a decision-making compass to direct organisational strategy in the context of satisfying both profit and social goals. But how mission, values, and organisational orientation achieve objectives

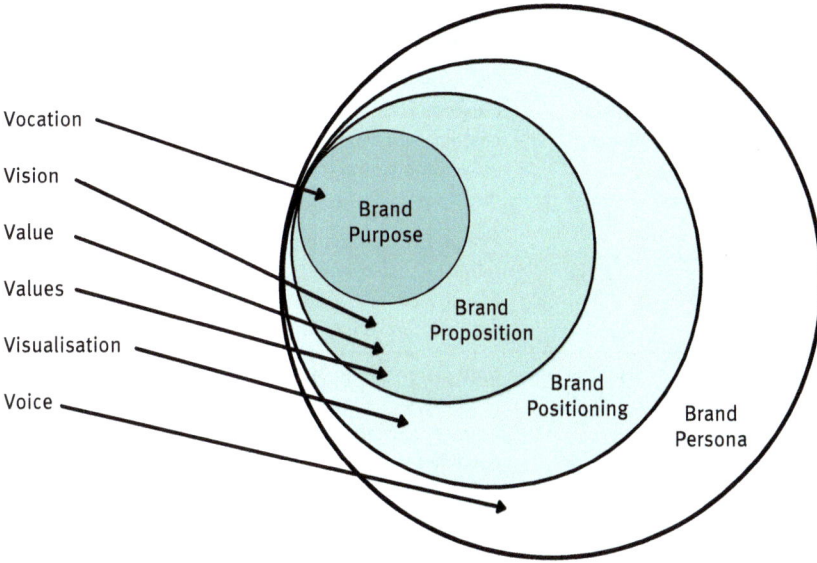

Figure 4.2: Components of brand strategy.
Source: Authors' representation (2022)

Table 4.7: Components of purpose-driven brand strategy.

Brand purpose Why an organisation exists beyond financial goals. An expression of credible and achievable meaning.	Vocation	*Raison d'etre*: Strategy is moving closer on the *customer-company continuum*, and companies have to assess their strategic raison d'etre, why they exist, and how organisational values align with their customers' beliefs.
		Mission: The organisation's purpose translated into achievable goals. This never changes and defines the business and its most important objectives and goals. It describes what a company does, how it is done, who it is done for, and what value is created in doing so.
		Meaning: There is no brand purpose if there is no brand meaning. The driving force for meaning, created through shared values, is very much a *socially* constructed phenomenon, acting as a communications conduit between company and customer, between customer and customer, and can bond organisations and stakeholders in symbolic symbiosis.

Table 4.7 (continued)

Brand proposition	Value Values Vision	*Value and Values*: Profit and conscience. Value is co-created. Values are the mutual principles which bond customer and company. The DNA of the company which conditions strategic priorities and influences strategic direction.
		Vision: Is time-bound and the result of purpose in terms of customer value and impact in the wider social and environmental context. It imagines where the organisation is heading.
Brand Positioning	Visualisation	*Data insights*: Market segmentation, customer profiling, target audiences, and stakeholders within brand eco-system determine brand image and identity, customer perception, and competitive market location.
Brand Persona	Voice	Projection and amplification of brand identity and image through brand narrative, omni-channel integrated marketing communications.

Source: Authors' representation (2022)

and how can this be measured? Does the old management aphorism "you can only manage what you can measure" still hold true?

Firstly, how do consumers measure purpose? The following list has been extracted from a survey of 30,000 consumers (Accenture Strategy Research Report, 2018).

When asked what attracts a consumer to buy a brand other than economic reasons, these were the responses:

- the brand culture delivered on its promise to do what is claimed (66%).
- transparency with employment policy and trading arrangements (66%).
- the company treats its employees well (65%).
- they believe in reducing plastics and improving the environment (62%).
- the brand has ethical values and demonstrates authenticity in everything it does (62%).
- the brand is passionate about the products/services it sells (62%).
- the brand stands for something bigger than just the products and services it sells which aligns with my personal values (52%).
- the brand stands up for societal and cultural issues they believe in (50%).
- the brand supports and acts upon causes they have in common (eg: social, charitable) (50%).
- the brand connects me to others like me and gives me a sense of opportunity (38%).
- the brand takes a political stance on issues close to my heart (37%).

Chapter takeaways

- Short-term value generation, with its shareholder primacy orientation, often seen as being at the expense of other stakeholders, is now set in a completely different context than originally envisaged.
- Most successful enterprises are purpose-driven, aligning leadership and strategy with organisational mission and values.
- A solid platform for creating and sustaining a *purpose-driven brand strategy* is based on an authentic, relevant, and consistent philosophy, and a strong point of view of what the company stands for and why it does what it does.
- Aligning purpose, values, and positioning, with a value system to support achieving organisational objectives, can provide a roadmap of organisational strategy.
- Value isn't what *goes into* the value proposition by the company, it is what is *taken out* by the customer.
- A vision statement is an aspirational roadmap pointing the way to customers and employees, imagining the distant future.
- A mission statement focuses on the present and the immediate future, is on-going and atemporal, describes and defines direction and destination.
- Brand positioning is about establishing a core promise within the marketplace and relevant to a target constituency which enables a brand to function on both a rational and emotional level.
- If vision is where you are going, brand an expression of who and where you are, and strategy is how you get there, then purpose is *why* you do what you do.
- Purpose is a fundamental bonding agent between company assets and customer aspirations, the fusion of corporate mission and the motivational drives of consumption.

Closing case

Patagonia walks the talk with product and purpose

With a growing orientation towards ecologically-friendly and ethical production, even 'fashion' items with sustainability credentials can suffer from an "eco/ego contradiction" (Smith, 2007, p. 325). *Patagonia*, a progressive American clothing company, make product with a purpose – sustainable outdoor clothing for those who aspire to step outside mainstream society and engage in personal transformation through extreme sports in wilderness landscapes. The appeal is in the quality of their product, enhanced by the adoption of recycling techniques in the fabrication of its products, and reinforced by the brand's authenticity. Its purpose is to minimise environmental damage and promote sustainability whilst encouraging their brand users to appreciate the wilderness experience. To seek to *do less harm but more good*.

Yet paradoxically, integrity of practices runs counter to the increased demand and consumption for their product: the popularity of 'green' products actually increases production. Hepburn (2013) refers to the "complication of greenness . . . where purchasers of "ecofashion" also buy in to a process that carries forward the very economic and ecological trajectory they would ideally curtail".

Founded in 1973 by Yvon Chouinard, a well-known environmental campaigner, *Patagonia's* purpose statement goes beyond profit to include the key components of: distinguished quality, improving lives, and saving the planet. Its raison d'etre is expressed in the consistent "use of all its resources to protect life on earth". Founder members of the 'One Percent for the Planet' organisation which encourages businesses to give a percentage of their profits to environmental charities. Examples include campaigns such as "Ocean As A Wilderness" and "Don't Dam *Patagonia*", the 'World Trout Initiative' for protected species, a recent campaign to fight against oil drilling in Alaska the "Alaska Wildlife Refuge". These campaigns are not just superficial PR activities, but a serious attempt at politically motivating their customers beyond buying their product. The award of 'Eco Brand of the Year' in 2008 at the *Volvo Eco Design Forum* in Munich was proof that *there is purpose beyond profit in business*. Even though there is complicated greenness to their value proposition, their social and environmental values are so embedded in their company.

Patagonia's core values are expressed in their purpose statement: "To build the best product to limit ecological impacts, cause no unnecessary harm in business practice, use business to inspire and protect nature, and not to be bound by convention". Walking the talk is embedded in all they do which is in service of their purpose. This is manifest in the transparency and authenticity of their operation and decision-making, sometimes at their own expense. One such example was kick-started in 1994 when organic agricultural activist Will Allen demonstrated that their conventional growing of cotton involved chemically poisoning soil, air, and groundwater. This resulted in *Patagonia* changing production to 100% organic cotton, at the time representing 20% of their total $100 million business.

© Galyna Andrushko – stock.adobe.com.

Examples of *Patagonia's* support of environmental activism can also be seen in the commitment of $1 million given to the "Vote Our Planet" campaign, fighting oil drilling, a self-imposed "1% for the Planet" tax used for supporting grassroots non-profits, as well as donating its entire 'Black Friday' sales ($10 million) directly to environmental organisations. In addition, employees use their roles in the sports community to be Global Sports Activists to drive social and environmental change. For over 45 years, 'Patagonia Action Works' have connected with and supported environmental activists to the tune of over $90million on projects such as fighting for the Vjosa, the first Wild River National Park in Europe. 94% of Albanian people have voted in favour of a national park stretching 300 km from Greece to the Adriatic coast in Albania, protecting against 30 dam projects on the river and its tributaries in danger of destroying the natural environment.

Patagonia have been true to their purpose to use their resources – voice, business, and community – to do something about the climate crisis and preservation of the natural environment.

Questions

1. Explain what is meant by an "eco/ego contradiction" and how consumers balance 'fashion' with sustainability.
2. *Patagonia's* purpose statement goes beyond profit to include the key components of: distinguished quality, improving lives, and saving the planet. How have they applied these principles in practice and is this strategy sustainable?
3. What impact does the various activist affiliations have on their brand equity?

Note: The photo(s) used in this case study is/are not connected and/or does not represent any brand(s) mentioned. It/they is/are used to make a visual discussion point by the authors.

5 Managing customer-company fusion: Customer experience management

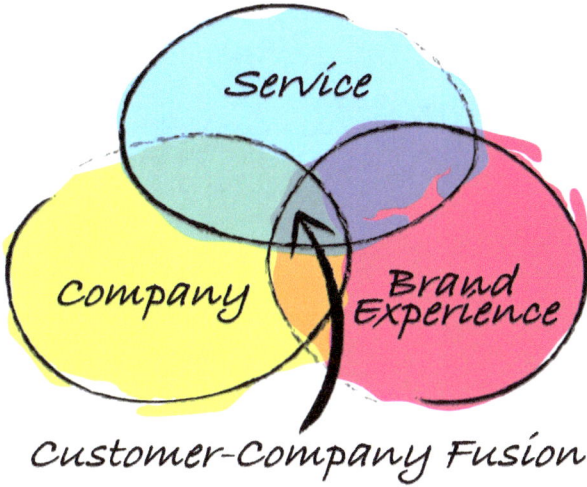

Customer-Company Fusion

https://doi.org/10.1515/9783110718638-009

Opening case

© Andrey Popov - stock.adobe.com

Absolut LGBTQ+ engagement or just Rainbow Washing?

Diverse demographic preferences play a significant part in targeting and engaging with specific market segments. It is critical to brand strategy that companies must connect with diverse multicultural audiences. In the 1990s, *Subaru* identified five specific target segments – 'teachers and other educators', 'technical professionals, 'engineers', 'rugged individuals', and 'female heads of households'. A large proportion of this last group had emerged from focus groups as 'women identifying as lesbian'. Although at the time the ads were not overtly aimed at trying to change minds or support the LGBTQ+ lifestyle, *Subaru* were admitting that they were selling cars to gay people. Ads featured subtle nods to sexuality and were accompanied by the tagline "It's not a choice. It's the way we're built". *Subaru's* success encouraged other companies to be more open in their communications.

The shift to consumer power has seen companies having to engage with their customers and stakeholders on *their* terms. For example, 'Millennials' and 'Gen Zs', and 'Gen Alpha',[74] born as digital natives, have been equipped with the technological and generational power to disrupt social norms, question authority, share opinions, and manifest values and behaviours in brand consumption. The imperative for companies to match up their value proposition with the customer's, and having simpatico social conscience makes this a driving force for societal change. The Covid-19 pandemic, extreme climate events, and a charged socio-political atmosphere have "reinforced people's passions and given them oxygen" (Deloitte, 2021).[75]

Research suggests that 81% of Gen Z are "passionate" about gender equality, whilst 63% "care deeply" about LGBTQ+ issues. Similarly, 55% of LGBTQ+ consumers would choose a brand and 70% would pay a premium to companies committed to supporting diversity. 78% of LGBTQ+ consumers would switch to brands that are sympathetic and supportive to the LGBTQ+ community. Of the *YouTube* viewers who self-identified as LGBTQ+, nearly 64% said they are more likely to buy from a brand that includes LGBTQ+ content in their ads.[76] Nearly three quarters of LGBTQ+ people visit social media 7–8 times a week, and brands are leveraging these platforms to better engage with this audience. From a company's perspective, this is a broad and growing demographic

---

74 Early 2010s – Mid 2020s age group.
75 "A call for accountability and action", The Deloitte Global/ 2021 Millennial and Gen Z Survey, deloitte.com/MillennialSurvey, 2021.
76 "YouTube LGBTQ Research figures" Pixability, "Purpose-Driven Marketing," May 2017.

worth engaging with. But what constitutes 'engagement' from a consumer's point of view is maybe different. Consumers are beginning to question whether engagement without authentic long-term purpose is really meaningful engagement or just 'rainbow washing'.[77]

One brand at the vanguard of engagement with the LGBTQ+ community is *Absolut*, the Swedish vodka manufacturer founded in 1879, owned by French firm *Pernod Ricard* since 2008. The brand is marketed in 126 countries (40% of vodka imported into the United States is *Absolut*), and is the world's third largest alcoholic spirits brand and, according to *Forbes Magazine*, was the number one luxury brand of 2002. *Absolut* have demonstrated their commitment to supporting LGBTQ+ (since 1981) by being the first to continuously present a major brand in gay media and fight the cause through more conventional channels. Like their iconic bottle design, engaging with this group was initially seen as being different from the norm, engaging with a trendy, growing demographic not necessarily identified with specific issues. The first exposure was followed by events in bars, the funding of LGBTQ+-oriented charities and causes, and sponsorship of a cable TV programme now gaining considerable mainstream traction – '*Ru Paul's Drag Race*' – as well as supporting *GLADD*, a non-governmental media group who monitor representation of LGBTQ+ people. Over $31 million has been spent on marketing to this community with over $40 million more in donations, but they still claim that the reason for LGBTQ+ engagement is not for political reasons. Their purpose is as potent as their product: "We don't take political stands but we believe in all people's rights to be who they are and express what they want. We believe in diversity and individuality. We do not believe in labels and prejudice" says CMO Kristina Hagbard.

Other brands such as *Casablanca Records, Yves Saint Laurent, Jägermeister, Coors*, and *Pernod Ricard* promoted to this group prior to *Absolut*, but this was all in the form of coded content or "gay vague" as Todd Evans of *Rivendell Media* puts it. *IKEA* and *Subaru* resisted the negative reactions to flying the Rainbow flag in the '90s. As the Aids disaster hit, many brands retreated; *Absolut* didn't waver but doubled down instead. Drinking is part of gay culture, so there was an obvious synergy, but *Absolut's* continuous and fully committed engagement with this community cemented an unbreakable bond. Todd Wilkie, curator of LGBTQ+ advertising, claims that: "*Absolut* maintained their presence for many years, building loyalty and name recognition, being known as one of the most gay-friendly brands of all time. Others got there much later". John McCourt, *GLADD*'s[78] Senior Director of Business Development & Integrated Marketing, suggests that "When brands authentically represent LGBTQ+ people and the issues that affect the community most in their marketing, then they can certainly expect to attract LGBTQ+ consumers. Authenticity is key". *Absolut* Vice President Regan Clarke claims that the key is permanent engagement: "We're here and we're not going away. We are committed to provoking dialogue that leads to cultural change every day".

Other brands have ventured into this sort of engagement. *Coca Cola's* 'Pool Boy' ad beautifully captures the inclusivity of the brand as well as sexual inclusivity and was well received by the LGBTQ+ community.[79] At a time when gay sex was illegal in their country, Indian clothing company *Anouk Ethnic* featured a lesbian couple preparing to meet one of the girl's parents for the first time. *Smart Communications*, a Philippines wireless and digital service provider, had the same theme

---

77 "Using rainbow colours and/or imagery to advertising, apparel, accessories, landmarks in order to indicate support for LGBQT+ equality (and earn consumer credibility) with a minimum of effort or pragmatic result". (Urban Dictionary).

78 *GLADD* is a US non-governmental media monitoring organisation founded as a protest against defamatory coverage of LGBTQ+ people and the issues that affect.

79 Google Survey, "LGBT Creative Best Practices," U.S., April 2017.

but this time with two males hoping to break barriers. However, when two men were seen kissing in UK brand *O2's* ad, many felt the sexual explicitness inappropriate for the time it was scheduled and offensive to their religious beliefs.[80] However, another UK company, *Lloyds Bank*, were voted by *Stonewall*, a gay rights charity, as the 2nd best LGBTQ+ employer for their "commitment to engage with LGBTQ+ people in the workplace" when their ad featured a same-sex proposal.

There are brands who are gradually engaging with non-mainstream social phenomena. Take the 'T' in LGBTQ+ – transgender. In 2014, *Johnson & Johnson's* dermatology brand aimed at young women *'Clean & Clear'* featured Jazz Jennings, a *YouTube* transgender teenage sensation for their #SeeTheRealMe campaign. Jazz had transitioned from being assigned a male at birth. This was a pivotal moment for gender transformation and for positioning the brand's 'self-confidence' essence to the teen market. Ellen Kahn, Director of the Children, Youth & Families Programme at the Human Rights Campaign in Washington said: "*Johnson & Johnson* is actually one of the corporations that scores 100% for inclusivity in HRC's Corporate Equality Index.[81] It's walking its talk. It fits into the company's commitment to diversity inclusion". Similarly, the *Marriott International* hotel featured a transgender model and advocate Geena Rocero in its #LoveTravels LGBTQ+ campaign.

Non-profits like the *Ad Council* reminded us that "Love Has No Labels". It's Superbowl 'Kiss Cam' iteration "Fans of Love" featuring non-traditional couples reached 6.7m *YouTube* views with the equivalent of 13.4m minutes 'watchtime' views (the equivalent of over 74k football games aired back-to-back). Significantly, the ad was 2 minutes of 'long form content' with 74% being viewed on mobile devices. The use of hashtags with cultural relevance is an effective engagement method. *American Eagle*, a lifestyle clothing company used #weallcan to celebrate individuality and inclusivity. Following the mass shooting in Pulse nightclub, *Jet Blue Airlines* hashtagged #westandwithorlando alongside free flights to victims' families. Others, such as *AT&T's* #attliveproud inviting "boldness" in exchange for a $1 donation, are acknowledged as being at the forefront of inclusivity. *Nike* developed a range of LGBQT-inspired designs featuring the rainbow gradient and a #betrue collection hashtag. However, not all brands superficially supporting LGBQT are authentic in their commitment to the cause. Organisations who temporarily display the flying the rainbow for self-promotion capitalising on short-term exposure are accused of "Rainbow Washing"[82] the gender equivalent of insincere environmental "Green Washing". It is surface-level solidarity, tokenistic, and has negative consequences for brands. It is seen as hypocritical and bad for business. So much so that some brands – like *Corona* in the United States – have eschewed the annual *Pride* celebrations to reinforce their emotional connection (predicated on action) on a permanent basis. That is "active outreach, not just saying as an organisation that we're supportive of you as an LGBTQ+ person but as an LGBQT consumer". That is real engagement.

Questions
1. Is it always important for companies to match up their value proposition and social conscience with that of the customer's?
2. Engagement without authentic long-term purpose isn't really meaningful engagement, it's just 'rainbow washing'. What damage, if any, does this do to brand equity?

---

80 The UK's Advertising Standards Authority.

81 HRC Foundation's Corporate Equality Index is a US benchmarking tool monitoring lesbian, gay, bisexual, transgender, and queer equality in the workplace.

82 David Brancaccio, Meredith Garretson, & Rose Conlon, "Rainbow washing during Pride hurts both brands and consumers", Marketplace Morning Report, June 23, 2021.

3. The UK brand *O2* suffered a backlash when some viewers were offended by the sexual explicitness featured in their campaign. When socially 'inclusive' IMC objectives exclude parts of
an audience, is this worthwhile?

Note: The photo(s) used in this case study is/are not connected and/or does not represent any
brand(s) mentioned. It/they is/are used to make a visual discussion point by the authors.

5.1 Outline of chapter

Management of interaction is moving away from being merely a company-oriented
'inside-out' organisational process to one where a customer-oriented experiential
'outside-in' perspective has primacy. Described by some as "the new frontier of
competitive advantage" (Rayport & Jaworski, 2004, p. 47), the *customer-company
interface* is where the brand experience, the service process which supports it, the
promise of company value proposition, and customer expectation and experience
are fused in mutually beneficial co-creation of value.

Over four decades ago, Ted Levitt (1981) strongly suggested that "When you ask
prospective customers to buy promises – as all service-oriented firms do – you must
provide metaphorical reassurances of quality and 'industrialise' the service-delivery
process". Just under two decades later, Bill Gates (2000, p. 15) advocated integrating
technology to energise customer-company relationships, employee involvement, and
the nature of service processes: "Most transactions will become self-service digital
transactions. Intermediaries will evolve to add value or perish". Latterly, emphasis
has shifted from a provider-dominant logic to a customer-dominant logic, where
multi-contextual value creation processes involve the company within the customer's
life and ecosystem (Heinonen, Strandvik, & Voima, 2013).

These statements mark out the territory of *Customer-Company Fusion*, the customer engagement/customer value interface where reciprocity, trust, and commitment are fused together to fulfil customer expectations and co-create mutually
beneficial value. The outcome of this is the Customer Experience (CX), the environment the customer encounters: the brand touchpoints in their individual customer
journeys, all the moments when the customer interacts with the organisation, the
brand, and service delivery.

Engineering a streamlined, frictionless customer service experience in order to
create mutually beneficial value is now an essential component of brand strategy. It
is becoming an increasingly digitised phenomenon, and with a gravitation towards
AI-powered Automated Customer Experience (ACX) the dynamic is changing even
further. For the purposes of clarity, discussion of the strategic approaches to managing the customer experience has been split into two distinct parts. *Chapter 7 Managing the Customer Journey: The Digital Consumption Experience* discusses how the

principles of service and customer centricity are applied and controlled both online and offline. This chapter looks at how the company is structured and organised in terms of strategic vision, leadership, corporate branding, how customer behaviour is analysed, how and why a culture of customer focus, innovation, and continuous improvement is implemented, and how performance is mobilised.

Learning outcomes

After reading this chapter, you'll be able to:
- Define and analyse what is meant by engagement at the customer-company interface.
- Understand why 'stakeholder orchestration', is a crucial part of brand strategy.
- Assess the impact of digital disruption on the customer experience.
- Establish the links between corporate identity and organisational culture, whilst evaluating how this impacts on the customer-company relationship.
- Explain why companies now have to go beyond corporate social responsibility compliance.
- Identify the key factors of how mutually beneficial relationships co-create value and help maintain brand longevity.

5.2 Introduction

Customer experience is a corporate driver of value and *the* test of customer engagement: how the value proposition is received, perceived, and encountered are the key 'moments of truth' of customer-company fusion. The interface between company and customer – the alignment between internal actions and external perceptions – is a key crucible of creation, communication, and commitment. The notion of 'service' is embedded in this, and is now applied to all organisations in all contexts. However, it is no longer a sustainable competitive advantage merely to offer quality service. Customers primarily buy the brand *experience* not just the product or service offer, and this impacts on perceived value, attitudes to consumption, and customer-company loyalty. Indeed, more often than not customer experience of a brand is as important as the actual product or service itself. "The secret weapon that differentiates exceptional, enduring companies is the quality of their customer engagement, encompassing the full set of activities through which companies build direct relationships with their customers".[83]

At its core, managing customer expectations and experience in service-oriented businesses, as well as manufacturers with applied service principles, is undoubtedly complex and challenging. Where customer-company interactions form a key element of customer experience, this complicates matters. As Hatch & Shultz (2010, p. 117)

---

[83] Bill Magnuson, CEO & Co-founder, "2021 Global Customer Engagement Review" *Braze*, July 2021.

assert: "It is one thing to brand products whose quality is at least predictable; it is quite another to invest in brands for which human variability is a significant factor". Therefore, it is imperative that companies strategically manage the actual and perceived experience that customers have, and that there is a streamlined and seamless "holistic process beginning with the relationship between the firm and its staff, coming alive during the *interaction* between staff and customers" (Dall'Olmo Riley & Chernatony, 2000, p. 137). The service provider is dependent on customer participation, but companies need to determine whether customer-*induced* or customer-*dependent* activities should be prioritised in constructing service blueprints (ie: a visual representation of interaction and relationships between service components).

Service marketing principles are the essence of customer centricity. "Ultimately, only one thing really matters in service encounters – the customer's perceptions of what occurred" (Chase & Dasu, 2001, p. 2). Creating and managing seamless customer experiences through processual service blueprints in order to plan the customer journey, measure interactions, inflection points, service encounters, or moments of truth, is therefore an essential part of brand strategy. Employees, particularly customer-facing service personnel, constitute the interface between a brand's internal and external environment and can have a powerful impact on how consumers perceive the brand and the service organisation.

Whilst managing the holistic customer experience can be the new competitive advantage, there is a difference between CEM and CRM: CEM focuses on *current* customer experience, unlike CRM which leans on the recorded history of the customer-company relationship. When companies talk about the *customer experience*, they are referring to any qualitative experiential aspect of all interactions at any time between a prospective, new, lapsed, or loyal customer and organisation: how the individual's relationship with the company makes them feel; what the company does and *how it does it*; as well as how the individual perceives service before, during and after use. Frontline service employees can have a powerful impact on how consumers perceive the brand and the service provided by the organisation in order to successfully manage and fulfil customer expectations. The 'digital nervous system' that Gates espoused and the notion of customer/company 'relationships' are both useful metaphors for the customer-orientation logic of service marketing, with its value-creation and the relational, systemised symbiosis between company and customer that Levitt championed. It is this integration, this *customer-company fusion*, increasingly mediated through technology, which is explored here.

According to Ambler *et al* (2002, p. 13) managing internal actions and external perceptions "are two sides of the same coin; one perspective without the other is unlikely to be effective". Internal organisational structures and cultures have to be aligned with external ecosystems (eg: a pharmaceutical company will have close links with hospitals, private patient organisations, governmental health infrastructures etc.) to maximise co-creative production of products and services. Internalising externalities makes the incorporation of purpose across these ecosystems challenging, but this way of looking at an organisation's stakeholders helps to define the role of *stake* in stakeholder co-creation.

Here, there is a true melding – or fusion – of areas focused on understanding and maintaining customer orientation which are quite often approached with a silo mentality and protected with a tight subject matter jealousy. Beyond the digital age, beyond the global pandemic, there will be an even greater need for customer-company fusion: knowledge of the customer, continuous process improvement, a service philosophy, co-created innovation, mutually beneficial relationships, Customer Experience Management (CEM), symmetrical B2C/C2B communications, symbolic symbiosis of meaning, organisational culture, and collaboration, are all essential aspects of the focus on a single goal: *customer centricity*. This dynamic interchange or interface places a growing emphasis on consistency between the internal projected brand identity and external customer image or perception of actual service delivery: the managing of the "service encounter" (Bachman, 2001, p. 42).

From its market diagnosis, once the company has articulated its purpose with clarity and conviction, the internal culture of the organisation has to be aligned with external stakeholders and operating environment. If employees behaviour is inconsistent and doesn't reinforce a brand's projected benefits, the credibility of the brand will be undermined (Samli & Frohlich, 1993, p. 145). Internal brand management strategy demands that brand equity be extended to account for the internal or employee perspective, so that there is accountability and increased comprehension of impact of employees on the brand on its implementation (King & Grace, 2009). Strategy, therefore, should be symbiotic, with customers and employees integrated in shared purpose and co-creation.

The impact of digitised interface facilitation, the fragmented digital remote work mediation (Prassl, 2008) of the post-COVID-19 economy, together with the growing socialisation of online purchase, and the enforced retail readjustment due to the pandemic restrictions, there has been a necessary re-evaluation of the notion of 'face-to-face' interaction. With the increased expansion in digital tools like e-Commerce, electronic payment processing, social media, mobile phones, apps, and even robotic AI media, 80% of company/customer interactions are now online. Call centre technology service provision is becoming the modus operandi of the sales and service functions of organisations in finance, retail, insurance, education, and a plethora of formerly brick-based sectors. The growing phenomena of remote 'screen-to-face' or 'voice-to-voice' interactions are becoming much more prevalent these days and have changed how companies can and do strategically manage the customer experience.

Electronic Data Interchange (EDI), for some time now a B2B computer-to-computer technological service facilitator, is a progenitor of the digital service disruption we are currently exposed to. For some time, routinised computer-to-computer re-ordering has been standard in the B2B sector. Subsequent developments such as the use of Artificial Intelligence (AI) platforms like Enterprise Resource Planning

(ERP), Systems Applications and Products in Data Processing (SAP) have extended this phenomenon. All these innovations have radically altered the customer/company interface, "employee experience management" with automated, remote numbers-oriented "algorithmic management" systems (Prassl, 2018, p. 55) beginning to affect the qualitative nature of service. This requires management of purchase processes, all interface communications, control through data analysis, social media interaction, and quality assessments at every touch point. Trust, tact, empathy, conformity, focus, and flexibility (Priola, 2009) are essential ingredients of customer interactions and this is at the heart of managing the new customer experience.

This digitally-infused interactive transformation is not an exact reproduction of the Direct Marketing model which, although it promoted 'precision targeted marketing', threatened to be just as (if not more) intrusive as the 'interruption' model of traditional broadcast media. This current technology has not just delivered intrusion but *seclusion*, where consumers lie beyond the control of organisations, communicating with other consumers, often providing user counter-narratives. Social media sites such as *TikTok*, consumer review sites such as *Epinions*, *Trustpilot*, and *Trip Advisor*, collaborative network sites like *Facebook* and *Instagram*, trading *EBay*, *Craigslist*, *Facebook Marketplace*, and *Gum Tree*, user-generated content sites like *YouTube* and *Cyworld*, as well as a plethora of independent influencer blogs are shifting the locus of control of meaning from company to consumer.

5.3 Engagement at the customer-company interface

It is an established fact now that engaged customers are a significant force in driving business revenues and profitability. From the customer's perspective, services are *experiences*; from the company's perspective, services are *processes* that have to be designed and managed to create the desired customer experience (Lovelock & Wirtz, 2011). Customer-company engagement is the crucible of value creation, "the new frontier of competitive advantage is the customer interface" according to Rayport & Jakowski (2004, p. 47). Online business, because of a range of reasons already outlined above, has superseded traditional bricks-and-mortar businesses in all aspects except one: the face-to-face human relationships of conventional business, turning the emphasis to human/technology engagement. As a consequence, building meaningful, long-lasting relationships with customers is more difficult in the less personal environs of often remote digitised ecosystems, but that is becoming the key challenge of our age: customer engagement with services and products, whilst being a process not an end state, can positively impact on outputs such as levels of acceptance, satisfaction, trust, commitment, and customer loyalty.

Managing engagement at the customer-company interface can help reduce customer churn, promote retention, shorten purchase cycles, enhance cross-selling and up-selling, foster positive WOM, and build brand sustainability. Research, such as that from *Bain & Company*,[84] suggests that in some sectors increasing customer retention by only 5% impacts profitability by more than 25%. The man responsible for that report, Fred Reichheld, championed the impact of creating a 'virtuous circle' based on building loyalty and repeat business through nurturing customer relationships managed through engagement processes for the benefit of the customer. Controlling customer churn through effective relationship loyalty programmes is helped by digital engagement. The digital employee experience is radically changing the role of the employee in the service operation and this has critical impacts for customer experience and the consequences of this on customer relationships, loyalty, and lifetime customer value.

'Loyalty' is more than a marketing metaphor but has different interpretations: from 'soft', emotive feelings towards a brand as a non-user, to the casual infrequency of the promiscuous repertoire user, to the hard-wired repurchasing behaviour of the repeat purchaser, retention is the goal and repetition is the driver. The company goal is to progress consumers through this affinity spectrum to become solid, loyal customers.

Customer engagement management gauges the quality (and often the quantity) of interactions between customer and company at all the important lifecycle touchpoints, measuring the strength of those human-to-human/human-to-technology connections. In strategic terms, it is the "psychological process that models underlying mechanisms by which customer loyalty forms, as well as the mechanisms by which loyalty may be maintained" (Bowden, 2009, p. 574). It is also about recognising that target audiences are heterogeneous and customers have to be managed as individuals with heterogeneous needs and expectations. Or put more simply: consumers are statistics; customers are people.

Principles in practice

Amazon tries a 'Fresh' approach to retail

Amazon Fresh, the first contactless, till-less grocery store outside of America opened in London in March 2021, offering *Amazon* customers a unique 'just walk out' self-service experience. Once inside, shoppers can pick up the goods they want without scanning them or even visiting a till. Sensors on the shelves detect when an item has been removed while cameras and other technology backed by artificial intelligence monitor individuals' movement around the store and the goods chosen. The bill is automatically charged to a shopper's *Amazon Account* when they leave the store.

Clive Black, an analyst at *Shore Capital*, said he believed *Amazon* would want up to 30 such outlets in the first phase of its expansion in the UK. The group already has more than 20 similar contactless grocery stores in the US under the name *Amazon Go*. Black said that the new store could be a "seminal moment in the history of the UK grocery market" and indicated *Amazon's* ambitions in the sector.

---

84 "Retaining customers is the real challenge", *Bain & Company*, January 20, 2006.

Upon entry, customers check in with a smartphone app and are automatically billed when they exit without needing to scan individual items. *Amazon* sells the vast majority of its goods online but owns the *Whole Foods Market* business, which has seven UK stores. It has previously opened 'pop up' shops for fashion and non-food items and has operated the grocer service *Amazon Fresh* for several years.

Source: *Amazon Fresh* opens first 'till-less' grocery store in UK, *The Guardian*, 24th March 2021

You can't manage customer experience without understanding the experience of the customer. Customer engagement doesn't only exist in the sales, support, or service functions of an organisation, it is an integrative brand management practice of anticipating customer needs, engaging in dialogues to encourage relationships and loyalty beyond transaction-only interchange. Mapping all customer encounters and behaviour that result in brand-focused consequences, CE has become an effective holistic strategy for understanding the nature and power of building close, emotional, and valued bonds between customer and company (Gummerus, Liljander, Weman, & Pihlström, 2012).

Another aspect of engagement which has changed the dynamic is the fact that the roles of user and provider – customer and company – are becoming increasingly indistinct. In service marketing parlance, this is referred to as 'simultaneity' where the production and consumption of services happen at the same time. More often than not, customers are complicit in co-production of product and service development and co-creation with user-generated content, peer support in product use, and customers often acting as communication C2C conduits. Customer engagement of this kind, in the context of a multi-user service ecosystem, is an amalgam of all the touch points and behaviours that may influence the organisation and can actually help business performance and enhances customer value.

Interactive customer experiences evidences a greater relational fusion beyond the transactional behaviour of the customer-provider dyad. Non-transactional consumer roles in the process can vary, such as: built-in co-production (label printing for product returns; home ticket printing for events or travel); voluntary partners (Bettencourt, 1997); be out of self-interest, (Ahearne, Bhattacharrya, & Gruen, 2005); as customer 'citizens' (Rosenbaum & Massiah, 2007); exogenously with consumer motives beyond the company's assumed value proposition; or as agents from recruitment or communication.

What is being described here is the *brand embedded in service processes and service being the essence of the brand*.

Processes are the architecture of services, the method and sequence in which service operating systems work and specify how they link together to create the value proposition promised to customers (Lovelock & Wirtz, 2011, p. 219). Customer involvement in service transaction and interaction can be seen in service antecedents such as the 'Servuction' model (Eiglier & Langeard, 1987) – a framework for analysing the role of the customer in the service production process – and the 'Servicescape' (Bitner, 1992) – the service ecosystem where service experiences are produced and consumed. Where companies have a product/service mix – particularly so within the industrial or B2B sector – the extension of the service offer alongside traditional physical products is known as 'servitisation'[85] a transition from a transactional product-centric provision to a service-oriented relational solutions orientation. Here, companies sell *outcome as a service*. For example, *Spotify* and *Netflix* have replaced the purchase of music and film in the form of product (eg: CDs and DVDs) by delivering media as the service. Kamalaldin, Linde, Sjödin, & Parida (2020, p. 306) identify four 'relational' components of this 'digital servitisation': "complementary digitalisation capabilities, relation-specific digital assets, digitally-enabled knowledge sharing routines, and partnership governance". Another phenomenon, combined with digitisation, which affects the customer-company interface, particularly B2B companies, is Industry 4.0. Frank, Mendes, Ayala, & Ghezzi (2019, p. 343) describe the dual effect: "Servitisation is mainly focused on adding value to the customer (demand-pull), while Industry 4.0 is frequently related to adding value to manufacturing process (technology-push)".

Customer-company engagement, therefore, can be beneficial in a number of ways:
– For the consumer, it can offer trust, empowerment, commitment, and social relationships with peers (C2C).
– For the company, improved loyalty, increased innovativeness, greater acceptance, adoption of new service products, premium pricing and so on can result.

From a resource perspective, the active role played by customers in the value co-creation process is both a challenge and an opportunity for companies. Indeed, as van Doorn *et al* assert "The concept of customer engagement behaviour in turn views customers exogenously, driven by their own unique purposes and intentions instead of originating from the firm" (2010, p. 253), manifest in behaviours which could have positive or negative impacts on the organisation.

5.4 Purposeful ecosystem orchestration

Creation and development of brand strategy depends on the complicity and coordination of internal and external stakeholders, interdependently linked in an economic and social network or 'ecosystem'. Ecosystems, according to Iansti & Levein are "organised around a keystone species . . . characterised by a large number of

---

85 Though formally introduced by Sandra Vandermerwe and Juan Rad in 1988,he concept of 'servitisation' has roots in the 1960s by Viper engines manufacturer *Bristol Siddeley* who offered a complete engine and accessory replacement service package.

loosely interconnected particpants who depend on each other for their mutual effectiveness and survival" (2004, p. 8). This is a useful analytical analogy. Viewing customers, employees, suppliers, competitors, and other stakeholders as 'member organisms' can help us visualise the dynamics of the customer-company interface. Similarly, defining an 'ecosystem' as an "affiliation" (Adner, 2016) views ecosystems as communities of associated actors defined by their networks and platform affiliations with the potential for symbiotic, interdependent relationships (eg: the 'Silicon Valley' ecosystem, an 'entrepreneurial' ecosystem, or a healthcare' ecosystem). An ecosystem (latterly macro- and micro-environments) comprises stakeholders like customers, intermediaries like distributors, suppliers, other manufacturers, and agents.

An 'ecosystem-as-structure' perspective views ecosystems as configurations of activity defined by " the alignment structure of the multilateral set of partners that need to interact in order for a focal value proposition to materialise" (Adner, 2016, p. 39). Here there is a difference between 'participation' and 'alignment' (satisfaction of engagement position by partners), and an emphasis on the value proposition as the foundation of the structure. Partners in brand meaning creation and maintenance are fused in symbiosis.

Pursuing strategies which are imbedded in 'purpose' can often be insular in their implementation and limited in stakeholder scope. Coerced compliance rather than company conscience can give strategy an 'inside-out' rather than 'outside-in' bias. Companies must take a broader strategic view – beyond the boundaries of the organisation – in order to make a positive social impact on communities outside rather than just focusing on inside the organisation. Remy *et al* (2021) propose purposeful *business ecosystem orchestration* (BEO) as a means of carrying out its higher purpose in addition to capturing new opportunities for value creation and profit. Whilst purpose can motivate internally, it must be authentic in its outward delivery. They argue that "Only once a company has a valid outward approach for pursuing purpose should it turn inward to aligning the organisation with this approach".

This implies a shift, even a transformation, from economic exchange linked to outside primary stakeholders to more sophisticated interactions with a much broader ecosystem. The emphasis is on value creation not mere transaction. The example cited of a car manufacturer working on electric mobility innovation – with stakeholders ranging from governments, power utilities, car part OEMs,[86] new technology providers, dealer partnerships, auto insurers, and so on – extends the *dependent* relationship (transactional exchange) to one where the emphasis is on *interdependent co-creation*. Here, value exchange is *in* the process. There is vertical collaboration but also lateral interaction. For example, flooring materials manufacturers in the 'Specification' market of the construction industry, engage with chemical suppliers (upstream) and a whole network of 'specifiers' like architects, building surveyors, client

---

86 OEM = Other Equipment Manufacturers.

users, floor layers and installers, and end-users like hospital committees and operatives (downstream). It can be seen in the development of computer software: *Microsoft* released *Windows 11* to a controlled 'beta' group of 'early adopters', "highly technical users" enrolled on their '*Windows* Insider Program', who get early access to new iterations and act as testers and facilitate 'diffusion of innovation' product adoption. As new models of *value creation and value capture*, engagement through the orchestration of extended ecosystems may be *in addition* to transaction, and offer greater stakeholder alignment potential (Adner, 2016).

5.5 Managing customer experience

Customer Experience Management (CXM or CEM) is a holistic approach taking a cross-functional, omni-channel, longitudinal, and attitudinal perspective. In her mind-shifting best seller *The Customer Revolution*, Patricia Seybold (2002) declared an essential truth of business today: "The power that had been flowing to customers is now rushing like a torrent. Traditional marketing is logistics-driven and product-focused, whereas experience is process-oriented and needs a strategic process solution. Now customers are driving business. Central now are the metrics that measure customer satisfaction and loyalty".

Today, in order to achieve competitive advantage through enhancing relationships and gaining sustainable customer loyalty, the most essential element of brand strategy is managing a customer's total experiences with a brand or a company. Customer experience is "the takeaway impression formed by people's encounters with products, services, and businesses, a perception produced when humans consolidate sensory information" (Berry, Carbone & Haeckel, , 2002, p. 114). Or as Meyer and Schwager put it: "the internal and subjective response customers have to any direct or indirect contact with a company" (2007, p. 118). Research by Grønholdt *et al* (2015, p. 90) provide evidence that those companies which incorporate superior customer experience are able to positively influence differentiation, market performance, and financial performance. Not only is CXM one of the most promising approaches to marketing, but some observers also contend it is *the* future of marketing (Klink, Zhang, & Athaide, 2020). And yet it requires collaboration between marketing, operations, human resources, design, and technology, and is 'out-to-in', integrated, and is as Schmitt suggests a "truly customer-focused management concept, a process-oriented satisfaction idea not an outcome-oriented one, and has a broad view of how a company can be relevant to a customer's life" (2003, p. 10).

Principles in practice

Socios' social sports scheme.
Coining it in with genuine or token engagement?

Emotion is the currency of brand engagement. For football fans, identity and group affiliation is the essential purpose of being attached to a favourite club. Sport is a global experience; engagement is almost entirely a digital, online phenomenon. For the clubs, the objective of creating emotional bonds with its customers is invariably to stimulate purchase intent and build loyalty. *Socios*, the world's first sports digital fan engagement platform selling cryptocurrency 'virtual tokens' in exchange for "a fan engagement platform that gives a digital pass to the teams you love", claims to do exactly that. It's a scheme which purports to connect supporters with their football club, "transitioning passive fans into active fans",[87] and even give them a democratic vote on club matters.

When the world's best player Lionel Messi signed for French football club *Paris Saint-Germain*, it captured the imagination as well as causing an explosion of headlines around the world. The fact that he was partly paid in $CHZ cryptocurrency fan tokens,[88] gave *Socios* social currency beyond their wildest dreams. But criticism from supporter groups about whether fan engagement is something that should be tokenised and monetised – club ownership through coin ownership – has fundamentally challenged this type of engagement. With some football clubs withdrawing from this scheme for fear of contaminating their brands, will this sort of promotion be seen as an own goal?

Socios.com's vision is for an extensive network of the world's leading sports organisations providing collectible digital assets in the form of 'fan tokens' minted on the *Chiliz (CHZ)* blockchain-powered fan interaction and incentives ecosystem. Partnerships include: football (*FC Barcelona, Atletico Madrid, Inter* and *AC Milan, Juventus, Valencia CF, Paris Saint Germain, Manchester City, Arsenal,* and *Everton,* as well as the *Argentinian* and *Portuguese* national teams); *Formula One*™ car racing with *Aston Martin Cognizant* and *Alfa Romeo Racing ORLEN;* the *NBA's New York Devils, 76ers,* and *Boston Celtics;* leading esports organisations like *Team Heretics, NAVI, OG,* and *Alliance;* and US Basketball giants, *Chicago Bulls* and the *Houston Rockets.* Over $150 million in revenues have been generated for over 40 major sporting organisations in 2021. 'Engagement' is evidenced in polls on *Twitter,* TV-visible signage at *Bulls'* home games, Half-Time fan presentation, score updates, and user rights to *Bulls* marks and logos.

Alexandre Dreyfus, CEO of *Socios.com* and *Chiliz,* describes *Socios'* role as "supporting clubs to generate additional revenue . . . moving sport from a passive fan to an active fan industry, where fans will have more influence". And yet despite claiming that "Creating opportunities for the fans" is their mission, critics question whether allowing a third-party to sell engagement is really fan engagement or merely monetising loyalty. Access to content via Pay-Per-View (PPV) channels, behind paywalls, or through digital membership is now standard practice in sport, and is, in effect, paid-for entertainment (and ergo engagement). But this scheme is perceived by some as being fundamentally different, seen as abusing the basic company-customer relationship of trust and mutuality.

Fans of teams in the *English Premier League (EPL)* have an obsessive relationship with their club. When fans of club *West Ham United* objected to their club monetising supporter loyalty, claiming that it contravened the engagement principles of the Department for Digital,

---

87 *Socios.com*

88 Cryptocurrency is both encrypted transaction data and a digital ledger of transaction data called a 'blockchain'. Tokens are cryptocurrency, both value tokens and strings of data. Native coin is a blockchain's inherent digital currency, CHZ in this case.

Culture, Media and Sport (DCMS), the *Socios* partnership abruptly ended. However, there is a view that this deal failed because of the ownership not the partner. Nonetheless, the idea that a privately-owned, Direct-to-Consumer (D2C) platform can have control and governance over club-fan relationships has been called into question and the prospects of being exposed to potential liabilities is a worry for clubs. 'Engagement' has been put under the microscope like never before.

Claims of fan 'influence' have been over-stated. A *Barcelona* spokesperson said: "Questions about which fans were asked are focused on the digital side, the creation of content and so on. In no case will token holders be consulted about the running of the sporting side of the club or business decisions". However, other clubs argue that regular engagement is not affected: these days there is more engagement not less. *Socios*, as a sponsorship partner, have legitimate rights to player appearances, experiences, hospitality etc. It could be argued that 'access' is being used for genuine fan engagement experiences as opposed to corporate entertaining.

There is no doubt that fans who engage with their club almost entirely through out-of-stadia interactions crave tangible evidence of intangible experiences. Whether the *Socios* scheme is seen as genuine or merely token engagement, they are both sides of the same coin.

Not surprisingly, *managing the customer experience* has its roots in the principles of Service Marketing:

- The company is the service *provider,* and the customer is the service *user.*
- There are perceptions of *expectation* by the user and *management of those expectations* by the service provider.
- The '*servicescape*' (becoming increasingly digitised) is often *remote*, even partly automated, and is a key focus for management.
- The service may involve elements of *intangibility*.
- The '*service encounter*' Touchpoints or '*moments of truth*' (Carlzon, 1987) in the customer journey are critical interactions or *encounters* which impact on customer's experience of service. In 2011, *Google* reset this traditional concept with what they referred to as 'Zero Moment of Truth' (ZMOT). Although the original referred to satisfaction *in use* – the 'critical incidents' in the service encounter where service provider meets service user – ZMOT has more recently been applied to product information search. The Second ZMOT can be another person's search using somebody else's original search (in the form of C2C recommendation). In a broader service marketing context, Critical Incident Technique (CIT) methodology is used for collecting and categorising such critical incidents in service encounters.
- The '*onboarding*' process is analogous of '*service encounters*' and '*service blueprints*'.
- Critical journey analysis is a development of '*gap analysis*' where the discrepancies between perceived and actual service delivery provide scope for process improvement.
- Aspects of service quality (SERVQUAL) are measured by reliability, responsiveness, competence, access, courtesy, communication, credibility, security, understanding the customer, and tangibles which help to measure the gap between customer expectations and experience.

This shows that the elemental logic of service and brand experience is *interaction*. Grönroos (2004, p. 100) makes this very point, describing service marketing as "a process consisting of a series of more or less intangible activities that normally, but not always, take place in interactions between customer and service employees and/or physical resources or goods and/or systems of the service provider, which are provided as solutions to customer problems".

[You can see echoes of this later on in *Chapter 7* as we explore what the digital customer journey is and why it's so important to user understanding and brand development.]

From a consumer's perspective, customer experience, is a cognitive and subjective assessment of the company's performance; from a company's perspective customer experience is a source of value creation and competitive differentiation. Therefore, it requires strategy to take into account its qualitative, phenomenological nature. Experience can be leveraged as part of the value proposition, but in order to do so "offering products or services is no longer enough: organisations must provide their customers with satisfactory experiences . . . and must manage the emotional component of experiences with the same rigour they bring to the management of product and service functionality" (Berry, Carbone, & Haekel, 2002, p. 120). This echoes Pine & Gilmour's seminal text in the late 1990s, placing customers as the centre of business activities and formalising customer experience as an economic principle in its own right "as distinct from services as services are from goods" (Pine & Gilmore, 1998, p. 50).

For companies with a high-touch, person-to-person dynamic, back-end (company) service processes must be aligned with front-end (consumer) experiences. As we have seen, this exposure to the corporate and brand image and service process is a complicated network of interactions and touchpoints – encounters across multiple channels and at varying points in time – which present customers with an opportunity to compare their prior perceptions and expectations of the business and form an opinion (Stein & Ramaseshan, 2016). Here, customer experience is conceptualised as the "the customer's subjective response to the holistic direct and indirect encounters with the firm and customer quality as its perceived excellence or superiority" (Lemke, Clark, & Wilson, 2011, p. 846).

The service process, once a key differentiator in markets with tight competitive parity, is increasingly becoming itself commoditised, with consumers demanding "engaging, robust, compelling, and memorable" experiences (Gilmore & Pine, 2002, p. 10) beyond expected standard levels of service. Medberg and Grönroos (2020, p. 509) identified seven empirical dimensions of positive and negative value-in-use: solution, attitude, convenience, expertise, speed of service, flexibility, and monetary costs.

5.6 Impact of digital disruption on customer experience

Against a backdrop of volatility and unpredictability, digital innovation is disrupting traditional marketplaces. It is disrupting but it is also *enabling*. Like the personal computer (PC) in 1981, the World Wide Web in the early 1990s, mobile from 2007, and then Cloud, disruption causes systemic and structural change by disrupting the legacy business models (Rauch, Wenzel, & Wagner, 2016) and market offerings of existing dominant companies. The change has been so dramatic that this phenomenon has been referred to as the Fourth Industrial Revolution (Industry 4.0). Digital transformation through the disruption of digital innovation and the rapidly changing economic landscape is now an established principal catalyst for change in how companies create and deliver relevant and mutually-beneficial experiences to its customers and stakeholders.

Digital disruption is often framed as environmental turbulence induced by digital innovation leading to the erosion of boundaries and approaches that previously served as foundations for the organising and capture of value (Karimi & Walter, 2015). Skog, Wimelius & Sandberg (2018, p. 434) describe disruption as "The rapidly unfolding processes through which innovation comes to fundamentally alter historically sustainable logics for value creation and capture by unbundling and recombining linkages among resources or generating new ones". It is a destructive creative force which will shake "the core of every industry" (Bonnet, Buvat, & Subrahmanyam, 2015) and "induce short fuse, big bang situations" capable of threatening entire sectors (Farrall, Harding, & Hillard, 2012).

Competition is heightened by organisations finding competition from outside their traditional sectors. Those organisations that are successful in understanding what constitutes disruption and how best to tackle it and also learn how to disrupt others, will have one key competitive advantage: resilience. The imperative to transform rather than stagnate is what Brown (2020, p. 10) refers to as the "innovation ultimatum". Technology has also expanded the challenge of competition. The increasing prevalence of AI-powered Automated Customer Experience (ACX) technology has made the customer-company interface more effectively but less personally managed. This is the corollary of the new. Enrichening of experience also increase expectation. Companies need to take a "holistically integrated approach to creating a memorable experience in which multidimensional value can be delivered through multiple, sequential stages of experience. The co-creation of experience can lead to a sustainable experience that can be life transforming or perspective transforming" (Homburg, Jozić, & Kuehnl, 2017, p. 380). Companies like *Starbucks*, *LUSH*, *Hotel Chocolat*, *Costa Coffee*, *Disney*, and *Amazon* put great emphasis on creating 'experience' brands.

What we are already seeing is a 'platform' ecosystem of new generation on-demand service providers offering highly-distributed, highly-virtualised customer experiences. How consumers and companies interact, engage, and develop commercially sustainable relationships is characteristic of the megatrend of digital transformation. Some time ago, *Apple* displaced technology-leading *Nokia* as market leaders in mobile technology because they had more appropriate customer-orientation and met market needs with more relevance. The likes of *Amazon, Apple, Uber, Netflix, Domino's Pizza, LinkedIn, Airbnb, Dropbox,* and *Spotify* represent the new frontier of on-demand, subscription, 'freemium'[89] business models. They have proved that positive customer satisfaction can be driven by a mainly digitised customer experience which impacts positively on revenues and loyalty.

Table 5.1 gives some examples of disruptive digital innovators who have used technology to help re-invent their value propositions. The use of smart technology, immersive technology, Big Data, Artificial Intelligence (AI), the Cloud, mobile technology, the Internet of Things (IoT) (ie: the interconnection via the Internet of everyday devices), the smart domestic products (SDPs) like water meters, online banking etc., the automation of traditional manufacturing, remote working with work/life dramatically reassessed, immaterial productivity, large scale Machine-to-Machine communication (M2M), data analytics, all to help analyse processes with minimal human intervention are all characteristic of this increasingly social but distant age. For customers, the data is not the experience; it is an enabler *for* the experience.

Table 5.1: Disruptive digital innovators.

Netflix	From its early US business model (a DVD rental business), *Netflix* reinvented itself as the major digital streaming service and production company, distributing product into homes over the internet.
Argos	Originally a conventional 'brick' retailer providing warehouse goods selected via catalogue over the counter as the primary retail channel. Became a digital retailer in 2012 with online catalogue and ordering, web browsers, apps, and free in-store wi-fi. In advance of COVID-19, *Argos* transformed stores into pick-up points for online orders. *Argos.co.uk* is the second most visited retail site in the UK.
Domino's Pizza	Another traditional retailer transformed into an online company (60% online sales; 30% from mobile devices), *Domino's* has introduced innovative digital ordering tools (iPad app with a 3D animated pizza builder; an Android app using *Google Wallet*; online real-time pizza production/delivery tracker).
Burberry	Traditional trench coat maker *Burberry* transformed itself into one of the coolest fashion brands by using digital technology to create an exciting brand image and massive following through social media exposure on *Facebook, Instagram, Pinterest,* and *YouTube*. A CRM system, linked to *iPads* and interactive videos triggered by RFID-embedded chips.

Source: Various

---

89 Internet business model establishing demand for a product or service by providing free basic services in the hope that users will trade up to paid for premium content or advanced features.

Other innovations which will continue to disrupt business models and force change are:

– *Influencer Marketing*, the use of mavens, opinion formers and opinion leaders, people who through celebrity or expertise explicitly or implicitly influence awareness, brand image and imitative behaviour, is growing rapidly, especially in the accelerated Word of Mouth of social media with built-in audience uptake.

– *Artificial Intelligence* (AI), such as the built-in algorithms of *Amazon* and *Netflix* that aid consumer decision-making, tailored content creation, voice, finger-print, and face-recognition, chatbots and digital assistants, will become more prevalent in strategies because of AI's ability to add value to personalised consumption experiences through more accurate data analysis.

– *Virtual Reality through the customer journey* (VRCJ) is the use of computer-mediated interactive environments capable of offering sensory feedback to engage customers, strengthen relationships, and drive consumer behaviour during the customer journey.

– *Personal Digital Assistants*, such as *Alexa* and *Google Assistant*, are designed to enrich the consumption experience and has business productivity application.

– *Chatbots* are devices designed to improve the personal and business user experience (UX) and are becoming ubiquitous in social messaging platforms such as *Facebook*.

– *Voice Search* (VS), *Speech Recognition* (SR), and *Search Engine Optimisation* (SEO) have expanded the search element of consumer decision-making by the use of long-tail keywords and search phrases that are much more detailed than early versions of search.

– *Blockchain Technology* is a list of records interconnected by cryptography designed for the safe exchange of money, property, contracts etc. without the use of an intermediary, which is 100% transparent and promotes safe data exchange and will be useful in brand building strategies based on trust.

Although consumer markets receive most attention, B2B markets also have a B2C dynamic which has been fundamentally changed. *Directline's* Head of Transformation, Claire Sadler, claims that "The salesman use to be the face of the insurance brand. Today, insurers have to tell their brand story through touchpoints including their website and B2B advertising".

The success of this disruption/transformation was a combination of internal organisational structure and orientation; relationships with key stakeholders; more appropriate business model; and how the market and competition are targeted. For companies learning to cope with this digital challenge, they must embrace and adopt digital technologies in order to gain competitive advantage or even merely achieve competitive parity, to keep existing customers happy or recruit new ones. The classic case of *Kodak*, unwilling to give up a hard-won market monopoly, hoping for status quo rather than planning for change, losing out to the digital camera

era of *Sony* and *Cannon*, is a stark reminder that resistance to changing customer needs and new technology can be fatal. Positive customer experiences in one sector are motivating consumers to demand similar service provision in other sectors.

The integration of digital technology into all areas of a business is a once-in-a-lifetime phenomenon describing 'technology and cultural shift' of processes, activities, and competences which is transforming every sector and every organisation in the world. User experiences are being transformed – both internally in changing its employee orientation and externally in terms of the new business models it must present to its customer base and outside stakeholders – as part of its altered value proposition. This digital transformation emerged because of changing consumer purchase dynamics, new world economic conditions and market realities, shifts in societal structure, existing and rapidly developing digital technology, the world ecosystem, and industry disruption. Generally speaking, disruption follows innovation: customer behaviour changes, expectations evolve; companies alter their value propositions (as seen in 'consumerisation of IT' discussed above).

In the digital era, with the traditional asymmetrical communications paradigm disrupted, power has shifted from company to customer, management's control has been diminished (Deighton & Kornfeld, 2009), the brand manager is "no longer a 'guardian' of the brand but becomes more of a brand 'host'" (Christodoulides, 2009, p. 141). Consumers use digital media disconnected from company's control in separated pockets of consumer-to-consumer collaboration: user-generated content (UGC) sites such as *YouTube*, *Cyworld*, and blogs; trading sites like *Ebay* and *Craigslist*; collaborative network sites like *Facebook*, *Instagram*, *Orkut*, and *Meetup*; and review sites like *TripAdvisor* and *Epinions*.

This transformation has four trajectories: digital technology, digital strategy, customer experience, and data-driven business models. Customer engagement, so often framed within a managerialist perspective of asymmetrical control, has now been affected by the logic of disintermediation and devolution of power. The new less directive model of digital customer experience offers a challenge to companies beyond the traditional disruptive engagement. Now people have the power, are more purposive, have become the medium, and the company is often an interloper in the conversation. Competitive advantage may lie in transforming customer experience through enhanced service provision, but it is digital technology that is both the driver and the effect of this.

The way an organisation chooses to interact with its customers and other stakeholders is referred to as the Customer-Company Interface (CCI), a visual representation of which is presented by Rayport & Jaworski (2000) in Figure 5.1. This essentially depicts the key elements which comprise currently the main servicescape. Digital environments are becoming relevant for this interaction and are becoming substitutive rather than supplementary.

The customer interface is interactive and dynamic and there needs to be an experiential platform built into the process which goes beyond the quantitative orientation

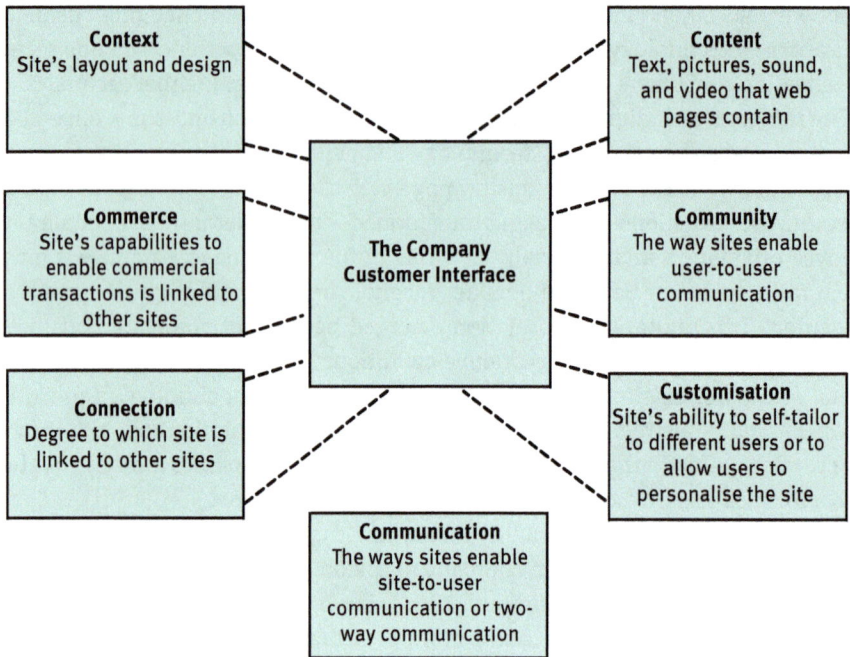

Figure 5.1: The 7Cs of The Company Customer Interface.
Source: Rayport & Jaworski (2000)

of CRM, incorporating intangible elements. Interaction with *the brand* can occur outside interaction with *the company*. C2C sentiment can affect company reputation, and this reinforces the imperative of 'outside-in' customer-orientation. Where customer experience and reputation management converge, this is referred to as reputation experience management (RXM). [This is covered in greater detail in *Chapter 9*].

Application of experience management has traditionally been adopted from a customer's perspective, but the 'customer' can be an industrial or institutional buyer as well as consumer. Witell *et al* (2020, p. 423) apply CEM principles to a B2B context and highlight three key challenges as:

– *Relationship expectations* (mismatches in customer relationships, siloed customer experiences).
– *Actor interaction* (mismatches across the customer's journey lack of touchpoint control).
– *Temporal challenges* (dynamics of the customer experience).

Embracing digital technology and investing in digital capability to mitigate economic and structural disruption, offering customers an enhanced experience is the stage that companies ahead of the curve are now in. The duality of dealing with the exigency of disruption, and preparing for the altered business paradigm of the 'new normal', describes how customer experinces are now being managed.

Principles in practice

McDonald's creates new 'customer experience' team

Customer experience is the most crucial element in service marketing, particularly so with fast-food restaurants. With dining rooms shut and digital eating habits changing (sales up by 60% for *Burger King* and 70% for *McDonald's* respectively), and likely to make up 50% of sales by 2025, the impact of the Covid-19 pandemic has dramatically affected the way consumers engage with restaurants. For operations like *McDonald's*, managing customer experience is becoming much more difficult. According to research, companies now need to ensure that the online eating experience is "just as carefully designed as the in-person one . . . Covid has forever changed the customer experience".[90]

To help deal with an increasingly worrying situation, they have created a new "customer experience team" combining the strengths of global marketing, global restaurant development and restaurant solutions, data analysis, and digital customer engagement. Meeting customers in terms of location and method of engagement – drive-thru, in their homes, on their phones – has meant streamlining the three teams, investing in restaurant modernisation with a greater focus on digital, delivery, and 'drive thru' operations. Customer experience personalisation is being enhanced through the new 'My McDonald's' loyalty app a tailored customer journey experience.[91]

5.7 Mutually beneficial relationships

Along with reorienting organisations to be purpose-led, how best to strategically encourage and leverage *mutuality* is the essence of brand strategy. Whilst the identification of "drivers that influence important outcomes for the firm and a better understanding of the causal relationships between these drivers and outcomes" (Hennig-Thurau, Gwinner, & Gremler, 2002, p. 230) is a key goal of relationship marketing theory and practice, mutuality is essentially encouraging a humanist approach to business, where the company joins with the customer in a reciprocal relationship to create common values and purpose. On one side there is company retention strategy; on the other is consumer loyalty.

This requires us to reflect on the notion of retention and examine "the degree of appropriateness of a relationship" (Hennig-Thurau & Klee, 1997, p. 747). The critical goal (and then strategy) of customer *retention* (as opposed to a fixation with customer acquisition) was a natural customer-oriented extension of the Total Quality Management (TQM) philosophy of 'zero defects': zero *defections* (Reichheld & Sasser Jr,

---

90 *Kellogg* School of Management at Northwestern University, 2021.
91 '*McDonald's* Creates New Customer Experience Team; Appoints Manu Steijaert as First Global Chief Customer Officer' *McDonald's* website, 26th July 2021.

1990). With the cumulative impact of all the disruption detailed above, managing customer-company relationships is as critically important in the 2020s than ever before. This new *purposeful relationship marketing* has roots in the precision of 'direct' marketing and targetted marketing, and the relationship-orientation of industrial business practices, and is "more process rather than outcome oriented, and emphasises value *creation* rather than values *distribution*" (Sheth & Parvatiyar, 1995, p. 397). The difference here is that the latter is 'inside-out' and the former is 'outside-in'.

In the midst of the Energy Crisis of the 1970s which resulted in stagflation, excess capacity and rising raw material costs, the *transactional exchange* paradigm was becoming increasingly inappropriate. Around the same time, Service Marketing, with its strategic focus on retention and the relational possibilities of encouraging the loyalty of customers, started to emerge and gain traction. During the Service Marketing explosion of the 1980s, led by Len Berry, Christian Grönroos, and the members of the European Industrial Marketing and Purchasing Group (IMP), progenitors to B2B marketing, Customer Relationship Management (or sometimes Customer Relationship Marketing) emerged as one of the most enduring marketing strategy stalwarts. CRM is "the intelligent mining of customer-related data for strategical or tactical purposes" (Buttle, 2009). The benefits of leveraging the loyalty of existing customers – estimated at 5 times the return on investment (ROI) of new customers – was a Eureka moment which is still true: retention of customers is more effective than the acquisition of new customers.

In addition, the imperative in the Business-to-Business (B2B) sector, where interdependence was the locus of maintaining and developing key accounts, consolidating supply partnerships, building networks, establishing the quality drive of Total Quality Management (TQM), and the continuous development philosophy of the Japanese *Kaizen*, engendered a partnership not partisan approach to business based on reciprocity, trust, and commitment. The subsequent impact of Information Technology (IT), Enterprise Resource Planning (ERP) and the widespread use of Customer Relationship Management (CRM) database systems, gave impetus to a more relational paradigm of interaction rather than transaction, and one based on *mutually beneficial relationships*.

Relationship marketing focuses on retention rather than the 'leaky bucket' strategy of customer churn and acquisition, providing value and satisfaction through trust, commitment, loyalty, and shared values. The strategic focus is on encouraging and nurturing company/customer fusion through partnership and the co-creation of value through relationship building and loyalty. Whilst the two are often used as synonyms, here, relationship building is generally the *process* and loyalty the *outcome* of brand strategy. This is an implicit and integral part of service marketing: consumption of a service is *process* consumption rather than *outcome* consumption. This is sometimes referred to as 'interactive marketing'; this is why the interface between production and consumption is always critical to the consumer's perception of the service and to his or her long-term purchasing behaviour.

When there is competitive parity of products consumed, this makes the service element, particularly the relationship content of that provision, a key differentiator on which to build loyalty. Grönroos (2000) claimed that the relationship marketing perspective is based on the notion that on top of the value of products and/or services that are exchanged, the mere existence of a relationship between provider and user enhances the value created. Like so many marketing concepts which find their way to adoption in marketing practice, relationship marketing has its roots in early research and development in service marketing (Berry, 1983), where the nature of quality is a critical focus for management control. Quality is a meta-construct with subjective individual interpretation (ie: heterogeneity) being a complicating factor. The relationship approach has internal value-generating processes of customers, not products at the centre (Grönroos, 2004, p. 102).

Drawing on the relationship metaphor, with its emphases on trust, commitment, co-creation, and, of course, mutuality, provides a framework for developing strategy. Examining relational benefits and relationship quality holds the key to developing how useful customers can be to companies and how companies can be of use to customers. Companies benefit from the economies of reduced costs of new customer acquisition, lower price elasticity, enhanced profitability, income stability, brand longevity, as well as the positive impact customers have on other users or potential users (eg: word of mouth); customers benefit from reliable consumption satisfaction, social benefits, and the confidence benefits of reduced purchase risk.

As customers are heterogeneous, their individual interpretation of what constitutes a 'relationship' will vary and, therefore, service provision (and relationship goals) must be differentiated. Moving a customer from *brand promiscuity* – the casual purchase of a range of suppliers from a number of product categories – to *brand loyalty* – repeated purchase of one brand in a single product category – to one of solid *brand advocacy* is a vital business objective. Segmenting customers by loyalty, understanding the nature of their commercial commitment and shared values, informs marketing actions.

Data insights into "relative attitude and repeat patronage" (Dick & Basu, 1994, p. 99) is a foundation upon which mutually beneficial relationships can be built and can highlight vulnerabilities in the customer base, identifying reasons for customer churn before mass migration occurs. Rowley (2005, p. 575) describes the differentiation between brand promiscuity and loyalty as "those customers that are inertial in attitude and behaviour, and those that have a positive orientation" and suggests a 'Four Cs' customer categorisation of: committed, contented, convenience-seekers, and captive customers. Iacobucci and Hibbard (1999, p. 13) describe three types of relationship: business marketing relationships (BMR), interpersonal commercial relationships (ICR) and business-to-customer (B-to-C). In Table 5.2, factors are illustrated in an ICR relationship.

Table 5.2: Business Marketing Relationship Factors.

Business Marketing Relationship Factors	Definition
Commitment	Implicit or explicit pledge of relational continuity between exchange partners; adoption of a long term orientation toward the relationship – a willingness to make short-term sacrifices to realize long-term benefits.
Trust	One party's belief that its needs will be fulfilled in the future by the actions undertaken bu the other party. Contingent on the presence of uncertainty.
Power	Ability of one party to get another party to undertake an activity that the other party would not normally do.
Control (part of power)	Outcome of power and results when a party is successful in modifying its partner's behaviour.
Balance of power (part of power)	Balance = symmetric power. Imbalance = hierarchical; one party has dictatorial abilities over the other.
Interdependence	Mutual state of dependence.
Communication	Formal and informal sharing of meaningful and timely information between firms.
Cooperation	Similar or complementary coordinated actions taken by firms to achieve mutual outcomes.
Idiosyncratic Investments	Sunk costs that would not be recoverable in the event of termination.
Conflict Resolution	Functionality of dispute resolution stimulates more creative and effective partnerships.

Source: Iacobucci & Hibbard (1999, p.13)

According to Grönroos (2004, p. 100), when implementing a relationship marketing initiative, a shift in focus is required involving:
- An interaction process as the core of relationship marketing.
- A planned communication process supporting the development and enhancement of relationships.
- A value process as the output of relationship marketing.

The core of relationship marketing therefore is the *interaction* process where the solution is often the relationship itself: process not outcome. Critical to this is the fact that customers' views of relationships are holistic – a sort of *gestalt* perspective where cumulative singular experiences project an organised whole perceived as more than the sum of its parts. Consumer perceptions of total service quality, and therefore, the nature of the relationship, can be skewed by single service faults (eg: delivery, packaging, badly handled complaints, after-sales care) which can affect overall product/service satisfaction. In an iterative and interactive exchange process, analysis must be made of critical incidents, service encounters, and all touchpoints of service be they interaction with another human or programmed machine.

5.8 Corporate identity and organisational culture

Another way in which an organisation engages with its customers and other stakeholders is through the projection of corporate identity. Businesses of all kinds are facing identity issues; balancing a firm's perception of itself with how external constituencies view it is a key managerial challenge. The evolution in many industries from integrated, self-suffcient firms to networks of interdependent organisations blurs organisational boundaries and brings identity issues to the fore. Boundaryless organisations with supplier hubs and outsourced 'Just-in-Time' delivery systems – where the demarcation lines in the customer-company interface is increasingly fused and confused; where strategy is both convergent and divergent, purposively designed but only enviromentally emergent – distort traditional organisational configurations and make a cohesive, constant company image a most difficult strategic challenge.

As one of the firm's most pivotal valuable assets, corporate identity has become a critical determinant of achieving successful corporate strategy. Corporate brands are valued as strategic resources and provide the primary synthesis for aligning what the organisation is, what it says about itself, and what it does to express its values (ie: corporate vision, organisational culture, and stakeholder perceptions). As well as incorporating the strategic vision, corporate identity is also "based on the tacit reality of the organisation and its culture the definitive characteristics which give specificity, distinctiveness, and strategic coherence" (Melewar & Storrie, 2001, p. 21). Turning the brand promise into experiential reality is achieved through an organisation's culture; culture is expressed through customer experience. If internal culture and external image are managed properly, it can positively impact results.

According to Bouchiki & Kimberley (2008, p. 60), "Companies can have a variety of phenomena in which their identity is anchored: it may be a brand, it may be a mission, it may be a particular form of business. But every company has a constellation of things which, together, provide an answer to the question 'Who are we?'" Identity can also be anchored in other aspects such as core business, knowledge base, nationality, business philosophy, etc. Because identity is an important social construction, any aspect that key stakeholders view as core, enduring, and distinctive about an organisation is its identity. This will vary with each organisation dependent upon the strategic, communicational context, organisational culture, and market positioning of the corporate brand (eg: *Virgin* is personality, *Toyota* is nationality, *Apple* is social technology). Therefore, corporate identity gives a sense of belonging and can be a major source of competitive advantage. It makes values visible.

Corporate identity, described by Olutayo & Melewar (2007) as "where the firm is going", "how the firm is different", "what the firm does" and "how the firm carries out its business" (p. 428), is how the organisation presents itself to its many and varied stakeholders. Consistency reinforces culture and communication across channels and messages, but how does an organisation maintain consistency in a volatile, dynamic environment where change is the only constant? Corporate identity and company culture are inextricably linked. The values that corporate identity makes visible are the organisational culture; organisational culture is essentially the corporate identity. There is some debate as to whether organisational culture is a determinant of corporate identity or the result of organisational culture. Either way, alignment of corporate identity with external and internal stakeholders involves organisational culture. The extent to which organisational members' identify with their employing organisation's espoused organisational culture and projected brand identity will influence brand behaviour and customer's experience (Stuart, 2003).

An organisation projects its character and personality through values and beliefs – its culture – through *internal* processes and people, and builds its identity through interaction with the outside world. It can project an organisation's competitive position and value proposition. These days, there is a growing urgency to also project a company's purpose, the consciousness of company culture. This 'conscious culture' is described as "the ethos – the values, principles, practices – underlying the social practice of a business which permeates the atmosphere of a business and connects the stakeholders to each other and to the purpose, people, and processes that comprise the company. All companies have a culture, but not all companies intentionally develop a culture that promotes their values and purpose".[92]

Balmer & Thomson (2009, p. 17) describe the following characteristics of corporate brands:
- Multidisciplinary in scope.
- Strategic in orientation.
- Underpinned by a coprorate brand covenant.
- Derived from identity.
- Can be viewed as a distinct identity type.
- Require alignment with other identity types.
- Multifarious in their benefits.
- Personnel are of crucial importance.
- Have attendant brand communities.

---

92 *Conscious Capitalism, Inc. (CCI)* is a US-based non-profit organisation whose purpose is to build a movement of business leaders improving the practice and perception of capitalism with a purpose.

The evolution in many industries from integrated, self-suffcent firms to networks of interdependent organisations blurs organisational boundaries and brings identity issues to the forefront. Boundaryless organisations with supplier hubs and outsourced 'Just-in-Time' delivery systems, where the demarcation lines in the customer-company interface is increasingly fused and confused, strategy convergent and divergent, purposively designed but enviromentally emergent, distort traditional organisational configurations and make a cohesive, constant company image a most difficult strategic challenge. The key to this, as with marketing strategy and innovation in general, is balancing status quo with transformation – managing and maintaining brand identity through consistency whilst retaining relevance or changing to become relevant. Corporate brand identity has many faces. Balmer (2008, p. 879) suggests five "identity-based views of the corporation relating to identity and identification (what he calls the 'quindrivium'):

- *Corporate identity*: the identity *of* the organisation.
- *Communicated corporate identification*: identification *from* the organisation.
- *Stakeholder corporate identification*: an individual or stakeholder group's identification *with* the organisation.
- *Stakeholder cultural identification*: an individual or stakeholder group's identification *to* the organisation.
- *Envisioned identities and identifications*: how an organisation or group envisions how another corporation or group characterises their identity or mode of identification.

Consumer's affective as well as cognitive knowledge of an organisation affects what is believed about a company's product and service value proposition. And yet corporate branding requires taking an internally-focused view, analysing the employee's role in the organisation's brand building strategies. The corporate brand is "the visual, verbal, and behavioural expression of an organisation's unique business model" (Knox & Bickerton, 2003, p. 998). It has a meaning for all internal and external stakeholders, representing the organisational value and values. A comprehensive definition, with wide-reaching inference is "a systematically planned and implemented process of creating and maintaining a favourable image and consequently a favourable reputation for the company as whole by sending signals to all stakeholders and by managing behaviour, communication, and symbolism" (Einwiller & Will, 2002). This suggests strategy, process, stakeholders, marketing constituencies, and hints at how a company behaves, communicates, and what the negotiated meaning is between all active partners. It necessitates alignment of strategic vision, organisational culture, and corporate image. Expanding on this, Chattananon *et al* (2007, p. 234) describe corporate image as "the totality of a stakeholder's perceptions of the way an organisation presents itself through its corporate identity mix either deliberately by controllable sources or accidentally by uncontrollable sources". Interaction to demonstrate action is an essential part of customer-company fusion.

Aligning employees with corporate identity therefore also involves alignment with organisational culture. When an organisation is aligned with a desired culture, "there is a more unified [brand] identity presented to different stakeholders and greater likelihood that staff will act in a more consistent manner" (de Chernatony, 2006, p. 158). There are different perspectives on organisational culture: organisations *have* cultures; organisations *are* cultures; or cultures are *emergent* in organisations. This contrast is between integration and differentiation: culture is something the organisation *has* compared with culture being something the organisation *is*. This implies that culture can be strategically managed. The strategic cornerstones of purpose, vision, mission, and philosophy are mobilised, supported, and reinforced by factors such as integrated marketing communications, corporate branding, executive leadership, operational location, CSR programmes, and of course organisational culture.

The Chartered Institute of Management (CMI) define organisational culture as:

> *The way that things are done in an organisation, the unwritten rules that influence individual and group behaviour and attitudes. Factors which can influence organisational culture include: the organisation's structure, the system and processes by which work is carried out, the behaviour and attitudes of employees, the organisation's values and traditions, and the management and leadership styles adopted.*

The management imperative is to try and control and manage brand consistent behaviour and consistent brand image through diffusion of organisational mission, values, and purpose. Schein's (2010) Organisational Culture Model is featured below in Figure 5.2.

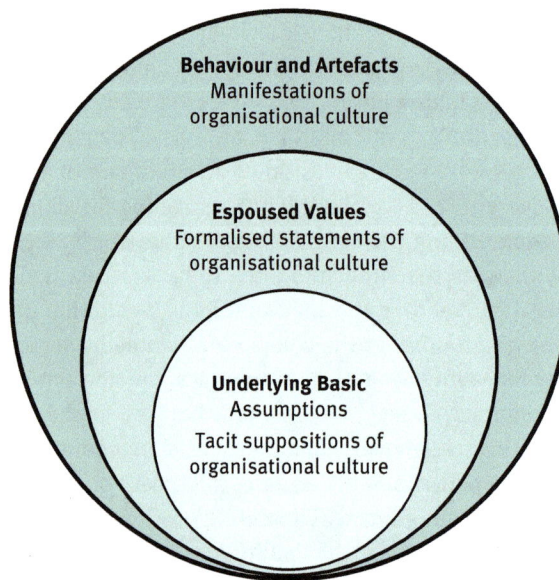

Figure 5.2: Organisational Culture Model.
Source: Schein (2010)

Schein defines the culture of a group as "the accumulated shared learning of that group as it solves its problem or external adaptation and internal integration; which has worked well enough to be considered valid and, therefore, to be taught to new members as the correct way to perceive, think, feel, and behave in relation to those problems. This accumulated learning is a pattern or system of beliefs, values, and behaviors that come to be taken for granted as basic assumptions and eventually drop out of awareness" (2017, p. 45).

Organisational *climate* is described as being "the meanings people attach to the policies, practices and procedures employees experience, and the behaviours they observe getting rewarded, and that re supported and expected"; organisational *culture* is described as the basic assumptions about the world and the values that guide life in organisations (Schneider, Ehrhart, & Macey, 2013, p. 362).

Managing and influencing customer perceptions is of vital importance because this can be a critical strategic asset and provide a key source of competitive advantage. The power of a strong corporate image can enhance a competitive value proposition, improve reputational value, positively influence customer decision-making and patronage. Often, the two key corporate associations used by customers to evaluate companies are *corporate ability* (expertise and experience in producing and delivering its products and services), and *corporate conscience* (the demonstration of a corporation's fulfilment of its societal obligations in terms of ethics and social responsibility). Corporate Social Responsibility (CSR) has been a concept which frames the business contribution to sustainable development. In recent years corporate social responsibility (CSR) has become increasingly important as the concept which frames the business contribution to sustainable development (Commission of the European Communities 2002) where the 'triple bottom-line' of social, economic, and environmental (aka People. Profit. Planet) impacts. It dramatically affects how a company projects its principles, raison d'etre, and sustainable strategic approach. The criticism of enlightened self-interest – competitive advantage rather than altruism – is balanced by those advocates who point to the added value to business and society and cite it as a source of innovation. CSR marks out a progression of value-creating measurement from shareholder to stakeholder to societal.

Balmer (2006) offered a 'corporate marketing mix' including:

- *Character* (corporate identity): tangible and intangible assets, corporate ownership, corporate philosophy, structure, markets served.
- *Culture* (organisational identity): employees define themselves in terms of organisational membership especially if values, beliefs, and assumptions about the organisation are shared.
- *Communication* (corporate communications): outbound B2C channels deployed by the firm as well as internal communications.
- *Conceptualisations* (corporate reputation): perceptions of the corporate brand by customers and key stakeholders.

- *Constituencies* (stakeholder management): groups that customers also belong to (employees, investors, local community).
- *Covenant* (corporate brand management): *emotional ownership* (aka 'customer equity') form an informal 'contract' with the organisation and the brand.

Biraghi & Gambetti (2013, p. 1) suggest a crucial crossroad between internal and external stakeholders acting as a 'bridge' among key intangibles and as an 'inside–outside' interface between company and stakeholders. The organisational structure of the portfolio of products, brands, sub-brands, and services – the brand architecture – exists on three basic levels: corporate, business unit, and product or service level. Muzellec and Lambkin describe the concept of brand architecture as a "useful diagnostic framework to help map the often-complex collection of brands owned by large companies" but, as a static framework which provides a snapshot (2009, p. 39), does not offer much understanding of the "vertical interaction among levels within the brand hierarchy nor does it really the fundamental variations of the corporate brands emanating from those levels".

Product and corporate brands are often considered as equivalent because they are "context independent" (de Chernatony, 2002, p. 114), and share a commonality of communication objective in terms of needing to create differentiation and selection preference. Yet, as Muzellec & Lambkin (2009, p. 41) suggest, the "complexity of the corporate context has fundamental implications for the nature of the corporate brand", going beyond product branding by focusing on a well-defined set of values.

There is separation but there is mutuality; it is the enactment which is different.

The 'House of Brands' perspective – individual brands being distinct from the corporate brand (eg: *P&G* have a whole range of consumer brands which add up to the portfolio) – benefits by consumer brand not affecting corporate reputation. Where corporation and consumer brands share the same name (a 'branded house' perspective), the master brand (eg: *Virgin*) becomes the 'umbrella' brand and is the key driver for brand image and reputation, although values from the rest of the portfolio can affect corporate values.

Because this impacts on external and internal stakeholders, the role of management and employees is crucially important in transmitting the brand values (Balmer & Gray, 2003, p. 972). It is imperative that vision, culture, as well as corporate identity are aligned with external positioning and corporate image.

5.9 Corporate social responsibility and beyond

All businesses contribute to, and impact on, society, and must interact with internal and external stakeholders in the social ecosystem of the organisation's operating context. Equally, all businesses, and indeed all stakeholders, carry some responsibility in that creation and impact. How an organisation manages interaction with customers, regulators, legislators, and the general public in acknowledging and demonstrating its responsibility is how it is perceived by its stakeholders and society in general. Strategy must incorporate stakeholder interaction in every decision the organisation makes. Traditionally, Corporate Social Responsibility (CSR) has been the strategic platform for businesses to respond to social and environmental threats and opportunities, going beyond coerced compliance to enhance business opportunities as well as creating social values. As the interface between the organisation and the external environment, it has been the conduit for communications and the manifestation of a company's purpose, ethics, and values.

At best, CSR is embedded into the soul of the organisation's being; at worst it is a superficial projected brand image of how the organisation assumes its target customer base interprets its credentials. In principle, company, consumers, and the focal social issues all benefit from CSR (Bhattacharya & Sen, 2004). It can be used to create *moral capital* (the outcome of a company's philanthropic judgement or ethical activities); as an insurance against potential damage from negative stakeholder evaluations; to gain a unique competitive advantage; and to support a company's idiosyncratic intangible assets such as credibility and reputation (Godfrey, 2005). Consumers may have an enhanced perception of product or service quality because they signal greater management competency (McWilliams & Siegel, 2001).

Hur, Kim and Woo (2014, p. 76) discuss "corporate brand credibility which is based on consumer trust as a mediational pathway linking CSR perception to corporate reputation and brand equity". In other words, CSR has a significantly positive effect on corporate brand credibility. Furthermore, brand credibility plays a mediating role on the CSR-corporate reputation relationship and the CSR-corporate brand equity relationship. Other research focuses on resource-based perspectives (RBP) demonstrating the relationship between a corporation's internal characteristics and its performance (Branco & Rodrigues, 2006), specifically, "fundamental intangible resources such as corporate reputation, culture, or capabilities contribute to the enhancement of financial performance because they are rare and cannot be imitated or substituted" (Hur, Kim, & Woo, 2014, p. 76). However, stakeholder engagement may or may not involve a moral dimension and, hence, is primarily a morally neutral practice (Greenwood, 2007). Porter and Kramer (2006) summarise the dissatisfaction experienced with CSR as an integrated component of strategy referring to it as "a hodgepodge of uncoordinated CSR and philanthropic activities disconnected from the company's strategy that neither make any meaningful social impact nor strengthen the firm's long-term competitiveness" (p. 80).

Currently, the view is that companies need a new approach to engaging and managing the external environment. To be fair, organisations have never been under so much pressure to "incorporate interaction with stakeholders into decision-making at every level of the organisation" (Browne & Nuttall, 2013, p. 30). That pressure beyond the economic partnership between customer and company, beyond compliance, beyond positive relationships of mutuality, is being replaced by a kind of government by proxy akin to the role which non-for-profit (NFP) organisations fulfil where solutions to economic, social, and environmental problems have to be part of strategy. Like effective marketing starts with having a detailed knowledge of customers, good external relationships must start with a comprehensive analysis of stakeholder requirements and possible impacts. Integrated external engagement (IEE) is a vital element of a company's competitiveness. Corporate Social innovation (CSI) as a model of value creation looks at how external relationships are configured and integrated into strategy as a hybrid of "shared value" (Porter & Kramer, 2011) and "social contract" (Davies, 2005).

5.10 Measuring corporate culture impacts

Successful corporate strategy is dependent on corporate culture. In volatile, complex markets, company culture and responsibility is becoming increasingly important in order for business to regain its social standing and maintain its sustainable franchise. The *Institute of Business Ethics*[93] (2021) defines corporate culture as "the combination of factors that drive behaviour within an organisation". The *Financial Reporting Council* on corporate culture underlines the seriousness of this. Successful corporate strategy is dependent on corporate culture. As with all aspects of strategy, 'What gets measured, gets managed'. Ergo, corporate culture must be measured.

Corporate culture, often viewed through a qualitative lens, can be difficult to be quantified but must have the same empirical examination as all other aspects of strategy. 'Shared meaning and values' may not be metrics that can necessarily translate into key performance indicators (KPIs) expressed in numbers. Foster Back states that "There can be no effective oversight of corporate culture unless boards have first set and promulgated a statement of values and purpose against which expected behaviours can be defined and measured (Foster Back, 2020).

The *Institute of Customer Service* (ICS) has established a clear connection between customer satisfaction and financial performance and that employee engagement is critical to customer satisfaction. For example, only 11% of customers would repurchase from an organisation following a bad experience with an employee, while 43% of would actively dissuade others. For every 1-point increase in employee engagement, customer satisfaction rises by 0.41 points.

Customer satisfaction leads to greater revenue and loyalty (Kriss, 2014) higher shareholder returns and sales growth (Morgan & Rego, 2006), greater profit margin (PM), return on assets (ROA), return on equity (ROE), proxies of a firm's profitability, and in the market value added (MVA), a proxy of firm value (Sun & Kim,

---

93 *FRC* (2018) The UK Corporate Governance Code.

2013). Customer satisfaction also boosts the efficiency of future advertising and promotion investments and has a positive influence on a company's excellence in human capital (employee talent and manager superiority) (Luo & Homburg, 2007).

Greater customer satisfaction, service quality and loyalty lead to increases in customer profitability (Eklof, Podkorytova, & Malova, 2020). Employee satisfaction has a positive influence on customer satisfaction which in turn positively influences financial performance.

NPS is widely used as a key measure, but in comparison to various customer satisfaction models it is less effective, with no clear link to improving a firms financial performance. NPS has been criticised on the basis that:

- "Loyalty is too complex to be measured with a single metric.
- NPS outperformed by *Norwegian Consumer Satisfaction Barometer (NCSB)* and the *American Consumer Satisfaction Index (ACSI)* in predicting firm revenue growth.
- 'Intention to recommend' valuable but not the 'only' metric of true value.
- Loyalty attitudes do not necessarily translate to loyalty behaviours.
- NPS provides no data on what to do to improve.
- NPS focuses only on keeping customers, not on winning new customers.
- There is no such thing as a "passive" customer.
- NPS provides no competitive data.
- NPS is internally focused not externally focused."
  (Keiningham, Cooil, Aksoy, & Andreass, 2008; Fisher & Kordupleski, 2019)

Among the possible indicators for customer satisfaction (and therefore positive customer engagement) are:

- '*Net Promoter Scores*', used by Retail companies measuring how likely a customer would be to recommend a company/ its products to friends and family.
- Social Media Interaction.
- Customer survey data.
- Call centre records on resolving customer queries.
- Complaints, including the success with which they were resolved.
- Repeat Purchase/Renewal Rate.
- Average Time On Site/Page.
- Open And Click-Through Rates.
- Number Of Form Fills.
- Calls to action responses
- Direct User Feedback (NPS with driver analysis / TOP 2 CSAT Scores Or Online Reviews).
- Market share.
- Repeat Visit Frequency.
- Customer Referrals.

Chapter takeaways

- Management of interaction is moving away from being merely a company-oriented 'inside-out' organisational process to one where a customer-oriented experiential 'outside-in' perspective has primacy.
- From the customer's perspective, services are *experiences*; from the company's perspective, services are *processes* that have to be designed and managed to create the desired customer experience.
- Creation and development of brand strategy depends on the complicity and coordination of internal and external stakeholders, interdependently linked in an economic and social network or 'ecosystem'.
- Interactions are 'moments of truth', service encounters or customer experience touch points across multiple channels and at varying points in time, which present customers with an opportunity to compare their prior perceptions and expectations of the business and form an opinion.
- Digitised customer behaviour has a significant impact on the way companies manage their relationships with customers and how value is present in more transparent, democratic, and seamless interaction.
- Corporate brands are valued as strategic resources and provide the primary synthesis for aligning what the organisation is, what it says about itself, and what it does to express its values: corporate vision, organisational culture, and stakeholder perceptions.
- Corporate identity and company culture are inextricably linked. The values that corporate identity makes visible are the organisational culture; organisational culture is essentially the corporate identity.
- There are different perspectives on organisational culture: organisations *have* cultures; organisations *are* cultures; or cultures are *emergent* in organisations.
- Often, the two key corporate associations used by customers to evaluate companies are corporate ability and corporate conscience.
- All businesses contribute to, and impact on, society, and must interact with internal and external stakeholders in the social ecosystem of the organisation's operating context.

Closing case

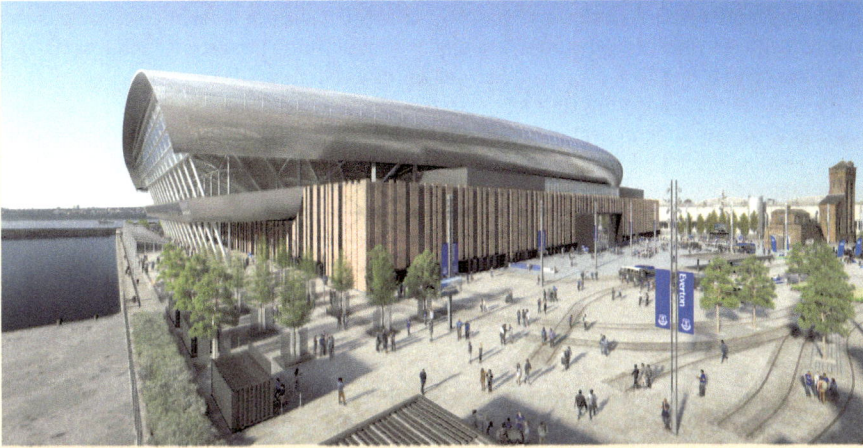

Exemplar engagement from enterprising *Everton*

Ever since a former manager inadvertently positioned *Everton Football Club* as *"The People's Club"*, listening to the 'voice' of the fans and communicating to a wider stakeholder franchise has been the hallmark of this prominent *English Premier League* organisation. Its credentials for acknowledging its social purpose is evident in the values which underpin the long-established charitable arm of the club *Everton In The Community* (*EITC*), and this, according to CEO Denise Barrett-Baxendale, is something which had to be true for this project: "Listening, consulting, and collaborating on all important club matters".

A robust, transparent, and creative two year campaign – branded as *'The People's Project'* – was aimed at achieving planning permission for a new state-of-the-art stadium, built on the Banks of the River Mersey. This resulted in the highest recognition: being named winners in the prestigious "Stakeholder Engagement in Planning (Development Management)" category at the recent National Planning Awards. Held annually, the Planning Awards recognise excellence in planning, regeneration, economic development, and urban designs across the UK. Judges described the consultation conducted as "a great example of cross-cutting engagement at all levels".

The omni-channel pre-planning consultation, conducted in two phases across 2018 and 2019, for a 52,888 capacity waterfront stadium at Bramley-Moore Dock, together with an innovative community-led 'legacy project' on the site of the current stadium Goodison Park, was one of the largest engagement programmes ever. A fully integrated marketing communications strategy included a permanent online presence in the form of *'The People's Project'* website, a geo-targeted social media campaign, email and postal surveys, focus groups, and an ambitious touring exhibition which visited 21 locations and attracted 20,000 people.

Stunning visualisations of the new stadium – designed by world-renowned architect Dan Meis and *BDP Pattern* – were made possible through a unique immersive experience including 360-degree virtual reality 'stadium tours' via roadshows, architect-led design consultation workshops, and the use of a unique *People's Project* 3D home viewing app which contains a range of interactive materials.

Assisted by global real estate advisor *CBRE*, the project has been heralded as the largest consultation in the City of Liverpool's history and a blueprint for future projects. Colin Chong,

Stadium Director at *Everton*, said: "This award is testament to the planning and hard work put into what is widely acknowledged as an exemplar public consultation". Engagement on a global scale across world-wide *Everton* supporters was extended to include other non-*Everton*ians and non-football fans who showed almost unanimous support for the transformational socio-economic and cultural effects of the project, as well as the aesthetics of its modern design.

The new stadium, upon the start of construction, was recognised as the largest civic and commercial construction project in the UK. This transformational scheme will have a catalytic effect resulting in a £1.3 billion boost to the local economy and the wider regeneration of the region estimated to be worth at least £650 million, creating more than 15,000 jobs and attracting over 1.4 million visitors annually. Over 43,000 people responded to the 2nd Public Consultation stage, nearly twice that of the 1st phase, making a total of over 63,000 respondents, hailed as exemplar by leading experts in civic engagement, sports business, and marketing.

Further engagement was made with the wider business and football communities, as well as politicians from all parties. *Premier League* Chief executive, Richard Masters, Professor Michael Parkinson, Associate Pro-Vice Chancellor for Civic Engagement at the University of Liverpool and an advisor to national governments and the European Commission on Urban Affairs, Steve Rotheram, Metro Mayor of the Liverpool City Region, and even Lord Michael Heseltine, former Deputy Prime Minister have all applauded the level of engagement and endorsed the project. Because the proposals are within Liverpool's World Heritage Site, the influential heritage group *The Merseyside Civic Society* were included in the consultation. Senior business leaders, such as Andy Snell, Head of Strategic Partnerships at the *Wirral Chamber of Commerce* and former director of the *Liverpool Chamber of Commerce*, applauded "the Club's commitment to its widespread engagement". Chris Brady, Director of the *Centre for Sport Business at Salford University*, as well as being an independent commissioner on the *Football Regulatory Authority* said: "The terms 'engagement' and 'consultation' are often bandied about as soundbites, but *Everton* have actually taken the terms very seriously in developing their plans for the new stadium".

The strongest praise, however, came from a man to whom branding is of the utmost importance – Chris Daly, Chief executive of the *Chartered Institute of Marketing (CIM)*. He enthused that "Strong brands put their customer at the heart of everything they do, and *Everton*'s stadium consultation is a shining example of that. The club has not assumed but *asked* fans what it is they want. Its choice of engagement channels has marked the club out as an innovator. Whilst the stadium is changing, *Everton FC* has made it clear that its values will not, confirming its authenticity and securing loyalty through this period of change". It was no surprise that *The People's Project* was named 'Best Property and Construction Campaign' at the *Northern Marketing Awards* 2019, and a finalist for 'Marketing Campaign of the Year' in the *CIM Awards* 2020, with *Everton's* social presence *EITC* also extending exemplar engagement with 'Best Foundation' at The Corporate Engagement Awards 2021.

On February 23, 2021, Liverpool City Council unanimously approved *Everton's* Stadium and community-led legacy project at Goodison Park. Automatic referral to the Secretary of State for Housing Communities and Local Government resulted in another positive outcome. After 24 months of the largest engagement process ever on Merseyside, *Everton* broke ground in the summer of 2021, making the new stadium their fans have always dreamed of a step closer to reality.

Questions
1. What are the chief characteristics of 'engagement' and why would *The People's Club* consultation be an exemplar?
2. Is it necessary to have such a wide consultation with stakeholders for a project which will only be used by a small minority of customers?
3. How are the club's values evident in this engagement campaign?

6 Managing strategic segmentation: Customer insights from data

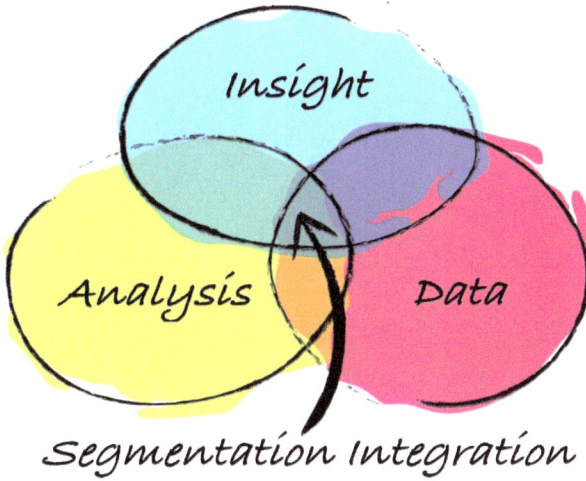

https://doi.org/10.1515/9783110718638-010

Opening case

Ava bridges gender data gap
producing insights into reproduction

The *Office for National Statistics (ONS)* acknowledge that gender issues are influenced by misinformation and assumption instead of a clear evidence base: there is a "gender data gap" of disproportionate male-oriented research and disaggregated information. *Women Deliver*, a leading non-profit global advocate for women's health, rights, and well-being, claim that there is "a significant gender gap in health innovation". In her book *Invisible Women*, Caroline Criado Perez, British journalist and feminist activist, claims that medical researchers say that "the female body is too complicated to measure". One company attempting to bridge this data gap and offer women a "long-term technological companion" is *Ava*, a women's digital health company. Launched as a Swiss start-up in September 2014 by Pascal Koenig, Philipp Tholen, Peter Stein, and Lea von Bidder, and boosted by a $2.6 million investment by *Zürcher Kantonalbank* and *Swisscom*, *Ava's* mission is to advance women's reproductive health by combining data-driven insights from scientifically-proven clinical research and artificial intelligence applied to all stages of their reproductive lives. Specifically, they aim to "understand the menstrual cycle in depth, not only so that we can develop products that will improve women's lives, but also so that we can educate, empower, and arm women with critical information about their health".

Ava were convinced that algorithms and technology could be harnessed to help combat these inherent data biases and help deepen our understanding of women's health. One such project to assist this goal was a peer reviewed paper in the *Journal of Medical Internet Research* which revealed that temperature is not the only physiological signal during the menstrual cycle, demonstrating that there are, in fact, changes evident in 5 physiological signals. The study (Goodale, *et al.*, 2019) found that by tracking these 5 signals simultaneously, 'fertile days' can be detected in real-time. The longitudinal study recruited 237 Swiss women, all wearing the *Ava (Ava AG)* 'Bracelet', syncing the device to a corresponding smartphone app, storing details of their 24-hour activities in an electronic diary, and recorded alongside regular urinary luteinising hormone tests.

Data extracted by using ambulatory wearable technology detected multiple physiological parameters including phase-based shifts in pulse rates and wrist skin temperature (WST).

Wearable sensor technology, initially developed for domestic sports monitoring and primarily providing individual physical activity data collection, is finding a greater amount of health care applications. Sensors embedded in head bands, chest straps, wristwatches, and clothing can now track a whole range of data. Wearable technology makes medical monitoring available to everyday consumers, facilitating longitudinal tracking and allowing users to see very personalised patterns in the data. It could fill the gap between high-cost, high-accuracy ovulation detection and free, less-precise fertile window approximation. There are period tracker apps available which predict fertility – LH tests, retrospective temperature tests – but the *Ava Bracelet*, a wearable phase-shift detector, has both temperature and photoplethysmographic (blood volume) sensors, an 'accelerometer' (sleep detection), is worn during sleep and provides data on fertility, pregnancy, and general health, delivered in a convenient and non-invasive way. *Ava* were the winners of the *Women's Health Femtech Award* in 2018. As well as European Medical Device Regulation (EU MDR) certification, US *Food and Drug Agency (FDA)* clearance was received in February 2021 making it the first and only FDA-cleared wearable fertility tracking device and accompanying app the *Ava Fertility Tracker*. By March 2019, 20,000 pregnancies had been recorded and the status in women's health care was firmly established.

Positioning amongst conception and contraception competitors was thought to be limiting in brand scope and potential. Purpose positioning played a big part in adopting a 'scientific' narrative and positioning rather than 'women's lifestyle' femcare. There are other brands (like *Apple Watch*) which use wearable technology to measure personal fitness metrics (eg: in 2019 *Google* changed their brand to *'Fitbit'* from the previous company *Healthy Metrics Research Inc*). *Ava's* brand agency defined a new brand promise: "Driving the progress women deserve, one cycle at a time". This echoes CEO Lea von Bidder's bold statement about *Ava's* purpose: "We'll remain steadfast to this vision [being a "long-term technological companion" for women] until we live where data collection and scientific understanding of human health mirrors the population: equal parts women and men". For *Ava*, insight from data does not just inform its brand strategy but its purpose.

Source: Extracts from *Ava* website and Goodale *et al* (2019) observational study

Questions
1. Explain what is meant by "gender data gap" of disproportionate male-oriented research and disaggregated information and how this impacts on brands at females.
2. Differentiate between purpose positioning and 'women's lifestyle' femcare positioning.
3. Why does insight from data not just inform *Ava's* brand strategy but its purpose?

Note: The photo(s) used in this case study is/are not connected and/or does not represent any brand(s) mentioned. It/they is/are used to make a visual discussion point by the authors.

6.1 Outline of chapter

Diagnosis precedes and conditions strategy. Strategic choice comes out of this: what an organisation will do and will not do, and who is to be targeted. If targeting and positioning is the start of strategy, segmentation is the end of diagnosis. Well, the start of the *initial* diagnosis. The focal point of strategy always has to be the customer – that is, *customer centricity* – and the needs of the customer are constantly changing. Understanding customer expectations, needs, perceptions, and experiences along the path of their buying 'journey' is vital in converting, satisfying, building long-term relationships, maintaining customer lifetime value (CLV), sustaining loyalty, and spreading brand advocacy. Understanding your customer is understanding your business and this is the role of strategic segmentation.

The old adage "The customer is always right" is now an anachronism. Rather, as Fader (2012, p. 5) suggests: "The customer isn't always right; the *right* customer is always right". Acknowledging that customers are heterogenous is a fundamental pillar of segmentation; segmenting customers into homogenous groups is the *sine qua non* of data analytics. This implies a focus on strategy that is customer-driven; strategy that is customer-driven has to be *data*-driven. Converting customer data into meaningful, actionable strategy involves predictive analysis, and is as much about understanding customer lifestyles, analysing customer expectations and experience, curating precisely tailored communications, and projecting likely future consumption behaviour as it is about collecting aggregated transactional data like recency, frequency, and monetary value (RFM) of customer purchases. The process of segmentation is central to this: predicting buyer behaviour drivers by identifying and examining targetable homogenous groups from heterogeneous individuals in order to align a strategic fit between internal resources and capabilities and external opportunities.

The rapid diffusion of global marketing has encouraged companies to deploy segmentation to facilitate better management of complex markets in terms of strategic brand management (Hassan & Craft, 2012). Strategically, segmentation allows better assessment and selection of market attractiveness, deeper analysis of customer-company congruity, more mutually beneficial value proposition creation, and helps develop successful customer engagement and communication. Failure to grasp this fundamental marketing principle is, according to Christensen (1997), why 90% of new products and services fail. Indeed, because of the customer's demand for information in markets of abundant choice and increasing fragmentation, because of the customer's demand for personalised service, an implicit form of segmentation is mandated by customers.

This chapter discusses how segmenting target markets and profiling existing customers into categories with potential for growth and development gives strategy a vital focus for ensuring time is better allocated and customer's experiences are enhanced. Segmenting customer data to reveal deep, actionable customer insights can enhance retention and customer development, monitor for indications of unwanted customer churn and lost patronage, examine potential for leveraging loyalty or re-motivating lapsed users, and continuously innovate customer-centric brands. Klein (2013) defined insight as "an unexpected shift in the way we understand things.

Intuition is the use of patterns they've already learned, whereas insight is the discovery of new patterns". That's what this chapter is about.

Learning outcomes

After reading this chapter, you'll be able to:
- Understand the concept of 'customer-centricity' and explain why customer insights from data is the fundamental driver of brand strategy.
- Critically apply why segmentation and profiling are essential elements of short-term survival and long-term development.
- Explain why reliance on Big Data might lead to confusion in segmenting customer bases to aid decision-making.
- Establish the links between strategic segmentation and improving the customer experience in encounters with the company.
- Analyse how narratives built from data can be beneficial in improving the customer experience.
- Assess the impact of 'datafication' in the age of the social customer.

6.2 Introduction

All strategic decisions should be based on insight from data. Companies that are data-driven, make well-informed decisions. Insight from data is like a customer insight visualisation platform, allowing companies to view the delivery of the value proposition through the customer's eyes. The relationships that customers have with the company are critical. The biggest and most significant strategic shift in terms of the tools companies use to deliver superior customer experience is the use of advanced predictive analytics to drive data-driven customer experience decisions.[94] For example, data from segmenting and profiling customers by how they evaluate unique individual service encounters and interactions with employees can provide useful insight into 'critical service incidents', their role in service production and delivery, the effects that tangibles and the physical environment play in analysing individual customer evaluation of service encounters, and are crucial in improving the value created in the customer-company interface. Equally, the values reflective of the relationships the customer has in the external environment must be embedded in the company's values.

Companies have access to more consumer data than ever before. However, in order to deliver a better customer experience, to exceed customer expectations, companies must leverage customer data. Insight from data is becoming universally accepted as a crucial ingredient of strategy. And if 'purpose-driven brand strategy' is becoming the paradigm shift in today's organisations, "digital data-driven insights

---

94 'Closing the Customer Experience Gap: How IT and Business Can Partner to Transform Customer Experiences', Research Report, *Harvard Business Review Analytic Services*, 2017.

are the new currency of business".[95] For example, *Danone*,[96] the Spanish food manufacturer, used actionable insights (or "near-to-immediate pulse checks") through deep social listening (some 225 million online conversations) which resulted in a major change in strategy. Insights are created in the analysis of information. When their customer base declined from a peak of 20 million to 5 million, *Netflix* transformed their original business model – a subscription mailing DVDs direct-to-customer proposition – to become the world's largest streaming service. This metamorphosis, grown out of insights from customer data and market research, now shows 203.66 million subscribers generating $25 billion in 2020 with 64% of customers based outside the US and Canada. *Netflix's* mobile app for *iOS* and *Android* was downloaded over 19 million times in 2021 alone.

Another global brand, furniture retailer *IKEA*, has a network of franchise outlets whose designers are informed from centralised customer insight data. Data-informed decisions are extracted from actionable insights. The quantity of data isn't the issue; "what matters most is how you discover and implement digital insight into the fabric of your business. To do this, you don't need more data; you need systems of insight".[97] The real driver for this of course is customer-centricity, and as a foundational element of understanding customers, segmentation has "the largest impact on marketing decisions" (Roberts, Kayande, & Stremersch, 2014, p. 127).

Dividing customers into discernible, manageable groups of individuals with similar characteristics – managing strategic segmentation based on advanced analytics – can give deep customer insights which can strengthen existing relationships and help develop new ones. Insight into active and lapsed customer disposition, acquisition, retention, defection, reactivation, performance, and customer journey movement analyses, can help in managing customers. And yet, as access to meaningful data improves, "many businesses suffer from a kind of segmentation paralysis" (Chaubey & Subramanian, 2020, p. 2349) where the application of generic segmentation may not provide accurate customer insight. According to Venter, Wright, & Dibb, (2015, p. 62), "traditional studies address segmentation as an epistemological issue: segments objectively exist and it is the task of the marketer to unveil them".

However, segmentation cannot just be a retrospective, static process because modern customers are not static in their buying behaviour. They can migrate to other segments or leave without notice. There is a disconnect as Dibb & Simkin (2009, p. 219) warn: "Despite its long academic heritage, segmentation may be failing to achieve its original objectives".

From a philosophical perspective, "segmentation has shifted from a simple focus on understanding customer's needs to an intricate exploration of customer

---

95 Ted Schadler, "Digital insights are the new currency of business", *Forrester*, April 28th, 2015.
96 This is presented in detail in *Chapter 6* in the *Danone* case.
97 Brian Hopkins, "Think You Want To Be 'Data-Driven'? Insight Is The New Data", *Forrester*, March 9th, 2021.

lifestyles . . . . On a practical level, the multiplicity of real-time, digital data about customers has paved new ways of understanding them" (Chaubey & Subramanian, 2020, p. 2349). Taking a performative perspective, framing market segments as an ontological descriptive statement, views segmentation in terms of the reality of who a company's customers actually are and how best to serve them. This unfolds through a conversation (human) and materiality (non-human) dialectic (Kjellberb & Helgesson, 2010). The focus on performative research – how practitioners actually *do* segmention – is essentially relational, describing the "strings of association" (Cooren & Fairhurst, 2009, p. 49) between customer and company, and revealing what segmentation actually is. And it is in those clues of association and linkage where insight and value is mined. Segmentation can only be seen as a customer-centric strategic platform for growth if it is aligned with corporate strategy and integrated with the marketing processes, and can only be seen as strategically useful if it provides meaningful insight.

Management decision-making needs to be supported by an accurate assessment of customer behaviour, competitive activity, and continuous environmental monitoring. Matching the generation of insights through deep analytics, creative data gathering, and defining accurately what the problems and areas of strategy focus are is essential. Smarter target marketing through accurate segmentation may not just be beneficial to companies but demanded by the marketplace, a fact that has been heightened by dynamic changes in the macro and micro environment. This has been highlighted as the most important marketing priority in the current economic post-COVID-19 period by the UK's leading Marketing Education provider, the *Chartered Institute of Marketing* (CIM). COVID-19 has shown us that consumer motivations and purchasing patterns can evolve, and brands must adapt their approach to segmentation accordingly. Traditional consumption methods of researching, selecting, and buying have changed. Buying in more economic quantities, stock piling, increased online buying, new brand trialling, moving to new channels such as online and touchless. Engagement touchpoints have altered necessitating better insight into consumer preferences, pain points in order to implement more targeted communications. Static segmentation models have been challenged and replaced with more dynamic consumer segmentation, using real-time consumer data. A good example of this is in the food sector where evidence of the splitting of the traditional segments of 'culinary enthusiast' and 'cuisine connoisseur' into cohorts comprising 'flexitarians', 'healty-conscious vegetarians', 'vegans', 'passionate daily cooks', 'food activists', 'meal-kit spenders', and 'organic foodies'.[98]

Having superior products and services is no longer sufficient to guarantee survival. Profiling can identify significant customer characteristics and provide insightful

---

[98] Andrew Smith and Tanya Anand, "Advancing consumer segmentation during COVID-19 and beyond", *The Drum Network*, 29th July 2020.

knowledge about an organisation's strengths and weaknesses and strategic fit. Effective strategy comes from insightful analysis. Successful organisations know how to define and select the most attractive markets which are appropriate to their resources, capabilities, and competition. Strategic success depends on an organisation's ability to cultivate and maintain loyal customer relationships, co-create sustainable mutually beneficial value, expand the customer base, design, and develop customer-appropriate offerings, micro target sales opportunities, improve cross-selling and up-selling, and realise full profit potential. Analytics have to be:

- *Descriptive* (retrospective analysis of activities to help contextualise results and inform future decision-making).
- *Predictive* (projecting trends beyond current data).
- *Prescriptive* (relating possible action from models).
- Engage by asking for feedback from the target audience.

Early versions of the concept of segmentation saw criticism of the premise of homogeneity inherent in models of 'perfect competition' (Smith, 1956). The Segmentation Targeting Positioning (STP) triad became a stalwart of marketing plans, applying the analysis of customer information to profiling targeted existing and potential customers with appropriate positioning of value propositions. Attractive segments were seen as homogeneous, measurable, accessible, and substantial. As Weinstein (2004, p. 4) claims, "Segmentation means knowing your customers, giving them exactly what they want or may want, building strong relationships with channel affiliates and co-marketing partners, and communicating via highly targeted promotional media". Traditional definitions nearly always featured classification or categorisation: demographic, geographic, cultural, user purchase behaviour and loyalty levels, or psychographic and benefits sought (domestic markets); geographic, cultural, demographic, purchasing approaches, situational factors (industrial markets). Characteristics can be *hard* such as socio-economic and demographic, and *soft* such as values, attitudes, and lifestyle (VAL). They can be *objective* such as frequency of usage, sensitivity of pricing, response to communications, the levels of loyalty, or *subjective* such as benefits sought or brand perceptions.

As we have discussed, segmentation is a creative and iterative process, a primary strategic element in a company's brand development. Yet whilst brands are a company's greatest asset, time is its most valuable resource. Inefficiencies in the application of resources can be more easily identified, and more appropriate products developed and more effective campaigns can be communicated.

Principles in practice

New ways to connect for brands through Connected TV

Reaching target audiences with conventional TV ads through conventional linear TV scheduling is fast becoming ancient history. These days, it may not even involve cable or satellite subscription or involve a traditional TV with the majority of content served via the internet. Today's consumers have a rich diversity of viewing options across multiple types of screen and device: Smart TV sets, laptops, smart phones, game consoles, tablets, operator devices like *Sky* and *Virgin*, and streaming devices like *Amazon Fire, GoogleTV, Google Chromecast, Roku*, and *Apple TV*. Connected TV (CTV), is an innovative disruptor, but its status is in contention: TV, digital, or new media sector?

For brands, connecting via fast-emerging innovative digital formats presents an exciting opportunity to reach a new and unique audience. Projections for the US market forecast 48.6% year-on-year growth, expected to double by 2025. In 2020 in the UK, 63% of people by Ofcom's Technology Tracker[99] had an internet-connected TV set at home, with 41% via a games console and 11% through a streaming stick. Connected TV adoption is expected to grow from 40.9m users in 2020 to 44.4m in 2025.[100]

Sophisticated methods of reaching audiences such as 'addressable' advertising – appropriate specific media or message content targeted to a specific device – via the likes of *SkyAdSmart* dynamic ad replacement (DAR) on broadcast TV enabled by *Virgin* and *Sky*, and ads on CTV device user interfaces (eg: *Samsung First Screen Ads* and *LG Home Launcher Ads*) are opening up opportunities for companies to connect with potential customers. Forces driving CTV advertising are: TV audiences migration to CTV; media owners are focusing on growing CTV audiences; growing demand for data-driven targeting; market for CTV buyers to include digital buyers/SME advertisers and fear of missing out.[101]

Amazon Advertising Head of Measurement, Maggie Zhang,[102] outlines four crucial ways to provide seamless streaming experiences and reach these new emerging audiences:

- Brands must aim to appear on the primary viewing device, the TV. An *Ipsos* study found that 30% of connected consumers are more likely to pay attention to video content on a TV screen compared to 21% via a social media feed.
- Provide relevant content with 'first party signals': 61% preferred ads based on their interests and 57% said they find ads which are relevant to be most helpful.
- Position brand as exclusive sponsor of exclusive premium content aimed at audience's strong affinity and offering reciprocal value. 40% said they preferred a customer-first approach with brand sponsorship in limited commercial interruptions.
- Innovative ad techniques (such as interaction via using the remote, having the option to have information sent to their email upon viewing the ad; shoppable video ads), is an effective method of achieving both advertiser and user needs.

99 *Ofcom* technology tracker, 2020. Fieldwork conducted 9th January – 7th March 2020.
100 https://www.emarketer.co/content/uk-digital-video-2020.
101 "Connected TV advertising market dynamics: Report for Ofcom" by *SparkNinety*, November 2020.
102 Maggie Zhang, "*Amazon Advertising's* Head of Measurement on how to own streaming", *The Drum*, 17th August 2021.

Traditional methods of segmentation – which tend to be static 'moments in time' snapshots – need to be used with contextual, data-integrated methods which give dynamic insight in order to have learning from customers as an embedded part of the process.

Therefore, whilst customers may appear to be similar, in order for marketing information to be meaningful and actionable, knowledge of expectations, perceptions, and indeed purchase potential has to be granular. As consumer needs have become increasingly fragmented and diverse, the process of identification has become more complex and challenging. The counter-intuitive concept of 'mass-customisation' became a marketing mantra, with 'differences and similarities' being the foundation for analysis. The benefits of accurate strategic segmentation are: better allocation of resources; more appropriate product and service match; greater exploitation of customer potential; improved competitiveness; and enhanced knowledge of the influence of customers and stakeholders on the business.

These days, whilst still having customer-centricity as its focus, correctly implemented data-driven customer segmentation is less a sequential tactic, more a holistic strategy, shifting from a concept rooted in theory to one with real-world applicability. What exactly is customer-centricity?

6.3 Customer centricity

Moving 'customer-centricity' from the column marked 'Mission' to the one marked 'Strategy' is akin to changing from a noun to a verb. It is one of the most fundamental marketing constructs and is the philosophical stance and strategic approach to focusing organisational resources towards serving and servicing the customer. It involves aligning value propositions with the needs of the company's most valuable customers to maximise customer life value (CLV) and delivering optimal service to a heterogeneous customer base. Value for customer-centric organisations derives from identifying the most valuable customers and creating mutually beneficial value propositions based on a deep understanding of the customer's perception of value.

Customer-centricity is not a new phenomenon, but is a marketing construct which is organic, constantly evolving, and subject to reiteration throughout various contexts: company internal culture; customer-orientation; service delivery and customer expectation; customer life cycle management; relationship marketing; customer experience management; and, latterly, the dynamics of digital transformation. At the heart of this is customer analyses that have valuable impacts, analysing the customer base by segmentation to identify replicable (customers with similar needs) scalable service and valuable opportunities.

It has been a cornerstone of marketing for quite some time now, and is becoming the most useful model for predicting behaviour and analysing customer needs in today's data-driven climate. Understanding buying states and communication needs are strategy imperatives for which digital innovations have made consumer knowledge and ubiquitous connectivity powerful tools. Leveraging data for competitive advantage and enhanced customer experience through customer insight is a significant trend.

For companies, there are benefits of increased efficiencies in buying predictability, production capacity, more accurate targeting, better sales conversion ratios, enhanced customer satisfaction, decreased churn, and better communications; for consumers, it is risk-free decision-making, greater product knowledge, and closer involvement in brand development. According to the Pulse survey, "brands that gain the ultimate analytical advantage – by unifying the analytics life cycle from data to discovery to deployment – will also gain *competitive* advantage through brand preference" (Wilson, Malik, & Kanioura, 2018). In their view, the most effective strategies are ones which derive insights from analytics through:

- *Unified customer platforms:* the synthesis of online and offline customer data.
- *Proactive analytics:* purpose-built data collection and analytics capabilities integrating service, operations, and support.
- *Contextual interactions:* interrogation of customer digital journey tracking.

This survey, (taken from 560 high and middle-ranking executives in various key industry sectors), found that 58% of respondents claimed that their companies experienced a "significant increase in customer retention and loyalty as a result of the use of customer analytics" (2018, p. 1). 60% stated that the ability to use real-time analytics "to improve customer experience across touch points and devices is extremely important today". They refer to this as "contextual customer engagements across their journey" (2018, p. 2). Omni-channel, self-serve, personalised recommendations, and increasingly automated processes ensure customer journeys are a holistic, value-added experience.

The following performance areas were seen as being dramatically improved:

- Customer retention/loyalty (58%).
- Understanding/strength of the customer journey (51%).
- Growth/revenue generation (44%).
- Customer lifetime value (33%).
- Ability to quantify marketing ROI (29%).
- Profitability (26%).
- Employee satisfaction/engagement (25%).

When asked which new technology tools were most important, respondents say "CRM, predictive analytics, social media monitoring, content management systems, and marketing operations management are the technologies and capabilities most important to their real-time customer efforts today" (Pulse 2018, p. 5). Other technologies, (including IoT, intelligent assistants, text/speech/ voice analytics, mixed reality, content management, and cloud computing) were seen as becoming even more important in the years ahead.

The following were seen as being Critical Success Factors (CSF):
- Clear strategy/goal (42%).
- Actionable data/visualisations (39%).
- Collaborations across roles/functions (33%).
- Data hygiene reliability (32%).
- Strategic alignment (29%).

Understanding your customer is understanding your business. To reiterate, "The customer is always right" is now an anachronism. Rather, as Fader (2012, p. 5) suggests: "The customer isn't always right; the *right* customer is always right". Well, additionally, to find out about the right customer, then the *right* tool needs to be used to find them, with an acknowledgement of an appropriate market orientation based on overall goals. Segmentation by customer needs, for example, can be responsive (eg: explicitly known) or proactive (latent needs, hard to articulate) both of which can be argued as a form of segmentation, ideally a holistic approach that deploys qualitative and quantitative means it can provide a rounded view. It is not a binary choice. One is not better than the other. More the right tool for the job.

Customer centricity focuses on the profitable creation and maintenance of superior lifetime customer value while considering the interests of other key stakeholders and providing norms for behaviour regarding the organisational development of a responsiveness to market information. Holbrook's evaluation of consumer value as being an "interactive relativistic preference experience" (1999, p. 5) describes customer-company interaction, which fluctuates relative to consumption contexts. Some have argued that it is limited in its practical application, marketing complexity demanding multi-level customer interaction, businesses having to service the interests of many stakeholders, a "network-based stakeholder approach – *balanced centricity* – epitomised by the concept of many-to-many marketing" (Gummesson, 2006).

It can be viewed from three perspectives:
- The nature of how companies formulate customer-driven strategy; as a transformative.
- Company value-creating catalytic programme.
- A collaborative venture with supply chain companies as partners in delivering value to the end user.

Customer centricity is a mindset and a way of doing business that focuses on creating positive experiences. Grieger & Ludwig (2019, p. 473) describing original equipment manufacturers (OEMs) in the automotive B2B market, claim that digitalisation drives change to value propositions, opening up to closer collaboration and customer integration, implying a transformational change from product- towards customer-centricity.

Principles in practice

Steve Jobs: Market research myth busting

Apple Co-founder Steve Jobs once famously said: *"Some people say give the customers what they want, but that's not my approach. Our job is to figure out what they're going to want before they do. I think Henry Ford once said, "If I'd ask customers what they wanted, they would've told me a faster horse". People don't know what they want until you show it to them. That's why I never rely on market research. Our task is to read things that are not yet on the page."*

This quote often gets misinterpreted on a number of levels. On the one hand, this is a generalisation and doesn't capture how immensely broad market and social research is. The UK's *Market Research Society* (The World's leading research association) defines it as:[103]

> *Research is the collection, use, or analysis of information about individuals or organisations intended to establish facts, acquire knowledge or reach conclusions. It uses techniques of the applied social, behavioural, and data sciences, statistical principles and theory, to generate insights and support decision-making by providers of goods and services, governments, non-profit organisations and the general public.*

On the other hand, Steve Jobs is referring to a certain type of research and customer insight, with a different outcome. Namely, an approach that is more aligned to a responsive-market orientation, where explicit customer needs, preference and wants are known. Inherently, this lends·itself to a quantitative approach. This methodology allows for the critical stages of test, measure, and validate, the nuance of which is imperative in developing customer insight from data. The sentiment of the Job's quote is that it is a binary choice: one way is better than another. But that is not the case; there are a number of dynamics that influence this choice, for instance, the purpose, targeted outcome, sample population and context should dictate the appropriate methodology. There are immensely powerful segmentation variables that can be used in evaluating customers (and their market orientation) in many contexts and purposes such as psychographic and profile, attitudes, motivations, interests, sentiment, perceptions, and satisfaction. The point being: applying the right methods, tools and techniques to fit the research objectives and outcomes. Job's quote rightly highlights that this approach is not best suited for 'big-bang' step-change innovation break-through, but more toward incremental continuous improvement and customer insights that are more inherently qualitative:

> *The problem with market research is that it can show you what your customers think of something you show them, or it can tell you what your customers want as an incremental improvement on what you have. But very rarely can your customers predict something that they don't even quite know what they want.*[104]

Effectively, this quote betrays the fact that Jobs is articulating the very definition of proactive market orientation, whereby a key aim of customer and consumer market research is to identify and address latent and tacit needs, meaning that a customer or resident is unable to clearly articulate a 'known' need as it is emergent, and the problem and known solution is yet to present itself. The key point of difference is that Jobs was well known to undertake a deeper qualitative approach to

---

103 https://www.mrs.org.uk/about.
104 https://www.businessinsider.com/steve-jobs-quote-misunderstood-katie-dill-2019-4?r= US&IR=T.

market research, arguably a form of ethnography. In many ways, in this context, that methodology suited the purpose, research objectives and all too often criticisms toward market research are on shaky ground. Katie Dill, the former Head of Design at *Lyft* as well as the former Director of Experience Design at *Airbnb*, highlights this point:

> *I agree with that quote, but I think it is often misinterpreted . . . I agree with the sentiment that we can't just ask for what customers want; they don't always know how to articulate it. But I am a firm believer in the power of understanding our community. I'm a firm believer in the power of user research and qualitative insight gathering.*[105]

6.4 Big Data can lead to big confusion

There is an argument that the 'Big Data' and analytics dream has not yet been realised by all organisations. At best, many businesses are simply using data for historical analysis but very few are leveraging its full potential. Often, more data can simply mean more confusion for those making decisions. The *IBM* Big Data and Analytics Hub[106] identified four key issues at play:

- *Volume (scale)*: Too much data and it is overwhelming for business leaders. 90% of today's data was created in the last 2+years, which equates to 2.5 quintillion bytes of data.
- *Velocity (speed with which it is created)*: Every 60 seconds, 204m emails are sent. This can create confusion, overload, and unproductive work practices. It is no longer the case that emails always enhance productivity. Data provided quickly does not make it more valuable.
- *Variety (forms of data)*: There are many different forms of data (video, textual, tweets, pictures). Knowing how best to capture and use this is a challenge.
- *Veracity (uncertainty of data)*: 1 in 3 do not trust the information they use to make decisions. In fact, poor data quality costs the US economy $3.1 trillion a year."

Although 'data-driven' decision-making has become a current buzz phrase, this often relies on secondary sources which can be poor quality, not credible, or not targeted/specific enough to really make a difference. There is a clear need for more accurate and meaningful data to support success: *"The 'Big Data' challenge shows that more, different, connected data does not equate to value or insights, just volume"* (IBM).

The principles of this 'Big Data' challenge are very relevant and a useful lens to assess the various segmentation models, approaches and use of technology (eg: AI-based needs-based approaches). Ideally, each model should be assessed

---

105 https://www.businessinsider.com/steve-jobs-quote-misunderstood-katie-dill-2019-4?r=US&IR=T.
106 *IBM* Big Data & Analytics Hub, online at https://www.ibmbigdatahub.com/.

for robustness, credibility, relevancy and continuity; it shouldn't necessarily be a static picture, undertaken once a year, every 3 years or more, but ideally an ongoing basis. The model should be balanced between qualitative and quantitative approaches so that nuances and points of differences are captured on a continuous basis. In other words, business, brands, customers, emerging customer segments, and society are always changing and developing. As such, critically reviewing models and adopting a holistic approach that only uses technologies as a catalyst and not the primary driver is fundamental for success. There is a danger that businesses and decision-makers are seduced by new technologies (eg: 3D digital printing, or VR), that may offer some superficial tactical wins but don't deliver strategic value or impact. There is a danger that the next big thing, which at best causes decision-makers and planners to become distracted, and at worst, means they forget the key principals for success. This is an ongoing dynamic that will continue to be raised with the emergence of machine learning and human-centred design and cuts across all aspects of a businesses' digital transformation. In relation to the Big Data vs Big Confusion – just because it can be collected and analysed, doesn't necessarily mean that *everything* will add value in decision-making. For instance, the quality, veracity and coverage of what data CEOs need to make decisions is more important than ever. In a *PwC* Global CEO 2019[107] survey, the following data priorities were highlighted:

- 94% consider data about their customers' preferences and needs as critical or important.
- 90% feel that having data about their brand and reputation is critical for long-term success.
- 86% consider data about their employees' views and needs to be critical to run their business.
- 55% said they are not able to innovate effectively.

There is a significant gap between what is considered critical for decision making and the comprehensiveness of the data available. This is particularly significant across brand, customers, competitive environment, employees, and innovation. The evidence supports this assertion. For instance, *PWC*'s 10-year review clearly demonstrates that CEOs hold customer data as a critical information need, but the level of quality and scope (ie: Is the data comprehensive enough?) demonstrates that the gap has actually worsened in a time where data and AI tools are flooding the market – 2019 (79%-gap) vs. 2009 (74%-gap).

What constitutes an Insight Driven Organisations (IDO)? As defined by *Deloitte*,[108] "An insight driven Organisation (IDO) is one which has succeeded in embedding

---

107 23rd Annual Global CEO Survey (2019), *PWC*, online at https://www.ibmbigdatahub.com/.
108 Insight Driven Organization Survey (2019), *Deloitte*, online at https://www2.deloitte.com/content/dam/Deloitte/it/Documents/deloitte-analytics/IDO_Survey%202019_Deloitte%20Italia.pdf.

analysis, data, and reasoning into its decision-making processes. . . . an IDO 's capability goes far beyond technology considerations. It considers strategic alignment, talent and leadership, business processes, and the entire information lifecycle and systems associated with it to elevate the effective generation and application of insights in all areas of the enterprise. They see analytics as a core capability across their organisation rather than as a project with a start and end date." Crucially, these IDOs tend to rely on secondary data, which as highlighted previously, is limited as it is often not relevant, contextual and there is no chance to align it with an organisation's and/or key decision maker's priorities.

Top level findings from the *Deloitte* IDO 2019 survey finds that most executives do not believe their companies are insight-driven. Fewer than four in 10 (37%) place their companies in the top two categories of the IDO Maturity Scale, and of those, only 10% fall into the highest category. The remaining 63% are aware of analytics but lack infrastructure, are still working in silos, or are expanding ad hoc analytics capabilities beyond silos. However, 67% of the executives surveyed say that they are not comfortable accessing or using data from the company tools or resources.

In order to succeed in becoming a data-driven company, leveraging big data to strengthen a business, develop a culture of continuous learning, and break down silos, it is not enough to have data. It needs to be the *right* data.

6.5 Segmentation and profiling

It is important to note that 'segmentation' is a broad area. It can be applied in many different ways and at different stages of a customer relationship: from wider market assessments, non-users and potential customers, through to different stages of customer life cycle such as advocacy. For instance, various segmentation models are vital in understanding how to explore perceptions and attitudes of non-users, build up an understanding of potential customers (with a clear criteria of who NOT to target and why), and how customers experience and invest meaning in a brand.

[*Section 3* includes a number of *FUZE* cases that are all underpinned by tailored and contextual *customer, potential* and *non-user* segmentation models which cover a range of these stages].

At a macro-level, segmentation models should include an assessment of 'potential customers', which is quite often derrived from a national/global/external 'consumer classification' database/set. The company *Experian* offers a range of different products and services, that sit under its *Mosiac 7* brand:

> *Mosaic 7 is a powerful cross-channel consumer classification system built for today's multi-channel world. It has evolved to help you understand your customers' likely characteristics and communicate with them in the most relevant ways. It allows you to ensure you are relevant to them, so you can reach the right people with the right message at the right time – every time.*

Being effective across all channels – from traditional offline to digital TV and online display – the Mosaic consumer classification system enables accurate and consistent targeting, so consumers receive marketing relevant to them.

Mosaic creates an easy to understand segmentation that allocates individuals and households into groups and detailed types allowing you to make sure that you can send relevant communications.[109]

This type of approach would potentially use a post-code (or other consumer classification ID) and then provide a 'matched classification' overview against the multiple sources of data at a national representation: *"use variables from a combination of Experian proprietary, public and trusted third-party sources – including research findings and behavioural data – to build a picture of the latest UK consumer and social trends".*[110]

This offers a useful and varied mix of top-level segments, with sub-segments that often have generalised 'profiles' or pen-portraits. For example, where an organisation can supply a list of customer postcodes and these can be classified and matched against a national representation of consumer profiles. This allows organisations to have some form of understanding about customers across a range of key planning insight such an technology use and behaviour, media use and consumption, holiday and leisure planning and spend, attitudes towards certain topics like money, family, travel, education, to name but a few. There are multiple benefits to this approach: (1) it allows businesses of all sizes to access insight to aid their planning, which arguably offers more value than tailoring/accessing a consumer panel; (2) the strength of the model is the robust national / representation of the multiple data sets and secondary sources that the profiles / sub-profiles are drawn from; (3) these models have the useful capability of matching key customer segments based on provided data, and then identify geographically, so that planners and campaigns can locate customers that most fit their segments.

The main challenges/caveats of this approach are that it does not allow an organisation to tailor variables and deep-dive into certain areas, that are relevant to that sector or context. The pen-portraits tend to be useful, but often relatively top-level generalised intelligence. Additionally, this model includes an *'assumption'* gap of sorts, in that there is an assumption that the models and back-end databases are an accurate portrayal of that customer. All datasets have caveats and assumptions, (good quality organisations will highlight these), but there are often layers upon layers of datasets and caveats. The question is, are all these caveats factored in for all end-users to assess the veracity and quality of these foundational layers? For instance, a post-code (or other generalised ID) is a true reflection of that consumer, as opposed to tailoring and gathering data specifically and asking a non-

---

109 https://www.experian.co.uk/business/platforms/mosaic.
110 https://www.experian.co.uk/business/platforms/mosaic/whatismosiac7?.

user, potential customer, or actual customer. Another example would be value and volume segmentation models in economic modelling in tourism segmentation, which are excellent means of estimating at a macro-level county-level, regional and national economy profiles, including customer segments with spend, employment levels, break down of business types etc. The outputs to these are very useful, but carry the caveats that there are assumptions made about spend, overnight and day visits, employment levels, business profile, and stock. These caveats are clear and allow decision-makers to assess the back-end datasets and sources. This example highlights the need for awareness and acknowledgement.

Another approach includes undertaking a specific research project (often combining qualitative and quantitative methods) and accessing relevant online panels (eg: online surveys, behavioural tracking etc) and/or recruiting specific participants (eg: focus/discussion groups ethnography, interviews etc). This allows an organisation to develop a highly targeted and contextual segmentation model, and often allows companies to target those who best match their sample criteria (eg: non-users, 'ideal', potential customers etc), and provide data that is likely to be more relevant when planning and better understanding potential customers and non-users. For instance, the models allow businesses to weave in essential 'need-to-knows' that could unlock purchasing triggers, identify perceptions and attitudes to overcome barriers/friction on a pathway to purchase or reframe brand positioning and tactical communication decisions. The challenges of this approach *can* relate to the robustness and representation of the sampling, the quality of responses and engagement with the research methods, and the overall cost could be prohibitive for SMEs, and cost-focused larger organisatons.

Customer segmentation can be differentiated from market segmentation and has a more insightful orientation in terms of value creation: classifying current, potential, and lapsed customers based on their market reactions. A major factor facilitating company's pursuit of *customer centricity* is the ability to segment and profile customer databases, refining customer interactions at various touch points. Knowledge from behaviour can be replicated in a process applied to simulate how other customers with similar traits may behave in certain customer-company interactions.

Digital interaction affords new touchpoints, and this gives users much more flexibility (even empowering customers to self-design personal buying 'journeys'); this makes the service provision much more complex. As we have seen, users may have multiple service encounters as part of their service experience. Schmitt, Brakus, and Zarantonello (2015) suggest, every service exchange leads to a customer experience, regardless of its nature and form. One way for companies to manage this complexity is by the segmentation of customers by analysing:
- The use of specific touchpoints.
- The use of specific touchpoints at certain stages of the service process.
- The use of specific touchpoints at certain stages of the buying process.
- The digital devices used in interaction.
- How users' interpretations of satisfaction at each stage can be measured.

Research done by Herhausen *et al.* (2019) looks at how retailers can develop segment-specific customer journey strategies, identifying five *time-consistent* segments: store-focused shoppers, pragmatic online shoppers, extensive online shoppers, multiple touchpoint shoppers, and online-to-offline shoppers, and how companies can learn about how customer loyalty formation occurs at each point of segment. Similarly, Yachin (2018) explores the opportunity to learn from 'experiential discourse' of firm-customer encounters (user-generated content) in the micro-tourism sector suggesting that "the possibility to generate knowledge about experiential purposes is conditioned by the firm's ability to bestow encounters with an experience-like quality and promote the customers' transformation into participants" p. 216. The potentially powerful influence of "distal social others" or "travelling companions" in the shared social experience of consumption – motivation, search, evaluations, decision, and post-decision – is described as "the social customer journey, which extends prior perspectives on the path to purchase by explicitly integrating the important role that social others play throughout the journey" (Hamilton, Ferraro, & Haws, 2020, p. 68). This is peer-to-peer (C2C) influence.

Benefits can be:

- More focused value propositions.
- Differentiated competitive value propositions.
- Building competitive barriers or protection.
- Market surveillance of trends and competitive offers.
- Allocation and use of resources is more efficient due to deeper analysis of customer needs and wants.
- Enhanced internal clarification of inter-departmental functions which comes from established purpose, mission, strategy, and goals.
- Better customer retention and reduced churn.
- Increased revenues and profitability from existing customers.
- Enhanced performances from target segments.
- Targeting relevant audiences through accurate profiling.
- Improve customer response rate to campaigns, new products, behavioural prompts.
- Profiling from segmentation can improve customer acquisition and retention.
- Improved market penetration.

Principles in practice

Reframing neurodiversity via 'brand' *Dyslexic Advantage*

The word 'brand' traditionally lends itself to sales and marketing promotions. However, this textbook demonstrates how brands have become social mechanisms to connect individuals, organisations, and society, in creating brand purpose and fostering stakeholder value. Using perception to create social meaning through brands is a tried and tested strategy for building brand equity. However, using branding to change social perceptions of Dyslexia where 'learning differently' is generally misunderstood, is an altogether different proposition. Yet this is exactly what *Dyslexic Advantage*, a brand movement that is tackling neurodiversity head on, have done: *repositioning perceived disadvantage to celebrate difference and potential*. It must be noted that Dyslexia is just one form of neurodiversity to be celebrated in this way; others include ADHD, Autism, Dyspraxia, Dyscalculia, Dysgraphia, and Tourette's syndrome. However, for the purposes of the case, its focus is on Dyslexia. That being said, the advantages of learning and thinking differently apply to all, and that includes those who are neurotypical (Neurotypical means someone whose brain behaves in the same way as the majority of society).[111]

In the US, an early definition developed by the *National Institute of Child Health Development (NICHD)* and later adopted by the *International Dyslexia Association (IDA)* viewed dyslexia through a narrow lens of it being "a specific learning *disability* resulting from a deficit in the phonological component of language". It didn't, however, examine skills or capacities or *potential*. It didn't examine the *processing challenge* of Dyslexia. More importantly, it didn't acknowledge that people with Dyslexia may also excel at spatial reasoning, interconnected thinking, and display amazing creativity."[112] Whilst decoding the written word may be problematic, 'reasoning' skills such as 'mechanical', 'interconnected', 'narrative', and 'dynamic' can be the exact opposite. People like Albert Einstein, musician John Lennon, entrepreneur Richard Branson, architect Richard Rogers, novelist Vince Flynn, actors Anthony Hopkins and Tom Cruise, actress Kiera Knightly, cell phone pioneer Craig McCaw, and film maker Bryan Singer prove there is a link between dyslexic processing and having special abilities.

Enthused by their findings, they launched magazines, a Dyslexia library, talent awards, college scholarships, a website, and a dedicated online course for teachers. Their commitment to offering prescriptive advice to individuals, parents, teachers, and educational institutions quickly expanded into the creation of a non-profit organisation providing teaching and content with a scientifically-validated approach underpinned by data and insight via their purpose-built screener:

> *Neurolearning Social Purpose Corporation was founded in 2014 by learning specialists Drs Brock and Fernette Eide and technology innovator and entrepreneur Nils Lahr. They came together to address the need for accurate, accessible, and affordable tools that could help children and adults with different learning and cognitive styles, including dyslexia, to flourish.*[113]

The *Dyslexic Advantage* organisations in this group, along with other organisations such as *'Made by Dyslexia'* [114]based in the UK, all share a common purpose: building up brand positioning and value around the *strengths* of Dyslexia, rather than 'perceived' weaknesses. This is an insight-driven brand strategy inclusive of all types of people and a celebration of neurodiversity:

> *Scientific research shows that dyslexic children and adults process information differently from non-dyslexics and some of these changes may account for strengths in creative problem solving, entrepreneurial thinking, and certain types of learning and memory. An understanding of the advantage side of dyslexia is important for children to discover how they learn and remember best as well as for adults to find careers and work environments that allow them to work to their highest abilities.*[115]

---

111 https://www.healthassured.org/blog/neurodiversity/.
112 https://www.dyslexicadvantage.org/.
113 https://neurolearning.com/about-our-founders/.
114 https://www.madebydyslexia.org/.
115 https://www.dyslexicadvantage.org/.

Their book provides a comprehensive insight into what dyslexia is, but their organisation is a learning network, a social ecosystem, for everyone suffering with or providing support for dyslexia. In so doing, they have effectively 'positioned' Dyslexia as a brand, recognising the pattern of strengths, abilities, and talents which develop in people with Dyslexia, particularly in adults. This is what some people identified as the *dyslexic advantage*.

In 2011, there was recognition that Dyslexia is not a lack of intelligence. Leading experts in the fields of dyslexia and brain-based learning (neuro-learning), Brock and Fernette Eide – authors of '*The Dyslexic Advantage: Unlocking the Hidden Potential of the Dyslexic Brain*' – set about exploring how intelligence could be creatively harnessed. They knew from their work that dyslexia is quite common (over 20% of the UK population have this learning difficulty), and they discovered that those with this condition share a unique learning difference that they claim can create advantages in the classroom, on the job, or at home.

They see the 'advantage' of harnessing the positive sides of this neuro-diversity: "Cutting-edge research shows how dyslexic people perceive the written word differently, but also may excel at spatial reasoning, interconnected thinking, and display amazing creativity."[116]

6.6 Segmentation and the customer journey

Developing a successful omni-channel, multi-stage brand strategy rests on the foundations of insight from segmentation. Customers have a wide range of options with which to personalise their journey. Journey analytics uses information about the customer's *interaction choices* – how the customer navigates through touch points in the service encounter before, during, and after any purchase activity – and the reasons behind those interaction choices to build loyal relationships. User perceptions of value-in-use is a key determinant. "Omnichannel customer journeys are inherently individualistic but driven by effects that apply to any single interaction, sequencing effects, and customer journey patterns" (Barwitz & Maas, 2018, p. 116). For example, Alt, Săplăcan, Benedek, & Nagy (2021, p. 659) examine how digital technology facilitates insurance companies reaching customers via multi-channel access, and how users can be segmented by information search, purchasing channels, and personal characteristics in the digital environment. Information channel preferences were the most important clustering variables and the following segments were identified: 'Young Fully Offliners' (23.7%); 'Mature Fully Offliners' (31.5%); Committed Online Searchers (23.2%); and Cross-Channel Onliners (21.6%).

Dell Technologies, who had revolutionised the PC market with its configure-to-order (CTO) direct supply model and its 'inventory velocity' just-in-time (JIT) model,

---

116 https://www.dyslexicadvantage.org/.

found that this challenged their 'singular supply chain' strategy. They responded to the challenges of changing customer needs, the commoditisation of products, global pressures, and low-cost competition, by using segmentation to transform their supply chain into a portfolio of offerings focused on speed of delivery, product customisation, and cost efficiencies all derived from customer insights.

6.7 Narratives and knowledge from data

According to Dykes (2020, p. ix), the use of data as a marketing tool "has become one of the most valuable business assets". When data and stories are used together, they resonate on both an intellectual and emotional level (Smith, McCarthy, & Aaker, 2013) and act as "intentional artefacts that present data in an interesting, evocative, and informative way" (Feigenbaum & Alamalhodael, 2020), turning data into insights and insights into knowledge. As a vital enabler in driving change, storytelling is not just a core pillar of data literacy but a powerful strategic tool. Data is employed as enabling a "theorised storyline" (Golden-Biddle & Locke, 2007) where theorising is the product of abstracting, generalising, relating, selecting, explaining, synthesising, and idealising (Sutton & Straw, 1995). Duffy (2021) advocates the power of empathy and perspective in using data analytics: "Data and tactics do the most good when they feed insight and inform strategy. For that to happen, you will need more than research and analytical skills. You and your team will need to cultivate the skill of thinking from your target's perspective – to see the world as the buyer does" (p. 45).

6.8 Societal impacts of datafication in the age of the social customer

Traditional segmentation methods are still relevant in the socio-digital era: targeting influencers can enable cost-efficiencies in selecting appropriate platforms and delivering personalised messages; interactive individualised customer communications result from individualised customer analytics and purchase propensity modelling. Research has been done on the social implications of the widespread diffusion of digitisation. The ability of companies to track and manipulate individuals' digital data trails has both benefits and problems. Strategically exploiting digitised technologies by capturing digital data which drive "algorithmic decision-making" has created a "tension between businesses – that increasingly profile customers and personalise products and services – and individuals who are 'walking data generators' often unaware how the data is being used" (Newell & Marabelli, 2015, p. 3). Decision-making based on relationships suggested in the data might not be so obvious to the brand user and might actually narrow choices from the 'provoked' and 'considered' decision sets (Mayer-Schonberger & Cukier, 2013). This area is the 'Big

Data' analytics concept originally defined by Gartner (2001)[117] as having: *volume* (the amount of data determines the value); *variety* (cross-referenced data from different sources); and *velocity* (data are rapidly generated). One change imposed by data analytics is this: decision-making used to be path-dependent, affected by past knowledge and learning; following digitisation, decisions are past-determined. An example of business efficiency played off against individual freedom is *Edgerank* used by *Facebook* as trace data to weight 'likes' and modify a user's page. Compare the trade-offs and discriminations illustrated in Figure 6.1.

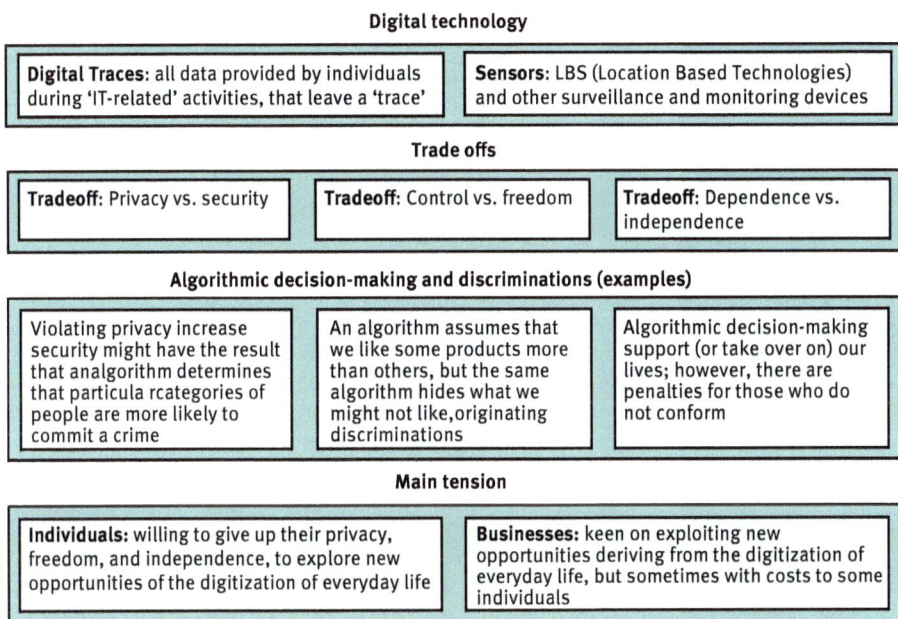

Digital technology

Digital Traces: all data provided by individuals during 'IT-related' activities, that leave a 'trace'	**Sensors**: LBS (Location Based Technologies) and other surveillance and monitoring devices

Trade offs

Tradeoff: Privacy vs. security	**Tradeoff**: Control vs. freedom	**Tradeoff**: Dependence vs. independence

Algorithmic decision-making and discriminations (examples)

Violating privacy increase security might have the result that analgorithm determines that particula rcategories of people are more likely to commit a crime	An algorithm assumes that we like some products more than others, but the same algorithm hides what we might not like,originating discriminations	Algorithmic decision-making support (or take over on) our lives; however, there are penalties for those who do not conform

Main tension

Individuals: willing to give up their privacy, freedom, and independence, to explore new opportunities of the digitization of everyday life	**Businesses**: keen on exploiting new opportunities deriving from the digitization of everyday life, but sometimes with costs to some individuals

Figure 6.1: Digital trade-offs and discriminations.
Source: Newell & Marabelli (2015, p.11)

As we have seen, digital technologies present businesses and brands with an opportunity to amass huge amounts of data across a wide range of sources. This leads to businesses and brands looking for ways to be more efficient and effective using algorithmic automated decision systems. This, of course, potentially turbo-charges a business ability to segment and profile customers and potential customers. This significant opportunity also carries a higher than ever regulatory risk. To the extent, that article 22 in the UK GDPR has provisions on: "(1) automated individual decision-

---

117 In 2001, Doug Laney (then at Gartner Research & Advisory) articulated the definition of Big Data as consisting of the 3 V's - volume, velocity and variety.

making (making a decision solely by automated means without any human involvement); (2) and profiling (automated processing of personal data to evaluate certain things about an individual). Profiling can be part of an automated decision-making process."[118]

Castets-Renard (2019) succinctly summarises the pitfalls and considerations when applying technologies to (customer) segmentation and profiling:

> *Digital technologies collect massive amounts of data and evaluate people in every aspect of their lives, such as housing and employment. This collected information is ranked through the use of algorithms. The use of such algorithms may be problematic. Because the results obtained through algorithms are created by machines, they are often assumed to be immune from human biases. However, algorithms are the product of human thinking and, as such, can perpetuate existing stereotypes and social segregation. This problem is exacerbated by the fact that algorithms are not accountable.*

Chapter takeaways

- Understanding your customer is understanding your business and this is the role of strategic segmentation.
- Segmenting customer data to reveal deep, actionable customer insights can enhance retention and customer development, monitor for indications of unwanted customer churn and lost patronage, examine potential for leveraging loyalty or re-motivating lapsed users, and continuously innovate customer-centric brands.
- Profiling can identify significant customer characteristics and provide insightful knowledge about an organisation's strengths and weaknesses and strategic fit.
- Customer-centricity involves aligning value propositions with the needs of the company's most valuable customers to maximise customer life-time value (CLV) and delivering optimal service to a heterogeneous customer base.
- CRM, predictive analytics, social media monitoring, content management systems, and marketing operations management are the technologies and capabilities most important to their real-time customer efforts today
- There is a danger that businesses and decision-makers are seduced by new technologies, that may offer some superficial tactical wins but don't deliver strategic value or impact.
- Customers have a wide range of options with which to personalise their journey. Journey analytics uses information about the customer's *interaction choices* – how the customer navigates through touch points in the service encounter before, during, and after any purchase activity – and the reasons behind those interaction choices to build loyal relationships.
- When data and stories are used together, they resonate on both an intellectual and emotional level and act as intentional artefacts that present data in an interesting, evocative, and informative way, turning data into insights, and insights into tangible actions.
- Strategically exploiting digitised technologies by capturing digital data which drive algorithmic decision-making has created a tension between businesses that increasingly profile customers and individuals who are walking data generators often unaware how the data is being used.

---

118 https://ico.org.uk/for-organisations/guide-to-data-protection/guide-to-the-general-data-protection-regulation-gdpr/individual-rights/rights-related-to-automated-decision-making-including-profiling/.

Closing case

Causeway Rescue: **From rescue and tragedy to micro-brand strategy**

When Shaun Heath, Founder of *Causeway Rescue*, was in the Middle-East helping a specialist NGO (Non-Governmental Organisation) train rescuers in Urban Rescue and Training, he was moved and inspired in equal measure. He knew full well that many of those rescuers would be putting their training into practice in the most harrowing of places, where communities had been ripped apart by natural disasters and wars. He had first-hand experience of how this type of train- ing was being deployed in war zones, where the 'rescuing' would include innocent women and children, and all too often this would also, sadly, include 'recovery'. And yet, in this most tragic of circumstances, he had an inspirational idea. *Causeway Rescue* – helping to improve Safety and Rescue standards in the UK, Ireland, and as part of international projects, building awareness and capability – if not yet officially formed, had been conceived, and Shaun set about turning his expertise and experiences into a micro-brand with the same purpose and meaning.

Heath explains how the principles of the very serious nature of what they do underpins the micro-brand strategy: brand credibility, service provider/service client trust, ensuring their clients invest meaning in their purpose, as well as being able to identify the marked difference of 'manual-ready' vs. 'first-hand' experience and capability of *Causeway* compared to their competitors:

> *Causeway is staffed and operated by rescue professionals. All personnel are either serving, have served, or retired from frontline operational roles as trainer responders within a specialist rescue team of a statutory rescue organisation based in Northern Ireland. Our staff have direct specialist rescue experience across a wide range of disciplines and incident types – Training operations and rescue at height, in collapsed structures, confined spaces, water (static and swift flowing) and first responder assistance, safety and rescue.*

> *Our staff also have experience on a strategic level, both within Causeway and their main employment. Their staff have developed and delivered Emergency Response Planning regarding Flood Response, Confined Space and Urban Search and Rescue.*

> *We have seen many training organisations offer services and products that are delivered by people who just don't have the experience in emergency situations. Our clients really connect with the fact our team and approach comes from a place of real-life situations and hard learning. We have always put brand at the heart of what we do, and really focused on the rescue elements, and the peace of mind our clients have in investing in our services. Even if it is a case of a 'What If?' scenario.*

> *We actively engage with our clients (and seek out clients who are willing to engage) in order to design and deliver training that meets their safety and rescue needs, develops their staff, and increases their preparation for and response to negative events.*

Causeway Rescue is a great example of how a start-up can construct a micro-brand strategy over many years – of being a statutory emergency responder, absorbing all the experiences, training and know-how, and sharpening this into a clear focused value proposition of fulfilling a basic and fundamental human need: *'certainty of existence'*. In a taxonomy of needs,[119] this goal (ie: *'safety and security'* delivering end-states of reassurance and peace of mind for their clients spanning public and private sectors) is the 'apex' position. An example of this is that in the UK, by 2021 (mid-year) of the 142 workers killed in work accidents in 2020/21, over half were in the Agriculture, Forestry and Fishing and Construction sectors (which was similar to earlier years), with the highest proportion being 35 coming from falls from a height.[120]

The question is, can a start-up develop an iterative and insight-based micro-brand strategy with limited resources and without the help of professional expertise?

---

119 Riess and Havercamp (1998) Toward a Comprehensive Assessment of Fundamental Motivation: Factor Structure of the Riess Profiles 'in' Franzen and Moriarty (2008) Art and Science of Branding, M. E. Sharpe.

120 https://www.hse.gov.uk/statistics/pdf/fatalinjuries.pdf.

Time and time again, start-ups and small organisations (as well as large in some cases) fall into the trap of taking an extremely narrow view on what 'brand is' and not considering its customers/potential customers in this dynamic. Sometimes, a limited approach, often overly product-driven, lacking any type of customer insights/feedback, and only having a name, logo design, and website constitutes a minimal 'brand identity' strategy. This is usually because the need to tackle the day-to-day running of the business, where resources are limited and cashflow control is critical, more often than not restricts appointing expensive creative and brand agencies, leaving the initiative squarely at the feet of the Founder or if they are lucky, a co-founder.

With a nod to its Northern Irish heritage and positive associations of outdoor imagery, Heath reflects how *Causeway's* own micro-brand strategy has been years in the making, and how its core brand values run right through the business:

> *I have been fortunate to work in a number of rescue NGOs and at height training companies. This was invaluable experience in defining Causeway's unique brand proposition. I learnt lots of useful things and also how some businesses don't actually match what the brand says it is about and what it delivers. When setting up Causeway, I was determined to spend the extra time in evaluating what we stood for and what we could/would deliver, against what our customer's actually value and need. We continually assess and manage our brand against the feedback we get from our customer, potential clients, our team and other stakeholders. At the start of the journey it was clear that safety and security, was really important. Over the period we have been operating, it has been further reinforced that fundamentally we are aligned to deliver peace of mind, confidence and capability for our clients and their team on the ground. They know that if something goes wrong there is a plan in place that could save a life. A really, simple but compelling purpose.*
>
> *The Causeway Rescue team are amazing, and I am very proud to have had feedback from our clients that when things have gone wrong – as they can do – the training kicks in and that has ensured a positive outcome.*

Recent client feedback from one of *Causeway's* corporate clients underlines this point:

> *Causeway Rescue have carried out 'confined space entry and rescue services' for us on nu-merous occasions. They are exceptionally professional, diligent and always prepared to go the extra mile for us when needed. Their background in professional rescue reassures me that if something were to go wrong, we have the right people on site ready to react.*

> *The Causeway team have also delivered many confined space courses for Whitemountain (part of Breedon Group Plc). These were bespoke to suit our specific confined space needs and delivered to the highest standards. Causeway can do what most other training and ser-vice providers can't.*

The critical factor in determining how Shaun achieved his ambition of turning his meaningful ambitions into a brand reality was to start with a 'feedback' mind-set which helped inform a micro-brand approach, simply starting with the 'need-state analysis'. This is a great starting point for any Founder/start-up as it allows a simple, universal value-proposition focus to iden-tify customer needs and wants. 'Needs' tend to be push processes;[121] 'wants' are pull pro-cesses. In the case of *Causeway* this was a basic but powerful anchor which guided many aspects of their business.

For instance, their training and development programmes, sales and marketing collateral, digital content strategies, advertising campaigns, the core values of the brand, and how that dictates the type of people they recruit, the standards upon which they want their employees to behave and deliver to, are all critical in laying strong foundations from which an emerging cus-tomer-company brand culture can be created. This is particularly relevant for 'high-growth scale-ups' as it allows them to grow rapidly, aligning brand identity (internal company view) with brand image (external-customer view).

For a start-up, if this anchor is not in place, it is highly likely short-term necessity of day-to-day business survival can distract from long-term brand development and growth. Brand strat-egy may become more generic, overly product-driven, lack distinctiveness; the 'brand', as such, may barely be recognised, and, even more concerning, customers may be unable to discern their brand value in relation to their competitors.

Questions
1. What are the advantages for small start-ups such as *Causeway Rescue* in constructing a brand strategy ahead of actual launch?
2. Research what is meant by a taxonomy of needs and explain how *Causeway Rescue* have ap-plied this to their value proposition.
3. List the key ingredients of a successful customer-company relationship for micro-brands.

---

121 Franzen and Moriarty (2008) Art and Science of Branding, M. E. Sharpe.

7 Managing the customer journey: Strategic service approaches to the consumption experience

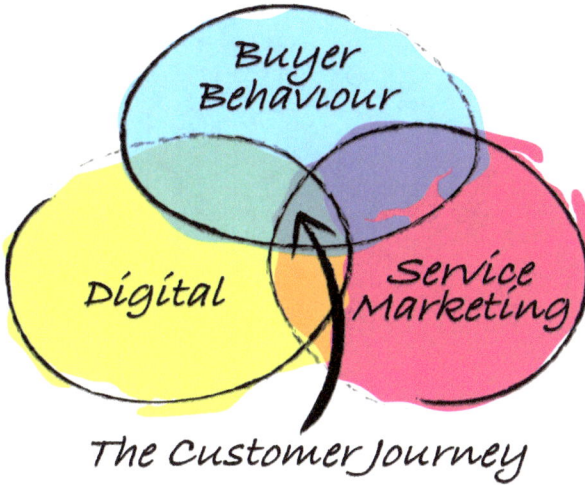

https://doi.org/10.1515/9783110718638-011

Opening case

Premier League Fantasy: Tribal boundaries cast aside for points

'Gamification' is an online marketing technique designed to encourage engagement by simulating the experience of real game dynamics and mechanics in non-game contexts. One such example is a growing App-based phenomenon that is changing the way football (soccer) fans are engaging and consuming the *English Premier League* – it is called *'Fantasy Premier League'* (*FPL*) football. Such is its power, and subsequent diffusion, that there are scenarios, stretching all over the world where staunch and multi-generational fans, who may have culturally inherited *'their'* real team, often with season tickets, express group affiliation by life-time support and often animosity towards rival teams and their players. The actual *Premier League* is a real powerhouse in terms of brand value – "hitting €8.5bn in brand value in 2020, 19% more than La Liga and Bundesliga combined. Besides leading in brand value, the Premier League also generates the highest revenue of all the European football leagues and has the highest operating profit."[122] This gamification has effectively added a new dimension to the *Premier League's* overall brand value and meaning, via an enthralling and engaging App-based game.

Tribalist lines emanate from the 'real' game of *Premier League* football. And, yet conversely in the virtual world of *FPL*, the power play of the game, with its immersive customer engagement and journey, means that these rivalries are abandoned and players that are cast as the villain in real stadia on a Saturday become the hero on the virtual game of *FPL* and innate passion is replaced for points.

The following outlines the broad rules and appeal of the game:

> *The (physical) Premier League consists of 20 teams, each of whom play each other twice, resulting in a season of 380 fixtures split into 38 unique game weeks, with each generally containing ten fixtures. A manager in FPL has a virtual budget of £100m at the initiation of*

---

122 https://londonlovesbusiness.com/premier-league-hits-e8-5bn-in-brand-value/

the season from which they must build a squad of 15 players from the approximately 600
available. Each player's price is set initially by the game's developers based upon their per-
ceived value to the manager within the game, rather than their real-life transfer value.[123]

For over 7 million users, the game of *Fantasy Football* has transformed historically mundane fixtures to the casual fan, into a knife-edge fixation of, for example, what if a goalkeeper has kept a
clean sheet or some obscure midfielder has potentially scored a hattrick? Surely the prize of such
a pull, dedication, and transformation should be significant? A luxury, once in a life-time holiday?
Life-changing cash prize? No. If a user beats the other 7 million users, it is a modest, all-inclusive
7-night stay in the UK and a VIP hospitality trip away to *Premier League* games, as well as a *Nike*
manager coat, as well as other perhaps less inspirational prizes.[124] Arguably the size of the prize
doesn't align with the time, energy, research and dedication required to excel in the game. For
the rest, the glory resides in the bragging rights, where the narrowest of margins in points can
make all the difference is the difference between success and failure within their private leagues,
which span work and social circles, and geographical regions of the world.

For instance, in 2018–19, two-thirds of *FPL* managers were from overseas. Indeed, the success of players on the pitch, teams and the brand value of the league overall, tends to positively
impact the customer engagement in the game, be it player-specific, region or even gender:

This year's edition saw fans in Egypt register almost 700,000 teams, representing the most
managers in a country outside the UK and nearly 10 per cent of all participants, as the na-
tion's hero Mohamed Salah was joined by compatriot Trezeguet in the Premier League. The
game also grew elsewhere in Africa, as numbers in Nigeria rose 57 per cent, while there was
an increase of 60 per cent in Kenya. There was also a noticeable rise in female managers,
with 24 per cent more women and girls taking part compared to the previous season.[125]

The customer journey of *FPL* parallels that of the actual *Premier League*: the latter having successfully designed and developed a brand-customer engagement strategy that hooks casual
users into a more compelling brand relationship based on self-identification and group allegiance to a specific football club; the former expanding this, going beyond traditional and tribal
boundaries. The critical factors of success lie in the strategic interactivity with the App and how
meaning is created in their *FPL* customer journey both at an individual and social-group level.
'Meaning' is elevated where players simulate the role of being a manager by choosing their
team, making transfers, and effectively adding meaning to fixtures that historically were mean-
ingless. The processes of group formation and social identity are key to understanding human
behaviour in any social domain, and even though it is principally a virtual customer journey, the
interactive, social dynamic in *FPL* is no different. It has fostered a customer journey experience
of virtual gamification where interactions with explicit rules and norms, acceptable and unacceptable group behaviour, are analogous to service processes. For some, this has affected their real-life
engagement with real football. The following encapsulates the change in how *FPL* 'managers' view
the brand and are interacting with *FPL*. Holly Shand, founder of the Fantasy Football Community:

123 O'Brien JD, Gleeson JP, O'Sullivan DJP (2021) Identification of skill in an online game: The case
of *Fantasy Premier League*. PLoS ONE 16(3): e0246698. https://doi.org/10.1371/journal.pone.
0246698 https://fantasy.premierleague.com/prizes
124 https://fantasy.premierleague.com/prizes
125 https://www.premierleague.com/season-review/the-fans/1749131?articleId=1749131

I'm constantly making notes on substitutions, injuries and set-piece takers – FPL has completely changed how I follow football. Last-minute winner . . . Moments later, millions of phones flash with WhatsApp messages, pinged between FPL-dedicated group chats. Twitter and Reddit are alight with tales of joy and despair. The conversation isn't centred on the goal, nor the Premier League title race. Instead, it's all about doubled captain totals, squandered points and mini-league ramifications.[126]

Fundamentally, the *FPL* and the *Premier League* brands have found the sweet spot of digital engagement, with a smooth customer journey, rooted in the interactivity of users and the co-creation of value and meaning, reinforcing private and public group interactions that reinforce the brand so as to strengthen emotional, psychological, or physical investments (Chaffey, 2011). The game creates habitualised behaviour, with its key features and appeal of the wider *Premier League* brand acting as a catalyst in the success of its gamification. Mark Griffiths, a psychologist and director of the International Gaming Research Unit at Nottingham Trent University, agrees: "Fun, excitement and competition are the three most rewarding features of gaming. So, if you enjoy Fantasy Football, find it stimulating and are doing better than your friends, endorphins and other pleasure chemicals will be released into the body."[127]

Casting aside real tribal boundaries for virtual points is one thing, but the excitement of engagement in the simulated customer journey of the online gaming world of *EPL* is no fantasy at all. It is not football as we know it, but for its millions of players, it is real engagement.

---

126 https://www.wired.co.uk/article/fantasy-premier-league
127 https://www.wired.co.uk/article/fantasy-premier-league

Questions
1. Identify five ways within which the *FPL* gamification helps improve the overall brand value of the *Premier League* globally?
2. What role for interactivity play in the continued success of the *FPL*?
3. To what extent does brand meaning and social identity play in *FPL*?

Note: The photo(s) used in this case study is/are not connected and/or does not represent any brand(s) mentioned. It/they is/are used to make a visual discussion point by the authors.

7.1 Outline of chapter

Value is not embedded in the product at the moment of transactional exchange, but obtained through consumption processes (Tynan, McKechnie, & Chhuon, 2010) *at the point of interaction.* Indeed, how the customer experiences a brand through encounters with the company via service processes is almost as important as the actual product or service itself: it is an essential test of the value proposition. It is also a complex phenomenon. Customer experience (CX) – creating memorable moments of engagement – is a key arena of strategy development for organisations. Better service provision is based on knowing the customer better. What the customer experiences of the brand in the interface with the company, and how the company manages customer expectations and service encounters, is crucial in creating value and understanding individual and often complex buyer behaviour.

One way for companies to manage CX is to take a *process* view in order to model interactions, touchpoints, pain points, customer decision points, and idiosyncratic consumption behaviour. Companies try to create satisfactory end-to-end customer experiences matched to customer expectations. When there is a perceived break-down in expected service, pain points are basically customer subjective interpretation of 'problems' that may occur at interaction, customer journey, or relationship levels. Pain points may be usability issues, confusing self-service instructions, lack of problem resolution, no personal communication, inconsistent experience across channels, irrelevant Q&A responses, or lack of agent knowledge. They may incur time or financial costs to the customer, or result in a lack of confidence or trust in the process, the company and ultimately the brand.

Although this is generally a 'consumer' service problem, customers in B2B markets, (where nearly 50% of purchasing is now online), are reportedly disillusioned with the online customer experience. Research suggests that 52% of B2B buyers experience frustration with online buying resulting in 53% switching supplier for all purchases. Lack of functionality (61%), slow load speeds (60%), and finding it hard to find products (32%) were the main reasons cited.[128]

Identifying and resolving pain points is essential to enhance customer journey experience. They can be examined and resolved by extracting qualitative data through employing Critical Incident Techniques (CIT). There is increasing C-suite recognition that "outside-in businesses recognise that digital marketing and customer success are really two sides of the same customer journey coin".[129] Mapping customer experience against expectations – the *customer journey* – is a method of systemising the value creation process, and an optimisation point to impact the customer's decision-making.

With roots in 'flowcharting' and 'blueprinting' in service marketing, managing the customer journey is a service instrument for detailing individual customer decision process cycles. Indeed, progenitors for the 'customer journey' are the 'service encounter' with its moment of truth bullfight metaphor (Normann, 1984), and the 'servicescape', originally a conceptual framework developed by Booms & Bitner (1981) to analyse the physical environment within which consumption takes place.

According to *Data Trends*,[130] 80% of marketers claim that the customer journey is a key factor in successful customer-centric brand strategy. This chapter is about understanding who customers are; how audiences are effectively targeted and provided for by segmenting existing and potential customers into groups through 'personas'; how customer relationships with the organisation, brand, and service are affected by individual perception and experience; and what companies have to do to design and implement an appropriate value-in-use customer journey.

It analyses what organisations need to understand to compete in the increasingly digital world of service, how it affects consumption, and how AI-powered platforms enable automation of the customer experience (ACX), effectively and efficiently providing seamless customer engagement. It explains why technology is not the actual customer experience but an *enabler* of the customer experience; it recognises that although customer experience is part of the brand, the brand is not more valuable than customer experience.

Learning outcomes

After reading this chapter, you'll be able to:
- Define and understand what the concept of the 'customer journey' is and explain why customer insights from data help companies to improve it.
- Establish the critical links between buyer behaviour, service marketing, and brand strategy.

---

128 Report by Wunderman Thompson, featured in "B2B, values, convenience: 5 interesting stats to start your week", *Marketing Week*, 27th Sep 2021.
129 Joe Fuca, President and CEO of Reputation.com, Forbes Technology Council, "Why Customer Experience Matters Now More Than Ever", *Forbes*, January 14th, 2021
130 *Data Trends*, June, 2021.

- Evaluate why having a strategic 'service' approach to managing the customer experience underpins the customer-company relationship.
- Explain what 'touchpoints' are, why they are critically important to understanding and enhancing customer experience management and the decision-making 'journey'.
- Critically analyse how and why digital engagement is becoming the established norm of customer experience management.
- Demonstrate how 'listening' to the customer's 'voice' is essential to enhancing the customer journey.

7.2 Introduction

In the wake of the COVID-19 pandemic, digital expectations and consumer shopping habits have changed irreversibly, with 78% of consumers saying that the online experience is better and easier (*2021 Digital Consumer Trends Index*)[131] than the 'physical' experience. In addition, consumers have been forced to engage with companies online because of 'Lockdown' restrictions, resulting in a greater level of complexity that consumers are now willing to undertake online.

Mark Evans, Managing Director of *Direct Line Group*, the UK's biggest provider of insurance, supports this: "Insurance claims are a complex, sequential process but we've seen more customers willing to go through it. Expect more complicated journeys to take place online".[132] Evans is referring here to the time-logical sequence of positive and negative touchpoints his customer's experience during engagement in the purchase process with his company. Fixing 'pain points' as part of the customer journey experience has an impact on customer lifetime value and loyalty. Managing 'backstage' service actions to support customer satisfaction is an integral part of brand strategy.

How the company *conceives* value and how the consumer *perceives* value affects the digital consumption experience, not only impacting on short-term perceptions of transactional satisfaction but conditioning long-term brand loyalty. There can be a difference in perception. For example, in a survey[133] of 362 companies, 80% of senior executives claimed that their companies provided an excellent service. Only 8% of their customers agreed. Evaluation must be done through the eyes of the consumer.

This is the *customer journey* (sometimes referred to as the 'buyer journey'), the service experience which is an amalgam of multiple customer-company encounters

---

[131] "2021 Digital Consumer Trends Index", Cheetah Digital & Econsultancy, *Marketing Week*, 2021
[132] Mark Evans, Managing Director, *Direct Line Group*, speaking at the DX Summit 2021 *Festival of Marketing*, June 2021.
[133] *Bain & Co* Senior Executive Survey, 2019

in the user experience. It is a record and a blueprint of the customer's experience and may focus on a specific part or look holistically at the totality of experiences.

Customer experience is a complicated construct and it requires a broad definition here. Homburg Jozić, & Kuehnl provide us with a comprehensive description: "Customer experience is the evolvement of a person's sensorial, affective, cognitive, relational, and behavioural responses to a service offering by living through a journey of touchpoints along pre-purchase, purchase, and post-purchase situations and continually judging this journey against response thresholds of co-occurring experiences" (2015, p. 384).

In some respects, the customer journey has become the product. It can guide a customer through a company's product and service processes; it can provide a company with customer knowledge to help that process such as consumer perceptions of 'risk', process, and lifestyle convenience.

Customer satisfaction is the driver behind development of the customer journey concept, but the tools have been marketing research and service design. Some of that research has focused on: analysing customer behaviour (Lemon & Verhoef, 2016); testing experience-centric services (Zomerdijk & Voss, 2010); and evaluation of service perceived quality (Halvorsrud, Kvale, & Følstad, 2016). Making a competitive difference by engineering a better customer journey – experience differentiation – is at the heart of success stories of the likes of *Amazon, Directline, Google*, or *Apple*. It is why *Paypal, Apple Pay, Clearpay*, and *Klarna* have made inroads into the competitive, mature finance sector. *PayPal*, the online payments giant with over 400m worldwide active accounts, bought *Paidy*, a Japanese 'Buy Now, Pay Later' (BNPL) company for $2.7bn in late 2021, reflecting the BNPL point-of-sale loans boom during the COVID-19 pandemic.

According to Deloitte (2013),[134] "The digital age is disrupting traditional customer service models – new customer touch points are appearing the world over at breakneck speed and against a backdrop of rising expectations". Digital disruption has forced companies to enhance, transform or create entirely new business models. The phenomenon of omni-channels – brand strategy that integrates all available channels to create a seamless shopping experience that increases customer convenience and engagement during the purchase process – affects a wide variety of retail: marketing, commerce, communications, and information systems (Mosquera, Olarte Pascual, & Juaneda Ayensa, 2017).

Michelle Roberts, Group Marketing Director at car giant *BMW*, claimed that *the* COVID-19 pandemic has effectively compressed 10 years digital acceleration into one. Speaking at the *CX* Summit, she said: "We know that customers absolutely want to have the choice between on- and off-line experiences, but they want them

---

134 "The Digital Transformation of Customer Services: Our View", *Deloitte Touche Tohmatsu Limited*, 2013

to be humanised. We know they're happy for those experiences to be transactional, straight-forward, seamless".[135] However, this is not uniformly the case; consumers are heterogenous, and their expectations differ: some require speed; some require care. Evaluating data (eg: sales, e-commerce metrics such as retention, customer lifetime value, digital touchpoint reaction to availability, accuracy of deliveries, relationship NPS) to assess customer service needs is critical. Quantitative measurement can result in greater qualitative customer satisfaction. For example, correlating 'NPS to retention' is an important measure in the Insurance market. An insightful comment from Roberts is key here: "Two years ago, we put our staff through a "best for customer" training programme so we could recalibrate around what the premium experience looks like and how they can shift the dial. Within my team, I've set up individuals who are customer journey managers looking at the product from end to end".

Customer journeys now mainly begin, and sometimes end, online. In today's digital world, every consumer is exposed to some form of digital technology, and every company must understand what it is to be a digital organisation. There are many examples of disruption (mainly through digital technology but not exclusively) which have changed customer expectations and organisations' value propositions. A new approach to customer service strategy is required as this digital disruption is redefining the consumption experience, and companies must provide a fuller service with a greater purpose in the battle for customers. Two common denominators which are the central focus of buyer behaviour, service marketing, customer relationship management, branding, and the application of segmentation in the Digital Age are firstly, the *heterogeneity of consumption* – not all customers are the same and require differing degrees of service – and, secondly, *human experience drives business*. Whilst branding is still a vital cog in the marketing machine, it is the heterogenous customer experience which has been gaining traction with academics and practitioners alike, and it is the management of this which is the driving force of strategy.

Companies like *Google*, *Facebook* and *LinkedIn* spend relatively little on traditional advertising but have grown through offering valuable customer experiences which are passed on to and shared with other customers. The digital consumption experience is a hybrid process of analysing, profiling, and servicing individual customer needs at all *touchpoints* on the journey from prospective buyer to loyal brand ambassador, providing appropriate, relevant support for brand users and lifetime customer value of organisations. Customer satisfaction is an evergreen, on-going goal of any organisation. One way to monitor and manage this is by following customers on their buying journey through each touchpoint.

---

135 Michelle Roberts, UK Group Marketing Director, *BMW*, speaking at the DX Summit 2021 *Festival of Marketing*, June 2021.

7.3 Defining what a 'Customer Journey' is

As an integral part and foundation of a customer engagement strategy, an empathetic, customer-oriented approach – how, when, and why typical customer engagement occurs – needs to be taken. In other words, plotting and analysing the *customer journey* in every 'moment of truth' touchpoint at all stages of interaction from the initial state of unawareness, navigating websites and apps, through the conversion vortex of persuasion and purchase, to the cognitive dissonance stage of brand rejection or reinforcement. Tracking and analysing customer behaviour across omni-channel interfaces will provide opportunities to enhance customer experience, reinforce loyalty, and drive continued engagement.

Customer expectation is constantly changing and companies have to be agile in their response. For example, according to research, while shopping online, 45% of consumers would like to be able to filter products by the values that matter to them, such as sustainability and diversity. This rises to nearly two thirds for shoppers aged 25 to 34.[136] Drilling down for insights by interrogating data to identify user motivation, customer churn, migration, where engagement peaks and when disengagement happens, where assistance is required to unblock engagement, helps provide a better customer experience by making the customer journey appropriate and useful.

Tools which provide rich data insights (eg: visual 'heat maps' representing customer activity) can be linked to analysis of goals and corresponding key performance indicators (KPIs). Segmentation of the customer base by the use of primary and secondary 'personas' created from behavioural attributes and interests, and simulating relevant experiences through 'scenarios' can help align appropriate communications based on customers' needs, behaviour, and purchase/search history and so on. Buyer personas are data-driven fictional customer profiles of actual and 'ideal' target customers, a tool which helps assess likely service requirements and decision-making stages. These are inserted into an imaginary customer journey experience, providing an 'outside-in', customer-centric focus.

As discussed in the previous chapter, there are multiple ways within which segmentation variables, sample groups, and indeed customer journey stages can be applied. Figure 7.1 below has been adapted from Kotler, Pfoertsc, & Sponholz (2020, p. 183) which originally showed how market segmentations (macro-level) can connect with persona mapping (micro-level) aligning to empathy mapping, skills attitudes, behaviours, mental modes, and user experiences etc. It could be argued that there is significant value in creating highly contextual and tailored customer personas.

---

136 *Data & Marketing Association*, featured in *Marketing Week* 27th Sep 2021.

Some of the application of this is evidenced in the *FUZE* Chapters later on in *Section 4* relating to *Freedome*, *Inspired Villages*, *Festival of Thrift*, and the *University of Cumbria*, showing different perspectives of how this principle is applied. Whilst they all have specific foci based on the outcome of that related book chapter/mirrored theoretical section, each one has adopted this hybrid version of segmentation, customer personas mapped against the specific customer journeys. For instance, the *University of Cumbria* and *FUZE* applied a unique 'learning expectations and experience model' that also mapped the dual-student customer journey. This refers to the complex dynamic of students who undergo dual journeys at University, and how they perceive and experience the learning and customer elements at different points of university life whether that is formal and/or informal learning and whole-person development. This had a significant bearing on: developing personas that informed the University's (and Institute's) brand positioning and awareness building; updating the pathway to purchase via a strategic website; development through to conversion strategy; and a student experience and satisfaction programme design and development. This was extended all the way through to building alumni brand loyalty.

However, the model and personas were only relevant to *this* University, based on their key strategy, place offering, people, brand heritage and local economy/typology, and other key macro-factors. This context must inform the segmentation model, development of personas, and potentially fusing this context with empathy mapping.

Kotler *et al.* (2013) go some way to combining these views, but arguably applies it from a UX perspective, which is inherently applied qualitatively, rather than using it as a useful framework to bridge the unique context required at micro-level. There is no set 'formula' but merging, developing, and applying segments to personas to the specific contexts (and in some cases mapped to customer journeys) provides a useful approach that is tailored. Figure 7.1 is simply applied to the *University of Cumbria*, and summarised this visually:

Principles in practice

Predicting digital trends in 2021
Forrester Research predict the following likely digital trends in 2021:

Products. Digital products and services are the way you will reinvent your business models and customer relationships. By the end of 2021, we expect 30% of Global 2000 companies to have a significant digital product portfolio and 20% to stand up digital divisions dedicated to launching disruptive products to accelerate their transformation to full ecosystem participation.

Practices. In 2021, every new digital division will embrace innovation through ecosystems, and we expect a further 50% of enterprises to make cloud-centric transformation a priority, moving business-critical operational apps and all experience apps into the cloud. Agile practices will infuse every facet of planning and execution, spanning business, operations, and technology teams.

Platforms. In 2020, enterprise resource planning became digital operations platforms (DOPs), reconceived as the agile, AI-based backbone of your digital core. In 2021, vendors will tailor DOPs with more industry-specific functionality. Enterprises will also expand their use of bridging systems such as product information management or marketplace platforms to accelerate the digital shift and boost operational excellence.

Partners. The pandemic forced an existential decision: What's the least you could do and the most you could get from partners? In 2021, this innovation through ecosystems, once the exclusive superpower of start-ups, will become the strategy for every digital initiative. In 2021, service providers will seek to be your co-innovation partner and support value exchange through adopting outcomes-based pricing.

Places. In 2021, brands will broaden where they place a "buy" button. For digital leaders, it won't just be a decision between *Shopify+* and custom-coding a headless commerce solution – or *Facebook Shops* and *Amazon Business*. It will be about experimenting and unifying all these channels, supported by investments in personalization, digital asset management, and even augmented and virtual reality, which will accelerate as sellers look to stand out on the digital shelf and boost search rankings.

Source: *Forrester Research* 2021

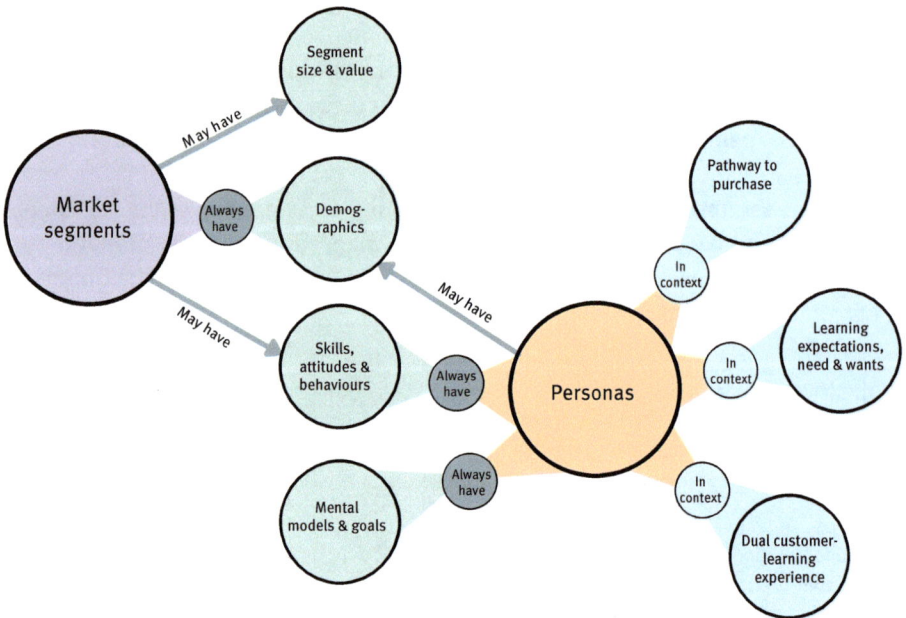

Figure 7.1: Overlaps & blindspots between market segments & personas.
Source: Adapted from Kotler (2000)

There needs to be a distinction made between the customer journey and the consumption experience, and the fact that reaction to interaction may be multi-faceted – "cognitive, affective, emotional, social and physical" (Verhoef, *et al.*, 2009).

These interactions or touchpoints have the ability to influence a consumers buying or intent to purchase, all throughout the five stages of the buyer purchasing decision-making process: problem recognition, information search, the evaluation of alternatives, purchase decision, and post-purchase behaviour (Kotler, Burton, Deans, Brown, & Armstrong, 2013). A target audience (or market) is a group of consumers a company has decided to organise its marketing strategies to reach with their message (Kurtz, 2010). One method of effectively segmenting for digital audiences is simplifying existing and potential customers into groups through *personas*. Essentially, a persona is "a detailed profile of a particular subset of people within the broad target audience" (Barker, Barker, Bormann, & Neher, 2013, p. 48). Personas comprise: demographics such as age, Internet experience and spending habits; constraints such as technological limitations, language barriers; and needs and wants, customer requirement that may be turn a 'persona' into real-life customer (Lurie, 2006).

Precisely targeted marketing is essential for both company efficiency and to add value to customers. As Scott (2009, p. 32) advises: "If we break the buyers into distinct groups and then catalogue everything (that) we know about each one, we make it easier to create content targeted to each important demographic". Segmenting by purchase potential, social media usage rate, family structure and so on, is a much more accurate way of analysing potential customers. Next, assessing people by constraints does not necessarily make them inaccessible but will require a shift in approach or media used. Then, taking into account the personal desires, needs and wants of individuals gives better accuracy. Using imaginary, fictitious personas helps to model in order to communicate with real people fitting that persona. Creating personas from scratch entails: identifying persona roles; listing all needs and situational triggers from concerns to symptoms; and creating messaging objectives suited to each persona's needs that you have the experience to address (Golden, 2011, p. 87). In order to combat the *spam* of communications (unnecessary, intrusive advertising due to poorly targeted mass communications), social media messages have to be very accurately targeted. Figure 7.2 illustrates that even though all of these spheres show all of the target audience, the *optimal target audience* is located where need, interest, and money intersect.

Eric Schmidt (of *Google*) claimed some time ago in 2010 that "It would be very hard for people to watch or consume something that has not in some senses been tailored for them". Whilst this may have social issues of privacy, control, and independence, it demonstrates the shift in buyer behaviour as a result of the digital transformation. This phenomenon has been accelerated by the COVID-19 pandemic, changing the traditional business model, and putting the emphasis on a streamlined, convenient online consumption experience:

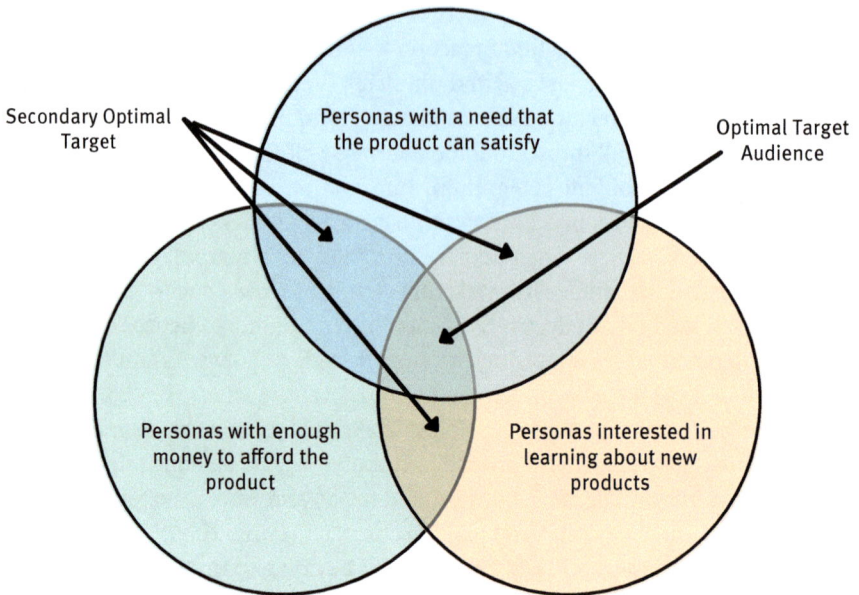

Figure 7.2: Relationship between types of persona.
Source: Lurie (2020)

- The consumer decision-making process (DMP) has become more fragmented and can occur in non-contextual situations (ie: not now always in store, before the actual product, in the company of salespeople, in more relaxed situations).
- A non-linear decision-making process.
- Asymmetric purchasing power has been reversed online with the consumer in the seller's position of being empowered with immediate access to deeper and broader product knowledge.
- Individualised heterogenous consumption with maximised customisation and optimum choice variation.
- Online browsing facilitates Reverse Showrooming (search online/purchase in-store).
- The conduit of mobile technology connects, searches, purchases, tracks, and reinforces consumption conveniently and quickly. Mobile has now exceeded desktop for search. *Google* factors mobile-orientation in its search algorithm.
- Search and selection process is a remote, controlled experience.
- Fewer steps needed in the decision-making process (DMP).
- Trust and loyalty is an essential ingredient of purchase.
- Peer-to-peer recommendations can affect brand selection. 77% of customers use online reviews prior to purchase; 93% of purchases are influenced by social media.

- The bi-directional communication capabilities of the Internet to create accelerated Word of Mouth on a scale not known prior to digitisation impacts on brand awareness, brand building, customer retention, service, and product development, and can reinforce quality control through user C2B and C2C feedback.
- Payments made by mobile provide a seamless experience.
- Content marketing via social media can be relevant, add value and reinforce recommendation.
- The convenience of using Voice Enabled Search (eg: *Amazon's Alexa, Google's Assist* or *Apple's Siri*), has changed retail search.
- Virtual Reality (VR) and Augmented Reality (AR) which allows virtual use and simulated application.

Accompanying the customer journey can be a channel 'roadmap' of engagement with an omnichannel holistic strategy that drives customer engagement. Progenitors of the customer journey are the service 'flowchart'. Flowcharting the nature and sequence of service delivery helps us understand the totality of the customer's service experiences. Experiencing the firm's value proposition may involve all or some of the components of the service for the customer; processes have to be designed to offer coherency, compatibility, and reinforcement of service elements. Flowcharting can help service providers to do this.

In addition, insight into how customer's perception varies between the four categories of service – people processing, possession processing, mental stimulus processing, and information processing – will provide insight into the nature of customer involvement and engagement. A more sophisticated version of flowcharting is *service blueprints*: the former is a static representation of an existing process; the latter is detailed real-time plan of how the service process should be constructed and what parts are visible to the customer. Blueprints can provide a common cross-functional, inter-departmental perspective aimed at maximising customer satisfaction and operational efficiency.

As processes are the architecture of services (Lovelock & Wirtz, 2011, p. 219), blueprints detailing processes involving flows, sequences, relationships, and dependencies (Shostack, 1992, p. 76), is an apposite metaphor. Blueprints are a framework which allow closer examination of customer-company interaction – the interface between internal actions and external perceptions. This practical concept allows managers to identify potential *fail* and *pain points* where there is risk of the service provision failing, and can help determine the role of customers as passive recipients or as active co-producers in service provision. Whilst it is axiomatic to suggest that "value is always uniquely and phenomenologically determined by the beneficiary" (Vargo & Lusch, 2006, p. 19), it is nonetheless an essential truth: customer experience is subjective and involves intangible factors which requires us to acknowledge that we must learn from customers to understand the customer's perception of value.

As a consequence, product and service development has to be managed with customer complicity (Kumar, *et al.*, 2010). Yachin (2018, p. 201) suggests that "the possibility to generate knowledge about experiential purposes is conditioned by the firm's ability to bestow encounters with an experience-like quality and promote the customers' transformation into participants", facilitated by involving customers in customer journey planning, using user-generated content (UGC), learning about customers' subjective perception of value, adopting an experiential discourse, and utilising in-situ supporting moments to socialise. In the context of tourism, he describes a three-stage journey of prospective pre-trip period phase, an active tourism experience, and a reflective post-trip phase:

- *Prospective phase*: involves information search, decision-making and the booking process itself. This phase also includes the time after the experience was booked and before the actual trip. The value created is in the 'anticipation'.
- *Active phase*: both the customer and the firm are at the same place at the same time. The experience (the core of the activity) is preceded and followed by in-situ transition moments. At this phase, the interactions between the firm and customer are arguably most intense, and value is created through participation.
- *Reflective phase*: value is created through a recollection of the experience, using a nostalgic reinterpretation of events, satisfaction, and enhanced self-image.

Sørensen & Jensen (2015, p. 336) differentiate *service* and *experience* encounters: service encounters are standard service process one-way deliveries designed to satisfy functional customer expectations; whereas experience encounters address latent desires and experiential purposes. The former is relatively easy to provide, but the latter, involving personalised and dynamic interactions, are much more difficult to predict and understand.

7.4 Strategic service approaches to the customer journey

Strategic marketing has two key objectives: achieving company goals and building long-term relationships with customers. Both are inextricably linked to the point at which they are fundamentally the same thing. In order to deliver a positive and value-added brand experience, it is incumbent on companies to engage with customers every step of the way and integrate multiple business functions. The use of 'customer journey maps' devised through customer journey analysis (CJA) – data documents analysing service interaction processes, customer's expressed consumption and communication preferences, expectations and perceptions – can present an honest externalised customer perspective if viewed in the context of consumer experiences of service within the service encounter as well as in a multichannel environment. This empathetic approach to process – seeing the system through customer's eyes – in the context of consumer experiences of service within the service encounter as well as in a multichannel environment is dependent upon having comprehensive knowledge of individual consumption preferences.

As has been stated at the start of this chapter, value is not embedded in the product but at the point of interaction. Indeed, how the customer experiences a brand can be dependent upon the individual interpretation of value. To reiterate Prebensen (2014), value has four dimensions: functional value (perceived quality and performance); emotional value (well-being, excitement); social value (status, self-identity, image); and epistemic value (gaining new knowledge, adventure).

Lemke, Clark & Wilson (2011) propose a useful framework of customer experience, conceptualised as the customer's subjective response to the holistic direct and indirect encounters with the firm and the impact that this has on customer relationship outcomes. We can see this illustrated in Figure 7.3 showing the *arcs of interaction and engagement between company and customer* where exposure to organisational processes and expertise creates an image of the company to the user. This is a structured portrayal of a basic customer journey.

In their research, Lemke, Clark & Wilson find that customer experience quality is judged with respect to its contribution to *value-in-use*, and this is not solely determined by evaluation of the firm's product and service offer but also the broad range

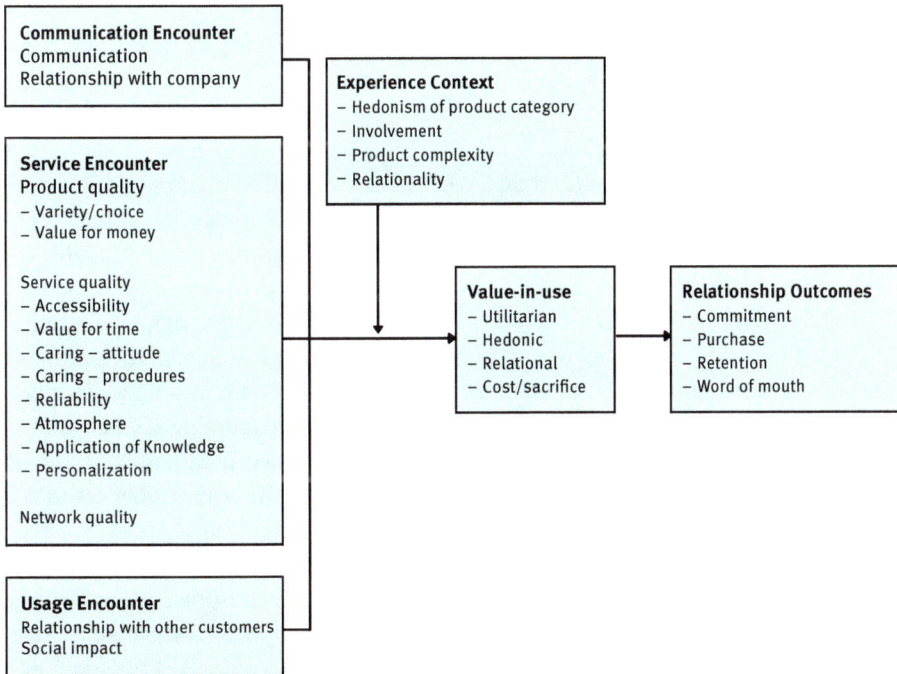

Figure 7.3: Customer experience quality model.
Source: Lemke, Clark & Wilson (2011)

of encounters with communications, relationships with the company, relationships with other customers, the product category context, and individual consumption motivations. As illustrated above, the tourism experience is characterised by intensive encounters between tourist service providers and users involving customer journeys which are physical and virtual involving pre-trip, the tourism experience itself, and a post-purchase phase (Shaw & Williams, 2009). Other consumers act as a useful experiential knowledge source in the customer journey of holiday buyers. For example, user-generated content by customers in Swedish micro-tourism firms were shown to enhance or distort company-customer encounters by providing subjective holiday consumption experiences (Yachin, 2018).

Customer journey mapping was originally developed for commercial use, but, more recently, has been used in the Public Sector, for example, to analyse citizen's experiences of public services. Crosier & Handford (2012) discuss the first use of mapping as an advocacy tool by a national charity which lead to improved access to goods and services for disabled people. A study by Ponsignon, Smart & Philips (2018) in the Healthcare sector demonstrated that adopting a patient journey approach could improve the practitioner perspective of the service delivery system (SDS), achieving higher quality patient care throughout the patient journey. Their research revealed heterogeneity in user experience across the customer journey not normally accounted for in standard 'homogenous' SDS designs.

Deloitte suggest a framework which describes this process as providing "new capabilities",[137] depicted in Figure 7.4.

This illustration describes a customer service delivery model which puts service operations into tiers characterised by:

- *Omni-channel customer interactions:* In the course of the customer life cycle, users interact with cross-channel, multi-touchpoint services designed to engage with and request services. Service providers must construct a differentiated unified, pro-active, seamless customer experience and fully understand individual preferences. With omni-channel service provision, the business model has transformed from single-channel to multi-channel, to channels being used in combination and simultaneously. Omni-channels systems should offer flexibility of service and consistency throughout the individual's journey, adapting to changing consumer needs, and providing a blended experience which integrates traditional channels such as branches and call centres with digital apps like mobile and social media. Touchpoints may be complementary and used simultaenously. Click n' brick shopping is a good example of this where search and selection may be at two separate touchpoints. Understanding heterogenous consumer preferences is why segmentation (see 'Personas' above) is so important to customising customer

---

137 "New capabilities for the service delivery method", *Deloitte*, April 2013.

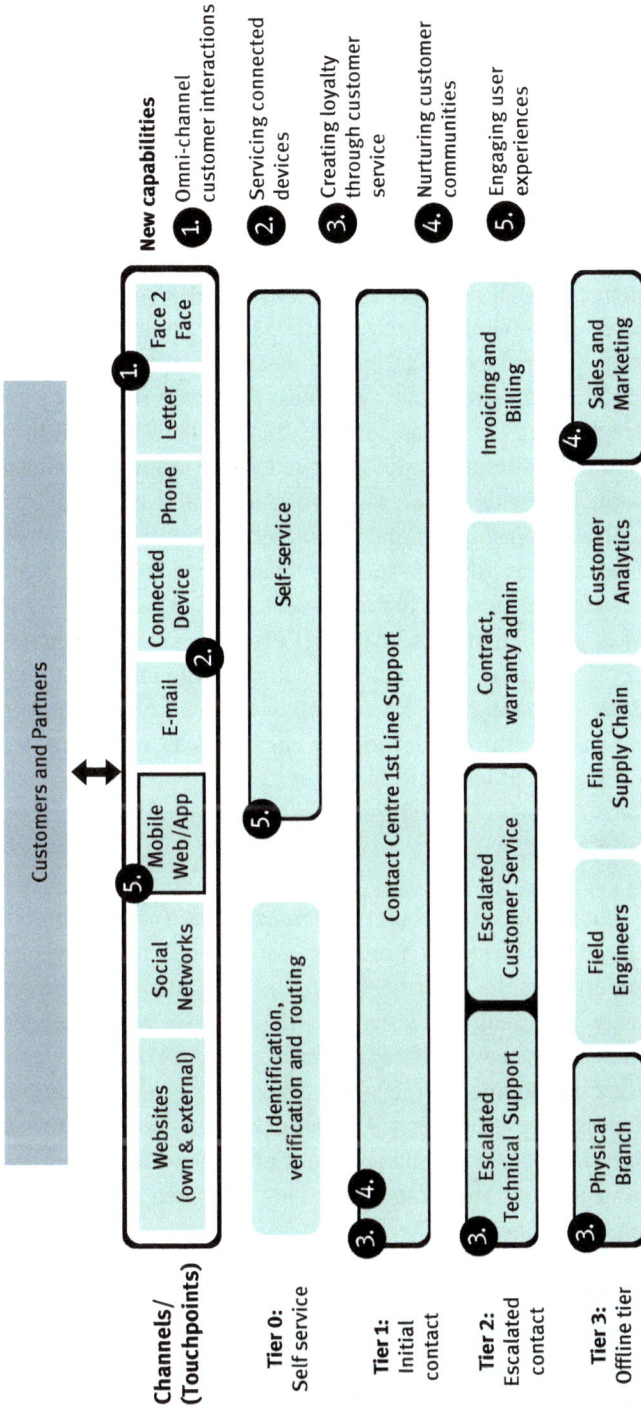

New capabilities

1. Omni-channel customer interactions
2. Servicing connected devices
3. Creating loyalty through customer service
4. Nurturing customer communities
5. Engaging user experiences

Channels/ (Touchpoints)

Tier 0: Self service

Tier 1: Initial contact

Tier 2: Escalated contact

Tier 3: Offline tier

Customers and Partners

Websites (own & external) | Social Networks | Mobile Web/App | E-mail | Connected Device | Phone | Letter | Face 2 Face

Identification, verification and routing

Self-service

Contact Centre 1st Line Support

Escalated Technical Support | Escalated Customer Service

Contract, warranty admin | Invoicing and Billing

Physical Branch | Field Engineers | Finance, Supply Chain | Customer Analytics | Sales and Marketing

Figure 7.4: New capabilities for service delivery method.
Source: Deloitte (2013, p.10)

journeys. Using customer channel preference to pre-empt service changes or even failures can alleviate customer anxiety and also impact positively on costs.

- *Servicing connected services:* The use of connected service devices to facilitate better service provision through remote service monitoring and device data analysis can enhance customer experience and extend company growth opportunities. For example, the *British Gas* initiative of helping user consumption cements customer-company relations and its 'predictive maintenance' approach has preventative cost-savings for the company.
- *Creating loyalty through customer services:* It is a traditional adage in service marketing that it is more cost-effective to retain rather than acquire customers. Digital communications, particularly social media where instant transparency and digital amplification are the dominant dynamics, has made retaining customers that much more difficult. If handled correctly, it also allows the ability to develop loyal relationships. Traditional reactive service provision has expanded to the point where service providers are proactive relationship builders, and support channels like *Twitter, Instagram* and *Youtube* have become communities of experience for consumers. Also, because companies can track and trace customer activity so much more accurately now, 'end-to-end' experiences – the customer journey – key performance indicators (KPI) such as Net Promoter Score (NPS) and Customer Lifetime Value (CLV) can change the emphasis from *measuring provider efficiency to customer-orientation.*
- *Nurturing customer communities* through leveraging customers as a resource, encouraging user-generated content and self-help.
- *Creating engaging user experiences* through online channels, quality interfaces, and investing in the user experience.

What is implicit in this is that managing customer experience links two vital components of strategy: brand building and service processes. Any alteration to provision or any part of it which undermines the customer-company relationship will impact on the brand and ultimately brand equity. Clatworthy (2012, p. 212) underlines the importance of aligning the customer experience to company brand strategy during the front end of new service development (NSD). He advocates the development of a *service personality* and consideration of service touch-point behaviours achieved through tighter integration between brand management and NSD. This should be reflective of how the brand identity and brand image are managed and how the 'personality' of the brand is positioned.

The classic service personality of *Avis*, the car rental company, originally positioned as the challenger brand to *Hertz*, was embodied in the slogan "We Try Harder". As we have seen above with outdoor clothing manufacturer *Patagonia* is their purpose may be "We're in business to save our home planet", but the alignment of brand, manufacturing, and service provision is still aligned with their mission statement "To build the best product, cause no unnecessary harm, use business to inspire and implement solutions to the environmental crisis", reflecting the personality of the brand. Strategically then, brand strategy and service processes must not just be linked but aligned.

Indeed, a company's goal must be to align its business strategy and the experiences that create most value for customer. Norton & Pine (2013) advocate strategically analysing and stage managing the customer journey – the sequence of events that customers go through to learn about, purchase and interact with company offerings – using it to road test and refine business models. When approached as a strategic design process, the customer journey, can provide all the elements of a business with a unifying organisational map. Kuehnl, Jozic & Homburg assert that in increasingly complex and digitalised consumer markets, an effective customer journey design (CJD) constructed in a thematically cohesive, consistent, and context-sensitive way can be an important source of customer value and loyalty over and above the effects of brand experience. They claim that "an effective CJD more strongly influences utilitarian attitudes, while brand experience more strongly affects hedonic attitudes" (2019, p. 553).

Having the customer at the centre of business, as the driver of CXM, can be done by viewing existing and potential customers through the metaphorical profile of data-constructed 'personas'. This allows an empathetic as well as economic profile from which to segment from. However, we need data to help evaluate what consumers actually experience. The customer experience begins before the transaction stage of the customer/company interface: it can be a state of unawareness of company, brand or even category need, or it can be the total pre-purchase, consumption, and post-purchase behavioural responses – cognitive, affective, and conative – of exposure to the service. It encompasses "the *total* experience, including the search, purchase, consumption, and after-sale phases of the experience" (Verhoef, *et al.*, 2009, p. 32). The static snapshot 'moments in time' data extracted through traditional methods of segmentation must be contextually relevant giving dynamic insight in order to have the actual experience of customers embedded in the process.

Consistent with the dramaturgical metaphor (Gardner & Avolio, 1998) often used in service marketing, interrelated acts or 'episodes' (such as shipment of goods, 'front of house' waiter service in a restaurant, payment facilities, and extra 'customer delight' value-added options) are all service sequences which form part of the service encounter, and therefore affect service perception. Because of the sequential nature of service experience, "this implies that the analysis of a sequence may contain all kinds of interactions related to a particular year when a particular project was carried out" (Holmund, 1996, p. 49), and it is not always obvious that sequences may overlap and perceptions may blur perceptions of other elements of the overall interaction. Figure 7.5 illustrates the interaction levels in a relationship, here split into four levels of aggregation: the act, episode, sequence, and relationship.

With the aid of digital technology, companies can focus best practice of customer engagement, that is, (CRM). Analysing data for greater customer insight – for

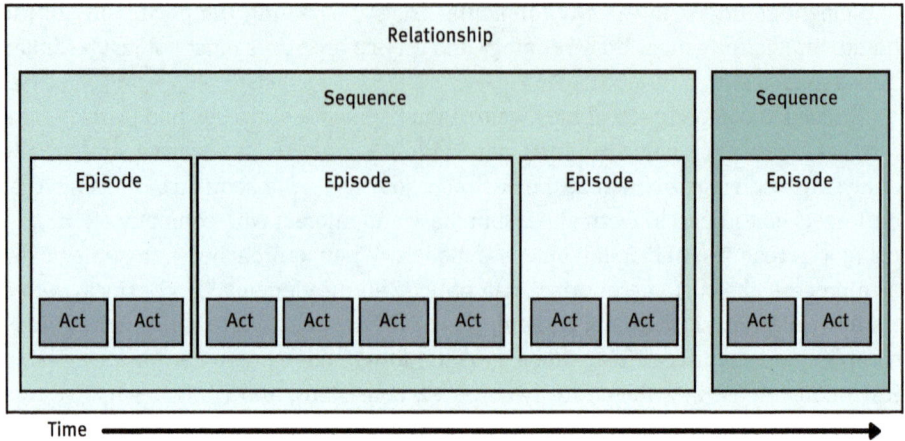

Figure 7.5: Interaction levels in a relationship.
Source: Holmund (1997, p.36)

example, data analytics and data visualisation powered by AI – can help make better decisions to enhance the customer experience. Similarly, the mining of social media using such tools as social media monitoring and sentiment analysis can assist engaging customers in marketing, sales, and service. The easy access and flexibility provided by mobile technology and mobile apps (eg: Virtual Live Assistant and co-browsing support), and the faster response of automated software and apps (email campaigns, welcome emails, lead generation, call scheduling, chatbot assistants, and self-service), together with omni-channel presence (integrating text, instant messaging and social) can help apply digitally the principles of CRM and deliver a unified customer experience of the brand.

One way of visualising the customer journey, as illustrated in Figure 7.6, is through a metaphorical 'vortex' of conceptual threads which direct activities and progressively expose the customer to increasing layers of communication and service provision. These threads describe both the parallel stages of consumer exposure to the company (ie: 'service encounters'), and the key elements of company strategy: managing the consumer decision-making process; the processes which assist the service provision; and the cumulative process of brand building.

– *The consumer decision-making process:*
  Category need arousal
  Information search
  Consideration and evaluation
  Decision and purchase
  Advocacy

– *The service support processes:*
  Pre-purchase touchpoint
  Decision-making touchpoints
  Post-purchase touchpoints

– *The cumulative process of brand building:*
  Unawareness
  Awareness
  Brand usage
  Brand adoption
  Brand loyalty

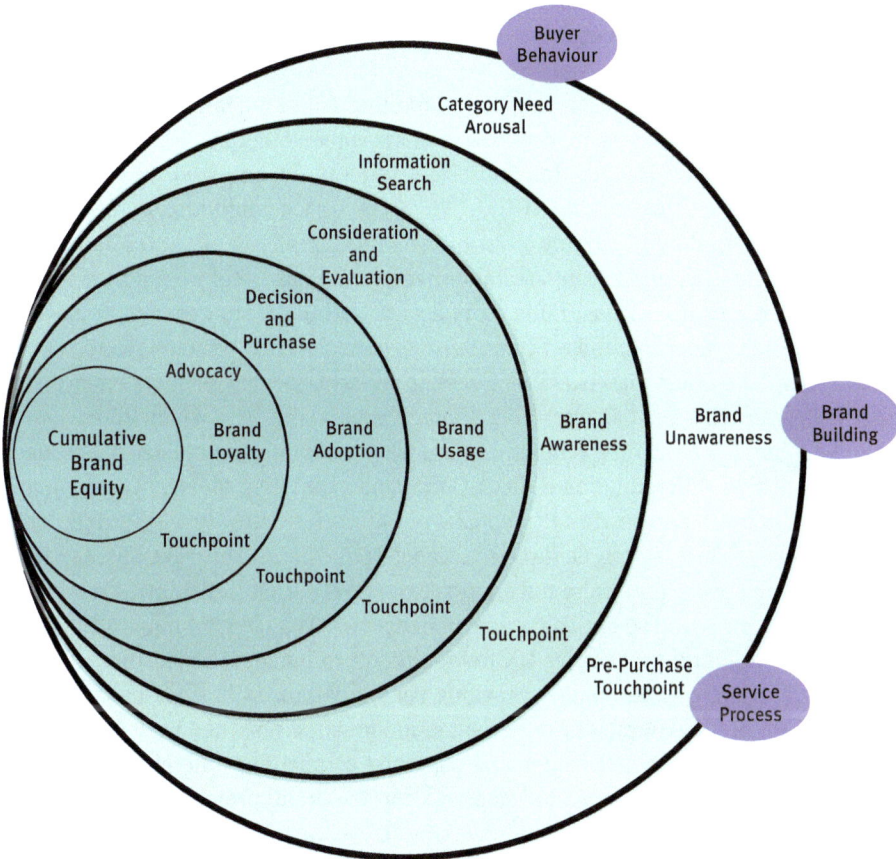

Figure 7.6: The Customer Journey.
Source: Authors' representation (2022)

This illustrates a multi-discipline approach to understanding the customer journey which shows the process from both customer and company perspectives. The goal of strategy and processes is to move customers seamlessly through the stages of exposure and experience, maximising satisfaction and building brand loyalty and confidence. The customer's 'journey' starts way before the decision-making process and may begin, from point of view of the application of integrated marketing communications, may start from a position of unawareness.

As we have already discussed, data analytics can help create 'customer personas', plotting where the customer is at each stage of their individual journey, ensuring that appropriate and relevant communications are targeted dependent upon 'buyer state' (eg: category or brand awareness, knowledge, consideration sets, preference, conviction), and the journey stage the customer is at. The overall goal is to build mutually beneficial value from loyal, sustainable relationships, building brand equity for the company and value for the customer. One very important aspect of this vortex is that it is not a funnel, the customer needs attention at all the levels of engagement. Traditional funnels tend to apply most of the marketing communications budget at the front end – where customers are *acquired* – whereas the vortex has a cumulative and even spread of spend to cater for individual touchpoint and holistic experience needs – customer *retention.* Lurie (2006, p. 6) discusses "accumulation marketing . . . relatively indiscriminate . . . grows out of broad assumptions about audience and strategy that are both unsubstantiated and inaccurate. Because of that, accumulation marketing can rack up serious traffic numbers and fail utterly to generate any useful business". The vortex can build on cumulative experiences and cement loyalty.

All companies must understand and seek to enhance the customer experience; the customer experience is what marketing strategy is all about. The commoditisation of mature markets – where there is little variation between competing brands in a product category – makes differentiation difficult. Companies must see the service encounter from the customer's perspective. Perceptions of brands have always been subjectively based on non-product factors. Quite often, service *is* the brand. This is heightened with online channels were the brand experience can convey trust, reliability, credibility, ease of use, returns, and so on. The user experience (UX) is a blend of human and computer interaction, and that makes UX more difficult to manage, especially as future user experience is conditioned by previous user experience. Strategy must be customer-centric; processes must prioritise signature touchpoints, the 'customer delight' moments which enhance satisfaction and maximise competitive differentiation. These proof points of interaction remind customers what the brand promise is, reinforce the emotional connection of brand positioning, and deepen the relationship.

One of the peculiar challenges for managing services is the need to standardise a heterogenous experience; service consistency of delivery right across all touchpoints is the key. Ballantyne & Varey (2006, p. 336) discuss the customer service experience in terms of three value-creating activities: relationships to give structural support for the creation and application of knowledge resources; communicative interaction to develop these relationships; and the knowledge needed to improve the customer service experience.

Customer journey analysis – investigating how, where, and why customers navigate their purchase experience journey – is crucial to fully assess customer needs. According to Norton and Pine (2013, p. 12), "the customer journey, when approached as a strategic design process, can provide all the elements of a business with a unifying organisational map". Aligning strategy with the experiences that create the most customer value is imperative. Managing the customer journey is really the structured analysis, implementation, and maintenance of service delivery. Halvorsrud, Kvale, and Følstad (2016, p. 844) advocate customer journey analysis (CJA) for investigation into individual service experiences in a multichannel, cross-functional environment. Modelling the service process in terms of touchpoints, they identify four types of deviations during service delivery:

- Occurrence of ad hoc touchpoints.
- Irregularities in the sequence of logically connected touchpoints.
- Occurrence of failures in touchpoints.
- Missing touchpoints.

CJA seems effective in revealing problematic and incoherent service delivery that may result in unfavourable customer experiences. In addition to their list, a common fault is the assumption of homogeneity of service, and also that it is assumed that customers experience the same organisational touchpoints, and their needs are homogenous, and they perceive touchpoints as equally important. A user experiences varied exposures to the service – multiple service encounters – and their journey may not be linear but looping and involve a mixture of cognitive, affective, and conative behavioural responses. Research reveals heterogeneity in experience quality in health care customer journeys evidencing the need for multiple, stage-specific service delivery system (SDS) using a critical incident analysis (Ponsignon, Smart, & Philips, 2018). Similarly, Voorhees *et al* examine variation of use and perception of service experience at the "pre-core service encounter, core service encounter, and post-core service encounter as distinct periods within a service experience" (2017, p. 216).

Principles in practice

The *Netflix* customer journey that revolutionised TV viewing

The practice of watching the latest movie in the comfort of your own home has been a well-established practice all around the world for some time now. At its peak, *Blockbuster LLC*, a giant 'bricks and mortar' US retailer, dominated the home entertainment business, providing video rental (and then latterly DVD-by-email) through over 9,000 stores employing about 85,000 people. In 2000, its closest rival, *Netflix*, with only 300,000 subscribers to its direct mail service, was fighting for survival and turned to *Blockbuster* for help. As a start-up, *Netflix* were offering a 50% stake in their business. *Blockbuster*, reflecting on their market dominance and know-how, declined the offer. Today, Bend, Oregon is the site of the only remaining *Blockbuster* store, and *Netflix*, now with over 150m users worldwide,[138] has an estimated net worth of over $1 billion.

The secret of their success – now expanded into media streaming and original content creation – is down to three factors: independently-funded product; understanding the dynamics of digital transformation; and providing users with a tailored customer journey that suits individual tastes and decision-making.

Although the *Netflix* value proposition was pre-digital, its premise was based on dissatisfaction with the existing *Blockbuster* customer experience. CEO Reed Hastings understood only too well the frustration with lengthy queues, out-of-stock product, and the curse of late fees. Face-to-face interaction was not necessarily a positive. Developing a customer journey which was computer-based and user-friendly, the first 'disruption' model offered a mail-order DVD subscription service. However, predicting the future demand for instant-access with personalised, Internet-streaming convenience, and, by 2013, being agile enough to quickly respond to the trend for 'binge watching' and alternative content, *Blockbuster* filed for bankruptcy and the *Netflix* customer journey as we know it today was firmly established as a model of customer experience.

A 'smart content recommendation system', (an innovative 'Profiles' feature), based on utilising AI machine learning technology to analyse personal preference, guarantees that users have individualised customer experiences which allows users to watch product (TV shows and movies) without commercials. This has the advantage of enhancing customer satisfaction but also making the process 'sticky' enough to encourage frequent usage and reinforce customer satisfaction.

Wary of its own parity competition (such as *Amazon Prime*), the constant response to changing customer viewing preferences, *Netflix* has responded to omni-channel customer usage by augmenting and strengthening its customer journey flexibility with a number of cross-channel partnerships. Extended access via telecommunications and media organisations like *Sky, BT,* and *Vodaphone* in the UK offers even more flexibility to the viewer. Access can also be via *iOS, Android,* or *Windows 10* and devices without Internet connection. Smart technology – such as voice-activated devices like *Google Home* and *Amazon's Alexa* extends this even further.

The strength, and indeed the success, of *Netflix's* digital customer journey paradigm is that it has a data-driven mapping process and co-creates value with its customers.

7.5 The voice of the customer

Along the customer's journey from prospect to advocate, the root to delivering replicable satisfaction is watching what the customer does but also listening to what the customers says. Power has shifted in the Information Age, the consumer's former passivity transformed by a myriad of knowledge and influence making stakeholder democracy a growing phenomenon in the customer-company interface and the *customer's voice* becoming louder than ever before. When customers vocalise their views of their experience, they demand companies listen, act, and communicate those actions back.

---

[138] *Netflix* allows users to share with non-subscribers which increases the customer base by a factor of 2/3 times.

Successful marketing is reliant on accurate market-sensing in order to integrate company strategy with customer perceptions of their assessment of the value proposition. And as the location of 'value' is increasingly intangible, relational, and customised in nature, the importance of customer-company interactivity, particularly dialogical, cannot be under-estimated. Improved competitiveness and sustained growth is the goal of customer-centricity. Customer journey management is really about *strategically managing customer expectations and experience* so that brand promise and service provision meet and exceed basic relationship requirements. Turning data from customer feedback and service queries into actionable knowledge to facilitate change can help this process. As we have seen in *Chapter 6*, presenting data as a 'narrative' or a "theorised storyline" (Golden-Biddle & Locke, 2007) can turn data into insights, and insights into knowledge. 'Theorising' is the product of abstracting, generalising, relating, selecting, explaining, synthesising, and idealising (Sutton & Straw, 1995) and allows the company to think from the customer's perspective. Brown (2010) describes this narrative approach as "Maybe stories are just data with a soul".

The notion of the 'Voice of the Customer' (VOC) is both philosophically-oriented – input provided by the customer to the company in its alignment with the organisational foci of 'customer centricity' – and process-driven – with its roots in the Quality Function Deployment (QFD) movement in Japan. It is both attitude and application. VOC research can create a tangible customer connection by analysing often intangible experience along the customer journey path; co-creation of processes and propositions can be the outcome. This is an in-depth process capturing the customer's perspective through direct feedback on preferences, blockages, reasons for migration, expectations of service, and experience of the brand which can reveal themes and trends which can be codified and turned into actionable process changes, conducting surveys to gauge buyer attitudes, intentions, and expected behaviour, constructing representations of customer, buyer, or user types ('personas' or 'pen portraits') which resonate with insights from segmentation and customer data can help frame a user-centred customer experience.

Gathering information from a range of data may involve individual in-depth interviews, focus groups, ethnographic techniques, contextual inquiries, content analyses, cloud services. Kwon, Cha & Lee (2015) compare hierarchical value maps (HVMs) for portal sites, smart phones, and social network services (SNSs) to evaluate satisfaction levels of consumers, querying their opinions on the attributes, functional and psychological consequences, and perceived value of each media product. VOC metrics can include Net Promoter Score (NPS), Customer Satisfaction (CSAT), and Customer Effort Score (CES), and the ultimate financial measure – Customer Lifetime Value (CLV). Lam & Mayer (2014) discuss the positive association between employee job autonomy and customer-focused service process in a hospital context where employees articulate patients' voices.

This has precedents in the perennial 'product life cycle' and Vandermerwe's (1993) 'customer activity cycle', the former a static representation of stages in customer 'maturity', the latter a process map for evaluating company match to customer expectation. Customer-centricity is a company commitment to designing customer experience processes in order to engender buyer preference and customer delight. Woodruff & Gardial (1996) provide a model of customer satisfaction, a hierarchical representation of value assessment plotting three levels: attributes, consequences, and desired end-states. These become increasingly more intangible, and therefore more abstract, the further up the customer goes in the journey cycle. The purchase of anti-virus software, for example, involves a customer's description of the value proposition's *attributes* (eg: "Protection from cyber fraud and data attack" extendable across 5 devices); the *consequences*, the results of possession, could be psychological comfort from reassurance form perceived risk; and the *desired end-states* of being able to use a PC safely.

Applying text-mining analytics to general historical customer data can yield actionable insight (eg: a taxonomy of key words in customer comments). Managing customer voice by using real data consisting of 'sentiment' expressed, particularly across social media platforms and apps such as *Twitter* and *Facebook*, is used to evaluate customer care. Singh, Nambisan & Bridge (2021, p. 42) claim that "Machine-age technologies, including automation, robotics, and artificial intelligence, are profoundly expanding the variety of service interfaces and therefore the possible ways that customers and firms can interact across customer journeys". They refer to "one-voice" seamless, reliable interactions with three themes:

- *Service interaction space* to capture the interrelationship among devices, interfaces, interactions, and journeys.
- *Learning* and *coordination* as core capabilities for generating and using intelligence, respectively, to enhance customer engagement in subsequent interactions.
- *One-voice strategy* to configure *learning* and *coordination* capabilities in combinations.

7.6 Customer journey touchpoints

Companies have become 'customer lifestyle marketing platforms' using attribution-based data models to profile and plot the consumption journeys at every touchpoint one-on-one at scale. Touchpoints are all the customer-company interactions before, during, and after purchase; conversely, customer journeys are made up of many touchpoints (or 'pain points') where customers directly or indirectly experience the brand. Customers may make many different brand journeys, and each may not be linear each time and may be influenced by different elements at different points. Even with the accuracy of 'personas' constructed through segmentation data, target audiences are different, and customers are heterogeneous. Taking a proactive, action-oriented approach to understanding how customers interact throughout their consumption journey will provide helpful insight, allowing the company to modify service provision to match customer expectation and experience. The better this is managed, the more chance there is to achieve strategic goals like improving awareness, consolidating preference, encouraging purchase, maintaining loyalty, upgrade a service, recommend to another customer.

Quality control of the touchpoints is crucial. There are a number of encounters which constitute customer experience touchpoints: all methods of advertising, company website, social media, emails, technological, process, billing, physical stores, customer service, customer support, subscription renewals, peer reviews, point of sale, influencer recommendations customer onboarding, physical events, online events. Touchpoints between provider and user are referred to as 'owned media'[139] and can even include the 'physical evidence' of (for example, in the case of a pub or restaurant), drink optics behind the bar, shelf displays, pump promotions, in-house posters, music events, touch display payment, ordering apps, website, beer mats, displays, menus and so on. The company has some measure of management and a limited amount of control. 'Paid For' media such as TV, external posters, and other media are rented spaces. However, 'Earned Media' – which tends to be peer-to-peer (C2C) can include peer observation of users, post-purchase peer approval, recommendation or criticism in the online or offline conversations of word of mouth (WOM) – can aid purchase intention, usage satisfaction, social bonding, build brand relationships (sometimes even communities). Good press coverage and editorial recommendation, whilst still 'earned' is fast-becoming of secondary importance to the digital world of *TripAdvisor* and the influence of the influencers. [All covered in Chapter 8].

Principles in practice

Danone: staying relevant by staying attentive

Social media monitoring (or social media *listening* to be more to the point), is used to find out what customers are saying about companies, brands, and individuals online. Whilst face-to-face feedback is still important, social media listening and text techniques such as *KDD* (Knowledge Discovery in Databases), *text analytics*, and *text mining* (extracting information from texts) is quickly becoming a useful customer intelligence tool. Encouraging your customers to talk about your brand is one thing, but listening closely to what they say is taking engagement to the next level. Ever since the Covid-19 pandemic hit, it is something *Danone*, the Parisian food corporation giant founded in Barcelona, has been doing to a phenomenal degree. Using social media to 'listen' to customers has helped gather social insight and consumer attitudes to the brand and food consumption in general, which is shaping product innovation and how the company communicates with its customers. CMO Valérie Hernando-Presse claims that "listening to people through this type of approach is a condition of being relevant to them. Deep social listening allows us to

---

139 There is an extensive discussion on 'owned', paid-for', and 'earned' media in *Chapter 7*.

take a near-to-immediate pulse check on what people are discussing when they talk about these changes online".

Gathering social insights has been part of *Danone's* approach to getting close to its customers, something they have done through its 'Food Revolution Barometer' since 2018 in partnership with agency *Futerra* and tech start-up *Bloom*. 225 million online conversations with over 33 million messages across every social media platform (which tripled in 2020/21) have been analysed. Insight into not just brand consumption but attitudes to health, bodily intake, production processes, fair trade for farmers, environmental impact concerns, and social use in context have resulted in a different approach to how data extraction has shifted from asking people to really listening to people. Hernando-Presse pinpoints the Covid pandemic as being a major factor in consumer attitude change: "The pandemic has, of course, shaken our lives. It has also shaken up our relationship with food, and that led to a breakthrough in conversation from farm to fork to fight". She highlights listening to the overwhelming rise in people talking on social media about their change in attitude to "pursuing planetary diets by eating with purpose" as the key factor which has driven *Danone* to reassess its approach to brand strategy. Not only has the data from listening attentively (and extensively) given *Danone* a call to action to champion sustainability and social progress, but it also presents the company with a "gold mine for innovative ideas". As Hernando-Presse states: "It really is something new this new activism. If I don't look at what matters to people in their conversations, how will I stay relevant as a brand?"

Source: Extracts from Manny Pham, "From asking to listening: How *Danone* is using social insight to stay relevant", *Marketing Week*, July 20, 2021

With over 59% of the World's population actively online,[140] customer journeys are partly if not wholly online; service encounters can be a seamless, 24/7, omni-channel experience where multi-channel service switching can complement or replace traditional face-to-face service encounters. Big Data is morphing into Fast Data; instantaneous 'personas' are calculated based on assumed demographic, psychographic, and behavioural customer data. The COVID-19 pandemic has coerced people to work remotely, and companies have been forced to find more appropriate and relevant ways to deliver products and services. Post-pandemic has dramatically changed this to the point where not being digitally engaged is the exception. Table 7.1 shows the likely strategic and operational changes to service provision.

Today, service provision must take a central role in integrating all customer engagement processes, and the experience which companies must offer – the holistic customer journey – must be interactive, immediately responsive, and personalised. For companies to accompany customers, to influence and engage, to fulfil expectations and add value to drive the consumption experience, and build thriving communities, strategy must be based on real-time data, and communications must be precisely targeted and relevant at all touch points along the route of their journey. Customers interact with companies at many touch points in the digital ecosystem

---

140 2020 figures.

Table 7.1: Transition in Services.

	Today	Tomorrow
Strategic	Operational efficiency Service transaction Reactive response Revolving issues Information silos	Customer advocacy Managed journeys Pro-active advice Nurturing communities
Operational	Emails and phone calls Informative websites Information systems Desktop based	Information consistency Social interactions Engaging applications Connected experiences Touch-based, Voice-based

Source: *Deloitte* (2013, p.8)

through multiple channels and ever-changing media, communication now having a much more social aspect to it. A digital ecosystem is "a sociotechnical network of interdependent digital technologies and associated actors that are related based on a specific context of use" (Kallinikos, Aaltonen, & Marton, 2013, p. 357). (Nacchira, Dini, & Nicolai, 2007) define a digital ecosystem as "the technical infrastructure, based on a P2P distributed software technology that transports, finds, and connects services and information over Internet links enabling networked transactions, and the distribution of all the digital 'objects' present within the infrastructure". They make the point that the definition of a *business* ecosystem (Moore, 2003) – interacting organisations and individuals producing goods and services of value to customers who themselves are members – was used as a basis for the new digital perspective. This is analogous of the 'consumerisation of IT' – the proliferation of personally-owned digital product in the workplace which migrated from the vast consumer market – which has impacted on the adoption of digital technology in organisations. With the individual as the driver (as had previously been seen with migration from mainframe to personal computers), the encouragement to 'bring your own device' (BYOD), the use of social media, adoption of cloud bridging systems such as product information management or marketplace platforms to accelerate the digital shift and boost operational excellence.

At a time when sustainable customer advantage is becoming increasingly difficult, with enhanced business transparency through C2C adoption of social platforms, digitalisation is a catalyst for rapid change, making innovation in terms of how customers are engaged an imperative for strategy. The dynamics of disruption evidence: increased connectivity, easier usability, and affordable technology leading to *rapid technological adoption*; new business models, lower barriers to entry, more powerful customers, and new business models leading to a *greater competitive micro-environment*; and, diminishing brand loyalty, tech-savvy users leading to altered *customer behaviour*. The volatility of global marketplaces, exacerbated by the disruptive impact of the COVID-19 pandemic, has forced all organisations in all sectors to accelerate the rate at which companies become digitised; in turn, digital transformation has become a major driving force of business strategy. According to a report by the *Boston Consulting Group*, 80% of global business leaders intend to rapidly increase digitisation in their organisations. It has thrown the spotlight on how employees, customers, and other stakeholders engage with the organisation and how the organisation engages with them.

The diffusion of digital devices, with digital technology having the ability to monitor the minutiae of our everyday lives (Hedman, Srinivasan, & Lindgren, 2013), has made it vitally important for organisations to be agile in response to changing customer expectations. One of the impacts of the pandemic has been to make digitising the customer experience a top priority for organisations, offering information, choice, and convenience as part of a reimagined value proposition. Remote customer contact with increasingly digital rather than face-to-face engagement is already reshaping retail, banking, education, and a whole plethora of sectors. Contactless transactions have morphed into contactless interaction, presenting opportunities for some organisations but real problems for others who are not 'future set' structurally or culturally aligned to adapt. Whilst omni-channel digitisation may have been the norm for a few innovative customer-obsessed companies, it may become the new norm post-COVID-19.

7.7 Digital engagement

Companies use brand-generated content on social media in order to engage prospective, lapsed, and existing customers at all stages of the customer journey. Digital engagement is a phenomenon which has been rooted in the interactivity of service marketing and the co-creation of value and meaning, designed around consumers' interactions with a brand to strengthen emotional, psychological, or physical investments (Chaffey, 2011) as part of the consumer decision-making process. It is strategically important because it focuses on how the customer's brand experience – all the touchpoints with the company and fellow users – can be improved and how this can be leveraged to produce loyalty, income flow, and profitability. (Drummond, O'Toole, & McGrath, 2020, p. 1247) derive a range of digital social media marketing capability: connection, engagement co-ordination, and collaboration. Users classify activities into: 'fun' practices, 'learning' practices, customer feedback, working for a brand or talking about a brand, but these are all differently related to the three buyer motivational states of cognitive, affective, and conative (Eigenraam, Eelen, van Lin, & Verlegh, 2018). Consumer engagement has been heralded as strategic in facilitating sales growth, competitive advantage, and profitability but this has to be extended to the broader perspective of multi-stakeholder digital engagement (Viglia, Pera, & Bigne, 2018).

Many companies track customer interactions and user-generated content and then design online content to coincide with customers experiences, attempting to influence the sentiment (sentiment analysis looks at consumers' perception of a brand), of subsequent B2C communications (Meire, Hewett, & Ballings, 2019).

Determining the nature of brand loyalty and brand promiscuity is important because companies need to understand why customers repeat purchase or do not. Brand loyalty, and therefore consumer behaviour, has three components: commitment, preference, and repeat purchase with four levels: *cognitive* (conscious mental process of evaluation); *affective* (emotional often irrational element of evaluation, liking or even love of a brand); *conative* (purposeful striving for action); and *action* (conative stage but with a desire to overcome obstacles to purchase, block alternative purchases, repeat purchase).

Coyles and Gokey (2002) differentiate between three types of 'loyalty segments':
- *Emotive loyalists:* not as much purchase deliberation due to satisfaction with current choice.
- *Inertial loyalists:* due to high switching costs or because of lack of involvement with the brand, inaction and/or repeat purchase decisions based entirely on inertia.
- *Deliberate loyalists:* due to their perception of current brand's actual or perceived superiority, their rational purchase is solidly loyal, but may reassess if alternatives offer better proposition.

These loyalty patterns are influenced by: how often purchases are made; the frequency of other kinds of interactions (eg: service calls); the emotional or financial importance of the purchase; the degree of differentiation between competitor offerings; and the ease of switching. Achieving attribute superiority required for a deliberative loyalty strategy is difficult to pursue for product categories where there is little differentiations among brands (Dillon, Madden, Kirmani, & Mukherjee, 2001).

Digitalisation is driving the need for a new perspective on service marketing where consumer behaviour has dramatically changed. Figure 7.7 charts the impact technology has had on customer service.

Technology-enabled interaction is becoming an increasingly prevalent part of the customer-company relationship instilling a greater concentration on customer experiential, communication, and engagement needs. Even though there is a distinction between traditional product-oriented and customer-oriented perspectives, all economic exchanges have always involved some sort of service involvement. Indeed, the distinction should be the transition from innovation *in* services and the notion of service *innovation*, particularly the role played by digital transformation. This is a hybrid fusion involving not just Information and Communication Technology (ICT) but other 'operant' resources such as human capabilities such as intangible skills and knowledge, as well as 'operand' resources like tangible, physical assets. Traditional service provision has been changed by emergent technologies. Barrett *et al.* (2015, p. 136) claim that "digital innovation facilitates the disintegration

| 1960s | 1970s | 1980s | 1990s | 2000s | 2010s |

In 1967, AT & T creates the 1-800 number, allowing customers to call companies directly at no charge.

Continental Airlines were automatic call distributors. This allows calls to be re-wired to agents.

Interactive voice response goes mainstream allowing companies to route calls using speech recognition.

The fist email is transmitted.

The first mobile phone calls made.

AOL creates online messaging system for personal computers proliferating use of live chats and instant messaging.

Expanded use of the Internet and growth of call centres increases automated interactions with customers.

Customer Service Management (CRM) software improves ability to cross-sell products and obtain repeat business.

Twitter, Facebook connects companies with customers on a global scale. First iPhone becomes available.

YouTube makes distributing product videos less expensive. Facilitates relationships with customers.

Omni channels enable multiple social media channels to interact simultaneously with customers.

Companies use artificial intelligence to assist customers Chatbots and virtual agents provide 24/7 interactive support.

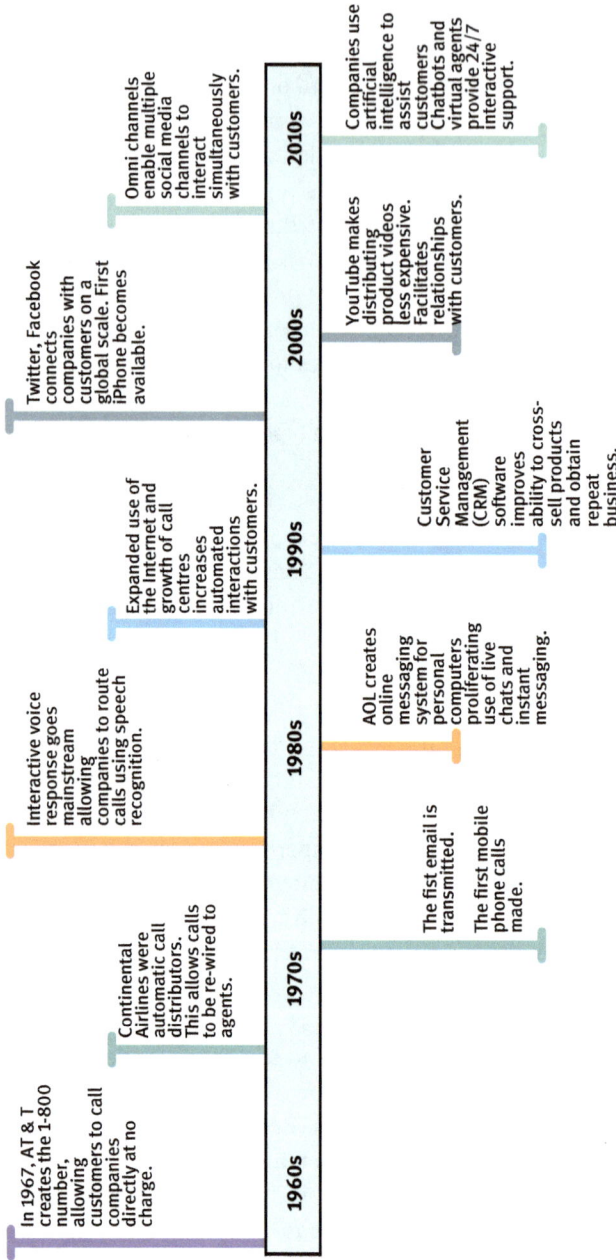

Figure 7.7: How Technology has shaped customer service.
Source: Jordan, (2019)

of global value chains by understanding how firms apply modularity or break down their value chain with the rapid growth of new service providers".

Service innovation, according to Miles (2008, p. 117) should be examined as emergent, interactive, and dynamic, as well as knowledge and information intensive as information flows between company and customer. Providers may apply *ad hoc* innovation or develop new areas of knowledge and innovation, may be *anticipatory*, or have standardized procedures formalised across omni channels and varied client interactions (Gallouj, 2002, p. 20).

Using Hertog's classification, Barrett *et al.* (2015, p. 139) service innovations have developed in the following areas:

- *The service concept* (categorising information services; measures of information services; automated/autonomous personalised information services).
- *Client interface* (human-computer interaction in ICT-enabled service systems; process design and automation in customer/provider interactions.
- *Intra-organisational service delivery systems* (ICT-enabled knowledge processes in firms; ICT implications in service organisations).
- *Inter-organisational service delivery systems* (sourcing and outsourcing of services in markets and networks; ICT effects in networked interactions; ICT effects on value creation in markets and networks).
- *Technology* (digital innovation); digital infrastructure and standards; platforms and ecosystems).

Some companies use 'augmented reality' (AR) – technology which supplements real world product views with a computer-generated image to project a possible product use – to enhance consumer experience. Particularly relevant to a retail shopping experience, research has shown consideration sets are broadened, product curation is aided, and choice sets are narrowed, and cognitive dissonance is amplified when AR is incorporated into the customer experience (Romano, Sands, & Pallant, 2020).

Chapter takeaways

- Value is not embedded in the product at the moment of transactional exchange, but obtained through consumption processes *at the point of interaction.*
- The customer journey has become the product, guiding customers through a company's product and service processes, providing a company with customer knowledge to help that process.
- Tracking and analysing customer behaviour across omni-channel interfaces provides opportunities to enhance customer experience, reinforce loyalty, and drive continued engagement.
- The use of 'customer journey maps' devised through customer journey analysis (CJA) can present an honest externalised customer perspective.
- Customer experience quality is judged with respect to its contribution to *value-in-use* through its product and service offer but also the broad range of encounters with communications, relationships with the company, and relationships with other customers.
- The notion of the 'Voice of the Customer' (VOC) is both philosophically-oriented and process-driven.
- Touchpoints are all the customer-company interactions before, during, and after purchase; conversely, customer journeys are made up of many touchpoints (or 'pain points') where customers directly or indirectly experience the brand.
- The use of customer experience maps (CXMs) or customer buying maps (CBMs) are used to capture activity or behaviour at each touchpoint, with CXMs extending beyond buying.
- Service provision must take a central role in integrating all customer engagement processes, and the experience which companies must offer – the holistic customer journey – must be interactive, immediately responsive, and personalised.
- Digitalisation is driving the need for a new perspective on service marketing where consumer behaviour has dramatically changed and technology-enabled interaction is becoming an increasingly prevalent part of the customer-company relationship.

Closing case

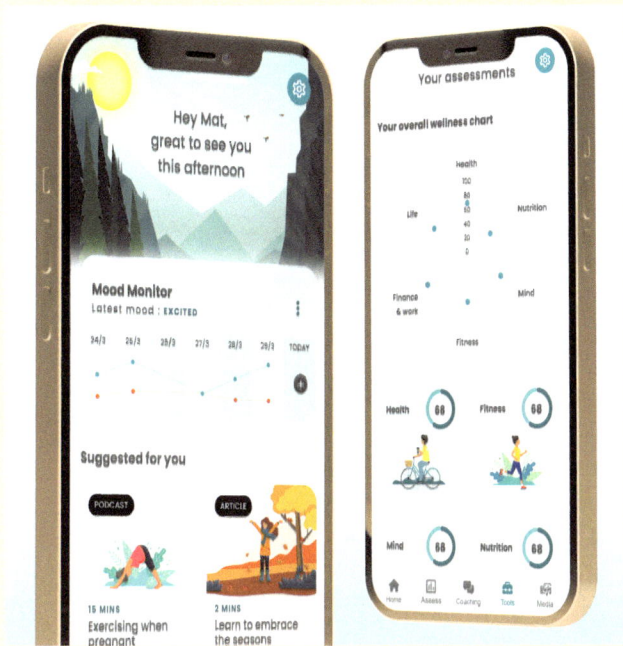

Raiys: Repositioning wellness to help wellbeing

In 2020, when Matthew Shaw took the helm as Managing Director of app-based *PAM Life*, part of the largest privately-owned Occupational Health and Wellbeing company in the UK, *PAM Group*, he was faced with a branding dilemma: How could he transfer *PAM Life's* (and the *PAM Group's*) B2B market success into a compelling consumer-facing solution? The answer was re-rationalising what the brand stood for, and how this internally projected brand identity would align with the external brand image. No easy feat. More so, in this context, when considering the complex and serious nature of health and wellbeing outcomes like the deployment methods of cognitive behavioural therapy to tailor programmes for users. In addition, there was the challenge of ensuring that there was an effective user experience (UX) to help aid the technology adoption process, complemented by a smooth customer journey. All in all, could Shaw and his team rise to the challenge?

The sector in which the *PAM Group* competes – the broader health and beauty market – is almost immune to recession: in terms of consumer spend, it remains a priority in budgets. 'The Lipstick Index', a phrase coined in 2004 by Leon Lauder, Chairman of *Estée Lauder* to describe how cosmetic sales boom during economic uncertainty, perfectly describes this phenomenon. Fast forward to 2021, the health and beauty sector is now part of a much larger Health and Wellness industry boom which encompasses all activities which promote physical and mental wellbeing: from yoga to healthy eating, personal care and beauty, nutrition and weight-loss, meditation, spa retreats, workplace wellness, and wellness tourism.[141] Health and Wellness is now worth up to £2.8 trillion worldwide, according to the Global Wellness Institute. The sector is growing rapidly. By 2022, British consumers are forecast to spend £487 per head annually on "wellness", according to analytics firm *Global Data*.[142]

The launch of a new growth and wellbeing 'hub', *'Raiys'*, designed to enhance the coaching experience for individuals with an array of supporting tools and digital resources, effectively reframed the brand *'PAM Wellbeing'* whilst at the same time leaning on the *PAM Group's* long established brand credibility, trust, and expertise. The group's collective services include: physiotherapy services, psychological services, wellness solutions, employee support like a confidential 24/7 phone line, and cognitive behavioural therapy, supporting more than 700,000 employees across more than 1,000 (B2B) clients.[143] The brand's credibility is underpinned by a strength in clinical experience and proven a track record.

There is significant brand equity in the B2B market in relation to the wider Group and *PAM Wellbeing*, and the decision was not an easy one to re-brand the B2C solution and use this as a platform to engage the booming B2C market opportunity. Shaw describes his dilemma of trying to find a balanced brand solution:

---

141 https://globalwellnessinstitute.org/press-room/press-releases/wellness-now-a-4-2-trillion-global-industry/
142 https://www.telegraph.co.uk/business/tips-for-the-future/future-of-health-wellbeing-beauty/
143 https://www.pamgroup.co.uk/about-us

The PAM Group is very well-established, and the original brand name was PAM Life. There was a strong link to parent company (PAM Group) who have established reputation in the B2B market, but the challenge was that PAM Life was relatively unknown in consumer market. The evidence identified that the name didn't really emotionally connect with our purpose and didn't lend itself to signify the link of wellbeing to consumers.

Raiys is the all-in-one mobile app designed by wellness professionals to promote a healthy lifestyle. Customers use Raiys to help in three key areas: optimising health, losing weight sustainably, and boosting mental wellbeing.

Satisfaction derived from health and wellbeing consumption, whilst it has a functional and social value, has a significant emotional value. Given the important health and wellbeing outcomes, the brand re-framing and re-naming needed to have a more meaningful emotional connection. As covered throughout this book, where there is a compelling and meaningful brand purpose, there often requires a brand strategy that includes fulfilling a universal need but also fosters a strong emotional connection. *Raiys* were diligent to know that this element had to be incorporated into their brand strategy.

This is an intangible experiential element. Therefore, it was imperative that *Raiys* took a strategic approach in embedding this right across their customer journey. This effectively follows a pathway to purchase across the following stages:

1. Awareness building via omni-channel marketing and promotion (i.e. word of mouth/recommendations, search engine ads, social media etc).
2. Registering an account and paying a subscription cost, dependent on whether the user wants to only use the app and/or a professional service (health, coaching/therapy etc.).
3. Customer then downloads the app, signs in, and then goes through an onboarding process.
4. The customer can also connect their account via the website that has additional features.

This of course is a rudimental overview, but it does acknowledge the fact that all customers are different and have varying needs, and may approach the pathway to purchase via different routes. The brand plays a significant role in this process.

The wellness sector is hyper-competitive, awash with tech start-ups. In comparison, *Raiys* (with the strength of the *PAM Group* behind them), have a competitive advantage in being clinically and scientifically underpinned and have a solid brand equity to draw on. The crux of building brand equity is via strong customer relationships characterised by credibility and trust. Shaw highlights that the practical foundations of any brand building exercise rely on making positive associations, whilst also acknowledging the challenges of developing brands and obtaining relevant domains:

Our customer insight highlights how the name 'Raiys' lends itself to positive connotations and associations, in terms of its use as a stylised-replacement for the word 'raise' (ie: 'raiys up', 'raiys your profile', 'raiys of sunshine', 'getting a pay raiys', 'raiys the bar' etc). Obviously, it is always a risk, and a bold one, to change things grammatically, but we are in the age of this occurring more and more. Our target consumer market and insights pointed to the risk being outweighed by the potential benefits. Ultimately, the app is there to help elevate someone as a person, so the name Raiys works very well in this sense. It's succinctness, added to our ability to secure raiys.com, allows us to have a consistent digital presence. The fact it's differently spelt than 'raise' gives us a bit of an edge/modern feel as

https://www.telegraph.co.uk/business/tips-for-the-future/future-of-health-wellbeing-beauty/
https://www.pamgroup.co.uk/about-us

> long as this is explained in our marketing communications. Building brand awareness and ensuring all touch-points on the pathways to purchase are smooth and mitigate risk, for example, ensuring that misspelt domains are owned so that we can direct traffic via those routes as well.

Additionally, to ensure there was sufficient company buy-in, Shaw and his team collectively insisted that the re-framing was underpinned by a clear and simple value-proposition framework that reinforced the *'Raiys'* switch, summarised by Shaw as:
- *Technology-led wellbeing, designed by wellbeing professionals.*
- *Holistic approach to wellbeing (covers 6 pillars: nutrition, physical health, fitness, mental health, financial wellbeing and lifestyle/social).*
- *Unique algorithm for personal 'Raiys score' following range of health assessments.*
- *Range of proprietary digital tools enabling users to be more educated, resilient and motivated.*
- *All-in-one app (ie: covers a breadth of areas a user would usually have to download multiple apps for).*
- *Professional services for a more personalised support package (health coach and therapy).*
- *AI chat bot for mental health.*

Clearly technology adoption, via a smooth customer journey, go hand in hand – the stages almost mirror themselves – awareness, usage, adoption, loyalty resulting in brand value and equity (tangible and intangible). Broadly, key factors around perceived usefulness, ease of use, key alignment on attitudinal value and overall intention to use, help drive the success of app adoption, when mapped against a 'customer journey' they should also reinforce the process. Particularly in that customer engagement strategy, that an empathetic, customer/user-oriented – how, when, and why typical customer engagement occurs. *Raiys* align these critical stages in the development of their own in-app metrics:
- *User demographics.*
- *User interests/motivations.*
- *Areas of attention.*
- *Lead sources.*
- *Login regularity.*
- *Average time spent on platform.*
- *Average wellness scores (and improvement over time).*
- *Average mood (and improvement over time).*
- *Most popular tools/resources.*
- *Goal achievement and habit completion.*

This all acts as a means of tracking and analysing user behaviour/attitudes across omni-channel interfaces so that the brand re-frame and re-name can exploit opportunities to enhance customer experience, reinforce loyalty, and drive continued engagement.

Questions
1. Undertake a cost-benefit analysis of *Raiys'* re-frame and re-name brand strategy.
2. Think about the last time you download and subscribed to an App. What were the critical stages of this customer journey? Identify three strengths, three weaknesses, and three improvements.
3. To what extent are in-App metrics important to *Raiys* in technology adoption and customer journey analysis?

8 Managing the conversation: Integrated marketing communications

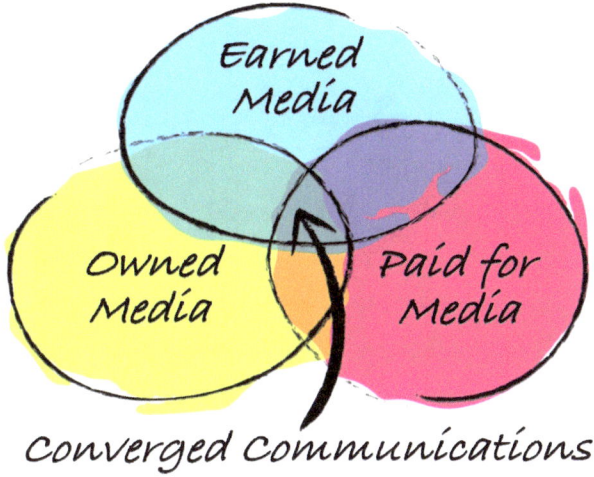

Earned Media

Owned Media

Paid for Media

Converged Communications

https://doi.org/10.1515/9783110718638-012

Opening case

© Jasmin Merdan – stock.adobe.com

Gillette: Managing a Man's Conversation

The era of targeted, participative, interactive dialogue has largely replaced the broadcast model of communicating *to* rather than *with* customers. Informing, persuading, and reminding is not as applicable, and more to the point, not as effective as demonstrating, engaging, and empowering in social communications. Jaffe (2005) analogises traditional marketing communications campaigns being fireworks: spectacular, exciting, attention-getting, big bang displays. And then zero follow-up. Conversation, on the other hand, is 'short head', where the critical factor is sustainability, engagement, buy-in, relationship building, and the staying power of the idea and commensurate long-term positioning of the value proposition.

Gillette's perennial positioning of their essentially product-oriented value proposition has for decades clearly reflected their competitive superiority, specific target audience, and implicit 'maleness' – 'Gillette, the Best a Man Can Get'. As an almost constant market leader in the safety razor and men's personal care sector, copycat 'Me Too' positioning is not something *Gillette* has had to contemplate. But the younger consumer expects brands to stand for something or, as often the case nowadays, stand *against* something. In the aftermath of the #Metoo movement (intended to empower women through empathy), *P&G's Gillette* found itself with a machismo image with undertones of toxic masculinity and even misogyny.

Rivals *Unilever* had *Axe*, a male grooming range positioned with similar stereotypical machismo appeal that had been transformed with the 2017 campaign "It's OK For Guys" aimed at giving their brand image a less aggressively masculine appeal. The subsequent *'The Best A Man Can Be'* campaign was their attempt to spark a conversation, to get men talking about the unacceptable cultural elements of 'being a man', and to try and repel a growing wave of perceived

anti-men public opinion. With an inspiring film, a landing stage website celebrating male advocates, and a social media hashtag #thebestmencanbe to encourage user participation across all
social channels, it certainly got people talking, particularly a younger audience, but how much
damage it did do to the brand by alienating its core users is the subject of debate. Can product
be successfully mixed with politics? Was the goal of starting a conversation really an own goal?
It got huge female support but provoked a lot of male anger.

The data which came out of the focus groups (with men and women) mirrored *Bodyform's*
focus on the female image of "Like A Girl". Times had changed in the 30 years since "Gillette,
The Best A Man Can Get". Challenging the accepted social more that "Boys Will Be Boys", often
used as an excuse for anti-social behaviour, became the conversation starter.

The campaign began on social media with a short film entitled "We Believe: The Best A Man
Can be", confronting negative behaviour amongst men – sexual harassment, bullying, sexual
misconduct, toxic masculinity – and asking the question "Is this the best a man can get?" This
time it wasn't about product superiority but male attitudes. It was met with controversy becoming one of the most disliked *YouTube* videos with accusations of "virtue signalling" and calls to
ban *Proctor & Gamble* and *Gillette*. The promise of donating $1 million a year to organisations
that "help men achieve their best" did little to quell the anger (such as Boys and Girls Clubs of
America). The ad, complete with companion website, pleaded with men to "do the right thing"
but *Gillette's* own customers were beginning to question whether they were doing the right
thing by them.

As an example of CSR, the responsibility of addressing social issues was being expressed
and acted upon. Whilst it did receive praise (most notably by Martin Luther King Jr's daughter,
Bernice), for being "pro-humanity" and demonstrating "that character can step up to change
conditions", it also received heavy criticism from those who saw the emasculation of men and
was giving in to the undercurrents of feminist influence and the woke culture of those who were
driving a war against masculinity. It compared unfavourably to the authenticity of *Nike's* campaign which featured Colin Kaeprenick which was uplifting not accusatory.

But was this *Gillette's* intention all along – to generate controversy as a kind of 'outrage marketing'. Some credit was clawed back with the follow-up "First Shave" on *Facebook* and *Instagram* which featured acknowledgement of transgender issues. There was certainly evidence
that the brand was at least trying to be redefined as relevant and values-oriented and was partly
proving to be valuable in provoking conversation which, after all, is what marketing communications is all about. Gary Coombe, President of *P&G's* Global Grooming said: "By holding each
other accountable, eliminating excuses for bad behaviour, and supporting a new generation
working toward their 'personal best', we can help create positive change that will matter for
years to come".

However, for men who were coming under a lot of scrutiny, it felt like a betrayal, a stereotyping of all men, and not being consistent with its previous stance of perceived indifference. Of
the 40 million who have viewed the *YouTube* video, over 2 million people have disliked it, twice
those who have liked it. However, although the backlash from conservatives and Men's Rights
Activists (MRA), (in some ways a sort of counterpoint to feminism), characterised the polarisa-
tion of opinions, it was clear that this was to be the result of the campaign's segmentation objective. Aimed at a younger more liberal demographic based on education levels, political
beliefs, and a sympathetic orientation towards gender equality, the tropes used in the ad were
designed to appeal directly to Millennials, Generation Z, and, perhaps just as importantly,
mothers. Whilst the latter group are the biggest influencers on purchase (and the chief gate
keeper on all other *P&G* products), the former is the group embracing the drive for change in
perceptions of 'masculinity'.

Addressing gender stereotypes was not the only marketing communications objective. Subverting harmful racial stereotypes is present in the support of African American fathers supporting their daughters, educating other men, protecting women from catcalling, and even featuring Terry Crews' Congressional testimony about sexual abuse by his Hollywood agent.

Exposure to stereotypes comes from the media, family, and cultural influences. The *Gillette* campaign inadvertently gave credence to the notion that masculinity is inherently toxic, that bullying is a solely male phenomenon, that learned toxic behaviour is primarily from the father. This is just as likely to be a mother's influence, defence, and justification as it is men in the family. Maybe expertise in the quality of product doesn't transfer to determining the quality of a man.

These days, it is not enough just to sell product. It is the job of marketing communications and brand strategy to 'read' and influence the social context within which brands compete. Organisations must have a purpose: they must stand for something. *Gillette* may have been trying to sell razors but they were also trying to challenge the notion of masculinity and change the dialogue. Research show that authentic brands that have a positive purpose are rewarded with customer loyalty. Even if *Gillette* have lost a few MRA activists and core conservative customers, they may have gained a new customer base. A different type of razor user rather than a different type of razor may prove to be the best *Gillette* can get.

Questions

1. Compare the effectiveness of marketing communication campaigns of targeted, participative, interactive dialogue with the traditional broadcast model of communicating to rather than with customers.
2. With over twice as many men disliking the campaign, the existing loyal customers viewed the stereotyping of all men as a betrayal. How dangerous is alienating one demographic for long-term 'purpose' objectives?
3. Discuss the view that positioning a brand based on relevance and values is now seen as more effective than one proposing a rational value orientation.

Note: The photo(s) used in this case study is/are not connected and/or does not represent any brand(s) mentioned. It/they is/are used to make a visual discussion point by the authors.

8.1 Outline of chapter

The role that marketing communications plays in creating and protecting brand identity and sustaining brand equity is one of the reasons for its growing importance in successful marketing strategy. It is the vocal and visual representation of the brand proposition. In their ground-breaking text on the strategic imperative for communication integration, Shultz, Tannenbaum, and Lauterborn's (1993) advocacy of "customer-focused marketing" didn't only radically transform marketing communications but has become the "new paradigm" of contemporary marketing logic: a holistic fusion of interaction, interrelation, and integration.

What emerged – Integrated Marketing Communications (IMC) – is "a way of looking at the whole marketing process from the viewpoint of the customer" (Kotler, 2003, p. 50), echoed in the service marketing mantra 'everything and everyone communicates'. Grönroos captures this well: "What employees say, how they say it, how they behave, how service outlets, machines, and other physical resources look, and how they all function, all communicate something to the customer" (2015, p. 312). In addition to what the firm says and does, what *others* say and do represents the total integrated marketing communications 'triangle' originally espoused by Grönroos & Lindberg-Repo (1998, p. 10). Similarly, Shultz (2004) claimed that "every place and every way in which the organisation touches its customers, employees, and stakeholders, . . . IMC has moved towards a more holistic view of communication as the backbone of the entire enterprise" (p. 52). Co-creation, mutually beneficial relationships, and interactive dialogue is the essence of this customer-to-company, cross-functional fusion. This chapter explains why *strategic integration*, a convergence of messages and media, added brand value, and augmented company symbolism, acts as a range of varied relationship conduits between customer and company, and is "the defining construct of IMC" (Kerr & Patti, 2013, p. 2). It is a dialogic form designed to be audience-centric, a process of engagement and interaction aimed at stimulating conversation. Given the heightened urgency in the context of the new globalised highly competitive economy infused with the dynamics of digitalisation, omni-channel connectivity, and the gravitation towards customer power, it discusses why the vigilance with which customer engagement and experience must be managed, presents organisations with considerable challenge.

Learning outcomes

After reading this chapter, you'll be able to:
- Define what the concept of 'integrated market communications' is and evaluate why it has had a wider impact on marketing strategy and corporate philosophy.
- Identify and explain the reasons why the transition to communicating with, rather than promoting to, customers has changed perspectives for both company and customer and elevated marketing communications from being just a part of the marketing mix.
- Examine the symbiotic relationship between IMC and brand equity, explaining why successful IMC rests on strong branding but also strengthens the brand.
- Explain why content, connectivity, and convergence are the essential ingredients of integration and strategic consistency.
- Analyse the impact digital dynamics and the changing contexts of IMC have had on customer-company conversations.
- Differentiate between 'permissive' and 'interactive' marketing and assess how they have transformed customer-company communications.

8.2 Introduction

In marketing communications (as with a common thread throughout this book) the importance of *fusion* has emerged as a significant factor in the successful application of strategy. Integration, cohesion, convergence, synthesis, combination, assimilation, and yes fusion, or, as Kerr refers to it, "fruit salad": "Once, we thought that comparing advertising and public relations was a bit like comparing apples with oranges. While they both belonged to the broad general category of communications, they looked and sounded different and were even very different in practice. Then in the 1980s, someone suggested fruit salad" (2011, p. 44).

A gradual re-focusing of marketing communications from a disparate collection of siloed, specialist subjects with an almost trade-like approach by professional practitioners, to one of cohesive fusion is characterised and defined by its *integrative impact* not just on its communication components but on customers and companies also. Early perspectives of marketing communications define it as an internalised management controlled 'communications mix' with external promotional objectives. The transition to communicating *with* rather than promoting *to* customers has changed perspectives for both company *and* customer.

Company control over communications with target audiences has changed. The disruption brought about by the convergence of telecommunications, media, and the Internet has "required both traditional and new media to reposition themselves or enhance their competitive edge at both strategic and operational levels . . . has led to a customer-focused marketing approach where the old way of implementing marketing strategies may no longer be as effective as before" (Liu & Picard, 2014, p. 2). As a consequence, brand communication strategies have changed from traditional 'reach and frequency' of mass media advertising to those based on audience engagement. As Jaffe (2007, p. 197) suggests, the traditional mass-mediated "trifecta of reach-connect-effect" has been reinforced by a stronger trinity of "exposure-engagement-experience" based on engagement with context, predicated on permission-based partnerships, relationships, and customer-centric connectedness.

Some would argue that the epicentre of IMC is its ability to create and curate conversation. According to Ballantyne & Varey (2006, p. 228), "marketing's unused potential is in the *dialogical* mode" with ongoing dialogue being the basis for a learning relationship based on *mutuality* and communication *between* not *to* parties. Communications between organisations and their stakeholders have witnessed a move away from the asymmetrical, one-way transmitted monologues of 'interruption' communications (B2B) to dialogic business-to-customer communication, two-way dialogues of 'negotiated' communications between customers and companies (C2B) and between customers (C2C). Analogous to this, in the context of service ecosystems, the use of the terms 'actor' and 'actor-to-actor' (A2A) relationships reflect this dynamic.

Ethical communication management, therefore, should be more dialogical than monological. Roper (2005) argued that symmetrical communication can actually lead to greater power for the organisation. Indeed, as Pettigrew and Reber (2010) claim, one of the features of a dialogic act is its power, and that, as Dialogic Theory suggests, it is not the outcome that is important but the process. As Smith suggests, the company intended 'meaning', mediated meaning (marketing communications), and the conversational capital of negotiated meaning (2007, p. 326) provides a new model of social interaction.[144] It is imperative for successful marketing communication to be grounded in social interaction (Varey, 2000), and this is instrumental in building brands as social constructions (Peñaloza and Venkatesh, 2006).

The focus of IMC has to be in the crucible of social meaning. However, proponents of contemporary Marketing Communications Strategy reject 'inside-out' thinking and extol the virtues of building and leveraging customer relationships in order to drive value. Whilst the early emphasis on *planning* is still entirely relevant and indeed necessary, enhancing value by driving relationships features high in current definitions. The *American Marketing Association (AMA)* recognises the added value which derives from comprehensive, cohesive communications, and IMC has moved from being about "how the organisation co-ordinated and aligned its external communication to an approach and a process whereby the firm aligns and manages its *brand contacts* and *customer touch points*" (Schultz, 2003, p. 318).

As Duncan posits, it has a broader appeal beyond an agency perspective: "A cross functional process for creating and nourishing profitable relationships with customers and other stakeholders by strategically controlling all messages sent to these groups and encouraging data-driven purposeful dialogue with them" (2002, p. 8). There is acknowledgement, albeit not explicitly, that marketing *communication* and *service* marketing are like marketing Siamese twins, supportive and complementary, conjoined by purpose and process. This is an increasingly dominant characteristic of purpose-led, customer-centric brand strategy. Customer-centricity means exactly that: "a genuine understanding of the customer and their views begins with a direct understanding of their world" (Schembri, 2006, p. 88). Indeed, Kitchen, Kim & Schultz (2008) refer to IMC as a concept, a strategy, and a set of programmes; its strength lies in providing organisations with an integrating framework for managing relationships with target audiences.

The transition from promotional to functional co-ordination, through a cultural orientation of values-driven customer-facing strategy to integration (Fill, 2002, p. 469) has changed IMC to be more than a just a managerial process; it is also a philosophical perspective.

IMC is "a system of belief or engagement, embedded in an organisation's culture, underpinned by communication and driven by technology and senior management" (Luck & Moffatt, 2009, p. 311). It is a fusion of systematically integrated multiple messages across omni-channel exposure, synthesised into a cohesive, consistent 'one-message' marketing communications mix. Even 30+ years later, Schultz, Tannenbaum & Lauterborn's (1993) blueprint for integration – beginning with

---

144 This is covered extensively in *Section 3.5 above.*

detailed customer information, building a synchronised, multi-channel communications strategy that reaches every market segment with a single, unified message – still holds true.

For consumers, IMC provides a heuristic short cut to assimilating, interpreting, and understanding what a company stands for, what a brand's values are, and where it is positioned against the competition. It makes consumer purchase decisions easier, reduces perceived risk, and even expands lifestyle expectations. If consumers have affective ties to brands, they are susceptible to communications (Moor, 2007). From a company's perspective, it can demonstrate not only a brand's authenticity, but an organisation's credibility and professionalism. It can add depth and amplification and give a unique voice to dialogue between brand owner and brand user. Whilst digital technology has shifted the tectonic plates of communication between company and customer, it can neither create nor destroy relationships; it is not the outcome but the dialogic process itself that is important (Kent & Taylor, 1998).

Marketing communications must be captivating and engaging, but there must be a solid, relevant underlying strategy underpinning it. To paraphrase Cuomo's American adage, marketing communications strategy must *campaign in poetry, implement in prose*. The *magic* of brand creativity, vision, passion, and the projection of meaning has to be balanced with the nuts and bolts *mechanics* of brand strategy, analysis, planning, implementation, and control. But consumers do not necessarily understand or are even aware of communication objectives, positioning, one voice multi-media campaigns, or a brand's suitability to fulfil category needs or psychological wants. And yet, although they may be "unaware of the concept, they recognise integration and see it as making it easier for them to build an overall *brand picture*" (Yeshin, 2007, p. 329). That's the result of good Marketing Communications Strategy: to make the links between messages coherent and understandable, providing a holistic environment within which a relevant and meaningful brand narrative can exist.

Principles in practice

Like brands only cheaper. Every *Lidl* helps with #lidlsurprises

In the 1990s, when the German family-owned discount supermarket giant *ALDI* entered the UK market, aiming at dominating the lower-priced sector between *Netto* and *Kwik Save*, competition was polarised between 'quality-positioned' and 'price-positioned' value propositions. *ALDI's* positioning strategy was ostensibly 'no frills'. Research done by Wood & Pierson (2006) compares *ALDI* with a supermarket diagonally opposite in the UK market – *Sainsbury's*. Both are described as "holistic brands" offering different marketing mixes and serving two distinctly different customer profiles: *Sainsbury's* to an ABC1 customer profile; *ALDI* to the lower C2Ds. Marketing communication approaches for this sector at this time (almost 20 years ago) were positioning 'quality' through promotion compared to *ALDI's* by tight control of product, store format, and price positioning (Brandes, 2004). In 2008, the global financial crisis affected economies the world over, and dramatically changed consumer perception of 'value-for-money' brands. The time of the discount retailer was here and *ALDI* was heading the queue.

In 2011, determined to realise their distinctive brand assets, they began to strengthen their 'real reflections of real life' positioning as a counterpoint to campaigns of the 'quality' end of *M&S* 'food porn' ads and *Sainsbury's* Jamie Oliver celebrity endorsement. The original *ALDI* ads, in stark contrast, did not feature actors or celebrities but instead a range of 'ordinary' people seen comparing prices AND quality under the brilliant tagline 'Like brands only cheaper'. This elevated the German retailer in both market share, brand awareness, but also authenticity. It boosted pre-tax profits by 124% to £158m in 2012, attracted over 1 million more shoppers, as well as winning over 25 national and international awards for creativity and effectiveness. Adam Zavalis, Marketing Director at the time, claimed that they had to dispel the *'ALDI myth'* by claiming that their brands "were just as good, if not better, than the brands people know and love". The 'Like Brands Only Cheaper' campaign, to quote Zavalis again, "pricked the conscience of the British consumer to re-evaluate *ALDI*".

From its humble beginnings in 1973 with only 3 employees, another German supermarket chain *Lidl*, with over 12,000 stores in the US and Europe, including 600 in the UK, has also decided to take on the 'Big Four' of *Tesco, ASDA, Morrisons,* and, of course, *Sainsbury's.* Ever since they opened stores in the UK in 1994, their positioning has conditioned the perceptions of their brand as a low-cost outfit. They knew they were misleading; they had quality too. So, they played on this in their *#lidlsurprises* campaign aiming at subverting that misconception. They made a conscious effort to minimise any traditional communications media. The hashtag/tagline was a clever positioning ploy against the competition above them, particularly *Tesco's* 'Every Little Helps'. The campaign was launched primarily through social media and attempted to engage with prospective and existing customers online, in store, and in a series of 'surprise' events.

On *Twitter*, using London-based social media 'foodies' blogger influencers, people were invited to an exclusive 'farmer's market' event in the trendy East End, where they had the opportunity to sample food ranging from steaks and cheese to fruit and vegetables. A local leaflet push enhanced the numbers of attendees. There were two 'surprises': one was the low pricing; the other was the produce the stallholders packing up their purchases in bags adorned with the *Lidl* brand name! Other 'surprise' events were rolled out to emphasise the *#lidlsurprises* theme and help get social media traction. Home County residents in wealthy Hertfordshire were invited to a tasting event at a plush mansion which actually turned out to be a Gourmet Christmas Dinner, all prepared from *Lidl* produce. The TV campaign was reinforced by huge exposure on *YouTube* with WOM pushed through post using the hashtag *#lidlsurprises*, repeated on billboard ads and instore posters. A special *#lidlsurprises* website was created adding to the exciting 'surprise' theme.

The campaign was a huge success, with over 10 million views for the 'Farmer's' video, *Twitter* followers doubling and social media 'buzz' beyond *Lidl's* wildest expectations. In these sort of campaigns, the online conversation, where the customers actually become campaigners, spreading the communication voluntarily and repeating the hashtag even on other topics. The *Lidl* Christmas ad proved to be a massive success with a score of 3.27 (out of 5) for persuasion.[145]

Both brands had excellent integrated marketing communications campaigns with consistent images across multimedia platforms which helped re-position perceptions by connecting with people through authenticity, using real people just like the target audience, and emphasising the experiential nature of purchase.

Both supermarkets face a Goliathan task in competing with the Big Four, but with campaigns like '*#lidlsurprises*' and 'Like Brands Only Cheaper', every *Lidl* helps.

---

145 *Millward Brown Research Agency.*

8.3 Digital dynamics and the changing contexts of IMC

Marketing communications has changed dramatically from the days of asymmetrical, interruption, one-way, broadcast media, mainly because of the dynamics of digital media: we can engage with our customers in two-way discourse. Once digital technology had migrated to the mainstream, and shifted the communications paradigm from monologue to dialogue, 'conversation' became part of the conversation.

All communications are culturally contingent, set in and subjected to the influence of many contexts: *global* values, attitudes, and ecological concerns have impacted, and are impacting, on all organisations' operating environments; the external *macro* (political, economic, legal, and immediate societal influences) environment; *micro* (intermediaries, and media) environment affecting and affected by all agencies and stakeholders; the *internal* context of organisational core values, attitudes, culture, behaviour, and external alignment; and, perhaps most importantly, the customer context of perceptions, motivations, attitudes, lifestyles, and behaviour.

Engagement between companies and customers is, and will continue to be, the touchstone of effective strategic brand management, and should mirror the market and the social context within which it operates (Kapferer, 2014). The communication contract between companies and customers – the means by which organisations speak to target audiences and the methods by which consumers get what information they need to make informed purchase decisions – is now characterised by the most radical shift in dynamics marked by three key game-changing realities: audience and media fragmentation; an increasing real and virtual connectedness between consumers and between consumers and companies; and the growing ineffectiveness of traditional communication methods on target audiences. Speaking on the eve of a proposed $45bn acquisition in 2008 of *Yahoo!*,[146] a US web services provider, *Microsoft* CEO Steve Ballmer claimed that "Offline advertising will all be online within 10 years".[147]

Table 8.1 shows a comparison between traditional 'classic' and integrated marketing communications.

'Integration', 'retention', 'relationship', 'targeted', 'relevance', 'circularity', and 'customer satisfaction' are the hallmarks of brand strategy; the two pillars which support it are new brand communications and the essence of service marketing.

The digital era, therefore, has affected consumer's relationships with brands: they can engage directly with companies and between each other, and this has affected how brands should be managed (Hatch & Shultz, 2010, p. 912). For companies, the democratisation of communications, facilitated by the conduit of social media, has moved the focus away from jockeying competitive positioning for brand awareness

---

146 Actually now owned 90% *Apollo Global Management*/10% *Verizon*.
147 *Wall Street Journal* 2008, B1.

Table 8.1: Comparison of Classic and Integrated Marketing Communications.

Classic communications	Integrated marketing communications
Aimed at acquisition	Aimed at retention and relationship
Mass communications	Selective communications
Monologue	Dialogue
Information is sent	Information is requested
Information provision	Information self-service
Sender takes initiative	Receiver takes initiative
Persuasive 'hold-up'	Provide information
Effect through repetition	Effect through relevance
Offensive	Defensive
Hard sell	Soft sell
Salience of brand	Confidence in brand
Transaction	Relationship oriented
Attitude change	Satisfaction
Modern, linear, massive	Post-modern, cyclical, fragmented

Source: Yeshin (2007, p. 327)

and category preference, no longer just about visual representation, but also about vocal presence.

The contexts within which IMC operates are where brand awareness, perception, attitudes, knowledge, exposure to "moments of truth", and brand experiences all occur, influenced by company, society, and other agencies. All are points of contact – planned and unplanned, formal or informal – where the brand 'talks' to its audiences and with its customers. This reflects the 'service' dynamic and the need for the 360° planning and control of integrated marketing communications. These 'brand interactions' or 'service encounters' take place in a partly-controlled environment where not all communication can be managed:

- *Explicitly planned brand encounters*: campaigns which are objectively researched with communication mix elements like advertising and direct marketing applied. There is some element of control with transmitted messages which can be tested beforehand and adjusted with feedback from the market to ensure *planned* messages get through.
- *Implicitly planned brand encounters*: interactions which have a degree of subjective interpretation like the physical evidence of a reception or the ambience of a retail store, and so on are more difficult to control.

- *Solicited planned brand encounters*: The brand's 'narrative' is projected second-hand through stockists, retailers and other intermediaries through, for example, displays and merchandising, and can be only partly controlled by organisations. Manufacturers attempt to control their image and brand messages by offering free-of-charge displays and merchandising units, discounts on products displayed, merchandising teams to dress shops in a uniform fashion, staff training and so on.
- *Unsolicited unplanned brand encounters*: Word of mouth, miscommunications, or misrepresentation by competitors or uninformed parties in viral ads, for example, may present a distorted impression of the brand.

Digital media covers a whole range of channels and platforms – websites, social media, digital print content, direct email marketing, mobile apps, and streaming video content – and has injected a different dynamic into IMC. The lines between traditional media, personal contact, and digital media have become interchangeable but they are differences which affect the effectiveness of integating the various components: the flow of communication, the response mechanism, the nature and quantity of content, and the control over its delivery.

When traditional media and digital media are planned and implemented in conjunction as part of a cohesive IMC strategy, they can connect with and complement each other to add value to marketing communications. Furthermore, the shift from traditional marketing communications means that traditional approaches to brand strategy are too limited to be effective; search, social negotiation, and peer-to-peer brand assessments give better scope but require methods to make communications more measurable and, therefore, strategy more accountable. Content, and in particular 'user-generated' content, is characteristic of the new democratic dynamic of digital, but it has also and blurs the lines. Consumers are actively encouraged (not that they can be stopped!) from talking about brands they use or even in some cases brands they don't use. Quite often, in a digital context, comments that consumers make about brands are considered to be 'advertising' in the sense that these comments are essentially content relevant to a brand (Rodgers & Thorson, 2017).

Trust is a major issue in customer-company relationships. Credible sources who have likeability and authority can be effective disseminators of communication. Opinion Leaders (OL) and Opinion Formers (OF), the key actors in word of mouth communications in the 80s and 90s, have given way to a new intermediate force, in the form of *Influencer Marketing*, a direct result of its audience: Millennials, Generation Z, and, increasingly, Generation Alpha. The principles are the same but the role of the influencer is now more explicit: disrupting consumer behaviour, 'Influencers' have an authentic voice and the power to engage with 'followers' (audiences) and influence brand sentiment and purchase decision-making.

In order to prepare for marketing communications strategy, we need to analyse the context within which the organisation is operating and within which the brand is created:
- *External context*: Global influences, intermediaries' requirements, media agendas, societal influences, and market conditions.
- *Internal context*: brand and organisational core values, attitudes, company culture.
- *Customer context*: user attitudes, motivations, perceptions, and behaviour.

Principles in practice

The Autocomplete Truth: *Google Search* sparks a discrimination conversation

Digital communications is increasingly becoming an essential part of any integrated marketing communications strategy. However, the 'Autocomplete Truth' campaign was one which was deliberately different in order to make a difference. With gender inequality as a hot button issue, the *UN Women's* 2013 campaign used *Google Search* to provoke a social media conversation about discrimination against women and sexist attitudes in society.

It contributed to the women's right campaign of the United Nations Entity for Gender Equality and the Empowerment of Women' (ie: *UN Women*). With offices in Europe, the US, Africa, the Arab States, the Caribbean, Asia, North Africa, and the Pacific, *UN Women* has a mission to protect gender equality, enhancing women's economic empowerment and increase their leadership but that all females live in peace.

Using actual *Google* searches, typing in just the words "Women should . . . ", the results of phrases generated from *Google Search's* 'autocomplete' feature were pasted over the mouths of women from all different cultural backgrounds. The messages used – ranging from "Women shouldn't HAVE RIGHTS", "Women shouldn't VOTE", and "Women shouldn't WORK" – symbolised the silencing of women's voices. Four separate images were created and distributed for use on billboards, in print, and on social media with the hashtag *#womenshould* and its single objective – to provoke a global online conversation – was achieved. A special 'tribute to women' video was produced juxtaposing women's achievements in history alongside the autocomplete phrase and posted on *YouTube*. As the campaign caught fire, TV and radio stations began extending the conversation and various news websites and blogs amplified this. The campaign team extended this with PR sessions in schools and universities, pushing for women's rights issues to be part of school curricula.

The 'Autocomplete Truth' exceeded all campaign targets, achieving over 150 million impressions on *Twitter* by the end of 2016, with nearly 800 million world-wide views in over 50 different countries, achieving the accolade of 'Most viewed ad on *Facebook*' with over 116,000 shares and mentioned in the media over 600 times. It created headlines and started a conversation on gender equality in news outlets, magazines like *Time* and *Elle*, online newspapers like *Le Figaro, Metro Sweden, Times of India,* and *The Guardian*, and websites like the *BBC, CNN, Huffington Post, Mashable,* and *Buzzfeed*. The *Ad Council* voted it 'Social Campaign of the Year' for 2013, and in the following year it won two *Clio* awards in both the 'PR' and 'Content & Contact' categories and a whole host of 'Best Use of a Hashtag on Twitter', 'Best Viral Campaign' and 'Best Social campaign' *Shorty Award* nominations. Up to 50 variations of the campaign theme was used with minority groups and the general public borrowing the '#. . . . . should' hashtag to raise awareness for fighting racism, bigotry, and discrimination.

It may have been autocompleted, but this campaign started a discussion about a universal truth.

The importance of digital technology, as with antecedents like the printing press, radio, cinema, magazines, and TV before it, is not just the impact it has had on helping the awareness and positioning of products and services, but how it has radically changed the way companies communicate with consumers, and how consumers communicate with each other. And yet this isn't only about technology; it's about people. B2C to C2B to C2C). "Technology is only interesting, from a marketing point of view, when it connects people with other people more effectively" (Ryan & Jones, 2008, p. 4).

In 2020, over 59% of the World's population were *actively* online. Our way of life has been disrupted by inexorable forces of technology and a Global pandemic. Waves of digital innovation have changed our lives more than many previous innovations:

- *Web 1.0* in the 1990s, often referred to as the 'Hypertext Web', introduced e-commerce and was characterised by relationships based on reciprocity and trust.
- *Web 2.0*, the 'Social Web', infused with the accelerated WOM of C2C, shifted the dial away from broadcast media to a more symmetrical dialogic communications.
- *Web 3.0*, the 'Semantic Web', welcomed in the era of smart phones, mobile applications, expanded access to advanced high-speed Internet access, wearables, domestic smart home gadgets, online retail experiences, the Internet of Things (IoT), smart domestic products (SDPs), and Big Data, with an increasing emphasis on privacy concerns as data breaches have a negative effect on sales confidence.
- *Web 4.0*, the 'Symbiotic Web' exposed us to the vast potential of Cloud-based technology, artificial intelligence (AI) and augmented reality (AR), where the anthropomorphised landscape of service robots are taking the concept of remote, non-human service provision to the next level of hybrid interaction of human-to-human as well as digital customer engagement.

The nature of online relationships is one of a seamless, 24/7, omni-channel experience where consumers can easily switch between devices and even between devices for one company via websites, *Facebook* page, *Instagram*, or company mobile applications. There are less and less obstacles to purchase, online relationships are networked C2C relationships can be dangerous to companies, much more personalised, and more transparent. This has provided a more collaborative, multiuser opportunity for value creation and analytical capability.

What we have witnessed in the past few decades has been the democratisation and socialisation of branded media. The components of this (shown in Table 8.2 *Digital Dynamics*) are: Influence, Intelligence, Integration, Interrogation, and Insight.

- *Intelligence*: the mechanics and measurement of social, sentiment, search, and site behaviour. Data is collected from multiple sources: secondary and primary; data processing occurs, to order, structure to add meaning. In other words, this then becomes meaningful for a business or brand when it is applied in that context, synthesised to solve a problem, applied as defensive or competitor intelligence (etc).
- *Influence*: the power of peer-to-peer influencers, user-generated content, the impact of experiential brand communities.

- *Integration*: Online and offline integration.
- *Interrogation*: Big analytics (AI-powered analysis and interpretation) that is applied and contextual intelligence.
- Insight derives as 'wisdom' that requires change, improvement, action evidence-based decision-making.

Table 8.2: Digital Dynamics.

Intelligence	Identifying key influencers: research methods for WOM, opinion leader analysis.
	Targeting consumers in the Web 3.0 era: profiling, targeting, and positioning online Marketing Communications.
	Digital dynamics: the mechanics and measurement of social, sentiment, search, and site behaviour.
Influence	The rising power of the consumer: from passivity to interactivity; focus on the 'social' in communications. 'Influencers' have an authentic voice and the power to disseminate information.
	Online consumer behaviour: the dynamics of C2C WOM influence.
	The disruptive digital environment: paradigm shift in Marketing Communications.
Integration	Beyond traditional Marketing Communications: migration from transmission to permission.
	Community and network building: affiliate marketing and strategic partnerships; 'natural' and 'brand communities'.
	Online and offline integration: paradigm shift in Marketing Communications; new models of convergence and connectivity; mobile marketing.
	Acquisition, conversion, and retention strategy: online customer development, service, and relationship marketing.
	Brand building in the digital era: social media and online consumer engagement; online PR and reputation management.
	Content management: the generation and control of online company and user-generated content; collaborative content and consumption.
	Channel/ platform management: 360-degree media neutral planning and the dynamics of C2C WOM influence; Email marketing.
Interrogation	Online Quantitative Research: web survey systems, designing online surveys, working with panels and databases.
	Social Media metrics: Search Engine Optimisation, Social Media Optimisation, participatory blogs as research tools, and measurement and evaluation of digital performance.
	Online Qualitative Research: online focus groups, bulletin board groups and parallel IDIs, other qualitative methods.
	MROCs: Market Research Online Communities.

Source: Authors' representation (2022)

The key drivers of digital are:
- *Speed:* The expectancy of immediacy facilitated by incredibly fast and ubiquitous global network.
- *Adaptability:* Complex algorithms, software updates, experiences and preferences automatically across all touchpoints changing content.
- *Adjacency*: Externally, all of the competition globally is visible/clickable at the same time in the same space; internally, departments are more inter-connected which promotes collaboration and coherence in offering a comprehensive service.
- *Scale:* Content can diffuse on a much wider scale and doesn't cost any more.
- *Precision:* 'Big Data' etc. can bring much better rationality to decision-making.
- *Digital adoption*: The adoption and adaption of new software by an individual user or group of users into their routine workflows or consumption habits

Lurie (2006, p. 7) describes the Internet as "the only two-way marketing medium outside of a face-to-face meeting, a telephone call, or a video conference" making it more efficient, profitable, and much more complex. Companies use brand-generated content on social media in order to engage prospective, lapsed, and existing customers at all stages of the customer journey. The term 'branded content' is used (perhaps rather obviously) to denote content relevant to a brand and present on channels such as branded mobile apps, messages from companies in short or long-form blogs, tweets, posts on *Facebook* and *Instagram*, texts, or any message on social media. Digital engagement of this sort is a phenomenon which has been rooted in the interactivity of service marketing and the co-creation of value and meaning, designed around consumers' interactions with a brand to strengthen emotional, psychological, or physical investments (Chaffey, 2011) as part of the consumer decision-making process. It is strategically important because it focuses on how the customer's brand experience – all the touchpoints with the company and fellow users – can be improved and how this can be leveraged to produce loyalty, income flow, and profitability. The 'vortex' of conceptual threads illustrated in Figure 7.6 *Customer Journey* in the previous chapter describes how the consumer is progressively exposed to the key elements of company strategy: managing the consumer decision-making process; the processes which assist the service provision; and the cumulative process of brand building.

There is a distinction to be made between Internet marketing and social media marketing: social media is the aggregate of primarily user-generated content not specifically direct from the brand owner. Its strategic importance is in the following characteristics: replicating a message (not necessarily about the product but usually brand-related) via consumer-to consumer communication (C2C) to cause a 'buzz' and create a 'viral' campaign; creating ways to engage users in C2C communications which can lead users to talk to users; and communications not controlled by companies. Unlike with traditional marketing, companies can't really control the conversation. They can build trust through relationships with users. Positively influencing consumers to spread word of mouth (WOM) in order to convert to interest, sales, loyalty etc. is the end goal. Barker *et al* (2013, p. 35) list the 8Cs of strategy development:

- *Categorise* social media platforms by target market relevancy.
- *Comprehend* the rules, policies, and behaviour of specific platforms.
- *Converse* as a contributor not a promoter, gaining trust through knowledge and concern for users' topics of interest, solving problems.
- *Collaborate* to mutual benefit with platform participants, building connections, real relationships by emphasising human not financial partnerships.
- *Contribute* 'thought leadership' content to build a reputation and be a valued contributor to the community.
- *Connect* with the influencers to enlist them through exemplar service to help shape opinion.
- *Community* creation and participation can elicit insightful feedback and valuable suggestions for user-advocated product and service improvement.
- *Convert* strategy execution into desired outcome such as brand building, increasing customer satisfaction, driving WOM recommendations, producing new product ideas, lead generation, handling crisis reputation management, increasing site traffic and search engine ranking.

8.4 Marketing communications strategy and planning

Whilst there are plenty of planning structures to describe the different approaches to researching, creating and managing a Marketing Communications Plan, Kotler's failsafe summary of: analysis, planning, implementation, and control (APIC) still provides a backbone to most academic and practitioner Marketing or Communication Plans (Dahlén, Lange, & Smith, 2010). The *CAMPAIGN* Marketing Communications Planning Framework© featured here in Figure 8.1 essentially emphasises this. It differs from the standard IMC frameworks because of its circularity as opposed to the unrealistic linearity of other models. Campaigns can be short-term or medium-terms bursts of activity, but strategy is an on-going, iterative process, adjusted for context and adapted to suit customer needs, and this is reflected in the *CAMPAIGN* Marketing Communications Planning Framework©.

This is an instructive and summative structure designed to illustrate the following elements of Marketing Communications Strategy:

- A reinforcement of the core components consistent with Marketing Plans (ie: analysis, planning, implementation, and control).
- An outline of the various planning and implementation stages in the development of marketing communications.
- A visual demonstration of the integrated and coherent aspect of campaign planning as a continuing process.

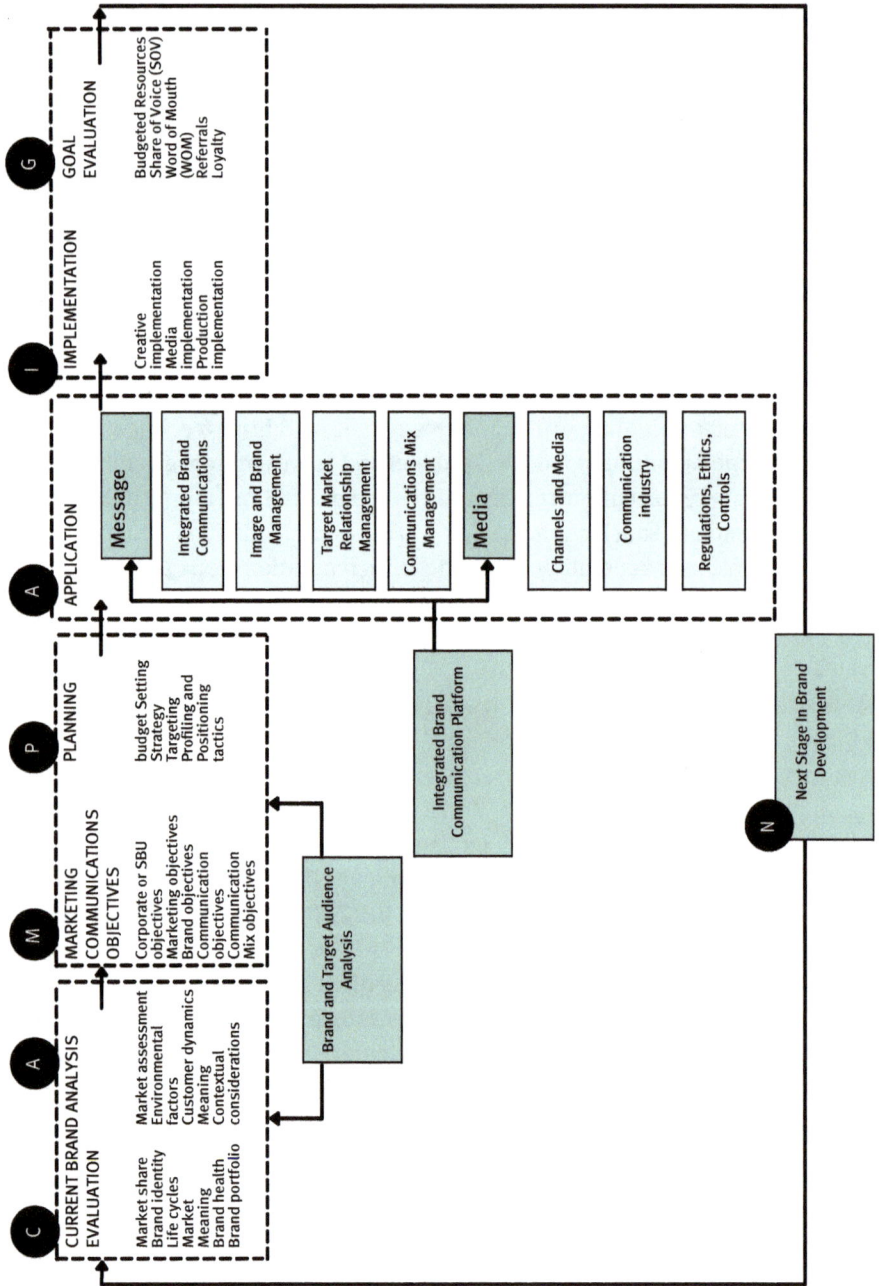

Figure 8.1: CAMPAIGN Strategy Framework.
Source: Dahlen, Lange, & Smith (2010)

- A reinforcement of an over-arching brand narrative thread which all communication strategies, tactics, mix elements, and resources create and contribute to.

It is an aide memoire using the acronym CAMPAIGN which will help students and
managers understand and apply this strategic structure.
- *Current brand evaluation*: research into market share, brand and company history, brand health, strategic role within brand portfolio, market meaning.
- *Analysis*: market assessment, environmental influences, target market and customer dynamics, and other contextual considerations.
- *Marketing Communication Effects and Objectives*: corporate (or SBU), marketing,
  brand and communication effects and objectives.
- *Planning*: strategic framework, segmentation, targeting and positioning, tactics,
  techniques, and budgets.
- *Application*: all message (communications mix, branding, reputation management,
  relationship management) and media (channels and media, intermediaries, communication industry).
- *Implementation*: creative, media and production implementation.
- *Goal evaluation*: budgeted resources, share of voice, awareness, purchase, referrals, market share, customer retention.
- *Next stage of development*: the future of the brand narrative, direction of brand
  development, feedback from the marketplace into the start of the next cycle of
  planning.[148]

What are the successful ingredients of IMC? Shultz and Kitchen (2000) describes
these as the '5 Rs' of communication planning:
- *Responsiveness*: Asymmetrical communication is geared towards talking not listening, monologue not dialogue. The reverse should be the case if companies are
  to understand buyer behaviour and respond to the informational needs of the
  consumer.
- *Relevance*: This is the interruption vs. value issue. 'Interruption' marketing (eg:
  TV 30-second spot advertising, print advertising) is not as effective and in some
  cases not relevant. Added value communications which enrich the information
  search experience, entertain, and educate, but which addresses consumer not
  company needs is essential.
- *Receptivity*: Information of value must be communicated when and how consumers need it.

---

148 Some of the detail is extracted from one of the author's previous textbooks *Marketing Communications: A Brand Narrative Approach, 2010, John Wiley & Sons*

- *Recognition*: Brands which build affiliation can differentiate from the competition. Ongoing communications and brand encounters are the source of unique relationships between company and customer.
- *Relationships*: Retention marketing and the customer-company interface are vital elements of the relationships that are built up and the importance of a customer service-oriented organisation is of paramount importance.

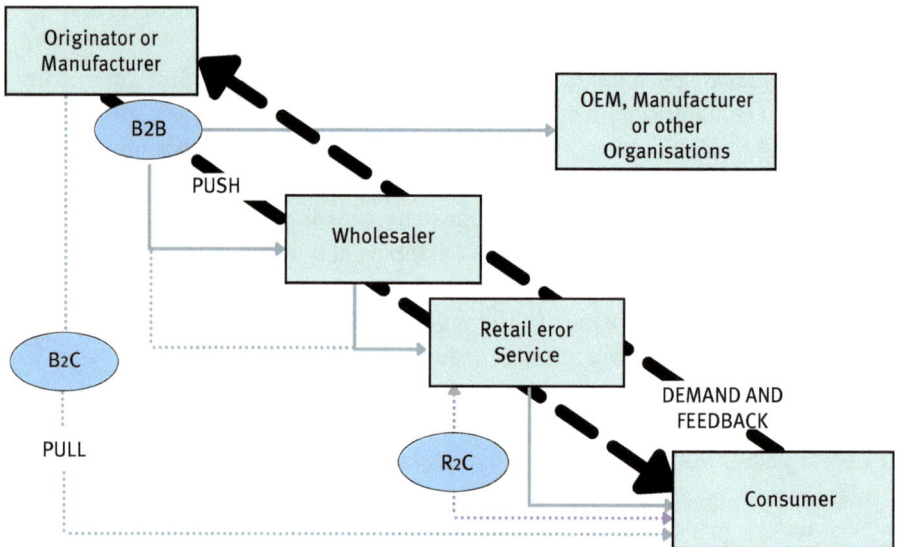

Figure 8.2: Communication flow and communication agent dynamic.
Source: Dahlen, Lange, & Smith (2010)

Figure 8.2 shows the communication flows and communication agencies involved in the dissemination of IMC messages. The flow of communication can be based on: an inside-out perspective aimed at influencing end-user customers by moving people from a state of 'unawareness' of either product category or brand by appealing to fulfilling a desired or latent need ('Pull' strategy), or driving communications through the channels of intermediaries ('Push' strategy). The former involves the creation of content – ads, editorials, paid influencers, viral campaigns etc. – to gain attention, raise awareness, stimulate interest, instil desire, and initiate a 'call to action' like information search, enquiry, traffic into store, trial, and so on. Personal and professional appeals which resonate with customers' lifestyle needs, manufacturing specifications, or service requirements are designed to pull the flow of communication into the organisation's control. On the other hand, a 'push' strategy looks to drive product stocking and create opportunities to see (OTS) through obtaining a presence in intermediaries' and retailers' physical (warehouse) or virtual (website) sites.

The communication agency dynamic is given below:

- *Pull Strategy (or positioning)*: Often referred to as 'B2C' (Business-to-Consumer or company to end user customer). This might involve TV advertising, digital campaigns (eg: content strategy), and direct marketing campaigns aimed at the consumer, which is a circular communication flow, since feedback allows for two-way dialogue.
- *Push Strategy (or positioning)*: B2B (Business-to-Business). Some Manufacturers will deal with other manufacturers (OEMs) or through intermediaries who provide bulk-breaking and cost advantages as well as access to markets for the company. They offer time, choice, location, and added-value utilities to end-users.
- *Push/Pull Strategy (or positioning)*: A circular B2C. Some companies (eg: *Dell Technologies*) do not deal through intermediaries and have a direct link with their end-customers and have a direct Business-to-Customer (B2C) flow of both transaction and communication.
- *R2C Push/Pull Strategy (or positioning)*: Retailer-to-Customer (R2C) flow of communication illustrates the switch of power to retailers. Has made the Business-to-Customer (B2C) relationship much more meaningful than ever before and retailers invest heavily in sustaining this.
- *B2B Push/Pull Strategy (or positioning)*: Some companies supply direct to other businesses and organisations on a contract basis (eg: *Dell Technologies* has a B2B Division) or sell components to other manufacturers or other equipment manufacturers OEM (eg: *Michelin* tyres to *Ford Motor Company*).

Push and *Pull* strategies have their roots in marketing communication goals and objectives, brand ownership, and the need to 'try' and control the brand message channelled to and through an ecosystem of customers, stakeholders, influencers, intermediaries, and other interested parties. All elements need to be co-ordinated and integrated to retain some measure of management of brand identity and customer relationships. These also have to be integrated with the third part of Marketing Communications Strategy – concerned with the management of internal and external stakeholder perceptions in order to maintain corporate reputation and brand equity – usually referred to as a *Profile* strategy (Fill 2002. p.339), and is essentially a synthesis of Public Relations (PR), Corporate Branding, and Image and Reputation Management (IRM).

As we have seen, an organisation's image is not just down to product fit or service process satisfaction; it now covers expressions of conscience and commitments to purpose. Retailers must demonstrate that they have corporate and social responsibility, an ethical supply chain, and a deep understanding of customers' values. Relations with the media, digital influencers, and the user-generated content which can make or break an organisation's reputation must be managed.

Managing online reputation is increasingly sophisticated. That ugly word 'findability' is a recent addition to the brand manager's lexicon. Search engines such as

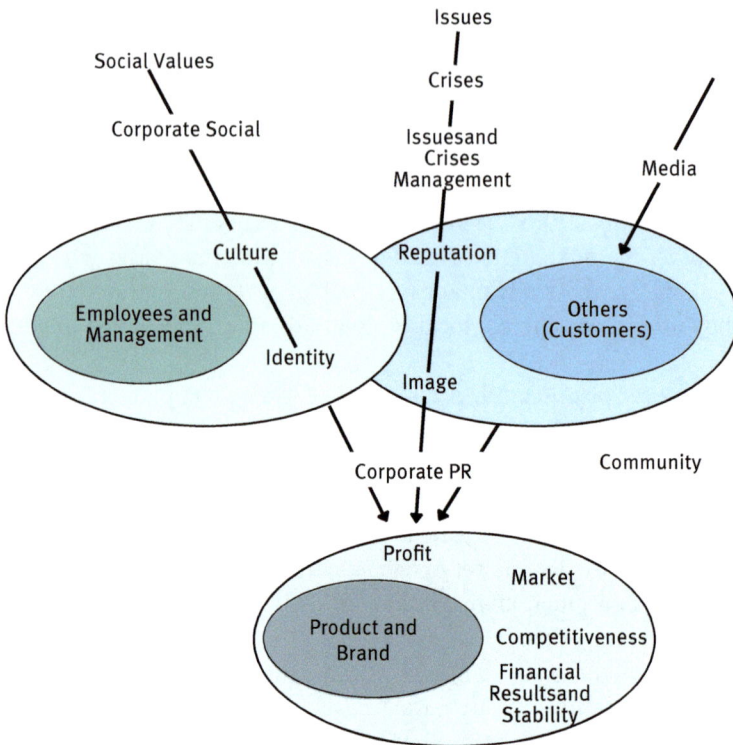

Figure 8.3: Profile Strategy.
Source: L'Etang & Pieczka (2006, p.291)

Google provide Search Engine Results Pages (SERPs) which help companies record data across all digital touchpoints. Reviews, ratings, and feedback on Google, the company website, and third-party sites, influence search ranking, and, more importantly, gives an opportunity to positively influence the customer experience, learn about perceptions of company positioning, and so on.

The three domains of profile strategy (See Figure 8.3) include the *internal*, *micro*, and *macro* environments, product and brand, employees and managers, and the wider community respectively (L'Etang & Pieczka, 2006, p. 290).The projection of values, culture, and identity of the organisation are mainly expressed through employees. The broader societal context has taken on a greater corporate and individual significance with position on ecological and ethical consideration crucial.

Principles in practice

Conversation, community, and cookies.
Oreo flies the LGBTQ+ PFLAG flag.

People buy brands that they can identify with, or relate to, or whose message carried in the conversations of communication campaigns resonates with their individual values and beliefs. To stay alive, therefore, some brands have to stay relevant to its audience's social conscience as well as its consumption needs. The decision to target a different segment, or focus on a particular value, may be because there is more sales potential, or it gives an opportunity to reinforce the social synergy between customer and company. However, when a brand reassesses its value proposition – and, for that matter, positioning on values – to reflect that of a new or changing demographic, this may alienate the brand's original core buyers.

For example, when *Volvo* targeted a new more lucrative demographic, it changed its central platform of 'Safety' (primarily a product-orientation positioning) because it had negative social connotations with a new targeted younger audience. Similarly, when *Oreos* introduced their *Pride*-themed multicoloured cream biscuits, made with a purpose – to celebrate and support the lesbian, gay, bisexual, transgender, and queer (LGBTQ+) community – it was hailed as both "a rainbow capitalist moment" and "normalising the LGBTQ+ lifestyle to brainwash children and adults alike by desensitising audiences". When brands become allies, they can unite or risk alienating their customer base.

Oreos, like parent top-ranking *HRC's 2020 Corporate Equality Index* company Mondelēz International formerly *Nabisco*, has been celebrating 'family' social themes for over 100 years, and have supported 'gay' themes for more than a decade. It is a favourite brand of Gen Z and Gen Alpha,[149] the most liberated and diverse generation in history. As a brand which has always been socially aware, acknowledging segment heterogeneity but also recognising individual identity has been (and continues to be) a central communication conversation platform for this brand. The introduction of *Pride*-themed rainbow-coloured cream biscuits, with product pronoun packs, celebrate all the diverse social groups of homogeneity and gender-neutrality. However, when the appeal was extended to include parents, families, friends, and allies of LGBTQ+ people, this proved to be inclusive but divisive.

PFLAG (Parents, Families, and Friends of Lesbians and Gays), the first and biggest US organisation of its kind, has over 400 US 'chapters' and affiliates with 200,000 members and supporters, with many organisations and activists around the world utilising the 'family and ally' model doing similar work. *Oreo* joined with *PFLAG* to produce a film 'Proud Parent' and revealed that there would be Limited Edition *Pride*-themed Rainbow biscuits (10,000 packs only) as rewards for posting acts of "allyship" with the LGBTQ+ community on *Twitter* and *Instagram* with hashtags *#ProudParent*. "This *#ProudParent* platform is aimed at empowering and inspiring parents, families, and allies of LGBTQ+ to come out in loud support", said Brian Bond, Executive Director of *PFLAG,* "because every time they do they inspire others to do the same, making the world a more accepting, affirming and compassionate place. Having a supportive family and committed allies is crucial for the health and well-being of lesbian, gay, bisexual, transgender, and queer people". However, sparking connections with one group alienated another.

---

149 Generation Alpha (Gen Z), the demographic succeeding Generation Z, are those born entirely in the 21st Century (2000 or 2001 dependent on calendars).

OneMillionMoms.com, a division of the American Family Association, an organisation whose moral crusade is "to stand against immorality, violence, vulgarity, and profanity in the media" is a frequent boycotter of pro-LGBTQ+ initiatives. Campaigns against the "pushing the LGBTQ agenda to brainwash children as young as toddler age and adults alike by desensitising audiences" have included *Hallmark* gender-neutral cards, gender-inclusive *Mattel* dolls, as well as *Disney Junior's* cross-dressing *'Gonzorella'*.

For *Oreos*, the loss of certain customers has to be balanced against building relevance and loyalty through the community conversations of integrated marketing communications.

8.5 Permissive and interactive marketing

A direct result of the change away from company-dominated asymmetrical communications is *permissive marketing* (Godin, 1999), a communications strategy that, unlike traditional invasive or interruption marketing, promotes and communicates once advanced consent is given so that target audiences will willingly accept messages. Engagement was often thought of as merely being strategically placed TV, magazine, or billboard ads, carefully targeted to hit captive audiences with well-researched messages and product information. In over-crowded marketplaces, with communication 'noise' at saturated levels, the 'silver bullet' effect of broadcast communication was starting to be blunted. Many business owners still stick to their default 'Push' strategies and remain staunchly product-oriented instead of being customer-centric.

Traditional media, undermined and replaced by new digital media and changing communications consumption, has been placed under the microscope and its cost-effectiveness and efficacy questioned. Social media has fractured the fabric of traditional methods, changing the dynamic to a more *permissive* (aka 'Pull' strategy) form of marketing communication. York (2018) advocates customer-centricity, designing "permissive content to attract, to engage, to support information/education needs, to dialogue with other customers, to engage with the company, and provide an accessible path to acquisition" (p. 7). Engagement with consumers – at every stage of the decision-making process from 'unawareness' to 'post-purchase brand reinforcement – is a critical element of brand strategy. Indeed, the cognitive, emotive, and conative components have been augmented with social and experiential dimensions. *Experiential* phenomena embraces physical, corporeal (Christodoulides, 2008), and multi-sensory elements of encounter (Schmitt, 1999); *social* comprises consumer interaction, active participation, negotiation of meaning, dialogic communication and co-creation.

With a nod to Shostack's seminal service-shifting paper, Christodoulides encourages both academics and practitioners to 'break free' from the industrial age of openness and creation (2008, p. 292). Engaging with consumers can be seen by practioners as "a dynamic and process-based concept evolving in intensity on the basis of a brand's capability of increasingly intercepting consumer's desires and expectations using all possible physical and virtual touchpoints between brand and consumers" (Gambetti, Graffigna, & Biraghi, 2012, p. 660). For practitioners to adapt strategy successfully, they believe three key elements must be employed:

- Strategy must be in sync with consumers *value-based affinity* (a container or 'value system' of thoughts, perceptions, and meanings).
- The brand should have a *point of reference in consumers' lives* (functional, aesthetic, and symbolic).
- There has to be *leverage of consumer's protagonism* (creating and spreading brand values through active participation, socialisation, co-creation, and total enactment of the brand in their daily lives).

Brand engagement research using insightful data analysis can help assess the effectiveness of communication by tracking how brand strategy has affected 'sentiment' towards the brand, and how this can be converted into long-lasting loyalty and lifetime customer income.

8.6 Integration and strategic consistency

As we have seen, the scope of IMC has broadened to include all stakeholders, all channels, and every written, verbal, symbolic, planned or unplanned, utterance from the company. In order to maintain corporate integrity with an organisation's social ecosystem and help build a foundation for integrated marketing communications, it is important for strategic brand management to be consistent in terms of maintaining positioning and image, but particularly so with regard to reinforcement of core brand values, business philosophy, and corporate mission (Dewhirst & Davis, 2005). Consistency of message through 'one voice' integrated communications can help: form bonds of unbreakable customer loyalty; enhance stakeholder trust; improve brand perception and competitiveness; and facilitate continual brand development and longevity. According to Duncan, IMC is "a cross-functional process for creating and nourishing profitable relationships with customers and other stakeholders by strategically controlling or influencing all messages sent to these groups and encouraging data-driven purposeful dialogue with them" (2002, p. 7).

 IMC strategy, by its very nature, should have a 360° planning to be objective. Some would argue that a 'media neutral' approach – selecting media channels without prejuice which the brand objectives dictated – should be adopted. Others would disagree that this force fit creative work and communications relevance was compromised. Having flexibility to change in response to platform and message changes is vital however, and the 'de-siloing' aspect of media neutral planning (MNP) certainly does that. Tapp's view on media selection hits the nail on the head: "Which media to choose is best done once one knows what the firm is good at, what the proposition to the customer is, what market one wishes to go for, how to segment that market and how to position the company against the competition" (Tapp, 2004, p. 133).

What type of media selection is appropriate depends upon the nature of the sender and the perspective of the recipient. Communications sent directly from a company tend to be perceived as least likely to be trusted; those from a 'neutral' fellow consumer the most credible. A framework which provides a useful guide to this sometimes goes under the title of 'PESO' standing for 'paid', 'earned', 'shared', and 'owned' media (See Figure 8.4).

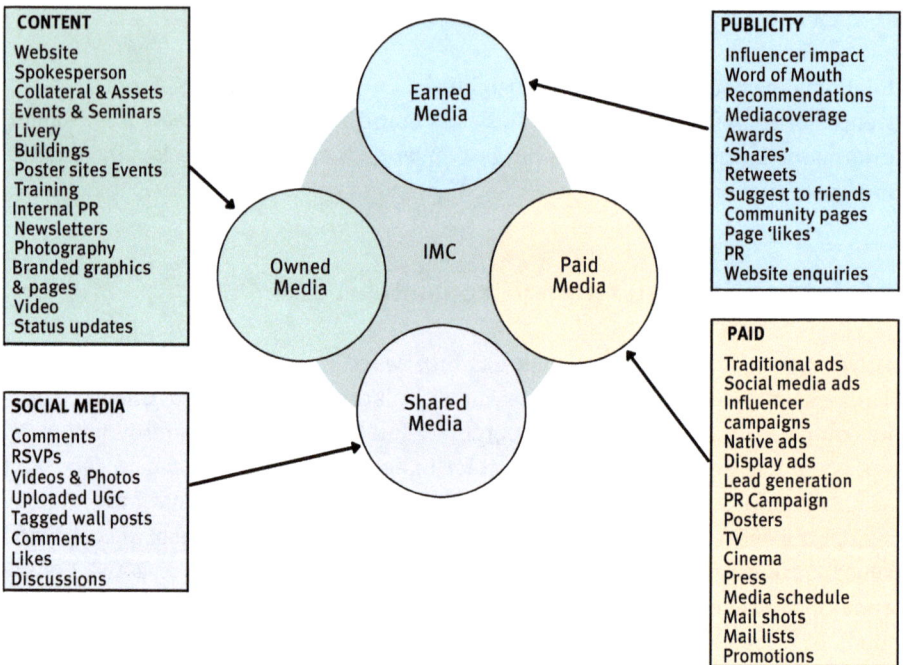

CONTENT
Website
Spokesperson
Collateral & Assets
Events & Seminars
Livery
Buildings
Poster sites Events
Training
Internal PR
Newsletters
Photography
Branded graphics
& pages
Video
Status updates

PUBLICITY
Influencer impact
Word of Mouth
Recommendations
Mediacoverage
Awards
'Shares'
Retweets
Suggest to friends
Community pages
Page 'likes'
PR
Website enquiries

SOCIAL MEDIA
Comments
RSVPs
Videos & Photos
Uploaded UGC
Tagged wall posts
Comments
Likes
Discussions

PAID
Traditional ads
Social media ads
Influencer
campaigns
Native ads
Display ads
Lead generation
PR Campaign
Posters
TV
Cinema
Press
Media schedule
Mail shots
Mail lists
Promotions

Earned Media — Owned Media — IMC — Paid Media — Shared Media

Figure 8.4: Media components of IMC.
Source: Authors' representation (2022)

There are essentially four ways a company can communicate with their customers and stakeholders:

- *'Owned Media'*: The company has full control over the message (eg: company websites, webinars, company-generated content). May be inexpensive but may lack reach, impact, and be poorly received in terms of trust.
- *'Paid For'*: where the company pays a media owner or influencer for channel leverage has some control over the message (eg: other companies' websites, paid-for-generated content, boosted content, advertising, 'native' advertising or advertorials). May get exposure but can be costly, and be poorly received in terms of trust.

- *'Earned Media'*: The company has earned the opportunity for exposure due to media relations (eg: positive sentiment on social media); and customers 'become the channel'.
- *'Shared Media'*: The company intends content to be shared but has little control over it (eg: WOM marketing content, organic social, review sites, media sharing sites, brand community, user-generated content).

Paid and Owned media may get more exposure, but the two types of Earned media – traditional such as good publicity and mentions in the press not paid for, and the socially earned online WOM from brand community and independent blog posts – may have more impact.

Owned media can use GIFs, infographics, video content, and so on to engage audiences with tools such as search engine optimisation (SEO) used to analyse results. Because of the impact of *TIVO* ad-skipping devices, and the decline of newspapers, Paid Media has taken a different complexion and become more digitised (eg: *Google Ads*). Earned media is unsolicited content acquired from others (eg: journalists, bloggers, vloggers, and influencers, online customer reviews, recommendations) which provokes the brand being positively talked about. There are a plethora of media tool kits used for analysing 'sentiment' and 'mentions'. Earned and Shared media are unpredictable and more difficult to control.

8.7 Content, convergence, and connectivity

Clutter, creativity, the changing cost-efficiencies of media, together with a focus on consumer-orientation constitute a complex and challenging communications landscape, where advertisers are no longer in control of their brands. Modern consumers hardly ever read a newspaper, use a landline phone, are not 'captive' in front of a TV, download their own choice of programme, trust unknown bloggers, and have a communal experience on-line through the plethora of social media. Marketing Communications has moved beyond traditional audience interruption to a new era of audience brand engagement. Technology has affected both company and customer: companies are better equipped to talk with customers through omni-channel, one-voice communications, but customers are more in control of that conversation.

The key features of innovation and transparency have been "enhanced by the altered relationship of stakeholders recognised as partners and co-creators not just consumers" (Chua, Goh, & Ang, 2012, p. 176). The efficacy of traditional transmissive monologue approaches to reaching target audiences through "interruption mass-communications" (Shultz 2005, p.34) have been undermined by a dialogic, cross-platform integration of simultaneous media consumption experience of permissive, communality. It is customer-centric and customer-driven. The era of "open-source marketing", the rise of social media, the imperative of brand narratives, and the focus on co-authored communications, is moving towards a brand landscape where 'media' is seen as 'content' and 'communication' as 'conversation'. Solis (2011, p. 9) captures this well: "Social tools facilitate the online conversations, but the people who are the instigators of change".

Consumers consensually 'opt-in' with user-generated and co-authored 'long-form' content, helping to create or re-create the brand experience. It is this essentially experiential approach to branding, based on use which is related to situational benefits, which creates affinity and a sense of brand community. From a consumer perspective, the rich media (sound, video and even touch) of the "social web" (Weber, 2009) enhances impact and engagement as it aggregates consumers and allows discourse within the environmental context of the brand: pharmaceutical companies engage in debate about diseases; car companies discuss pollution and the need for hybrid cars; and even chocolate confectioners raise the nature of fair-trade supply. There are four forces which are accelerating the rate of change in the digital revolution and causing the advertising industry to rethink: the ubiquitous "24/7/365" connectivity of broadband; the emphasis on receiving messages via wireless communications; search engines which are "the key gateway for most users to reach online content; and networks which offer the promise of community and the empowerment that comes from being informed, connected and unified" (Weber, 2007, p. 153). The transition from passive reception to democratic negotiation marks out a new era of content and connectivity.

Kimmel (2010, p. 290) offers five key lessons relevant to "engaging with consumers and leveraging their conversations":
- *Connections have different values.*
- *Different connected marketing tools for different marketing goals.*
- *No connected marketing effort stands on its own.*
- *Open, honest, and ethical connections for long-term value.*
- *Everything must be measured.*

Looking at these 'lessons' in detail:
- *Connections have different values*: Not all communities of consumers have the same value for achieving different marketing objectives and it is therefore imperative for consumer targets to be carefully identified. Peppers and Rogers (2004) describe most valuable customers as "those who the proponderance of business with the enterprise relative to the costs of acquiring them, yield the highest margins and are likely to remain loyal", (p. 56). In Figure 8.5, a useful model has been suggested by *Forrester Research* illustrating how networks differ in terms of scale ('proximity') and dynamics ('community'). The varying potential values associated with consumer networks which differ in terms of *scale* ('proximity' in the model) and *dynamics* ('community' in the model). The network with the highest potential value is seen in the top right-hand corner whose members are 'entwined' with another and whose connections are 'intimate' rather than 'public'. They stay in touch and have

relationships based on trust. Those that are most cohesively linked together ('entwined') and whose connections are 'intimate' rather than 'public' offer the most value. These demonstrate regular contact and a high degree of trust and peer references are highly credible. The high value quadrant depicts entwined communities whose connections are more public with active online participants. Companies target these sort of brand communities through engagement programmes (eg: *Starbuck's 'My Starbuck's Idea'; Dell Technologies' 'Ideastorm'*). The medium quadrant sees a more loosely connected group less trusting brand advocacy; the quadrant with the lowest potential value are a loosely-bonded, often anonymous community.

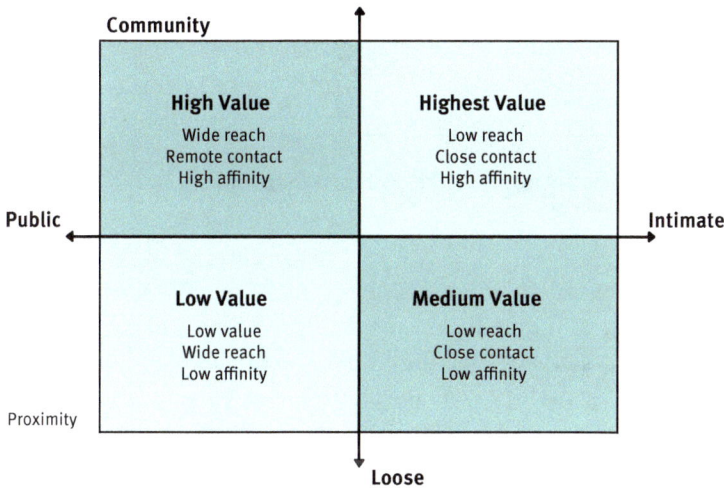

Figure 8.5: Connections have differing relative values for marketing.
Source: *Forrester Research* (cited in Kimmel, 2010, page 291)

- *Different connected marketing tools for different marketing goals*: Engaging with customers and leveraging the WOM potential of conversations can be achieved using many different tools, dependent upon a number of factors: competitive environment, resources, customer characteristics, media usage habits, and so on. As Oosterwijk L and Loeffen (2005) suggest, different marketing communication tools can be used for different marketing goals (See Figure 8.6).
- *No connected marketing effort stands on its own*: It is a truism that all tools have to be appropriately selected and applied, and that integration with other communication mix components (and indeed all the other elements of the marketing mix) is essential.
- *Open, honest, and ethical connections for long-term value.*
- *Everything must be measured.*

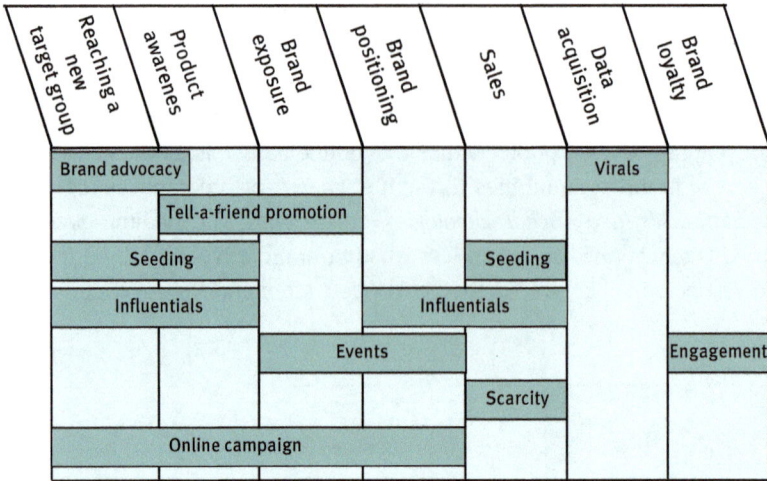

Figure 8.6: Matching connected marketing approaches with marketing goals.
Source: Oosterwijk L and Loeffen (2005)

Convergence is the over-riding characteristic of today's media environment, with consumers interacting with brands through multiple online and offline channels. The Internet is a portal, an aggregator for linking companies and customers. The plethora of portable technology such as smartphones and tablets, and the range of platforms like *Twitter* and *Facebook* has precipitated a convergence into the online domain and resulted in 'media neutral' planning and multi-channel brand strategy. There is no doubt that the COVID-19 pandemic has disrupted the work/life balance of most people across the world. The use of alternative news, on-demand content, video streaming entertainment, 'non-navigational' linear and 'navigational' non-linear multi-media, live broadcasting, the acceleration of e-commerce, and social distraction have changed media consumption 'norms' and impacted on media owners, planners, and advertisers. In this continuing state of uncertainty and transformation, brand building is much more of a challenge. Brands need to remain relevant and communications tone of voice has to be consistent; strategy has to be even more cohesively implemented.

8.8 Benefits of integrated marketing communications

The benefits of a marketing communications strategy which is integrated, cohesive and consistent across the elements of the mix are shown in Table 8.3.

There is a lot of research to support the view that practitioners don't use integrative strategies for marketing communications; some even argue that there is a misunderstanding of the word 'strategy' (Steyn, 2004). Either way, both focus on two

Table 8.3: Benefits of integrated marketing communications.

Increased impact of communications dialogue	All programmes deliver the same message.
	All communications speak with the same 'voice'.
	Overall strategy for the brand rather than individual tactical use of communication tools.
	Reinforcement of message helps recall and recognition.
	reduces confusion in the minds of the consumer.
	Cumulative effect adds to brand equity.
	Consistency of message delivery.
	More control over unplanned communications.
Corporate cohesion	Used as a strategic tool in communicating its corporate and brand image for both external and internal cohesion
	Aids operational efficiency.
Interaction	Better flow of communications between company, intermediaries and end-user consumer.
	Better flow of communications between creative agencies and media.
	Easier working relationships.
Participation	Two-way dialogue encourage co-authorship of brand narrative.
	Communication complicity with employees and intermediaries.
Resource efficiencies	Greater control over communications budget.
	Measurability.
	Reduces cost because of cohesion of communication mix components.
	Maximises strengths of individual components.
	unbiased marketing recommendations.
	Media schedules not agency-led.

Source: Derived from Linton and Morley (1995), Kitchen and Schultz (1999), and Yeshin (1998)

key areas: the target audience and how perceptions of the value proposition (positioning) are received, interpreted, and negotiated. Segmentation and data analysis are pre-requisites to, and provide a framework for, successful targeting which underpins positioning which is the primary concern of strategic brand management. Positioning applies to all brands in all organisations in all sectors. Positioning is the outcome of marketing communications. Some would argue that "marketing communications strategy is essentially about positioning" (Fill, 2009, p. 294). Maintaining an authentic, strong competitive position, and repositioning if market conditions dictate, is the primary concern of brand strategy.

Chapter takeaways

- Value is not embedded in the product at the moment of transactional exchange, but obtained through consumption processes *at the point of interaction*.
- The customer journey has become the product, guiding customers through a company's product and service processes, providing a company with customer knowledge to help that process.
- Tracking and analysing customer behaviour across omni-channel interfaces provides opportunities to enhance customer experience, reinforce loyalty, and drive continued engagement.
- The use of 'customer journey maps' devised through customer journey analysis (CJA) can present an honest externalised customer perspective.
- Customer experience quality is judged with respect to its contribution to *value-in-use* through its product and service offer but also the broad range of encounters with communications, and relationships with other customers.
- The notion of the 'Voice of the Customer' (VOC) is both philosophically-oriented and process-driven.
- Touchpoints are all the customer-company interactions before, during and after purchase; conversely, customer journeys are made up of many touchpoints (or 'pain points') where customers directly or indirectly experience the brand.
- The use of customer experience maps (CXMs) or customer buying maps (CBMs) are used to capture activity or behaviour at each touchpoint, with CXMs extending beyond buying.
- Service provision must take a central role in integrating all customer engagement processes, and the experience which companies must offer – the holistic customer journey – must be interactive, immediately responsive, and personalised.
- Digitalisation is driving the need for a new perspective on service marketing where consumer behaviour has dramatically changed and technology-enabled interaction is becoming an increasingly prevalent part of the customer-company relationship.

Closing case

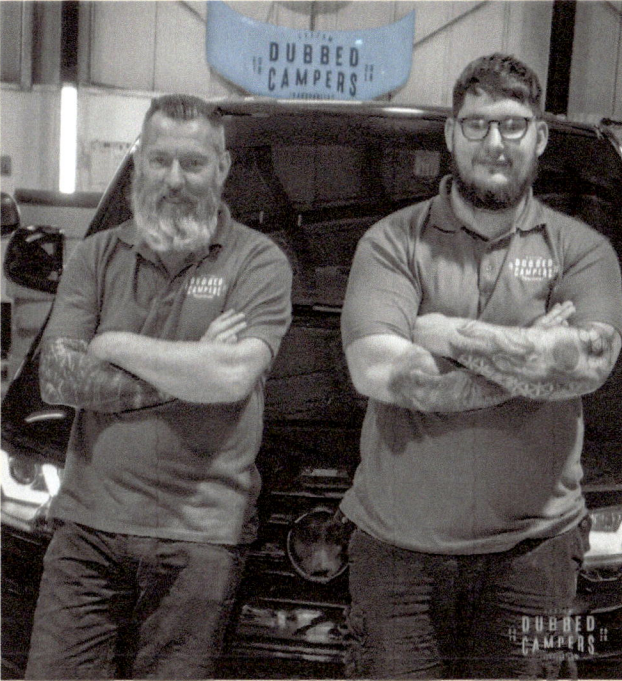

***Dubbed Campers* – big lessons on the road to building a micro-brand through camper conversations**

On the road to building a business, what role does an integrated marketing communications approach play for a micro SME? For *Dubbed Campers*, a family-run business set up just as the world was becoming aware of a spreading pandemic, January 2020 presented a daunting double challenge. From the worries of pre-start up through to the challenging 18-month "valley of death",[150] starts-ups must navigate a treacherous path before they are able to reach the sustainable growth stage. By September 2020, over 1,000 start-ups had collapsed – the highest level in over 10-years[151] – amid the ensuing chaos of COVID-19. But though the journey to building their business would be a precarious and difficult one, the passion and expertise they had pushed them down the road to re-building camper vans and building brand equity. The key to *Dubbed Campers'* success was that the construction of both carriage-conversion and campaign planning had already started.

---

150 https://www.forbes.com/sites/martinzwilling/2013/02/18/10-ways-for-startups-to-survive-the-valley-of-death/?sh=63b2a51e69ef
151 https://sifted.eu/articles/startup-deaths-hit-record-level/

Like a lot of SMEs, the small acorn of a hobby grew into a sustainable business. *Dubbed Campers* started as a father and son's obsession with repairing and maintaining their *VW Transporter* vans to become an established business that offers a range of products and services from custom modifications, an online retail shop through to high-specification campervan conversions. Co-Founder, Luke Appleby, pinpoints the moment he and his father John decided to try and build a micro-brand from their developing re-building business:

> *My dad and I both had VW transporters that we had a passion for customising, so it came naturally to want to work on them. I started an Instagram page posting different vans and at the same time opened a small online business selling VW-inspired clothing and stickers in my spare time. My dad had been working on his own transporters for years and we eventually agreed it would be a shared dream to work on them together.*

When micro-brands set up, often the impetus is the initial manufacturing or service idea; the business and marketing communications strategy develops as a necessity *after* orders are achieved. *Dubbed Campers*, however, are an example of how taking a holistic view of brand communications can actually provide the backbone for an entire operation, irrespective of size (Grönroos & Lindberg-Repo, 1998, p. 10). When done effectively, that process of co-creation, mutual benefit, and interactive dialogue between customers and company can help build a business through the relationships of positive customer to company conversations.

At the heart of Luke's simple but effective strategy was the building of a strong loyal following and with a clear focus of purpose expressed through *interactive* dialogue via strong social media activity. This not only established the value proposition to a growing target market, but also mitigated the risk that all start-ups face: establishing a presence and critical mass of customers before an official 'launch'. They knew that the curation of brand awareness and loyalty in parallel with slowly building business would give them the confidence to believe their business would be sustainable.

> *In 2018 I started an Instagram page called Dubbed Campers – I began by posting pictures of other people's vans that I thought looked great. I genuinely hand-picked interesting vans rather than spamming average vans. I also made and started using the hashtag #dubbedcampers with the intention of this being a hashtag used to describe customised transporters (to date this hashtag has been used just shy of 4,500 times). For around 1.5 years I spent at least 2/3 hours a day on Instagram posting, searching for vans to post, commenting and replying to messages. I managed to build up to around 10k followers which were highly active on my page.*

Creating a conversation between brand users and suppliers is not a common trait of SME start-ups, but Luke achieved this with an interactive dialogue with *Dubbed Campers'* audience, hooking into the visually appealing/aspirational nature that embodies the *VW* T5/T6 brand subculture. In March 2018 that had 10 likes, when they had 60 followers, and by January 2020 (when they launched the physical aspect of the brand) they had just over 11,000 followers. As a start-up this level of engagement is very powerful and demonstrates the simplicity and effectiveness of engaging in the *right* conversation with the *right* audience can build something special. Matching *Dubbed Campers'* credibility with the user experience is evident in the early targeted advertising campaigns which personified their foundations and emergence of their early brand loyalty:

> *I did a hard advertising push using only Facebook and Instagram which led to us being nearly fully booked for our 2nd month of opening. We even had a guy travel 5 hours to have his suspension fitted by us as he had followed our Instagram for quite some time. After*

> *launching is where we reaped the benefits of the hours I had poured into brand awareness via Instagram!*

Prioritising this 'start-position' allowed them to generate an audience prior to starting up the business formally which required significant capital and resource outlay, in terms of garage units, people and resources, equipment, and all the administration/back of house operations any business requires.

Dubbed Campers has one singular brand purpose to only serve *VW* Transporters vans, specifically T5 and T6 models. This niche targeting allows for multiple benefits in terms of developing a brand identity that is clear, compelling and creates a two-way conversation not by talking to *everyone*, but with the *right* selection of users. Interestingly, *Dubbed Campers* bravely used this selective focus to create boundaries of communication, prohibiting some business in order to engage in much more meaningful interactive dialogue with an audience that belongs to a growing *VW* Transporter/Campervan brand subculture (2018, Wilson).[152] Additionally, favourable market conditions have seen a domestic boom in UK tourism, but more broadly a growing appeal and increase in campervan, caravanning and motorhome ownership for new markets. With younger campers driving the surge in caravan sales amid UK's 'staycation' boom, with leading motorhome and caravanning companies seeing a quarter of sales from the under 40s market.[153]

Because of the foresight shown in establishing early traction in brand awareness by their niche and loyal following, the foundation would not be in place to maximise this market opportunity. Here, thorough integrated marketing communication planning worked hand-in-hand with their main business. It is clear from reading how both Luke and John collectively have absolute clarity on what makes their brand and how they integrate their brand identity and communications across the business in all forms:

> *We've had a saying ever since we started: 'Would I be happy if this was on my van?' This is something we've stuck to and on many occasions we have stripped out our own work and started again to maintain that high standard (also earning me the satirical nickname 'QA' [i.e. quality assurance' as I ensure this high standard is met consistently).*

> *I always try to remain on brand for everything I possibly can – down to advertising, any media we create, packaging for our items and even the colour of equipment for the workshop. We aim to provide a professional customer service approach whilst still maintaining the small family run business feel. We've built some fantastic relationships with our customers since we started, and I believe our genuine passion for what we do shines through.*

One of the cornerstones of *Dubbed Campers'* success has been integrating its holistic customer journey using insights to help their decision making in developing their website, through to offering personalised design services and offering post-conversion check-ups. All of this really strengthens all aspects of their customer relationships and brand value. The use of website technology identified:

---

152 Wilson. S (2018) *VW* Campervan Subculture: Tourism Mobilities and Experiences, Published PhD, retrieved: https://sure.sunderland.ac.uk/id/eprint/9314/1/Final%20Submission%20PHD%202018%20%28S%20Wilson%29.pdf
153 https://inews.co.uk/inews-lifestyle/travel/younger-campers-surge-caravan-sales-uk-staycation-boom-1045413

- How users first heard about the brand (to aid brand awareness/channels intelligence) – 33% – *Facebook*; 32% – *Google* search; 15% – *Instagram*.
- Why users are visiting their website (motivational profiling) – 38% online retail/shop visitor, 31% – Upgrade/modification information (e.g. body kit/suspension) 18% – Planning a conversion.
- Overall website experience (user satisfaction) – 63% – 5-Star; 24% – 4-Star; 7% – 3-Star

(Top 3 – response base: 371, *FUZE* data, 2021)

Note: These insights help inform their brand and marketing communication strategy (content focus, website customer journey, advertising, website development etc) on a continuous basis. Applying this resource to their business is unusual for a micro-SME, and is something that not all large organisations do, proving it's the size of ambition not the size of business that matters.

Questions

1. Identify three key elements of marketing communication strategy that *Dubbed Campers* deployed in the setting up this family-owned micro-brand.
2. Is it risky to "build a conversation" before launching a company?
3. What are the strengths of using this approach?

9 Managing brand equity: Tangible results from intangible assets

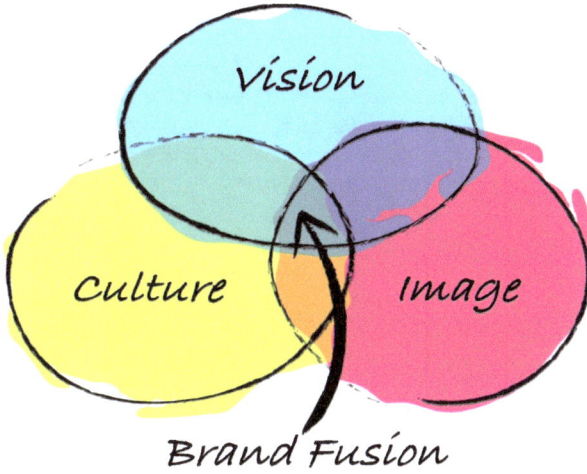

https://doi.org/10.1515/9783110718638-013

Opening case

ESG problems for *Ben & Jerry's*
Brand purpose, politics, and equity

Brand equity is implicit in the associations and relationships customers have with a brand or with an organisation. It is the 'good will' in the customer-company connection, present in the intangibility of perceptual positioning. When Howard Shultz positioned *Starbucks* not as merely a coffee shop but as a social "third space" between home and work, the impact was phenomenal for *Starbucks'* business and transformational for the coffee retail sector. When changing social dynamics cause contemporary readings of original value propositions to threaten brand equity built up over many years, legacy brands often have to reposition. When *Kentucky Fried Chicken* rebranded to *KFC*, they successfully obscured the negative social connotations of unhealthy living. Similarly, *Weight Watchers*, acknowledging that definitions of health and wellness had changed dramatically since its post-2nd World War inception, changed to "*WW* – Wellness That Works". However, although strategically shifting to 'wellness' is not inherently a bad move, they made the mistake of talking *to* and not *with* their audience. Confused positioning, inappropriate celebrity endorsement, the odd name change, and a new purpose which didn't resonate with loyal customers resulted in 50 years of brand equity being dangerously diluted.

Creating conversations of authenticity, relevance, and purpose as an integral part of marketing communications strategy, particularly through the accelerated phenomenon of digital word of mouth (WOM), is now crucial to building brand equity. One company which has purpose as the most defining part of its brand DNA is *Ben & Jerry's*, formerly an independent ice cream manufacturer whose social conscience, environmental concern, and political beliefs now sit alongside a range of products in the *Unilever* brand portfolio. Since forming in 1978, *Ben & Jerry's* have supported global issues such as the safety of refugees, the rights of LGBTQ+ citizens, and peace building posted all over their ice cream tubs. Whilst supporting '420', a day designated to fight for the legalisation of cannabis, they continued the 'Black Lives Matter' narrative of dismantling White Supremacy by focusing on the racial inequalities of black arrests – "Legalisation without justice is half-baked". Significantly, this statement of brand purpose had nothing to do with ROI; it wasn't about selling pints of ice cream but getting 15,000 people to write to Congress asking for representatives to support the More Act (Marijuana Opportunity, Reinvestment, and Expungement), legalising cannabis use, and expunging previous convictions. 65,000 messages sent to legislators and 120m impressions online proved their customers had a huge appetite for activism as well as ice cream consumption.

In fact, there is actually a dedicated Global Head of Activism (since 2012), Christopher Miller, who expounds that "There are moments in the course of history when it's important to stand up and be counted, and that's true of individuals and brands alike". He harnesses the expertise of an ice cream manufacturer "knowing how to market stuff" with the company's authentic credentials in social activism. Some brands are accused of 'virtue signalling' but not *Ben & Jerrys'*. Miller again: "The strongest bond you can create with your customers is a shared sense of value, but that's not why we do this". Creating financial value through shared social values is the *Ben & Jerry* formula for building brand equity.

With a fine line between brand purpose and brand politics, can we distinguish clearly between the two? When does the marketing communication objective of 'recall' become a *call to action*? In today's volatile markets, how and why do these key contemporary brand strategy components contribute to the creation and maintenance of brand equity? Marc Pritchard, former *P&G* CMO, aligned purpose with brand building some time ago when his statement on brand strategy – "This is not the time to be unclear on what your point of view is and what side of history you choose to be on" – could have been confused with political electioneering rather than brand positioning.

Brand equity is the generation of product value from associations with company values. When consumers attach prestige and purpose to a brand, premium pricing, competitive protection, higher profits, relationship loyalty, and assurance of new introductions accrue. The positioning of superior quality and moral high ground are virtually interchangeable ingredients. In the unpredictable, post-COVID-19, post-truth world we live in, where compassion and competitive advantage are often confused and misused, aligning your brand with purpose is an essential condition. Positive brand equity can build brand longevity but do altruistic associations represent short-term tactical gains or long-term sustainable strategy?

P&G's support of transgender rights (*Secret* deodorant), LGBT rights (in an ad for haircare product *Head & Shoulders*) align with their stated purpose of "improving the lives of the world's consumers". Serving the world's consumers whilst being committed to being one of the most socially responsible companies certainly shows that it is working for them. *Unilever's* 'Sustainable Living Brands' – including those with the biggest brand equity such as *Dove, Knorr, Omo-Persil, Rexona/Sure, Lipton, Hellmann's,* and *Wall's Ice Cream* – grew 69% faster than the rest of their business in 2018. *Unilever* CEO, Alan Jope, claimed that:

> Two-thirds of consumers around the world choose brands because of their stand on social issues. We believe the evidence is clear and compelling that brands with purpose grow. Purpose creates relevance for a brand, it drives talkability, and builds brand equity. The fantastic work that Dove has done in helping 35 million young people with self-esteem education; Lifebuoy reaching 1 billion with handwashing campaigns; Ben & Jerry's campaigns for social justice and climate change; Vaseline reaching 3 million people living in poverty and disaster with skin healing programmes. But talking is not enough. It is critical that brands take action and demonstrate their commitment [to a cause], to making a difference.

Other brands with purpose judiciously mixed into their recipes for building brand equity – *Tumblr* (supporting 'planned parenthood' and women's care); *Tony's Chocolonely* (pushing for legislation on modern slavery and illegal child labour); *Nike* (social stance of supporting Colin Kaepernick's "taking of the knee"); *Heineken* (#OpenYourWorld petitioning for social change); *H&M* ('Beyond the Rainbow' *Instagram* LGBT campaign) – all managed to balance social purpose and brand positioning at the same time as building equity.

Which brings us back to *Ben & Jerry's*. A conflict with parent company *Unilever* evolves around brand politics, something which is bound to negatively affect the brand equity of both parties. Following a unilateral decision to withdraw sales to Occupied Palestinian Territory (OPT) – which is consistent with their purpose "to make the world a better place by seeking ways to improve the quality of life locally, nationally, and internationally" – *Ben & Jerry's* have clashed with *Unilever's* legal franchise obligations to continue trading across Israel (including the West Bank). Pressure on *Unilever* came from investors with corporate governance and/or stewardship policies. The 'ESG' conundrum is this: Can *Ben & Jerry's* social mission decision not to renew the contract of an Israeli licensee be reconciled with *Unilever's* governance obligations to its investors? *Unilever* have sought to distance itself from *Ben & Jerry's* subsidiary autonomy on social issues, but this is viewed as odd from a governance perspective. *Unilever* had offered to accommodate alternative distribution arrangements, but Anuradha Mittal, Chair of *Ben & Jerry's* Board of Directors, claims that this contravenes the original acquisition agreement of 2000 which accommodates subsidiary autonomy. The violations of "the spirit and the letter of the acquisition" refer specifically to *Ben & Jerry's* "social mission and brand integrity". In other words, the investment in brand equity and brand purpose will be negatively affected.

Questions
1. Is there a distinction between brand purpose and brand politics?
2. Will Ben & Jerry's brand purpose be effective in creating brand equity if it fails to reconcile its parent's governance obligations?
3. Do all brands have to contribute to 'social good', to be aligned with values, mission, vision, and the organisation's purpose?

9.1 Outline of chapter

Marketing, with its customer-centric focus, is a source of multiple resource and value-creating potential. The chief source of that value are the assets within a company. Assets which are market-based and customer-facing can be leveraged to give organisations superior customer value, competitive advantage, and help sustain brand longevity. According to Srivastava (2001, p. 4), market-based assets are principally of two related types: external *relational* assets (customers, channels, strategic partners, providers of complementary goods and services, outsourcing agreements, networks, image, and eco-system relationships), and internal *intellectual* assets (explicit and tacit knowledge, process-based capabilities, experience, knowledge, cross-disciplinary, and intraorganisational knowhow). The former assets are 'available' but not owned by the organisation; the latter are knowledge assets that the firm has about its competitive environment. The biggest market-based assets of any company are its brands – as valuable intangible assets to the organisation, and as social, psychological, and experiential enrichment to the customer.

The balance of shareholder value has shifted irrevocably from tangible to intangible assets (Pringle & Field, 2008, p. 5), and as Keller & Lehmann suggest, "branding has emerged as a top management priority in the last decade due to the growing realisation that brands are one of the most valuable intangible assets that firms have" (2006, p.740). Managing brands is not just a managerial imperative or a product-oriented output of an organisation, but represents the management of meaning. "If brands exist as cultural, ideological, and sociological objects, then understanding brands requires tools developed to understand culture, ideology, and society, in conjunction with more typical branding concepts, such as brand equity, strategy, and value" (Schroeder, 2009, p. 124). The two key components of brand equity – brand *identity* and brand *image* – are linked but separate and must be managed in order leverage the organisation's most intangible of assets.

This chapter analyses how brand management is strategic and visionary as opposed to tactical and reactive, analysing the role branding plays as the most significant part of an organisation's value creation process, and as the driving force of marketing communications strategy. Our discussion describes how strategic brand marketing has to be a balance between the cumulative long-term brand building of equity and customer relationships, and the immediacy of short-term sales activation.

Learning outcomes

After reading this chapter, you'll be able to:
- Explain why managing brands is not just a managerial imperative or a product-oriented output of an organisation, but represents the management of meaning.
- Differentiate between brand strategy as being instrumental in achieving marketing communication objectives and also being focused on projecting visual identity and sociocultural meaning.
- Understand and discuss why brand equity is about viewing the intangible value of assets of the organisation as a driver of value creation, and also as a strategic connection between customer and company.
- Analyse the reasons why companies are facilitating the development of compelling relevant and authentic narratives as part of brand strategy.
- Analyse the impact digital dynamics has had on asymmetrical, interruption, one-way, broadcast media, shifting the dial on the communications paradigm from monologue to dialogue.
- Understand and discuss why strategic brand marketing has to be a balance between the cumulative long-term brand building of equity and customer relationships and the immediacy of short-term sales activation.

9.2 Introduction

Despite the best efforts to categorise brands, they often have an ontological ambiguity, an imprecision of definition somewhere in a mixture of corporate intention, social construction, and consumer interpretation. There is a lot of academic research and practitioner experience to support the view that consumers use brands as social frames of reference. Organisations who build strong brands which are relevant and meaningful to their customers "consistently outperform their markets" (Mudie & Pirrie, 2006, page 40). Brands are perceptions, promises, expectations, experiences, ideas, myths, and beliefs held by the brand user. A brand is a living system consisting of three poles – a value proposition, semiotic variants such as name and symbols, and a brand/service experience. It exists when it "has acquired power to influence the market" (Kapferer, 2008, p. 12). Some brands like *Google, Skype, Uber*, and *Netflix* (like *Hoover* before them) have so much power to influence their respective markets that they become verbs!

Brand 'labels' have ranged from: *product-orientation*, for example "referent" (Aaker, 1996) and "guarantee" (Kapferer, 2012), to *experiential phenomena* such as "emotional relations" (Fournier, 1998) and "social linking value" (Cova, 1997). We have witnessed a steady migration from brand value being inherently in the product to one where socially constituted peer-to-peer meaning dominates. The socially-embedded nature of consumption elevates the product attributes due its symbolic social connectivity and projection of self-esteem which give it meaning and the potential for competitive advantage.

Nonetheless, the different *types* of brands cover a broad field: corporate (eg: *Apple, Nike, Unilever, P&G, Coca Cola*); nation (eg: *"Incredible India"*, *"Uniquely Singapore True Asia"*);[154] charity or Not-for-Profit (eg: *Amnesty International, Breast Cancer Care, Mind mental health*); celebrity or personal (eg: *Oprah Winfrey, Pink Floyd, Cristiano Ronaldo*); destination or place (eg: *'New York The Big Apple', 'Visit Wales', 'Tourism Australia'*); luxury or premium (eg: *Gucci, Louis Vitton, Moët et Chandon, Porsche*); private label (eg: *M&S's 'St. Michael', Tesco 'Venture', Macy's 'Alfani'*); ingredient (eg: *Intel Inside, Nutrasweet, Gortex*); fashion (eg: *Prada, H&M, Zara); and activist brands (eg: Patagonia, Ben & Jerry's, Dove*).

De Chernatony & McDonald define a successful brand as: "an identifiable product, service, person, or place, augmented in such a way that a buyer or user perceives relevant and unique added values which match their needs more closely than the competition" (2003, p. 25). Consumers seek ways to reduce purchase risk and anxiety, connect with other groups and individuals, combat illness, change lifestyles, have political affiliation, and have services appropriate to benefits sought and desired. Brands are vehicles of meaning, and meaning is a product of internal consumer perceptual processing of external images and messages. Indeed, some have claimed that "the brand is the marketer's most advanced emotional tool" (Hastings, 2008, p. 100).

9.3 What is brand strategy?

Because the development and management of brand equity is long-term, is constantly evaluating customer expectations and satisfaction, determines value proposition positioning, gives protective competitive advantage, and produces value for the organisation, it is strategic. The focus of strategy is to encourage loyal customer relationships and maintain value by encouraging ritualistic consumption that soothes consumers' identity anxieties (Holt & Cameron, 2010). "Once the brand is thought to convey what the French call 'sens' – a term meaning various things including 'meaning' itself – it becomes a unique resource that's hard to copy" (Berger-Remy & Michel, 2015, p. 1). Elliot & Percy (2007, p.4) suggest that "as brands only exist in the minds of customers, then the management of brands is all about managing perceptions".

How can we begin to define brands? Brands need contextualisation as much as conceptualisation. As a "contested, cultural, managerial, and scholarly arena" (Schroeder, 2009, p. 125), analysing the concept of brand can be understood from different perspectives:

---

154 According to 'Nation Brands 2020', *Brand Finance*, the top 100 nation brands lost US$13.1 trillion of brand value in 2020 due to the impacts of the COVID-19 pandemic.

- Essential source of differentiation in consumer choice.
- A cultural melting pot of meaning construction.
- How a company presents its value proposition to prospective users.
- A consumer buying heuristic.
- An aid to reduce perceived social, psychological, monetary, or safety risk.
- A socially constituted language.
- A key source of company value.

Brands can provide a co-creative framework for developing and sustaining customer-company fusion.

Hedling, Knudtzen, & Bjerre (2020) offer us an excellent framework from which we can take a number of approaches:

- *The economic approach*: the brand as an essential part of the traditional marketing mix tools deployed to achieve strategy.
- *The identity approach*: the brand as linked to the projected corporate identity of an organisation and which embodies its value proposition.
- *The consumer-based approach*: the brand as linked to consumer associations. Linear communication based on cognitive psychology where the assumption is of management controlling consumer's intended action.
- *The personality approach*: the brand as a human-like character. Rooted in human personality psychology, this anthropomorphic approach is based on endowing brands with human characteristics.
- *The relational approach*: the brand as a viable relationship partner. Building on the above, the relationship metaphor in marketing fundamentally changed the way brands are viewed and is rooted in the philosophical tradition of existentialism. The dialogic element extends the instigated in the personality approach.
- *The community approach*: the brand as the pivotal point of social interaction, a dominant force in fusing social networks and relationships.
- *The cultural approach*: the brand as part of the broader cultural fabric, interwoven with social meaning and is a universal language of consumption.
- *The sensory approach*: the brand as experienced through our senses. Human physiologies, a biological consumer perspective linked to brand experience, brand identity and brand touchpoints.

The most innovative brands change, develop, and sustain relevancy by reflecting and being reflective of the cultures they are created in, like "condensates of complex changes in time and culture" (Hedling, Knudtzen, & Bjerre, 2020, p. 10). Brand 'business' drives company culture, company operations, and customer experiences: it is the central organising idea of any operation and, as such, should be operationalised.

Ownership is at the centre of understanding brand management, and is the essential platform of the two predominant brand paradigms of the past 40 years:

- *Positivist perspective*: From the early 80s, a 'positivist', managerialist perspective, based on the brand being organisational property, owned by the marketer, its positioning created by company-constructed association and linkage.
- *Interpretivist perspective*: The alternative socially constructionist 'interpretive' paradigm which emerged in the 1990s, where the brand is owned by and controlled by the user (Hedling, Knudtzen, & Bjerre, 2020).

Allen, Fournier & Miller (2008, p. 783) refer to this positivist/interpretivist dichotomy as, respectively, 'a received view' and an 'emerging paradigm':
- "The *received* view on branding is squarely grounded in the disciplines of psychology and information economics.
- The *emergent* paradigm encapsulates the relational, community, and cultural approaches and the development towards the interpretative paradigm"

The two are compared in Table 9.1.

Table 9.1: Central tenets of the Received View vs the Emergent Branding Paradigm.

	Received view	**Emergent paradigm**
Brands	Informational vehicles that support choice processes; risk reduction tools and simplifying heuristics	Meaning rich tools that help people live their lives
Guiding metaphor	Information	Meaning
Role of context in research	Context is noise	Context is everything
Central constructs of interest	Knowledge-based cognitions and attitudes	Experiential and symbolic aspects of consumption
Focal research domain	Purchase	Consumption
Guising tenets	Simplification and control	Co-creation and complexity
Marketer's role	Owner and creator brand assets	One of several bran meaning makers
Brand positioning assumptions	Consistency, constancy, simplicity	Complexity, mutability
Primary units of analysis	Individual consumers	Individuals, people in groups, consumers in cultures, cultural production in mechanisms
Consumer's role	Passive recipient of marketer information	Active contributor to brand meaning making
Consumer's central activity	Realising functional and emotional benefits	Meaning making

Source: Allen, Fournier, & Miller (2008, p. 783)

Strategically, branding is focused on projecting visual identity and sociocultural meaning through well-targeted marketing communications: in other words, the management of perceptions. However, brands are not just mediators of cultural meaning; they themselves "have become ideological referents that shape cultural rituals, economic activities, and social norms" (Schroeder, 2009, p. 124). Of course branding is also about the hard-nosed proposition, positioning, and perception behind strategy, where attention has shifted from "brand producers and products toward consumer response and services to understand brand value creation" (Muñiz & O'Guinn, 2001, p. 412).

That last element – "response and services to understand brand value creation" – is crucial for our understanding of why brand management and service processes are interrelated isomorphic parts of the same thing: purpose-driven brand strategy.

Although the best brands are co-created, ultimately they are related to individual interpretation and are therefore subjective: "The brand is created in the mind of a customer following a flow of brand contacts – interactions between customer and service provider in the on-going relationship between the two parties" (Grönroos, 2007, p. 337). This link between the dynamics of branding and service marketing hinges on the shared experience characteristics of perception, expectations, intangibility, perishability, heterogeneity, and the notion of 'encounter'. This is captured well by Keller: "Any potential encounter with a brand – marketing initiated or not – has the opportunity to change the mental representation of the brand and the kinds of information that can appear in consumer memory" (1993, p. 3). Here, 'brand contacts' are really interactive service touchpoints, the 'moments of truth' or 'pain points' which have to be managed as part of the processing of brand user experience.

Because experience necessarily is subjective and part of a larger frame of reference, competitive comparison has to be part of the branding process. Where there is competitive parity, with identical product and pricing, or where service is the core value proposition, *the company is the brand*. Differentiation based on creating intrinsically emotional relationships with customers – turning 'moments of truth' into 'customer delight' – can provide a longer lasting connection above competitive parity as well as protection against customer defection. That is, brand equity is created.

To some extent, this subjective comparison isn't just an end product of strategy, but one conditioned by demand side of consumer production, influenced on the customer supply side by intermediaries, beyond the control of the organisation. As we have seen, ownership is a central debate in brand management (ie: organisational property owned by the marketer or owned by and controlled by the user). Brands are organic and have a life beyond the factory, beyond the product, in what Sherry (1987) refers to as "personal brandscapes". This is a key point for brand-driven organisations: brands are independent of products and much more valuable to customer-company co-creation. Kapferer put this well: "At birth, a brand is all potential: it can develop in any possible way. With time, however, it tends to lose some degree of freedom; while gaining conviction, its facets take shape delineating the brand's legitimate territory" (2000, p. 1006). Branding can show "the human ability to create an ethical surplus, a social relation, a shared meaning, an emotional involvement that was not there before . . . as a direct basis of [the brand's] economic value" (Arvidsson, 2005, p. 237).

9.4 The concept of brand

Brands are embedded in every aspect of an organisation's purpose and process, and are central to every aspect of a consumer's social ecosystem. They are not static entities but are organic, evolving to adapt to changing environments and customer needs. Think of your company and your brand as a living entity that, as described by former *Disney* CEO Michael Eisner, "is enriched or undermined cumulatively over time, the product of a thousand small gestures."[155]

A brand is a synonym for customer-centricity and is a conduit for creating mutually beneficial meaning between customer and company, corporation and stakeholders, bonded by promise and loyalty, value and values. A brand is "a cluster of meanings" (Batey, 2008), a "guarantee" or "referent" (Kapferer, 2012), a "covenant" between company and customer, a promise, "the set of expectations, memories, stories, and relationships that, taken together, account for a consumer's decision to choose one product or service over another" (Godin, 2012). Or as Kapferer says: "a name with the power to influence" (2014). According to de Chernatony & McWilliam (1989), there are five possible categories of brands:
- An ownership device to show control, a trustworthy badge of origin and heritage.
- A differentiating device.
- A means of communicating a promise and guarantee of satisfaction through the experience of use.
- An aid for consumers' rapid decision-making.
- A symbolic device to enable consumers to express about themselves.

Understanding of brand strategy relies on understanding of the mechanics of meaning – "the semantic logic" (Franzen & Moriarty, 2008, p. 20). They argue that "in order to systemize brand strategy, we need a semantic logic that sorts out these concepts and groups them based on their related dimensions". Their content analysis, featured in Table 9.2, produced the following logic:

---

155 *Disney* CEO Michael Eisner.

Table 9.2: Semantic logic of brand.

Nature or deep structure	Core concept, essence, soul, character, core vision
Strategy (intention)	Identity, function, mission, focus, segmentation, differentiation, position, promise, culture
Meaning (perception)	Awareness, function, image, associations, personality, position, charisma, picture, values, culture
Relationship	Reputation, covenant, promise, contract
Structure	Architecture, physique, extensions, portfolio, bandwidth, brandsphere
Power or leadership	Strength, saliency, equity, loyalty

Source: Franzen & Moriarty (2008, p. 20)

Essentially, a brand has two functions: differentiation from its competitors in a product category; establishing its origin, heritage, salience, and, increasingly importantly, its provenance. As Doyle states, a successful brand is built on four pillars: "strong consumer value proposition, integration with the firm's other value-creating assets, be positioned in a sufficiently attractive market, and be managed in order to maximise the value of the brand's long-term cash flow" (2001, p. 255). The value proposition of a brand consists of three essential parts:
- The product or service offered to fulfil a customer need or want.
- A brand name which aids positioning, recall, reputation, and is the sum of customer experiences.
- A 'concept'.

Just look at how this definition of branding has moved on in 60 years: "A brand is a name, term, sign, symbol, or design, or a combination of them, intended to identify the goods and services of one seller or group of sellers, and to differentiate them from those of competitors" (*American Marketing Association*, 1960). It implies that production and control of a brand's image and positioning is a managerial initiative only. It doesn't recognise any element of negotiation of brand meaning between company and customer. It focuses on organisational input not the co-created consumption process. Here, input is brand identity (that which is engineered and disseminated by the organisation) and process is brand image (that which is mediated by users and communication channels).

A useful way of looking at this is determining what a product is and what a brand is. It is almost impossible to think of a product which doesn't have some sort of association to a brand. A generic brand may not have an expensive advertising campaign or fancy labelling to make it scream out from the supermarket shelves, but it carries the clothing of 'category' by being positioned next to the leading brands. When does a

banana become something more than a simple item of fruit? When it has *'Growers'
Selection'* in *ASDA* or *'Organic Fair Trade'* in *Tesco*.

As always, Kapferer (2008, p. 40) has a useful way of looking at this, describing
what he refers to as the 'Brand/Product Halo Effect'– the juxtaposition of customer
expectations of 'product satisfaction' against 'brand aspiration'. In Figure 9.1, you
will see that the product's visible and differentiating characteristics consist of:
– Design
– Performance
– Ingredients or components
– Size and shape
– Price
– Marketing Communications

The brand's intangible values and imagery consist of:
– Values
– Brand imagery
– Image of stores where sold
– Perceptions of brand users

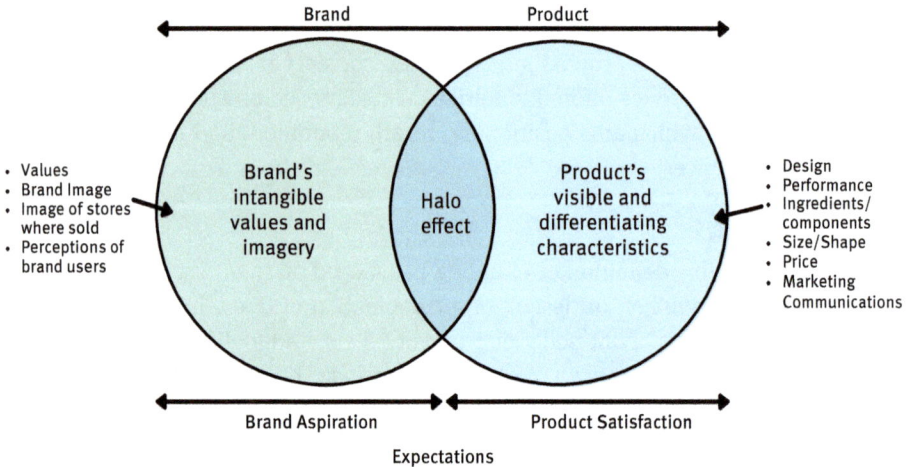

Figure 9.1: Product/Brand Halo Effect.
Source: Kapferer (2004)

This is an apposite image for this book which uses the ubiquitous Venn Diagram to
illustrate separation and fusion. Thorndike's original conceptualisation of 'the halo effect' described the inability to differentiate between conceptually distinct and potentially independent attributes. In Kapferer's interpretation, the symbolic value of a
brand can mask inadequacies of the product. We can see this when problems with

product attributes are 'accepted' because of the strength of the brand: the 'halo effect' is when rationality and emotion become blurred. This is analogous with the blending of corporate brand identity and customer brand image discussed below in *Section 9.4*.

As we have seen in *Section 3.10* above, brands are semiotic marketing systems (Conejo & Wooliscroft, 2014, p. 287), which project meaning through a brand culture of cultural codes such as myths, self-identity, group affiliation, associations, images, narratives. The 'value' is a social one, influencing the brand's meaning and what it symbolises in a social sign system. Brands occupy the space between strategic goals and consumer perceptions (Schroeder & Salzer-Mörling, 2006), and the 'halo' effect is the fusing of product and brand, but it is also between customer and company.

We can explore this a little further below if we examine the symbiotic relationship between brand and individual. In Figure 9.2, a brand platform model devised by Hart & Murphy (1998).[156] The overriding constant purpose of the organisation is interpreted into the vision and then, in turn, the action obligation (the mission) is imposed by the nature of that vision. This gives brand strategy a directional energy translated into the brand's value system. The two parallel hierarchies describe the customer-company brand interface: the brand and brand user's functional, expressive and central values of the brand's value proposition.

The expressive values of a brand match what type of person the consumer wants to be or thinks she is. *Starbucks* positioned their coffee brand in the 'third space' between home and work, appealing to the social values attached with the brand. *Costa Coffee* extended their social contract by "helping communities grow" by improving the welfare of communities through their ethical "fair trade supply" policy, and purchasing their beans through their *Costa Foundation*. This reflects the desired "socially responsible" conscience of the consumer beyond the product of coffee. The brand/consumer central values is what the brand and the purchaser share at a moral or philosophical level: what the brand is associated with in terms of symbolic meaning resonating in the brand's positioning. Brand values must link with consumer values.

The first step in creating a differentiated and appropriate brand platform is to create a brand vision of the competitor/customer context of the category or consumer experience which is unique to the brand. The vision should be distinctive and be dislocated from how the market is served and current category thinking if possible.

In *Section 5.8* above, we discussed the internal symbiotic relationship between corporate identity and organisational culture. Here, we look at how the internalised projection of the 'brand' as initially conceived in line with the brand owner's intentions is negotiated externally by users in contextual brand meaning. In order to understand the ramifications of this for brand management, let's first look at the two sides of the brand coin: brand identity and brand image.

---

156 Figure 9.2 has been developed to accommodate the contemporary place of purpose in the mechanics of branding. It is significant that this was absent from the original model.

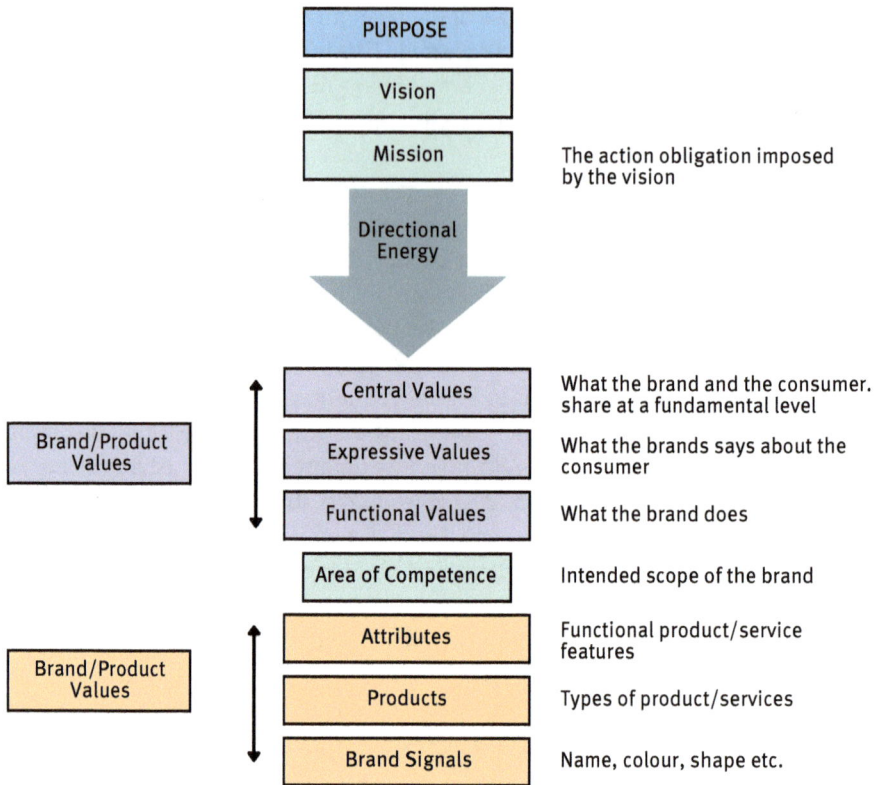

Figure 9.2: Brand Platform Structure.
Source: Hart & Murphy (1998)

9.5 Brand identity, brand image, and reputation management

Brand strategists must be cognisant of the impact that all stakeholders – external and internal – have in creating brand meaning as it is conceived and perceived. "Brand meaning is not the sole province of marketers, but also draws on the institutional environment surrounding the brand" (Lindgreen, Beverland, & Farrelly, 2010, p. 81). In building successful, valuable brands, two of the key concepts – brand identity and brand image – are inextricably linked but quite separate entities. Together, they form a synthesis of the conception and perception of reputation.

Brand identity originates from the brand owner and is the intended, authentic personality of the brand, created internally before presenting the brand to external audiences (Balmer & Greyser, 2006); it is what the company wants to create. Brand image originates from the brand user and reflects negotiated brand meaning; it is the image formed in the customer's mind and is inseparable from their concept of 'the brand' (ie: brand and brand image are synonymous). Because it is experiential perception, it is perhaps a truer representation of the brand, and because brand identity is an internal *projected* perspective and brand image is an external *perceived* one, essentially, they are how the company and customer see the value proposition.

Corporate identity represents the timeless essence of the brand, with associations which are intended to be constant across new customers and markets, projecting unique value and values. *Nike* repeats images of performance, success, and life-enhancing achievement, whilst demonstrations of service, cleanliness, and quality project *McDonald's* brand identity. Both are oriented around company as well as product.

The corporate brand here can be seen as a unifying construct: "the mechanism that allows for the alignment between desired identity and how stakeholders see the identity" (Abratt & Kleyn, 2012, p. 1053). In their "VCI Model", Hatch & Schultz state that this requires the alignment of vision, culture and image: "the strategic stars of the corporate brand" (2001, p. 128). Similarly, Harris & de Chernatony (2001) declare that there needed to be a synthesis between identity components (vision, culture, positioning, personality, and presentation) and between these and corporate reputation. Balmer (2009) formalised this into a "theory of identity alignment", and then in 2012 introduced a diagnostic model – the "AC⁴ID Test" comprising the "corporate identity constellation" of Actual, Communicated, Conceived, Covenanted, Cultural, Ideal, and Desired" (Balmer 2012). The most interesting thing here is that he advocates *fusion* – a shift from a "centrifugal" approach (a bilateral alignment between the distinct internal and external brand identities) to a "centripetal" one (ie: the alignment under corporate brand identity of all the identities). In addition, he draws on the service quality 'Gap' model (Parasuraman, Zeithaml, & Berry, 1985) from Service Marketing to assert that alignment of brand promise and delivery is key.

The term 'brand building', therefore, is misleading. It is not something the company can do alone; it is a joint venture, not always collaborative and not always synchronously created. The role that 'image' plays in strategic branding is important: it communicates expectations, moderates experience(s), is a function of both expectations and experiences, and has an internal impact on employees and an external impact on customers. Grönroos (2015, p. 339) posits that "If anybody builds a brand, it is the consumer". As reported by Gyrd-Jones & Kornum (2013, p. 1489), this is echoed in practice by *LEGO*: "We own the brand name; our customers own the brand".

Rindell (2007) points out that consumers have an 'inherited' image based on previous experience with the brand or organisation, and this has to be managed. Disconnect between projected company identity and negotiated user image can be destructive. For example, the premium identity constructed for the *Stella Artois* premium lager brand through the extensive 'Reassuringly Expensive' campaigns was destroyed by the negotiated meaning of its users who referred colloquially to its actual consumption as "Wife Beater". *Volvo*'s unshakable brand identity and reputation for 'safety' became a psychological barrier when the brand was re-positioned for a younger audience because 'safe' had negative connotations of 'boring' to a younger target group. Brand identity can therefore become distorted by 'brand reality'. Both examples demonstrate that ability to try and manage how the brand is perceived is vitally important to strategy. It is the key goal of brand strategy (through marketing communications) to maintain congruence between the two. As we will see, alignment of identity and image might, for example, be achieved externally by using IMC to alter how the brand is positioned in the customer's mind, or it might be achieved internally by focusing on employees' values and behaviours to become more congruent with the company's desired brand values. It might be a product of both. Analogous to service marketing principle and process, customers compare perceptions with expectations; managing the 'gaps' between identity and image is rooted in understanding customer expectations. As Grant (2000) says: "It's not what you do.

It's what they do with what you do". All companies can do is create a frame of reference – providing quality physical product and service supported by appropriate marketing communications – within which users can construct their image of the brand. It is in the interaction with the brand, in continuously developing relationships, that brand image is formed.

Aaker describes brand identity as being "what the organisation wants the brand to stand for in the customer's mind" (Aaker, 1996, p. 25). It is the 'vision' of strategy, the personality and image projected from company to customer, and often viewed as so-called 'softer' branding in terms of competitive differentiation. This softer delineation is implicitly embedded in organisational culture and bonded in the symbolic relationship between brand and consumer, projected through intangible attributes such as consistency, uniqueness, reliability, innovative value, transcendence, credibility, and the mental associations implicit in perceptual positioning. In contrast to 'hard' branding attributes (which are tangible features such as text, sounds, images, logos, taglines, slogans, music, jingles, songs, colour, value mantra, etc.), emotional connections are essential in owning the brand and offering reasons above functionality to build loyalty.

Therefore, the difference conceptually and in practice is that brand identity is how an organisation's brand wants to be perceived, and brand image is how the brand is actually perceived. Brand management must take into account the active negotiation of meaning socially constructed in the context of user discourse. The theoretical space between the company conception of brand identity and consumer interpretation of brand image is brand culture (Schroeder, 2009, p. 125). Two models of brand identity – Kapferer's (2004) 'Prism of Identity' model and Aaker's (1996) 'Brand Identity Planning System' – help illuminate this 'theoretical space' and are discussed in detail below.

Kapferer's (2004, p. 34) model describes a 'Prism of Identity' (Figure 9.3) to illustrate how the internal projection of brand identity relates to the outside environment and features 6 brand identity facets viewed from 4 perspectives ('Sender' and 'Receiver' of brand identity; 'Internal' and 'External perspective').

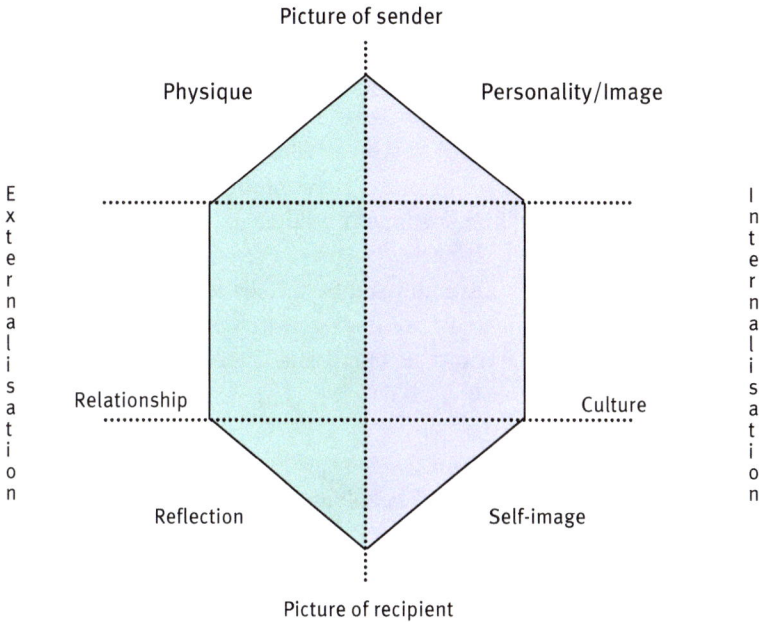

Figure 9.3: Product/Brand Prism.
Source: Kapferer (2002)

Externalisation covers:
- *Physique*: Relates to the concrete, tangible or objective features of the brand encompassing product features, symbols and attributes. The tactile features like product and packaging are essential components in brands like *Orangina, Budweiser, Absolut Vodka, After Eights*. These elements are considered the basic purpose of the brand in terms of what the brand is, what it does and how it looks. It is significant that in service-centric businesses, physical evidence (eg: premises, architecture, location, and interior décor) tries to give tangible cues for intangible value propositions and contribute to an organisation's visual identity.
- *Relationship*: A relationship perspective of brand identity extends 'exchange' beyond a purely functional, rational domain and infuses an emotional element (eg: the 'caring' positioning of *Fairy Liquid* or 'status' brands like *American Express*).
- *Reflection*: Brands which are aspirational project an image of who their customers would like to be. The use of the product projects the element of the brand which relates to the actual or desired self.

Internalisation covers:
- *Image*: Relates to how the brand is viewed introspectively. Brand associations such as *Body Shop* and *Virgin*. Or metaphorical ones like *Frosties*' Tony the Tiger, *McDonald's* Ronald.
- *Culture*: The organisation's values such as *Apple's* 'think outside the box', conspicuous capitalism of *American Express* or the ethics of the *Co-op*.
- *Self-Image*: The inner dialogue which feeds into self-image is evident in brands like *Weight Watchers*.
- *'Physique'* and *'Personality/Image'* are controlled by the sender whilst *'Reflection'* and 'Self-image' are consumer-oriented from the receiver. 'Culture' and *'Relationships'* are the bridge which link the corporate brand (the sender) and the consumer (the receiver).

In addition, Aaker & Joachimsthaler (2000, p. 44) provide a comprehensive framework for constructing brand identity (Figure 9.4), divided into:
- *Brand as product*: product scope, product attributes, quality/value, uses and users, country of origin.
- *Brand as organisation*: organisational attributes such as innovation, trust, consumer concern, purpose, local V global.
- *Brand as person*: personality such as genuine, energetic, customer/brand relationships.
- *Brand as symbol*: can provide cohesion and structure to a brand and make it easier to gain brand recognition and brand recall. Brand as symbol: visual metaphors and image, brand heritage.

These are alternative propositions of identity which traditionally form the basis of perceptual positioning. Even without the qualification of user brand image, projecting identity into often volatile and competitive-intensive markets can be fraught with danger. Aaker (2004) claimed that there were four brand identity traps:
- *Brand Image Trap*: If this isn't controlled, this can become the brand identity. Should be about the soul of the brand but also about how the brand is perceived by users. *Snapple* enjoyed an anti-establishment brand image but this was contaminated when the acquisition by *Coca Cola* destroyed that perception. This could be true also of brands like *Green & Blacks* and *Innocent Smoothies* whose challenger brand authentic 'ethical provenance' positioning could be contaminated by the reputations of their new owners *Cadbury* and *Coca Cola* respectively. *Tommy Hilfiger* removed the logo as an experiment on a brand extension and the innovation failed miserably as customers bought the status the logo symbolised more than the material.
- *Brand Position Trap*: Where the emphasis is too much on one functional aspect, this may limit the potential for developing brand identity. *'Volvo'* signified SAFETY, a reassuring message to an older age group. The 'cage' of safety had negative connotations and brand image suffered when the brand was re-positioned to try and

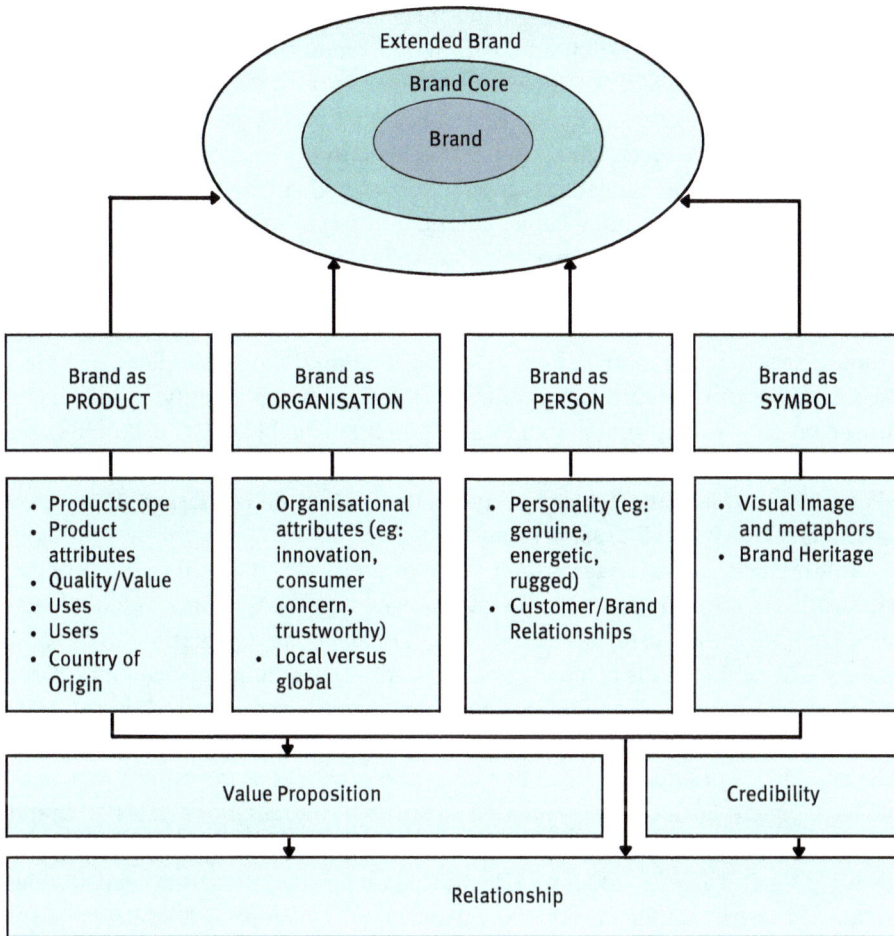

Figure 9.4: Brand Anatomy.
Source: Aaker & Joachimsthaler (2000, p. 44)

capture a younger audience. When the search for brand identity becomes the
search for brand position.
- *External Perception Trap*: Internal markets (such as employees) must buy into the
  organisational brand narrative. *BA* employees never bought into '*The World's Favourite Airline*' campaign and an internal communications campaign had to be
  implemented in order to combat disconnect between external promises and internal realities.
- *Product/Attribute Fixation Trap*: Fixation with features not benefits. Fountain
  pen sales suffered because quality engineering of the product was not perceived
  to be a benefit alongside the inexpensive and functional *Bic* Ballpoint Pen ideally suited to the new 'throwaway culture'.

Because brands are created in the dynamic of socially constituted meaning – where individual and group affiliation are expressed in brand community participation – there is a tension between the three affected elements – company, customer, and brand – and there is often a confusion between what exactly we mean by 'identity'. Beverland, Napoli & Green (2007) apply this logic to a B2B context, claiming that brand identity comprises: relational support, coordinating network players, leveraging brand architecture, adding value, and quantifying the intangible, underpinned by 5 company capabilities of entrepreneurial, reflexive, innovative, brand supportive dominant logic, and executional abilities.

A major social phenomenon – brand communities – have a major impact on meaning negotiation and, therefore, brand co-creation (France, Merrilees, & Miller, 2015), and this can distort the organisation's intended brand identity. Research has focused on bilateral processes: brand's effect on individual identity (Belk, 1988), on groups (Veloutsou, 2009), and the relationship between consumer and brand (Cova & Pace, 2006). This brand/self-congruity (Smith, 2011, p. 25) is a fusion of projected brand image and individual self-identity.

Any relationship an organisation (B2B) or consumer (C2B) has with a brand starts with a state of unawareness being changed and the start of a potential customer-company relationship seeded. It is the function of an organisation to devise a strategy – attaching to the company's value proposition a brand personality – to try and position a brand in the mind of a possible buyer to encourage positive associations with category use and suitability of the brand to meet user needs within that category. This is *positioning* – affecting perceptions as well as targeting a particular market segment. Positioning is regarded as "the manifestation of a 'facet' of brand identity in relation to competitive offerings as opposed to being a part of brand identity per se" (Kapferer, 2004, p. 117) and "identity is more stable and long lasting, for it is tied to the brand roots and fixed parameters" (2004, p. 102). Whilst positioning and brand identity are related, the former is not a dimension but a consequence of the latter. The brand promise is what the company claims the user can expect will be the benefits of using the brand. A definition of the corporate brand is slightly more holistic: "The visual, verbal and behavioural expression of an organisation's unique business model" (Knox & Bickerton, 2003, p. 998).

One of the ways in which this can be better understood is by seeing how the overlapping spheres – the elements which affect brand strategy – are separate but interrelated and integrated. In Figure 9.5 the following elements Brand Fusion components are described:

- *Purpose-Driven Brand Vision*: (the core mission; the reason why the organisation exists; the intended brand perception and organisational narrative projected into stakeholder markets; strategic value alignment; the visualisation of company character, personality; authenticity and integrity).

- *Company Brand*: (core values in operation; the service culture embedded in all processes; customer-focussed operations; continuous innovation development; continuous learning and improvement; employee behaviour guided by cultural values, and customer expectations and experience; employee humility, engagement and satisfaction; who the company is; internal market-orientation)
- *Customer Brand Image*: (the brand experienced by individual and group users; C2C communication between users; induvial/brand congruity; aggregate user and influencer perceptions; consumer disposition to purchase; loyalty forged in repetitive use).

Where Company Brand Culture and Purpose-Driven Brand Vision intersect, that shows Brand Identity, the corporate brand philosophy, brand practices and brand personality originating internally from the organisation and is the intended, meaning, values, authenticity and personality projected externally and also to internal markets.

Where Purpose-Driven Brand Vision and Customer Brand Image intersect, that shows the Articulated Brand Promise, the strategic and tactical brand positioning, the brand value proposition, projected by through the intended brand communications, stating the contract between company and customer within which the brand's potential and meaning will be expressed.

Where Company Brand Culture and Customer Brand Image intersect, that shows Brand 'In use' encounters, the actual company customer-orientation in practice, the actual delivery of internal brand service, relationship management programmes etc., the positive associations of customer equity, and how this is mediated by influencers, external brand intermediaries, brand communities, internal and group consumption experiences, and Word of Mouth of other users' experiences. To reiterate from above, brand image is how an organisation's brand is actually perceived.

Where all spheres – Purpose-Driven Brand Vision, Company Brand Culture, and Customer Brand Image – intersect, this describes the point at which brand strategy is aligned with organisational values and customer expectations – Brand Fusion.

Quite often, brands are part of a portfolio "where the [strategic] goals are to create synergy, leverage, and clarity within the portfolio and with relevant, differentiated, and energised brands" (Aaker, 2004, p. 13). In determining what constitutes a "strong brand", Keller (2001, p. 14) lists the following attributes which the best and most enduring brands have:
- the brand excels at delivering the benefits customers truly desire
- the brand stays relevant
- the pricing strategy is based on consumers' perceptions of value
- the brand is properly positioned
- the brand is consistent
- the brand portfolio and hierarchy make sense

- the brand makes use of and co-ordinates a full repertoire of marketing activities to build equity
- the brand managers understand what the brand means to consumers
- the brand is given proper support, and that support is sustained over a long time
- the company monitors sources of brand equity

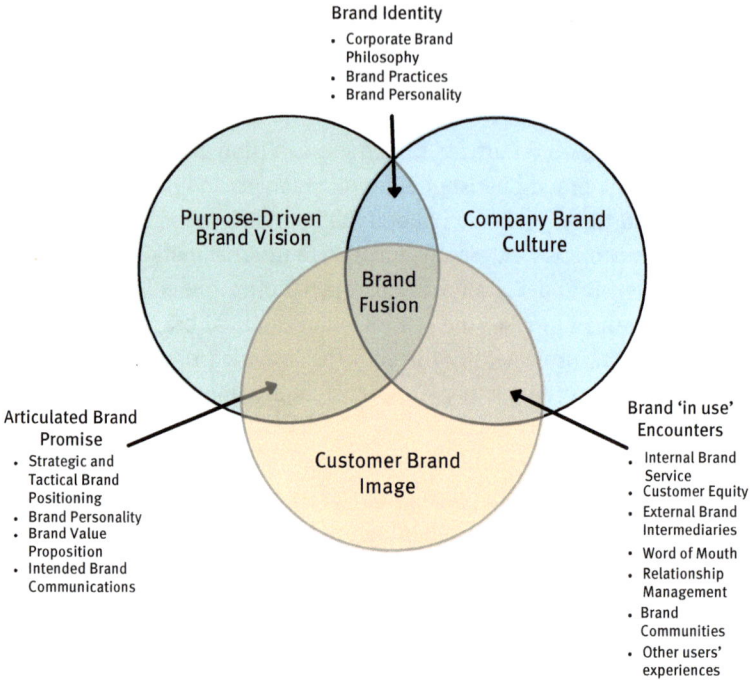

Figure 9.5: Brand Fusion Components.
Source: Authors' representation (2022). Developed from Dahlen, Lange, and Smith (2010).

To further complicate matters, there is sometimes conflation between the terms brand identity and brand reputation being used interchangeably as if they were the same thing. They are separate entities not synonyms. As we have seen, brand identity is an internal perspective. As with brand image, brand reputation is the perspective of external stakeholders (Basedo *et al*, 2006), and is generally the aggregate set of public judgements whose valence may change over time (Siano, Vollero, & Palazzo, 2011). Reputation may partly be drawn from consumer interpretation of a brand's positioning or product salience (Veloutsou & Moutinho, 2011). With its user perception orientation, it is much more akin to brand image than brand identity.

According to Bernstein, there has to be alignment of corporate brand between rhetoric and statements (ie: what the company says) and behaviour and performance (ie: what the company does) in order to avoid "corporate dissonance" (2009,

p. 603). Companies enjoying a positive reputation experience significant market value premium, superior financial performance, and trust with customers and other stakeholders. Consumers are no longer passive participants in meaning creation but empowered players in the development of brands (Payne, Storbacka, Frow, & Know, 2009), who may influence the perceptions of other users (Cova & Pace, 2006), or affect the reputation (and therefore brand image) through the memetics of imitative behaviour and Word of Mouth (Hutter, Hautz, Denhardt, & Füller, 2013). Memetics is "the imitation of consumer behaviour – cultural material propagated by an imitation process" (Williams, 2002, p. 162). 76% of consumers are influenced by ratings and reviews when deciding on a purchase. 60% are less likely to react to a negative review if the company has responded to it.[157] This is one of the reasons why the dominant logic in marketing is social.

This phenomenon of spreading information/misinformation (online image dissemination is accelerated Word of Mouth) enhances consumer empowerment in brand reputation and image creation (Quinton, 2013). In the new 'feedback economy', customers now have a powerful platform to express their views about an organisation and its brands. The impact of social media, in an environment radically shaken by COVID-19, gives publicly expressed and publicised sentiment a persuasive power which can positively or negatively impact on a company's reputation. Companies now employ a synthesis of customer experience and reputation management referred to as Reputation Experience Management (RXM). Reputation Experience Management means obtaining customer feedback, responding to it, and acting on that feedback to improve the company's services, optimise the Customer Experience, and thus enhance the reputation of the brand. It includes not only the evaluation of self-gathered, structured data (eg: from customer surveys), but also the unstructured "data in the wild" that people leave on the internet about a company – and is much more difficult to find and capture. Only if you are able to listen, understand and act, can you set yourself apart from your competitors and be truly successful. The majority of companies are most likely to measure the impact of a positive Online Reputation in terms of customer relationships, specifically increased sales (59%), higher conversion rates (57%) and better marketing ROI (46%).[158]

9.6 Brands and the notion of value

If definitions of branding, brand strategy, brand identity, and brand image have broad scope for interpretation and misinterpretation, brand equity is just as complex. The commonality is that 'experience' and 'value' are central themes. In essence,

---

157 A survey by *London Research and Reputation.*
158 Status Report *Online Reputation Management* 2020.

there are two distinct sides of a definition of brand equity: one is the value of the relationship a consumer has with a brand or organisation; the second is the financial value brands have to the organisation.

From a consumer's perspective, personal, social experience and value are the driving forces. Keller describes this as the power that "lies in what customers have learned, felt, seen, and heard about the brand as a result of their experiences over time" (2003, p. 10). Aaker claims that it "affects the customer's confidence in the purchase decision and the quality of user experience" (1996, p. 15). From a company's perspective, the value is in managing awareness, image, quality, loyalty, and the cultural meaning of brands. In a nutshell, that is what brand equity is.

Traditional methods of measuring asset value in an organisation – focusing on traditional ROI financial results – can often be limited in terms of exploiting intangible assets which can provide sustainable competitive advantage. However, against a backdrop of intense competition, increasing costs, consumer promiscuity, and flattening demand, brand equity can produce improved productivity, enhanced value, and longevity. It is the *notion of value* which is key.

Kaplan & Norton (2001) argue that this can present difficulties because of the following factors:

- *Value is indirect*: Improvements in intangible assets may impact indirectly and slowly on financial outcomes of revenue and profit through cause-and-effect relationships involving two or three intermediate stages. For example, investment in employees through training will eventually improve service quality. Higher service levels lead to customer satisfaction. Higher customer satisfaction leads to loyalty. Enhanced loyalty resulting in improved sales and profits. But like we will see below in *Section 9.14*, short-term activations may have an immediate impact on the long-term goal of brand building.
- *Value is contextual*: The value is dependent on how the organisational context and strategy is deployed, and the competitive comparison made by the user.
- *Value is potential*: Tangible assets which convert raw material into product have immediate, straight-forward measurability. Converting intangible assets into realizable value is much more unreliable.
- *Assets are bundled*: Except for brand names which can be sold by themselves, generally value does not reside in a single intangible asset, but must be bundled with other assets in order to create value.

Nonetheless, it is fair to say that brand equity is the added value implicit in brand name, brand perception, and brand awareness, and is translatable into tangible results like customer preference, loyalty, competitive security, regular income streams, repeat purchase, and brand longevity.

The value 'on the balance sheet' of this intangible asset can be most dramatically demonstrated when it is seen to be the key factor in transfer of ownership between companies. In 1988, Swiss foods giant *Nestlé* agreed a $4.5 billion buyout of the British confectioner *Rowntree* making it the second biggest confectioner behind *Mars Inc*. This was largely attributable to the market dominance and consumer love of their *KitKat* brand. Swedish furnishing manufacturer *IKEA* recently sold the *IKEA* name to one of its subsidiaries for €9 billion. *Louis Vitton – Moët Hennesey* (LVMH), a French multinational luxury goods conglomerate, took over *Bulgari* in 2011 for €4.3 billion, four times the turnover and 86 times the company's net income (Les Echos, 2011).

The added value that brands represent for the company is manifest in good will, accruing incremental cash flows, customer relationships, market share and market valuation, established brand associations and competitive protection, and a means of survival and growth; for the customer, brands represent the added value given to products or services beyond their tangible functional application and category appropriateness.

From a consumer's perspective functional values refer to the basic level of economic or time utility required in order to fulfil hunger or safety physiological needs, convenience of use, ease of purchase or minimising cost. What type of product is expected? Natural? Technological? The aftermath of the 'lock downs' of COVID-19 emphasised a stripped-back aesthetic. Online social media platforms like *Instagram* and shopping channels like *ASOS* facilitate a more functional brand where consumers are more savvy, and are focused on information about product ingredients, product usage, dimensions, and so on. The phenomenon of 'sofalising' and *Google* search has put more emphasis on extensive information search on the functionality of brands as part of the consumer decision-making process. The product or service must reflect this in providing the benefit of use, cost or composition. *Allinson's* bread boasts "bread w' nowt taken out"; and *Ronseal* "does exactly what it says on the tin".

Principles in practice

Did the *Science Museum* kill irony (and their own reputation)?

With over £163m support given – from *BP*'s support of the National Portrait Gallery and Royal Opera House through to thousands of local sponsorships – corporate sponsorship of the arts has been an astonishing success in the UK.[159] Whilst it is meant to be a mutually beneficial arrangement of positive value association and enhanced image for the sponsor, it can also damage reputation and have a negative impact on brand equity.

When Greta Thurnberg, a climate and environmental activist with over 5 million followers, tweeted that "The 'Science' Museum just killed irony (and their own reputation)",[160] in response to the news that the *London Science Museum* had signed a 'gagging agreement' not to publicly criticise sponsors *Shell* as part of a sponsorship deal (for an exhibition about carbon capture 'Our Future Planet'), it highlighted the dangers of mismanagement of corporate image and reputation.

---

159 artsandbusiness.org.uk, 2019.
160 @GretaThurnberg, Jul 29, 2021.

Culture Unstained, an environmental campaign group, leaked an email exchange between Ian Blatchford, Museum Director, and *Shell* seeking help in securing support from the *Oil and Gas Climate Initiative* (a group of the largest fossil fuel corporations). Oil and gas industry support for British cultural institutions has been subject to attack from environmentalists, and the *Science Museum* is accused of allowing *Shell* to "greenwash" its public image. Ecologist Dr Emma Sayer, a contributor to the exhibition, withdrew her name from installations claiming she felt "embarrassed to be involved". Youth climate protestors disassociated themselves with their climate change placards featured in the exhibition.[161] This not only highlighted The *London Science Museum*'s hypocrisy and exposed *Shell*'s sponsorship motives, but almost certainly damaged the brand equity of both parties.

The classic example of *Lucozade*'s metamorphosis from being associated with old-age tonics to become a leading isotonic 'sports' drink brand demonstrates this. The "above systems and structures" *Apple* narrative illustrates the brand's unique view of itself and brand users, what *Interbrand* refer to as "a new reality".

The brand's direction and thrust – the brand's mission – is conditioned by the vision and the constant, long-term purpose of the brand. *Benetton*'s vision – or brand narrative – to "celebrate diversity and colour of product through challenging the beliefs and ethical values of consumers globally" is evident in all brand encounters between customer and company.

9.7 Brands as capital

Critically for organisations, brands can be seen as a form of capital, an integral part of marketing strategy for building brand equity by encouraging selection over competition by producing value and values through immaterial assets, and as a method of securing and maintaining loyalty. Strategically, brands are "monetisable symbolic values" (Gorz, 2003, p. 60), an amalgam of tangible product attributes and intangible group identification and self-expressive benefits. Indeed, the notion of connections with external symbolic or *representational value* to enhance internal value is a relatively new perspective in business since it identifies hidden wealth in the form of intangible assets.

What exactly do we mean by 'intangible assets'? This concept has its origin in financial analysis and is a companion to 'intellectual capital' in the world of knowledge management. Both are referred to as 'immaterial resources' (eg: ideas, sensations, feelings, and experiences), not financial assets as such, but, as a factor of production, play a crucial role in the creation of value. Intangible assets comprise:

---

161 Fatima, Manji, "Revealed: Science Museum signed gagging clause with exhibition sponsor *Shell*", *Channel Four News*, Jul 29, 2021.

- *Human Capital:* (sometimes referred to as 'operant assets') such as physical, social, and cultural knowledge skills, individual professional expertise and skills, workforce social skills, ability to innovate, responsiveness to change, entrepreneurial engagement.
- *Relational or Customer Capital*: Customer and stakeholder relationships, customer databases, brand relationships, business partner capital with other equipment manufacturers (OEM), and intermediaries and suppliers, relationships with investors, banks, financial service organisations, and pressure group relationships.

The above is similarly described as Corporate Social Capital, the virtual or intangible resources from stakeholder or social relationships.

- *Structural Capital*: Business infrastructure, processes, information systems, intellectual property (eg: copyrights, patents, trademarks), design patents and expertise, location advantages, and organisational culture.

In the same vein, Saint-Onge (1996) claims that intangible assets are composed of human capital, structural capital, and customer capital. Sveiby (1997) describes 'knowledge capital' as comprising: customer capital, structural capital, and human capital. The concept of 'customer capital' can be used to build a bridge between the inputs of business and marketing strategy and the outputs of revenue growth, profitability and shareholder value (Pringle & Field, 2008, p. 9). However, Ambler (2000) cautions against replacing the asset of brand equity with the resource (capital item) of customer capital as this will shift attention to the short-term and detract from the long-term mission of building brand equity.

To have real financial worth, brands must produce Economic Value Added (EVA), and part of this must be directly attributed to the brand itself. Intangible assets give companies the capability of creating economic value in the form of customer value as well as shareholder and stakeholder value, and are the primary source of capacity to innovate and create differential added value. As such, brands have a balance sheet value, but the process of creating that value has to be supported by production capacity and capability, a customer service structure, the logistics of warehousing and delivery, and of course a feasible, sustainable business model.

Therefore, Brand Equity is the subjective added value the brand gives to the objective quality of a product or service, enhancing price premium for the organisation and minimising perceived user risk for the consumer. It is the "differential effect that brand knowledge has on consumer response to the marketing of that brand", the accruing financial value being "the financial representation of a business's earnings due to the superior demand it creates for its products or services through the strength of its brand" (Keller., 2003). A brand strength, specific to a moment in time in terms of user relevance and competitive advantage, can be higher market share, secure positioning, customer loyalty, price inelasticity, premium pricing, easier new product or service introductions, expansion into diverse markets, and other behavioural competitive indicators.

The intangible brand value accruing from these strengths must be managed in order to produce tangible results.

Managing Brand Equity is one of the most critical aspects of organisational strategy and relates the value of goods or services to the organisation. If managed properly, this could link company and customer in loyal, mutually-beneficial relationships (or 'fusion') which can enhance consumer lifestyles and create reliable income streams and secure brand longevity. Ambler's (2000) simplistic definition of brand equity – "what we carry around in our heads about the brand" – is succinct but incomplete. In order to understand brand equity, we must have a comprehensive understanding of what is meant by 'assets'.

9.8 Equity from intangible assets

Brand equity is about viewing the intangible value of assets of the organisation – both positively as assets and negatively as 'liabilities' – as a driver of value creation and a strategic connection between customer and company. It is what the company promises it stands for, and it implies trust, consistency, and expectation of experience. It is the aggregate value of all brand assets, with all the connotations of customer association, company reputation, and competitive positioning, the monetary value of the brand as a singular asset. Brand Equity is the customer's cognitive and affective relationship – the brand's ability to satisfy functional and representational needs – with and of the brand due to direct or indirect experience.

To some, brand assets are "learnt mental associations and effects acquired through time from direct or vicarious, material or symbolic interactions" (Kapferer, 2000, p. 15). It gives customers confidence to overcome the perceived risks of purchase, encourages long-term relationships, and presents an implied frame of reference for what the brand is about and how it answers purchase problems. For the company, it provides competitive protection, projects perceptual and market positioning, lends credibility and trust for new product additions or innovations, allows premium pricing, builds repetitive income streams and profitability. Loyalty, for example, can offer a company protection against adversity. The customer loyalty of *Apple* and *Samsung* customers protected them against negative backlashes to the *iPhone* and *Galaxy Note* recalls, whereas *Toyota* and *Volkswagen* suffered in comparison.

Brand Equity has become an important issue from a variety of perspectives: mergers and acquisitions, evaluation of strategies, and management (in terms of its impact on value creation, brand extensions, enhancement, and exploitation of brand strengths, and so on (Srivastava & Shocker, 1991). There have been many iterations of techniques which attempt to build competitive advantage from company resources, some with reducing effectiveness with common adoption and diffusion. However, organisations with agility and foresight acknowledge the role that brands have as long-term, value-creating strategic assets. Brand equity is both the driving force and corollary of all marketing activities: the process and the result of co-creation manifest as intangible value, and yet the real value "lies outside the organisation in the minds of potential customers" (Kapferer, 2000, p. 14). When a company purchases another company because of the 'equity' in its brands, it is essentially buying the promise made by all of its representations and relationships built with its customers. It is buying the 'good will' built into the brand.

Aaker (1991, p. 15) refers to Brand Equity in terms of the concept of brand associations, being "the set of assets and liabilities linked to a brand, its name and symbol, that adds or detracts from the value provided by a product and/or service to a firm and/or to the firm's customers". He characterises brand equity as a 'perceived' or 'behavioural' value and included loyalty, perceived quality, associations, as well as price premiums accrued as a result of this differentiation. Brands constitute 'added value' – economic added value (EVA) – which is endowed by the brand onto the product in the form of both intangible assets (balance sheet value) and conditional assets (the need to work with other material assets such as production and service processes to facilitate them). Berry (2000, p. 28), emphasising this, claimed that "In packaged goods, the product is the primary brand. However, with services, the company is the brand".

Aaker's (Aaker, 1996) model includes four aspects which have mutual customer-company value-creating benefits:
- *Brand loyalty*: Reduced costs of marketing, trade leverage, easier acquisition of new customers and competitive protection for the company; the bonuses of relationship and co-creation for the consumer.
- *Brand awareness*: Familiarity, visibility, signal of substance, anchor for other associations for the company; easier purchase facility in category for the consumer.
- *Brand associations*: Differentiation and positioning, purchase justification, and user attitude creation for the company; the social benefits of group affiliation and self-esteem, and the psychological benefits of meaning for the consumer.
- *Perceived value*: Positive links with brand experience, brand extensions and introductions easier for the company; purchase confidence, and choice reinforcement for the consumer.

Brand Equity measurement can be split into two strands: Customer Based Brand Equity (CBBE) and Corporate Brand Equity, the former value based on customer's associations and derives from Keller's (2001) definition, and the latter being determined by stakeholder's perceptions to the brand in the context of the competition and category need. It can offer companies protection through performance, social image, trustworthiness, commitment, and loyalty, and this in turn facilitates extension of product range and new product acceptability. Table 9.3 details the composition of brand asset value.

Table 9.3: Brand Asset Value.

Brand assets ───────────▶	Brand strength ─────────▶	Brand value (financial equity)
Brand awareness	Market share	Net discounted cashflow
Brand reputation (attributes,	Market leadership	attributable to the brand after
benefits, competence,	Market penetration	paying the cost of capital
know-how, etc). Emotion	Share of requirements	invested to produce and run
Perceived brand personality	Growth rate	the business and the cost of
Perceived brand values	Loyalty rate	marketing
Reflected customer imagery	Price premium	
Brand preference or	Percentage of products the	
attachment	trade cannot delist	
Patents and rights		

Source: Kapferer (2008, p.14)

Ever since the 1980s, when a spate of high-profile mergers and acquisitions put branding at the centre of discussion and negotiation, Brand Equity became recognised as an organisation's most valuable intangible asset, and a Holy Grail for marketers. Although there are numerous descriptions of what it actually means, Brand Equity definitions focus on financial value or consumer perception of a brand. However, any definition has to link financial performance with consumer behaviour. Untangling intangible brand value is anchored in the phenomenological social meaning and competitive advantage analysed in *Section 1 The Foundations of Theory and Practice*. The roots of this as a marketing strategic tool lies in customer engagement: as Smith suggests, Brand Equity "resides in culturally constituted meaning, in the brand experience, . . . is bonded in strategic and tactical dialogues which consumers co-create, disseminate, and advocate" (2011, p. 25).

Salinas (2009, p. 2) reviews three concepts of brand based on accounting, and management-oriented perspectives.

Accounting perspective
- The brand as a recognisable intangible asset: marketing-related assets (eg: trademarks, trade names, internet domain names); contractual assets (eg: licensing agreements); technology-based assets (eg: patented technology, databases); customer-related assets (eg: customer lists; customer relations); and art-related assets (eg: books, films).
- Non-recognisable intangible assets (eg:internally generated brands).
- Trademark, brand and branded business (eg: a name, logo, and other associated visual elements; a broader scope including intellectual property; holistic company or organisational brand).

Economic perspective
– Economic vs accounting criteria.

Management perspective
– Brand corporate reputation
– Brand and visual identity
– Brand, intangible assets, and intellectual capital
– Brand equity and intangible assets
– Brand, intangible assets, and intellectual capital

9.9 Leveraging brands as assets

Whilst assets reside inside the organisation, direction for application has been outside the traditional confines of marketing, with theoretical perspectives from sociological, psychological, anthropological, and philosophical domains of knowledge in meaning creation. However, unless the brand as an asset can be leveraged to create actual value, a brand has no worth. As Kapferer states: "A brand has no financial value unless it can deliver profits" (2014, p. 15). The resource-based view (RBV) of strategy is that organisations can derive sustainable competitive advantage (SCA) not from industry characteristics but from owning and utilising their resources. Advantages stem from the heterogeneity of resources applicable and leverageable by each separate company. SCA isn't inherently in possession but in appropriate management of those resources (Sirmon, Hitt, & Ireland, 2007). The most commonly used, according to Kraaijenbrink et al, are: "financial, reputational, or human; tangible or intangible; fungible [exchangeable] or non-fungible" (2010, p. 352). However, according to Barney (1991), resources are only strategic (and therefore can be leveraged) when they are valuable, rare, inimitable, and non-substitutable (VRIN). Brands are a vital resource for leveraging value in any organisation.

In the 1980s, the recognition and the subsequent change to re-aligning brands as assets, as strategic drivers of the business rather than tactical market mix tools, was as transformational to how marketing was perceived and how it functioned as was segmentation, mass marketing, and globalisation. Brands are more than mere resources; they may not be physical entities, but they are assets which have real value for companies and provide meaning for customers and, like other assets need long-term investment to achieve longevity. Brand assets are the sources of influence implicit in user relationships, emotional and positional associations, patents etc. which can be turned into brand strengths. As Aaker says, "Connecting 'brand' to the concepts of 'equity' and 'assets' radically changed the marketing function, enabling it to expand beyond strategic tactics and get a seat at the executive table" (2021).

The bridge between the resource-based view (RBV) – strategically exploiting internal resources to leverage external competitive advantage – and the many service-oriented perspectives – managing internal processes to enhance the customer experience and create value – is the strategic approach of managing brand equity. Davis advocates "brand asset management . . . to manage the brand as an asset, with every strategic and investment decision an organisation makes either impacting or being impacted by the brand" (2002, p. 6). The implication here is that brands should be managed higher up in the organisation rather than demoted to a tactical, operational level, Brand Equity being the purview of the CEO and Board, and that brand management is strategic, combined with business strategy, reflecting the same strategic vision and corporate culture.

9.10 Leveraging employees as assets

Whether organisations are product-oriented or service-oriented, or whether they are based on human or technology-facilitated exchange, competitive advantage through the relationships between employees and customers (and between employee and employee) represents a key asset in terms of sustainable differentiation and competitive advantage, especially when competition becomes more homogenous (Mosley, 2007). Despite research linked to internal brand management strategy, such as brand-oriented HRM, brand-centric leadership, the link between internal and external integrated marketing communications (Burmann & Zeplin, 2005), an understanding of EBBE is now an established requirement.

Articulating and managing customer expectations is a key employee interchange function, particularly so with front-line customer-facing service employees, and it is the contextual interpretation of needs and expectations where employees are most useful. With antecedents in service productivity and quality, in tandem with HRM, the "triplets of quality, productivity, and profitability, all serve the purpose of making service operations efficient" (Gummesson, 1991, p. 113); it is the element of process which is key. The role of the employee in the evaluation of the service experience links crucially into the service-profit chain where the service encounter is a pivotal relationship moment, and the employee skill base (ie: 'operant resources') as a vital brand experience input can provide a competitive advantage.

Irrespective of how well a brand is presented, nothing can salvage a weak brand experience (Berry, 2000). As de Chernatony and Cottam (2006, p. 616) argue, "ultimately, *what* is delivered is less important than *how* it is delivered". 'Living the brand' is what employee equity is based on. The view that the behaviour of employees lies at the heart of any brand is strongly endorsed by Burmann, Zepli & Riley (2009, p. 265) who "proponents of internal brand management maintain that it is the entire body of employees, regardless of their hierarchical or functional role in the company, who play a crucial part in building competitive advantage through strong branding".

Despite the emerging focus on the notion of the 'internal market' with employee as customer and the acknowledgement of the role played by the employee in the service-profit relationship throughout service marketing research (Zeithaml, Berry, & Parasuraman, 1993), brand equity has traditionally been analysed from a market-facing orientation, with consumer and financial perspectives dominating. The emphasis on the employee contribution to the internal intangible value creation – Employee Based Brand Equity (EBBE) or 'employee branding' or 'employee brand identification' – is getting increasing traction. With antecedence in service marketing, this concept was introduced by King & Grace (2009) and is derived from a connectionist perspective, part of the context-based cognitive psychology paradigm. Strong brands and service quality are premised by employees' ability to deliver on customer expectation (Lings & Greenley, 2005).

This perspective suggests that the meaning created in brands can affect employee attitude and behaviour (whether positively or negatively) eliciting either company evangelism or animosity. In turn, it can affect Firm-based Brand Equity (FBBE) and Customer-based Brand equity (CBBE). More and more companies are coming to realise that at the crucial customer-company interface, the employee is a vital component of internal brand management; it is a necessity.

Burmann, Zeplin & Riley (2009) state that the internal brand management model covers brand commitment, brand citizenship, and the brand-customer relationship:

– *Brand commitment:* the psychological attachment to the brand comprises 'obedience' (individual willingness to adjust own views to the brand or company requirements), 'identification' (the extent to which the employee believes in being a constituent of the brand and the organisation), and 'internalisation' (the degree to which the employee has incorporated the brand into his or her thinking and behaviour).
– *Brand Citizenship Behaviour (BCB):* A marketing extension of the general term Organisational Citizenship Behaviour (OCB), described as "extra-role behaviour". According to Burmann, Zeplin & Riley (2009), BCB is significantly different to OCB in that it goes beyond OCB to strengthen brand-customer relationship factors like satisfaction, loyalty, and retention. An antecedent of brand citizenship is the 'psychological contract' employees demonstrate over-and-above standard job description. Brand citizenship is the intention to voluntarily identify with brand identity outside the formal role expectation, how an employee aligns with the corporate identity and values. This type of employee engagement has been referred to "brand ambassador" (Vallaster & de Chernatony, 2006), "living the brand" (Burmann & Zeplin, 2005), and "delivering the brand promise".
– *Brand promise:* How an organisation commits to being perceived. An employee's brand-favouring behaviour (ie: 'living the brand') and brand citizenship behaviour become pivotal factors in communicating the brand to its customers through employee interactions (Ind, 2007). As Burmann, Zeplin & Riley (2009, p. 267) suggest, "key variables for fostering brand commitment are brand-centred human resource management, brand communication, and brand leadership measures . . . [which] must coincide with two contextual factors – aligning the corporate culture and corporate structure fit with the identity of the brand".

Service experience is a direct corollary of the organisation's culture as well as the skills, experience and attitude of the employee. The building and maintenance of customer-company relationships becomes an inextricable essential part of the service value proposition, acting like a virtuous circle, demonstrating that productive employees act like catalysts for satisfaction, loyalty, and profitability. Delivered brand experience has to be consistent with communicated brand promise; the essential component of managing the internal brand is influencing and managing the attitudes and behaviour of employees.

Some organisations actively encourage employees to embrace their role as brand ambassadors (de Chernatony, Cottam, & Segal-Horn, 2006), their commitment increasing if they know how they can and are contributing. Cultivating EBBE is a product of human capital, how internal stakeholders (employees) can affect other internal stakeholders (other employees) as well as external stakeholders (customers). Here, service provision achieves the same ends as delivering the brand promise. Implicit in this is that employees understand what the brand strategy is intended to achieve and their role in that. Employees provide an essential ingredient in building brand meaning and brand equity (Berry, 2000). Indeed, this internalisation of the brand means that employees are customer-facing and better placed to fulfil the explicit and implicit brand promise because ethe desired brand values, practices, and behaviours are clarified and defined proving a service and brand blueprint providing a clear direction for all organisational efforts (Tosti & Stotz, 2001).

EBBE is not the creation of a separate employee brand identity, but rather the reinforcement of it, reflecting the employee's brand knowledge and the differential effect that brand knowledge has on an employee's response to their role in the brand strategy. Employee knowledge and experience is key to contextual credibility, none more so than in a B2B service setting. Biedenbach & Marell (2010) describe how employee knowledge and experience has a positive effect on the four key dimensions of brand equity: brand awareness, brand associations, perceived quality, and loyalty.

9.11 Leveraging customers as assets

Customer equity is a data-driven, outside-in approach which essentially operationalises the fundamental marketing concept of customer-centricity, and links customer equity to corporate evaluation (Gupta, Lehman, & Stuart, 2001).

Throughout the last 60 years, the 'marketing concept' has migrated from product-orientation to market-orientation, but the transition to customer-centred approaches, with the changing emphasis from short-term transactional to long-term relational strategies, has had the most lasting impact. The one major link between all of the key developments in marketing conceptual thinking and practical application, is strategy orientation and business process implementation being centred not around products but *customers*: customer satisfaction, market orientation, and customer value. The migration from a product economy with product-orientated thinking as its axis to one of a service economy with its customer-orientation, has emphasised the need to put the customer at the heart of the company as a realisable asset.

However, there is a difference in passively declaring this as a part of organisational philosophy, and actively putting the focus on the value of the customer as a real source of value – maximising long-term profits by leveraging customer retention through cultivating profitable customer relationships and growing the business by extending loyal CLV. True customer-centricity is about organising tangible and intangible assets around maximising Customer-based Brand Equity (CBBE), considered a good proxy for the value of a firm. Keller's definition – "the differential effect of brand knowledge on consumer response to the marketing of the brand" – has three key elements: differential effect is a competitive comparison; brand knowledge refers to brand image and brand awareness; and consumer response to marketing stimuli (eg: acceptance of brand changes, product extensions, negative PR). Rust, Lemon & Zeithaml's definition as the "total of the discounted lifetime values summed over all of the firm's current and potential customers" (2004, p. 109), suggests that customers and customer equity are more central to many firms than brands and brand equity.

Rust, Zeithaml and Lemon (2000) describe three key drivers of customer equity:
- *Value equity*: the customer's objective mainly cognitive assessment of the utility of the brand in terms of price, convenience, quality based on a rational evaluation.
- *Brand equity*: not explained by objective assessment, this is the customer's subjective, irrational, often emotional and intangible assessment of the brand built through image and meaning, influenced by brand awareness, brand image, consumer's attitude to the brand and the company's disposition to corporate citizenship.
- *Retention equity*: the tendency of the customer to stay loyal to the brand over and above the objective and subjective assessments, whether through brand switching inertia, purchase heuristics, repeat purchase based on satisfaction.

Based on the early work of Blattberg & Deighton who advocated a retention strategy based on the premise of "attracting and keeping the highest value customers being the cornerstone of successful marketing" (1996, p. 136), Rust, Zeithaml & Lemon (2000) extended the concept of Customer Equity as a convergence of three perspectives: the financial impact of service quality (Return on Quality); service quality measurement and customer value; and customer retention. Maximising customer equity is the balance between acquisition and retention and transferring product management into customer management. This is the product of strategically successful customer relationship management, and, as such, is of one of the most important metrics for managers to measure and manage company performance, a key driver of shareholder value. This perspective differs from retrospectively valuing customer's past performance by looking at future cash flows arising from investment in customer relationships. Implicit in this approach is segmenting customers based on profitability.

There are three aspects to this:
- *Customer Lifetime Value*: (the discounted sum of cash flows or net present value of future profits from a customer or segment of customers over a lifetime of the customer/company fusion).
- *Static Customer Equity*: (the sum of the CLVs of a particular group or cohort of customers).
- *Dynamic Customer Equity*: (the discounted sum of both current and future cohorts) (Kumar & Shah, 2015).

Customer Equity is similar to Brand Equity in that they are both long-term measures of the intangible values of marketing assets, but they differ in a number of ways: CE is quite standard whilst BE varies between practitioners; unit of analysis (product versus customer); whilst BE usually measures consumer attitudes, CE measures observed behaviours; BE models can be descriptive, whereas CE models are analytical; brand value and CE in the way that they drive financial performance; CE drivers are easily defined whilst BE definition more complex and grounded in consumer psychology.

For companies like *Apple*, *Facebook*, and *McDonalds* the high level of customer equity they enjoy is a major source of competitive advantage. According to Blattberg and Deighton (1996, p. 143), "brands don't create wealth; customer do". Brands are just one instrument among with which to build customer equity, but they are never more important than the customers they reach. Indeed, brand management may actually impede customer management.

Kim and Ko (2012) found in a study on luxury fashion brands that the relationship between social media attributes – entertainment, interaction, trendiness, customisation, and WOM – had a "significantly positive on purchase intention with value equity, brand equity, and relationship equity", although brand equity had a significant negative effect on customer equity, whilst the relationship between purchase intention and customer equity had significance.

Wiesel, Skiera & Villaneuva (2008) report that "firms that aim to increase the value of their customer base should report forward-looking customer metrics because such reports align customer management with corporate goals". The concept of evaluating customer potential through existing customer segmentation (rather than potential market segmentation) – 'The Customer Pyramid' – (Zeithaml, Rust, & Lemon, 2001) views customers as resources that can be cultivated in 'profitability tiers'. This strengthens the link between service quality and profitability resulting in more effective, efficient, and profitable strategies for serving the customer.

Venkatesan, Rajkumar and Kumar (2004) evaluate the usefulness of CLV as a metric customer selection and marketing resource allocation and show that marketing contracts across channels influence CLV non-linearly with customers selected on the basis of the CLV providing higher future profits than customers selected on other criteria. However, in a study in a B2B context, Ramasehan, Rabbanee and Hsin Hui (2013) found that whilst value equity and relationship equity have a significant influence on customer loyalty through the mediating effect of customer trust, it was found that brand equity had no effect on customer trust or loyalty.

9.12 Building through narratives of relevance, authenticity, and love

When there is evidence of consumers having a deep emotional connection with a brand or an organisation, company brand identity and customer brand image can be bonded in symbolic symbiosis – a fusion of co-creation and mutually beneficial harmony. The more successful brands help this process by facilitating compelling narratives sealed in company promise and owned by the customer. Building narratives of relevance, authenticity, and love within evolving sociological contexts, reliant on the subjectivity of relative experience, is an evolutionary, organic approach to brand strategy based on forging profitable relationships between customer and company by fostering emotional attachment. Indeed, Beverland challenges the view that marketers provide brand meaning, arguing that it is derived from day-to-day interactions between brands and sub-cultures: "authenticity requires brand managers to downplay their overt marketing prowess and instead locate brands within communities and sub-cultures . . . appealing to timeless values" (2005, p. 460). 'Attachment' to brands and organisations is evidence of consumer socialisation and of meaning being transferred, and this can be instrumental in the emotional consequences which influence purchase decisions, disposition to company ethics, and building brand loyalty. This individual brand attachment phenomenon can be reinforced turning customers into 'fans', especially when they connect with consumers' culture. Brand managers must "evaluate, emulate and infiltrate the core culture of their customers" (Blackwell, Miniard, & Engel, 2006, p. 435).

One element of consumer emotional attachment is 'brand love' which has antecedents in brand identification and the group affiliation associated with brand community. It is anchored in the metaphor of relationship, where bonding goes beyond the transactional. An example of this is the emotional bond with a brand experienced through social-interactive engagement such as habitualised users of *Facebook* (Vernuccio, Pagani, Barbarossa, & Pastore, 2015, p. 706). Their research shows how "the positive influence of social-interactive engagement on brand love is mediated by the psychological effects related to how members [of online communities] perceive their self-concept based on belonging to the social group of a brand fan page". Batra, Ahuvia & Bagozzi argue that brand love needs to be conceptualised from the ground up, built on a deep understanding of how consumers experience it . . . best represented as a higher-order construct including multiple cognitions, emotions, and behaviours which consumers organise into a mental protype" (2012, p. 1). They identified 10 major components of the 'brand love prototype': high quality, linkages to strongly held values, beliefs that the brand provided intrinsic rather than extrinsic rewards, use of the loved brand to express current and desired self-identity, positive affect, a sense of rightness and a feeling of passion, an emotional bond, investments of time and money, frequent thought and use, and length of use. Implicit in this emotional attachment is the resonance it has with the brand user.

Principles in practice

Weight Watchers rebranding takes the eye off the ball

Staying relevant as a brand, re-aligning brand strategy, attracting different clientele, re-positioning original value propositions, or even re-branding to change perceptions of a company's image, can be a complex undertaking. If not managed properly, it can be a big mistake and cause severe or even irreparable damage to growth prospects and brand equity.

In 2019, on the back of the 'body positivity' movement, *Weight Watchers*, a global company with a well-established reputation for "weight loss and diet maintenance", decided to make a sea change decision to rebrand. Dropping the negative connotation of 'weight' from its brand name, and aiming at broadening their clientele, '*WW*' – linked to "*Wellness and Wellbeing*" – was introduced. This approach had proved very successful for *Kellogg's Special K*, who had previously used a "shape management" narrative as a euphemism for 'weight loss programme'. Not so for legacy brand *Weight Watchers*. They couldn't have imagined their new image would impact so badly on their bottom line, stock market earnings, and, in some ways most importantly, deterioration of brand equity. With "Diet culture" generally discredited and the number of dieters falling, weight loss still represents a multibillion dollar industry. But W*eight Watchers'* business was faltering. Adopting a more holistic approach to health, in a market reportedly worth $3.4 trillion, and with a partnership with 'meditation and mindfulness' company *Headspace*, seemed a more sustainable strategy.

In the second half of 2018, loyal customers voted with their feet with a loss of over 600,000 members. A marketing truism is the fact that acquiring new customers is far more costly than retaining loyal customers. The biggest mistake was not the realignment of target customers or the redefinition of what 'healthy' had become ("*Wellness That Works*" is ostensibly a better brand platform for repositioning the brand), it had been the perception of name change (the most familiar name in the weight loss category since 1963), and the lack of pre-launch efforts to generate awareness to core customers. Their core customer base were there for one main reason: to lose weight. As the social tides turn, and 'wellness that works' replaces 'losing weight' as their value proposition, "*WW* – *Weight Watchers Re-imagined*" may be best placed to take advantage and make a full recovery. But listening to customers might have saved a lot of dollars!

Another element of this brand bondage is the 'authentic' nature of the brand or organisation and the relationship the user has with it. Post-modern consumers use brands as social linking mechanisms and attribute authenticity which resonates with individual values of the 'self', and connects with time, space, and culture. The inauthentic nature of some of today's brands is a legacy of branding strategies focused on the individual's functional product needs, often without the wider sociological and ecological context from which the extended debate on 'identity' has been raging ever since Naomi Klein lit the fuse some 20 odd years ago (Klein, 1999). The interaction between company, customer and environment is becoming an increasingly important landscape in which to examine possible strategies. A study amongst SME CEOs reveals that "brand authenticity is operationalised as consisting of three factors: brand consistency, brand customer orientation, and brand congruency . . . which fosters brand trust, which in turn drives SME growth" (Eggers, O'Dwyer, Kraus, Vallaster, & Guldeberg, 2013).

Beverland (2009, p. 115) identifies 6 strategies for successfully creating and maintaining authentic brands:

- *Embedding the brand in a community*: When brands become a part of a community, as 'entrenched locals', purchasing them becomes an act of loyalty and identity. Authentic brands tend to stand up for the local community.
- *Challenging conventions*: Going against the way the market is served. Embodying the contrarian, rebellious spirit of the artist, is often a trait of authentic brands.
- *Sticking to one's roots*: Staying true to the original essence of the brand reinforces the mission and enhances credibility.
- *Loving the craft behind the product/service*: Authentic brands are staffed with people passionate for the product/service.
- *Downplaying one's market expertise*: Modest positioning can strengthen credibility.
- *Ignoring direct customer input into innovation*: This may enforce genuine brand reputation.

Consumer trust and respect, earned through relevance and authenticity, are the solid foundations of building mutual brand value. Brands signal position credibly, and credibility is projected through reinforcement of relevance. Brands with reputational relevance are more successful. At each touch point in the customer journey, the customer experiences a moment of truth, an experiential encounter with the brand promise. The authenticity of that brand promise is examined and tested, and the customer-company relationship is either reinforced or undermined. Experience expectation is implicit in the brand promise; authenticity is a consumer's perception. Brands which are rated as "authentic partners" are more likely to have higher levels of brand equity (Keller 2003). Consumers want authenticity because brand choices are an extension of their desired self (Belk, Wallendorf, & Sherry, Jr., 1989), and since traditional markers of identity such as race, religion, and culture are weakened symbols of lifestyle or personality, consumers achieve individual/brand congruity through self-authentication. In an increasingly fake or simulated world, where societal fabric has fragmented into a secular and cellular dynamic, consumers seek, and indeed demand, brands which have a measure of authenticity (Arnould & Price, 2000).

This can be a better predictor of purchase intentions than trust and credibility; brands which have authenticity can have higher levels of brand equity in their category than comparable brands (Beverland, 2009), are more likely to attract big spending consumers and gain word-of-mouth support (Principals-Synovate, 2008), and are more cost-effective in terms of promotional spend. Belk, Wallendorf, & Sherry, Jr. argue that "the sacralisation of the secular"– putting meaning over and above the brand's authenticity – is evidence of consumers achieving a transcendent experience through consumption of 'special' objects or experiences.

Authenticity can wrap a brand in a shield of protection which can enhance competitiveness and augment longevity. It is of critical importance, therefore, for brand managers and academics to understand the nature of authenticity when positioning a brand's purpose (Newman & Dhar, 2014). Grant (2000, p. 6) proclaimed it to be "the benchmark against which all brands are now judged". A conceptualisation of this includes:

- *An objectivist perspective*: where 'indexicality' (where a sign points to an object in the context it occurs) perceptions arise from evidence-based reality which can be verified through brand information such as labels of origin, age, ingredients, or performance.
- *A constructivist perspective*: a personally or socially constructed phenomenon, providing a schematic fit with consumer's expectations as opposed to the brand's objective properties.
- *An existentialist perspective*: which refers to a brand's ability to reflect an individual's true self through consumption
  (Morhart *et al*, 2015, p. 201),

Some of the other cues consumers use to identify and select brands which may be authentic are continuity, credibility, integrity, and the brand's use of symbolism to resonate with user's perception of the self.

- *Continuity*: Reflects a brand's ability to transcend trends because of its timelessness and resembles the concept of pedigree (Beverland, 2006).
- *Credibility*: Delivering on promises, transparency and honesty are all essential ingredients of authentic brands.
- *Integrity*: The values projected through branding, the virtue reflected in the brand's intentions, moral purity, and responsibility (Morhart, *et al*, 2015, p. 202). It's what Holt (2002) refers to as "commercial disinterestedness", similar to "staying true to one's morals" (Beverland & Farrelly, 2010).
- *Symbolism*: Based on consumption occurring in a socially constructed mediated marketplace, plays an important function. Perceived brand authenticity, therefore, is described as "the extent to which consumers perceive a brand to be faithful towards itself (continuity), true to its consumers (credibility), motivated by caring and responsibility (integrity), and able to support consumers in being true to themselves (symbolism) (Morhart, *et al*, 2015, p. 203).

Building brands through relevance necessitates constructing and maintaining a brand ecosystem which is co-created and socially constructed. Relevance represents more than product or service category appropriateness: relevance is social salience. Social salience and permanent engagement is critical for brand longevity; all Marketing Communications are bonded in strategic and tactical brand dialogues which consumers co-create, disseminate and advocate. Social salience in the context of marketing relates to the relevance and value of brands or organisations in providing offers which resonate socially amongst appropriate groups (Smith 2011). The social 'fit' of a brand, the individual/brand congruity, is implicit in the stories created and diffused amongst a brand's users, fans, followers, opinion formers and opinion leaders, and advocates. In simple terms, all that matters is that "consumers buy into the mystery of the brand story and can conform enough of it fits their desired Truth" (Beverland & Farrelly, 2010, p. 112). This overarching phenomenon – building brand narratives – is a co-created, socially-constructed ecosystem of meaning structure of perceived brand authenticity and trust within which meaning is negotiated.

Extending Aaker & Joachimsthaler's (2000, p. 52) conceptualisation of how brand extends the boundaries and thereby the value of the product, Figure 9.6 shows the additional brand narrative components. The second layer illustrates how the brand gives social and psychological substance and meaning to the product. As Kapferer (2000, p. 46) says, enduring loyalty will not come from "transforming the product category" Kapferer (2000, p.46), but must be rooted in engaging audiences in salient, social narratives. If the brand is the full market offering that makes the product competitive, the brand narrative is the on-going connecting dialogue between company and customer. The components of the brand narrative are explained in Table 9.4

Like metaphor and analogy, the use of narrative to communicate often complex subject matter has dominated most of the social sciences – philosophy, psychology, anthropology, sociology, political theory, literary studies – and yet had lesser impact in marketing strategy. Constructing narratives which are authentic, salient, and enforce experiential consumption can be a useful platform for companies, communicating company strategy in customers' contexts, both practically and andragogically. Transmitting values from business to customer (B2C), business to employee (B2E), and then through the brand telling its own story by the word of mouth conduit of peer-to-peer or C2C communications, meaning is transferred and negotiated socially.

Transmedia story telling can be a persuasive strategic mechanism, acting as a lifestyle lock-in parallel to product life cycles, protecting brand longevity, aiding brand recall and recognition, providing reliable income streams for organisations and, most importantly, constructing meaning for consumers (Smith, 2011). Narratives built around company history, environmental ethics, product reliability, brand provenance, and symbolic association can provide experiential relevance and value which strengthen bonds of loyalty and meaning. Applying the cultural logic of social construction to marketing strategy, operating in a field of social invention and

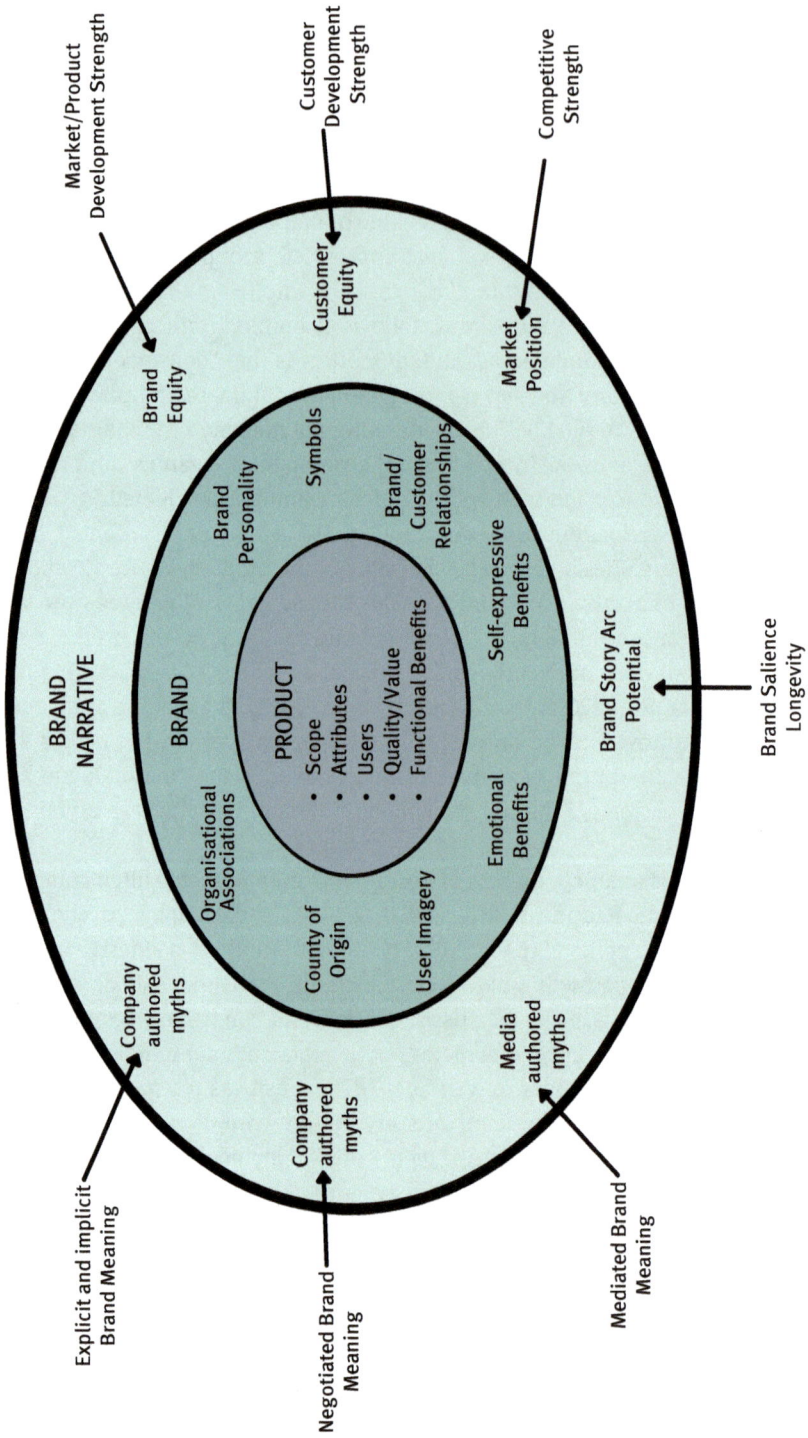

Figure 9.6: Brand Narrative Components.
Source: Dahlen, Lange, & Smith (2010)

Table 9.4: Components of Brand Narrative.

Brand Dimension	Explanation	Example
Company Authored Myths	Planned, company-controlled explicitly and implicitly projected corporate and brand communications.	*Coke* – symbolises American values *Virgin* – Anti-establishment *Arctic Monkeys* – Music label released downloadable material before the band was established to build up word of mouth and create a buzz.
Customer Authored Myths	User negotiated image and meaning.	*Stella Artois* – user projected 'Wife Beater' image aligned to USE.
Media Authored Myths	Brand meaning mediated through channels of communication such as media, intermediaries and agency either through planned dissemination of communication or voluntary word of mouth.	
Brand Equity	Total positive and negative connotations communicated by and about the brand.	Cumulative multiplier effect of IMC and environmental communications.
Customer Equity	Total positive and negative customer experience with the brand.	Assets of customer loyalty from which brand can grow.
Employee Equity		
Market Position	Strength of competitive market share.	Power in market.
Brand Story Arc Potential	On-going brand narrative.	Longevity of brand and ability to engage audience in on-going dialogue.

Source: Dahlen, Lange, & Smith (2010)

transformation, brands are like "map-making devices which situate consumers within symbolic networks of symbolic resources, as transmediated marketing accomplishments, created through rituals of transition, belonging, intimacy, and affect" (Kerrigan, Brownlie, Hewer, & Daza-Le Touze, 2011, p. 1504). Zaltman (2003, p. 89) calls these "consensus maps . . . networks of abstract understandings that constitute part of our mental imagery" Zaltman (2003. p.89).

The *Nike Community Impact Fund* (*NCIF*) is a good example, exclaiming its 'purpose' narrative by supporting grassroots organisations in 'lifestyle partnerships' with the likes of *Apple*, *Headspace*, and *ClassPass*. These type of social narratives focus on strategies which build long-term relationships with mutual purpose and emphasise co-creating shared value, engaging customers through providing brand experiences which resonate with their lives and values and help construct social meaning. This is achieved by aligning internal company culture with external customer context. Consumers are actively engaged in co-creating brand stories. *Harley Davidson*, with the dedicated commitment of a loyal customer base, transformed the 'driving experience' into a mystical, spiritual event. Another example – consuming coffee – is given 'purpose' by *Starbucks* who "connect with transparency, dignity and respect through the lens of humanity". Similarly, *LEGO* gives purpose to children's toy building blocks demonstrated in narratives of "inspiring and developing the builders of tomorrow". Purpose here goes beyond positioning: it is a social bonding mechanism with relevance rooted in the contemporary meaning. The strategic challenge for companies is to leverage real-time consumption data to create empathetic living brand experiences. Meaningful interactions between customer and company based on brand relevance delivers greater business impact and enhanced user satisfaction. Value-driven organisations like *IKEA* express social salience through economic, social, environmental, and communication-based values (Edvardsson, Enquist, & Hay, 2006).

Some brands have migrated from their own authentic brand narratives – *Snapple* drink, *Green & Black's* chocolate, *Innocent Smoothies* drinks all created in original, ethical brand spaces – and been absorbed into the respective portfolios of *Quaker Oats*, *Cadburys*, and *Coca Cola* with varying degrees of success. Often, the authenticity of the smaller niche brands has become contaminated by the inauthenticity of the new parent brand. Certainly the perceived amateurish marketing of *Snapple*, ignored by *Quaker*, caused a calamitous failure resulting in the writing off of $1.4 billion from the original $1.7 billion purchase. This is because authenticity is a subjective positioning bestowed on brands by customers who experience consumption individually and collectively in a social context, as acts of self-authentications if you will. These are user-generated myths, partly based on consumer experience, partly created by consumer perception.

9.13 Relationship between IMC and brand equity

The relationship between IMC and brand equity is symbiotic: successful IMC rests on strong branding; successful IMC strengthens the brand. Described as "one of the most influential marketing management frameworks of our time" (Schultz & Patti, 2009, p. 75), the primacy of IMC as the chief customer-company conduit is unquestioned. It can be defined as "the notion and the practice of aligning symbols, messages, procedures and behaviours in order for an organisation to communicate with clarity, consistency and continuity within and across formal organisational boundaries" (Christensen, Firat, & Torp, 2008, p. 424).

IMC has evolved from a tactical set of communications 'mix' tools, to being a part of the strategy for building and enhancing brand equity. Both IMC and brand equity are crucial components of building brand longevity. Analogous to the service marketing mantra of 'everything and everyone communicates', every point of contact between consumer and company has an impact on brand equity (Duncan & Mulhern,

2004). Customer contact at any stage in the customer's exposure to the organisation, by any element of communications can positively and negatively affect brand equity. Brands are 'live' 24/7, brand image is susceptible to sentiment, and sentiment affects brand equity.

However, Schultz (2004) points out that brand equity is not just built through random communications but is generated by managing brand equity contacts via IMC. The synergy between IMC components, according to Chang & Thorson (2004), could potentially create the greatest effect in consumers' encounters with brand contacts. These brand 'contacts' are both 'service encounters' in the process of interaction, and the stages of brand awareness and development of brand image. Brand knowledge culminates from these experiences and the responses build brand equity. And of course at the heart of this is the development and maintenance of reciprocal relationships forged in managed customer-company engagement. The presence of multiple brand stakeholders and the proliferation of digital media increases the amount of brand information generated exponentially.

When a firm fails to harness this information, to manage the conversation, it risks misalignment between identity and brand image, which, in turn, can tarnish brand equity (Orazi, Spry, Theilacker, & Vredenburg, 2017). Jaffe (2007, p. 3) refers to IMC as "a two-way dialogue or a stream of messaging between two or more parties with like-minded or shared beliefs, wants, needs, passions, or interests. Conversation is not initiated by any one person, side, or organisation. It is organic, non-linear, unpredictable, and natural".

Principles in practice

Negative brand image results in negative brand equity

Intended brand communications doesn't always translate into positive consumer sentiment. For example, in an attempt to deal with the social problem of children missing out on having a school meal, *Kellogg's* embarked on a laudable *Twitter* campaign 'Give A Child Breakfast', donating one breakfast for every retweet they received. However, this was perceived as blackmailing consumers into thinking kids would starve without the social media engagement. The ensuing *Twitter* 'fume' meant lost brand equity.

That was unlucky for *Kellogg's*, but some companies deserve their 'Gerald Ratner Moment'.[162] To celebrate 'International Women's Day', *BIC* aired a commercial to "promote gender equality" featuring the phrase *"Look like a girl. Think like a man"*. Previously, Ellen DeGeneres openly attacked the *"BIC: For Her"* campaign, claiming it to be misogynistic and undermining of gender equality. The inevitable happened.

Perhaps the worst example of all of PR brain contaminating corporate heart was *Coca Cola's* attempt to capitalise on the growing bottled water market. Success with their US brand *Dasani*

---

162 Gerald Ratner, former CEO of major British jewellery company *Ratners Group*, speaking at the 1991 *Institute of Directors Annual* convention, jokingly called the company's product "crap" and brand equity disappeared overnight.

encouraged expansion into the European market via the UK. The £7 million spent on introducing the "pure water" brand into the UK wasn't just wasted money, it failed to gain any traction, was withdrawn before it was fully rolled out (500 million bottles), and the ensuing PR disaster severely damaged the company's brand equity and ability to introduce a water brand into the UK. It was, in fact, tap water and contained illegal levels of bromate, a lethal carcinogen![163]

Using images of race, whether intentional or unintentional, which may have connotations of ambiguous social meaning, can be either unfortunate or just down to poor thought-through communications. German-based skin care brand *Nivea* launched its *'White is Purity'* campaign – aimed at the Middle Eastern target market – but was forced to retract after accusations of racism spread throughout an angry social media. This came only 6 years after a previous campaign using images of a black man throwing away a Neanderthal mask, accompanied by the tagline 'Recivilise Yourself', had caused a similar furore. The question of innocence or ignorance also applied to *Sony's 'White Is Coming'* campaign to accompany the replacement of its black *PlayStation Portable* with an all-white version. Set alongside an image of a white model aggressively clutching the face of a black woman by her chin, these naïve and insensitive images provoked accusations of stoking up inter-racial conflict and were seen as racially derogatory. Outrage was mainly in countries not directly affected by these campaigns. Similarly, Swedish fashion clothing brand *H&M* were accused of cultural insensitivity with its *'Coolest Monkey in the Jungle'* campaign featuring a black child wearing a sweatshirt.

An ad for Dutch beer brand *Heineken* featured a bartender sliding a beer to a white woman past three black people. Was the tagline *'Sometimes Lighter Is Better'* deliberate provocation or target positioning? However, there has to be relevance and a logic to positioning brands. *Pepsi's* attempt to "project a global message of unity, peace, and understanding" incurred the wrath of the public by using an image of Iesha Evans, an African-American woman who had resisted riot police during the *Black Lives Matter* protest in the US. However, *Estée Lauder's 'Double Wear'* range of makeup, with more than half of the shades aimed at women with 'very pale, light skin', was a kind of segregation by segmentation. Even when brands embrace a cause, this can sometimes negatively impact on brand equity. For example, *Starbucks's #Racetogether* initiative encouraging customers and baristas to discuss race relations backfired when they were accused of using racial politics for brand exposure.

All these examples demonstrate that negative brand image will invariably result in negative brand equity.

Branding is the driving force of marketing and as such is the central focus of marketing communications.

Fill (2006, p. 405) distinguishes three strategic dimensions to brands:

- Integration: all brand encounters have to be consistent and coherent, and the brand is the glue which binds the elements of integrated marketing communications.
- Differentiation: brands acts as a way of positioning away from the competition.
- Added Value: brands enable customers to derive extra benefits which may be functional, social, or even psychological.

163 https://www.theguardian.com/business/2004/mar/20/medicineandhealth.lifeandhealth

9.14 Links between brand building and brand activation

An apparent paradox of brand strategy is the mutually exclusive goals of immediate sales gratification and the long game development of brand equity. Pressure to make an immediate impact on sales has made short-termism an easy trap to fall into for CEOs and CMOs, producing strategies that are focused on half-yearly results rather than the goals of company vision and mission.[164] As Drucker warned back in 1993, "Long-term results cannot be achieved by piling short-term results on short-term results". However, one of the contemporary counter-intuitive truths of marketing strategy is that brand equity, a key philosophical and practical pillar of long-term brand building, paradoxically, should have a strong relationship to the urgent requirement of short-term sales. However, as we have already seen above, replacing the *asset* of brand equity with the *resource* of customer capital will shift attention to the short-term and detract from the long-term mission of building brand equity (Ambler, 2000).

The uncertainty of the marketplace in a post-COVID-19 economy, and the subsequent C-Suite impatience for commercial immediacy, makes the compatibility of these strategic goals a head and heart balancing act. Some have even suggested that building brand strategy is a global task and targeting product activations is a local one, but this perhaps is taking the dichotomy too far. Certainly the assumed binary choices of 'strategic and tactical', 'long-term and short-term', 'retention and acquisition', together with 'sales or brand' may actually offer a synthesis of strategy.[165]

Focusing on long-term goals whilst managing the here and now is not new in strategic philosophy. As we have seen in *Section 2.9* above, the Balanced Scorecard, developed as "a measurement system to help organisations expand their focus beyond the short-term cycles found in typical financial systems" (Russell, 2015) has been a compass of strategic direction. And yet, sustainable on-going success has often been trumped by the 'quarter-to-quarter' mentality of the capital markets, the "financial engineering of major corporations such as *Quest, Enron, World.com* and even *IBM*'s *Big Blue*" (Maltz, Shenhar, & Reilly, 2003, p. 187), and the 'new management orthodoxy' of adding shareholder value in lieu of key investments in the future. (Hayes & Abernathy, 1980). Shenhar & Dvir's (1996) 'Success Dimensions' included a broader time horizon; Hamel & Prahalad (1994) envisaged a new forward-thinking perspective on competitive strategy that focuses on "creating and dominating emerging opportunities".

Two more recent studies in the US and the UK show that long-term strategies deliver better performance than short-term tactical approaches. Over 600 publicly listed US companies were studied by McKinsey over a period of 15 years showing 47% more

---

164 Andrew Baxter, CEO, *Publicis Australia*, "Long-term vs short-term marketing campaigns, *Association for Data-Driven Marketing & Advertising (ADMA)*, 22nd February 2018.
165 Mark Ritson "The Long and the Short of It maps exactly onto the challenges of global marketing", *Marketing Week*, 9th Sep 2021.

top line growth, 36% more higher earnings, and added average market capitalisation of $8.67 billion. The UK study conducted by the *Institute of Practitioners* (*IPA*), analysing over 500 examples over 20 years, showed that for companies who pursued long-term strategies of brand building (not immediate sales) impact were 3 times more efficient, 3 times more likely to drive market share improvement, and 60% more likely to improve profit.

This 'long and short' perspective stems from the work of Binet & Field, (2013) who argue that there are TWO trajectories to growth: immediate activation and years of brand building. Following their meta-analysis[166] of 996 campaigns and 700 brands spread over 83 categories, their considered view is that whilst the two are different, there can be no long-term effects (growth-oriented brand campaigns) without short-term actions (efficiency-oriented direct campaigns). Mark Ritson (2021), a long-time champion of their work, claims that there are two undulating lines of immediate and incremental growth: marketing is becoming less effective and short- term in its nature (although ignoring 'brand' for 'sales' is a fallacy); and the promotion of "sophisticated mass marketing[167] has broken one of our discipline's most cherished principles – that you must segment and target in order to have the greatest marketing impact". The *Ehrenberg Bass* empirical evidence supports the view that long-term brand building needs "whole category" targeting rather than segmentation. Similarly, it is suggested that loyalty programmes can be deceptive. Companies assume they are necessary in order to maximise revenue streams from existing customers, and yet, Binet & Field found that they do not improve sales as much as new customer acquisition programmes. Plus, existing customer sales may be at saturation point anyway.

The approach that Binet & Field (2013) advocate is illustrated as in Figure 9.7.

This is based on Daniel Kahneman's (2011) *'Thinking Fast and Slow'* work on rational and emotional decision-making who refers to two systems as 'System 1' (automatic, emotional, fast) and 'System 2' (effortful, cognitive, slow). System 1 is the invisible majority whilst System 2 is the conspicuous minority. System 1 drives brand preferences and has a powerful 'priming' effect in assisting the decision at point of sale.

Binet & Field advocate a middle path; acquisition and retention strategies are not mutually exclusive objectives. Short-term activation or *re*activation of the existing customer base is narrower and may have smaller paybacks; long-term brand development has a broader scope, an extended time frame, and will have bigger paybacks. Their research shows that short-term metrics can be misleading: very large immediate effects have to be balanced against cumulative large profits. Aiming at *all* prospects is a long-term task with a 'combined' strategy targeting existing, new, and then all customers. Rational product and pricing effects depend on brand building, the impact of IMC decaying quickly; building long-term brand preferences through 'priming'

---

166 Data from 'Marketing in the Era of Accountability', *IPA* Effectiveness Databank, 2007.
167 *Ehrenberg Bass Institute.*

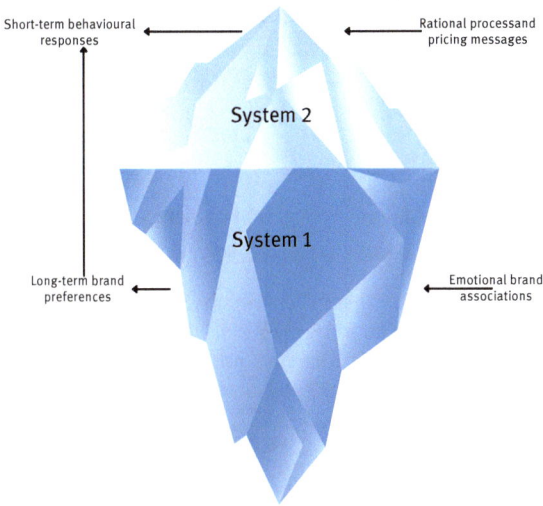

Figure 9.7: Long and short brand strategy.
Source: Binet & Field (2013)

through emotional brand associations (eg: purpose, narrative, customer-brand congruity) has smaller impacts on sales but decays slowly. Rational approaches have an immediate impact on sales but brand perceptions are relatively unchanged; the brand grows stronger with emotional priming and there is a much bigger uplift in volume, price elasticity increases, and profitability is enhanced in the long-term. Sales spikes may not actually produce sales build. Both strategies are needed.

A common observation in traditional survey brand trackers was that KPIs, wave after wave, only shifted marginally, the cumulative development of customer relationships and brand value moving with glacial pace. Understandably, fuelled by an abundance of digital and behavioural data, the drive over the last few years for a focus on a narrower range of evidence-based bottom-line performance has seen a concerted push for activity with ROI that's easier to demonstrate a proven relationship to financial outcomes. Marketers became more commercially credible in the boardroom, their activities generating a definite sales return, and a rounded approach to strategy more pragmatic. Now the imperative for brand strategy was not just about balancing purpose with profit, but also managing both the *emotional* campaigns which produce considerably more powerful long-term effects than *rational* campaigns which have considerably more powerful short-term impact on sales. Brand experience is an integral part of brand activation as it allows an emotional connection with the brand which may lead to consumer brand satisfaction and brand trust (Marist, Yuliati, & Najib, 2014).

Binet and Field, supported by Ritson, propose a rule of 60/40 split in terms of activity (ie: resource effort, budget spend) directed towards sales (brand activation) and long-term brand building respectively. They explain the rationale for deciding upon the most efficient way to split %-channel spend:

> *In 2007, prior to the start of the new communications strategy, all expenditure went behind short-term promotional activity. Over the following four years the proportion spent on brand building rose gradually to 28%.*

> *Sales grew strongly following the introduction of the new strategy and continued to grow as the proportion of brand building activity rose towards the optimum 60:40 split.*

> *The econometric model revealed that the majority of long-term growth was driven by the brand-building pillars and the pattern of growth suggests that further rebalancing in favour of brand-building activity would promote yet more growth. This is consistent with the 60:40 rule as the brand still allocates considerably less than 60% of its budget to brand building.*[168]

Addressing the *Advertising Research Foundation's (ARF)* 2019 Conference, in reference to the "60/40 Rule" which he and Field advocate, Binet reminded his audience: "Share of voice matters, but [what also matters is] how you allocate share of voice between brand building and activation." Optimum effectiveness is the nub. In 2009, *Aldi*, a combined German family-owned discount supermarket chain with over 10,000 in 20 countries, deployed this strategy when they started to lose market share. The pressing need to increase foot fall and short-term sales meant that their activation advertising efforts had to double as a brand campaign. *Axe/Lynx* combined a TV 'Fallen Angels' brand campaign with clever app activation.

Other splits were investigated across a range of spend for sales activation and brand building scenarios: "For the group of campaigns with activation share of budget in the range 30–50%, with groups where it is lower and higher, efficiency appears to be more than double, with the balance in the right range. Too little brand activity and the brand equity needed to drive sales in future will not accumulate. Too little activation activity and the brand will not be exploiting the full sales potential of brand equity as it accumulates.

This ratio is not definitive, and will vary with each category. If, for example, in a category with a high degree of innovation, activation is easy. The activation tilt can be split more 70/30. In categories where there is a big element of online search involved in the decision-making process, activation is straight forward and spend can focus more on brand. In the tourist industry, consumer decisions may hinge on pre-booking research (which is often a key and integral part of the holiday experience) provided by search engines like *Google*, *Booking.com*, or *TripAdvisor* (or a combination of sites). The tilt may be as much as 75/25 skewed towards emotional brand objectives.

B2B companies face a challenge because of the narrow nature of focusing on delivering short-term sales from existing customers. Yet Field & Binet's research on

---

168 https://jeanallary.files.wordpress.com/2016/07/the_long_and_short_of_it_pdf_doc.pdf – page 40.

storytelling and brand building has given this sector encouragement that growing business and remaining competitive are compatible objectives.[169] Colin Lewis, CMO at *Open Jaw Technologies*, claims that "Big B2B brands such as *IBM*, *Microsoft* or *Intel* have always needed a proper and evolving brand story because they operate in such a dynamic market, but for other companies the challenge can be getting the sales function to buy into the importance of long-term brand building".

What is 'brand activation'? Looking at Figure 9.8, at the first contact points of the brand/customer journey vortex, the customer is in a state of 'unawareness', either in terms of the category or the brand. *Engagement authenticity* via a multiplicity of channels and touchpoints through brand experience in order to increase awareness, create interest, and trigger sales is the first job of strategy. The overall strategy is to move customers progressively through a 'journey' from unawareness to advocacy. In so doing, the brand is moved from one state to another. *Activation*, therefore, refers to igniting the potential of the brand to spark a sales transaction that might lead to an emotional connection, loyalty, and regular income streams. Experiential marketing, using simulated or actual usage of the brand, often in a relevant consumption context, through giving physical samples, with in-store promotions, sponsorship, or experiential events, can be an effective method if brand touchpoints are linked. If handing out samples seems a bit 'analog', the digital equivalent of emails, online ads, social media, and free downloads as free product trials can be useful in providing feedback and generating WOM. Activating some sort of dialogue with potential customers is important. Activation through emotional connection can hit short- and long-term goals.

The examples of *Pirelli Tyres* sponsoring *Formula One* and *Red Bull* sponsoring the annual 'Flutag' demonstrate how brand associations are created by brand events. Blending digital and physical experiences (eg: mobile apps, VR simulations, games, experience reinforcement like post-ride photographs) aims at reaching consumers on multiple levels: emotional, taste, tactile. Public Relations (PR) has evolved from activities based on encouraging media relations to an effective brand activation tool with engaging consumers and using 'call to action' social media and content marketing campaigns. Segmentation analysis provides insight into the range and stages of customers in relation to their customer journey. A 'reactivation' campaign aimed at the following groups can re-ignite their interest or reveal their dissatisfaction and/or reasons for not purchasing: Existing customers who we need to *retain* and inactive or 'dormant' customers who may have left or for some reason haven't purchased for a reasonable period of time who may be '*reactivated*'. Brand activation is not a means to activate the brand; it is a means to activate the *customer*.

---

169 Steve Hemsley, "Why B2B brands need to invest in brand marketing", *Marketing Week*, 5th June 2019.

The way we measure and improve on effectiveness and efficiency of brand strategy continues to come under intense scrutiny. It appears that the dependency on short-term metrics, sometimes as a substitutive rather than supplementary activity to continuous year-on-year improvements, is self-defeating. Assuming immediate impacts will have lasting effects is a fallacy and detrimental to growth and damaging to profitability. Whilst long-term brand building will produce impacts in the short-term, the reverse is not true. Single brand extended campaigns have been proven to be more effective over the long haul than short, sharp tactical expediencies.

Binet & Field describe the optimum solution to balancing short and long-term perspectives: "Ideally a campaign will be designed at the outset around an idea that can accommodate brand and activation ideas, ie: a brand response campaign". That is, a rounded approach is to develop highly creative 'fame' campaigns supported by powerful activation to drive short-term sales whilst the brand effect gains momentum. Their definition of 'fame' campaigns is those which provoke positive feelings towards a brand in a way that inspires them to share with other people and amplify the positive attributes of emotional involvement in terms of profit growth.

As we have seen, "marketers need to drive both short and long-term effects, continually feeding the funnel with new prospects who may buy for some time, as well as stimulating purchase amongst existing customers. This requires "two different kinds of marketing activity" (Binet & Field, 2013, p. 27). Accenture claim that "Winners will combine the sprint on COVID-19 response with the marathon of longer-term socio-economic impact".[170]

9.15 Purpose-driven brand strategy

Organisational transformation built on the successful implementation of sustainable purpose-driven brand strategy must have a customer-centric holistic approach, operationalised across the whole of the organisation and the broader stakeholder ecosystem, with customer experience as its orientation, with a mindful connection with employee experience, and a cohesive synthesis of 'inside-out'/'outside-in' customer-company interface at its centre.

Franzen & Moriarty (2008, p. 8) sum this up beautifully: "Both corporate and consumer forces contribute to the identity of the brand through a delicate dance between intended meanings sent by the company and the perceived meanings

---

170 "A brand. New. Purpose. Navigating the human and business impacts of COVID-19", *Accenture*, April 2020.

elicited through consumer response. The interactive nature of brand identity follows logically from the view of a brand as a message and brand strategy as a dialogue".

Continuous learning and improvement, contingent on the volatilities of the macro environment, the unpredictability of competition, and the ever-changing demands of the precious customer base, requires a fusion of long-term building of brand equity and short-term activation. Therein lies the significance of fusing market orientation as an ongoing practice to drive brand orientation. Whilst the promise and delivery of the value proposition must be reinforced at every customer touchpoint experience, *purpose-driven strategy must be aligned with the long view of customer values.* Outside-in, customer-centric organisations recognise that successful brand strategy is a two-sided customer journey coin: satisfied, loyal customers on one side; the sustainable growth of brand equity on the other.

There must be a blending of building mutually beneficial emotional brand structures between customer and company and the sustainability of rational income streams; both must be consistent with an ongoing, developing narrative which reinforces customer-company meaning, but with organisational purpose as a constant guiding North Star: a fusion of purpose and the pragmatism, where the gaze remains fixed but the translation is responsive to fluxes in the macro environment.

At the centre of the philosophy and practice of brand fusion is the recognition, and indeed the reinforcement, of the natural synthesis of three often separated strands of marketing:
–   The purchase decision-making journey of the customer from a position of indifference to advocacy.
–   The service processes which support and enhance that experience.
–   The cumulative build-up of 'equity' or value in the brand.

They work *in fusion*. They work *with purpose*.

Companies who are in sync with this, and indeed in sync with their role(s) in maximising and sustaining satisfaction of the customer journey, will inevitably succeed. Figure 9.8 puts this in context. For those three central pillars to work together cohesively – the objective of brand strategy – there has to be a sustainable centripetal force moving prospects through a vortex of increasing trust and commitment from a state of *unawareness* through the various strengthening positions of loyalty. This is a view of the cumulative brand equity process from the customer's perspective, whereby employee and cultural aspects impact this process but sit outside this model and yet are acknowledged as a critical catalyst in these multiple processes.

Fused with this sequential route to brand loyalty is the consumer decision-making process – from latent needs to consistent, repeat purchase – supported by a service system that is designed with consumer insight and customer complicity.

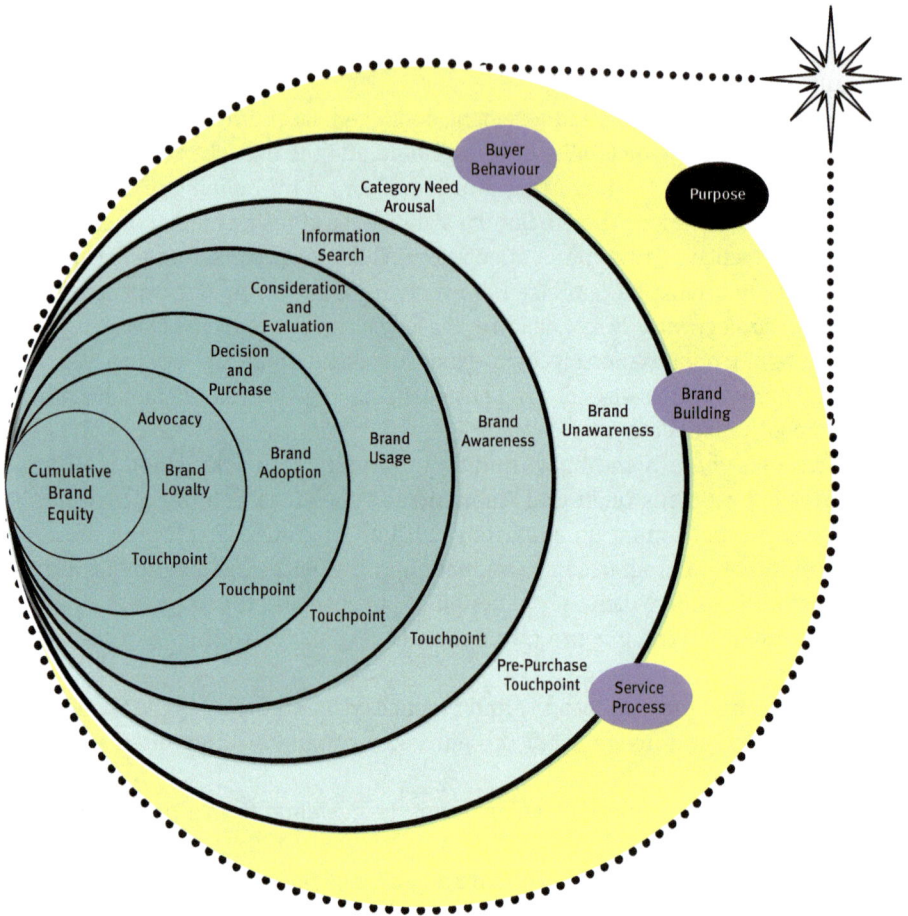

Figure 9.8: Purpose-driven brand strategy.
Source: Authors' representation (2022)

The stages of loyalty progress from:
– Establishing brand identity with depth and width of brand awareness.
– Eliciting positive, unique brand responses to build brand recognition.
– Promoting brand recall through creating associations with possible use within a category need.
– Creating brand meaning through a combination of brand identity and negotiated image.
– Reinforcing positive associations with the brand in order to cement brand loyalty and repeat purchase.
– Forging brand relationships with customers that are characterised by intense, active loyalty. Building cumulative brand equity strengthened by customers becoming brand advocates.

Nuclear fusion is one of the most powerful but simple processes in the Universe. Energetic atoms collide and are transformed into one potent atom. Our marketing analogy – the strategy of *Brand Fusion* – energises the customer journey, the decision-making process of buyer behaviour, the dynamics of service marketing, and the co-creation of value and values through social meaning, and, ultimately, sustainable brand equity.

The journey of the consumer from a position of being unfamiliar with the brand or even the product category charts the application of integrated marketing communications, the forging of relationships, the co-creation of meaning by customer and company, the cementing of competitive protection, and the very substance of brand longevity – *purpose-driven brand strategy*.

9.16 Coda

So far in these first 9 chapters, we have examined the changing philosophical and practical dynamics of the customer-company relationship: how the market myopia of shareholder primacy is being progressively transformed into both co-created value and values of responsibility, inclusiveness, and mutuality. We have advocated the efficacy of embedded, long-term strategy over short-term tactical communications campaigns. We have taken a 'fusion' approach which is omni-subject, integrative, and topical, presenting a wide-ranging intellectual and practical debate about the *purpose of purpose*. Furthermore, whilst there is a social meaning pivot underpinning the book, the exposition of the mechanics and magic of purpose-driven brand strategy which transcends profit-only goals puts it in the vanguard of a radically changing marketing environment over the next few years.

There is a growing awareness that the climate crisis is influencing consumer expectations and behaviours. According to Steve Varley, *EY* (*Ernst & Young*)[171] Global Vice Chair for Sustainability, "Businesses have an opportunity to create value and grow revenues by responding to the trend for sustainable consumption". The *EY Future Consumer Index*,[172] predicted that consumers willing to pay a premium for sustainable products will make up a third of the consumer base as we move beyond COVID-19, and this trend is likely to be accelerated post-*COP26*. A clarion call from Nigel Topping, *COP26* High Level Climate Action Champion representing the *World Energy Council*,[173] exhorted businesses to "stand up and be counted by setting truly

---

[171] Steve Varley, *EY* Global Vice Chair – Sustainability, "Five reasons why business should care about COP26", 8th June 2021, *Reuters Events, Sustainable Business.*

[172] *EY* 'Future Consumer Index' is based on regular global surveys (covering 18 countries)conducted exclusively for *EY*, providing data on consumer behaviour, sentiment and intent.

[173] Nigel Topping, COP26 High Level Climate Action Champion, *World Energy Council*, "Race To Zero: What More Can Companies Do?", November 2021.

ambitious science-based net zero targets to reduce greenhouse emissions. A global energy system transformation is underway . . . Companies can either drive this transition and be masters of their fates or be reactionary and behind the curve". Tony Danka, Director General of the *Confederation of British Industry* (*CBI*), addressing the *COP26 Climate Change Conference* in Glasgow in November 2021, claimed that "This is a moment in history where every firm needs to step up and lead. For some of you, I know, this is a moral obligation; a commitment to business as a force for good or to leaving a sustainable legacy to future generations."[174]

Taking a bold stance is not without criticism, however. For our part, any critical opprobrium of the effectiveness of *purpose-driven brand strategy* has been counterbalanced by a wealth of contemporary and extant theoretical knowledge, alongside detailed discussions of exemplar practice of how and why organisations are aligning purpose, positioning, and proposition.

Companies featured above in extensive case studies like *Patagonia, Gillette, Absolut Vodka, Ava, Danone, Chester Zoo, Marks & Spencer, The Co-op*, and *WW (Weight Watchers)*, to SMEs and micro-brands like *Tirtyl, Causeway Rescue, Dubbed Campers, Pact, Raiys, and Dyslexic Advantage* are all *living* authentic organisational purpose.

Brands have become causes for inclusive capitalism, feminism in the media, culturally-constituted social meaning, sustainability, the positioning of dyslexia, LGBQT+ inclusivity, social mobility, gender equality, and much more.

Institutions like the *CMI, CIM, Harvard Business School, Deloitte, Forbes*, the *Regenerate Trust, Mars Catalyst, B Corps, Oxford University*, and *Säid Business School* are all flying the flag in support.

The results from research and the evidence of practice are clear – if a business, a brand, their leaders and employees, collectively *define-align-execute a brand purpose* they will outperform those that don't. According to analysis from the *IPA Effectiveness Awards Databank*,[175] in metrics associated with distinctiveness, of those brands that had a strong purpose case,

- 70% built *differentiation* (versus 33% all non-purpose cases).
- 61% built *image* (versus 34% all non-purpose cases).
- 59% *improved employee satisfaction* (compared to 23% of non-purpose cases).
- 82% *increased media coverage* (which dropped to 56% among non-purpose cases).

This study highlights the *power of purpose*. But why does this matter? It matters because it goes beyond branding and marketing. Whilst *purpose-driven brand strategy*

---

174 August Graham, "Companies can deliver Net Zero regardless of *COP26* outcome, says *CBI* boss", *Evening Standard*, 4th November 2021.

175 "Criticism of brand purpose is 'naïve and unjustified claims Peter Field". Michaela Jefferson in an interview with Peter Field, *Marketing Week*, 12th October 2021.

is the catalyst, purpose has to be all-pervasive for it to be fully transformative. It must be integrated into core business strategy. It must connect meaningfully not just with customers but with all other key stakeholders.

The results are predicated on one essential characteristic of this new paradigm: brand strategy has to be authentic, credible, and meaningful with clear evidence to show how organisations and stakeholders are investing meaning in purpose. It is a key strategic choice and driver in stakeholder management: consumers, customers, employees (and future employees), private and institutional investors, society, the planet, and future generations – all of whom have a *stake*.

When it is superficial and unconnected without any real meaning to those stakeholders, then brand purpose will not garner the same results and likely flounder and fail. When brand purpose doesn't work it is usually because very little thought has gone into evaluating that purpose and meaning in relation to these outcomes and stakeholders.

If there is no purpose, then what is the point? If there is no meaning, there is no purpose.

When it works, *purpose-driven brand strategy* is a *customer-company fusion*, providing a road map to remain competitive, deliver clear outcomes of long-term value and embedded values, and extend its influence beyond its products and services to a broader social and environmental franchise. Purpose is now considered a "core business strategy practiced by B2C and B2B companies around the world. How it empowers and powers organisations to embrace extraordinary new stakeholder responsibilities is profound when developed, embedded, and activated authentically".[176]

In the next section, we document the detail of how some companies like *Legal & General, Dell Technologies, Headspace, Inspired Villages, Freedome, Festival of Thrift,* and the *University of Cumbria* are *living* authentic organisational purpose, embedding it into their long-term corporate strategies and operational plans, and how they and their customers are benefitting from this mutuality.

---

176 Carol Cone, "What Will Be Your Organisation's Authentic Purpose in 2021?", *Sustainable Brands*, April 2021.

Chapter takeaways

- Brands have an ontological ambiguity, an imprecision of definition somewhere in a maelstrom of corporate intention, social construction, and consumer interpretation.
- If brands only exist in the minds of customers, then the management of brands is all about managing perceptions.
- Strategically, branding is focused on projecting visual identity and sociocultural meaning through well-targeted marketing communications.
- Brands are semiotic marketing systems which project meaning through a brand culture of cultural codes of brands such as myths, self-identity, group affiliation, associations, images, and social narratives.
- A brand platform structure has two parallel hierarchies which describe the customer-company brand interface: the brand and brand user's functional, expressive and central values of the brand's value proposition.
- Brand identity originates from the brand owner and is an internal projected *intended* perspective; brand image originates from the brand user and reflects *negotiated* brand meaning. They are how the company and customer see the value proposition.
- When there is evidence of consumers having a deep emotional connection with a brand or an organisation, company brand identity and customer brand image can be bonded in symbolic symbiosis – a fusion of co-creation and mutually beneficial harmony often in the creation of compelling narratives sealed in company promise and owned by the customer.
- An apparent paradox of brand strategy is the mutually exclusive goals of immediate sales gratification and the long game development of brand equity.
- Organisational transformation built on the successful implementation of sustainable purpose-driven brand strategy must have a customer-centric, holistic approach, operationalised across the whole of the organisation and the broader stakeholder ecosystem, with customer experience as its orientation, with a mindful connection with employee experience, and a cohesive synthesis of 'inside-out'/ 'outside-in' customer-company interface at its centre.
- The strategy of *Brand Fusion* – energises the customer journey, the decision-making process of buyer behaviour, the dynamics of service marketing, and the co-creation of value and values through social meaning, and, ultimately, sustainable brand equity.

Closing case

Chester Zoo: The Not So Secret Life of Building Brand Equity

When *Chester Zoo*[177] were assessing an alternative route to develop their brand strategy, little did they know that they would capture the hearts and minds of a nation. '*The Secret Life of The Zoo*' and its curious cast – customs-seized two-horned Cameroonian Chameleons, pregnant Orangutan sisters Emma and Subis, randy meercats, snoring aadvarks, baby vampire crabs, Lochley, a buffy-headed capuchin, a two-year-old female capybara with dubious parenting skills, and Sumatran tiger Kirana, a much better mother – would provide customer engagement on a grand scale. The gripping drama ensured it was a TV phenomenon, but even by the end of Series 1, the series was a hit on all social media platforms and it was obvious that the Zoo would be a secret no more!

Home to 20,000 animals and more than 500 different species, many of whom are endangered in the wild, *Chester Zoo* also supports field projects around the world and closer to home, preventing the extinction of highly threatened species. Welcoming more than two million visitors a year, it is the UK's most visited zoo and England's most visited tourist attraction outside London. Originally in 2015, in an effort to gain some media coverage for the build of their 'Islands' project, they engaged with a number of production companies discussing the idea of a 'behind-the-scenes' documentary about the project development. Little did they know that it would grow immensely, into 9 successful series, summarised by *Channel 4* as an "Observational documentary series capturing, in incredible detail, the remarkable behaviour of the animals at *Chester Zoo*, and their relationships with their keepers".[178] The 'Secret Life of the Zoo' has continued to be phenomenally successful, highlighted by viewing figures peaking at 2.88m UK viewers[179] for Series 2, Episode 4 'Save the Elephants', and receiving a BAFTA award nomination for its production in 2018.[180] Caroline Sanger-Davies, Director of Marketing, at *Chester Zoo,* explains how momentum built:

177 (www.chesterzoo.org)
178 https://www.channel4.com/programmes/the-secret-life-of-the-zoo
179 https://www.barb.co.uk/viewing-data/most-viewed-programmes/
180 http://awards.bafta.org/award/2018/television/features

> *Blast! [production company] approached us with an idea to do something wider than Islands and create a "behind-the-scenes" documentary. We are always keen to work with established producers and broadcasters, and the opportunity to have a high-profile series on Channel 4 was something we were delighted with. At that stage we, of course, didn't know that one series would turn into many!*

As we will see, it has had a significant impact on *Chester Zoo's* brand both domestically and internationally. The Zoo reported an increase in international visits. Indeed, by 2019, 'Secret Life of the Zoo' had sold into over 110 territories, including sales into all regions of Spain and Italy, and, most notably, to include Vatican City. Sanger-Davies notes:

> *We regularly received anecdotal feedback via social media comments and Trip Advisor posts saying people have visited from around the world because they love the show and wanted to visit as a result.*

The reach and popularity of the series has continually allowed the Zoo and its stars of all species to connect with new audiences. It has proved a great vehicle for brand awareness (covering those unaware of the Zoo, visitations, converting new brand advocates, as well as re-engaging audiences who were perhaps aware of the Zoo but had not visited and had a repeat visit). Sanger-Davies highlights this impact, but also the innate charm of the *'Secret Life of the Zoo'* (affectionately known as *'SLOTZ'*) internally:

> *People have an overwhelming demand to know personal details about the animals. SLOTZ serves this need really well. Within our research we ask about reason for visiting. "Coming to visit some personal favourite animals" grew by 15% as a motivating factor for a visit in 2017, which we attributed to the SLOTZ effect. One of the biggest things we've noticed since SLOTZ is that people have more knowledge of previously unappreciated species and the personalities of individual animals within each species. We've been aware over the years of people coming specifically to see Mr Parsons the chameleon after it featured in an episode, to name just one example.*

At the end of Series One, the Zoo's average monthly *Facebook* followers increased by more than 1000% during the two-month period that the programme was announced, aired and then repeated on Sunday evening. Their average monthly *Twitter* followers increased more than 522% during the same two-month period, an astonishing PR impact widely acknowledged across the zoo. Visitor figures were 21% up in February compared to 2015 (itself a record-breaking year). Visitor numbers were then up 60% in March compared to 2015. To put this into context, the real terms 400,000 additional visits (an increase of 19% from 2015 to 2019) is greater than the resident population of Cheshire West and Chester (Local Authority of where *Chester Zoo* is located) estimated in 2018 to be 340,500.[181]

Indeed, whilst there are many attributable factors that have seen footfall and membership grow, *SLOTZ* continues to be a key catalyst for creating and fostering long-term brand equity. The growth in both key areas is clear in the following table:

Table 9.5: Footfall & Membership Number.

Chester Zoo – Footfall and Membership Number

	Footfall	Membership
2015	1.7m	76358 members at the end of the year (57835 at the start)
2016	1.9m	88152 members at the end of the year
2017	1.8m	94905 members at the end of the year
2018	1.9m	114,680 members at the end of the year
2019	2.1m	129,483 members at the end of the year

Source: *Chester Zoo* (2021)

It is clear that '*SLOTZ*' had a significant positive impact on brand equity but also highlights a key theme throughout the book: how an effective brand strategy can fuse customer-company dynamics with a clear cultural buy-in. It takes an organisational culture and leadership team that embodies bravery, transparency and trust to open the doors of your business up to behind-the-scenes documentary team, Jamie Christon, CEO of *Chester Zoo*, highlighted that rather than perceive the programme as a risk, it was in fact a collegiate form of cultural bonding:

> *The programme required a significant investment in time and energy right across the organisation, so it was vital that we took a team approach. Prior to embarking on each series representatives from each department met to ensure we were happy to continue and had resource to do so. As a result, we shared in the delight when each episode aired, and thanks to Blast! we were able to get together as a team to watch the first episode of each series and celebrate appropriately!*

---

181 https://inside.cheshirewestandchester.gov.uk/find_out_more/datasets_and_statistics/statistics/population

We approached the filming in a fully transparent way. There was nothing that we weren't happy for the cameras to see, and what shone through by doing that was the care and passion of every one of the Zoo team.

Chester Zoo's brand, mission, and impact to 'Prevent Extinction by connecting people with animals' by empowering, enthralling, and championing conservation'[182] has been instrumental in the success of *SLOTZ*, and, in turn, this helped deliver a real boost to brand equity. The branding strategy echoes Aaker & Joachimsthaler's (2000, p. 44) definition:

- *Brand as product:* in terms of increased visitation and revenue allowing for 'product development' and develop further product attributes/extending its mission and reach
- *Brand as organisation:* organisational cultural attributes of innovation, trust, transparency, purpose-driven environmental concern, far reaching local and global audiences.
- *Brand as person:* allowing visitors to connect and build customer/brand relationships, and also arguably via affective connection with 'animal personalities'.
- *Brand as symbol:* can provide cohesion and structure to make *Chester Zoo* easier to gain brand recognition, recall, visitation and loyalty; based on credibility and a stronger relationship.

For *Chester Zoo*, 'The Secret Life of the Zoo' has certainly shown that there is no secret to building brand equity.

Questions
1. What are the risks and benefits to *Chester Zoo's* brand by undertaking the '*Secret Life of the Zoo*' TV documentary?
2. What part did social media play in helping to build brand equity?
3. How has the Zoo's repositioning as conservationists affected their brand strategy?

---

182 *Chester Zoo's* Mission, brand values and quotes, unpublished documents supplied to *FUZE*, 2021.

Section 4: **The application and purpose of practice**

Section 4 showcases some of the work of *FUZE,* a data-driven insight-tech-learning company which specialises in using technology to evaluate customer-culture-employee experiences against an organisation's branding strategy, and empower individuals, teams and organisations to learn and develop. The objective of this section is to demonstrate various examples of brand fusions in-context, to support wider learning and application, so that students, instructors, practitioners, decision-makers and founders, are able to connect and apply learning to context/role and learning journey.

Chapters 10 to 17 include both in-depth living cases and featured cases, analysed and applied in their very specific contexts, showing how the application of proven theoretical brand strategy and practical experience can help enhance competitive performance, build brand equity, and create value for brands, customers and society. Applying a theory-application-practice approach, this section evidences how the emerging brand fusion theoretical framework can be successfully adopted and applied to companies of every size, offering a contemporary solution in a variety of contextual settings.

The cases are a good balance between primary/empirical data and secondary data/public sources from a variety of sectors and organisational perspectives. The 'live' primary data-driven cases feature clients – *Inspired Villages, Freedome, Festival of Thrift,* and *University of Cumbria* – who have commercial relationships and/or have commissioned *FUZE,* and presents a unique and valuable inside/applied view of real organisations in real contexts. *FUZE* have themselves also undertaken an exploratory SME study with the intention to lay the foundations to support SMEs and brand strategy, collaborating with *Be the Business.* This provides robust and credible qualitative and quantitative data/evidence upon which to develop brand fusion. The 'featured' cases (using secondary data and public-facing materials) are an interpretation of brand strategy via the lens of brand fusion. These brands include companies such as *Dell Technologies, Headspace,* and *Legal & General.* Whilst being very detailed analyses, they do not represent the view, opinions and/or an endorsement of these organisations.

The core-proposition that has developed the relationship, understanding and perspective of these 'live cases' is that *FUZE* use the insights to develop key improvement drivers and have a unique action-plan methodology that help partners deliver high-impact actions to deliver continuous improvement, learning and growth, cross-functionally and at all levels of these businesses.

FUZE use peer-reviewed research to inform the construction of their research design and methodology (always combining mixed-method approaches), which they blend and develop in collaboration with their clients to ensure they conduct valid research that is targeted to the specific needs of that client, brand, organisation, context and sector. The targeted outcome gives non-users, customers, and employees a chance to independently express their feelings, wants, and needs, highlighting their preferences, triggers, and barriers on various pathways to purchase. Additionally, *FUZE* map and evaluate customer journeys (post-purchase through to long-term

https://doi.org/10.1515/9783110718638-014

relationships), analysing experiences in a way that goes beyond the 'immediate' brand encounter to assess how customers and employees invest meaning and value in brands, via a framework that is unique to that organisation. This allows *FUZE* to develop a more detailed picture of the issues clients and brands may face whilst delivering comprehensive insights from a holistic perspective.

The work presented is also representative of *FUZE*'s *iMPACT Learning Academy* which offers tailored and insight-driven learning programmes with credit-bearing qualifications, providing a creative value creation framework linking theory to practice across a number of disciplines and levels (eg: *Institute of Leadership and Management* Levels, 2, 3, 5 and 7 qualifications).

10 Legal & General: Inclusive capitalism – change, sustainability, and purpose

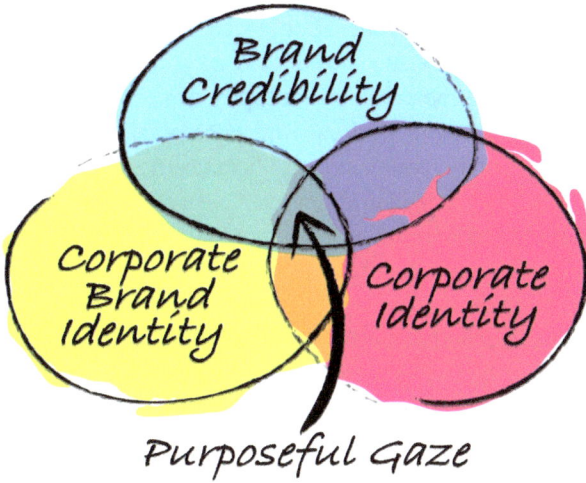

https://doi.org/10.1515/9783110718638-015

10.1 Outline of chapter

As highlighted in *Chapter 2 Developing strategy: roots, resources, relationships*, there is an urgent call for capitalism to reinvent itself around the concept of shared value and social consciousness (Porter & Kramer (2011, p. 64). The challenge to prioritise the need for global corporations to combine monetary, social, and environmental activities in a mutually beneficial process of value creation and exchange across a diverse collection of internal and external stakeholders is now a critical strategic imperative. The following case highlights the importance of a purpose-driven corporate brand strategy as an area of responsible business and investment, and illustrates how reframing capitalism as a catalyst for social good and long-term change has been applied in practice. The chapter is a *featured* case study and is based on secondary evidence and public-facing materials. The organisation under focus – *Legal & General Group Plc* (*Legal & General*) – are tackling this challenge head on, delivering what they believe is a key catalyst for delivering meaningful and sustainable change for employees, investors, customers, communities and the wider macro and micro environment: *their* 'inclusive capitalism' agenda. As we will see, this is far reaching in scope, ambition and is grounded in change.

This chapter demonstrates how *Legal & General*, have captured – at a corporate level – an ability to deliver clarity and accessibility, so that its purpose transcends typical corporate boundaries. More so, as with any brand purpose, it engenders and fosters a rich socio-emotional ecosystem. That is to say, it creates a value exchange dynamic that allows stakeholders to invest *their* meaning in a unified purpose, building a form of intangible corporate value or brand equity. This exemplifies how they are applying an enlightened view of inclusive capitalism through a brand strategy that it is helping tackle *real life issues* that are directly impacting *real people* across a diverse range of communities.

Learning outcomes

After reading this chapter, you'll be able to:
- Distinguish the arguments regarding shareholder primacy and stakeholder democracy.
- Understand the importance of assessing the macro-environment and identify how that can influence (corporate) brand strategy, specifically, how macro trends have influenced inclusive capitalism and ESG.
- Identify and assess how a purpose-driven corporate brand strategy can be a catalyst for change, shareholder and wider societal value creation.
- Differentiate between tactical/operational CSR initiatives versus building long-term corporate brand equity via ESG outcomes.
- Examine and assess the importance of brand credibility and corporate-brand identity – by analysing the importance of meeting 'deeds and actions'.
- Evaluate the key strategic decisions and stakeholder value when delivering a long-term inclusive capitalism agenda, particularly in dynamic market conditions.

10.2 Introduction

Some argue purpose-driven brand strategies are merely positioning strategies: a PR tactic rather than embedded strategy. Whilst that is undoubtedly true with some organisations, this case demonstrates how purpose has driven brand strategy, adopting this orientation as company culture throughout *Legal & General's* multiple stakeholders with complete a corporate level alignment and execution. This gives strength of clarity: an inherently complex corporate identity has been crystalised into a clear and compelling long-term strategic vision. This allows all manner of stakeholders (internal and external) to invest meaning in the proposed outcomes, in this case prioritising a positive contribution to environment, social, and governance (ESG) outcomes. The quotation below (extracted from *Legal & General's* "Sustainability and Inclusive Capitalism 2021 Report") illustrates this:

> *Legal & General's vision of inclusive capitalism is founded on the belief that investment which delivers both positive economic and positive social outcomes is the best way to achieve progress at scale, enabling more people to benefit from economic growth and financial opportunities. By delivering this vision, Legal & General seeks to accelerate meaningful change for employees, investors, customers and wider society.*[183]

The crucial role that corporate brand strategy plays when connecting purpose, profit, and an organisation's social ecosystem (see *Chapter 3 Managing meaning: social dominant logic*) is examined below. Whilst there are criticisms that being a socially responsible business is sometimes merely a list of stated intentions which rarely deliver the results (often the cynicism of lip-service CSR-based programmes) it espouses, it is fair to say that some organisations continually evolve and learn from attempting to implement this type of strategic initiative. The manner in which *Legal & General Group Plc* have elevated its importance across the organisation is testimony that, in their case, the means and the ends are in sync. They have demonstrated that such an approach is a strategic imperative and a central growth driver for the business where *their* measure of success is directly targeting and delivering ambitious ESG outcomes in a way that has influenced many others in the sector and wider economy (eg: via its diverse investment portfolio, business activity and supply chain etc).

---

[183] https://group.legalandgeneral.com/media/icwnfxwn/sustainability-report-final-press-release.pdf

The photo(s) used in this case study is/are not connected and/or does not represent any brand(s) mentioned. It/they is/are used to make a visual discussion point by the authors.

© jan_s - stock.adobe.com.

10.3 Case orientation and context

Established in 1836, *Legal & General* has a rich brand heritage that has allowed it to become one of the UK's leading financial services groups "for corporate pension schemes and a UK market leader in pension risk transfer, life insurance, workplace pensions, and retirement income", and a major global investor with international businesses across the world in the US, Europe, Middle East, and Asia. As of 31st December 2020, it had almost £1.3 trillion in total assets under management.[184]

Discussing the group's business philosophy in 2020, Sir Nigel Wilson, Group Chief Executive from *Legal and General Group Plc*, described the basic principles as:

> *30 years of unbridled capitalism have left many questioning the fairness of an economic system that has created huge wealth, while leaving so many people behind.*

> *Our business strategy is based on 'inclusive capitalism' but it can be a difficult concept to understand. We want to protect our customers' financial lives and add value for shareholders, but we want to do that by investing in things that are good for society as a whole. In this way, more people can benefit from economic growth.*

His 10 fundamental principles guidelines for making Capitalism more inclusive are listed below:

---

184 https://group.legalandgeneral.com/media/icwnfxwn/sustainability-report-final-press-release.pdf.

1. *Inclusive Capitalism is patient – sometimes capitalism is short-term and transactional. We aim to fund large-scale, long-term projects, which are both economically productive and socially useful.*
2. *Inclusive Capitalism benefits a broad range of people – while delivering a financial return for investors, investments and initiatives must also carry a broader social benefit.*
3. *Inclusive Capitalism creates new initiatives – companies must undertake initiatives and projects that lead to new assets and new jobs. A company practicing inclusive capitalism might invest heavily in making a regional city a better and more technologically appealing place to live.*
4. *Inclusive Capitalism helps solve market or policy failures – for example, an exemplary company might not only invest in making the healthcare system at large more efficient and effective, it might also take steps to tackle, say, wellness in later life.*
5. *Inclusive Capitalism should be politically agnostic – the opposite of divisive or 'populist.' Companies might finance local or regional growth by partnering with leaders of all political shades. Regardless of political leanings, we are collaborating with local authorities across the country, to build homes, carry out major regeneration projects as develop science and technology centres.*
6. *Inclusive Capitalism supports environmental, social, and governance measures (ESG) – investing in urban regeneration, affordable housing, clean energy and small business finance is the mark of a socially and environmentally conscious business. But it's important for investment managers to practice what they preach.*
7. *Inclusive Capitalism strives to use technology for broader benefits – Taking financial inclusion as one example, companies practicing inclusive capitalism might employ technology to expand the use of auto-enrolment to get employees to save for a rainy day.*
8. *Inclusive Capitalism requires that we break the cycle of combined educational, financial, and digital exclusion – Lacking access to decent education creates social exclusion and isolation. The same is true of being unbanked or not being able to afford basic technology.*
9. *Inclusive capitalism strives to break the cycle of intergenerational inequality – Studies have shown that younger generations lack sufficient assets and access to capital to get a start in life. Last year, we provided lifetime mortgages to the over-55s worth £965m. This releases money older people have tied up in property and, according to our Bank of Mum and Dad surveys, many use it to help their children onto the housing ladder*
10. *Inclusive capital need not involve making hair-shirted sacrifices – There's no reason why a business has to be less profitable because it's also socially useful. Focusing on our inclusive capitalism strategy, in 2019 Legal & General achieved a total return of more than 40% for shareholders and an operating profit of £2.3 billion.*

Legal & General – Principles (2020)[185]

Note the juxtaposition of latest results in terms of investment, key results and outcomes alongside each inclusive capitalism principle. As clear an application principle in practice as you are likely to see. Whilst the vision has significant scope, the following summarises, very succinctly how they propose to tackle this at a high-level:

---

185 *Legal & General* – Principles (2020) 10 guidelines for inclusive capitalism: What makes capitalism inclusive and how is *Legal & General* practising what it preaches?: retrieved from https://brand.legal andgeneral.com/building-infrastructure/10-guidelines-for-inclusive-capitalism/.

> – *Rethinking and reframing retirement by tackling ageism head on.*
> – *Tackling the climate crisis by raising the importance of ESG credentials to shape investment decisions.*
> – *Investing for good illustrated by the commitment of "When we invest our customers' money, we want the companies we invest in to demonstrate the highest standards of corporate behaviour".*
> – *Building infrastructure by levelling up the UK and its key infrastructure needs.*
> – *Harnessing technology to help individual improve their own personal finances and "creating innovation networks across the UK is essential to boost the economy".*
>
> (*Legal & General* – Purpose, 2021)

Further reinforcement of purpose is shown below:

> *Our purpose is to build a better society, while improving the lives of our customers and creating value for shareholders. To do this we're investing in long-term assets that benefit everyone, from housing to renewable energy – we call it inclusive capitalism.*
>
> *The future of our planet and economy has never been so critical. Using money as a force for good, businesses, communities and individuals can help to make society stronger, creating a world of inclusive capitalism. With the UK still facing issues such as housing, climate crisis and an ageing demographic, discover more about the strategies that could be employed to tackle such matters. We are taking action against companies that are not acting responsibly and investing in urban infrastructure, clean energy, research into how to improve later living and technology to improve lives*[186]

10.4 Matching deeds with actions: Going beyond 'tactical CSR' to delivering corporate brand purpose and brand equity

The notion of responsible business in terms of corporate social responsibility (CSR) is not a new one. Historically, previous research highlights that companies can benefit greatly by effectively executing CSR activities, going beyond favourable consumer awareness, positive attitudes and associations, and create a stronger attachment, whilst also building a positive corporate image and a good reputation (Bhattacharya & Sen, 2004; Bhattacharya, Korschun, & Sen, 2009; Du, Battacharya, & Sen, 2010; Melo & Garrido-Morgado, 2012). A key strategic driver for companies to invest in CSR initiatives is to create and foster positive moral capital, so that the company can develop intangible assets such as credibility, goodwill, and reputation (Godfrey, 2005). The perceptions of consumer and wider stakeholders is immensely important in the dynamics of corporate brand trust and credibility. Godfrey (2005) argues that developing moral capital goes some way in mitigating the potential of negative stakeholder evaluations. For instance, consumers assess the sincerity of CSR

---

186 https://www.legalandgeneralgroup.com/inclusive-capitalism/.

initiatives, from the outset as they "do not want a Company to take advantage of its relationship with them nor do they and feel cheated to egoistic CSR motivations" (Alcaniz, Caceres, & Perez, 2010, p. 169).

Successfully executed CSR initiatives are underpinned by brand trust and credibility. The crux of this trust dynamic is based on consumers and stakeholders assessing a company's intentions to demonstrate sincere moral behaviour. This must go beyond words and be measured in actions, results and outcomes, and communicated in such a way that they are able to connect emotionally, personally, and as a group-community, investing meaning in these outcomes. Moreover, it is argued that brand credibility is a mediating pathway that links CSR perception to corporate reputation brand equity (Hur, Kim, & Woo, 2014). In this case, it is crucial for *Legal & General* to effectively build corporate brand credibility – the way within which a brand *signals* its intent as well as the believability consumers have in the company's trustworthiness and expertise (Erdem, Swait, & Louviere, 2002). Indeed, trust is often founded upon personal levels in terms of value-based trust, whereby the perceived benefit of a company that engages in CSR initiatives, fosters a favourable impression with consumers, investors, communities and wider society. Indeed, if they are able to clearly see social issues being addressed by CSR initiatives (Pivato, Misani, & Tencati, 2008). This further supports the trust-relationship. Given *Legal & General*'s rich brand heritage, its strong market presence/track record, and building on its existing brand equity in areas such as finance, pensions and insurance, this all adds further credence in developing goodwill, trust and credibility in delivering their inclusive capitalism vision.

As evidenced throughout the book, cultivating brand equity in any organisation, size or type, is one of the most powerful strategic assets a firm can develop. It can often be the catalyst for achieving sustainable competitive advantage, particularly so in financial, investment, and insurance markets where products and services are very similar in terms of features (ie: price, terms and conditions, length of service, cover, return on investments etc). Therefore, it is imperative to develop intangible brand value through clearly defined benefits and positive associations of reputation, credibility, and trust.

More broadly, of course, there will always be criticisms aimed not just at corporates but all businesses in relation to their motives, decisions, and activities when embarking on the journey of becoming an outcome-focused, trustworthy, socially responsible business. For instance, some argue that CSR initiatives do not have the strategic importance to truly unleash the full resources and capabilities large corporations have at their disposal (Polonsky & Jevons, 2009). Historical criticisms must also be acknowledged, as many organisations endeavour to deliver social good, in that such activity should not be viewed as another promotional opportunity to be leveraged (Carroll, 1999)(McAlister & Ferrell, 2002). Some organisations "mistakenly try to use CSR in a superficial tactical fashion, which can often be justifiably criticised as being opportunistic rather than meaningful" (Polonsky & Jevons, 2009,

p. 329). More worryingly, more firms are engaging in greenwashing, misleading consumers about their environmental performance or the environmental benefits of a product or service, and this "can have profound negative effects on consumer and investor confidence in green products" (Delmas & Burbano, 2011, p. 66). The repercussions toward corporate and brand reputation when motives and actions are seen as disingenuous can be seriously damaging. Younger generations, like millennials, are more socially responsible and have a high level of environmental awareness and understanding (Ospina, 2021), and therefore have a more informed view on assessing sincerity of corporate activities and outcomes.

Therefore, developing an all-encompassing, tightly defined and yet compelling CSR-related corporate brand purpose is anything but simplistic: organisational stakeholders (internal and external) will always have ever-changing and varying views on key issues that are in themselves complex to define and ever-evolving (Schlegelmilch & Pollach, 2005). CSR initiatives have been shown to have a positive impact on brand equity, for example, as related to the persuasive advertising effects in the life insurance sector (Hsu, 2012). It could be argued that the power of purpose is in responding to a wider socially responsible dominant logic.

Legal & General's broader corporate brand strategy goes beyond the realms of typical CSR boundaries, key corporate level brand performance metrics and outcomes, centralising inclusive capitalism with the upmost of importance. Typical CSR measures, are at best, often restricted to campaign or operational which drives marketing outputs as opposed to effective centralised strategic brand management capbability, decision-making and is evaluated with related outcomes (such as ESG indexes). More recently, it has been (re)highlighted that effective CSR activities, which includes ESG priorities, are vastly challenging on the basis that there is insufficient known about how to define and value CSR (more broadly) (Zein, Consolacion-Segura, & Huertas-Garcia, 2020). The fact that consumers, employees, and other stakeholders have more awareness and understanding of these issues, increases the pressure for stronger alignment and execution of a purpose-driven corporate strategy. In other words, one that does not cause friction and create gaps between identity, image and reputation, but instead aligns these factors so that the company's identity garners credibility, trust, and increases both tangible and intangible assets.

Embracing corporate socially responsible business requires global organisations to think outside existing models of operation (Doanne, 2005), and Sir Nigel Wilson, *Legal & General*'s Group Chief Executive, has certainly taken on that mantra, not only raising inclusive capitalism's strategic importance, but also bringing the corporate brand purpose to life by weaving these key ESG outcomes as a central measure of business success and contribution for the betterment of society. This is matching *words* with *deeds*:

> *Our inclusive capitalism agenda has never been more urgent or important. The unforeseen consequence of the pandemic has been more inequality and we risk a K-shaped economic recovery;*

we're matching words and deeds to help level up society and build back better. Our purpose sets us apart in our response to COVID-19. *The human and economic cost of the pandemic reaffirms our commitment to inclusive capitalism as the only way to do business responsibly.*[187]

10.5 Frictionless foundations: Credibility is the driving force for success

The previous sections identified how historically there has been a tendency for CSR initiatives to be limited to tactical and operational boundaries. The evidence cited of how *Legal & General* have applied principles to practice highlights that whilst corporate brand strategies are often far-reaching, complex, ambitious and multifaceted, if a purpose is clear, compelling and inspiring, with tangible results assigned to its success, it can seamlessly connect customers, consumers, employees, investors, communities and wider society. However, a simultaneous challenge is whether corporate brands can foster a symbiotic relationship that doesn't cause friction and break the 'brand equity' chain. Tensions will always exist with people, (sub)cultures, and the pressures of allocating resources; the challenge is in the execution and (re)alignment. Purpose and values need to become real for stakeholders, to transcend all manner of boundaries such as geographical, brand, business, sectors, and remove organisational silos.

Resolving this simultaneous challenge lies in developing an effective structure which embeds and connects shared values, clearly identifies ownership, responsibility and accountability, whilst also integrating marketing communications, all of which is underpinned by an effective system that allows for the evaluation of results and outcomes (Balmer & Gray, 2003). For *Legal & General*, clear points of difference and a nuanced separation between (multiple) product-brand identities and ongoing reconciliation with the overarching corporate brand identity needs to be created and maintained (Aaker & Joachimsthaler, 2000; Hill & Lederer, 2001; Keller, 2001). In addition, it is necessary to find a point of connection, association and in some cases, elevation, whereby the corporate brand is able to positively influence and reinforce brand equity for the product-brand identities and vice versa.

---

187 https://group.legalandgeneral.com/media/icwnfxwn/sustainability-report-final-press-release.pdf.

10.6 Corporate identity-based? An affirmative gaze

The following section posits that deploying an identity-based view of corporate brands can offer considerable utility in the analysis of *Legal & General*'s execution of inclusive capitalism (Balmer, 2008, p. 1065). There are multiple ways within which brand roles are defined, structured, and operationalised. These are usefully summarised, across a brand relationship spectrum "that applies a methodology for classifying brand roles that shifts between applying a 'strategic approach' (eg: with master brand as driver, co-driver, strong endorsement, token endorsement, and shadow endorser) and applying a 'naming approach' (eg: with same identity, different identity, linked name, and not connected)" (Olsen, 2002, p. 432). *Legal & General Group* arguably apply a number of these approaches to best suit the varied conditions of which stakeholders they are serving. That being said, there remains one core and compelling 'North Star': a corporate brand purpose anchoring these multiple approaches, driving decision-making and continually evaluating its progress, taking the long view from brand nurture and gestation.

For instance, a key focus is evident in this description of an "inclusive future":

Our journey to net zero – The transition to a low carbon future is both a risk and an opportunity. It shapes every part of the Legal & General business, from proprietary asset investment strategy and influence over investee companies, through to day-to-day operations[188]

---

188 https://www.csrwire.com/reports/724741/pioneering-inclusive-future-inclusive-capitalism-delivers-positive-change-through.

Clearly, this a long-term challenge that society, countries, and organisations face, but, to their credit, *Legal & General* have set a number of targets in their 'Sustainability and inclusive capitalism – 2020–21' report which are assigned and aligned to the Group's long-term (financial) balance sheet targets, with clear deadlines and recognition of strategic importance – a key long-term corporate brand metric of success. As an example, the following is extracted from the 'Sustainability and inclusive capitalism – 2020–21' (2021, p. 68) detailing a small selection of the many targets and deadlines that underpin the purpose-driven corporate brand strategy:

  – *We have set Group balance sheet carbon intensity targets to monitor alignment with the Paris objective and will reduce 2030 our portfolio carbon emission intensity by half by 2030 and targeting net zero by 2050.*
    [Deadline – 2030]

  – *Our retirement businesses, covering c.90% of our Group balance sheet, has further committed to reduce portfolio carbon 2025 emission intensity by 18.5% by 2025 as part of a wider published ESG policy.*
    [Deadline – 2025]

  – *As a large UK housebuilder, we will enable all new homes we build from 2030 to operate with net zero carbon emissions. 2030 In addition, we're seeking to understand and monitor the embodied carbon associated with the construction of our homes.*
    [Deadline – 2030]

10.7 A purposeful gaze navigates uncertainty, allowing for an inclusive stake

According to Sir Nigel Wilson, *Legal & General*'s stance on inclusive capitalism is "a balanced vision, where profits and purpose co-exist, and everyone can build their own *stake* in our economy" (2021, p. 5). Balmer suggests that adopting identity-based perspectives for corporate brands enables a clear and discernible means to assess their multifaceted nature (2008, p. 893). A corporate brand purpose acts as a clear compass to navigate the inevitably unpredictable path. This applies particularly to SMEs who navigate the complexities of an uncertain cashflow, but equally important is that it allows large corporates to pivot in times of flux: the gaze remains steadfast in its focus, but the translation can be fluid and responsive when required (for the characteristics of effective hybrid market orientation see *Chapter 11*). For instance, the impact of COVID-19 will reverberate for years to come; many governments and corporations were taken aback by its unprecedented disruption and dangerous reach. This notion of having a fixed gaze on a core brand purpose, with a responsive translation to its wider environment as well as the organisational interpretation has been informed by Renshaw (2019, pp. 216–218) and extended in this analysis to incorporate marketing orientation theory. *Legal & General* were able to deploy such a pivot, which effectively did not deviate from the inclusive capitalism agenda and committed initiatives/developments (pre-COVID -19). This highlighted that whilst their purpose, path, and gaze never changed, the interpretation of corporate social response delivered action and impact on its corporate brand promise. Below is an extract from their report on the response to 'COVID-19':

> *We've launched a range of initiatives to help meet the growing social needs arising from the coronavirus disruption. With the virus disproportionately impacting the health and wellbeing of older populations, we believe our £20 million partnership with Edinburgh University's research into elderly care is more important than ever. As such, we are accelerating components of this arrangement.*
>
> *Another of our [existing] partnerships has helped create a UK network of Bruntwood SciTech innovation districts, dedicated to driving the growth of the science and technology sector. One of these, Alderley Park, in Cheshire, has recently become the home of one of the government's three national 'Mega Labs' to facilitate mass testing for coronavirus.*[189]

The capricious nature of change and the fact that stakeholders hold varying perceptions and expectations means that each key group invests their own meaning into a corporate brand. What is fascinating with regards to *Legal & General*'s corporate brand purpose is its use of inclusivity, collective consciousness, and shared values – articulated pertinently by Sir Nigel Wilson's use of the term '*stake*': "Inclusive capitalism is a balanced vision, where profits and purpose co-exist, and everyone can build their own *stake* in our economy." (2021, p. 5).

Indeed, whilst there is a fine balance in the need to build and exploit corporate brand credibility across product-business-brand portfolios, this notion of empowerment for change is a powerful driving force that underpins the corporate distinction. Balmer (2012, p. 1065) summarises the key challenges (2012, p. 1065):

> *This is because there is a good deal more flexibility in terms of the meanings which can be accorded to product brands vis-a-vis corporate brands on the part of customers and other stakeholders. For instance, as I have long-argued, the brand meanings assigned to product brands by an organisation are, to a large extent, contrived. Corporate brand values, in contrast, are innate (or need to be innate). Successful corporate brands are credible because there is a symbiosis between corporate brand identity and corporate identity: the latter relates to an organisation's defining and differentiated identity anchors (attributes).*

Therein lies the challenge: there is a need for a symbiotic relationship between corporate brand identity harnessing brand equity, suitably distinct from product brand identity portfolios, where conditions of success remove friction, and support the overall positioning, to exploit corporate brand trust and credibility. For example,

---

189 https://www.legalandgeneralgroup.com/media-centre/press-releases/our-response-to-covid-19-the-coronavirus/.

Legal & General Group plc, has four businesses, all of which have significant scope, resources, and many layered elements to their businesses. The following summarises these businesses, and provides an overview of their highlights from the 2020 reported in the Inclusive and Sustainability Report – 2020–21:

(1) *Retirement – We take on pension scheme liabilities from corporate schemes in the UK and the US to bring certainty to companies over their liabilities and provide guaranteed retirement income to individuals. We help our customers accumulate pensions savings and transform them into income to have a colourful retirement life.*
   2020 Highlights – £8.8bn institutional retirement sales / £910m individual annuity sales
(2) *Investment management – Our savings and investment plans enable our clients to take control of their financial future. As one of Europe's largest asset managers, Legal & General Investment Management (LGIM) offers investment solutions to clients globally and influences the companies it invests in to behave in a responsible way that benefits everyone. We are the UK market leader in providing pension asset management services to institutional clients and manage the assets our clients hold to cover their pension scheme liabilities and generate returns.*
   2020 Highlights – £1.3tn assets under management
(3) *Capital investment – We channel our customers' pension assets and the Group's shareholder capital towards long term investments in specialist commercial real estate, clean energy, residential property and SME finance. Our £3.1 billion direct investments generate returns for pensions and on the Group's capital while benefitting society through socially responsible investing.*
   2020 highlights £3.1bn direct investments
(4) *Insurance – As the UK's number one individual life insurance provider with 5.5 million customers, we help our customers protect themselves and their families, and plan for the unexpected. We provide life insurance to 1.3 million people in the US and our group protection business in the UK offers life insurance and income protection products to 1.8 million people through group protection schemes with their employers."*
   2020 Highlights – £2.8bn gross written premiums (2021: 7)
   This highlights the sheer scale of Legal & General Group Plc operation, which consists of four key businesses, with immense financial, social and environmental resource base and wider impact. If we consider, that within the business of Legal & General Capital (ie: Capital Investment stated above has an investment approach that consists of a residential property housing platform (which includes businesses/partners, with varying control and structures) – but effectively consists of various sub/product brand relationships with key verticals – these brands include Legal & General Affordable Homes, CALA Group (both Build-to-sell); Suburban and Urban (both Build-to-rent); Inspired Villages (featured in Chapter 11) and Guild Living (Later Living); Modular Homes (Modern construction).

The point is that there is a multitude of dynamics at play, with many branching areas and considerations that highlights the complexity-clarity dynamic upon which underpins the inclusive capitalism agenda.

In summary, it is clear that the corporate brand strategy holds a distinct identity-based approach guiding product-brand dynamics with various forms – what is telling with *Legal & General* as evidenced in this Chapter and further corporate resources/results, it is clear that the critical factors that Balmer (2012) highlighted are very much present with this purpose driven corporate strategy (the concluding section of this chapter further supports this): "Authentic (reflects the firm's identity); believable (reflects the firm's culture); durable (sustainable); profitable (creates stakeholder and shareholder value); and responsible (reflects the firm's purposes and the CSR and ethical requisites expected by society)" (2012: 1065). The crux of this is underpinned by the importance of establishing brand credibility, which was explained in the earlier sections, the consistent delivery against purpose, allowing stakeholders to invest meaning develops both tangible and intangible brand value.

10.8 The corporate brand Gaze: Lazer focus – ESG

In recent years, the importance of responsible investment has grown – a topic which is very prevalent throughout this book. In many ways, the investment approach that focuses on key ESG factors in investment and management, is also most likely related to the rise of purpose-driven corporate brand strategies. It has become a global phenomenon: "In fact, global sustainable investment has increased a 67% in the last four years from $18,276 billion in 2014 to $30,683 billion in 2018 in the five major markets" (Alliance, 2018).[190] Clearly, as highlighted throughout this chapter, Zein *et al* pertinently summarise the importance of ESG focused market orientation in global branding: "This popularity of sustainable investment may be viewed as investors becoming aware of environmental sustainability, the treatment of companies to their employees and society as a whole, as well as in business policies such as the diversity of the board of directors and ethics business. . . . In fact, ESG factors may improve a business's image for its stakeholders and engage its clients, boosting brand value" (2020, p. 3).

Legal & General have undertaken a significant shift in the definition, alignment, and execution of its inclusive capitalism strategy, arguably going beyond typical CSR and branding strategies that quite often exist independent of each other, both caught in operational silos/limits. Of course, the crux of this case has been how *Legal & General* have maintained a fixed gaze on its core purpose; even in times of flux, the translation has been fluid and responsive. This flexible framework can only be effective if the corporate brand strategy is continually scanning and to its markets and diverse stakeholder groups. One such example of their corporate change-agent status is the drive to, and investment in, extending the current ESG paradigm to include 'Health' as an important component in levelling up health inequality in the UK, and more broadly deliver on the ESG framework that is weaved globally throughout many purpose-driven brand strategies in some form. Sir Nigel Wilson, clearly articulates their intention:

> *We are delighted to have partnered with Sir Michael Marmot [Director of the University College of London (UCL) Institute of Health Equity (IHE) and professor of epidemiology] to bring forward*

---

190 *Alliance, G.S.I.* (2018) Global Sustainable Investment Review. Available online: http://www.gsi-alliance.org/wp-content/uploads/2019/03/GSIR_Review2018.3.28.pdf (accessed on 11 July 2021).

this ground-breaking research and multi-million pound funding partnership. Reducing health inequalities is part of levelling up: literally a matter of life and death.

Businesses and ESG (Environment, Social, and Governance) investors are proving key to reducing carbon emissions. ESG's "E" is working, but the "S" is further behind – the impact of corporate activity on population health and its associated costs is not currently adequately addressed. Post-COVID-19, there is a strong case to consider health and health inequality as crucial to the "S" of ESG – or even to explicitly call out health within a new "ESHG" framework.[191]

In summary, there are critical factors that allow corporations like *Legal & General* to deliver purpose-driven brand strategies, adapting Polonsky and Jevons' (2009) key factors of complexity that can inform ESG and CSR initiatives in relation to corporate brand strategies. This Table 10.1 extends this analysis and has been updated with an ESG lens (not specific to *Legal & General* but nonetheless informed) and applied generally to purpose-driven corporate brand strategies more broadly.

Table 10.1: Critical factors that help deliver CSR/ESG corporate brand strategies.

Complexity type	Definition
Issue	
Social issues	Determination of the scope of issues to be considered in global organisation's ESG/CSR activities is diverse, tackling key global issues for the betterment of communities, society, and the environment whilst adding stakeholder and shareholder value.
Heterogeneity	Determination of the specific definition of issues within a social area to be considered is varied, underpinned by a robust evidence base to inform the need for critical change.
Measurement	Agreement on the appropriateness of metrics to be used to assess performance can be difficult. These may cut across brand, business, financial measures, and ESG outcomes.
Interpretation	Determination of what level of performance is "acceptable" is dependent on stakeholders' interpretation and how these standards are communicated as part of an ESG/CSR corporate brand strategy.
Organisation	
Corporate brand	Determining the degree to which ESG/CSR is a core platform of the organisational corporate brand identity, and how that aligns effectively with corporate brand image (particularly where there is a complex stakeholder mix).

---

191 https://www.legalandgeneralgroup.com/media-centre/press-releases/legal-general-establishes-partnership-with-sir-michael-marmot-to-address-uk-health-inequality/.

Table 10.1 (continued)

Complexity type	Definition
Multiple products and Brands	If there is no clarity in the corporate brand relationship and overall positioning with clear 'meaning behind the purpose' and how that is being delivered by product/different brands and sub-brands, and if these dynamics are not aligned, it could cause confusion in some consumers/stakeholders minds (brand image).
Site and functional activities	International activities and corporate brand purpose may span national boundaries and functions may face different sets of regulatory environments that must be dealt with. Likewise, there will be cross-cultural nuances in terms of delivering corporate intangible brand value (emotional). Therefore, choosing global issues that are relevant to the degree upon which the issues are relevant to the stakeholder mix (eg: national only, national predominantly, with an element of international/territory relevance and/or global issues).
Supply chain management	Expectations on global firms that they are "responsible" for ESG /CSR activities of suppliers, and the standards and expectations that required, linked to interpretation (issue).
Communication	
Intensity of positioning	The degree to which ESG is leveraged in global communication activities will vary, but is positioning clear and compelling for a broad spectrum of stakeholders (eg: customers, employees, investors, communities, NGOs, governments and so on)?
Communicating actions	The type of information provided will vary across activities (eg: the extent to which these activities are strategically integrated, providing the right blend between local (operational businesses/product) and global (corporate messaging).
Implementation/ change issues	The degree to which integrated marketing communication is consistently delivering the same message (eg: depending on principles/priorities ensuring the ESG/CSR 'issue' and connected purpose are clear, there is a 'need' based on evidence to 'change').

The following quote from Sir Nigel Wilson, taken from *Legal & General*'s 'Sustainability and inclusive capitalism – 2020–21 report', it summarises the importance of acknowledging the three levels of complexity in relation to corporate brand strategy, whereby the key issues and principles, govern and influence organisational and communication issues:

We are not afraid to call out companies that are not doing enough, whether it is on delivering inclusive capitalism, tackling climate change or addressing environment, social and governance issues.[192]

(2021: 5)

Chapter takeaways

- *Legal & General* is an exemplar of a corporate, purpose-driven, embedded, and sophisticated approach to branding.
- *Legal & General's* 'inclusive capitalism' vision is ambitious, far reaching, and complex which has been communicated into a clear and compelling long-term strategic vision.
- An effective corporate brand purpose allows multiple internal and external stakeholders to invest meaning in proposed outcomes, in this case prioritising a positive contribution to environment, social, and governance (ESG) goals.
- This chapter highlights an applied view of how corporate brand strategy plays a crucial role when connecting purpose-profit and an organisation's social ecosystem to which *Legal & General* are key catalysts for change in this global agenda.
- This case demonstrated why a key long-term strategic driver for companies is to invest in CSR initiatives in order to create and foster positive *moral capital* from which intangible assets such as credibility, goodwill and reputation can be developed.
- As a corporate brand, *Legal & General* are able to lean on a rich brand heritage, building on its existing brand equity in areas such as finance, pensions, and insurance, adding credibility when developing stakeholder goodwill, trust, and credibility in delivering their inclusive capitalism vision.
- Cultivating brand equity in any size or type of organisation is one of the most powerful strategic assets a firm can develop and is often a catalyst for achieving a sustainable competitive advantage.
- Sir Nigel Wilson, *Legal & General's* Group Chief Executive, has not only raised inclusive capitalism's strategic importance, but also brought the corporate brand purpose to life by weaving key ESG outcomes as a central measure of business success and the contribution to the betterment of society. This is matching *words* with *deeds*.
- Brand credibility is a key driving force for success. If a purpose is clear, compelling, and inspiring, with tangible results assigned to its success, it can seamlessly connect customers, consumers, employees, investors, communities, and wider society. However, a simultaneous challenge is whether corporate brands can foster a symbiotic relationship that doesn't cause friction and break the 'brand equity' chain (internally and externally, between identify and image).

──────────

192 https://group.legalandgeneral.com/en/sustainability/sustainability-reporting-centre/sustainability-and-inclusive-capitalism-report-2020.

11 Inspired Villages: Purpose, values, & alignment

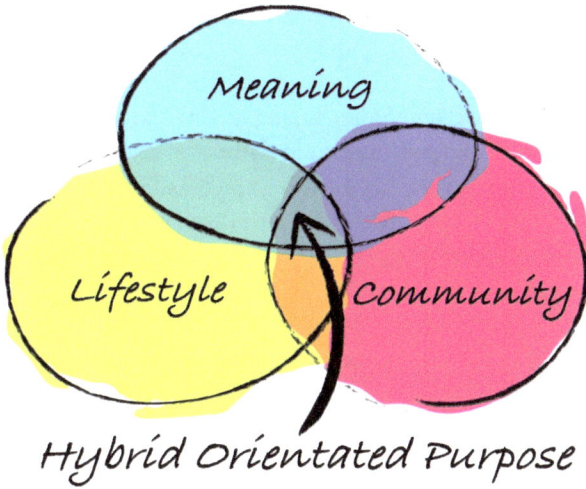

Meaning · Lifestyle · Community · Hybrid Orientated Purpose

https://doi.org/10.1515/9783110718638-016

11.1 Outline of chapter

The Ecological Theory of Aging (ETA) (Lawton, Nahemow, & Eisdorfer, 1973) examines the effects on person-environmental ecology and interaction during later living (Hu, Xia, Skitmore, & Buys, 2015), and it is overwhelmingly confirmed within gerontological research that 'aging well' is a product of both personal and environmental resources. Changes in Government policy, together with the changing differentiated social nature of ageing, suggest that there will be an expectation of individual responsibility for the consumption of health in later life in the 21st century, with the emphasis being on the maintenance of the self (Rees Jones, et al., 2008). One of the responses to these trends in recent years has been the 'marketisation' of aged care services, with an emerging acceptance and demand for retirement villages and communities (Bernard, Liddle, Bartlam, & Scharf, 2012). For example, in Australia, almost 63% of the population was found to prefer living in retirement villages and communities (Judd, Olsberg, Quinn, & Groenhart, 2010) which provide purpose-designed and built residential and lifestyle environments.

The following chapter is a detailed exploration into how one of the UK's leading operators in retirement communities, *Inspired Villages*, have been able to position themselves as a community-driven lifestyle brand that delivers overall health and well-being for their customers. This empirically evidenced case study demonstrates how their employees (referred to as 'colleagues') and customers (referred to as 'residents') invest *meaning in their shared brand purpose*. This extended case study demonstrates how *Inspired Villages*, working in partnership with *FUZE*, applied years of continuous proactive and reactive market orientation diagnosis (or a hybrid approach) in order to convert 'customer' intelligence into value across their business model.

As the appeal of retirement communities grows in the UK, this case illustrates how *Inspired Villages* deliver a truly cross-functional, resident-driven culture of improvement, and in the process strengthen their brand position and equity. As we will see, this is a complex area, and the power of purpose has been proven to inspire an ever-evolving employee base to ensure high-growth plans are being delivered, and, crucially, fostering an authentic relationship with consumers (and community) based on attachment, authenticity, and trust (Kramer, 2017, p. 432).

Learning outcomes

After reading this chapter, you'll be able to:
- Critically analyse the changing dynamics of *Inspired Villages'* environment, and the vital role a purpose-driven brand strategy can play.
- Determine the importance of strategic brand management in defining, aligning and executing brand strategies, whilst identifying key drivers for success.
- Assess the strategic and operational impact of merging customer experience and brand management (ie: the integration of customer journey mapping and experience management).

- Explain the significant role that market orientation plays in developing brands.
- Apply and assess the significance of a hybrid version of market orientation to *Inspired Villages* (and other contexts).
- Identify the ways within which *Inspired Villages* connect and align their purpose to their operations through brand meaning, by delivering on community, improved lifestyle, and health and well-being.

11.2 Introduction

The *Inspired Villages* business model is complex involving the procurement of land, planning and building integrated retirement communities and properties, selling houses, delivering on promises of improved quality of life, health, and well-being. Crucially, a culture of improvement with a continuous feedback loop (from potential customer, residents, and colleagues) is embedded to help improve customer and employee experiences, using this insight to refine and strengthen its purpose. The case highlights how the organisation, driven by a collective ownership of senior leaders, has demonstrated how effective brand management is critical to success, and how it has far-reaching benefits across an organisation including increased revenue, higher customer retention and loyalty, higher propensity for premium pricing, higher employee engagement and satisfaction, and managing risk more effectively in terms of entering new market expansions (Aaker, 2014; Beverland, Wilner, & Micheli, 2015; Lee, O'Cass, & Sok, 2016; Tavassoli, Sorescu, & Chandy, 2014). This exemplifies the core proposition of this book: cultivating an ever-evolving, dynamic marketing/branding capability, capturing, and exploiting mutually beneficial value that is grounded in delivering brand purpose and meaning-making.

Based on this unique hybrid market orientation approach, the critical success factor here is for the organisation to continuously *review, reflect, refine, and re-calibrate* their brand purpose over a number of years. These well-established outcomes are in addition to other benefits which include: effectively 'orientating' and 'refining' a brand purpose can lead to a strategic differentiation and long-term advantage; delivering a brand purpose to immediate customer needs and satisfaction leads to improved business performance; balancing other market and societal needs (direct and indirect), can not only lead to business success (ie: doing well) but and also have a lasting positive impact across a host of environmental spheres such as social, cultural, health and well-being at an individual and community level etc (ie: doing good) (Bonchek & France, 2018). It is now well established that companies pursuing strategies based on purpose – doing well and doing good effectively woven into the fabric of an organisation – can achieve superior performance, and a new way to acquire differentiation (Biraghi, Gambetti, & Quigley, 2020, p. 403). However it must be emphasised that this will only be successful if there is: an effective orientation towards a holistic market view; a mindset of continuous evaluation and refinement throughout brand management process; the building up of effective marketing capability so that customer intelligence (from predicting latent/future needs and exploiting existing customer knowledge structures) and dynamic capability can be grounded in the strategic process of defining, aligning, executing, and evaluating the brand purpose strategy.

The key discussion point covered is the *paradox of purpose,* a purpose which is rooted in the goodwill of society whilst on the other hand requiring a brand culture of continuous learning and improvement, with a senior management team committed to a process of honest reflection and assessment laid-bare by customers and colleagues. Biraghi et al eloquently summarise the challenge in the quest for purpose:

> *Achieving a strong brand purpose means for a company setting off on a long journey, purpose cannot be found in isolation inside corporate headquarters, it must be generated in and with society. It cannot be written in the stone once and for all. It must be discussed and lived by daily. It is in others words a profound co-construction effort.* (2020: 404)

11.3 Case brief

Inspired Villages worked with *FUZE* to develop and execute a continuous research project that covered a diverse customer-base across a complex 'eco-system' of Villages, all with a unique proposition, culture, brand strengths, and key priorities. The strategic environment highlights a competitive landscape of providers attempting to capitalise on the market opportunities arising from the ageing population in the UK, with *Inspired Villages'* value proposition already delivering on a very strong aspirational and distinctive 'sell' of independent living, peace of mind, safety, and security, together with belonging to a community. Ultimately, the brief was clear: To help *Inspired Villages* to continue to build, measure, and respond to 'priority' customer and brand benchmarks, with a focus on providing meaningful action-orientated insights that are strategic levers to deliver key outcomes such as increase resident satisfaction, improve health, quality of life, and community outcomes, as well as strengthening brand equity.

11.4 Case orientation and context

Before delving into the theory-application-practice discussion, it is necessary to introduce the case context. The term 'integrated retirement communities' is by its nature, relatively challenging to define; it sits within a broader catchment term of the retirement communities and villages. The *Associated Retirement Community Operators (ARCO)*, the UK's represented governing body, defines a retirement community as:

> *Integrated Retirement Communities combine high quality housing options for older people with tailored support services. They allow residents to rent or own a property and to maintain their privacy and independence, with the reassurance of 24-hour on-site staff, communal facilities, and optional care and support as needed. Integrated retirement communities may also be referred to as retirement housing, retirement villages, extra care housing, housing-with-care, assisted living, close care apartments, or independent living settings.*[193]   *(ARCO, 2021)*

It is important to further note, that *Inspired Villages* is not a care home nor sheltered accommodation/retirement housing; it offers a fully integrated retirement community, with a focus on improving quality of life, high-quality properties, services and facilities, such as a clubhouse, gym and swimming pool, restaurant and bar, onsite shops and even cinemas. Figure 11.1 identifies the differences when segmenting the wider retirement market:

---

193 *ARCO* (2021) https://www.arcouk.org/ retrieved 20th February 2021.

Living Options for Older People

Figure 11.1: Segmentation differences with broader demographic.
Source: *ARCO* (2021) https://www.arcouk.org/

As highlighted in Figure 11.1, there are many similarities across the accommodation market for the later living sector:

> *Integrated Retirement Communities offer older people the opportunity to live independently in their own home as part of a wider community. Lifestyle, wellbeing, and care services are available to support people's independence and aspirations. ARCO says these communities are the fast-emerging 'lifestyle option' for older people, sitting between 'sheltered housing' where minimal support is provided, and 'care' or 'nursing' homes, which are increasingly focussed on supporting people with higher levels of care needs. The term also reflects the fact that such provision tends to have both an active and well-integrated community onsite and its increasingly likely to be integrated into the wider town or community within which it operates.*

> *Research shows that 8 out of 10 older people are interested in housing and care options which will help them to retain their independence, enjoying a fulfilling lifestyle as part of a wider community. People want facilities such as cafés and restaurants, optional activities and social links, with care available if they need it. Integrated Retirement Communities provide this choice at a range of price points, but awareness remains low.[194]*

At a glance, retirement housing appears very similar; they both offer housing specifically designed for older people with the desire to live an independent life-style. How-

---

194 *ARCO* (2021) visual supplied *ARCO Organisation* https://www.arcouk.org/press-release/housing-with-care-sector-announces-new-term-to-categorise-sector

ever, integrated retirement communities tend to have a more enhanced offer in terms facilities, wrap-around hospitality services, and housing specification. Some even offer a lower-level additional care on-site, these differing greatly in terms of the 'Care Home' offer (highlighted in Figure 11.1) and the subsequent complexities in terms of care.

In the upper end of the market, due to the enhanced offer, integrated retirement communities, on offer from the likes of *Inspired Villages*, tend to be more aspirational and expensive in terms of property price. In these types of retirement communities, the properties range from 1 or 2 bed cottages or apartments, 2 bathrooms, living room and a high specification kitchen, with large spacious rooms and a real focus on interior design and finish. A key point of difference in the retirement property market compared to other markets is that the properties tend to be sold as leasehold (between 99 years and up to 250 years) as opposed to free hold. This influences all aspects of the customer journey, from delivering transparent and all-encompassing information during the buying process, which is typical with high-involvement purchases; as we will see, this process is a primary focus for *Inspired Villages* and their brand management strategy in that effectively managing and exceeding the new resident experience helps strengthen the long-term brand loyalty. For example, overall customer satisfaction was 24% higher in respondents who stated their expectations had been 'exceeded' compared to those who stated their expectations had been 'fully met' (100% v 76%) – (References: *Inspired Villages* (2019) Resident/Customer Research, FUZE Research).

11.5 Challenging the cultural status quo: Delivering social impact

The basic elements of any successful brand management function is the ability to find a balance between consistency in terms of brand image and tactical execution, but also delivering strategies to benefit the medium to long term. All of which is built upon a continuous process of customer-centric evaluation in terms of image and positioning, in the context of a macro-environment (Kotler & Keller, 2012; Santos-Vijande, del Río-Lanza, Suárez-Alvarez, & Diáz-Martin, 2013). In practice, for *Inspired Villages*, at a macro-level this requires the brand to exploit the emerging market opportunity in the UK, whilst also tackling the UK's cultural stigma of ageing with and delivering social impact (*STOP Ageism*, 2021). For instance, the UK's retirement community market faces a significant imbalance between supply and demand, with specialist 'later living' accommodation. The growth in demand is expected to double in a relatively short timeframe; in housebuilding construction terms, it is estimated that there are currently 12m over 65s in the UK, with this figure expected to increase by 50% over the next 20 years.[195]

Therefore, the short-fall of supply, identifies why retirement communities and properties are a key focus, with only 7,000 age-appropriate homes delivered in the 'later living' market each year.[196] Additionally, the UK's integrated retirement community market is relatively immature in comparison to other international markets and represents a significant market opportunity for the right brand to position itself. *Inspired Villages* is a limited company, formed in 2017 as part of *Legal & General*'s long-term investment into the 'later living' housing market, which as highlighted is one of the most underserved sectors in the UK's housing market. Phil Bayliss, Executive Chairman of *Inspired Villages* highlighted that:

> *Internationally, we have seen countless examples of how active, community-focused living can change people's lives. Over 5% of over-65s in the US, New Zealand, and Australia now opt to live in 'later living' communities. In the UK, it is only 0.6%. We have a wonderful opportunity to create vibrant, inclusive communities enabling each retiree to live their best life.*[197]

There are multiple benefits for belonging to a community such as this, including: improved health, social connection, reduction in isolation and life-style, and community benefits. *Legal & General* (2021) highlight these benefits based showing that:

> *Each person living in 'later living' community enjoys a reduced risk of health challenges that leads to a 46% decrease in the number of planned GP visits among other benefits. This contributes to fiscal savings to the NHS and social care of £3,500 per person per year (Holland, 2015: 7). With its focus on holistic wellbeing, and the option of flexible, discreet support in residents own homes, Inspired Villages is particularly well placed to deliver 'later living' communities that transform life for over 65s and help them enjoy healthy, independent lives for longer.*

---

195 *Legal & General* (2021) https://www.legalandgeneralgroup.com/media-centre/press-releases/legal-general-s-later-living-business-accelerates-development-pipeline-as-works-start-on-six-acre-site-in-bedfordshire/
196 'Retirement Housing: Residents' Experiences' report by *NHBC*.
197 *Legal & General* (2021) https://brand.legalandgeneral.com/rethinking-retirement/rethinking-retirement/: retrieved 20th February 2021.
  ² Holland (2015) https://www2.aston.ac.uk/migrated-assets/applicationpdf/lhs/245545-final%20report1.pdf

11.6 The purpose paradox: Market dynamics

In order to develop competitive advantage through improving marketing/brand capability, *Inspired Villages* have been able to develop through continuous market orientation diagnosis an intuitive 'brand framework'. Brand management can often be
about balancing opposing forces: on the one hand maintaining consistency through
delivery (tactically); on the other, the ability to adapt to environmental changes
(macro/strategically). This requires a fluid and iterative knowledge management
system, that centres on customer insight. All organisations often prioritise short-
term financial targets through commercial necessity whilst requiring to be proactive
strategically (Lee, O'Cass, & Sok, 2017). *Inspired Villages* are no different and face
these same challenges. A key point of difference is their ability to define, align, and
execute a clear brand purpose from a set of values, which sit within their brand
framework. The theoretical arguments are clear in that there is an inherent tension
which brings about the need to further explore a deeper understanding of (a) developing marketing/ branding capabilities as a source of competitive advantage (Day,
2014; Gregory, Ngo, & Karavdic, 2017; Hult & Ketchen, 2017), and (b) evaluating
how the development brand management processes can further improve brand performance, meaning-making and equity (Aaker, 2014; Lee, O'Cass, & Sok, 2017).

Following discussions with Jamie Bunce the Chief Executive Officer about *Inspired
Villages*' strategic brand management function, how to builld in an emotional connection that can connect and inspire potential customer, customers, colleagues, suppliers, investors and other important stakeholders, it was clear that the importance of
stating what the brand is and how best to define it had to be at the centre of the organisation's mindset. Using the brand framework is a key vehicle to set strategic

intent and then deliver effectively market orientated strategic choices, but there is a paradox.

When Mackey introduced the notion of 'conscious capitalism', he described a balance between financial value and social values, a more humane form of sustainable capitalism. As we have seen above, it has four pillars: spiritually-evolved, self-effacing servant leaders; a conscious culture; a stakeholder orientation; and a higher purpose beyond profit. However, to some, 'maximising profits by not making profits the primary goal' has an inherent contradiction: are these corporate goals competing binary opposites or compatible objectives sat on a 'purpose-profit' continuum? The tension between the two can risk a lack of authenticity, a bias of tactics over strategy. The customer-company relationship is based on mutual trust and a legitimacy of purpose. Purpose has to be built-in not added-on. Companies with 'human-centred' design or who have 'cathedral thinking' approaches to enlightened company vision, have *meaning* at the centre of their strategic vision, where often 'why' is a central driving force. Meaning can connect and bind; purpose can be essential for commercial success. Adhering to strong principles is vital to sustain that mutuality; following a course with a higher purpose is of paramount importance. Protecting the patent not the planet can be a paradox, a trap of 'shareholder primacy'. As *Inspired Villages* are proving, being a forward-looking organisation, taking a balanced approach, and having sustainability as a developing goal means that this is scalable and therefore achievable. Another purpose paradox is 'inherent sameness' due to all brands trying to be 'purposeful'. Purpose must help position a company, but choosing the values which resonate with **your** target customer base can help differentiate from the competition. Choosing conscience with commerciality, value with values – that purpose paradox – is a balance *Inspired Villages* continue to embrace.

The crux of continuity and successful ongoing execution seems to be through harnessing the power of emotion (Gobe, 2009) and how this is not only a tactical tool to communicate importance of the brand to customers and employee alike, but it is also a key strategic hook to ensure a brand has more meaning than just profit. Indeed, two functions of brand management (strategic brand management and internal branding) are highlighted as critical in achieving medium to long-term success (Keller, 2003; Santos-Vijande, del Rio-Lanza, & Suarez-Dias, 2013). Additionally, as argued in this case study, the critical success factors relate to fusing market orientation diagnosis, refining and calibrating purpose, in order to deliver a dynamic capability. Jamie Bunce the Chief Executive Officer at *Inspired Villages* highlights these points:

> With Inspired Villages we have been able to build and connect emotion (on a number of levels) right across the business and our activities. This allows us to drive all aspects of our brand strategy right through the business from our LinkedIn posts, our wordplay in all our sales communications, through to the Village designs and so on. The critical success factors are:
> – Simplicity is the key: We undertook continuous market analysis and then linked our purpose to our brand, so every time you see our logo it has 'The Best Years of your life?' – it links and tells people what the core of our business is.

- *All levels of the business understand and articulate the brand purpose: The acid test is, does it bring your brand to life in simple terms so that everyone can see and connect with it.*
- *Emotional hook: There has to be a clear emotional hook, quite often tapping into a set of needs. This drives how potential customers follow a path to purchase, customers invest meaning in a product or service experience, and how the team will connect with meaningful work – be more engaged, satisfied and loyal defenders of the brand and its reputation.*

Inspired Villages' approach has challenged the status quo and effectively re-positioned what many other operators are now attempting to imitate: a clear focus on community in terms of physical village centre and associated atmosphere, life-style, and activities to meet retirement goals, safety and security, specific design of properties to be inclusive of all ages. There is a clear brand purpose to deliver and improve quality of life, health, and well-being outcomes. Bunce adds:

Our ethos is simple. We put the health and happiness of our residents at the heart of everything we do, with the promise of a life less ordinary for today's generation of retirees. Everything we do is motivated by the admiration and respect we have for our residents, their families, and the life-style they desire and deserve from the service levels of our team through to the planning and design of the village itself.

Ben Renshaw, who supports the senior leaders of *Inspired Villages*, helps build pur-poseful partnerships with leading organisations to develop leadership capability, high performing teams and transform organisational cultures.[198] Renshaw contex-tualised the importance of purpose:

The purpose is epitomised by Jamie Bunce CEO and his burning desire, his obsession and energy to genuinely improve the residents lives, by making this the best years of their life. And in doing so, as a team, making their best years of life in achieving this.

Renshaw identified some critical success factors:

We did an executive (eg: C-suite/senior decision makers/stakeholders) session with Inspired Villages. At that stage, it was focused on individuals, knowing their own purpose and sharing this purpose with the others so that meaningful relationships could be formed [with these colleagues]. It allows people to connect and define what success looks like and encourages others to be purpose-led.

Generally, CEOs and other C-suite leaders are the key driving force for successful purpose-led organisations. They are the primary cultural carriers of change, in terms of role modelling, communicating and connecting the importance, encourag-ing and developing an 'authentic' culture powered by purpose-vision-values. This becomes a critical catalyst right across three different levels: (1) personal, (2) team and (3) organisational levels (Renshaw, 2019). Renshaw notes, it must start at per-sonal level, followed by team and then organisational-wide; an effective brand pur-pose – and its core essence – should be timeless to inspire people at all levels of the

---

198 https://benrenshaw.com/about-ben-renshaw/

business: "the purpose shouldn't change, how it is translated should". This relates strongly with how *Inspired Villages* response to its dynamic environment. As we will see, the translation changes can be both responsive and proactive in nature, evidenced by *Inspired Villages* and *FUZE* partnership, a form of hybrid market orientation is best suited.

11.7 Strategic brand management: Holistic business model

In hyper-competitive and dynamic markets like those which *Inspired Villages* operate in, the importance of effective brand management cannot be understated. However, it is often challenging given its perplexing nature of finding clarity of purpose, effectively executing strategies, and then maintaining consistency across offerings, all the while being able to respond and adapt to turbulent market changes. Brand management for integrated retirement communities is no different. It is argued that to successfully develop the brand, organisations are required to strategically invest in developing marketing processes and exploiting (developed and emerging) capabilities so that relevant information about (a) customers (ie: insight gathered and 'known' through existing structures like customer experience evaluation strategies and/or identifying latent needs from prospective customers or assessing wider market trends), (b) competitors, (c) investors, and (d) other stakeholders, with a clear objective to convert any changes into brand value in the short and long-term (Iyer, Davari, Srivastava, & Paswan, 2020).

From a business model perspective, *Inspired Villages* arguably operate three distinctive business models:
1. Land acquisition, design, and planning as a developer.
2. Construction/housebuilding management including estate agency and management.
3. Hospitality, wellbeing, and property services that are flexible to resident needs and enhance their lifestyle.

The point here is to demonstrate that these business models are diverse, with complex supply chains, dynamic planning and delivery programmes, all of which require constant market orientation diagnosis aligned to an ever-refining purpose, with a focus on finding an effective balance between 'customers in the now' (eg: achieving resident satisfaction in current service levels via the hospitality model) and 'customers for the future' (eg: identifying latent needs and features for homes and *Village* designs often 3–5 years ahead). Whilst there is no consensus of how to define a business model, the following is useful as a robust anchor for this discussion: "a business model describes the rationale of a how an organisation, creates, delivers, and captures (customer) value" (Osterwalder & Pigneur, 2010).

If we consider these diverse business models, there is one commonality that binds them – generating and capturing customer (and stakeholder) value across many of their activities, whether it is the construction of a wide range of property types including cottages, apartments, village centres and offices, fulfilling and managing fitness suites, maintaining the garden management and rural appeal of the Village centre or meeting health care needs. In all of these contexts, *Inspired Villages*' brand strategy is grounded in effectively applying a long-term resident-first, relationship-based approach. In other words, from a strategic, operational, and tactical perspective, their brand purpose guides all aspects of operations, cross-functionally, creating a rich emotional economy that allow their residents to invest meaning in customer experiences right across the critical stages of their resident journey. Table 11.1 shows the following pathway to purchase, highlights how *Inspired Villages* aim to add-value to the process from a customer-centric/empathy perspective, highlighting what success looks like:

Table 11.1: Resident Journey.

1. Dream – evaluation of the retirement village market, property types and building consideration of purchasing criteria and financial budgets/implications: Customer-centric view: *'I'm looking for a new home to make my life easier. I want to be near family, have friends, keep active and feel safe & secure'*
2. Plan – decide on the right option: Customer-centric view: *'I have thought long and hard about what I want and have all the information I need. I understand all the financial implications as well as the benefits.*
3. Reserve – committed to moving: Customer-centric view: *'I've made my decision and I am excited about it. Inspired Villages have been patient and reassuring and made the process clear and simple.'*
4. Move-in day and settling in: Customer-centric view: *'there was so much to do but Inspired Villages made moving very easy. The move was amazing and better than I expected. I have met my neighbours and already feel my life has changed for the better.*
5. Enjoying Village life – Settled in and living the best years of their life: Customer-centric view: *'I love my new life. The people here make it so special – they understand what matters most and how to help me. I'm happy and healthy.*

Source: *Inspired Villages* (2021)

The strategic imperative has been to capture this customer value, evaluate where value is being lost and then *aim* to improve their relational model so that *Inspired Villages* is able to build long-term brand equity in a continuous loop of resident and colleague feedback with applied learning and improvement. For example, if we focus on the context of the wider housebuilding sector, there is strong evidence that have been quality issues with new homes from 2006 to 2020. 90% of respondents to a national survey on new homes build quality consistently reported faults to their builder about their home. From 2016 to 2020, 25% of respondents consistently reported 16+ problems to the builder about their new home (*House Building Federation*, 2006–2020). Other new home house builders have applied a transactional approach to customer experience, with limited scope on quality, after sales service, long term satisfaction and fundamentally an effective means of building brand equity (Craig, Boothman, & Sommerville, 2018). Indeed, it has been argued that the current system has not seen any improvement, to the extent that a 'New Homes Ombudsman' has been set up to ensure build quality and that customer rights are upheld. Hence, a key issue in the sector is that "the private housebuilding sector has not tried to define what its customer's expectations and priorities are despite an increase in overall customer awareness and sophistication" (Craig, Pilcher, & Boothman, 2020).

Inspired Villages, on the other hand, have been able to ensure an effective transition across these business models, from property to people, people to community, where their brand management and performance is evaluated on what that allows residents to invest meaning that goes beyond solely financial ROI measures (ie: property purchase and service charge). Instead, there is a focus on evaluating resident experiences, measuring areas such as satisfaction, quality of life drivers, community cohesion, retirement lifestyle goals, health, and well-being outcomes, as defined by their residents and colleagues. From a practical perspective of knowing how to define, align and execute brand strategies, Jamie Bunce pertinently adds (specifically applying a service logic):

> When we think of executing a brand purpose in the realities of a business, the diversity of cultures at specific villages, the corporate dynamics etc – how do we do that? It really needs a simple purpose, one that emotionally connects from the CEO down to the housekeepers . . . can we [as senior leaders] explain it in simple terms, so that the team can emotionally connect with it and everyone can live that purpose in their own world/role and therefore contribute to the overall purpose . . . .?

An area that *Inspired Villages* has focused on strongly is ensuring that they have a clear brand framework and that the brand management cuts across all aspects of the business. Where it becomes real for colleagues tangibly and intangibly, top to bottom, this has been fundamental in the business in developing their brand management capability, which relates to a positive influence on an organisation's overall performance (Orr, Bush, & Vorhies, 2011; Lee, O'Cass, & Sok, 2017; Vorhies, Orr, & Bush, 2011).

For instance, in the following two examples Jamie Bunce explains the importance of effective strategic brand management and how that translates in practical, cross-functional teams, at all levels of the business:

> If we take a business case for gym facilities to the Board, you need an effective brand framework. One that is clear and that is connected with Inspired Villages purpose (aligned with corporate objectives), but the initiatives (and results) are built upon the soft activity . . . but before any such investment we must have a 'look in the mirror moment'. The communication and connection must be real and exampled "up and down" if we want residents to exercise, be healthier, take more walks around the villages, then we need great gardens. For example, if we invest in this particular type of gym and equipment, then residents will be 35% strong after using it for a year following a programme that it specifically designed for them. This all helps deliver our holistic

well-being outcomes . . . you will always need a tangible ROI, but this goes beyond a typical 'hard' calculation – and it does evidence our brand purpose to our colleagues and residents.

The second example, builds upon the point highlighted earlier in terms of construction and housebuilder quality and the way within which *Inspired Villages* are operationalising and managing their purpose-driven brand strategy:

'Construction Contractor Framework' – The Construction Director developed a framework document to use with potential contractors that totally aligned with our brand purpose and values said: "you have to align with this if you want to work with us". This is a crucial signal to the people that want to work with us, (a) how we want them to work clearly linked to our purpose (Best Years Of Your Life?) (b) everybody has a role to play with delivering that; whether it is the team in the Villages, or back office, right through to the contractors and sub-contractors on the building site . . . you want them to be asking themselves the finish on this needs to be amazing, as we are going to change the lives of older people!

Inspired Villages has an ambitious growth plan. Therefore, there is great emphasis on ensure the organisation's continued development of brand management capability is embodied by an organisation's ability to operationalise core processes, specifically strategic brand management and internal branding processes, which are expected to drive customer knowledge and expectations into effective positioning and image strategies (Orr, Bush, & Vorhies, 2011).

11.8 Strategic imperative: Finding dynamic capability through hybrid market orientation and internal branding

Inspired Villages operates in a complex environment that is influenced by many social, cultural, political, economic, and technological trends. As we will see, on the one hand, the UK's retirement living sectors represents a significant market opportunity for growth and expansion; on the other hand, it relies solely on a commodity that is one of the scarcest in the World: land. A strategic imperative is to ensure the brand is effectively garnering intelligence right across its macro environment, and narrowing its focus on customer's needs, wants and expectations now, and in the future. The average retirement community 'build to completion' will often span up to 4–5 years (or even longer). Given the long lead-in time for product development and delivery, in what is a highly competitive market, to be able to go beyond merely 'surviving' and prioritise gaining a competitive edge over it rivals, it is essential that *Inspired Villages'* brand strategy is able to harness intelligence and insight so that they are able to deploy their resources to match the business environment (Ambrosini & Bowman, 2009; Lamore, Berkowitz, & Farrington, 2013). The crux of *FUZE*'s contribution has been supporting *Inspired Villages* continued efficacy in marketing orientation, defined as the cultural and behavioural processes through which an organisation targets and generates market intelligence, disseminates, and deploys the intelligence via relevant knowledge management structures, departments and individuals, right across that organisation, and with one clear outcome, so that it takes appropriate actions in response to that intelligence (Jaworski & Kohli, 1996). It is established that there are two discrete market orientation constructs: proactive and responsive (Atuahene-Gima, Slater, & Olson, 2005); (Lamore, Berkowitz, & Farrington, 2013); (Narver, Slater, & MacLachlan, 2004); (Slater & Narver, 1998). The rationale for these typologies is based on the fact that there are two types of customer needs: latent/tacit needs (eg: hidden/value of which have not been uncovered, challenging to articulate) vs explicitly expressed needs (eg: grounded in lived customer experiences easily articulated) (Jaworski & Kohli, 1996); (Slater & Narver, 1998).

For the purpose of this case, we contextualised these typologies in relation to brand strategy, and applied to the case of *Inspired Villages*.

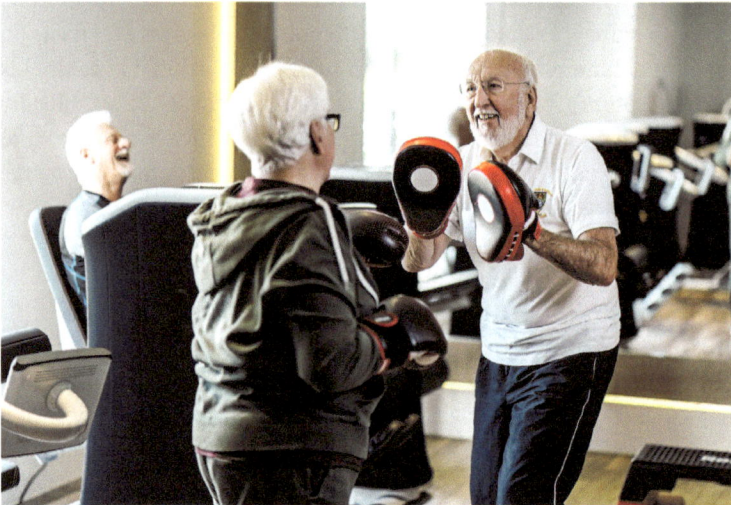

11.9 Responsive market orientation (RMO)

Responsive market orientation (RMO) prioritises being responsive and receptive to existing customer needs (Saini & Johnson, 2005; Slater & Narver, 1998). *Inspired Villages* are characterised as a customer-oriented organisation and have invested heavily in the structures, processes, and importance of collecting and evaluating all aspects of their resident's customer experience. There are key measures related to business wide key performance indicators, this has ensured that all village managers and staff are focused on delivering on their value proposition (community, lifestyle, and holistic well-being) and brand promises and embedding a customer-driven mindset, which contributes towards improved brand performance (O'Cass & Viet Ngo, 2007). At an organizational level, RMO allows an *Inspired Villages* to improve absorptive capacity

(Cohen & Levinthal, 1990) by identifying customer expectations at critical points of the resident journey, and then ensuring the customer experience, service and product levels meet or exceed this on a consistent basis; allowing for functional, emotional, and social needs to be fulfilled and allow residents to invest meaning in the overall brand experience. Another key attribute is that RMO promotes exploitative learning (Atuahene-Gima, Slater, & Olson, 2005), which is demonstrable by an embedded culture of continuous improvement.

11.10 Proactive market orientation (PMO)

The primary focus and key point of difference is that proactive market orientation (PMO) sets an agenda to identify and address customers' latent and tacit needs, meaning that a customer or resident is unable to clearly articulate a 'known' need as it is emergent, and the problem and known solution is yet to present itself. In the context of *Inspired Villages* this may relate to SMART home and health solutions or environmentally friendly home features, which are perhaps indicative of future needs of residents (ie: future generational needs) rather than explicitly known in the present. Therefore, PMO is heavily research-driven, dynamic, and iterative in nature, there needs to be a continuous process to explore, develop, and validate. Organisations that successfully implement this orientation approach require a learning mindset and be market-driven (Narver, Slater, & MacLachlan, 2004). If applied effectively, it enhances brand-positioning strategies (such as brand differentiation and design-based differentiation) which is positively associated with the PMO (Lyer & Srivastava, 2020).

Inspired Villages have been effective in developing a dynamic capability, which has been built-up overtime, and often make use of converting some level of tacit and idiosyncratic knowledge into explicit brand capability; otherwise known as brand management, the effective use of the firm to build purposeful and sustainable brands (Keller, 1993; Keller & Lehmann, 2006). It is important to note, that being more aligned to RMO or PMO is neither a negative or positive trait, it is merely reflective of the market environment, brand strategy, and organisational culture. However, the literature suggests that organisations tend to be one construct or the other (Lyer & Srivastava, 2020) but *Inspired Villages* have seemingly successfully developed a hybrid version, adopting a PMO for certain long-term activities, and RMO for continually evaluating customer needs, expectations, and experiences in the short-term. For instance, in the PMO construct, whereby they undertake a design-based approach to exploring and identifying latent needs for future village and property designs by undertaking programmes of research to assess what future resident segments may want and need to help feed the product-cycle (in some cases 5-years in advance). This simultaneously occurs whilst the RMO construct of orientation is in play, whereby each stage of the resident journey is evaluated from new resident experience from move-in, through to a continuous research programme of feedback to improve service-levels in areas in the hospitality, service, and facilities operations.

In other words, *Inspired Villages'* customer-centric approach has ensured that the brand management capability has found a balance between long-term strategic future proofing, and short-term incremental improvements in the here and now; this has been underpinned by their internal branding processes so that the colleagues right across the organisation have a shared experience, with clear processes, and ways of doing things, routines, and culture (Nelson & Winter, 1982).

FUZE play a crucial role in evaluating whether the resident experience is being met at critical points in the year and over each resident journey. This is achieved by evaluating each village across a number of tailored and focused brand metrics. The outcome of this research then drives clear action plans to maintain standards and improve the resident experience at both village and group level, allowing the business to develop and upskill colleagues based on customer priorities; crucially, this insight is converted into 'explicit' knowledge and is shared cross-functionally across the business, whether that is sales, village management, garden services, construction, and so on. Moreover, all company teams are aware of its importance, are accountable and evaluated against these brand metrics in some form or another. The success of this comes from a clear brand framework that is executed, where the strategic decision-makers have drawn clear brand boundaries of ownership, activity, and alignment. It has been argued that to truly exploit tacit knowledge in a branding context, it must not only be transferred but understood right across an organisation (Spender, 1996). Often, brand capability is built exploiting tacit knowledge, which is a challenge if the correct system, structure, and mind-set is not in place. Therefore, relatively few companies are able to successfully capture this knowledge and then 'convert' this value into a dynamic capability and resulting brand equity. *Inspired Villages* have been able to define, align and execute their brand strategy effectively the extent it has become a dynamic capability. The crux of this success was shared stake and ownership cross functionally. In other words, all colleagues no matter the level or role at *Inspired Villages* own the brand and are responsible for bringing it to life and defending it. The conditions for success relate the way within which the brand culture is formed around colleagues connecting, delivering and accountable in how the brand activity list is executed – whether that is design thinking for the village centres and facilities, the quality and finish properties, the health and well-being programme, or how the operations team bring the resident experience to life in the village community and so on.

The efficacy of executing and aligning brand strategy is the emphasis of the internal branding process. Internal branding is defined as "the set of strategic processes that align and empower employees to deliver the appropriate customer experience in a consistent fashion" (Ahmad, et al., 2014, p. 27). Furthermore, *Inspired Villages* ensured that their brand framework had a continued 'launch event' and continued evaluation that ensured all activities are aligning employees to "brands to create symbolic relationships that can lead to higher levels of brand identification, commitment, and citizenship behaviours" (Baumgarth & Schmidt, 2010; Burmann, Jost-Benz, & Riley, 2009; King, Grace, & Funk, 2012; Löhndorf & Diamantopoulos, 2014). This initiative is fundamentally a 'brand-orientated' employee experience strategy which included a range of activities such as workshops, training sessions, and communication programmes that were developed and implemented across the organisation, with a primary outcome: to create the employee–brand relationship (Santos-Vijande, del Rio-Lanza, & Diaz-Martin, 2013).

11.11 Customer journey, brand meaning, and equity: Community, life-style and purpose

Inspired Villages have worked in partnership with *FUZE* since 2018. Over that period, *FUZE* have helped shape the hybrid market orientation approach to help define and segment a unique and diverse customer-base across a complex 'eco-system' of *Villages*. The research established a clear resident framework and programme of helping the Board, Senior Management, and Operational staff team identify 'strategic levers' that can be prioritised to help ensure residents feel connected with the brand, its staff and that they are able to help shape their *Village* experience so that it is one that crucially meets and often exceeds their expectations, and ultimately, feels like they have found a new home and feel that they belong within the *Village*. The goal being to achieve a continued shift of increased resident satisfaction, with residents actively promoting and advocating the *Inspired Villages* brand. The following Table 11.2 highlights the various insights across the resident experience, allowing both customers and colleagues to invest meaning in the brand's purpose:

Table 11.2: Delivering on brand purpose.

Delivering on brand purpose	
Compelling purchasing 'triggers'	Delivering on core-brand proposition > Independent living + close to family + feeling safe & secure.
Strong positioning with a key brand advantage	Fulfilling very powerful needs at purchase such as autonomy and freedom, less stress, and the chance to enjoy other activities, the challenge as always is consistent brand delivery over the full customer journey (operationally).
Challenging assumptions, age is just a number	73.8% of residents rated their health as good, very good or excellent. Only 5.2% rated it as poor. Self-rated health is a key driver of general well-being. This represents a strong foundation to help *Inspired Villages* deliver on their strategic aims cultivate communities that challenge norms about ageing.

Table 11.2 (continued)

Delivering on brand purpose	
People are (still) making the difference	92.3% rated the customer service from village staff as good, very good or excellent.
Delivering on core purpose – holistic well-being and community	In 2020 the number 1 'Brand Advocacy' driver related to the broad definition of well-being, and how the facilities and lifestyle make a positive contribution to community and the resident's lives, which given the overriding challenges in 2020 and the context of COVID provides the brand with a very positive foundation for the future.
Social participation results demonstrate Inspired Village's impact	Overall group results show respondents are engaging more frequently across all the important activities that help deliver 'holistic well-being' in comparison to where they lived previously. However, there are key target improvements to be made at Village level.
Safety and security – still a stand-out result	91% of residents agreed to some extent that 'I feel safe and secure where I live' (at the Village). A key factor is finding the balance of feeling safe and secure, connected and not isolated, but having sufficient privacy. Positively, 88% of residents agreed to some extent that 'I have the privacy I want'.
Home is where the heart is	79% of residents agreed to some extent 'When I am in my property, it feels like I am at "home"'. The importance of this result cannot be understated – to belong and feel at home is a fundamental objective for *Inspired Villages*.
Holistic well-being as a key value proposition and the route to a competitive edge	There are clear conditions, characteristics and factors emerging per village that build a 'unique village culture' – and this will be a long-term competitive advantage.
A sense of 'belonging' remains steadfast in a year of flux	Overall, across the Group, 96% of respondents indicated they felt they belonged in their respective *Village* (the same as 2019). The reasons for belonging – community, friendship, atmosphere, and people – highlight *Inspired Villages* brand strength. The sense of belonging for new residents in 2020 was 98%. This is a clear brand advantage factor, belonging to a 'community' is fundamental in brand meaning.
Social participation for well-being impact	The highest rated aspect of the social activity programme was the quality of the well-being classes/activities with 64.2% of respondents rating this as excellent.
Delivering on property promise	The suitability for the residents' lifestyle was the highest rated property aspect with 89% rating this as positive (good-very good or excellent).
Peace of mind	In terms of overall village environment satisfaction, cleanliness of the *Village* shines through as the highest rated 71.3% (top 3 scores).

11.12 Key drivers for brand meaning and equity

A core brand purpose driver is the need to cultivate and manage the dynamics of a typical 'village community' (specifically for over 65s and all that entails) via a unique organisational culture at *Village* and group level. Each *Village* has a location based 'sub-brand' that is connected to a group level brand, which also is connected to a larger corporate brand. The complexity of these business models and brand relationship cannot be understated. However, the point here is that *Inspired Villages* are able to capture the uniqueness of each *Village* brand and respective culture so that residents are able to connect with the specific village offer, invest meaning in its overarching purpose and effectively attach and feel that they belong 'at home' and within the *Village* community, which is guided by the wider 'group-level' brand. As we have seen, the consistency in delivering a brand purpose rests on ensuring that the resident experience meets expectations (RMO), but also *Inspired Villages* are able to identify latent needs and proactively meet them in the future.

As we have said, purpose has to have meaning, and there is no meaning without value and values. Indeed, if we consider the context of *Inspired Villages'* brand purpose – *to deliver community, lifestyle, and health & well-being* – it is necessary to assess how customers are able to invest meaning in their resident experiences. At a strategic level, *FUZE* identified using validated predictors of well-being, which act as key brand quality drivers. In many ways the following Table 11.3 summarises these with interpretation and vignettes that have been weaved using various insights across multiple sources:

Table 11.3: Benefit & Belonging Since Moving to the Village – Well-being Drivers (Qualitative Vignettes).

Well-being Drivers	In what ways have you benefitted since moving to the *Village*? To what extent do you feel like you belong in the *Village*?
Meaning making	
– Social environment and 'community' – Interpersonal relationships – Networking	– Peace of mind: Residents cite that knowing their home is secure allows them to feel liberated and free to go venture out, meet friends and try new activities: *"I feel safe and secure, but not isolated, One has a feeling of security. Also, opportunity to join groups for different interests. The bottom line is that I am safe with help at hand 24/7"* – Beyond support: There is a real strength of 'community-driven support' that seems to characterise each *Village*, with many examples of a caring and supportive community (exampled by the challenges faced in the bereavement and illness of partners/ spouses): *"I was widowed last year, and I thank god that I live in the village – my life would have been very lonely if I had not."* – Strength in numbers: Residents feel their life has benefitted by meeting new people, which has been a catalyst to try new things and 'participate' in new activities. – Connecting with like-minded 'souls': The core drivers to tackle isolation that are prevalent in each village are community, friendships, and the companionship residents have found and benefited from: *"There are plenty of like-minded souls to do things with, I feel I have someone to turn to if I have a problem. But I feel have more company and have made new friends."* – Overcoming barriers, through a welcoming cultural 'habit' (resident-driven): Residents cited a clear recognition of each *Village* team doing their upmost to ensure those new to the village in 2020 were made to feel welcome, which given the challenging COVID context, is a real brand strength: *"settling in takes time and with the lock downs it is not very easy to socialise, but Inspired Villages are doing all they can to encourage us to belong to the village community. This is influenced by the welcoming and supportive attitude of staff. And the way there is a tradition (cultural) amongst long-standing residents of welcoming newcomers."*
– Identity and 'purpose' – Self-rated esteem and achievement	– New life, new confidence: The daunting challenge of starting a new life in an 'established' community should not be understated: *"Although my social life was curtailed when I moved from the place where I had lived for nearly 50 yrs.; I am now beginning to build a new life, but it is quite hard when you are older. But living here has brought me out of my shell, which has been a good thing."*

Table 11.3 (continued)

Well-being Drivers	In what ways have you benefitted since moving to the *Village*? To what extent do you feel like you belong in the *Village*?
	– Quality of life enhanced: The strong aspirational selling points are still prevalent: *"Overall moving to the village has improved my quality of life by relieving the stress and strains of running a home and garden."* – *Village* initiatives making a difference across these drivers: In general, there was an acknowledgement that for those who felt like they belonged, there have been various villages initiatives that have made a big impact, particularly at a time when there have been many restrictions.
Activities and participation	– Habitual connection: Connecting with like-minded people on a regular basis enables the formation of strong bonds and allows people to forge new friendship groups and feel confident to contribute to life and activities in the *Village*. – Power of green and rural 'third' space: It was clear throughout 2020, in various forms of feedback from the survey and interviews/discussion groups that gardens were a key priority/quality of life driver in the *Village*. This was noted in 2019 as a key driver, but over the lockdown periods these green spaces have been the residents' key outlet.
Voluntary work and 'engagement'	– The richness of volunteering: Social engagement in volunteering offers much more than a 'job': *"Volunteering in the bar and shop I have got to know many lovely people. Almost like having an extended family."*
Retirement lifestyle & goals achieved by living at the Village	– Living 'my' desired life: Overall *Villages* are fulfilling the aspirations of residents of living their version of supported independent living that maintains and enhances their quality of life; on their terms. – Stress-free living, with lots of options: Residents across the villages state how living at the *Village* is delivering on a stress-free life and allowing them to focus on enjoying themselves – on their terms: *"The benefit of living at the Village has taken the stress out of managing a large house and garden. Less time to work. More time to rest and play . . . Many more interests/opportunities right on my doorstep, many of which are free."* – Safety and security: In general, there was an acknowledgement by those who felt like they belonged and had seen some form of benefit since moving to the village, that safety and security was the key driver.

Table 11.3 (continued)

Well-being Drivers	In what ways have you benefitted since moving to the *Village*? To what extent do you feel like you belong in the *Village*?
Stimulation and physical activity	– Stimulation and physical activity is making a difference: There has been a recognition across the 2019 dataset that activities, stimulation and physical activity are tonics to a number of challenges that can be faced in later living, and the Village has benefitted those that engage: *"A wide range of activities are offered in the Village and I am enjoying taking full advantage of the opportunities offered when I am in residence. Physical, social and mental activities, improving wellbeing."* – Stimulation and physical activity is making a difference: The chosen lifestyle, and ability to participant in new interests: *"The Village has enriched my life and taken away many of life's pressures and provides varied choices"* – The pandemic situation has been a challenge, but out of crisis comes opportunity: *"My social life has changed, funnily for the better. I seem to have more 'friendly' contact with other residents, doing new activities or walking more."* Positive impact on health: *"Contact with other people has been better/I exercise more and have managed to lose some weight"*

Source: *FUZE Research*, 2019–2020 Total sample size n=586

Chapter takeaways

- *Inspired Villages* effectively adopt and continually implement market orientation by tackling the cultural perceptions of ageing and delivering far-reaching infrastructure, community, and social impact.
- Different types of market orientation are applied: *responsive* market orientation (RMO) which prioritises being responsive and receptive to existing customer needs; and *proactive* market orientation (PMO) which sets an agenda to identify and address customers' latent and tacit needs.
- *Inspired Villages* undertake both continuous proactive and reactive market orientation diagnosis (or a hybrid approach) in order to convert 'customer' intelligence into value across their an intuitive 'brand framework' and business model(s).
- Brand management can often be about balancing opposing forces: on the one hand maintaining consistency through delivery (tactically); on the other, the ability to adapt to environmental changes (macro/strategically).
- *Inspired Villages* have found a key point of difference with their ability to define, align, and execute a clear brand purpose from a set of values which sit within their brand framework, a key vehicle to set strategic intent and then deliver brand value and meaning.
- This case demonstrates the importance of brand meaning: effectively positioning the company as a community-driven lifestyle brand that delivers overall health and well-being for their customers and colleagues, and, in turn, customer and colleagues invest meaning in *their* shared brand purpose.
- Market orientation sets a broad agenda to identify and address customers' latent and tacit needs.
- *Inspired Villages* have successfully developed a hybrid version of market-orientation, adopting a PMO for certain long-term activities, and RMO for short-term evaluation of customer needs, expectations, and experiences.
- This case demonstrates the power of a culture of continuous improvement with a cyclical feedback loop, evidencing purpose and meaning in the integrated retirement communities context.

12 Small is beautiful: Big ambitions for SMEs

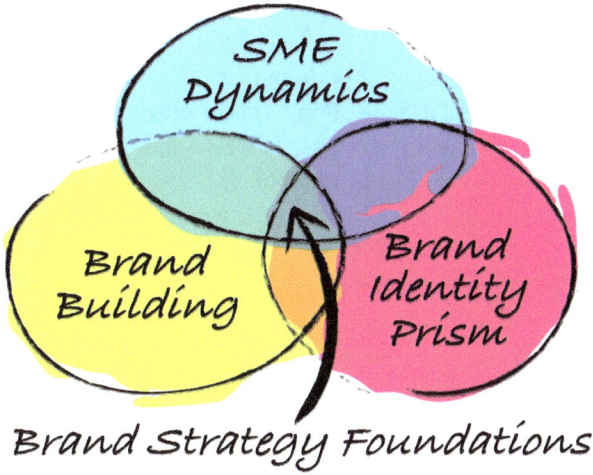

Brand Strategy Foundations

https://doi.org/10.1515/9783110718638-017

12.1 Outline of chapter

Historically, some SME owner-drivers have been accused of being "strategically my-opic", lacking a "long-term vision as to where their company is headed" (Mazzarol, 2004). More broadly of course, it is a business truism that strategic planning leads to increased business and financial performance. There is, however, a paradox for some SME owner/operators, a trade off in terms of prioritising strategic brand management and overall business performance, which has been argued to often rank "far behind intangible goals such as autonomy, personal satisfaction, lifestyle . . . and strategic planning may therefore have little value" (Wang, Walker, & Redmond, 2007, p. 2). As Berry (1998) suggests, neglecting strategic planning and the application of sound brand strategy principles may affect their growth potential and even survival. But whilst some SMEs operate as "extensions of their owner-managers" (LeCornu, McMahon, Forsaith, & Stanger, 1996, p. 2), as we have seen throughout the book, there are micro-brands and SMEs laying the foundations to adopt a more sophisticated and embedded approach to brand strategies.

The chapter further supports the need for improving brand management in SMEs, arguing for a contextual and fluid analysis by identifying an emerging continuum. Furthermore, it is underpinned by a *FUZE*-driven exploratory qualitative study, using primary data gathered and supported by *Be the Business,* an independent, Not-for-Profit organisation, whose mission is to centralise the importance of branding in helping SMEs become more productive. This throws the spotlight on how this new wave of micro-brands and SMEs are in fact developing the foundations of sophisticated and embedded brand strategies, where aligning brand identity and image is amongst the paramount tasks an SME brand should face. The outcome suggests that neglecting strategic planning and the application of sound brand strategy principles affects their ability to grow and scale, improve investment potential and crucially lay the foundations of a sustainable brand and even survival (Biraghi, Gambetti, & Quigley, 2020, p. 403). This chapter examines the role that a purpose-driven, cross-functional, customer-company brand fusion can play for micro-brands and brand-orientated SMEs even with resource/capability constraints and a restrictive 'strategic' mind-set.

Learning outcomes

After reading this chapter, you'll be able to:
- Explain the role that SMEs play in the global economy by assessing the critical issues and benefits that effective brand management can have for SMEs/aspiring micro-brands.
- Assess the potential impact a (micro/SME) purpose-driven brand strategy could have for high-growth organisations, whilst acknowledging the challenges and opportunities of size, resource, capability, and adaptability.
- Apply and explain the brand identity and image pitfalls SMEs face when developing and executing brand strategies, irrespective of size.

- Explain the core arguments that underpin the rigid assessment of brand management for large organisations and SMEs, and contrast this with the argument that brand management is a fluid and dynamic continuum.
- Contextualise the importance that effective brand orientation and management could have for SMEs.
- Evaluate the role organisations like *Be the Business* play in developing brand leadership and management capability/mind-set for founder/decision-makers in helping tackle the UK's productivity (wider environment) puzzle.

12.2 Introduction

The importance of small and medium size enterprises (SMEs) in the global market ecosystem cannot be understated. "Across the OECD, SMEs account for 99% of all businesses and between 50% and 60% of value added generated. Almost one person out of three is employed in a micro firm with less than 10 employees and two out of three in an SME" (OECD, 2019).[199] A key driving force in the development of the global economy is the success of building sustainable brands, irrespective of the size of the organisation. And yet despite this, brand management studies in the context of SMEs have received much less attention in comparison to larger and corporate organisations (Abimbola & Vallaster, 2007; Krake, 2005; Wong & Merrilees, 2005).

This chapter presents a unique focus on how effective brand management for SMEs can unlock growth and help strengthen the sustainability of these types of organisations. A 'micro' organisation can be defined as 1–9 employees; a 'small' business can be defined as 10–49 employees; a 'medium-sized' business has 50–249 employees; and a 'large' organisation has 250+ employees (OECD, 2019).

Much of the founding research around branding and brand management is grounded in the context of larger organisations (Aaker, 1991; Aaker & Keller, 1990). Larger organisations, typically, have a larger pool of resources, potentially greater expertise, and the ability to develop strategic brand capability. However, whilst the wider marketing literature for SMEs is well-developed (Carson, 1990; Carson & Cromie, 1990; Carson & Gilmore, 2000; Gilmore, Carson, O'Donnell, & Cummins, 1999; Gilmore, Carson, & Grant, 2001), it is argued that there is a need to focus on brand management in the context of SMEs (Spence & Hamzaoui-Essoussi, 2010).

In addition to effective market orientation (responsive, proactive, or hybrid), this is a fundamental building block, an integrated internal branding approach, of developing strategic brand management (eg: structure and function), continual assessment of competitive intensity, and overall brand orientation. A greater appreciation and evaluation of any perception gaps between brand identity (internal) and image (external) allows for a more holistic customer-driven, company fusion in

---

199 https://www.oecd.org/industry/smes/SME-Outlook-Highlights-FINAL.pdf

delivering customer experiences and value (short-term), and converting this value into brand equity (longer-term), whether that is B2B or B2C.

© Brett Jordan from Pexels via canva.com

12.3 The case for brand management in SMEs

Founders, directors and decision-makers who run successful and sustainable SMEs face both challenges and opportunities. Their success and sustainability comes from prioritising the importance and value of fostering a *collective purpose* that becomes the driving force of a meaningful brand. A core proposition of this book is to ensure that SMEs are able to translate, transfer, and apply a broader purpose-driven brand strategy to their organisational context. One critical success factor is the creation and maintenance of customer-company fusion whereby stakeholders, customers and employees are able to invest meaning, so that their key activities become focused on delivering their 'purpose'. A central platform for achieving this is prioritising brand management, which offers considerable benefits and opportunities for growth (Biraghi, Gambetti, & Quigley, 2020, p. 403).

Indeed, to reap these benefits, there are a number of key factors that allow SMEs to deliver stronger brand-orientation, which lead to improved brand performance and increased success in areas such as expansion (Spence and Essoussi, 2010). It is argued that the principal benefits of adopting a purpose-driven brand strategy are just as applicable to SMEs as they are to larger organisations, particularly in a time where many founders are driven by their own personal purpose.

Whilst some entrepreneurs set up a business through necessity (eg: a redundancy or at the end of an employment relationship), the majority do so after identifying a market opportunity and/or seeking greater autonomy and freedom in a given area of interest/personal motivation.[200] As we have seen with larger organisations (See *Chapter 10 Legal & General: inclusive capitalism – sustainability, change and purpose*), purpose-driven brand ESG strategies are becoming more prevalent and arguably more important in creating cross-stakeholder value. For start-ups seeking investment, it could be argued that creating a compelling brand narrative allows founders / decision makers to attract employees that connect with its purpose at the crucial early stages of growth, as well as evoking interest from investors or venture capitalists. For instance, 45% of Gen Zs want to work for a company that makes a positive difference to the world, with 65% stating they have the desire to personally create something world-changing.[201] This scenario provides an opportunity for purpose-driven micro brands/SMEs to attract talented people, who are more motivated to make a difference to the world than monetary returns alone, and thus improve the chances of early-stage growth and innovation.

Given the growing prevalence of conscious consumerism, it is inevitable that a new breed of start-ups, SMEs, and founders are responding to ESG challenges by building sustainable brands that deliver wider impact beyond financial performance. We have seen that there is much focus on conceptualising brand purpose, vision, and developing core values, but often this is done without sufficient care and attention of alignment, execution, and continuous monitoring/improvement, and this creates significant gaps that block the potential to exploit emerging brand equity.

12.4 Mind the gap: Brand identity prism

In organisations with smaller and 'flatter' structures, quite often the owner/founder and/or key decision-makers have a powerful influence on decisions which directly influence brand strategy (McCartan-Quinn & Carson, 2003). Whilst SMEs face challenges in terms of limited resources and expertise, developing a brand strategy presents a significant opportunity to embed robust brand management foundations, capability and knowledge to support decision-making and provide a competitive edge. When a start-up / SME is born, there is a significant focus on the name, logo, and website design, with the former being fundamental for the process of incorporation as a limited company (a common route), and equally as important when searching for distinctiveness as a sole trader.

For some start-up founders, they launch with a logo and accompanying website, the relevant business domain is purchased, the social media channels are launched

---

200 http://publications.aston.ac.uk/id/eprint/25172/1/Understanding_motivations_for_entrepreneurship.pdf
201 https://www.forbes.com/sites/markcperna/2019/12/10/gen-z-wants-to-change-the-world-at-your-company/?sh=513d13783c56

and this often becomes the main tool for building brand awareness and generating revenue (eg: e-shops). And yet, paradoxically, beyond the momentum from the initial creative design project, this is often where the brand identity strategy ends. Brand enthusiasm is at its peak, there is clarity, focus, and meaning, but often it is not codified, captured and continually evaluated. Founders lose focus and clarity and are often seduced by product-driven, day-to-day tactical issues, which are important, but so is building a strategic branding system that captures this value from day-to-day wins, over the long term. The brand image trap is set, the *internal company view* (brand identity) is often under-developed, or put aside, and there is very little strategy put in place to acknowledge and cultivate the brand image – the *external customer view* of that brand – and align this with what is espoused and hoped, versus what is signalled, communicated, and delivered for customers and potential customers. For instance, *Bain and Company* found that 80% of companies stated they deliver great service, from the same study, but only 8% of customers actually agreed.[202]

In simple terms, are SMEs and founders asking themselves whether the projected 'brand self-image' they reflect is what their customers actually see and experience (Kapferer (1992, p.38)? If not, then they are falling into the 'self-image trap'. Figure 12.1 applies a simple scenario with a B&B where there is alignment between the different perspectives of a founder and customer, and therefore an aligned reflection.

For some SMEs who find early success, the key focus is not long-term brand strategy but building investor momentum, prioritising high-growth returns, and often includes a road-map towards a successful exit or even initial public offering (IPO), leading to private to public company transition. However, as demonstrated throughout the book, developing and implementing a sophisticated brand strategy and capability can help gain the much-needed early traction and momentum. After all, investors make their decision on return of investment, total available market, and having a capable leadership team (amongst many other factors). Key drivers are its brand standing, value, and overall equity. Therefore, establishing an aligned identity-image with effective positioning will only strengthen the long-term development of the business (as we have seen in *Chapter 9 Managing brand equity: tangible results from intangible assets*). The prism of identity can either be a catalyst of success or a trap in waiting. The tonic is an effective brand strategy, irrespective of size and resource. However, this brand strategy needs to be a 'cultural mindset', often instigated by a founder/senior leader but lived by its employees and judged by its customers. For some, this mind-set is perhaps not prioritised to the extent that it should be.

---

202 *Bain and Company*, "Closing the Delivery Gap", 2005.

The photo(s) used in this case study is not connected and/or does not represent any brand(s) mentioned. It used to make a visual discussion point by the authors.

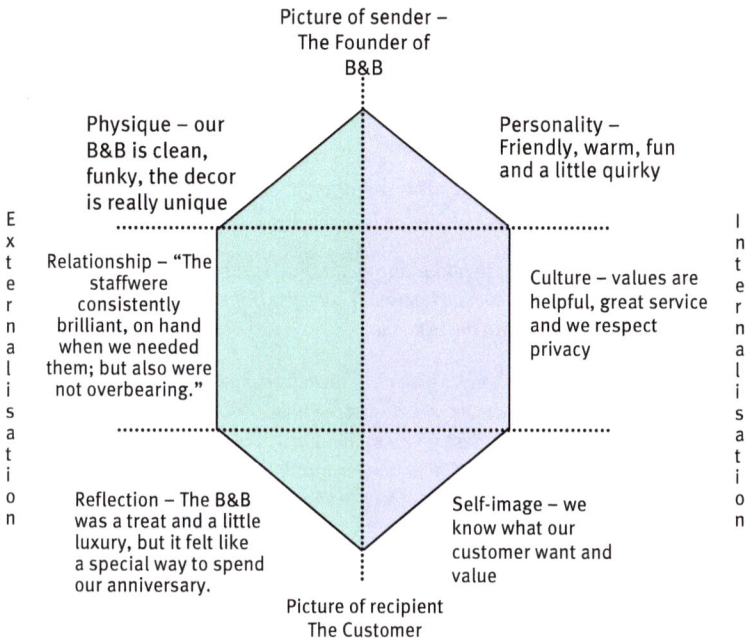

Figure 12.1: Identity Prism.
Source: Authors' representation (2022). Adapted from Kapferer (1998, p. 32)

12.5 The role of brand strategy in SMEs: Act small, think big

Let's look at the role brand strategy can play in SMEs and what can be learnt from applying a corporate mindset to micro-brand problems? Tom Lord, was previously the Head of Global Operations, for the *InterContinental Group*, which includes brands such as *Crowne Plaza, Regent, Holiday Inn,* and *Hotel Indigo* to name but a few. Lord holds over 23 years' experience in the leisure and hotel industry, where understanding and executing branding strategy spans over 5,000 operational hotels ranging from corporate level down to individual hotels. Here, for restaurants, gyms and spas, something akin to an 'SME brand strategy' would be required. Solving micro-brand strategy problems on the ground, (which could include scenarios like the positioning of a single hotel's restaurant brand in a local market), has given him an insight into what is needed from micro through to global group level.

Lord's reflections on his vast experience in the service industry offers a useful insight to *any* budding founder for a micro/start-up SME looking to lay the foundations of any emerging brand strategy, or, indeed, reversing the learning, large organisations that are perhaps applying the restrictive, reductive view of branding:

If you were starting a business tomorrow . . . . What would my golden rule be? . . . Start with your purpose. Why are we here? What are you going to do? How are you going to do it? Why are we different? What do our potential customers want, need and value? How are we going to bring the business to life? But we also have to emotionally connect with the team and customers so that they are proud of what we do.

After answering ALL this, then the do the last 20% – right, what are we going to name ourselves? Don't start with the name!

You start with what value you are going to add to the world. But, in a service world, you have to speak and connect emotionally with your customers. If the first thing they see is a word they don't understand, they will just move onto the next one!

If I were setting up a restaurant [in a hotel] – which I have over my time – as you design the restaurant, (traditionally) we will get a designer to design the hotel – they are amazing at designing hotel lobbies, bedrooms, and putting these lovely touches in . . . and we will get this designer to design the restaurant as well . . . but there is a danger that it just becomes a restaurant in a big room. And it connects with the hotel design and feel, brilliantly.

Then someone says, 'What is it going to do? What will this restaurant actually deliver and be about?' The answer, for example, would be, "It fits a bistro" . . . So we do a bistro. Then they walk outside and see next door is a bistro, and there are two more down the road and we have just designed something that cannot be anything but a bistro!

So, now we have done our market analysis and the best chance for success – would be, say, "An Italian restaurant". Yeah, but that design (brand identity) doesn't lend itself to being an Italian restaurant. You need to design from a place of what your customers are actually going to want, the market opportunity. And that brand identity needs to tell that story – reflecting that desired (brand) image of what customer perceive and want from an italian resturant.

So, now we have a new concept – right so it is an Italian, and that can be fine dining or a pizza shop – and then you do the name. You don't call it Papa Luigi's Pizza and do fine dining. If you have to work it all out and then devise the name after. It is easier to test, adjust, iterate after the analysis, rather than go with the name first. Otherwise, the design doesn't purvey the passion and emotion required, then the look and feel of the brand will be wrong."

If people just took the time to think, analyse, develop what goes into a brand strategy it would save time, money and resources in the long run – this is all underpinned by constant customer and employee feedback.

In this simple but clear example there are some underpinning factors that could help SMEs and micro-brands:

- Ensure any brand is not being solely *product*-driven. 80% of the activity (such as market orientation diagnosis, segmentation, targeting, preliminary positioning, and planning) could and should be undertaken prior to the last 20% (of choosing name and logo, and fine tuning the brand identity).
- Have a cultural mind-set to continually review and evaluate the alignment between what you say about your brand, and what your customer's actually perceive, experience, and value. It is an ever-changing dynamic, complex and

iterative process, building in the need for continuous feedback from customer, company and stakeholders.
- SME branding is high stakes, whereby resource is limited, and expertise is not always at hand. Following the 80–20 rule could (to some extent) help mitigate such risk and bridging a gap between brand identity (internal view) and brand image (external view).

Lord further shares some insights around how to approach the strategic brand management function, with the importance of stating what brand is and how best to define it must be at the centre of the organisation's mindset. Using the brand framework is a key vehicle to set strategic intent and then deliver effectively market orientated strategic choices. When asked how he would define a brand, the general gap between conceptualising and the effective execution becomes clear:

> *"I'll start with a question, what it should be or what it is?"* *The answer is two-fold:*
> 1. *What it should be – a brand should reflect the essence of the company, be linked with what your purpose is, and continually bring that to life. It should always be a reminder to all your team and your customers about what you do, who you are, and why you do it.*
> 2. *What it tends to be – Unfortunately, traditionally a lot of brands have been just a fancy logo, that just sits on a product and doesn't have any emotional strategy behind it. And, even if the brand is created / conceptualised with the emotion concept at the start, it doesn't necessarily factor in how you continually build in meaning and emotional value over time.*
> *More often than not, those that build the brand with the clear emotional connection do not execute and activate that strategy effectively. There is a disconnect. Fundamentally, brands should have an emotional connection with who you and what you do.*

What makes this a distinctive and pragmatic point, is that quite often the key fundamentals (such as purpose, alignment, and the essence of the company), focus on serving an added value to both team and customers and the key dynamics required to continually reinforce this on an ongoing basis. Holt (2002) argues that there are as many branding consultants as there are 'soulless' branding terms. This often builds barriers between those who conceptualise and those who are responsible and accountable for continually executing this value to the market. There is an incredible amount of focus, time, and resource (internal and external) on this conceptualisation stage. What is evident in these quotes is the need to focus on execution and evaluation in any such strategy.

Lord articulates the importance of asking some basic, but pertinent questions in executing brand strategy, irrespective of the size of the organisation, as brands, an employee base and organisational structure develops, the following principles could help SMEs lay the foundations toward a dynamic capability and also how to reduce the possibility of such a gap forming:

Who owns the brand? Every company should ask themselves this. However, the answer isn't simple . . . as no-one [or everyone?] owns the brand. The marketing teams decides on the toolkit so that runs through the marketing communications. If the marketing department owns the brand totally, it tends to create a 'silo' over protected guardian approach and just becomes an inflexible customer marketing piece. By that I mean, for example, that is not ever designed to bring the brand to life for the internal 'customers' (employees).

So, a good example, if you are trying to attract Over 65–75s with your external customer marketing, but 25-year-olds for your internal people and recruiting new roles. But you can't deviate from the external communications – but you are trying to convey the employee value proposition and all that entails from a branding perspective. If you kept to the external communication tone, then you are going to switch off the internal customer audience. You have got to be flexible [and the paradox is] that no one 'owns' the brand, but everyone needs to be passionate, defend it and responsible for bringing it to life in an aligned way so that it echoes with each other across the organisation, but doesn't jar against any internal-external customer piece.

So, revisiting that question, who owns the brand . . .? Everyone has a stake in it in some way or form. Then it is really the question of – who is accountable as part of their role/team outcome for the 'brand activity list' [ie: who is accountable for bringing the brand to life]?

a. Who owns how you market the brand to your external customer? Your marketing team.
b. Who owns how you bring your brand to life internally? Your people and culture team.
C. Who owns how you bring those customer experiences to life? The operations team.
d. And so on . . .

12.6 The role of brand management in SMEs

There is now a growing body of research in an SME context to suggest that brand management still has a vital role to play (Lin, Ansell, Marshall, & Ojiako, 2019; Krake 2005). Krake (2005) compiled a comprehensive list of key brand management aspects in relation to SME, repeated here but adapted to the context of this chapter:

- *Reductive concept*: Branding is not a priority in that this starts and ends with the logo, it is principally product-driven, with very little attention to the importance of brand management in daily tasks or business-brand performance measures (Krake, 2005).
- *Brand autocracy, but no central function/accountability*: The founder/senior decision maker determines brand policy, which can lead to a great focus on brand, but in many cases if the importance of brand management is not prioritised it can result in increasing the chances of its perception as a reductive concept. There is no ownership or accountability for the brand whether that is a dedicated employee or the founder/director, respectively. It tends to be product-only focus sitting in 'cultural silos'.
- *Brand identity, cultural congruence*: Brand-customer-company fusion has multiple benefits, but more specifically, brand identity strategy guides brand decisions, and therefore demands an alignment with organisational culture, bringing the core-values to life. Indeed, this is the focal point for many larger organisations, which has great potential for barriers. Krake (2005) argues that in SMEs, entrepreneurs are typically visionary characters whose own personality mirrors that of the brand personality. This is a potential source of advantage if a clear link between founder and brand can be established.
- *Clarity over cleverness*: In only 50% of SMEs, company and brand name are the same, and it is very common for these companies to use more than one brand name. SMEs face even greater challenges in developing brand awareness and being able to prioritise resources around single-point brand proposition is arguably a better use of precious resources and capability. Krake argued that if there is little connection between company, product/service, and brand there is a greater risk of a disconnect between brand identity (internal) and image (external), with company and product/service also competing for attention, comprehension and equity.
- *Collaborate or compete*: Krake found that many SMEs don't want to co-brand or collaborate with other organisations, which allows businesses to build partnerships and leverage potential brand value across ecosystems.

According to Davari, Srivastava and Paswan, (2020), effective market and brand orientation is proven to positively influence brand performance more than the size of organisation. However, other research suggests that there does tend to be brand building activities and characteristics that relate to organisational size. These should be interpreted as a continuum/spectrum, where some activities and characteristics are fluid and move between context; it should not be used as an 'either or list'. The exploratory study demonstrates how brand strategy is emergent in SMEs: there is no set path; it develops organically and is relevant to the context and culture of the business and sector which it operates within. Spence and Hamzaoui-Essoui (2010) throw some light on this by comparing brand building and management in large organisations and SMEs (highlighted in Table 12.1):

Table 12.1: Comparison of brand building and management in large organisations and SMEs.

Activity	Large Organisations	SMEs
Brand "culture" Brand identity	Sophisticated and embedded concept. Visionary strategic management with a systematic evaluation of alignment with image based on extensive market, brand and customer research, filling a gap in the marketplace	Reductive concept Visionary individual = the entrepreneur = opportunity for brand personality Intuitive/innate process as an embodiment of the entrepreneur's personality and values
Brand equity	Associations networked that is the fabrication of key consumer research and linked to consumer needs and product features Sophisticated evaluation and continuous learning system	Associations derived from the entrepreneur's personality and values as well as from consumer needs and product features Measurement of brand equity not a priority typically not on the measurement agenda/KPIs
Brand strategies	A multitude of strategies are being used locally and internationally, with the aim of maximizing market coverage and minimizing market overlaps – standardisation is the targeted outcome Corporate/group branding is part of the overall brand strategy development	A limited number of strategies are being used. Collaborative strategies as well as corporate branding not generally used – lack of leveraging ecosystems. Different levels of brand orientation have been observed
Organization structure	Brand responsibilities spread over several departments and functions	Brand responsibilities handled by the entrepreneur and the entrepreneurial team

Table 12.1 (continued)

Activity	Large Organisations	SMEs
Marketing mix	A wide range of highly visible and integrated marketing communication campaigns/programs	The emphasis is on the product A wide diversity of innovative and more or less integrated actions depending on the firm Search for low costs tactics that would maximize impact Internationally, minimum national requirements should be met and local adaptations are left to horizontal partners

Source: Adapted from Spence and Hamzaoui-Essoui (2010)

12.7 Drivers for success in SME brand building and management

As (Renshaw, 2021) states, "A purpose should remain timeless, but its translation is ever evolving". The process of developing a purpose-driven brand strategy requires an acknowledgement from the outset that, whilst the essence of a brand's purpose may remain constant and timeless, its translations must be dynamic in its response to the environment. As evidenced throughout the book, having a strong brand strategy alignment and customer orientation acts as an anchor for its customers and provides a foundation when market conditions are in flux, all of which are paramount to improving brand performance (Iyer, Davari, Srivastava and Paswan, (2020).

The following have been identified as key factors that could help support founders/decision makers in undertaking a 'pre-purpose assessment' to identify a market orientation typology (Narver, Slater and MacLachlan (2004):

Overall approach and effectiveness of branding and internal branding and strategic brand management.   (Santos-Vijande, del Rio-Lanza, Suarez-Alvarez, and Diaz-Martin, 2013)

Competitive intensity.   (Jaworski and Kohli, 1993)

Overall brand orientation.
          (Muhammad Anees-ur-Rehman, Ho Yin Wong, Parves Sultan, Bill Merrilees, 2018)

These factors have been used to inform an exploratory qualitative study undertaken by *FUZE* with 24 UK SMEs of varying size from micros (1–9 employees) through to larger medium sized (up to 250 employees), across a broad range of industries including IT/software, construction, professional services, publishing, real estate, retail, aerospace, legal and food manufacturing, engineering, hospitality and education. The seniority of participants were key decision makers, ranging from Founders, Managing Directors, CEOs and Senior Directors. Being exploratory in nature, this study may not be wholly representative of the UK's SME community, but as an indicative pilot to explore some key themes it does cover a number of useful contexts. Participants are responsible for making brand strategy decisions for their brand as well as a sizeable employee base, which spanned over 1,822 employees (for those who responded).

The following Table 12.2 summarises selective responses and themes, combining data-vignettes from two distinctive typologies: one that aligns more closely to 'Reductive' aspects; one with a more 'Embedded and Sophisticated' orientation.

Table 12.2: Emerging SME brand typologies.

'Reductive' Typology
Defining brand: – What is interesting, is that 50% of participants defined it from varying reductive viewpoints: "We don't have one, as we are just an accountants [50 employees]". "Non-existent – we are engineers [248 employees]". "No Idea [4 employees]". "the logo and name [30 employees]". – The remaining merely named the sectors in which their businesses worked in, the following quote capturing the challenge of breaking through this reductive mind-set: "Branding is not that important for us, we are too small and only have 25 employees, and we work in professional services, so it isn't relevant."
How does branding influence your strategy? – The responses indicate limited influence to varying degrees, with a lack of appreciation of it power and importance to overall business performance and sustainability, irrespective of market: "It doesn't influence it all, sits with marketing". "We market in the Middle East, so it is not as important". "I don't regard it as crucial as we are well established".
'Early' Stage – Embedded/Sophisticated – Typology
Define branding: There was a rich mixture of responses/themes, highlighting the complexity of defining brand and what it means. Nonetheless, the following is indicative of how these decision-makers are prioritising brand:
A journey from reductive to embedded: – "We are a 3rd generation family business. Taking over from the 2nd, 8 years ago, there was no understanding or engagement with the concept of "brand", even though the pride in our products, management style and customer engagement was unique and told a compelling story. Now, after a lot of rewarding work, we realise how lucky we are to be able to present ourselves to the world with an engaging and authentic story. For us, our brand tells the story of the impact that our values have right across our business: the relationships with suppliers, employees and customer [Manufacturer 100+ employees]".
Brand purpose and meaning-making: – "It's a combination of factors: (1) we are a well-established firm with a strong history in Manchester. [With] a reputation for high quality and standards for those who know us already but try to project this to the outside world for those newly engaging. We also put a lot of emphasis on our values as a fair, personable firm with genuine CSR credentials. These come to us naturally as a firm that wants to help effect people's lives positively [as a professional legal services – 150+ employees]."

Table 12.2 (continued)

Lived and real, codifying the brand implicitly?
- "We don't have a documented definition, but our brand is our identity, tone of voice, credentials, our promise to our customers. It reflects what we stand for, what we deliver and what customers can consistently expect from us [micro 6 employees – Engineering]"

How does branding influence your strategy?
The themes ranged from the importance if brand purpose, reputation management, embedding values and connecting these with customer and growth. The following indicates the maturity/ stages of this typology:

Early design and acknowledgement of assessing brand identity and image:
- "I confess we may not have verbalised this before. We did a lot of work about our Purpose hope our branding all reflects our purpose"

The emerging importance building strategic brand management capability and brand orientation (adopting an integrated brand system):
- "Our growth plans are influenced by market opportunity and our values which then flow out to form our brand strategy. we have never considered using brand to influence anything "upstream"
Brand strategy as customer-company fusion, highly connected and integrated, not siloed and 'separate', by symbiotic:
- "We don't have a brand strategy in its own right, bur brand plays its part in our 5-year plan where our vision is to become the world's leading provider of customer-centric fluid power solutions – an independent hub connecting a fragmented, product-led marketplace. We are working to continue to strengthen our brand and proposition to support the generation of higher margin income streams and further differentiate ourselves from our competitors as a quality, value-creating solutions."

How the branding acts as a North Star to navigate the challenging frontier of growth over time:
- "Leads to growth over time by staying true to our values. It is a central part of most decision making".
Top Barriers to innovation and growth:
Interestingly, it was noted that there were clear themes that emerged across the sample, in relation to:
- COVID pressures, Brexit and supply challenges, but also a lack skills within existing teams, retaining talented staff, being able to enter new markets (domestic and international) and attracting new customers. Clearly, an effective brand strategy can help alleviate some of these issues (political and economic macro-factors) around employer brand and reputation, growth and innovation culture that epitomises a customer-company fusion as well as building brand equity to provide a platform to launch into new markets.

Source: *FUZE Research* (2021).

The emerging themes and results highlight the complexity faced by SMEs and Micro brands in developing and executing brand strategies. Yet there is also evidence to suggest that there is a continuum emerging: a very reductive view-point is being applied (at one end); and also a more sophisticated approach which has a clear view of embedding strategic brand management, developing capability and 'mindset', and cultivating an internal branding culture (at the other end). Whilst these leaders, founders and decision-makers seem to be at different stages of developing and executing a brand strategy (in general) with some initial traction toward a purpose-driven brand strategy, it could be argued that there is an opportunity to use the early-stage framework of brand fusion to help catalyse the process of becoming more brand orientated. Embedding the principles of a sophisticated brand strategy can guide strategic decisions on: brand "culture"; brand identity; brand equity; brand strategies; organization structure; and marketing mix.

All this needs expertise, learning and support to design and deliver (ie: effectively applying), irrespective of the size of the organisation. At a basic level of knowledge, understanding and comprehension, the decisions and foundations can be laid to develop overtime to find efficacy in developing a purpose-driven brand strategy.

12.8 The productivity puzzle of SMEs

Generally, improving productivity has long been a challenge in the UK. UK businesses, and individuals within them, work more hours for the same output in comparison to other countries in the G7:

> Productivity is the efficiency and effectiveness of operating business. Economists use the term productivity to measure how effectively businesses use labour (ie: people/human capital) and capital (ie: the financial assets needed for a business to operate) to generate products and services for its customers.[203] (*OECD*, 2020)

In the UK Government 2019 *'Business Productivity Review'*,[204] two factors associated with *iMPACT* were identified as being directly linked to firm-level productivity:
- Leadership and management.
- Technology diffusion and adoption – specifically CRM (eg: customer relationship) software.

---

203 https://www.oecd.org/sdd/productivity-stats/40526851.pdf
204 *Business Productivity Review* (2019) UK HM Government, online at https://assets.publishing.service.gov.uk/government/uploads/system/uploads/attachment_data/file/844506/business-productivity-review.pdf
The photo(s) used in this case study is not connected and/or does not represent any brand(s) mentioned. It used to make a visual discussion point by the authors.

The *Business Productivity Review* (2019) states that even small improvements in management practices can be associated with up to a 5% increase in the growth rate of a business's productivity. As identified throughout this chapter and book, *branding, doesn't* and *shouldn't* sit in a neat, siloed box: an effective brand and brand strategy has a unique set of principles, and is (centrally) connected to a sophisticated ecosystem of customer-company fusion. It could be argued that an aligned and effective brand orientation and performance, with its strong link to improving business and financial performance provides:

> Effective management of brand loyalty, perceived quality, and brand image positively affect financial performance.　　　　　　　　　　　　　　　　(Hong-bumm, Woo Gon, & An, 2003)

> A stronger footing for competitive intensity.　　(Jaworski & Kohli, 1996) (Jaworski and Kohli, 1993)

> Overall brand orientation.　　　　　　　(Anees-ur-Rehman, Wong, Sultan, & Merrilees, 2018)

Additionally, there is a greater focus on technology adoption in terms of boosting productivity. Indeed, it was highlighted that adopting a range of basic technologies is associated with a productivity improvement of between 7% to 18%.[205] Analysis from the *Office of National Statistics* also shows the use of two or more business management technologies is associated with productivity gains of up to 25%. These technologies include accountancy software, customer relationship management systems (CRM), supply chain management and enterprise resource planning software. Low uptake of these existing technologies has been suggested as one of the reasons for the UK's relatively poor productivity performance.

This is a broader and more generalised business view; clearly, technology diffusion and developing leadership and management capability are significant levers to improve productivity levels, particularly for SMEs. However, evidenced throughout this chapter and book, deploying (or working toward) an embedded and sophisticated brand strategy, that prioritises purpose, profit and meaning-making could also be a key catalyst for micro-brands and SMEs that have high growth ambitions and being more productive.

---

205 *Business Productivity Review* (2019) HM Government, online at https://assets.publishing.ser vice.gov.uk/government/uploads/system/uploads/attachment_data/file/844506/business-productivity -review.pdf

12.9 Building productive brands in SMEs: Be the Business

There is an organisation that is endeavouring to be the tonic to the UK's wider SME productivity puzzle – *Be the Business,* an independent, Not-for-Profit organisation. Anthony Impey MBE, CEO of *Be the Business*, highlights their purpose:

> *Our goal is crucial for to the health of the UK's economy. The UK lags behind comparable nations in terms of productivity. But, by improving the performance of small business leaders, we improve the UK's position overall, and everyone benefits. We work with some of the UK's most successful businesses to provide small business leaders with the support, resources, and guidance they need to improve their productivity.*

Be the Business has far-reaching impact and scope and includes a '*Productivity Leadership Group*'[206] by some of the UK's senior leaders, from organisations like *EY UK&I (Earnst & Young), Nestle, Trinity Sky, Rolls-Royce, UBS, Amazon, KPMG, Accenture UK&I, Channel 4, BAE Systems* and *Facebook.* Their key activities covers:

> *We offer online support through our website, with business stories, action plans, and guides all freely available*

> *Our flagship programmes provide tailored, in-depth support for business leaders*

> *We publish research and studies from the frontline of small business, helping us to understand leaders and help them be more productive*

> *Our campaigns spread awareness of the productivity movement, demonstrating the benefits of moving forward, and tackling information gaps and fixed mindsets.*

---

206 https://www.bethebusiness.com/about-us/who-we-are/productivity-leadership-group/

This forward-thinking organisation champions the importance of brand strategy, and how being brand orientated is a key lever for improved business and financial performance and productivity. Shanni Elcock, SME Engagement Lead, highlights how *Be the Business* are catalyst for change, and how SMEs can adopt a 'big thinking and ambitious' brand strategy, has the potential positive impact businesses and the wider economy:

> *Our Ambassadors are a key part of the Be the Business movement. This network of business leaders exemplifies our productivity goal and the behaviours that we believe others would benefit from. As well as speaking on our behalf to other business leaders and to the Government, our Ambassadors are a crucial part of the day-to-day running of Be the Business – they help us decide on appropriate products and marketing from their invaluable perspective on the frontline of the small business sector.*

> *Our Ambassadors play an essential role in Be the Business' brand identity, key for business success small and large. Indeed, a core productivity practice is setting a vision and strategy for your business, and then sharing it internally with employees – once everyone is united under the same vision, they can work towards the same goal and increased productivity. Similarly, a vision directly correlates with a brand, which is the impression that customers have of a company. During my time as an SME Engagement Lead, I have witnessed, on multiple occasions, the moment that our Ambassadors realise the impression their business promotes is different from the one they want. This is largely because they haven't set a decisive vision, which has prevented them from communicating their brand identity with anyone else, internally or externally.*

> *To improve their performance and productivity, small business leaders must adopt a more sophisticated approach to defining and communicating their brand identity. Luckily, these businesses can play directly to their main strength: size. By being small, they can be reactive and agile. Any vision can easily be permeated across the business quickly and effectively, if done well, meaning that a small business leader can change their brand identity within a relatively small timeframe.*

> *However, it's essential that small business leaders recognise that a sophisticated approach doesn't mean hiring an army of graphic designers and content writers! Instead, business leaders must make sure that their vision is translated and adopted across the business first, influencing employee behaviours prior to external success.*

One key activity that *Be the Business* undertake for their 'ambassadors' is targeted content, support and action-plans. It is clear that *Be the Business* align strongly with the brand fusion framework and notion that being brand orientated can be a key driver for success for SMEs of all sizes, sectors and stages. The right mind-set in develop leadership and management capability, along with technology diffusion, is important, but so too is the context and the need to bond brand-customer-company, also. For instance, there following are two (vignettes) selective mini-examples that champion and 'embed' the key elements of this emerging SME brand fusion framework:

- *Brand advocacy should be embedded:* "Brand advocacy is built on a personal connection with the business: (1) Your brand can add value – an effective brand gives you an edge over competitors; (2) Education helps with brand buy-in (employees) – your employees need to know why your business exists – and why that matters – if they're going to champion it; (3) make your brand part of your culture – Factor your brand in everything you do, from customer service to recruitment." (Kinloch Anderson, Scotland, Retail & Wholesale).[207]

– *Bridging image and identity:* "Understanding what customers think you do, can improve your messaging: (1) Customers can inform your USP – The first step towards effective messaging is understanding what customers think your business does best; (2) Customer opinions should be embraced – Communicating why people choose your business can really help to improve messaging and make it resonate with new and existing customers; (3) Simplicity is key – Trying to squeeze too much into your messaging can confuse, overwhelm or bore customers. Keep it simple and focus on one key thing." (Fabulosa, Northwest England, Consumer Goods).[208]

Chapter takeaways

- SMEs play a vital role in the global economy. Therefore, the effectiveness of their associated brand strategies should be seen as important.
- Better understanding of the definition of a micro, small, and medium-sized organisations.
- In comparison to larger and corporate organisations, brand management studies have focused less on the SME context.
- There are significant opportunities for SMEs to translate, transfer, and apply a broader purpose-driven brand strategy to their organisational context.
- SMEs that prioritise brand management can offer significant benefits and opportunities for growth, improved reputation, brand performance, increased success in expansion, and positively impact financial performance.
- Some SMEs may focus on day-to-day tactical issues and lose sight of the imperative of building a strategic branding system that captures brand meaning, learning, and value.
- SMEs and founders of SMEs should ask themselves, whether projected 'brand self-image' reflects what customers actually see, experience, and say about their company.
- A useful framework discussed was that 80% of the activity (such as market orientation diagnosis, segmentation, targeting, preliminary positioning, and planning,) could and should be undertaken prior to the last 20% (of choosing name, logo, and fine tuning the brand identity). It should be an ongoing learning process.
- There are reductive versus sophisticated approaches to branding which are not binary choices. There is emerging evidence that in reality, SMEs are adopting an embedded and sophisticated approach albeit at different stages.
- Effective market and brand orientation has a crucial role to play in SMEs helping tackle the UK's productivity puzzle.

---

207 https://www.bethebusiness.com/real-business-stories/brand-advocacy-is-built-on-a-personal-connection-with-the-business/
208 https://www.bethebusiness.com/real-business-stories/understanding-what-customers-think-you-do-can-improve-your-messaging/

13 Festival of Thrift: Sustainability through brand community

https://doi.org/10.1515/9783110718638-018

13.1 Outline of chapter

Companies that extend their mission beyond 'selling goods' to 'doing good' can improve competitive positioning and enhance consumers' lives. 'Social purpose' can give a unifying community connection between company and customer, and be an effective way to change an organisation's mission. However, when the impetus comes from the community itself, one can lead to the formation of a company that embodies a community mission, that is authentic to a common goal. An exemplar of this is the *Festival of Thrift* (*FoT*), a community interest company (CIC) with a mission to "benefit the community and advance public awareness of sustainable living". They have a clear brand purpose and manifesto, grounded in creating a rich emotional economy, within which its community are inspired to make small, incremental attitudinal and behavioural changes in relation to sustainability.

Every penny they raise is reinvested into organising activities and engaging as many people as possible in improving people's lives and making a positive impact on the environment. Their aim is to reach new audiences and build new partnerships with individuals and organisations who share the company ethos – 'The Shift to Thrift' – showing how small personal changes can make a big difference to the future of the planet.

This chapter is devoted to discussing how the values of a group of like-minded individuals built a company with purpose from a collective conscience. As such, it is a model of a brand community being served by a joint mission and purpose, benefiting the individual and the collective. It demonstrates how the principles of social purpose, grown through the relationships of a brand community, can become a model of how brands can win from harnessing mission to growth, and how taking a social stand can having mutually beneficial outcomes beyond profit.

Learning outcomes

After reading this chapter, you'll be able to:
- Analyse why the *Festival of Thrift* have developed a brand purpose and manifesto, with clear objectives, in relation to their marketing environment.
- Assess the role that customer research and insight plays in evaluating and informing (planning) *Festival of Thrift's* brand strategy.
- Determine the value of brand community, attachment, and meaning in relation to the *Festival of Thrifts'* brand purpose.
- Evaluate how *Festival of Thrift* responded to external and internal environment conditions, to digitally optimise, innovate, and make effective strategic decisions.
- Identify and analyse how *Festival of Thrift* were able to integrate digital and offline marketing approaches.
- Assess how *Festival of Thrift* digitally enhanced their approach with effective stakeholder engagement.

13.2 Introduction

In September 2013, in Darlington, a small market town in the Northeast of England, thousands of people flocked to experience inspirational speakers who had joined forces with 'skill sharers' and 'ethical traders' and presented a platform "to place creativity at the heart of a shared, sustainable future and celebrate a new way of ethical living". From those humble beginnings, the *Festival of Thrift (FoT)* brand was born. Artists were positioned as inspirers to action, opinion leaders who encouraged change through workshops, exhibitions, and performances, and encouragement and confidence was given to families to create whilst having fun on a budget. From the huge success of that first festival, word-of-mouth spread, the gatherings got bigger, *FoT* formally became a community interest company (CIC), and a company *Festival of Thrift (CIC)* was established based in Redcar in 2015 with a mission to benefit the community and advance public awareness of sustainable living. All income that is raised via the Festival is reinvested back into organising and delivering its broad range of activities (such as skills workshops and community outreach programmes), endeavouring to increase brand awareness, engagement and building a solid foundation to deliver their mission.

FoT has a clear brand purpose and manifesto, grounded in creating a rich emotional economy, within which its community are inspired to make small, incremental attitudinal and behavioural changes in relation to sustainability. They state their aim as:

> *Our focus has always been on how we as individuals can make those small changes, the shift to thrift, that will add up to a big difference for the future of our planet, and encouraging others to join in.*

FoT's objectives are to:
- *Promote the concept of sustainable living and be a voice for sustainable issues, globally and locally.*
- *Build a unique and distinctive, fun and sustainable national event, drawing positive media attention to Redcar & the Tees Valley.*
- *Share the skills of artists and craftspeople, professional and amateur, to inspire people of all ages to learn old ways and find new ways to be creative in their everyday lives.*
- *Ensure wider economic benefit through encouraging visitor spend on travel, accommodation, restaurants & related businesses.*
- *Contribute to community cohesion through wide engagement in our programme, volunteering and participation.*
- *Celebrate the heritage and contribute to the future prosperity of Redcar & Tees Valley, and its business and industry.*

These strategic brand objectives act as a clear framework to design and deliver a festival, which includes pre-launch learning programmes with online learning and education outreach, a two-day festival typically held in September annually, and an emerging online marketplace. The *Festival* has consistently delivered excellent customer experience (both online and physically at the *Festival*) that has allowed its community members to bond with its purpose and invest meaning in its wider social value.

13.3 Case orientation and context

The *FoT* have developed an insight-driven brand strategy working in partnership with *FUZE* to help continually segment visitors using motivational and demographic approaches and evaluate each aspect of the *Festival* experience from the customer's perspective. This has allowed the CIC to continue to build upon the existing evidence base for the *Festival*, improve their marketing, customer experience and, consequently, foster a strong brand community and have consistent year-on-year attendance growth, which saw 50,000 in 2019 people attend, a 30% increase compared to the previous 2018.

From 2015 through to 2019 the *Festival* typically took place over two days in *Kirkleatham Museum & Grounds*, Redcar in September. It is now established as an integral part of the North East of England's cultural and environmental offer. *FoT* is primarily a family-orientated festival; in 2019 the largest proportion of 53.6% of attendees visited the festival with family, with 16.6% of respondents attended with their partner/spouse and 22.1% attended with friends. *FoT* centres on offering advice, inspiration, and workshops on how to live a value-driven, rich (eg: non-monetary), and environmentally conscious life, attracting festival goers from all of the country using powerful art, a diverse and eco-friendly retail marketplace and a high-quality food and drink offer. In 2019, the most popular reason for visiting the *Festival* was 'Having been before and wanting to return' (59.7%), which demonstrates very strong customer retention. This was followed by those who 'Visited as they attended a free workshop or demonstration' (47.8%) and 'Attended a talk or a debate' (11.8%). As highlighted in *Chapter 3 Managing Meaning: Social Dominant Logic*, a key strategic brand tool in the customer / company fusion is the development of brand community (Koh, Kim, Butler, Bock, & Woo, 2007). Indeed, in the case of *FoT*, they have continually been able to connect it's 'purposive value' (Dholakia, Bagozzi, & Pearo, 2004) with a broad range of audiences from right across the region and wider UK. In 2019, the largest proportion of respondents were from Redcar and Cleveland (35.3%); 24.3% of respondents were from the North East and 20.4% were from elsewhere in the Tees Valley. 19.6% of respondents were from the rest of the UK (which includes North Yorkshire, North West, West Midlands, Scotland, and elsewhere in UK).

13.4 Building a community through brand attachment

FoT has been effective in building up brand equity over a number of years, successfully delivering high-customer satisfaction, increasing visitor and brand loyalty, and laying the foundations of an authentic brand community. This case argues that a key driver in this dynamic has been developing a strong connection with visitors and thus, increasing overall brand attachment based on a connection with *FoT* mission and consistently delivering on brand promises and customer experience.

Brand attachment can be defined as the strength of the bond connecting the brand and the self, which is consistent with the wider understanding of the social functioning of attachment theory (Mikulincer & Shaver, 2007). In the context of this case, *FoT* have been able to communicate their brand purpose and deliver on their mission by developing a rich emotional economy through various channels, initiatives, and programme of activities. This has, in turn, fostered a strong positive response from visitors in the form of a rich and accessible memory network, involving thoughts and feelings about the *FoT* brand, the brand's relationship to the 'self', and desired brand outcomes. This is referred internally/within the community as being 'Thrifty', which further reinforces the connection and bond. To illustrate this, in 2019 *FUZE* profiled the key motivational reasons for visiting the *Festival*, with the results highlighting this strong self-connection with the 'Thrift' mission and brand ethos, whether that is being family-oriented, wanting to be inspired for change, interested in sustainability, or directly connecting with the brand community and mind-set of 'Thrifty living'. The following Figure 13.1 summarises the key festival metrics using *FUZE's* storyboard design approach.

FUZE. METRICS

THE FESTIVAL OF THRIFT

Visitor Evaluation The Festival of Thrift Storyboard

The Festival of Thrift held in Kirkleatham; the principal objective was to undertake an event evaluation of the Festival of Thrift held in Kirkleatham, Redcar from 14th – 15th September 2019. The total number of responses achieved was 237 (confidence interval 5.98% +/- 95% confidence level, using the total population of the previous attendance (estimated 50,000).

Fuze Metric 1: Understanding the Visitor

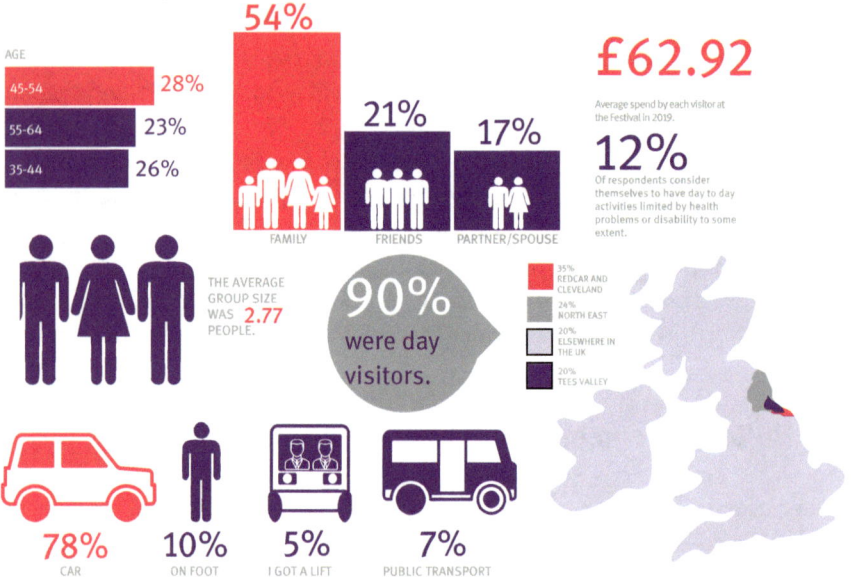

AGE
45-54	28%
55-64	23%
35-44	26%

54% FAMILY
21% FRIENDS
17% PARTNER/SPOUSE

£62.92
Average spend by each visitor at the Festival in 2019.

12%
Of respondents consider themselves to have day to day activities limited by health problems or disability to some extent.

THE AVERAGE GROUP SIZE WAS **2.77** PEOPLE.

90% were day visitors.

35% REDCAR AND CLEVELAND
24% NORTH EAST
20% ELSEWHERE IN THE UK
20% TEES VALLEY

78% CAR
10% ON FOOT
5% I GOT A LIFT
7% PUBLIC TRANSPORT

Fuze Metric 2: Visitor Behaviour and Motivations

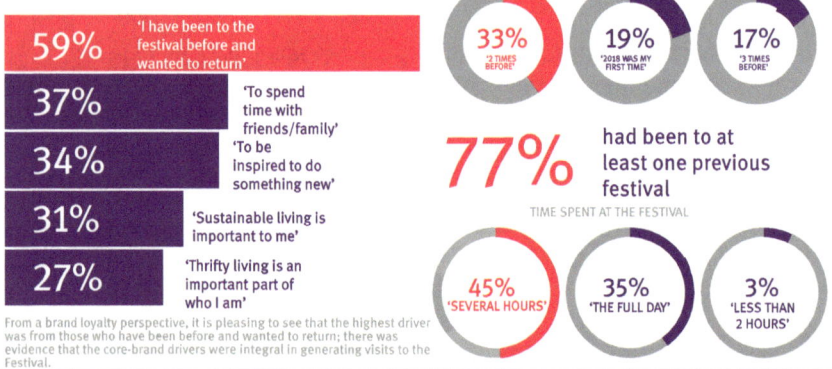

59%	'I have been to the festival before and wanted to return'
37%	'To spend time with friends/family'
34%	'To be inspired to do something new'
31%	'Sustainable living is important to me'
27%	'Thrifty living is an important part of who I am'

From a brand loyalty perspective, it is pleasing to see that the highest driver was from those who have been before and wanted to return; there was evidence that the core-brand drivers were integral in generating visits to the Festival.

33% '2 TIMES BEFORE'
19% '2018 WAS MY FIRST TIME'
17% '3 TIMES BEFORE'

77% had been to at least one previous festival

TIME SPENT AT THE FESTIVAL

45% 'SEVERAL HOURS'
35% 'THE FULL DAY'
3% 'LESS THAN 2 HOURS'

FUZE.

Figure 13.1: *Festival of Thrift* Visitor evaluation.
Source: *Festival of Thrift, FUZE Research* (2019)

Visitor Evaluation The Festival of Thrift Storyboard

FUZE. METRICS

THE FESTIVAL OF THRIFT

Fuze Metric 3: Marketing Effectiveness

HOW DID YOU FIND OUT MORE ABOUT THE FESTIVAL?

53%	70%	18%	18%	19%
Social Media	Website	Recommendation/ word of mouth	Email or e-newsletter	Leaflets

OVERALL MARKETING FOR THE FESTIVAL OF THRIFT WAS RATED

49%	19%	30%
'GOOD'	'EXCELLENT'	'NEUTRAL'

Overall there were many examples of the Festival's good or excellent marketing (100r), with respondents clearly engaging with the Thrift social media story from a very early stage and they felt 'connected' via various channels.

Fuze Metric 4: Visitor Experience and Satisfaction

48%
attended
a free
workshop or
demonstra-
tion

71 NPS
which is
considered to be
'excellent' and is
a 2.5-point im-
provement on
2018.*

93% RATED THE FESTIVAL AS 'GOOD-EXCELLENT'

80% RATED WHAT'S ON AS 'GOOD-EXCELLENT'

Fuze Metric 5: Strategic Aims

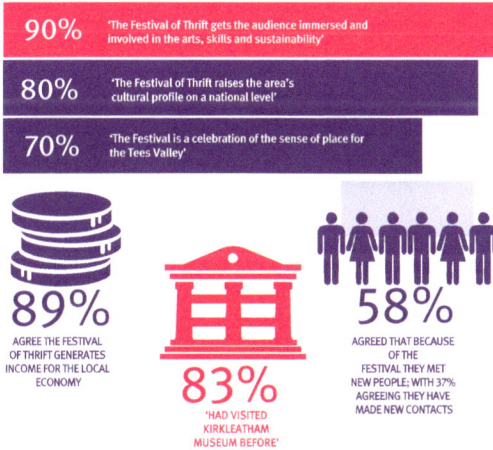

90%	'The Festival of Thrift gets the audience immersed and involved in the arts, skills and sustainability'
80%	'The Festival of Thrift raises the area's cultural profile on a national level'
70%	'The Festival is a celebration of the sense of place for the Tees Valley'

Visitors were:
• 60% strongly agreed that it is important to keep the Festival free
• 65% agreed in some way that they would be happy to make a donation whilst at the festival

89% AGREE THE FESTIVAL OF THRIFT GENERATES INCOME FOR THE LOCAL ECONOMY

83% 'HAD VISITED KIRKLEATHAM MUSEUM BEFORE'

58% AGREED THAT BECAUSE OF THE FESTIVAL THEY MET NEW PEOPLE; WITH 37% AGREEING THEY HAVE MADE NEW CONTACTS

71% agreed in some way that they feel inspired to save money by recycling, up-cycling or reusing

60% feel more informed about thrifty concepts and ideas.

Figure 13.1 (continued)

Findings were as below:
- 59% said they have been before and wanted to return (brand loyalty).
- 37% wanted to spend time with friend and family (social and family connection).
- 34% to be inspired to do something new (connect with a creative community).
- 31% sustainable living is important to me (brand self-connection).
- 27% Thrifty living is an important part of who I am (brand self-identity).

A key aspect of brand attachment is the way within which a customer has a positive recall of an experience (or product) which is highlighted by the strength in brand loyalty. Furthermore, for *FoT* some segments of visitors are arguably able to connect more strongly with the brand because it strongly represents who they are (eg: an identity connection), or because it is meaningful in light of their goals, personal concerns, or life projects such as spending time with friends and family and the value of sustainable living) as well as living a 'Thrifty' life. Brand connection (in terms of connecting with the 'brand' values of the visitors of *FoT* was also assessed.; asked to align the extent they agree with what the *Festival* espouses (from a brand purpose and mission perspective) versus what the customers to the *Festival* actually value. The alignment in terms of level of agreement, further demonstrates the strength of the *FoT* brand foundations. The results are highlighted in Table 13.1 illustrating how across a broad area there are certain brand strengths in alignment, but also areas that require further refinement and focus.

Table 13.1: Visit motivations.

Percentage	Motivational Reason to visit *FoT* (Response base, 2019 n=237)
90.3%	of respondents agree that the *festival* gets its audience immersed and involved in the arts, skills, and sustainability.
89.4%	of respondents agree the *Festival of Thrift* generates income for the local economy.
79.9%	of respondents agreed the *Festival* raises the area's cultural profile on a national level.
71.3%	of respondents agreed in some way that they feel inspired to save money by recycling, upcycling, or reusing more.
70.1%	of respondents agree the *festival* is a celebration of the sense of place for the Tees Valley.
64.7%	of respondents agreed in some way that they would be happy to donate whilst at the festival.
62.6%	of respondents agreed the festival celebrates the Tees Valley's local heritage.
60.6%	of respondents agreed in some way that they know more about businesses who have a sustainable ethos or products.

Table 13.1 (continued)

Percentage	Motivational Reason to visit *FoT* (Response base, 2019 n=237)
59.7%	of respondents strongly agreed that it is important to keep admission to the festival free.
59.6%	of respondents feel more informed about thrifty concepts and ideas.
49.1%	of respondents disagreed in some way that they felt Inspired to consider setting up their own business.

Source: *Festival of Thrift, FUZE Research* (2019)

Overall, the findings demonstrate brand attachment and the established out-comes of instrumental value to customers use of a brand (Park, Macinnis, & Priester, 2010, p. 7). In this case, this was: attending the *Festival* through developing skills, engaging in arts and creative crafts, feeling inspired to save money via various recy-cling methods, and hearing about best-practice from businesses, as well as connect-ing socially with like-minded people.

13.5 COVID-19 context: Key drivers for a sustainable, creative, and resilient community

In order for organisations such as *Festival of Thrift (CIC)* to reap the multiple bene-fits that an authentic brand community can offer, it is argued that there are number of relevant principles that must be followed (Fournier & Lee, 2009) applied in the context of case:

1. Brand community must be a business wide strategy, going beyond the boundaries of solely the marketing department (eg: *FoT*'s wider mission and activities in terms of education, learning, outreach, marketplace etc).
2. Brand community exists to *serve* the people/members of it, not to serve the business (eg: the *FoT*'s brand community serves its mission for the environment and sustainable practices through its programme of activities)
3. Successful brand communities build up momentum around 'social change/cause', or even controversial positions, with a definitive 'in-group' and 'out-group', they are not *"love fests only for faithful brand advocates"* (eg: the climate crisis is challenging people to change mindsets, attitudes, and behaviours).
4. Communities are strongest when all stakeholders play a role, over reliance in opinion leaders can create a false economy (eg: *FoT* have multiple stakeholders that co-create brand value from visitors, performers, teachers, stall holders, local government etc).
5. Digital social networks are not key to developing a community, digital networks only act as a catalytic tool when the correct principles are applied (eg: *FoT* 2020 Digital delivery only occurred because of the foundations previously built such as CSAT,[209] brand loyalty, bonding, and attachment).

FoT can boast very strong customer satisfaction scores, which lead to strong brand connection and bonding. In 2019, the Top 2 rated items (good and excellent) visitors rated for overall visitor experience was 93.2%, with a 70.5 NPS which is considered to be 'excellent' and is a 2.5-point improvement on the 2018 result. FoT have delivered meaningful and high-quality customer experiences consistently over a number of years so that customers are able to align strongly with a brand's aims. As a result customers feel more connected, which increases brand attachment and loyalty, and in doing so authentically builds a strong brand community, one which allowed them to not only 'survive' the 2020 COVID-19 restrictions, but to in fact thrive. The CIC relies on various public funding, which was reduced greatly in 2020, the team tends to be a collective of freelancers, many of the typical sponsors were not able to support, and there was minimal budget, with many of the freelancers losing vital income. Nonetheless, the team collectively decided to continue to deliver its brand purpose and mission in an innovative way. Emma Whitenstall, Executive Director of the *Festival of Thrift* CIC, highlights their resilience in ensuring the 2020 *Festival* was still delivered, aptly named *'Thriftfest Live'*:

> *2020 was a year of challenge and change, but that didn't stop our dedicated freelance team refocusing and expanding our reach to take our message wider. Our digital transformation has already begun. Going forward technology will be crucial for allowing us to campaign and offer year-round support as well as exploring how emerging technologies can enhance our*

---

209 Customer Satisfaction Score.

much-loved September weekend event, both at the event itself and to widen accessibility in a creative and immersive way for those who cannot attend in person.

"The climate crisis is growing, and we all need to take action, now. In our back yards, in our living rooms, in our communities, every day. So, we are no longer just an annual Festival *– though we are really looking forward to returning this September – but we are also becoming a campaigning organisation encouraging everyone to be a part of the solution – not part of the pollution!"*

The case has explored how *FoT* were able to 'repurpose' the Festival as an immersive online experience to the extent it was able to thrive and deliver its brand objectives, in new and creative ways. Over the period of the *Thriftfest Live* (held over one Sat 12th September 2020), the brand community was able to build on the strong brand attachment and co-create a successful programme, 4 live streams, 13 activities, 10 workshops, 6 talks, 4 demonstrations, across *YouTube, Vimeo, Facebook*, and their website, with an overall audience reach of 90,000, attracting people from New Zealand, the US, Scotland down to Cornwall. In a year when the high majority of festivals were cancelled, the success of this online digital experience fostered a highly engaged and committed brand community, one that has allowed the Festival to update its business model and develop a new online marketplace.

Chapter takeaways

- *Festival of Thrift* exemplifies how a brand with 'social purpose' can unify a community and brand.
- This case demonstrates how the *Festival of Thrift* brand reached new audiences and built partnerships with individuals and organisations who share the company ethos 'The Shift to Thrift', showing how small personal changes can make a big difference to the future of the planet.
- The importance of having a clear brand purpose and objectives provided a framework to guide their strategic decisions.
- Using customer insights and event evaluations allowed *Festival of Thrift* to create a culture of evidence-based decisions to inform operational improvements and strategic brand decisions.
- Building a community through powerful socio-emotive brand attachment and bonding was effective.
- *Festival of Thrift* scored strongly on key brand metrics relevant to their purpose.
- The strength of their brand came to the fore during COVID-19 and the development and delivery of a digital festival.
- Key drivers for developing a brand community were clearly aligned to the success of the *Festival of Thrift* digital festival.
- The brand's track record for delivering meaningful and high-quality customer experiences consistently allowed for customers to feel more connected, increase brand attachment, and loyalty.
- *Festival of Thrift* were able to authentically build a strong brand community, one which allowed them to not only 'survive' the 2020 COVID-19 restrictions but thrive, returning in September 2021 with over 50,000 visitors.

14 Headspace: Immersive digital meditation and mindfulness

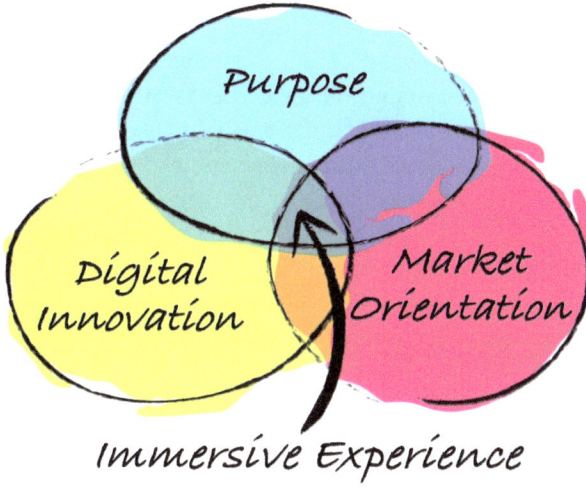

Purpose

Digital Innovation

Market Orientation

Immersive Experience

https://doi.org/10.1515/9783110718638-019

14.1 Outline of chapter

When *Headspace* was launched in 2010, initially as an events company, attendees at one of the meditation sessions at the London event were so impressed by what they had learned about the benefits of meditation that they wanted to experience it further . . . anywhere. From the first instance of making ideas and techniques available online, the *Headspace* formula – 'guided meditations', videos, animations, together with relevant mindfulness content – was conceived and its global meditation and mindfulness content app was launched. The *Headspace* app was launched so that as many people as possible could experience the benefits of meditation at their convenience, at any time, in any place. *Headspace*'s mission is clear yet ambitious: to improve the health and happiness of the world. With Headquarters in Santa Monica, California, and with offices in San Francisco and London,[210] it has now reached millions of users in more than 190 countries.

This case embodies how *Headspace* is able to cultivate and develop a rich emotional and spiritual economy. This economy is driven by guided meditation courses and mindfulness content that includes help with sleep, focus and even movement/exercise videos. Effectively, *Headspace* set the conditions so that users are able to connect and invest meaning in these tailored and highly personalised content, and in doing so foster deeply powerful experiences and deliver spiritual, health and well-being outcomes; or, through a brand equity lens, developing clear tangible and intangible brand value.

Based on secondary evidence/research and public facing materials, this chapter examines *Headspace* through a elements of the brand fusion lens, illustrating how they have followed a purpose-driven brand strategy with an effective approach to market orientation diagnosis and execution, with an aligned and clear raison d'etre, a deep understanding of user's needs, wants and preferences, and an effective delivery of a tailored and powerful digital customer experience.

Learning outcomes

After reading this chapter, you'll be able to:
- Analyse the ways within which *Headspace's* market orientation allowed them to align brand purpose, digital innovation, and wider sociological trends.
- Discover how *Headspace* are able to cultivate, connect, and develop a rich emotional and spiritual economy, via a distinct brand identity and (in-app) customer journey.
- Critically assess the ways within which *Headspace* are able to co-create customer and community value.
- Assess how *Headspace* endeavour to resolve any argued conflict between Buddhism, marketing innovation, and customer outcomes.

---

210 https://www.headspace.com/about-us.

- Evaluate how *Headspace* are able to develop long-term brand relationships with customers and community, from adoption through to advocacy via its immersive digital experience and innovation.
- Identify the ways within which *Headspace* deliver brand meaning, cultivate tangible (functional) and intangible (emotional) brand value (eg: health, well-being and spiritual outcomes).

14.2 Introduction

The following chapter presents an emerging argument that builds on the key themes throughout the book, but also presents a new branding dimension of meaning-making grounded in the 'self'. It is important to note, that there are tight boundaries upon which this chapter is framed: terms like the 'self' and 'spiritual' are highly-charged and often conflated, where studies tend to generalise the meaning of religious spirituality and the subjective milieu, merging faiths and religious ideals (Williams, 2014). These are part of an immensely broad and complex sociology of religion debates; therefore, the following summarises the *Headspace* case from a pragmatic brand strategy perspective. In other words, to reframe in the context of brand fusion, both strategically and sociologically, it is argued that the *meaning of marketing is the marketing of meaning*. Moreover, this *acute* example is revisited through the lens of the book's corollary arguments, that: (1) there is no brand purpose if there is no brand meaning; and therefore, (2) there is no meaning without value and values; (3) *Headspace* epitomises how the driving force of meaning-making is created through shared values (between users, companies and communities); (4) it is a co-created and socially constructed phenomenon, whereby an immersive digital experience acts as a conduit between customer-company meaning. That is to say, going beyond traditional functional and emotional brand value, into the realm of the subjective-life, bonding between company and customer and vice versa, in a process of symbolic symbiosis.

© sanderstock - stock.adobe.com.

14.3 Case orientation and context

Headspace in its purist form, is a mobile application that allows users to download and access guided meditation courses and mindfulness content. Founded in 2010 by Andy Puddicombe and Richard Pierson, it has one clear brand purpose or mission (*Headspace* – Mission, 2021):[211]

> *Headspace has one mission: to improve the health and happiness of the world. And with millions of users in more than 190 countries, we're well on our way. Headquartered in Santa Monica, California, we also have offices in San Francisco and London.*

Its accessibility and inclusiveness are real strengths, allowing anyone with a mobile phone access and offering a free trial where users can access bite-size courses to initially orientate users to the methods/visualisation and user experience. The range of courses – or as they referred to 'meditations' – cover a wide range of topics and allow users to tailor, and even personalise their own mediation and mindfulness preferences. These topics include balance, creativity promoting, finding *focus, happiness, kindness, managing anxiety, mindful eating, pain management, pregnancy, reframing loneliness*

---

211 https://www.headspace.com/about-us

The photo(s) used in this case study is not connected and/or does not represent any brand(s) mentioned. It used to make a visual discussion point by the authors.

and even *coping with cancer;* to name but a few. Its mindfulness content includes areas such as *sleep, move/exercise* and *focus.* All these support key aspects of users' life including improving sleep through guided sessions, toolkits for kids and parents, sleep music and even sleep radio. In the exercise content includes a wide range including *video-based workouts, mindful cardio, feel-good yoga* and globally inspired *dance moves.* The other key area is *focus* which again offer a wide range of content improve the *focus* of users, such as targeted exercises to reduce procrastination, improve prioritising, focus exercises, breathing and music. There is even a 'Mindful Earth' created with the BBC and '*Energy Shots*' that has Kevin Hart as the users' dedicated life coach.

A key benefit of *Headspace* is its guided meditation, which allows users to connect with the narrator/meditation guide in a deeply personalised way. Indeed, one of the prominent voices is that of co-founder Andy Puddicombe – who is synonymous with the *Headspace* as both the 'face' and the 'voice' of the brand. This association is clear when reviewing their brand origin story via their website (*Headspace* – About, 2021):[212]

> It's hard to talk about Headspace without talking about Andy Puddicombe . . . For over 10 years, his meditation training took him across the world to Nepal, India, Burma, Thailand, Australia and Russia. Eventually, he was ordained at a Tibetan monastery in the Indian Himalayas.
>
> After completing his monastic commitment, Andy returned to the UK with the huge-yet-simple goal of teaching meditation and mindfulness to as many people as possible. To demystify the mystical, Andy set up a meditation consultancy and began working with politicians, athletes (that sports science background finally came in handy), and business leaders.
>
> That's when Andy met Rich Pierson, who needed help dealing with the stress of the advertising world. Before long, Andy and Rich were skill-swapping meditation for business advice. That's when Headspace was born.

It could be argued that their background adds a level of authenticity in developing a unique brand identity. Reinforcing a brand personality through voice, tone and a calming nature. For example, the credibility of Puddicombe's voice builds a level of brand familiarity, which then allows casuals users to connect, comprehend and build trust toward the meditation process and importance of using mindfulness content. It is important to note that there are variety of male and female voices offering choice to users.

Therein lies a key strength and source of its brand equity and value. Moreover, this familiarity-credibility-trust dynamic allows customers to co-create highly emotional user experiences, and, in the process, fulfil immensely powerful needs with improved health and well-being outcomes. *Headspace* has been shown to have favourable outcomes of interventions including reduced stress (Economides, Martman, & Bell, 2018) improved focus (Bennike, Wieghorst, & Kirk, 2017) increased

---

212 https://www.headspace.com/about-us

The photo(s) used in this case study is not connected and/or does not represent any brand(s) mentioned. It used to make a visual discussion point by the authors.

compassion (Lim, Condon, & DeSteno, 2015), increased resilience (Champion, Economides, & Chandler, 2018; Champion, Economides and Chandler, 2018), reduced burnout (Morrison, Mahrer, Meyer, Gold, 2017; Morrison Wylde, Mahrer, Meyer, & Gold, 2017), increased positivity (Howells, Ivtzan, & Eiroa-Orosa, 2016) and improved satisfaction with life (Champion, Economides, & Chandler, 2018).

14.4 Market orientation: Embedding 'Buddhism' through digital innovation

Sociologically it is important to consider that marketing, and consequently, branding does not exist in a vacuum. It is embedded in an organisation's social context. Furthermore the way within which an organisation scans its immediate market environment is imperative to assessing future risks and opportunities. Crucially, this must extend its environmental gaze beyond traditional boundaries. Of course, the merits and challenges of reactive and proactive market orientation feature in all of the brand fusion cases, in some form or another; *Chapter 11* highlights the breadth of varying business models and the need for a fluid *hybrid* market orientation framework. Whilst it has a multifaceted offer, from a resource-based view, it could be argued that *Headspace* is a technology brand. Market orientation and innovation is a key driver for success in technology-based marketing and branding (Mohr & Sarin, 2009). Indeed, they pertinently argue using Drucker's position, that market orientation and innovation is fundamental to success in technology businesses that compete in highly complex environments. Consequently, they require sophisticated approaches to marketing and branding, but often companies have under-developed competencies in strategic brand management and lack the ability and understanding to prioritise customer needs. For brands like *Headspace*, those that do develop and implement market orientation, often allows for "sustained break-through innovations" (Mohr & Sarin, 2009, p. 1). In the context of Headspace, the case demonstrates and supports their argument – which is still relevant in the present day – that for technology innovation to be sustained, there are three main drivers:

(1) Ensuring a continuous market-orientation and action occurs.
(2) Customer co-creation.
(3) A focus on wider social responsibility and issues.

© Alexander Ozerov - stock.adobe.com.

Headspace is one of the category leaders. It is clear that purpose-driven brand strategies rely on continuously monitoring sociological (and other macro trends) identifying these opportunities and exploiting them by effectively 'hooking into' market shifts/changes, or in this case deploying a form of 'Buddhist Modernism' via technology innovation to reach a global mass market. Overreliance on solely focusing on the immediate needs of customers in terms of innovation and product development, lends itself to be imbalanced toward being reactive, and therefore can leave a business highly vulnerable (Narver, Slater, & MacLachlan, 2004). Drucker's foresight into the need to extend market orientation beyond existing customers, industries and even existential boundaries brings home the uniqueness of *Headspace*'s 'gaze':

> *It is always with non-customers that basic changes begin and become significant. At least half of the important new technologies that have transformed an industry in the past fifty years came from outside the industry itself.*   (1999, p. 121)

There has been critique of the argued McDonaldisation of mindfulness – "The exponential growth of mindfulness-based interventions (MBIs) in recent years has resulted in a marketisation and commodification of practice – popularly labelled 'McMindfulness'" – which is argued to divorce mindfulness from its spiritual and ethical origins in Buddhist traditions (Hyland, 2017). However, given the proven health and well-being outcomes and the growing evidence base highlighted previously, there is an argument, from a marketing concept perspective the commodification and development of a brand such as *Headspace*, whilst may receive criticisms from some quarters, academic marketing has theorised away any conflict between marketing and consumers. Conflict only occurs when a firm serves their internal interests rather than seeking to meet consumer wants and needs (Holt, 2002). The market will always decide. In this case the wider social and spiritual good is clear based on its proven evidence. The marketing concept declares that, with the marketing perspective as their guide, the interests of firms and consumers align (Holt, 2002).

At is core, Buddhism is presented as, "a path of human development that accorded with Western conceptions of the perfectibility of man through rational action, moral reflection, disengaged self-observation, and the attainment of control over the passions." (McMahan, 2008). The growth of meditation apps like (*Headspace, Calm, Insight Timer*) hook into socio-cultural trends that are effectively responding to the impact of secularisation and connecting with the wider spiritual revolution. Secularization can be defined as having three key components: the decline in religious institutions; the decline in the importance of religion in society; and the decline in the religious importance of religion for individuals (Davie & Woodhead, 2009, p. 254). Consequently, subjective religiousness, or subjectivized forms of religion or spirituality allow individuals to fashion their own type of religion or spirituality, which is a deeply personal collection of religious values moulded to fit their personal needs (Woodhead, Heelas, & Davie, 2003). Whilst *Headspace* is arguably drawing on *modern Buddhism* as a framework, it is also offering these sources of significance through chosen topics and content that fits the needs of users, consumers, companies (via its corporate offering), and wider society – this centres on meditation apps reflecting Western values for internal self-improvement (Gurewitz, 2020). Interestingly, McMahan highlights that the Western view often perceives and assumes that (Westerners) meditation is the central practice in Buddhism; when the reality is that the majority of Asian Buddhists practicing the *dharma* do so through ethics, ritual, and service to the sangha as well as meditation (2008). If we consider the meditation and powerful mindfulness content that embeds a form of ritual, service and positive habits and reinforces a positive ethical underpinning, then *Headspace* brand innovation, has built up brand value through strongly aligning customer (explicit and latent) needs, positioning around intangible brand value (ie: spiritual, health and well-being outcomes) even the brand name evokes and connect a powerful societal need of 'head space'.

14.5 Immersive digital experience

One of the key differentiators of *Headspace* is the way within which it allows users to tailor guided meditations and the broad range of mindfulness content; whilst leaning on the mystique of Buddhist principles. Additionally, it has a very distinct brand identity and immersive digital experience, one that uses animations/visualisations to help tell the story and act as an aid to support the meditations process with 'before and after reflection moments'. The brand identity in terms of its toolkit, characters and animation effectively means that the mass market are able to enjoy a creative and engaging user experience. Hence, are able to connect with this experience in a deeply personal way and where a broad range of choice in topics and content builds on the principles of inclusiveness and accessibility. This inclusivity and accessibility are key drivers in helping *Headspace* deliver its purpose/mission, as a reminded: "*Headspace* has one mission: to improve the health and happiness of the world". It is important to note, much of the intangible brand value is grounded in an aesthetic experience; that is to say, Wolfgang Welsch has argued that aesthetic experiences are not just sensuous, in that they also include cognitive elements. More specifically, where an initial experience may be sensuous, through stimulation it can evoke a powerful emotional response, which can lead to a process of reflection (Welsch, 1997, pp. 9–19). Indeed, the very nature of the *Headspace* user experience, aesthetically inspires this process of going beyond feeling, emotion and thought: *Headspace* has a clear 'end-state' meditation outcome for reflection and continuous self-improvement. Interestingly, Mohr's (2006) work suggests that individuals, particularly religious/ spiritual individuals, become embedded within their respective environments, which are "as culturally constructed as much as they are physically" (2006: 240). Users of *Headspace* connect with "internal mechanisms of information flow, its history, and its connections into the center of its reflection" (Mohr, 2006). This connects strongly with a key argument of the social dominant logic, in that, through the act of digital consumption there is a social meaning-making framework that consumers clearly value. Indeed, the value does not reside in the product and service purchased, or any materially owned possession (Holbrook, 2002), rather in the experience and what that means to them personally, connecting with their values and the way within which it can improve their lives. It is, in fact, the *interaction* that binds *Headspace* and its users and the *Headspace* brand community. The customer and company are operant resources, collaborative partners who co-create this shared value. *Headspace* even offers a 'Group Meditation' feature where people can connect virtually, connecting as a community but also sharing values and deeply personal experiences. This compatibility characteristic is a marker of successful innovation, whereby individual needs are connected with wider socio-cultural values (Kaminski, 2011).

Chapter takeaways

- The *Headspace* case study follows a framework of: effective market diagnosis and orientation evaluation; aligned with a clear raison d'etre; and a deep understanding of user's needs, wants and preferences; and effective delivery of a tailored and powerful digital customer experience.
- *Headspace* create highly personalised content, and in doing so, foster deeply powerful experiences, delivering spiritual health and well-being outcomes for customers with clear tangible and intangible brand value for the company.
- The case highlights how a pragmatic brand strategy approach that is both strategically and sociologically framed in the context of brand fusion, illustrates the adage that the *meaning of marketing is the marketing of meaning.*
- Given the context, this case highlighted the point that if there is no brand purpose there is no brand meaning, and, therefore, there is no meaning without value and values.
- *Headspace* epitomises how the driving force of meaning-making is created through shared values between users, companies and communities. This meaning is a co-created and socially constructed phenomenon, whereby an immersive digital experience acts as a conduit between customer-company meaning.
- The brand identity fostered created a 'familiarity-credibility-trust' dynamic which allows customers to co-create highly emotional user experiences.
- Purpose-driven brands such as *Headspace* are proven to improve health and well-being outcomes, deliver meaning which often fulfils immensely powerful needs.
- Market orientation and innovation is a key driver for success in technology-based marketing and branding.
- For technology innovation to be sustainable for brands, three main drivers have been identified: ensuring that a continuous market-orientation and action occurs; customer co-creation must take place; a focus on wider social responsibility and issues is required.
- *Headspace's* success is linked to its distinct brand identity and immersive digital experience, one that uses animations/visualisations to help tell the story and act as an aid to support the meditations process with 'before and after' reflective moments.

15 Freedome: Building franchise brand equity

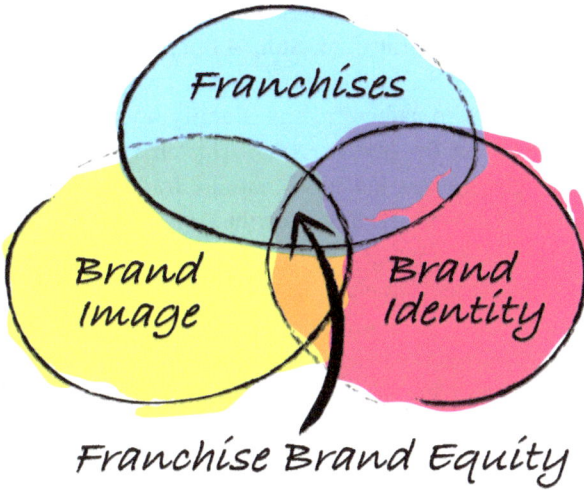

https://doi.org/10.1515/9783110718638-020

15.1 Outline of chapter

Where brand relationships are formed between franchisors and franchisees, brand resonance among franchisees holds tremendous importance for the brand equity of the franchised brand (Badrinarayanan, Suh, & Kim, 2016). Although neither party has complete control over the brand management process, they are mutually dependent on one another to safeguard the identity and image of the franchised brand (Pitt, Napoli, & Van Der Merwe, 2003). This chapter examines such a situation in which two parties operate in a complex franchise structure. 'Freedome Parks' is an immersive adventure park described as a "next generation mash up of fitness, sport, and entertainment"; it must balance local brand awareness with the brand equity demands of their franchisee *CircusTrix Parks (Freedome)*, an innovator and global originator of the trampoline park movement.

FUZE have worked with *Freedome Parks (Freedome)* since 2017 with a clear brief to evaluate the brand awareness and equity of the *Parks (Freedome)* brand and its direct impact on increasing sales and reduce barriers to visit (for potential consumers). The 2017 evaluation was a critical touch-point in the brand's first year of operations at the *Cheshire Oaks* venue. This particular site was strategically important to the wider group's international strategy in building a presence in Europe. In terms of its strategic corporate brand structure, the *Freedome Parks* brand identity arguably lends itself to a 'house of brand' taxonomy – which means it is connected to a group franchise but has an "independent standalone brand where it can maximise the impact of a market" (Osler, 2007, p. 430). However, the following case study demonstrates how in the practical realities of executing brand strategy (global to local) there is often a fusion of concepts: the unique conditions upon which *Freedome Parks* operates is independent, but draws on, combines with, and enhances the overall global brand equity of the original franchise model.

Learning outcomes

After reading this chapter, you'll be able to:
- Understand the complex (macro vs micro / internal vs external) stakeholder dynamics and brand relationship that relate to *Freedome* and its wider corporate (franchise) brand strategy.
- Distinguish the critical factors that impact strategic branding in a franchise context, highlighting the complexities of brand ownership, and the effective resource management in this context.
- Assess the importance of how *Freedome* used segmentation with key customer groups and non-users to assess pathway(s) to purchase, identify barriers to visit (for potential customers), and key customer perceptions.
- Appreciate the priority for *Freedome* to continually evaluate the gap vs alignment between brand identity (internal) and image (external).

- Evaluate how *Freedome* were able to use customer and brand insights to reposition the brand identity to better align with brand image, and 'product' offer and integrate this into their communications approach.
- Analyse how *Freedome's* robust approach to customer experience management helped provide foundations for this repositioning.

15.2 Introduction

This case and chapter relates strongly to '*Chapter 10 Managing Brand Equity: Tangible Results from Intangible Assets*' as a practical application of some key points in relation to how some brands represent value to both the organisation (group) and the customer. *Freedome* primarily targets the following customer groups: parents with various aged children, young adults, and a focus on offering children's parties. These are also known culturally known as 'buckets'. The UK market for trampoline parks is highly competitive. In 2017, there were over 15 established direct competitors (in 2021 this reduced to 8) within 2-hour drive time (as far as the Midlands), and a high number within North Wales and the rest of the North West of England. The trampoline leisure market is very price sensitive and currently operates on a 'last-minute' booking model, with the market being flooded with special offers and online promotional activity. Indeed, this 'last-minute, value conscious' market seems to be reflected with a high-proportion of *Freedome Park*'s customers booking on the same day as their visit. Additionally, within a local 40-minute drive time there are a number of large leisure and tourism attractions (arguably indirect competitors) all of which reinforces the need to continuously evaluate the brand benchmarked against its ever-changing competitive marketplace, identify ways to remain innovative in terms of product offers and prioritise high-levels of customer satisfaction and retention (eg: linking customer experience management with market orientation). One very well established view is that brand equity is comprised of dimensions of brand loyalty, brand awareness, perceived quality of brand, and brand associations and is, as Aaker claims, "a broad and complex concept it often varies from sector to sector and context to context" (1996, p. 103).

15.3 Case orientation and context

Formed in 2004 the Las Vegas Valley, *Sky Zone* is a chain of indoor trampoline parks based in 17 states and 3 provinces and has since expanded across 17 countries around the world, signing multi-unit franchise agreements in Saudi, Oz, Canada and Mexico. Facilities have been extended in some franchises to rock climbing walls, foam pits, Warrior Courses, Freestyle Courts, a 'fun-and-safe environment' for families and children. In 2017 a market consolidation, was initiated by *Circustrix LLC*, which combined two franchise groups (ie: *SkyZone* and *Rockin' Jump*). This group now operates franchises and joint ventures across all these territories. At the time of consolidation, the (former) CEO of *CircusTrix*, Fernando Eiroa said: "We believe strongly in the *Sky Zone* brand, and the opportunity to welcome these additional parks into the *CircusTrix* corporate family is highly appealing to us. Our industry is projected to grow to $3.23 billion by 2023 [Pre- COVID-19 projection], and as one of the global leaders in active entertainment with more than 45 million guests coming through our facilities on an annual basis." *SkyZone* is more widely known as a US-based trampoline park operator and has featured in films such 'The War With Grandpa' (starring Robert DeNiro) and successfully created innovative brand awareness campaigns, which grew its own form of sport category, such as the 'The Ultimate Dodgeball Championship'.

Initially in 2016, the *Freedome* brand represented the UK's presence for *Sky Zone*. In 2017, an American developer, operator, and franchisor the *CircusTrix* group with over 319 owned and franchised locations in the United States, Europe, and Asia acquired *Sky Zone* the corporate family of brands which includes *Sky Zone, Freedome, Superfly* and *Defy*. It is now one of the world's largest trampoline park operators, the biggest operator of extreme obstacle courses in the United States, and the operator of the largest trampoline park in Germany. This case focuses on the layered brand relationship between parent company franchisors (in this case *CircusTrix)* and franchisee (in this case *Freedome*), where ostensibly brand name and recognition are not overtly connected, but there is a network of shared brand knowledge, intellectual property (IP) and brand equity that is shared across the group. It examines how corporate brand equity can be transferred to a franchise operation in the form of "franchisee-based brand equity" (Nyadzayo, Matanda, & Ewing, 2011, p. 1104). Franchisee-based brand equity (FRBBE) includes: information sharing, brand architecture, franchisor support, channel power, conflict resolution, and bonding. Conversely, this case explores how equity built up by a franchisee can enhance franchisor brand equity (and vice versa). In addition, it explores why franchisee attraction and retention is a major motivation for franchisors as it enhances group brand awareness and market share as well as guaranteeing network survival and expansion (Perrigot, Basset, & Cliquet, 2011).

15.4 Strategic branding: Franchise foundations

The trampoline market was a relatively immature 'concept' in the UK In 2017, with general consumer awareness and comprehension about what a trampoline park actually was, in terms of activities and layout, fairly limited. Indeed, there were a number of (negative) associations that dominated top-of-mind perceptions. As we will see, these were more category related, but provided a useful foundation upon which to build. In the context of *Freedome*, being closely connected to an internationally recognised brand allowed for credibility to be in-built. Additionally, being part of an established franchise dynamic, and proven positioning with the group's other brands and competitors, the importance of building brand equity was a key requirement. The key element of a franchise arrangement, in broad terms, is the licensing of an established business value proposition with its operations, products, branding know-how and knowledge, in exchange for a franchise fee. There is a transfer of existing brand presence in a market, such as existing brand awareness and 'known' consumer experience, from the franchisor to the franchisee. This is, in effect, a conveyance of 'good will' – that is, brand equity, from company to company. Despite the challenges of finding a clear definition, there is consensus that brand equity is the incremental value of a product, as perceived by its users, over and above its tangible characteristics and uses, due its brand name, associations, experience of use, (Srivastava & Shocker, 1991).

In *Chapter 10*, it was highlighted how elements of brands become conflated with other (closely related) terms, such as brand identity and brand image. *Freedome* (and the *CircusTrix* group) prioritise the need to ensure that their brand building blocks and a clear structure upon which to launch new franchises are in place. Any blue-print (learning from the wider global business franchise model occurs on a regular basis) recognises the socio-cultural uniqueness of the local market, in this case the UK. There is a clear acknowledgement that *Freedome*'s brand identity comes from within the organisation such as values, culture, personality, and service-level standards etc. (internal perspective) and brand image reflects how the brand users (customer and non-customers) perceive and negotiate meaning in relation to this image (external perspective) – positively or indeed negatively. Pete Brown, Managing Director of UK & Europe of *CircusTrix* (which includes *Freedome*) identifies how customer insight is the key to fusing both inextricably connected spheres:

> *Better understanding our identity, and how and why our customers have visited us, and importantly, those who have not visited us yet, allows us to close the gap on any assumptions and misalignments between what we think (internally) our brand stands for, and what our customer/ potential customers (externally) see, think and feel about Freedome.*

> *It has allowed us to focus on our unique selling points and sharpen our brand identity, as well as to bridge some of the barriers which were preventing potential customers from visiting Freedome, which is how our potential customers were actually perceiving our brand image, from their perspective. Continuous evaluation of customer insight has been the backbone of how we communicate directly to our customers, stakeholders and potential employees.*

In a brand franchise context, this dynamic is arguably more complex in the sense strategic brand management functions are often about balancing global-territory-country-micro and local priorities, all the while endeavouring to balance and leverage group learning. The key component in successfully executing any brand strategy – which is potentially amplified in the context of a franchise – is again, the management of the strategic brand function as we have found throughout the book.

15.5 Brand ownership

The strategic question of brand *ownership* – controlling the integrity of the brand across a network of intermediaries, suppliers, media, opinion leaders, and indeed customers – is a critical one for any company. As Steve Forbes, Chairman of *Forbes Media* claims: "Your brand is the single most important investment you can make in your business". There may be some level of control over how an organisation *wants* to be perceived – brand identity – but not so much over how it is *actually* perceived – brand image. Key components of brand awareness, the communication of identity, the experience of use, the perception of the users (and stakeholders) and of course, word-of-mouth dynamics, the loyalty and trust in building corporate reputation. All of which condition how brand image is formed. The need to control this as much as possible across a wide brand ecosystem of 'agents' representing (and in some cases *mis*representing) the company's intended brand identity is an essential element of brand strategy. Achieving and maintaining brand consistency across a franchise network is imperative. Franchise brand protection relies on replication and consistency. Simpson (Simpson, 2021) puts this well: "It's that consistency that is the lifeblood of your franchise network – franchisees will join you and customers will come to you because of the surety factor of being part of an established and recognise brand". Echoing her thoughts, the following key principles of how to achieve this are applied in the *Freedome* case:

Building a brand equity framework: From a practical perspective, there is a need to resource and establish a full customer insight programme across various customer segments to inform the brand identity approach to ensure alignment (users and non-users), which continuously evaluates:

(i)   Brand awareness (top-of mind and recall, associations).
(ii) Drivers to visit and barriers not to visit.
(iii) Brand associations (positive and negative network).
(iv) Customer planning priorities (as per *their* brand image and meaning).

- *Consistent brand image throughout the network:* Clear guidelines, toolkit, process templates, communication campaign templates, 'on-brand' content, logos, fonts, colour palette, style guides, taglines, and standard 'tone of voice' in all marketing messages across all communications channels. This reinforces the franchise personality and brand identity, and should emphasise brand values, brand purpose, and franchise credibility to customers and stakeholders, as well as consolidating the previous equity framework.
- *Training and development:* Service process quality must be maintained to consistently high levels; customer touchpoints must follow a customer journey plan approach; ensuring the team and culture is 'on-brand'; customer satisfaction levels have to be consistent with the franchise business model framework.
- *Monitoring and evaluation:* Having an independent, customer-oriented evaluation of performance and user experience is essential. *FUZE* were heavily involved in helping to evaluate and align key aspects of the application of brand identity and image in *Freedome's* UK context.

Brown, aptly summarises how each stage is essential in the following quote:

> The latest project, specifically the customer persona mapping, not only helped us improve our targeting around reasons to visit, which resulted in a better marketing ROI, it also helped ensure

our customer experience was aligned effectively. It was a unique and tangible way to identify and manage desired employee behaviours and 'success', as defined by the customers. Understanding these desired staff behaviours has allowed us to manage the staff far more effectively and resulted in a much sharper and tighter, customer-driven culture.

Baselines, barriers, and brand awareness

In 2017, when the brand was relatively new, the crucial business imperative was to isolate insights around brand awareness and segmentation using areas such as 'Planning and motivation', 'Decision to visit' and clear barriers to visit across various sample groups (existing customers and non-users/prospects). In order to make a strategic choice in terms of priority focus, the key outcome was to segment these 'target buckets', ensuring there was more effective alignment between brand identity and image.

The following summary applies some of the key findings in the brand awareness assessment:

- *Actors in the decision-making process:* Given the context of key target markets (ie: children ranging from 2–15 years old, teenager 16–19 years old and young adults), brand awareness is the probability that users are aware and familiar with *Freedome's* brand capability of fulfilling a user need or want grandchildren. Therefore, in some instances these needs included two levels: the parent and/or guardian 'gatekeepers' (may not be the end user but very important in the process decision process); and the children or end-users. All are important in the brand awareness and service expectation assessment. The results highlighted how parents/guardians valued safety, value for money, cleanliness, whilst the end-user (ie: child, teenager and young adults) prioritised the need of fun, spending time with friends and exercise.

– *Brand awareness*: Measuring whether users had brand recognition (prior familiarity with or knowledge of *Freedome* as the type or level of visitation). In 2017, the results indicated that teenagers and young adults were more likely to be aware of *Freedome*, but less likely to have been converted into a visitation. Hence, the need for better understanding of barriers to visit across buckets (for non-users), as well as key drivers for those who had visited in order to help inform priorities in action plans.

– *Brand recall*: (having the ability to recover from memory the *Freedome* brand name and any positive or negative associations with category use). Overall, whilst there were those who were not aware specifically of the brand, they had a strong 'positive' association network and comprehension of what it could offer them and their families. The themes of being free, freedom, inclusive and family fun. For instance, some that related to some form of outdoor and adventure activity, underpinned by being active and energetic – ranging from climbing, parachute jumping, skate park, and skiing.

This broad association network gave *Freedome* a degree of flexibility in its positioning, in the sense it could lean toward the older target buckets (eg: teens and young adults), but also provided 'aspirational' angle so that *Freedome* could build further momentum in the target buckets that had greater success in converting higher brand awareness into visitations and then a sense of brand loyalty; and these have tended to be the parents with children. For instance, comparing 2017 to 2020, there was a refocus on the parents in terms of targeted communications and positioning using initiatives like special offers and a priority of parties as a key brand equity building tool:

– 44% of 'Parents of children aged 10–15 years old' were aware (including visited/ not visited) *Freedome*, grew to 46% in 2020.
– 37% 'Parents of children aged 5–9 year old' were aware (including visited/not visited) grew to 65% in 2020.
– 32% of teenagers had visited grew (including visited/not visited) to 48% in 2020 (which connects with the idea that younger buckets grew older who were loyal to *Freedome*).
– 21% of young adults having visited *Freedome* (grew slightly to 22%). This connects with the findings that the product offer/activities were not as appealing with this bucket.

As highlighted previously, in 2017, 'active attractions' was a relatively immature category in the UK. By 2020, there were more and more established brands in the UK such as more prominence of climbing walls, zip line attraction, outdoor surfing lakes and so on. As always, a hindsight analysis has the benefit of clarity and understanding of the known 'knowns'. In 2017, the *Freedome* brand faced a number of wider market challenges (one of which will be covered in the next section) including high competition, early-stage brand awareness and the overall comprehension and understanding of trampoline parks and its product offer. Whilst, *Freedome* had strengths in certain target buckets; teenagers and young adults had solid awareness, but in comparison to parent buckets, the conversion of a visit (and repeat visits) was not as strong. A clear strategic action in 2017 was to focus on the 'part pipeline' (which meant developing a competitive and attractive party offer targeting parents and various age groups; this brand awareness initiative in gaining momentum and building equity; as more children that attend parties increases, there is more exposure and understanding of the *Freedome* brand and offer to decision makers (ie: parents and guardians) and key influencers (ie: children).

15.6 Aligning brand identity and brand image

A golden thread throughout the book is the need to ensure there is a 'customer company fusion' which harnesses the potential of a business' brand strategy. As we have seen, brand identity is an internal perspective and brand image is the perspective of external stakeholders (Basedo, Smith, Grimm, Rindova, & Derfus, 2006), and it is important to align these two essential positional features. The *Freedome* case exemplifies that when developing brand equity there is a need to align identity and image at a strategic level. In other words, there is a required negotiation of brand meaning between company and consumer, it cannot solely be a one-way organisational *input* but rather an ongoing *process* of co-created consumption whereby the dynamics of identity (ie: *Freedome's* brand identity, which is engineered and disseminated by the company) and image by which visitors and non-users mediate this meaning based on their perceptions.

Freedome's 'product' is designed from a safety-first perspective, which includes high-level of staff training, strict rules of park build standard, monitoring the level and quality of supervision and even infrastructure upon which the trampoline park is built; all of which, reduces the risk of injury. For instance, *Freedome* only by using a chain structure between the trampolines so that there is flexibility and give, but sturdiness in terms of support. Additionally, the *Freedome* is a venue smaller in size comparison to other competitors and its activities tend align with younger age groups (as opposed to older groups like teenagers). A key finding in 2017 about the general perceptions of trampoline parks and outdoor active attractions (generally and not related to *Freedome*) in the UK and amongst other competitors, was a perception of a safety worry. Typically for parents, an overriding need was the fulfilment of safety. In general terms, for this category, this potential safety concern could be associated with perception of children being too small, worried about mixed ages of kids, and worries about potential injuries. The need for safety – is defined as absence of threats; order and control – defined as stability and the ability to control the environment; parenthood – defined as bonding, protecting, and nurturing. This was valuable insight in relation to the 'brand image' in terms of the potential perceptive barriers/associations from certain target buckets, aligning product and brand satisfaction. For instance, *Freedome*'s smaller venue was preferred by parents with younger children, a customer response highlights this: "I am overly cautious on safety and I prefer *Freedome* to others parks it is smaller, and easier to let my children play independently, but also I felt in control as I can see and get to them quickly. Other parks can be too big!".

If we reflect on the key ingredients of this chapter, there is evidence to suggest that the *Freedome* brand has a strong product-brand halo effect (Kapferer, 2004). Fundamentally, the core brand identity (this is what the brand espouses and its values) are safety-first, fun and exercise. The 'halo effect' is an alignment of the image with the perceptions of its user's role in co-creating value and meaning. This is further reinforced, by reviewing the 2020 brand performance metrics (in the context of this chapter) with safety, quality of staff and supervision, suitability of ages and size – all of which are present in each key three customer segments (Top 2 Satisfaction, n=675 – 2020):

- *Party Segment* (Top 5 Satisfaction Drivers)
  Safety (87.0%)
  Cleanliness (80.1%)
  Time allowed for activities (77.3%)
  Space (77.2%)
  Suitability for all ages (75.9%)

- *Midweek* 'Promotional Offers' (Top 4)
  Cleanliness (81.9%)
  Booking system (80.9%)
  Quality of supervision (79.8%)
  Amount of supervision (79.8%)
  Safety (77.6%)

- *Weekend* – 'Open Jump'
  Safety (84.9%)
  Time allowed for activities (81.1%)
  Booking system (80.6%)
  Location (78.6%)
  Friendliness of staff (75.9%)

Chapter takeaways

- *Freedome* reap the benefits of having a clear idea about their key customer segments and non-user market.
- Better understanding the dynamics and complexities of corporate and local brand strategies in a global franchise organisation, where brand name and recognition are not overtly connected, but there is a network of shared brand knowledge, intellectual property (IP) and brand equity that is shared across the group.
- Learnt that Franchisee-based brand equity (FRBBE) includes: information sharing, brand architecture, franchisor support, channel power, conflict resolution, and bonding.
- Understand the importance of strategic brand management in a franchise context.
- *Freedome* value the importance of brand identity and better understanding how their customers and non-customers perceive their brand (brand image). The brand recognises there is likely a misalignment between what they think and what customer/nonusers see, think and feel about *Freedome*.
- *Freedome* use these insights, specifically perceptions, barriers, and brand image, to inform their communication strategy.
- Brand consistency is the 'lifeblood' of a franchise – globally and locally.

- Building franchise brand equity for *Freedome* covered areas such as: brand awareness (top-of mind and recall, associations); drivers to visit and barriers not to visit; brand association; Customer planning priorities (as per their brand image and meaning).
- Other key drivers for success in delivering a consistent franchise brand experience are: delivery of the consistent brand image throughout the network; training and development; monitoring and evaluation.
- Establishing brand awareness, perceptions, and barriers to visit provide a unique foundation upon which to make strategic brand choices.
- The importance of aligning brand identity (internal view) with brand image (external view) and assessing this in the context of product offer and key segments.

16 University of Cumbria: Brand anchor, pledge, and persona

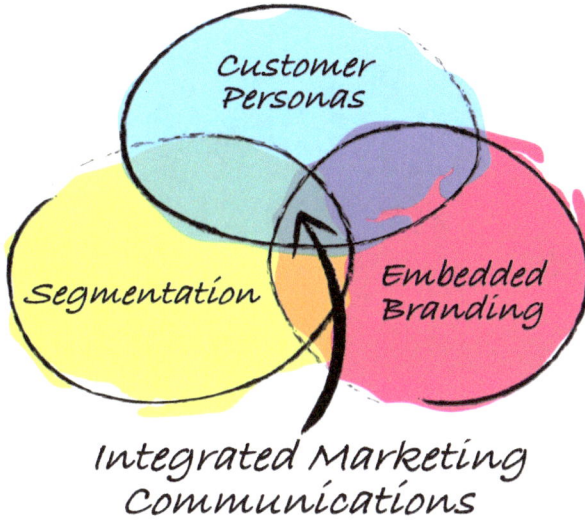

https://doi.org/10.1515/9783110718638-021

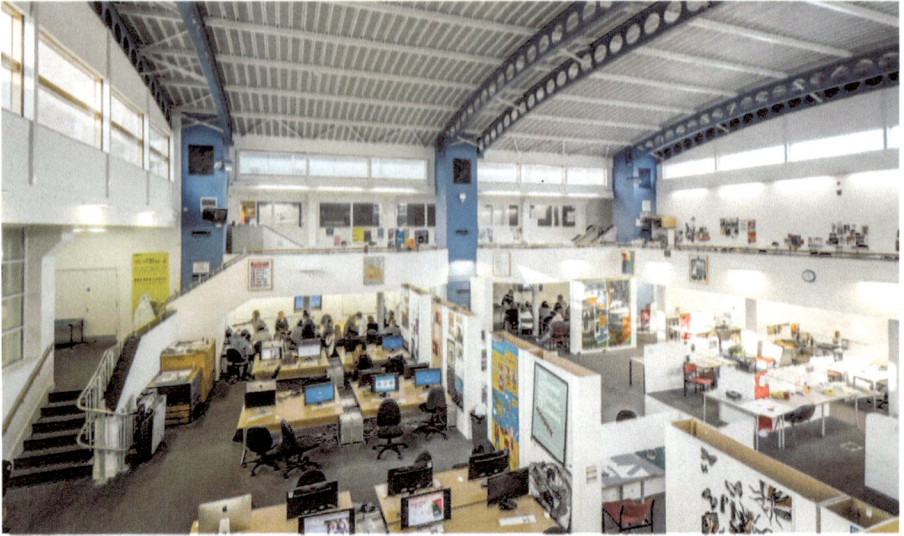

16.1 Outline of chapter

The globalisation of business has been embraced by the Higher Education sector in the UK, where the marketisation of education presents a difficult challenge for institutions offering tertiary provision. In a market where students are recognised as customers, universities have realised the role of corporate identity as a powerful source of competitive advantage (Melewar & Akel, 2005, p. 41).

As highlighted throughout this book, an effective market orientation strategy which is informed by primary research and data-driven segmentation allows for a tailored and contextual assessment and selection of market attractiveness. A grounded, evidence-based platform provides a stronger framework within which to view the environment that an organisation operates in. This increases the chances of making 'smarter' strategic choices in areas such as: targeting and positioning, brand (re)evaluations, customer-driven product development, and insight-driven tactical and integrated marketing communication campaigns.

The following case illustrates how *The University of Cumbria (UoC)* worked with *FUZE* to implement a University-wide strategic segmentation project that combined dual-perspectives per persona groups, relevant to *their* context (ie: 'learner student – learner customer'). This provided a 'deep dive analysis' – a thorough, comprehensive investigation – into the key drivers for 'course selection' and 'University selection', including: the decision pathway across all digital touch-points (eg: online research of course, booking campus visits, enquiries to course leaders etc) as well as traditonal (eg: campus visits and opens days, meeting course tutors, viewing accommodations etc.); 'Expectations of University life'; as well as mapping the full customer and learning journey from the perspective of 1ˢᵗ year entrants.

Learning outcomes

After reading this chapter, you'll be able to:
- Distinguish the important link between segmentation, targeting, and positioning in Higher Education, and how macro-environment drivers influenced *University of Cumbria's* brand strategy.
- Determine how brand strategy acts as an anchor to deliver brand purpose and 'pledges' in delivering brand strategy, whilst balancing the challenges and opportunities for customer, company and cultural change.
- Determine how brand strategy is interconnected with organisational culture, and vice versa.
- Assess how customer and brand insight offer challenges and opportunities for customer-learner, company and cultural change.
- Identify and assess how the use of personas were able to support, inform and reinforce the University's integrated marketing communications mix.
- Evaluate how data and insight was deployed across various points of the University's brand strategy, to help improve their communication approach.

16.2 Introduction

As Higher Education continues to grow, increased competition places more pressure on institutions to market their programmes (Adams & Eveland, 2007; Nguyen, Melewar, & Hemsley-Brown, 2017). Technological, social and economic changes have necessitated a customer-oriented marketing system, and a focus on developing the university brand (Judson, Gorchels, & Aurand, 2016). Researchers suggest that, in recent years, university branding has increased substantially (Melewar & Akel, 2005; Chapleo, 2007). These researchers propose a number of reasons, namely, a consequence to governmental demands on universities to attract and enrol greater numbers of students, rising tuition fees, the proliferation of courses on offer, the growing 'internationalization' of universities, escalating advertising costs, financial pressures, and, in many universities, heavy reliance on income from foreign students (Bennett & Choudhury, 2009) A university's brand is defined as a manifestation of the institution's features that distinguish it from others, reflect its capacity to satisfy students' needs, engender trust in its ability to deliver a certain type and level of higher education, and help potential recruits to make informed enrolment decisions (Nguyen, Yu, Melewar, & Hemsley-Brown, 2016).

In order to be competitive in terms of recruitment in the Higher Education sector, Universities must be able to examine the likely decision-making behaviour adopted by prospective candidates hoping to gain entry. There are many variables in student selection intention and institutions must match their value propositions (such as curricula and programme content) to the experience expectations and influential attributes valued by new applicants. Predicting future student selection criteria in order to secure successful intake requires the accurate analysis of existing student experience.

Director of Marketing and Recruitment at the *University of Cumbria*, Jayne Pugh perfectly sums this up:

> *"The personas really changed the way we operated right across the University. They really helped us to focus on improving conversion rates and income. The Action Plan also allowed us to help the academics plan and deliver a great student experience."*

16.3 Case orientation and context

The principal objective of the segmentation project was to provide the University and key decision makers from right across the University with accurate data in order to help all stakeholders (organisational level through to customer-students and prospects):

- Evaluate the student experience and identify relatable customer 'personas' for profiling and targeting.
- Inform the University's ongoing brand evaluation approach (which was a complete evaluation of the brand identity from core values through to campus level communications).
- Assess and align with the overall approach to learning and student experience.
- Deliver clear priorities and action-plans so that these decision makers (eg: University senior management, Institute Deans, Programme Leaders, Course/Unit leaders etc.) could identify areas of growth.
- Deliver a customer-centric culture that ensured that all levels and perspectives of the organisation were consulted and were able to shape this 'collective vision' and brand approach.

The impacts gained from achieving a better understanding of current students' experiences were:

(1) An improved digital and off-line sales and marketing approach, boosted student recruitment directly resulting from improved conversion rates.
(2) The improvements delivered a much stronger ROI.
(3) An evaluation of student satisfaction helped inform the learning experience, identify strengths, and isolate areas for improvement.
(4) Provided a strategic insight into how the University should be re-positioned and differentiated in a very competitive marketplace.

Higher Education continues to face a market in flux, where there have been seismic shifts which have changed student-customer dynamics. For example, the removal of the 'student intake cap' in 2015 meant larger Universities (with larger intake capability) were able to competitively 'squeeze' the recruitment/offers and recruitment targets in comparison to newer and smaller institutions (with a smaller intake capacity). The geographical region which the *University of Cumbria (UoC)* competes in – The Northwest of England – is a hyper-competitive marketplace with 12 Universities in the region alone. In the rest of England, there are a further 94, all of whom are competing with a variety of strategies of differentiation (such as research excellence, teaching excellence, student experience and 'niche' programmes/centres). Many of these Universities are executing well-defined national and international marketing strategies with effective integrated marketing communication (IMC) campaigns. *UoC's* overall strategic branding plan is about increasing brand awareness, gaining traction in brand equity, and effectively positioning their brand in the wider market. This is particularly applicable in those institutions who were granted University status post-1992 such as *Manchester Metropolitan University, De Montfort University* and *Coventry University*.

16.4 Emdedded branding: Finding an anchor to deliver a pledge

By unifying the analytics life cycle from *data to discovery to deployment*, brands that invest in a customer-centric, insight-driven approach are able to leverage the ultimate analytical advantage: gaining competitive advantage through brand preference (Wilson, Malik, & Kanioura, 2018). In practical terms, this must be developed on a bedrock of solid brand strategy, based on honest self-assessment, allowing an organic 'brand narrative' to emerge so that customer and community are able to connect diverse meaning with stories at all internal and external levels of the business.

Jayne Pugh aptly summarises her approach to developing and executing brand strategy, reinforcing the golden thread of this book: customer-company fusion, applying theory to practice, through battle tested strategies. She states:

> *Your brand is your culture, and your culture is your brand. A brand is a promise, or it is 'The Pledge' you make to your customers – current and potential – and you quite simply have to make sure you deliver on that pledge so that the reality matches the promise. And when you have dissonance and a negative pull-down on brand perception, that is when reality doesn't match the pledge! It goes deeper than that, if you have undertaken a brand strategy, and properly embed it across the organisations, then it should become an anchor to ALL decision making. It becomes the DNA of the organisation, when considering all business opportunities and challenges.*

The crux of this chapter – the challenges (and business imperative) is to ensure brand strategy is informed by and grounded in effective strategic segmentation, with continuous feedback loops and learning throughout an iterative approach – is highlighted in this statement from Pugh:

Challenges of brand strategy . . . before embarking on a brand strategy you need to make sure there is a true cross-section across all levels of the organisation, via consultation and their vital input. On long-term branding approaches, I think it is important to capture the natural storytelling of a brand – its contribution to customers, community and the wider world. And taking those stories from within the organisation that naturally come through and distil them down through an appropriate structure for that brand. It is a long-term approach and if it is a large organisation, or one that doesn't yet understand what a brand is, then it pays off massively. This was the exciting opportunity for University of Cumbria, to go beyond the logo and colour, and use storytelling as the bedrock for the brand.

If data is not applied to "use storytelling as the bedrock of the brand", the outcomes of any persona mapping often lose the immediacy and relevancy to ensure cultural buy-in of colleagues. In other words, there is credibility in the insights (eg: the team connect with the personas), and there is currency (eg: in the sense that they apply them in practical use to help them achieve their own individual and team goals – such as increased conversion and student experience scores). She continues:

It has become embedded across the organisation, and I have been blown away by the response. A really simple example: If we produce a PowerPoint template, there is a wave of Institutes wanting the new style. I have never worked in an environment where it has been so engrained in the culture. Even academic reports use the brand pillars of 'people, place and partnerships'. So, when there are new project initiatives or proposed degree programmes, the Institute team are using those brand pillars and values as part of the business case. That is the real acid test of a brand and being customer-student centric.

16.5 Strategic segmentation; tangible outcomes

The case demonstrates how segmentation allowed *UoC* to holistically improve their level of knowledge of customer-learner, so that they could implement action plans right across the organisation from learning approaches and content, learner support, building a community and atmosphere at its distinctive campuses, to endeavouring to build strong relationships with existing students, and also communicating more effectively via highly targeted promotional media to improve conversion rates.

It has been argued that a deeper analysis of customer-company congruence, is mutually beneficial in developing and validating value propositions that are aligned between *creator* and *user*. *University of Cumbria* represents an organisation that embodies how prioritising a customer-centric approach afforded the opportunity to improve its brand orientation and commercial objectives, improve customer experience and brand reputation, but also delivered more informed product-development (ie: programmes and courses) to ensure there is effective 'value exchange' in serving and servicing customers (Podsakoff, MacKenzie, & Podsakoff, 2016, p. 161).

Developing customer personas are the cornerstone (and in many ways also a catalyst) to successfully fusing market orientation and brand orientation with an integrated marketing communications approach. This is prioritising an 'organisational wide' brand culture of customer-centricity (or customer-company fusion), which is constructed from validated customer personas, heavily grounded in the 'micro' context upon which a product (or brand) is being positioned.

On occasions, secondary data sets are used to make assumptions about a certain 'customer profile' using such variables as postcodes, whereby these postcodes are mapped against a national dataset and aligned based on match criteria. The challenge of this approach is that they rely heavily on those datasets being regularly updated and a *dangerous* assumption that customer segments tend to be alike within a postcode area, which doesn't account for the diversity and mix of households, buying habits, attitudes toward money and lifestyle, family and education backgrounds. The approach adopted by *FUZE* had a number of key stages of primary data collection, both qualitative and quantitative, which was iterative and grounded in the reality of the University's student body with full engagement with the key stakeholders such as the student union and the diverse programme coverage and had clear boundaries focusing on 1st year students as primary sampling population, mainly full-time, as this was a clear business priority for future student recruitment, there was also a non-user sampling stream. For the study overall, there was 100% representation of all University Institutes, 89% representation at course level and 49% response rate of all 1st years (at that time). This book argues that segmentation is a creative, iterative and contextual process, where a top-level framework sets the priorities, but it is evidenced and informed from the bottom-up by customers and key stakeholders.

Jayne Pugh, who's role also includes Student Recruitment (effectively Sales as well as Marketing), highlighted how segmentation can act as a strategic catalyst whilst delivering tactical tangible outcomes, right across the organisation:

> *The depth of insight helped us to develop a more personalised approach to all elements of our marketing and engagement. Understanding the motivations and pain points changed how we think about potential students and has influenced content, messaging, campaign development and improvements to our website. We have crafted a prospect and conversion framework based on the research which makes it really clear what has to happen at each stage of the applicant journey to make it as effective, easy and enjoyable as possible for the applicant. The framework also enables us to be more precise when making further enhancements to ensure the journey is as personalised as possible.*

16.6 The student-customer personas: Overview messaging

The following Table 16.1 represents how the *personas in action* were used by *University of Cumbria* in terms buying/sales messaging; the fundamental messages informed all aspects of their integrated marketing communication strategy:

Table 16.1: Student Persona Benefits Message.

Student 'Persona 1'

Key themes:
- Local platform to build a new career and 'themselves', which focuses on personal development and growth.
- Learning is an exciting and new opportunity to (re)transform themselves and their lives.
- University is/should be a watershed moment in their lives (and for their family, potentially).
- All of the above needs to be underpinned by 'staying local' (live and work).
- Learning through collaboration with other like-minded people/professionals in the classroom and community.
- Personal growth, change and challenge is underpinned by subject interest to 'transform'.
- Transformation is primarily driven by career (retrain, refresh or switch) – personal growth/skill enhancement is a welcome by-product.
- Local employment opportunities are an aspirational selling-point.
- Persona 1 want to learn new knowledge, reconnect with themselves and pivot into a new career – all from a 'known' local base.

Student 'Persona 2'

Key themes:
- Persona 2 want to make a difference that matters to other people and society.
- Serving a greater good supersedes their individual needs.
- Key words around helping others to become better versions of themselves, support and 'heal' others, communities and wider society.
- Change the world, not from an idealistic perspective, but instead by practically applying themselves to these issues.
- Well-rounded and open to other people's perspectives.
- Belief in people power and connecting with others.
- Learning need through as a marketing proposition, be aware there is an expectation for the student to need a clear teaching and learning structure, with lots of supportive touch-points in place.
- Highlighted that students would welcome learning from research-active and expertise from their field.

Student 'Persona 3'

Key themes:
- This group are driven strongly by career-driven propositions, high tendency to value remuneration, rewards and career options.
- Likely to have a clear career plan – would respond well to professional development and career-road maps.
- Perceive themselves as competitive and consider themselves to be achievers, likely to be highly engaged and motivated students.
- Interestingly, highest scoring (56.6%) cluster to class themselves as a consumer, as opposed to a student.
- Likely to perceive tuition fees as an investment and would respond to a ROI message for certain career routes, for instance.

Table 16.1 (continued)

– Prioritise for personal growth and embrace the challenge of learning as on opportunity – although key motivator for this is an improved career prospect. – Open to change and new experiences as long as personal development focused on career/ future opportunities and job security.

Student 'Persona 4'

Key themes:
- Persona 4's key driver is for attending *UoC* is learning about a subject/new knowledge. The joy of learning. Hence, the 'Quest' of learning.
- More important to enjoy the degree, than chase £reward-driven courses/careers.
- Most likely to perceive themselves as a 'student', as opposed to a 'consumer'.
- Persona 4 'enjoyed' being inquisitive about a subject-area; it is likely they have held this subject interest for a long period of time.
- Persona 4 are not considering a career to the extent the 'Persona 3' do.
- They are experience-driven, living in the moment and 'enjoying' University life as a whole.
- Persona 4 hit all key satisfaction scores; getting good value for money, really enjoyed their studies, they feel they belong.
- Societies, events and socializing opportunities would appeal strongly to Persona 4 in marketing propositions.

Student 'Persona 5'

Key themes:
- Persona 5 – this group were most likely to have not enjoyed University in terms of learning and experience.
- Quite often had not aligned well with their chosen course or programme, and found learning frustrating and even boring.
- They had not found 'their' motivation driver or path.
- There was a lack clarity about why they are at University, and tend to coast through their experience.
- There was evidence (qualitatively) that some Path Finders will 'develop' or merge into other persona groups – when they discover their own path!

Source: *FUZE Research/University of Cumbria* (2018).

16.7 Impact: Benefits of using personas to drive IMC

The project overall allowed the wider *University of Cumbria* to 'refresh' its brand at a strategic level, adding evidence to help develop its overall brand capabilty at organisational levels, whilst providing a clear framework to enhance its integrated marketing communications approach at an Institute, department, and programme level (eg: tiered business units). It is important to note a caveat that the persona work only covered the 1st year cohort but has been updated and reviewed across varying levels. Overall the strategic segmentation project changed the way the brand was positioned in its hyper competitive market and how it influence its University-wide communication and campaigns.

The benefits of a marketing communications strategy which is integrated, cohesive and consistent across the elements of the mix are shown in Table 16.2 applied to the *University of Cumbria* and shown as examples in Figures 16.1 to 16.3:

Table 16.2: The benefits of *University of Cumbria's* application of the personas strategy and IMC – customer-company fusion.

Benefit	
Increased impact of communications dialogue	– Consistent delivery on the key University message – "Enrich" where each campus was able to have a clear brand identity but 'belong' and be consistent with the core University messaging. – This allows for campus/Institutes brand personality and communications to find a balance between 'UoC voice' but also a distinctive element at programme and department level. – The 'enrich' message and continuous reinforcement helped connect with various persona groups; the toolkit was described as bright and lively, and also distinctive to aid recall and recognition.
Improving resource efficiencies	– The project allowed for a clear path way to purchase across its customer journey, across multichannels; so that there was an effective measurement and evaluation of ROI and additional continuous learning to improve conversions.
Corporate cohesion Participation	– It became a strategic corporate tool across the University, to ensure brand identity and image was aligned and cohesive. – Additionally, as evidenced in this chapter, there was a strong cultural buy-in to the University brand, values, and identity down to how these elements supported academics in building business cases for new learning programmes, for instance.
Interaction	– There was a more effective communication flow University, Institutes, Departments and programmes – along with the students and key stakeholders (e.g. student union).

Adapted/Derived from Linton and Morley (1995), Kitchen and Schultz (1999), and Yeshin (1998).

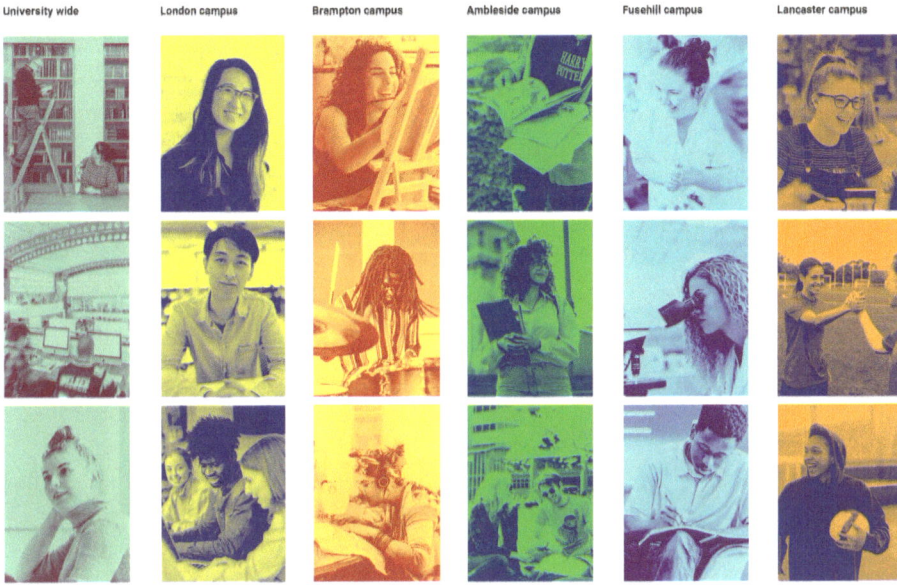

Figure 16.1: *University of Cumbria* Plate 1.

Figure 16.2: *University of Cumbria* Plate 2.

BRAND
IDEA

BEING.
ENRICHED.

OUR
STORY

WE INSPIRE, ENGAGE AND
ADD VALUE TO PEOPLE'S LIVES;
THROUGH EVERY STAGE OF LIFE
TO EVERY PART OF BEING;
OUR FOCUS IS PEOPLE,
COMMUNITY AND SOCIETY.
WE KNOW THE THINGS WE TEACH
WILL CHANGE LIVES...

Figure 16.3: *University of Cumbria* Plate 3.

These were the results of the persona mapping and how the University executed their IMC:
- Improved communications have seen prospectus requests grow by 349%.
- Improved conversion rate on the website from 21% to 40%.
- Lead generation grew by 192%.
- Website traffic grew by 750k in a year and 62% of that traffic was organic as a result of enhanced brand awareness.

16.8 Theory: The communication context

In order to prepare for marketing communications strategy, we need to analyse the context within which the organisation is operating:
- *External context*: Global influences, intermediaries' requirements, media agendas, societal influences, and market conditions.
- *Internal context*: brand and organisational core values, attitudes, company culture.
- *Customer context*: user attitudes, motivations, perceptions, and behaviour.

and within which the brand is created:
- Which market or markets do we want to target?
- What is the customer profile and behaviour of the target market?
- Who are or will be our main competitors?
- What do we want our brand(s) to stand for?
- How do we ensure that our target audience (or audiences) perceives our brand as the superior alternative?
- Can we ensure that we have a better position than our competitors?
- Do we use one brand or several brands to achieve effective market coverage?

Chapter takeaways

- Hyper competition in the Higher Education sector has led to Universities needing to improve their strategic choices in areas such as: targeting and positioning; brand (re)evaluations; customer-driven product development; and insight-driven tactical and integrated marketing communication campaigns.
- *The University of Cumbria (UoC)* case demonstrates the impact an organisation-wide strategic segmentation project can have on a brand strategy, combining dual-perspectives per persona groups, relevant to *their* context (ie: 'learner student – learner customer').
- *UoC* focused on a customer-centric culture that ensured that all levels and perspectives of the organisation were consulted and were able to shape this 'collective vision' and brand approach.
- This case personifies the adage that 'Your brand is your culture; your culture is your brand', reinforcing the customer-company fusions highlighted throughout this book.
- In order for the brand *pledge* (expressed to customers and employees) to be delivered, the brand strategy must be embedded and act as an anchor to decision-making.
- The development of a brand strategy needs to be cross-functional across all levels of the organisation, via consultation and with clear input. On long-term branding approaches, the natural storytelling of a brand – its contribution to customers, community and the wider world – should be central.
- This case demonstrates that segmentation and persona work needs an element of visual storytelling, so that it can be communicated to the whole of the organisation with immediacy, relevancy and applicable to helping them achieve their goals at individual, team and organisational levels.
- Through strategic segmentation, *UoC* were able to improve their learner experience, creating a community atmosphere at its distinctive campuses, and building strong relationships with existing students.
- Developing customer personas was the cornerstone (and in many ways also a catalyst) to successfully fusing market orientation and brand orientation with an integrated marketing communications approach. This allowed for targeting messaging based on the persona-brand-context and resulted in clear tangible results.

17 Dell Technologies: Person to person in B2B

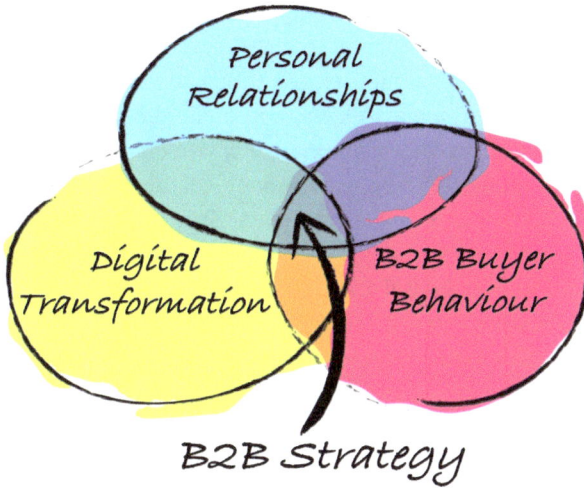

https://doi.org/10.1515/9783110718638-022

17.1 Outline of chapter

This case demonstrates the importance of corporate personality in decision-making, developing brand value, and strengthening brand relationships in the rational context of Business-to-Business (B2B) marketing. Creating trust, dialogue, loyalty, and behaviours that reinforce customer expectations relies greatly on underpinning brand relationships both at a macro-level (corporate identity) and through cultivating relationships at a micro-level (importance of personal aspects of the brand). In attempting a better understanding of 'company-customer collaboration' (Kotler & Pföertsch, 2006), there has been a paradigm shift from economic exchange to behavioural theory (La Placa & da Silva, 2016) which requires a unique balance of macro and micro forces at play. This chapter highlights how corporate brand relationships and personality can act as catalyst for innovation and digital transformation, applying a contemporary approach to the dynamics of a B2B customer journey, generating brand value through tangible (functional) and intangible (emotional benefits) delivery.

This chapter is a *featured* case study and is based on secondary evidence and public-facing materials research on the global technology company, *Dell Technologies*. It examines how brand value and innovative digital transformation can be developed through a B2B customer journey 'model'. This demonstrates that even within complex (B2B) buying ecosystems, the building of brand relationships and co-creating value is vitally important. The case reinforces many of the themes running throughout this book – having a clear (corporate) brand purpose, identifying the importance of customer centricity (whether that is direct or end user), the power of segmentation/customer persona and delivering a customer experience that exceeds expectations and allows direct customers (and in this case their end users) to invest meaning in that brand purpose and thus generate brand value.

> **Learning outcomes**
>
> After reading this chapter, you'll be able to:
> - Determine the complex dynamics of developing B2B corporate brand strategy, in the area of digital transformation.
> - Assess the importance of B2B brand management in the process of digital transformation.
> - Evaluate how long-term brand equity is a long-term basis for sustainable competitive advantage, via value exploration, value creation, and value delivery.
> - Assess the importance of *Dell Technologies* embedding a customer-company, embedded B2B brand strategy, going beyond product-driven/functional value, to connect purpose, personal and emotional value in a digital transformation context.
> - Analyse the influence of top-down drivers (eg: Founder dynamics such as corporate brand personality and entrepreneurial spirit etc) and bottom-up drivers (recognising the importance of end-user experience etc) in executing a B2B brand strategy.

- Identify and discuss the value of *Dell Technologies* deploying existing B2C strategic capabilities and customer personas to deliver brand-driven, digital innovation.
- Evaluate how the power of aligning purpose, values and relationships to deliver tangible and intangible brand value – co-created corporate identity.

17.2 Introduction

As competition increases in all markets, the power of brands to create value and differentiate is being accepted more and more. One of the key drivers in the value created between B2B customer and company is branding. Implicit in this is the emphasis not on just on the product produced and purchased or service provided, but the relationship between the parties. Development of B2B brand equity is critically dependent on individual perceptions about the human capital and mediating effects of mutually beneficial relational factors such as trust, commitment and shared purpose. It is a combination of *functional* (eg: technology, capacity, quality, after-sales service) and *emotional* qualities (eg: trust, reassurance, responsiveness, risk reduction). Research from the likes of Lynch & de Chernatony (2004, p. 403) advocate a better balance between functional and emotional values in B2B brands.

17.3 Case orientation and context

Technically speaking, 'organisational marketing' (derived from 'industrial marketing'), is a more all-embracing inclusive description of activities between *all* organisations including those not in the Private Sector such as charities, not-for-profit, and Governmental agencies. However, in the context of this case, where we draw comparison to business-to-consumer (B2C) principles, the term B2B is adopted. Because there are structural and buying behaviour differences in B2B markets, with demand not being direct but derived, with a higher concentration of demand, putting power into the hands of a few buyers, the dynamics of B2B are different. Some companies (such as technology, software, health) offer similar products to both commercial and business markets, but purchases and services from company to company (eg: accountancy service or website design), components purchased from various suppliers and other equipment manufacturers (OEMs), businesses selling directly to the end user/consumer (B2C), and complicated organisational decision-making units (DMU) make B2B buyer behaviour and pathway to purchase much more complex.

B2B brand management is the fluid and responsive organisational framework that prioritises the systematic stages of planning, development, implementation and the evaluation of the brand strategy; all of which involves all levels of marketing management. Given the many dynamics at play in B2B, (Kotler & Pföertsch, 2006, p. 9) argue that in order to build a long-term basis for competitive advantage and long-term profitability, companies must continuously identify:

- new value opportunities (*value exploration*);
- realise them in new and promising value offerings (*value creation);* and,
- use capabilities and infrastructure to deliver there is new value offerings efficiently (*value delivery*).

There are many buyer behaviour dimensions at play such as supply-chain, global social, cultural, economic, political and technological drivers to name but a few. Besides product leadership and operational excellence, one strategy relevant to B2B organisations is *customer intimacy*, a flexible, customer-centric approach to creating mutually beneficial value. Paradoxically, brand value and loyalty relies greatly in reinforcing brand relationships at a macro-level (corporate identity) through cultivating relationships at a personal/micro-level (importance of personal brand) that centres on trust, communication and customers seeing the behaviours that reinforce their expectations in customer experience.

A concept, and indeed a practical framework, which originated in B2C service marketing to describe the process of managing customer-company encounters is the "customer decision journey" (CDJ) (McKinsey, 2009) is being progressively utilised to further the notion of *customer-centricity* in B2B markets. This recognises that the traditional 'sales funnel' described a static, linear purchasing path, is no longer appropriate to the modern B2B purchase dynamic where control of customer and end user touchpoints is critical, replacing the metaphor with a 'loyalty loop'. Lingqvist, Plotkin & Stanley (2013) developed the model for B2B application claiming that its adoption has helped shift as much as 40% marketing spend to activities that generate higher ROI, boosting sales by an average 5–10%, one company yielding 8–10% higher revenues.

17.4 Branding in a B2B context

Corporate branding is contingent on the promise made to external stakeholders (Balmer & Gray, 2003), and the meaning created by those various parties. Therefore, a pre-requisite for B2B organisations to affect and manage interactions between the organisation and its stakeholders is having an in-depth understanding of the dynamics that shape their brand strategy formation (Lindgreen, Beverland, & Farrelly, 2010). Though there are limited academic studies concerned with the importance of brand value in a B2B context, some offer valuable insight. Vallaster and Lindgreen (2011) present "strategy-as-practice research identifying the brand actors who participate in corporate brand strategy formation, the construction of manifestations that subject the brand values to experience, and the situational context, all within a single, on-going recursive interaction process ". In other words, viewing branding through a practice lens (brand strategy as situationally accomplished), brand practices (actual activities by the organisation), and brand practitioners (skilled actors involved in brand strategy making). Ozdemir *et al* (2020) usefully explored this dynamic and identified how different types of corporate brand value, which centre on developing tangible and intangible value can be generated in B2B marketing relationships. Furthermore, it is argued that there is often more emphasis given in communicating the functional benefits of a brand in B2B relationships but with limited research attention on intangible or emotional aspects (Mudambi, 2002). This tends to be more prevalent in companies that are often drawn into a dominant product-orientated, approach, which is argued to contribute to a 'corporate zit', an antithesis of a marketing/branding as a philosophy – brand-company-customer (Sargeant, 2009). Furthermore, Ozdemir *et al* (2020) highlight the need to build and enhance different types of brand value, and its impact on B2B relationship initiation and maintenance strategies, re-addressing the balance so that intangible benefits are equally important, if not more in this dynamic. Additionally, there is a lack of identification and exploitation of the benefits of value-creation at a strategic, corporate level of branding activities, which can enhance brand relationships at a tactical management level from a supplier/customer's perspective (Gupta, Malhotra, Czinkota, & Foroud, 2016). Kotler and Pföertsch (2006) describe the B2B 'Branding Triangle' as being the basis "for competitive advantage and long-term profitability. The components – 'customer', 'company', and 'collaboration' – depict *customer-company fusion*. Below is an illustration of how these unique 'actors' and complex dynamics are applied in the B2B brand strategy context of *Dell Technologies*:

- *Company: Dell Technologies*, is one of the world's largest and well-known companies, helping organisations (B2B) and consumers (B2C) in providing computers, PC, laptops and all types of IT infrastructure required in the data era. It has a clear corporate brand purpose: "our purpose is to drive human progress, through greater access to better technology, for people with big ideas around the world." (*Dell Technologies* – Purpose, 2021).[213] In the context of this case, it focuses solely on its workforce solutions (B2B brand) to aid their customer's digital transformation.
- *Customer: BP* – the focus was on their Global Energy Business, which has a significant reach across the 'world's energy system'. They have just under 100,000 IT users and operate across many territories, including 78 countries. Moreover, their employees operate in a multitude of environments including those based in offices, trading floors, off offshore rigs and on ships. Much like *Dell Technologies*, *BP* has a clear (corporate) brand purpose: "Our purpose is re-imagining energy for

---

213 https://corporate.delltechnologies.com/en-gb/about-us/who-we-are.htm.

people and our planet. We want to help the world reach net zero and improve people's lives." (*BP* – Purpose, 2021).[214]

– *Collaboration*: It was clear that *BP*'s situation was immensely complex, due to that fact that there is such a large spread employee base, working in wide-ranging environments, all with different requirements for workplace solutions, in order to deliver their brand purpose. Likewise, *Dell Technologies*' own brand purpose focuses on digital transformation, which in this case can be translated to enabling *BP*'s Digital transformation. Indeed, the VP Enterprise IT&S at *BP* highlighted this strategic need and the conditions of success: "The energy industry is going through a remarkable level of transformation and it's happening an incredible pace and as we think about the role that technology has to play, he has to enable new innovations people have to work quite differently. This isn't an exercise in just replacing hardware it was it about really transforming the way we work, and then underpinning that with the right technology" (*Dell Technologies*, Customer Stories).[215]

© Science Photo Library via canva.com

214 https://www.bp.com/en/global/corporate/who-we-are/our-purpose.html.
215 https://www.dellemc.com/resources/en-us/asset/customer-profiles-case-studies/solutions/dell-bp-services.mp4
The photo(s) used in this case study is not connected and/or does not represent any brand(s) mentioned. It used to make a visual discussion point by the authors.

17.5 Digital transformation, pivoting a B2C model in a B2B context

As highlighted in *Chapter 7*, digital transformation acknowledges the fact that digital technology across the whole business ecosystem is such a priority for business growth that it transcends hierarchies, functions, operational borders, strategic initiatives and geographical boundaries. Indeed, it is argued that whilst customer-company fusion relies on human capital to execute purpose-driven brand strategy, the diffusion of digital and technology transformation requires an integrated strategy (rather than an add-on amendment) involving cultural change and company collaboration.

This case demonstrates the key target outcomes highlighted previously: (1) optimise and develop business processes; (2) change culture and enhance customer experience through innovative, (3) meaningful interactions and service to add value and foster brand loyalty; (4) and create a more fulfilling experience for employees.

Digital transformation is a very broad term and as a consequence needs to be framed the context of the case; *Deloitte* highlight its broadness and importance: "Digital technologies are accelerators of innovation. They can improve efficiency, power new products and services, enable new business models, and blur the boundaries between industries. Every successful enterprise will one day be a digital enterprise." *(Deloitte – Digital Transformation, 2021).*[216] Likewise, *Dell Technologies* have developed a seminal *Digital Transformation Index (DT Index)*, which is a global benchmarking indicator for businesses to assess their status, typology or stage of transformation across the globe, and how they are fundamentally performing in the digital age against their peers *(Dell Technologies – Digital Transformation Index*, 2020).[217] Their benchmarking typologies are as follows:
- *"Digital Leaders:* Digital ingrained in the DNA.
- *Digital Adopters:* Mature digital plans, investments and innovations in place.
- *Digital Evaluators: Gradual digital transformation and planning.*
- *Digital followers: Very few investments; tentative plans.*
- *Digital laggards – no digital plans; limited initiatives and investments."*

This form of 'company segmentation' provides a unique insight into 'customer' needs and wants, key barriers for technology adoption and fundamentally support brand positioning and developing brand equity and value across the broad spectrum of sectors, context, customer and end-user needs, in a true global context.

---

216 https://www2.deloitte.com/us/en/insights/topics/digital-transformation.html.
217 *Dell Technologies – Digital Technology Index (2020)* https://www.delltechnologies.com/en-gb/perspectives/digital-transformation-index.htm#pdf-overlay=//www.delltechnologies.com/asset/en-gb/solutions/business-solutions/briefs-summaries/dt-index-2020-executive-summary.pdf.

Dell Technologies, in partnership with the Futures Research Group Institute for the Future (IFTF) identified three key digital drivers that will "transform the future of work by 2030: (1) Inclusive talent – Human-machine partnerships will make it possible to find and match people's unique capabilities and compatibilities; (2) Empowered workers – Real-time and immersive collaboration will empower workers across the world; (3) AI fluency – A deep understanding of AI will unlock human potential and set workers apart."

(*Dell Technologies*, Future of Work, 2021).[218]

From a customer perspective – *BP* – they identified the challenges faced in company-wide digital transformations; whereby *Dell Technologies* provided an innovative pivot, utilising their world-renowned supply chain and deploying their B2C strategic capability, expertise and know-how by prioritising the end user (ie: *BP* employees) approaching it with a really simple, clear and empowering B2B customer journey. This was achieved by pivoting and developing an unique solution one, that focused on delivering tangible and intangible brand value. The Programme Director highlighted the principles that underpinned the 'customer-company-collaboration':

Typically customer (end-user) satisfaction rates were not running particularly high, a lot of performance issues, lots of end of service life issues (workplace equipment) and all of that impacts productivity. We wanted to move from a world where refresh was done 'To You' to a world where it done 'By You'. We absolutely wanted it to be user choice, we wanted this to feel like it was very consumer style service. We wanted our workforce to really be empowered so that they can leveraged the platform that had been laid down for them. We were looking for performance driven devices, robust devices and very cool devices to use; and when we looked at the Dell Technologies – that is exactly what offered to us.
Source: Programme Director, Workplace Transformation & PCaaS, Enterprise IT&S, *BP*.[219]

This personifies the importance of building brand relationships and co-creating value to achieve corporate brand success in B2B. In other words, even within large global companies the need to go beyond tangible brand value and leverage the power of intangible brand value is imperative. It is corporate branding truthfully originates from the aptitude to create genuine relationships encouraged as partnerships rather than purely transactional business (Erevelles, Stevenson, Srinvasan, & Fukawa, 2008).

---

218 *Dell Technologies* and *Institute for the Future* (2021), Future of Work: Forecasting emerging technologies impact on work in the next era of human-machine partnerships https://www.delltech nologies.com/en-us/perspectives/future-of-work.htm#pdf-overlay=//www.delltechnologies.com/asset/en-us/solutions/business-solutions/industry-market/realizing_2030_future_of_work_report_dell_technologies.pdf.
219 https://www.dellemc.com/resources/en-us/asset/customer-profiles-case-studies/solutions/dell-bp-services.mp4.

17.6 B2B relationship-driven tangible and intangible brand value

It is argued that the foundation of relationship-driven brand value (tangible and intangible) is grounded in different stages of the B2B relationship – in this case a familiarity of each other in collaboration. However, crucially, *Dell Technologies*' corporate brand is a powerful driver in building such a successful collaboration. This is evidenced here:

> The most significant benefit is that [BP] we transformed how are our people work, simply by giving them the right tool to do their job. They can choose how they work, where they work and when they work. It's critical that BP attracts and retains the right talent. The Dell Technologies services, expertise and capability we are able to save in the region 60% (that is $30 million) for us every refresh cycle. That is significant.
> Source: Programme Director, Workplace Transformation & PCaaS, Enterprise IT&S, *BP*.[220]

Here, the role of *Dell Technologies* corporate brand is fundamental, combining clear corporate personality and identity fostering the conditions for success. Corporate brand can be defined as the total sum of characteristics other company including intellectual and behavioural characteristics that serve to distinguish one organisation from another (Foroudi, Balmer, Chen, Foroudi, & Patsala, 2020). Often corporate identity is influenced by key senior figures and/or founder(s). For instance, *Apple* was (and arguably still is) synonymous with Steve Jobs 'design, nonconformity and creativity'; *Amazon*'s 'custom obsession and innovation' is synonymous with Jeff Bezos. The same could be applied with *Dell Technologies*, which is synonymous with Michael Dell, a personification of the case's thrust in a summary of the founding principles via their clear corporate purpose (website):[221]

> We create technologies that drive human progress.
>
> Our story began with a belief and a passion: that everybody should have easy access to the best technology anywhere in the world. That was in 1984 in Michael Dell's University of Texas dorm room. Today, Dell Technologies is instrumental in changing the digital landscape the world over.
>
> We are among the world's leading technology companies helping to transform people's lives with extraordinary capabilities. From hybrid cloud solutions to high-performance computing to ambitious social impact and sustainability initiatives, what we do impacts everyone, everywhere.[222]

The power of embedding corporate personality traits that mirror key figureheads is that they are positively associated with the corporate brand, imperative to strengthening brand relationships in a B2B context. *Dell Technologies*' strategic vision and acquisitions have built an end-to-end IT solutions and infrastructure that allows for

---

220 https://www.dellemc.com/resources/en-us/asset/customer-profiles-case-studies/solutions/dell-bp-services.mp4.
221 https://fortune.com/company/dell-technologies/.
222 https://corporate.delltechnologies.com/en-gb/about-us/who-we-are.htm retrieved 16th October 2021.

innovations highlighted in this case and beyond. Their truly global and far-reaching business capabilities are driving change and transformation for customers (B2B and B2C) from across the provision of personal computers and equipment, workplace solutions, IT infrastructure (end-to-end), security to name but a few. It is an all-encompassing value proposition, where 'direct' plays a central role in its corporate brand identity.

Of course, *Dell Technologies'* is one of the largest technology companies in the world, with 158,000 employees,[223] even with such a large employee base, corporate brand personality and association with Michael Dell is highlighted in this case, but also connecting his book 'Play Nice, But Win: A CEO's Journey from Founder to Leader' (Dell, 2021) where his insightful and candid analysis outlines his own journey as well as *Dell Technologies*. This case represents an inherent entrepreneurial spirit of innovation, growth through change and learning with a focus on improvement and customer-centricity, whilst leaning on strategic capability and, of course detailed execution. That is to say, this clearly aligns very closely to what is detailed in Michael Dell's summation of his guiding framework that arguably underpins this corporate brand personality. The following is a selection of this guiding framework that relate to this case [there were 21 in total]:

"Things I believe. The following, in no particular order, are principles, traits, ideals and lessons that have helped me and our company succeed:

- Curiosity. Have I mentioned curiosity already? It's so important, I'll say it again: Always be learning. You want to have big ears. To listen, to learn, and to always be curious. To be open to ambiguity. Design your company from the customer back.
- Used facts and data to make decisions. Be objective and humble and willing to change your mind if the facts and data suggest that's what is needed. The scientific method works in business.
- The rate of change in only increasing. It will not slow down in the future.
- Ideas are a commodity. Execution of them is not. Coming up with a great idea or strategy is necessary but not sufficient for success. You must execute. This requires detailed operational discipline and understanding.
- Be willing to take risks, experiment, test things. As the rate of change increases, small experiments will build a path to success.
- Find purpose and passion in your life by being part of something greater than yourself."

(Dell, 2021, pp. 322–324)

---

[223] https://fortune.com/company/dell-technologies/

The photo(s) used in this case study is/are not connected and/or does not represent any brand(s) mentioned. It/they is/are used to make a visual discussion point by the authors.

Indeed viewing this case via this framework provides a useful lens into the importance of a top down and bottom-up approach. For instance Founder / CEO dynamics such as corporate brand personality and entrepreneurial spirit are influencing values, culture and customer-company fusion, where bottom-up drivers meet top-down drivers to delivering tangible and intangible brand value by recognising the importance of (corporate) brand purpose that is driven by customer-centricity ('working backwards'), from the various needs and wants of customers, and a transformational end-user experience. These corporate personality traits guide employees in their decision-making, how they connect, and how they act with the customers and prospects. Usefully, Ozdemir *et al* (2020) identify this as: *"its 'heart' (passion and compassion), 'mind' (creativity and discipline) and 'body' (agile and collaborative) to guide employees with impact on how it will be seen by others"*. In addition, they build on a body of knowledge and cite how: corporate identity in this context can be identified as the key features, characteristics, traits or attributes in delivering *Dell Technologies* workforce solutions and transformation for *BP*. For example, collaboration underlines a holistic co-created corporate identity of both customer-company whereby there is a stronger alignment for both *Dell Technologies* and *BP*'s (individual and collective) expression of their company's philosophy, values, and mission, and communications; and corporate visual identity to all its audience (Ozdemir et al 2020; Balmer, 2001; Foroudi et al., 2020).

In practical terms, as we've seen, the customer wanted a smooth B2B customer journey for the end-users (ie: employees) which offer "back-end efficiencies across the whole supply chain, ordering, imaging shipping and delivery – which are laughing additional benefit of using *Dell Technologies* (ie: as-a-service)" Programme Director, Workplace Transformation & PCaaS, Enterprise IT&S, *BP*.[224]

As we have seen, transformation is an immensely complex task which can lead to an imbalance of only focusing on tangible/functional needs, such as technical specifications. The case demonstrates the need to also focus on the intangible emotional needs, and indeed, a customer-company fusion, deploying collaboration in a B2B context, as Doug Schmitt suggests:

> *Dell Technologies is very focused on making IT and workforce transformation very easy. Modernising is complex, especially on a global scale. As a large organisation going through our own transformation, we have a unique perspective and appreciation how to make it real. We work closely with BP to fully understand their culture, and how they do business, so we can provide that the personalised experience their employees are looking for.*
> Source: *Doug Schmitt – President of Dell Technologies*[225]

---

224 https://www.dellemc.com/resources/en-us/asset/customer-profiles-case-studies/solutions/dell-bp-services.mp4.
225 https://www.dellemc.com/resources/en-us/asset/customer-profiles-case-studies/solutions/dell-bp-services.mp4.

In the case of *Dell Technologies*, the need to be able to deliver a seamless B2B customer experience by innovating, effectively mapping customer and then user expectations, by promoting their own corporate brand values and delivering that purpose for *BP* in a clear collaboration, was of paramount importance. The four key elements in co-creating brand value, related to the 'End-user' buying portal, that mirrored a typical e-retailer:

> *There are four key elements the service that we [BP] jointly develop with them [Dell Technologies]:*
>
> *Choose the device*
>
> *Order and pay directly from the advice*
>
> *Receive that device directly.*
>
> *Set that device up very easily*
>
> Source: Programme Director, Workplace Transformation & PCaaS, Enterprise IT&S, *BP.*[226]

In many ways this could be perceived as a typical B2B functional/tangible benefits equation (eg: brand competence, economic benefits, assurances are likely to support their firms' business performances and profitability). However, the *BP* 'end users' highlight how the collaboration was able to build a brand relationship, a seamless customer experience, and deliver powerful intangible benefits such as empowerment, autonomy and feeling very valued. The following is a vignette of multiple end users, using a public facing source, when discussing the benefit delivering innovative digital transformation:

> *Having the autonomy and agency, in that this is the one I want [rather than this is the one I am getting!] – made me feel really valued as employee. Basically, it was easy as ordering on an online shopping store. Surprisingly, the great thing was how easy was to setup . . . I was able to setup the device according to my preferences and needs in just 15 minutes.*
>
> Selected vignette of End-users:
> *BP.*[227]

---

226 https://www.dellemc.com/resources/en-us/asset/customer-profiles-case-studies/solutions/dell-bp-services.mp4.

227 https://www.dellemc.com/resources/en-us/asset/customer-profiles-case-studies/solutions/dell-bp-services.mp4.

© wildpixel from Getty Images via canva.com

Clearly, as indicated, digital transformation is a very broad area, and the case has focused on a specific area so that the dynamics of branding in B2B can be evidenced and how corporate brand and relationships can deliver tangible and intangible brand value. Moreover, it clearly shows how *Dell Technologies* have "(1) new value opportunities *(value exploration)*; (2) realise them in new and promising value offerings *(value creation)*, and last but not least to (3) use capabilities and infrastructure to deliver there is new value offerings efficiently *(value delivery)* (Kotler & Pföertsch, 2006).

Indeed, it could be argued that the 'corporate' brand and relationships and value (tangible/intangible) in a B2B context is the 'glue' that binds/fuses the customer-company-collaboration, and personifies the corporate personality, aligning and co-creating *Dell-BP* corporate identity as a basis for competitive advantage and long-term profitability (Kotler & Pföertsch, 2006, p. 9).

The photo(s) used in this case study is/are not connected and/or does not represent any brand(s) mentioned. It/they is/are used to make a visual discussion point by the authors.

Chapter takeaways

- The B2B branding context is multi-faceted and complex, where corporate brand purpose, personality, and identity play an integral role.
- *Dell Technologies* demonstrates that there are multiple layers between customers and 'end-users', creating trust and loyalty relies greatly on the underpinning brand relationships both at a macro-level (corporate identity) and through cultivating relationships at a micro-level (importance of personal aspects of the brand).
- *Dell Technologies* highlight the importance of brand relationships and leveraging corporate personality to act as a catalyst for innovation and digital transformation, by applying a B2B customer journey, generating brand value through tangible (functional) and intangible (emotional benefits) delivery.
- In a hyper-competitive market, the relationship between customer and company is crucial in creating brand value and differentiation.
- Often B2B brand equity is overly focused on *functional* qualities (eg: technology, capacity, quality, after-sales service), *Dell Technologies* presents a strong case that highlights the important role that *emotional* qualities (eg: trust, reassurance, responsiveness, risk reduction) play. Long-term brand equity development has centred around new value opportunities *(value exploration)*, realised in new and promising value offerings *(value creation)*, and the capabilities and infrastructure needed to deliver their new value offerings efficiently *(value delivery)*.
- In a B2B context, brand value and loyalty relies greatly on reinforcing brand relationships at both a macro- and micro-level reinforcing trust, communication, and behaviours which reflect customers' expectations and enhance their experience.
- *Dell Technologies* ability to segment and develop targeted personas for customer and end-user, allowed for clarity in clear tangible (eg: functional) and intangible (eg: emotional) brand value and outcomes.
- The 'corporate' brand relationships and value (tangible/intangible) in a B2B context are the 'glue' that binds/fuses the customer-company-collaboration, and personifies the corporate personality, aligning and co-creating the *Dell Technologies-BP* corporate identity as a basis for competitive advantage and long-term profitability.
- The power, importance and influence of Michael Dell in the embedding corporate personality traits and guiding a cultural framework cannot be understated. There is clearly a positive balance and connection with the wider corporate brand and entrepreneurial spirit, imperative to strengthening brand relationships in this B2B context.

References

Aaker, D. A. (1991). *Managing Brand Equity: Capitalising on the value of a brand name*. New York: The Free Press.

Aaker, D. A. (1996). *Building Strong Brands*. Hoboken, NY: The Free Press.

Aaker, D. A. (1996). Measuring brand equity across products and markets. *Californian Management Review, 38*(3), 102–120.

Aaker, D. A. (2004). *Brand Portfolio Strategy*. New York, NY: The Free Press.

Aaker, D. A. (2014). *Aaker on Branding: 20 Principles That Drive Success*. New York, NY: Morgan James.

Aaker, D. A. (2021). What is Brand Equity? Aaker On Brands. *Prophet Thinking*.

Aaker, D. A., & Joachimsthaler, E. (2000). *Brand Leadership*. New York: The Free Press.

Aaker, D. A., & Keller, K. L. (1990). Consumer evaluation of brand extensions. *Journal of Marketing, 54*.

Abbott, H. P. (2002). *The Cambridge Introduction to Narrative*. Cambridge, UK: Cambridge University Press.

Abernethy, M. A., Horne, M., Lillis, A. M., Malina, M. A., & Selto, F. H. (2005). A multi-method approach to building causal performance maps from expert knowledge. *Management Accounting Research, 16*(2), 135–155.

Abimbola, T., & Vallaster, C. (2007). Brand, organisational identity and reputation in SMEs: an overview. *Qualitative Market Research: An International Journal, 10*(4), 341–348.

Abratt, R., & Kleyn, N. (2012). Corporate identity, corporate branding, and corporate reputations: Reconciliation and integration. *European Journal of Marketing, 7* (8), 1048–1063.

Accenture Strategy Research Report. (2018). *To Affinity and Beyond: From me to we: The rise of the purpose-led brand*.

Adams, J., & Eveland, V. (2007). Marketing Online Degree Programmes: How Do Traditional-Residential Programmes Compete? *Journal of Marketing for Higher Education*, 67–90.

Adjei, M. T., Noble, S. M., & Noble, C. H. (2010). The influence of C2C communications in online brand communities on customer purchase behaviour. *Journal of the Academy Marketing Science, 38*, 634–653.

Adler, P. S., & Kwon, S. (2000). Social capital: the good the bad and the ugly. In E. Lesser. (ed.), *Knowledge and Social capital: Foundations and Applications* (pp. 89–115). Boston, MA: Butterworth-Heinemann.

Adner, R. (2016). Ecosystem as Structure: An Actionable Construct for Strategy. *Journal of Management, 43*(1), 39–58.

Advertisers, A. N. A. (2018).

Ahearne, M., Bhattacharrya, C. B., & Gruen, T. (2005). Antecedents and consequences of customer-company identification: expanding the role of relationship marketing. *Journal of Applied Psychology, 90*(3), 574–595.

Ahmad, N., Iqbal, N., Kanwal, R., Javed, H., Dera, J., & Khan, G. (2014). The mediating role of employee engagement in relationship of internal branding and brand experience: case. *of service organizations of Dera International Journal of Information, Business, and Management, 6*(4), 26–41.

Akaka, M. A., & Chandler, J. D. (2011). Roles as resources: A social roles perspective of change in value networks. *Marketing Theory, 11*(3), 243–260.

Akaka, M., & Vargo, S. (2013). Technology as an operant resource in service (eco)systems. *Information Systems and e-Business Management, 12* (3), 367–384.

https://doi.org/10.1515/9783110718638-023

Alcaniz, E. B., Caceres, R. C., & Perez, R. C. (2010). Alliances between brands and social causes: The influence of company credibility on social responsibility image. *Journal of Business Ethics*, *96*, 169–186.

Allen, C. T., Fournier, S., & Miller, F. (2008). Brands and their Meaning Makers. In P. Curtis, P. Haugtvedt, P. Herr, R. Frank, & T. Kardes, *in Handbook of Consumer Psychology. Eds* (pp. 781–822). epublications https://epublications.marquee,edu/market_fac/98MarketingFacultyResearch.

Alliance, G.S.I. (2018). Global Sustainable Investment Review. Available online: http://www.gsi-alliance.org/wp-content/uploads/2019/03/GSIR_Review2018.3.28.pdf (accessed on 11 July 2021).

Alt, M. A., Săplăcan, Z., Benedek, B., & Nagy, B. Z. (2021). Digital touchpoints and multichannel segmentation approach in the life insurance industry. *International Journal of Retail & Distribution Management*, *49*(5), 652–677.

Alvesson, M. (1998). Gender relations and identity at work: a case study of masculinities and femininities in an advertising agency. *Human Relations*, *51*(8), 969–1005.

Ambler, T. (2000). *Marketing and the Bottom Line: The New Metrics of Corporate Wealth*. London: Financial Times/Prentice-Hall.

Ambler, T., Bhattacharya, C. B., Edell, J., Keller, K. L., Lemon, K. N., & Mittal, V. (2002). Relating brand and customer perspectives on marketing management. *Journal of Service Research*, *5*(1), 13–.

Ambrosini, V., & Bowman, C. (2009). What are dynamic capabilities and are they a useful construct in strategic management? *International Journal of Management Reviews*, *11*(1), 29–49.

Amit, R., & Zott, C. (2001). Value creation in E-business. *Strategic Management Journal*, *22*, 493–520.

Anderson, J., Narus, J., & van Rossum, W. (2006). Customer Value Propositions in Business Markets. *Harvard Business Review*, 91–99.

Anderson, L., Pass, N., Ager, T., & Spohrer, J. (2008). Science Service and Service-Dominant Logic. *Otttago Forum 2*.

Anees-ur-Rehman, M., Wong, H. Y., Sultan, P., & Merrilees, B. (2018). How brand-oriented strategy affectsthe financial performance of B2B SMEs. *Journal of Business & Industrial Marketing*, *33*(3), 303–315.

Anixter, J. (2003). Transparency or not? Brand Inside: Brand Outside. The most obvious yet overloaded next source for the brand's authentic evolution. In N. Ind, *Beyond Branding* (pp. 161–182). London: Kogan Page.

Anker, T. B., Sparks, L., Moutinho, L., & Grönroos, C. (2014). Consumer dominant value creation: A theoretical response to the recent call for a consumer dominant logic for marketing. *European Journal of Marketing*, *49*(3/4), 532–560.

Antorini, Y. M., & Schultz, M. (2005). Corporate Branding and the Conformity Trap. In M. Schultz, Y. M. Antorini, F. F. Csaba, & (eds), *Corporate Branding. Purpose, People, Processes*. København: Copenhagen Business School.

Ardley, B. C., & Quinn, L. (2014). Practitioner accounts and knowledge production: analysis of three marketing discourses. *Marketing Theory*, *14*(1), 97–118.

Arnould, E. (2005). Animating the big middle. *Journal of Retailing*, *18*(2), 89–96.

Arnould, E. J., & Price, L. L. (2000). Authenticating acts and authoritative performances. Questing for self community. In S. Ratneshwar, D. G. Mick, & C. Huffman, *The why of consumption. Contemporary perspectives on consumer motives, goals and desires* (pp. 140–163). London: Rutledge.

Arnould, E. J., & Thompson, C. J. (2005). Consumer culture theory: Twenty years of research. *Journal of Consumer Research*, *31*(4), 8686–882.

Arvidsson, A. (2005). Brands: A Critical Perspective. *Journal of Consumer Culture*, *5*(2), 235–258.

Arvidsson, A. (2007). The Logic of the Brand. *European Journal of Economic and Social Systems, 20*.

Ashcraft, K., Muhr, S. L., Rennstam, J., & Sullivan, K. (2012). Professionalisation as a branding activity: Occupational identity and the dialectic of inclusivity-exclusivity. *Gender Work and Organisation, 19*, 467–488.

Ashworth, G., & Kavaratzis, M. (2010). *Towards effective place brand managemennt: Branding European cities and regions*.

Aßländer, M. S., & Curbach, J. (2014). The corporation as citizen? Towards a new understanding of corporate citizenship. *Journal of Business Ethics, 120*(4), 541–554.

Atuahene-Gima, K., Slater, S. F., & Olson, E. M. (2005). The contingent value of responsive and proactive market orientations for new product program performance. *Journal of Product Innovation Management, 22*(6), 464–482.

Avallone, I. V., & Giraldi, J. E. (2012). Conscious Consumption: A Study on Plastic Bag Consumers in Brazil. *International Journal of Psychological Studies, 4*(1), 122–134.

Axelsson, B. and Easton, G. (1992). Industrial Networks (Routledge Revivals): A New View of Reality, London; Routledge.

Bachman, T. (2001). Welcome back to the branch. *Bank marketing, 33*(1), 40–47.

Badejo, F. A., Rundle-Thiele, S., & Kubacki, K. (2019). Taking a wider view: A formative multi-stream approach to understanding human trafficking as a social issue in Nigeria. *Journal of Social Marketing, 9*(4), 467–484.

Badrinarayanan, V., Suh, T., & Kim, K.-M. (2016). Brand resonance in franchising relationships: A franchisee-based perspective. *Journal of Business Research, 69*, 3943–3950.

Bagozzi, R. P., Batra, R., & Ahuvia, A. (2017). Brand love: development and validation of a practical scale. *Marketing Letters, 28*(1), 1–14.

Baker, M. J. (2013). Michael J. Baker: reflections on a career in marketing. *Journal of Historical Research in Marketing, 5*(2), 223–30.

Baker, M. J., & Holt, S. (2004). Making marketers accountable: *Marketing Intelligence and Planning, 22*(5), 567–578.

Balakrishnan, M. S. (2009). Strategic Branding of Destination. *European Journal of Marketing, 43*(5/6), 611–629.

Ballantyne, D. (2003). A Relationship Mediated Theory of Internal Marketing. *European Journal of Marketing, 37*(9), 1242–1260.

Ballantyne, D., & Varey, R. (2006). Introducing a Dialogical Orientation to the Service-Dominant Logic of Marketing. In R. Lusch, & S. Vargo, *The Service Dominant Logic of Marketing: Dialog, Debate and Directions* (pp. 1242–1260). Armonk, NY: M. E. Sharpe.

Ballantyne, D., & Varey, R. J. (2006). Creating value-in-use through marketing interaction: the exchange logic of relating, communicating and knowing. *Marketing Theory, 6*(3), 335–348.

Ballantyne, D., & Varey, R. J. (2006). Introducing a dialogue orientation to the Service Dominant Logicof Marketing. In R. F. Lusch, & S. L. Vargo, *The Service Dominant Logic of Marketing. Dialog, Debate and Directions* (pp. 224–235). Armonk, NY: M.E. Sharpe.

Balmer, J. M. (2001), "Corporate identity, corporate branding and corporate marketing-seeing through the fog", *European Journal of Marketing*, Vol. 35, No. 3/4, pp. 248–291.

Balmer, J. M. (2006). *Comprehending corporate marketing and the corporate marketing mix*. Working paper, Bradford School of Management, Bradford.

Balmer, J. M. (2008). Identity based views of the corporation: Insights from corporate identity, organisational identity, social identity, visual identity, and corporate image. *European Journal of Marketing, 42*(9/10), 879–906.

Balmer, J. M. (2013). Corporate brand orientation: What is it? What of it? *Journal Brand Management*(20), 723–741.

Balmer, J. M. (2008). Identity based views of the corporation: Insights from corporate identity, organisational identity, social identity, visual identity, corporate brand identity and corporate image. *European Journal of Marketing, 42*(9/10), 879–906.

Balmer, J. M. (2009). Corporate marketing: apocalypse, advent, and epiphany. *Mangement Decision, 47*(4), 544–572.

Balmer, J. M. (2012). Strategic corporate brand alignment: perspectives from identity-based views of the firm. *European Journal of Marketing, 48*(7/8), 1064–1092.

Balmer, J. M., & Greyser, S. A. (2006). Corporate marketing: Integrating corporate identity, corporate branding, corporate communications, corporate image, and corporate reputation. *European Journal of Marketing, 40*(7/8), 730–741.

Balmer, J. M., & Thomson, I. (2009). The shared management and ownership of corporate brands: The case of Hilton. *Journal of General Mangement, 34*(4), 15–37.

Barker, M., Barker, D., Bormann, N., & Neher, K. (2013). *Social Media Marketing A Strategic Approach*. South Western: Cengage Learning.

Barney, J. (1991). Firm Resources and Sustained Competitive Advantage. *Journal of Management, 17*, 99–120.

Barrett, M. I., Davidson, E., Prabhu, J. C., & Vargo, S. L. (2015). Service Innovation in the Digital Age: Key Contributions and Future Directions. *MIS Quarterly, 39*(1), pp. 135–154.

Barwitz, N., & Maas, P. (2018). Understanding the Omnichannel Customer Journey: Determinants of Interaction Choice. *Journal of Interactive Marketing, 43*, 116–133.

Basedo, D., Smith, K., Grimm, C., Rindova, V., & Derfus, P. (2006). The impact of market actions on firm reputation. *Strategic Management Journal, 27*(12), 1205–1219.

Batey, M. (2008). *Brand Meaning*. London: Routledge.

Batra, R., Ahuvia, A., & Bagozzi, R. P. (2012). Brand Love. *Journal of Marketing, 76*(2), 1–16.

Baudrillard, J. (1968). *The System of Objects*. Paris.

Baudrillard, J. (1988). *Selected Writings (Mark Poster, Trans.)*. Stanford, California: Stanford University Press.

Baudrillard, J. (1994). Simulacra and Simulations: The Precession of Simulacra. In E. G. Glaser.

Baumgarth, C., & Schmidt, M. (2010). How strong is the business-to-business brand in the workforce? An empirically tested model of 'internal brand equity' in a business-to-business setting. *Industrial Marketing Management, 39*(8), 1250–1260.

Bejou, D. (2011). Compassion as the New Philosophy of Business. *Journal of Relationship Marketing, 10*(1–6).

Belk, R. K. (1988). Possessions and the extended self. *Journal of Historical Research in Marketing, 7*(2), 184–207.

Belk, R. K. (1988). Possessions and the extended self. *Journal of Consumer Research, 1*, 139–168.

Belk, R. K., Wallendorf, M., & Sherry Jr, J. F. (1989). The Sacred and the Profane in Consumer Behavior: Theodicy on the Odyssey. *Journal of Consumer Research, 16*(1), 1–38.

Benkler, Y. (2006). *The wealth of networks*. Princeton, NJ: Princeton University Press.

Bennett, R., & Choudhury, R. (2009). Prospective Students' Perceptions of University Brands: An Empirical Study. *Journal of Marketing for Higher Education, 19*(1), 85–107.

Bennike, I. H., Wieghorst, A., & Kirk, U. (2017). Online-based Mindfulness Training Reduces Behavioural Markers of Mind Wandering. *Journal of Cognitive Enhancement, 1*, 172–181.

Berabou, R., & Tirole, J. (2010). Individual abd Corporate Social Responsibility. *Economica, 17*, 1–19.

Berger-Remy, F., & Michel, G. (2015). How brand gives employees meaning: Towards an extended view of brand equity. *Recherche et Applications en Marketing*, 1–25.

Bernard, M., Liddle, J., Bartlam, B., & Scharf, T. (2012). Then and now: evolving community in the context of a retirement village. *Ageing & Society, 32*(1), 103–129.

Bernstein, B. (1999). Vertical and horizontal discourse: an essay. *British Journal of Sociology of Education*, *20*(2), 157–73.

Bernstein, D. (2009). Rhetoric and reputation: some thoughts on corporate dissonance. *Managemnt Decision*, *47*(4), 603–615.

Berry, L. L. (1983). Relationship Marketing. In L. L. Berry, G. L. Shostack, & G. D. Upah, *Emerging Perspectives on Services Marketing* (pp. 25–38). Chicago: American Marketing Association.

Berry, L. L. (2000). Cultivating service brand equity. *Journal of the Academy of Marketing Science*, *28*, 128–137.

Berry, L. L. (2000). Cultivating service brand equity. *Academy of Marketing Science Journal*, *28*(1), 128–137.

Berry, L. L., Carbone, L. & Haekel, S. (2002). Managing the Total Customer Experience, *MIT Sloan Management Review*, 43, pp. 114–137.

Berry, M. (1998). Strategic Planning in Small High-tech Companies. *Long range Planning*, 31(3): 455–466.

Berstein, B. (1999). Vertical and horizontal discourse: an essay. *British Journal of Sociology of Education*, *20*(2), 157–73.

Bertilsson, J., & Rennstam, J. (2017). The destructive side of branding: A heuristic model for analysig the value of branding practice. *Organisation*.

Beschorner, T. (2013). Creating Shared Value: One-Trick Pony Approach. *Business Ethics Journal*, *1*(17), 106–112.

Bettencourt, L. A. (1997). Customer voluntary performance: customers as partners in service delivery. *Journal of Retailing*, *73*(3), 383–406.

Beverland. (2009). *Building Brand Authenticity: 7 Habits of Iconic Brands*. Palgrave-Macmillan.

Beverland, F. B., & Farrelly, F. J. (2010). The quest for authenticity in consumption: Consumer's purposive choice of authentic cues to shape experienced outcomes. *Journal of Consumer Research*, *36*(5), 838–850.

Beverland, M. B. (2005). Brand management and the challenge of authenticity. *Journal of Product & Brand Management*, *14*(7), 460–461.

Beverland, M. B. (2006). The 'real thing': Branding authenticity in consumption: Branding authenticity in the luxury wine trade. *Journal of Business Research*, *59*(2), 251–258.

Beverland, M. B., Napoli, J., & Lindgreen, A. (2007). Industrial Global Brand Leadership: A Capabilities View. *Industrial Marketing Management*, *36*, 1082–1093.

Beverland, M. B., Wilner, S., & Micheli, P. (2015). Reconciling the tension between consistency and relevance: Design thinking as a mechanism for brand ambidexterity. *Journal of the Academy of Marketing Science*, *43*(5), 589–609.

Bhattacharya, C. B., & Sen, S. (2004). Doing better at doing good: When, why, and how consumers respond to corporate social initiatives. *California Management Review*, *47*, 9–24.

Bhattacharya, C. B., Korschun, D., & Sen, S. (2009). Strengthening stakeholder-company relationships through mutually beneficial corporate social responsibility initiatives. *Journal of Business Ethics*, *85*(2), 257–272.

Biedenbach, G., & Marell, A. (2010). The impact of customer experience on brand equity in a business-to-business services setting. *Journal of Brand Management*, *17*, 446–458.

Binet, L., & Field, P. (2013). *The Long and the Short of It: Balancing Short and Long-Term Marketing Strategies*. The Institute of Practioners in Advertising.

Biraghi, S., & Gambetti, R. C. (2007). Is brand value co-creation actionable? A facilitation perspective. *Management Decision*, *55*(7), 1476–1488.

Biraghi, S., & Gambetti, R. C. (2013). Corporate branding: Where are we? A systematic communication-based inquiry. *Journal of Marketing Communication*, 1–24.

Biraghi, S., Gambetti, R. C., & Quigley, S. (2020). Brand Purpose as a Cultural Entity Between Business and Society. In J. Marques, & S. Dhiman, *Social Enterpreneurship and Corporate Social Responsibility* (pp. 401–422). Switzerland: Springer.

Biraghi, S., Gambetti, R. C., & Schultz, D. E. (2007). Advancing a citizenship approach to corporate branding: A societal view. *International Studies of Management and Organisation*, *47*(2), 206–215.

Birkinshaw, J., & Gibson, C. (2004). Buidling Ambidexterity Into an Organisation. *MIT Sloan Review*, pp. 47–55.

Bitner, M. J. (1992). Servicescapes: The imapct of physical surroundings on customers and employees. *Journal of Marketing*, *56*(2), 57–71.

Blackwell, R. D., Miniard, P. W., & Engel, J. F. (2006). *Consumer Behaviour, 10th ed*. Thomson South Western.

Blattberg, R. C., & Deighton, J. (1996). Managing Marketing by the Customer Equity Test. *Harvard Business Review*, 136–144.

Bonchek, M., & France, C. (2018). How To Connect Profit and Purpose. *Harvard Business Review*.

Bonnet, D., Buvat, J., & Subrahmanyam, K. (2015). *When digital disruption strikes: how can incumbents respond?* Cap Gemini Consulting.

Bonsón, E., & Ratkai, M. (2013). A set of metrics to assess stakeholder engagement and socil legitimacy on a corporate Facebook page. *Online Information Review*, *37*(5), 787–803.

Booms, B. H., & Bitner, M. J. (1981). Marketing strategies and organisation structures for service firms. In J. Donnelly, & W. R. George, *Marketing of Services*. Chicago, IL: American Marketing Association.

Bouchiki, H., & Kimberley, J. R. (2008). *The Soul of the Corporation: How to Manage the Identity of Your Company*. Upper Saddle River, N. J.: Wharton School Publications.

Bourdieu, P. (1985). The Forms of Capital. In Maureen T. Hallinan (Ed.), *Handbook of Theory and Research for the Sociology of Education* (pp. 241–258). New York: Greenwood.

Bourdieu, P., & Passeron, J-C. (1990). *Reproduction in Education, Society and Culture*. London: SAGE Publications.

Bowden, J. (2009). Customer engagement: A framework for assessing customer-brand relationships: The case of the restaurant industry. *Journal of Hospitality Marketing & Management*, *18*(6), 574–596.

Bower, M., & Garda, R. A. (1985). The Role of Marketing in Management. *McKinsey Quarterly*, *4*, 34–46.

Boyle, E. (2003). A study of entrepreneurial brand building in the manufacturing sector in the UK. *Journal of Product & Brand Management*, *12*(2), 79–93.

Brace-Govan, J. (2015). Faces of power, ethical decision-making and moral intensity. Reflections on the need for critical social marketing. In W. Wymer, *Innovations in social amrketing and public health communication* (pp. 107–132). London: Springer.

Branco, M. C., & Rodrigues, L. L. (2006). Corporate social responsibility and resource-based perspectives. *Journal of Business Ethics*, *75*, 97–113.

Brandes, D. (2004). *Bare Essentials: The Aldi Way to Do Retail Success*. London: Cyan Books.

Breitsohl, J., Dowell, D. J., & Kunz, W. (2013). Community of cuckoo's nest? A taxonomical update on online consumption communities. *Academy of Marketing Conference*. Bournemouth University.

Breznik, K., & Law, K. M. (2019). What do mission statements reveal about the values of top universities in the world? *International Journal of Organizational Analysis*, *27*(5), 1362–1375.

Brierley, S. (2002). *The Advertising Handbook*. London: Routledge.

Brodie, R. J., Glynn, M. S., & Little, V. (2006). The service brand and the service-dominant logic: missing fundamental premise or the need for stronger theory? *Marketing Theory*, *6*(3), 363–379.

Brown, A. W. (2019). *Delivering Digital Transformation: A manager's Guide to the Digital Revolution*. Exeter: University Press.

Brown, B. (2010). *The Gifts of Imperfection*. New York, NY: Penguin Random House.

Brown, S. A. (2012). "I have seen the future and it sucks: Reactionary reflections on reading, writing and research". *European Business Review*, *21*(4), 5–19.

Brown, S. A. (2020). *The Innovation Ultimatum: How Six Strategic Technologies Will Reshape Every Business in the 2020s*. Chichester: John Wiley & Sons.

Brown, S. A. (2005). *Writing Marketing: Literary Lessons from Academic Authorities*. London: SAGE Publications.

Brown, S., Kozinets, R., & Sherry, J. (2003). Teaching old brands new tricks: retro branding and the revival of brand meaning. *Journal of Marketing*, *67*, 19–33.

Browne, J., & Nuttall, R. (2013). Beyond Corporate Social Responsibility: Integrated External Engagement. *McKinsey & Company Home Strategy & Corporate Finance Reports*.

Brownlie, D., & Hewer, P. (2007). 'Concerning marketing critterati: Beyond nuance, estrangement, and elitism'. In M. Saren, P. MacLaran, C. Goulding, R. Elliott, A. Shankar, & P. Catterall, *Critical marketing: Defining the field*. Oxford: Butterworth-Heinemann.

Brownlie, D., & Saren, M. (2004). The Limits of Language: Marketing Praxis and Discourse Beyond Words. *Proceedings of the Academy of Marketing Conference, University of Gloucester*.

Brownlie, D., & Saren, M. (1997). Beyond the one-dimensional marketing manager: The discourse of theory, practice and relevance. *International Journal of Researcn Marketing*, *14*(2), 147–61.

Brownlie, D., Hewer, P., Wagner, D., & Svensson, G. (2008). Management Theory and Practice: Bridging the Gap through Multidisciplinary Lenses. *Special Issue of European Business Review*, *20*(6), 461–470.

Buker, E. A. (1991). 'Rhetoric in Postmodern Feminism: Put-Offs, Put-Ons, and Political Plays'. In D. R. Hiley, *The Interpretive Turn: Philosophy, Science, Culture* (pp. 218–244). Ithaca, NY: Cornell University Press.

Burmann, C. (2010). A call for user generated branding. *Journal of Brand Management*, *18*(1), 1–4.

Burmann, C., & Zeplin, S. (2005). Building brand commitment: A behavioural approach to internal brand management. *Journal of Brand Management*, *12*(4), 279–300.

Burmann, C., Jost-Benz, M., & Riley, N. (2009). Towards an identity-based brand equity model. *Journal of Business Research*, *62*(3), 390–397.

Burmann, C., Zeplin, S., & Riley, N.-M. (2009). Key determinants of internal brand management success: An exploratory empirical analysis. *Journal of Brand Management*, *16*(4), 264–284.

Buttle, F. (2009). *Customer Relationship Management*. Taylor & Francis.

Callingham, M. (2004). *Market Intelligence: How an Why Organisations Use Market Research*. London: Kogan Page.

Cameron, K. S., & Quinn, R. E. (2005). *Diagnosing and changing organisational culture: Based on the competing values framework*. New Jersey: John Wiley & Sons.

Campbell, N., O'Driscoll, A., & Saren, M. (2013). Reconceptualising Resources: A Critique of Service-Dominant Logic. *Journal of Macromarketing*, *33*(4), 306–321.

Carbone, L. P., & Haeckel, S. H. (2002). Engineering Customer Experiences. *Marketing Management, 3*(3).

Carlzon, J. (1987). *Moments of Truth: New Strategies for Today's Customer-Driven Economy*. New York: Balinger Publishing Company.

Carr, A. (2000). Critical Theory and the management of change in organisations. *Journal of Organisational Change Management*, *13*, 208–220.

Carroll, A. (1999). Corporate social responsibility: evolution of a definitional construct. *Business and Society, 38*(3), 268–95.

Carruthers, B. G., & Babb, S. L. (2000). Economy Sociology: Markets, Meanings, and Social Sructures. *Economic Sociology: European Electronic Newsletter, 1*(2), 22–23.

Carson, D. (1990). Assessing small firm marketing. *European Journal of Marketing, 24*(11), 8–51.

Carson, D., & Cromie, S. (1990). Marketing planning in small enterprises: a model and some empirical evidence. *The Journal of Consumer Marketing, 7*(3), 5–18.

Carson, D., & Gilmore, A. (2000). Marketing at the interface: not 'what' but 'how'. *Journal of Marketing Theory and Practice, 8*(2), 1–7.

Carù, A., & Cova, B. (2003). Revisiting consumption experience: A more humble but complete view of the concept. *Marketing Theory, 3*(2), 267–286.

Cassidy, T. (1997). *Environmental Psychology: Behaviour and Experience in Context*. East Sussex, UK: Psychology Press Ltd.

Castets-Renard, C. (2019). Accountability of Algorithms in the GDPR and Beyond: A European Legal Framework on Automated Decision-Making. *Fordham Intellectual Property, Media & Entertainment Law Journal*.

Cayla, J., & Arnould, E. J. (2008). A Cultural Approach to Branding in the Global Marketplace. *Journal of International Marketing, 16*(4), 86–112.

Cayla, J., & Eckhardt, G. M. (2008). Asian brands and the shaping of a transnational imagined community. *Journal of International marketing, 35*(2), 216–230.

Chaffey, D. (2011). *E-Business and E-Commerce Management: Strategy, Implementation and Practice*. London: Finacial Times/Prentice Hall.

Challagalla, G., Murtha, B. R., & Jaworski, B. (2014). Marketing Doctrine: A Principles-Based Approach to Guiding Marketing Decision Making in Firms. *Journal of Marketing, 78*, 4–20.

Champion, L., Economides, M., & Chandler, C. (2018). The efficacy of a brief app-based mindfulness intervention on psychosocial outcomes in healthy adults: A pilot randomised controlled trial. *PLoS ONE, 13*(12).

Chandler, J. D., & Vargo, R. L. (2011). Contextualisation and Value in Context: How Service Frames Exchange. *Marketing Theory, 11*(1), 35–49.

Chang, Y., & Thorson, E. (2004). Television and Web Advertising Synergies. *Journal of Advertising, 33*, 75–84.

Chapleo, L. (2007). Barriers to Brand Building in UK Universities. *Journal of Philanthropy and Marketing, 12*(1), 23–32.

Chase, R. B., & Dasu, S. (2001). Want to Perfect Your Company's Service? Use Behavioural Science. *Harvard Business Review*.

Chase, R. B., & Erikson, W. J. (1988). The Service Factory. *The Academy of Management Executive, 2*(3), 191–196.

Chattananon, A., Lawley, M., Trimesoontorn, J., Supparerkchaisakul, N., & Leelayouthayothin, L. (2007). Building Corporate Image Through Societal marketing Programmes. *Society and Business Review, 3*, 230–253.

Chatterton, P., & Hollands, R. (2003). *Urban Nightscapes: Youth Cultures, Pleasure Spaces and Corporate Power*.

Chaubey, D. S., & Subramanian, K. R. (2020). The Complexity of Market Segmentation Process. *Interantional Journal of Engineering Research and Management, 7*(5), 2349–2058.

Cheetah Digital & Econsultancy. (2021). 2021 Digital Consumer Trends Index. *Marketing Week*.

Christensen, C. M. (1997). *The Innovator's Dilemma: When New Technologies Cause Great Firms to Fail*. Harvard Businees Review Press.

Christensen, L. T., Firat, A. F., & Torp, S. (2008). The Organization of Integrated Communications: Toward Flexible Integration. *European Journal of Marketing, 42*(3/4), 423–452.

Christodoulides, G. (2008). Breaking free from the industrial age paradigm of branding. *Journal of Brand Management, 15*(4), 291–293.

Christodoulides, G. (2009). Branding in the post-internet era. *Marketing Theory, 9*(1), 141–144.

Chua, A. Y., Goh, D. H., & Ang, R. P. (2012). Web 2.0 applications in government websites: prevalence, use and correlations with perceived website quality. *Online Information Review, 36*(2), 175–195.

Clatworthy, S. (2012). Bridging the gap between brand strategy and customer experience. *Managing Service Quality: An International Journal, 22*(2), 108–127.

Cochoy, F. (1998). 'Another discipline for the market economy: marketing as performative knowledge and know-how for capitalism'. In G. Callon, *The Laws of the Market* (pp. 194–221). Oxford: Sage Publications.

Cochoy, F. (2011). Market Things Inside. In D. Zwick, & J. Cayla, *Inside Marketing: Practices, Ideologies and Devices* (pp. 59–62). Oxford: Oxford University Press.

Cohen, M., & Murphy, J. (2003). Sustainable Consumption: Environmental Policy and the Social Sciences (with Joseph Murphy), pp. 225–240 in *Exploring Sustainable Consumption: Environmental Policy and the Social Sciences*, Maurie J. Cohen and Joseph Murphy, Eds., New York: Elsevier.

Cohen, W. M., & Levinthal, D. A. (1990). Absorptive capacity: a new perspective on learning and innovation. *Administrative Science Quarterly, 35*(1), 128–152.

Collins, J. C., & Porras, J. I. (1996). Building Your Company's Vision. *Harvard Business Review*.

Cone, C. (2021). carolconeonpurpose.com

Conejo, F., & Wooliscroft, B. (2014). Brands Defined as Semiotic Marketing Systems. *Journal of Macrmarketing, 35*(3), 287–301.

Connolly, J., & Prothero, A. (2003). Sustainable consumption: consumption, consumers and the commodity discourse. *Consumption Markets & Culture, 6*(4), 275–291.

Constantin, J. A., & Lusch, R. F. (1994). Understanding Resource Management. *OH: The Planning Forum*. Oxford.

Cook, T. (2013). Goldman Sachs Technology and Internet Conference. Retrieved from www.mac world.com/article/2027900/this-is-tim-cook-at-the-2013-goldman-sachs-conference.html? page=0

Cooper, S., McLaughlin, D., & Keating, A. (2005). Individual and neo-tribal consumption: Tales from the Simpsons of Springfield. *Journal of Consumer Behaviour, 4*(5), 330–344.

Cooren, F., & Fairhurst, G. T. (2009). Dislocation and stabilization: How to scale up from interactions to organization. In I. L. (Eds.), *Building Theories of Organization: The Constitutive Role of Communication* (pp. 49–88). New York: Routledge.

Cornelissen, J. P., & Lock, A. R. (2005). The use of marketing theory: Constructs, research propositions and managerial implications. *Marketing Theory, 5*(2), 165–184.

Cova, B. (1997). Community and consumption: Towards a definition of the "linking value" of product or services. *European Journal of Marketing, 31*(3/4), 297–316.

Cova, B., & Cova, V. (2012). On the road to prosumption: marketing discourse and the development of consumer competencies. *Consumption, Markets & Culture*.

Cova, B., & Dalli, D. (2009). Working Consumers: The Next Step in Marketing Theory? *Marketing Theor, 9*(3), 315–339.

Cova, B., & Pace, S. (2006). Brand community of convenience products: New forms of customer empowerment – The case 'My Nutella is community'. *Eurpoean Journal of Marketing, 40*(9/10), 1087–11–5.

Coyles, S., & Gokey, T. C. (2002). Customer Retention Is Not Enough. *McKinsey Quarterly 2*.

Craig, N., Boothman, J., & Sommerville, J. (2018). The UK housing developers' fivestar rating: fact or fiction? *Journal of Facilities Management, 16*(3), 269–283.

Craig, N., Pilcher, N., & Boothman, J. (2020). The UK Private Housebuilding Sector: Social Media Perspectives. *International Journal of Housing Markets and Analysis*.

Crosier, A., & Handford, A. (2012). Customer Journey Mapping as an Advocacy Tool for Disabled People: A Case Study. *Social Marketing Quarterly, 18*(1), 67–76.

Csikszentmihalyi, M., & Rochberg-Halton, E. (1981). *The Meanings of Things: Domestic Symbols and the Self*. Cambridge: Cambridge University Press.

Dahlén, M., Lange, M., & Smith, T. (2010). *Marketing Communications: A Brand Narrative Approach*. West Sussex, United Kingdom: John Wiley & Sons Ltd.

Dall'Olmo Riley, F., & Chernatony, L. (2000). The Service as Relationship Builder. *British Journal of Management, 11*, 137–150.

Davenport, T., Delong, W., & Beers, C. (1998). Successful Knowledge Management. *Sloan Management Review, 39*(2), 43–58.

Davie, G., & Woodhead, L. (2009). Secularization and Secularism'. In L. Woodhead, H. Kawanami, & C. Partridge, *Religions in the Modern* World, *Traditions and Transformations, 2nd Edition*. London: Routledge.

Davies, A., & Elliott, R. (2006). The Evolution of the Empowered Consumer. *European Journal of Marketing, 40*(9/10), 1106–1121.

Davis, I. (2005). The Biggest Contract. *The Economist*.

Davis, S. M. (2002). *Brand Asset Management: Driving Profitable Growth Through Your Brands*. New York: John Wiley & Sons.

Davis, S. M., & Dunn, M. (2002). *Building the Brand-Driven Business: Operationalise Your Brand To Crive Profitable Growth*. Chichester: John Wiley.

Day, G. S. (2014). An outside-in approach to resource-based theory. *Journal of the Academy of Marketing Science, 42*(1), 27–28.

de Chernatony, L. (2002). Would a Brand Smell any Sweeter by a Corporate Name? *Corporate Reputation Review, 5*(2/3), 114–132.

de Chernatony, L. (2006). *From Brand Vision to Evaluation*. Oxford: Butterworth-Heinemann.

de Chernatony, L. (2010). *From Brand Vision to Brand Evaluation, 3rd*. Oxford: Butterworth-Heinemann.

de Chernatony, L., & Cottam, S. (2006). Internal brand factors driving successful financial services brands. *European Journal of Marketing, 40*(5/6), 611–633.

de Chernatony, L., & McDonald, M. (2003). *Creating Powerful Brands in Consumer, Service and Industrial Markets*. Oxford: Elsevier, Buterworth-Heinemann.

de Chernatony, L., & McDonald, M. (2003). *Creating powerful brands in consumer, service, and industrial markets (3rd edn)*. Oxford: Elsevier Butterworth-Heinemann.

de Chernatony, L., & McWilliam, G. (1989). The Varying Nature of Brands as Assets, International Journal of Advertising. *8* (4), 339–349.

de Chernatony, L., & Segal-Horn, S. (2003). The Criteria for Successful Service Brands. *European Journal of Marketing, 37*, 1095–1118.

de Chernatony, L., Cottam, S., & Segal-Horn, S. (2006). Communicating service brands' values internally and externally. *The Service Industries Journal, 26*(8), 819–836.

Deighton, J. A., & Kornfield, L. (2007). Digital Interactivity: Unanticipated Consequences for markets, Marketing and Consumers. *Harvard Business School Review*, Deighton, John A., and Leora Kornfeld. "Digital InteraHarvard Business School Working Paper, No. 08-017.

Deighton, J., & Kornfeld, L. (2009). Interactivity's Unanticipated Consequences for Markets and Marketing. *Journal of Interactive Marketing, 23*(1), 2–12.

Dell, M. (2021), *Play Nice, But Win: A CEO's Journey from Founder to Leader*, Portfolio / Penguin.

Delmas, M. A., & Burbano, V. C. (2011). The Drivers of Greenwashing. *California Management Review, 54*(1), 64–87.

Deloitte. (2013). *The Digital Transformation of Customer Services: Our View*. Deloitte Touche Tohmatsu Limited.

Deloitte. (2020). *Success personified in the Fourth Industrial Revolution: Four leadership personas for an era of change.*

Denzin, N. K. and Lincoln, Y. S. (2005), 'The Discipline and Practice of Qualitative Research' in The Handbook of Qualitative Research, SAGE Publications.

Dewhirst, T., & Davis, B. (2005). Brand strategy and integrated marketing communication (IMC). *Journal of Advertising*, *34*(4), 81–92.

Dholakia, U., Bagozzi, R., & Pearo, L. (2004). A social influence model of consumer participation in network and small group-based virtual communities. *International Journal of Research*, *21*(3), 241–263.

Dibb, S., & Simkin, L. (2009). Editorial: Bridging the segmentation tehory/practice divide. *Journal of Marketing Management*, *25*, 219–225.

Dick, A., & Basu, K. (1994). Customer loyalty: toward an integrated conceptual framework. *Journal of Marketing Science*, *22*(2), 99–113.

Dillon, W. R., Madden, T. J., Kirmani, A., & Mukherjee, S. (2001). Undertanding what's a brand rating: A model for assessing brand and attitude effects and their relationship to brand equity. *Journal of Marketing Research*, *38*, 415–429.

Dinnie, K. (2008). *National Branding: Concepts, Issues, Practice*. Oxford: Elsevier.

Doanne, D. (2005). Beyond corporate social responsibility: minnows, mammoths, and markets. *Futures*, *37*(2/3), 215–229.

Donaldson, T., & Preston, L. E. (1995). The stakeholder theory of the corporation: Concepts, evidence, and implications. *Academy of Management Review*, *20*(1), 65–91.

Doyle, P. (2000). *Value based marketing: Marketing Strategies for Corporate Growth and Shareholder Value*. Chichester: Wiley & Sons.

Doyle, P. (2001). Building value-based branding strategies. *Journal of Strategic Marketing*, 255–268.

Drucker, P. F. (1993). *Post-Capitalist Society*. New York: Routledge.

Drucker, P. F. (1967). *The Effective Executive*. Harper Collins.

Drucker, P. J. (1954). *The Practice of Management*. New York: Harper and Row Publishers.

Drucker, P. J. (1999). Management Challenges for the 21st Century. 121–123.

Drummond, C., O'Toole, T., & McGrath, H. (2020). Digital engagement strategies and tactics in social media marketing. *European Journal of Marketing*, *54*(6), 1247–1280.

Du, S., Battacharya, C. B., & Sen, S. (2010). Maximizing business returns to corporate social responsibility (CSR): The role of CSR communication. *International Journal of Management Review*, *12*, 8–19.

Duffy, S. (2021). *International Brand Strategy: A Guide to Achieving Global Brand Growth*. London: Kogan page.

Duncan, T. (2002). *Using advertising and promotion to build brands*. New York: McGraw-Hill.

Duncan, T. R. (2002). *IMC: Using Advertising and Promotion to Build Brands*. New York: McGraw-Hill.

Duncan, T., & Moriarty, S. (1998). A communication-based marketing model for managing relationships. *Journal of Marketing*, *62*, 1–13.

Duncan, T., & Mulhern, F. (2004). *A White Paper on the Status, Scope, and Future of IMC (from IMC Symposium sponsored by the IMC programmes of Northwestern University*. New York, NY: McGraw-Hill.

Dykes, B. (2020). *Effective Data Storytelling: How to Drive Change with Data, Narrative and Visual, 1st Edition*. New York: John Wiley.

Eagleton, T. (2006). Your thoughts are no longer worth a penny. *The Time Educational Supplement*.

Ebert, C., Hurth, V., & Prabhu, J. (2020). *The What, The Why and the How of Purpose: A Guide for Leaders*. Chartered Management Instititute (CMI).

Economides, M., Martman, J., & Bell, M. J. (2018). Improvements in Stress, Affect, and Irritability Following Brief Use of a Mindfulness-based Smartphone App: A Randomized Controlled Trial. *Mindfulness. 9*, 1584–1593.

Edvardsson, B., Enquist, B., & Hay, M. (2006). Values-based service brands: narratives from IKEA. *Managing Service Quality: An International Journal, 16*(3), 230–246.

Edvardsson, B., Tronvoll, B., & Gruber, T. (2011). Expanding understanding of service exchange and value co-creation: A social construction approach. *Journal of the Academy of Marketing Science, 39*(2), 327–339.

Eggers, F., O'Dwyer, M., Kraus, S., Vallaster, C., & Guldeberg, S. (2013). The impact of brand authenticity on brand trust and SME growth: A CEO perspective. *Journal of World Business, 48*(3), 340–348.

Eigenraam, A. W., Eelen, J., van Lin, A., & Verlegh, P. W. (2018). A Consumer-based taxonomy of Digital Customer Engagement Practices. *Journal of Interactive Marketing, 44*, 102–121.

Eiglier, P., & Langeard, E. (1987). *Servuction, le Marketing des Services*. Paris: McGraw-Hill.

Einwiller, S., & Will, M. (2002). Towards an integrated approach to corporate brnding – an empirical study. *Corporate Communications: An International Journal, 7*(2), 100–109.

Eklof, J., Podkorytova, O., & Malova, A. (2020). Linking customer satisfaction with financial performance: an empirical study of Scandinavian banks. *Total Quality Management & Business Excellence, 31*(15/16), 1684–1702.

Elkington, J. (1994). *Cannibals with Forks: The triple bottom Line of 21st century business*. Oxford: Capstone.

Elliot, R., & Davies, A. (2006). Symbolic brands and authenticity of identity performance. In J. E. Schroeder, & M. Salzer-Morling, *Brand Culture* (pp. 138–152). London: Routledge.

Elliot, R., & Percy, L. (2007). *Strategic Brand Management*. Oxford: Oxford University Press.

Elliott, R. (1994). Exploring the Symbolic Meaning of Brands. *British Journal of Management, 5*, 13–19.

Elliott, R. (1996). Discourse Analysis: Exploring Action, Function and Conflict in Social Texts. *Marketing Intelligence and Planning, 14*(6), 65–8.

Elliott, R., & Jankel-Elliott, N. (2003). "Using ethnography in strategic consumer research". *Qualitative Market Research, 6*(4), 215–223.

Elliott, R., & Wattanasuwan, K. (1998). Brands as symbolic resources for the construction of identity. *International Journal of Advertising, 17*(2), 131–144.

Ellsworth, R. L. (2002). *Leading With Purpose: The New Corporate Realities*. Stanford, CA: Stanford University Press.

Eraut, M. (2004). Informal learning in the workplace. *Studies in Continuing Education, 26*(2), 247–73.

Erdem, T., Swait, J., & Louviere, J. (2002). The impact of brand credibility on consumer price sensitivity. *International Journal of Research in Marketing, 19*, 1–19.

Erevelles, S., Stevenson, T. H., Srinvasan, S., & Fukawa, N. (2008). An analysis of B2B ingredient co-branding relationships, Industrial Marketing Management. *Industrial Marketing Management, 37*(8), 940–952.

Escalas, J. E. (2004). Narrative processing: Building consumer connections to brands. *Journal of Consumer Psychology, 14*(1), 168–180.

Fader, P. (2012). *Customer Centricity: Focus on the Right Customers for Strategic Advantage*. Philadelphia, PA: Wharton School Press.

Fafchamps, M. (2021). Building Social Capital. In C. Mayer, & B. Roche, *Putting Purpose Into Practice: The Economics of Mutuality*.

Farrall, F., Harding, C., & Hillard, R. (2012). *Digital disruption: shortfuse, big bang? In: Building the lucky country–business imperatives for a prosperous Australia.* Deloitte.

Feigenbaum, A., & Alamalhodael, A. (2020). *The Data Storytelling Workbook.*

Fill, C. (2002). *Marketing Communications: Interactivity, Communities and Content.* London: Prentice Hall.

Fill, C. (2006). *Marketing Communications: Engagement, Strategies and Practice.* London: Prentice Hall.

Fill, C. (2009). *Marketing Communications: Interactivty, Communities, and Content 5th Edition.* Harlow: FT Prentice Hall.

Fink, L. (2017). *A Sense of Purpose.* BlackRock 2017 Annual Report.

Firat Fuat, A. (1985). 'Ideology versus science in marketing'. *Changing the course of marketing, alternative paradigms for widening marketing theory; Research in Marketing, 2. 1*, 135–14.

Fisher, N., & Kordupleski, R. (2019). Good and bad market research: A critical review of Net Promoter Score. *Applied Stochastic Models in Business and Industry, 35*(1), 138–151.

Fitchett, J. A., & McDonagh, P. (2000). A citizen's critque of relationship marketing in a risk society. *Journal of strategic Marketing, 8*, 209–222.

Foroudi, M. M., Balmer, J., Chen, W., Foroudi, P., & Patsala, P. (2020). Explicating place identity attitudes, place architecture attitudes, and identification triad theory. *Journal of Business Research, 109*, 321–336.

Foster Back, P. (2020). *Measuring Culture: Goevernance in building societies.* Building Societies Association.

Foucault, M. (1980), '*Power/Knowledge: Selected Interviews and Other Writings* 1972–1977', trans: Colin Gordon, John Mepham, Kate Soper, & Leo Marshall, Pantheon Books.

Fougère, M., & Skålén, P. (2013). Extension in the subjectifying power of marketing ideology in organisations: A Foucauldian analysis of academic marketing. *Journal of Macromarketing, 33*(1), 13–28.

Fournier, S. (1998). Consumers and Their Brands: Developing Relationship Theory in Consumer Research. *Journal of Consumer Research, 21*(4), 343–373.

Fournier, S. (2002). Delivering on the Relationship in CRM. *MSI/ Duke Customer Relationship Management Conference.* Durham, NC.

Fournier, S., & Lee, L. (2009). Getting Brand Communities Right. *Harvard Business Review, 87*, pp. 105–111.

France, C., Merrilees, B., & Miller, D. (2015). Customer brand co-creation: A conceptual model. *Marketing Intelligence and Planning, 33*(6), 848–864.

Francke, A. (2018). *The What, The Why and How of Purpose: A Guide for Leaders.* Chartered Management Institute.

Frank, A. G., Mendes, G. H., Ayala, N. F., & Ghezzi, A. (2019). Servitization and Industry 4.0 convergence in the digital transformation of product forms: A business model innovation perspective. *Technological Forecasting and Social Change, 141*(1), 341–351.

Frankl, V. E. (1985). *Man's Search for Meaning.* Shuster and Shuster.

Franzen, G., & Moriarty, S. (2008). *The Science and Art of Branding.* M. E. Sharpe.

Freeman, K., Spenner, P., & Bird, A. (2012). Three Myths about What Customers Want. *Harvard Buusiness Review.*

Freeman, R. E. (1984). *Strategic Management: A Stakeholder Approach.* Boston, MA: Pitman.

Freeman, R. E. (2010). *Strategic Management: A Stakeholder Approach.* Cambridge: Cambridge University Press.

Freeman, R. E., Philips, R. A., & Sisodia, R. (2018). Tensions in Stakeholder Theory. *Business and Society, 59*(2).

Friedman, M. (1962). *Capitalism and Freedom.* Chicago: University of Chicago Press.

Frow, P., & Payne, A. (2011). A stakeholder perspective of the value prposition concept. *European Journal of Marketing, 5*(1/2), 23–240.

Frow, P., McColl-Kennedy, J. R., Hilton, T., Davidson, A., Payne, A., & Brozovi, D. (2014). Value Propositions. *Marketing Theory, 14*, 327–351.

Frow, P., McColl-Kennedy, J. R., Hilton, T., Davidson, A., Payne, A., & Brozovic, D. (2014). Value Propositions: A Service Ecosystem Perspective. *Special Issue of Marketing Theory*, 1–44.

Gabriel, Y., & Lang, T. (2006). *The Unmanageable Consumer: Contemporaray Consumption and its Fragmentation*. London: SAGE Publications.

Gallouj, F. (2002). *Innovation in the Service Economy: The New Wealth of Nations*. Northmpton, MA: Edward Elgar Publishing Inc.

Gambetti, S. C., Graffigna, G., & Biraghi, S. (2012). The Grounded Theory Approach to Consumer Brand Engagement: The Practitioner's Standpoint. *International Journal of Market Research, 54*(5), 659–687.

Gardner, B. B., & Levy, S. J. (1955). The Product and the Brand. *Harvard Business Review*, 33–39.

Gardner, W. L., & Avolio, B. J. (1998). The Charismatic Leadership: A Dramaturgical Perspective. *Academy of Management Review, 23*, 32–58.

Gates, B. (2000). *Business @ the Speed of Thought: Succeeding in the Digital Economy*. London: Penguin.

Gautier, F. (2008) *The Guru of Joy: Sri Sri Ravi Shankar and the Art of Living*, UK: Hayhouse.

Gergen, K. (1991). *The Saturated Self: Dilemmas of Identity in Contemporary Life*. New York: Basic Books.

Gerry. (2021). Microsoft.

Gilmore, A., Carson, D., & Grant, K. (2001). SME marketing in practice", Marketing Intelligence & Planning. *19*(1), 6–14.

Gilmore, A., Carson, D., O'Donnell, A., & Cummins, L. (1999). Added value: a qualitative assessment of SME marketing. *Irish Marketing Review, 12*(1), 27–35.

Gilmore, J. H., & Pine, B. I. (2002). Customer experience places: the new offering frontier. *Strategy and Leadership, 30*, 4–11.

Gladwell, M. (2000). *The Tipping Point*. Boston, Little: Brown & Company.

Gobé, M. (2001). *Emotional Branding: The New Paradigm for Connecting Brands to People*. New York: Allworth Press.

Godfrey, P. C. (2005). The relationship between corporate philanthropy and shareholder wealth: A risk management perspective. *Academy of Management Review, 30*, 777–798.

Godin, S. (1999). *Permission Marketing: Turning Strangers Into Friends and Friends Into Customers*. Schuster.

Godin, S. (2012). *This Is Marketing: You Can't Be Seen Until You Learn To See*. Penguin Books.

Golden, M. (2011). *Social Media Strategies for Professionals and Their Firms*. Hoboken, NJ: John Wiley & Sons.

Golden-Biddle, K., & Locke, K. (2007). *Composing Qualitative Research, 2nd ed.,*. Thousand Oaks: SAGE Publications.

Goodale, B. M., Shiliah, M., Falco, L., Dammeier, F., Hamvas, G., & Leeners, B. (2019). Wearable Sensors Reveal Menses-Driven Changes in Physiology and Enable Prediction of the Fertile Window: Observational Study. *Journal of Medical Internet Research, 21*(4).

Gordon, R. (2011). Critical social marketing: Definition, application and domain. *Journal of Social Marketing, 1*(2), 82–89.

Gordon, R. (2018). Critical Social Marketing. Reflections, introspections and future directions. In M. Tadjewski, M. Higgins, N. Dholakia, J. Denegri-Knott, & R. Varman, *The Routledge Companion to Critical Marketing* (pp. 83–97). London: Routledge.

Gorz, A. (2003). *The Immaterial*. Paris: Seagull Books.

Granovetter, M. (1985). "Economic Action and SoGranovettercial Structure: The Problem of Embeddedness. *American Journal of Sociology*, *91*, 481–510.

Grant, J. (2000). *The New marketing Manifesto: The 12 Rules for Building Successful Brands in the 21st Century*. New York: Business Essential Series, Wiley.

Grant, J. (2006). *The Brand Innovation Manifesto: How to Build Brands, Redefine Markets and Defy Conventions*. Chichester: John Wiley & Sons.

Greenwood, M. (2007). Stakeholder Engagement: Beyond the Myth of Corporate Responsibility *Journal of Business Ethics*. *74*, 315–327.

Gregory, G. D., Ngo, L. V., & Karavdic, M. (2017). Developing e-commerce marketing capabilities and efficiencies for enhanced performance in business-to-business export ventures. *Industrial Marketing Management*, *78*, 146–157.

Grieger, M., & Ludwig, A. (2019). On the move towards customer-centric business models in the automotive industry – a conceptual reference framework of shared automotive service systems. *Electronic Markets*, *29*, 473–500.

Grigorescu, A. (2006). Marketing of Public and Private Affairs. *A Link, Kybernetes*, *35*(7/8), 1179–1189.

Gromark, J. (2020). Brand orientation in action: A transformational learning intervention. *Journal of Business Research*, *119*, 412–422.

Grønholdt, L., Martensen, A., Jørgensen, S., & Jensen, P. (2015). Customer experience management and performance. *International Journal of Quality and Service Sciences*, *7*(1), 90–106.

Grönroos, C. (2004). The relationship marketing process: communication, interaction, dialogue, value. *Journal of Business and Industrial Marketing*, *19*(2), 99–113.

Grönroos, C. (2000). Creating a relationship dialogue: communication, interaction, value. *Marketing Review*, *1*(1), 5–14.

Grönroos, C. (2006). Adopting a Service Logic for Marketing. *Marketing Theory*, *6*(3), 317–333.

Grönroos, C. (2007). *Service Management and Marketing: Customer Management in Service Competition*. Chichester: John Wiley & Sons.

Grönroos, C. (2008). Service logic revisited: who creates value? And who co-creates? *European Business Review*, *20*(4), 298–314.

Grönroos, C. (2011). Value Co-creation in Service Logic: A Critical Analysis. *Marketing Theory*, *11*(3), 279–301.

Grönroos, C. (2015). *Service Management and Marketing: Managing the Service Profit Logic*. Chichester: John Wiley & Sons.

Grönroos, C., & Lindberg-Repo, K. (1998). Integrated marketing communications: The communications aspect of relationship marketing. *Integrated Marketing Communications Research Journal*, *10*(1), 10.

Grönroos, C., & Ravald, A. (2011). Service as business logic: implications for value creation and marketing. *Journal od Service Management*, *22*(1), 5–22.

Grönroos, C., & Voima, P. (2013). Critical service logic: making sense of value creation and co-creation. *Journal of Academy of Science*, *41*(2), 133–150.

Grönroos, C., & Voima, P. (2013). Critical service logic: making sense of value creation and co-creation. *Journal of Academy of Science*, *41*(2), 133–150.

Grove, S., & Fisk, R. (1997). The Impact of Other Customers on Service Experiences: A Critical Incident Examination of "Getting Along". *Journal of Retailing*, *71*(1), 63–85.

Guerin, B. (1993). *Social Facilitation*. Paris: Cambridge University Press.

Guidry, M. (2011). *Marketing Concepts that Win! Save Time, Money and Work by Crafting Concept Right the First Time*.

Gummerus, J., Liljander, V., Weman, E., & Pihlström, M. (2012). Customer engagement in a Facebook brand community. *Management Research Review*, *35*(9), 857–877.

Gummesson, E. (1991). *Qualitative Methods in Management Research*. Thousand Oaks: Sage.

Gummesson, E. (1995). *Relationship Marketing: From 4Ps to 30Rs*. Malmö, Sweden: Liber-Hermods.

Gummesson, E. (2006). Many-to-many marketing as grand theory: A nordic school contribution. In I. R. (Eds.), *The service-dominant logic of marketing: Dialog, debate, and directions armonk* (pp. 339–353). New York: M.E. Sharpe.

Gummesson, E. (2008). *Total Relationship Marketing*. Oxford, UK: Butterworth Heinemann.

Gundlach, G., & Gregory, T. (2007). Introduction to the Special Section: The American Marketing Association's New Definition of Marketing: Per spectives on Its Implications for Scholarship and the Role and Responsibility of Marketing and Society,". *Journal of Policy & Marketing*, *26*(3), 243–250.

Gupta, S., Lehman, D. R., & Stuart, J. A. (2001). Valuing Customers. *Marketing Science Institute Report No. 01–119*.

Gupta, S., Malhotra, N. K., Czinkota, M., & Foroud. (2016). Marketing innovation: A consequence of competitiveness. *Journal of Business Research*, *69*(12), 5671–5681.

Gurewitz, K. L. (2020). Mindful of a Profit? A Critical Analysis of Meditation Apps in the Context of Neoliberalism and Western Constructions of Religion. *Honours Program Theses*, *34*.

Gurrrieri, L., Cherrier, H., & Previte, J. (2013). Women's bodies as a site of control: Inadvertent stigma and exclusion in social marketing. *Journal of Macromarketing*, *33*(2), 128–143.

Gyrd-Jones, R. I., & Kornum, N. (2013). Managing the co-created brand: value and cultural complementarityin online and offline multi-stakeholder ecosystems. *Journal of Business Research*, *66*(9), 1484–1483.

Hackley, C. E. (2001). *Marketing and Social Construction: Exploring the Rhetorics of Managed Consumption*. London: Routledge.

Hackley, C. E. (2003). We are all customers now: rhetorical strategy and ideological control in marketing management texts. *Journal of Management Studies*, *40*(5), 1325–52.

Hackley, C. E., & Kitchen, P. J. (1998). IMC: A Consumer Psychological Perspective. *Marketing Intelligence and Planning*, *16*(3), 229–235.

Halverson, C. A. (2002). Activity Theory and Distributed Cognition: Or What Does CSCW Need to DO with Theories? *Computer Supported Cooperative Work*, *11*, 243–267.

Halvorsrud, R., Kvale, K., & Følstad, A. (2016). Improving service quality through customer journey analysis. *Journal of Service Theory and Practice*, *27*(4), 840–867.

Hamel, G., & Prahalad, C. K. (1994). Competing for the Future. *Harvard Business School Press*.

Hamilton, R., Ferraro, R., & Haws, K. L. (2020). Travelling with Compoanions: The Social Customer Journey. *Journal of Marketing*, *85*(1), 68–92.

Handy. (1990). What is a Company For? *Royal Society for the Encouragement of Arts, Manufactures and Commerce Conference*.

Haque, U. (2011). *The New Capitalist Manifesto: Building a Disruptively Better Business*. Harvard Business Review Press.

Harris, F., & de Chernatony, L. (2001). Corporate branding and corporate brand performance. *European Journal of Marketing*, *35*(3/4), 441–456.

Harrison, J. S., & Freeman, R. E. (1999). Stakeholders, social responsibility, and performance: Empirical evidence and theoretical perspectives. *Academy of Management Journal*, *42*(5), 479–485.

Hart, S. (1995). A natural resource-based view of the firm. *Academy of Management Review*, *20*, 986–1014.

Hart, S., & Murphy, J. (. (1998). *Brands: The New Wealth Creators, Interbrand*. London: MacMIllan Business.

Hartman, L., & Werhane, P. (2013). Proposition: Shared Value as an Incomplete Mental Model. *Business Ethics Journal Review*, *1*(6), 36–43.

Hassan, S., & Craft, S. H. (2012). Examining world market segmentation and brand positioning strategies. *Journal of Consumer Marketing*, *29*(5), 344–356.

Hastings, G. (2008). *Social Marketing: Why Should the Devil Have All the Best Tunes?* Oxford: Elsevier Burreworth-Heinemann.

Hastings, G., & Saren, M. (2003). The Critical Contribution of Social Meaning: Theory and Application. *Marketing Theory*, *3*(3), 305–322.

Hatch, M. J., & Schultz, M. (2001). Are the strategic stars aligned for your corporate brand? *Harvard Business Review*, *79*(2), 128–134.

Hatch, M. J., & Shulz, M. (2003). Bringing the corporation into corporate branding. *European Journal of Marketing*, *37*(7/8), 1041–64.

Hatch, M.-J., & Shultz, M. (2010). Toward a theory of brand co-creation with implications for brand governance. *Brand Management*, *17*(8), 590–604.

Haughton, J. (2019). *How to Define Your Business Purpose*. CMI.

Hayes, R., & Abernathy, W. (1980). Managing our way to economic decline. *Harvard Business Review*, *58*, 66–77.

Heding, T., Knudtzen, C. F., & Bjerre, M. (2020). *Brand Management, 3rd Edition*. Oxford: Routledge.

Hedling, T., Knudtzen, C. F., & Bjerre, M. (2020). *Brand Management: Mastering Research, Theory and Practice*. Oxford: Routledge.

Hedman, J., Srinivasan, N., & Lindgren, R. (2013). Digital traces or information systems: sociomateriality made researchable. *Proceedings of the 34th ICIS*. Milan, Italy.

Heilman, E. (2003). Critical Theory as a personal project: From early idealism to academic realism. *Educational Theory*, *53*, 247–274.

Heinonen, K., Strandvik, T., & Voima, P. (2013). Customer dominant value formation in service. *European Business Review*, *25*(2), 104–123.

Heinonen, K., Strandvik, T., Mickelsson, K. J., Edvardsson, K. J., Sundström, B., & Anderson, P. (2010). A customer-dominant logic of service. *Journal of Service Management*, *21*(4), 531–548.

Helkkula, A., Kelleher, C., & Pihlström, M. (2012). *Journal of Service Research*, *15*(1), 59–75.

Hennig-Thurau, T., & Klee, A. (1997). The Impact of Customer satisfaction and Relationship Quality on Customer Retention – A Critical Reassessment and Model Development. *Psychology and Marketing*, *14*, 737–765.

Hennig-Thurau, T., Gwinner, K. P., & Gremler, D. D. (2002). Understanding Relationship Marketing Outcomes. *Journal of Service Research*, *4*(3), 230–247.

Hepburn, S. J. (2013). In Patagonia (clothing): A complicated greenness. *Fashion Theory*, *17*(5), 623–645.

Herhausen, D., Kleinlercher, K., Verhoef, P. C., Emrich, O., & Rudolph, T. (2019). Loyalty Formation for Different Customer Journey Segments. *Journal of Retailing*, *95*(3), 9–29.

Herskovitz, S., & Crystal, M. (2010). The essential brand persona: storytelling and branding. *Journal of Business Strategy*, *31*(3), 21–28.

Hill, D. (2008). *Emotionomics*. London: Kogan Page.

Hill, S., & Lederer, C. (2001). Portfolio Dynamics. The Infinite Asset. *Harvard Business School Press, Boston, MA.*

Hills, G. E., Hultman, C. M., & Miles, M. P. (2008). The evolution and development of entrepreneurial marketing. *Journal of Small Business Management*, *46*, 99–113.

Hilton, T., Hughes, T., & Chalcraft, D. (2012). Service Co-creation and Value Realisation. *Journal of Marketing Management*, *28*(13–14), 1504–1519.

Hogg, M., & Vaughan, G. (2002). *Social Psychology*. Englewood Cliffs, NJ: Prentice Hall.

Holbrook. (1994). The Nature of Customer's Value: An Axiology of Service in Consumption Experience. In R. T. Rust, & R. L. Oliver, *Service Quality: New Directions in Theory and Practice* (pp. 21–71). Thousand Oaks: Sage.

Holbrook, M. (2005). "Marketing Education as Bad Medicine for Society: The Gorilla Dances". *Journal of Public Policy and Marketing*, *24*(1), 143–5.

Holbrook, M. B. (1999). Introduction to consumer value. In M. B. Holbrook, *Consumer Value: A Framework for Analysis and Research* (pp. 1–28). London: Routledge.

Holbrook, M. B. (2002). *Consumer value: A framework for analysis and research*. New York: Routledge.

Holden, N. J. (2002). *Cross-Cultural management: A Knowledge Management Perspective*. Financial Times Press.

Hollander, S. C., Rassuli, K. M., & Jones, B. D. (2005). Periodisation in Marketing History. *Journal of Macromarketing*, *25*(10), 32–41.

Hollensbe, E., Wookey, C., Hickey, L., George, G., & Nichols, V. (2014). Organisations with Purpose. *Academy of Management Journal*, *57*(5), 1227–1233.

Holmund, M. (1996). Perecived Quality in Business Relationships. *Hanken Swedish Business School of Economics Journal*, 49–60.

Holt, D. B. (1997). Poststructuralist Lifestyle Analysis: Conceptualizing the Social Patterning of Consumption in Postmodernity. *Journal of Consumer Research*, *23*(1), 326–350.

Holt, D. B. (2002). *How Brands Become Icons: The Principles of Cultural Branding*. Boston: Harvard Business School Press.

Holt, D. B. (2002). Why do brands cause trouble? A dialectical theory of consumer culture and branding. *Journal of Consumer Research*, *29*(1), 70–90.

Holt, D. B., & Cameron, D. (2010). *Cultural strategy: using innovative ideologies to build breakthrough brands*. Oxford: Oxford University Press.

Homburg, C., Jozić, D., & Kuehnl, C. (2015). Customer experience management: toward implementing an evolving marketing concept. *Journal of the Academy of Marketing Science*, *45*(3), 377–401.

Hong-bumm, K., Woo Gon, K. J., & An, A. (2003). The effect of consumer-based brand equity on firms' financial performance. *Journal of Consumer Marketing*, *24*(4), 335–351.

Howells, A., Ivtzan, I., & Eiroa-Orosa, F. J. (2016). Putting the 'app' in Happiness: A Randomised Controlled Trial of a Smartphone-Based Mindfulness Intervention to Enhance Wellbeing. *Journal of Happiness Studies*, *17*, 163–185.

HRH the Dalai Lama, & van den Muyzenberg, L. (2011). *The Leader's way: Business, Buddhism and Happiness in an Interconnected World*. UK: Hachette.

Hsu, K. T. (2012). The advertising effects of corporate social responsibility on corporate reputation and brand equity: Evidence from the life insurance industry in Taiwan. *Journal of Business Ethics*, *109*, 189–201.

Hu, X., Xia, B., Skitmore, M., & Buys, L. (2015). Conceptualizing sustainable retirement villages in Australia. *Thirty First Annual Conference 2015*, *7*, pp. 357–372.

Hult, G. T., & Ketchen, D. J. (2017). Disruptive marketing strategy. *AMS Review*, *7*(1/2), 20–25.

Humm, M. (1995). *The Dictionary of Feminist Theory, 2nd ed*. Hemel Hempstead: Harvester Wheatsheaf.

Hunt, S. D. (2017). Advancing marketing strategy in the marketing discipline and beyond: from promise to neglect to prominence to fragment to promise? *Marketing Theory*, *34*, 16–51.

Hur, W.-H., Kim, H., & Woo, J. (2014). How CSR leads to Corporate Brand Equity: Mediating mechanisms of Corporate Brand Credibility and Reputation. *Journal of Business Ethics*, *125* (1), 75–86.

Hutter, K., Hautz, J., Denhardt, S., & Füller, J. (2013). The imopact of user interactions in social media on brand awareness and purchase intention: The case of MINI on facebook. *Journal of Product and Brand Mangement, 22*(5), 342–351.

Hyland, T. (2017). McDonaldizing Spirituality: Mindfulness, Education, and Consumerism. *Journal of Transformative Education, 15*(4), 334–356.

Iacobucci, D. (1996). *Networks in Marketing*. London: SAGE Publications.

Iacobucci, D., & Hibbard, J. (1999). Towards an Encompassing Theory of Business Marketing and Interpersonal Commercial Relationships: An Empirical Generalisation. *Journal of Interactive Marketing, 13*, 13–33.

Iansiti, M., & Levien, R. (2004). Strategy as Ecology. *Harvard Business Review, 82*(3), 68–78.

Iansiti, M., & Levien, R. (2004). *The keystone advantage: What the new dynamics of business ecosystems mean for strategy, innovation, and sustainability*. Boston, MA: Harvard Business Press.

IBM. (2006). CEO Study.

Ind, N. (2007). *Living the Brand: How to transform every member of your organization into a brand champion, 3rd edition*. New York, NY: New York University Press.

Inoue, S. (1997). *Putting Buddhism to work: A New Approch to Management and Business*. Tokyo: Kodanasha International.

Institute of Business Ethics, 24 Greencoat Place, (2021).

iSMA. (2021). Retrieved from International Social Marketing Association.

Iyer, P., Davari, A., Srivastava, S., & Paswan, A. (2020). Market orientation, brand management processes and brand performance. *Journal of Product & Brand Management, 30*(2), 197–214.

Jackson, B. G. (1999). The goose that laid the golden egg? A rhetorical critique of Stephen Covey and the effectivesness movement. *Journal of Management, 36*(3), 353–377.

Jaffe, J. (2005). *Life After the 30-Second Spot: Energise Your Brand with Mix of Alternatives to Traditional Advertising*. New York: John Wiley & Sons.

Jaffe, J. (2007). *Join the Conversation: How to Engage Marketing Weary Consumers with the Power of Community, Dialogue and Partnership*. Hobkoen, NJ: Wiley & Son.

Jakub, J. (2021). Mutuality, The Roots of the Economics of Mutuality. In C. Mayer, & B. Roche, *Putting Purpose into Practice: The Economics of Mutuality*. Oxford: University Press.

Jaworski and Kohli. (1993). *Journal of Marketing*. 57(3), 53–70 Market Orientation: Antecedents and Consequences.

Jaworski, B. J., & Kohli, A. K. (1996). Market orientation: review, refinement, and roadmap", *Journal of Market-Focused Management*, Vol. 1 No. 2, pp. *1*(2), 119–135.

Jensen, M. C. (2001). Value Maximization, Stakeholder Theory, and the Corporate Objective Function. *Tuck Business School Working Paper No. 01–09; Harvard NOM Research Paper No. 01–01; Harvard Business School Working Paper No. 00-058*.

Jensen, M. C., & Meckling, W. H. (1976). Theory of the firm: Managerial behaviour, agency costs and ownership structure. *Journal of Financial Economics, 3*(4), 305–360.

Jones, T. M., & Wicks, A. C. (1999). Convergent Stakeholder Theory. *Academy of Management Review, 24*(2), 206–221.

Jordan, B. (2019). *Four Trends in Gartner Cycle for Customer Service and Customer Engagement*. Retrieved from https://www.gartner.com/smarterwithgartner/4trends-gartner-hype-cycle-customer-service-customer-engagement/.

Jørgensen, M. W., & Philips, L. L. (2002). *Discourse Analysis as Theory and Method*. London: SAGE Publications.

Judd, B., Olsberg, D., Quinn, J., & Groenhart, L. (2010). *Dwelling, land and neighbourhood use by older home owners*. Australian Housing and Urban Research Institute.

Judson, K. M., Gorchels, L., & Aurand, T. W. (2016). Building a University Brand from Within: A Comparison of Coaches' Perspectives of Internal Branding. *Journal of Marketing for Higher Education, 16*, 114–197.

Kahneman, D. (2011). *Thinking Slow and Fast*. Penguin.

Kallinikos, J., Aaltonen, A., & Marton, A. (2013). The ambivalent ontology of digital artifacts. *Management Information Systems Quarterly, 37*(2), 357–370.

Kamalaldin, A., Linde, L., Sjödin, D., & Vinit, P. (2020). Transforming provider-customer relationships in digital servitization: A relational view on digitalization. *Industrial Marketing Management, 89*, 306–325.

Kaminski, J. (2011). Diffusion of innovation theory. *Canadian Journal of Nursing Informatics, 6*(2), 1–6.

Kapferer, J-N. (2000). *The New Strategic Brand Management*. London: Kogan Page.

Kapferer, J-N. (2004). *The New Strategic Brand Management: Creating and Sustaining Brand Equity Long Term*. London: Kogan Page.

Kapferer, J-N. (2008). *The New Strategic Brand Management: Creating and sustaining brand equity long term, 4th ed.* London: Kogan Page.

Kapferer, J-N. (2012). *The New Strategic Brand Management: Advanced insights and strategic thinking (5th edition)*. London: Kogan Page.

Kapferer, J-N. (2014). *The New Strategic Brand Management: Advanced Insights and Strategic Thinking*. London: Kogan Page.

Kaplan, R. S., & Norton, D. P. (1992). The Balanced Scorecard: Measures that drive performance. *Harvard Business Review*.

Kaplan, R. S., & Norton, D. P. (2001). *The Strategy-focused Organisation: How Balanced Scorecard Companies Thrive in the New Business Environment*. Harvard Business Review Press.

Karimi, J., & Walter, Z. (2015). The Role of Dynamic capabilities in Responding to Digital Disruption: A Factor-Based Study of the Newspaper Industry. *Journal of Management Information Systems, 32*(1), 39–81.

Kay, J. (2010, March 8). Think oblique: How our goals are best reached indirectly. *The Independent*.

Keiningham, T., Cooil, B., Aksoy, L., & Andreass, T. (2008). Commentary on 'The Value of Different Customer Satisfaction and Loyalty Metrics in Predicting Business Performance'. *Marketing Science, 17*(4), 361–384.

Keller. (1993). Conceptualizing, measuring, and managing customer-based brand equity. *Journal of Marketing, 57*(1), 1–22.

Keller, K. L. (2013). *Strategic brand management – building, measuring and managing brand equity*. Harlow: Pearson Education.

Keller, K. L. (1993). Conceptualizing, measuring, and managing customer-based brand equity. *Journal of Marketing, 57*, 1–22.

Keller, K. L. (2001). Building Customer-Based Brand Equity. *Marketing Management, 10*(2), 14–19.

Keller, K. L. (2003). *Strategic Brand Management*. Upper Saddle River, NY: Prentice-Hall.

Keller, K. L., & Lehmann, D. R. (2006). Brands and branding: Research directions and future priorities. *Marketing Science, 25*(6), 740–759.

Kent, M. L., & Taylor, M. (1998). Building dialogic relationships through the World Wide Web. *Public Relations Review, 24*(3), 321–334.

Kerr, G. (2011). Apples, oranges and fruit salad: A Delphi study of the IMC educational mix. In D. Shultz, C. Patti, & P. Kitchen, *The Evolution of Integrated Marketing Communications: The Customer – Driven Marketplace*. London: Routledge.

Kerr, G., & Patti, C. (2013). Strategic IMC: from abstract concept to marketing management tool. *Journal of Marketing Communications*, 1–23.

Kerrigan, F., Brownlie, D., Hewer, P., & Daza-Le Touze, C. (2011). Spinning Andy Warhol: Celebrity brand theoretics and the logic of the celebrity brand. *Journal of Marketing Management*, *27*(13/14), 1504–1524.

Kim, A. J., & Ko, E. (2012). Do social media marketing activities enhance customer equity? An empirical study of luxury fashion brands. *Journal of Business Research*, *65*(10), pp. 1480–1486.

Kimmel, A. J. (2010). *Connecting with Customers*. Oxford: University of Oxford Press.

King, C., & Grace, D. (2009). Employee Based Brand Equity: A Third Perspective. *Services Marketing Quarterly*, *30*(2), 122–147.

King, C., & Grace, D. (2010). Building and measuring employee-based brand equity. *European Journal of Marketing*, 44(7/8), 938–971.

King, C., & Grace, D. (2012). Examining the antecedents of positive employee brand-related attitudes and behaviours. *European Journal of Marketing*, *46*(3), 469–488.

King, C., Grace, D., & Funk, D. C. (2012). Employee brand equity: scale development and validation. *Journal of Brand Management*, *19*(4), 268–288.

Kitchen, P. J., Kim, I., & Schultz, D. E. (2008). Integrated Marketing Communications: Practice Leads Theory. *Journal of Advertising Research, 48*(4).

Kitchen, P. J., & Schultz, D. E. (1999). A multi-country comparison of the drive for IMC. *Journal of Advertising Research*, *39*(1), 21–38.

Kitson, H. D. (1922). The Growth of the Service Idea in Selling. *The Journal of Political Economy*, *30*(3), 419–426.

Kjellberb, H., & Helgesson, C-F. (2010). Political Marketing. *Journal of Cultural Economy*, *3*(2), 279–297.

Klein, G. (2014). *See What Others Don't – The Remarkable Ways We Gain Insight*. Nicholas Brierley Publishing.

Klein, N. (1999). *No Logo*. New York: Picador.

Klink, R. R., Zhang, J. Q., & Athaide, G. A. (2020). Designing a Customer Experience Management Course. *Journal of Marketing Education*, *42*(2), 157–169.

Knox, S., & Bickerton, D. (2003). The six conventions of corporate branding", *European Journal of Marketing*. *37*(7/8), 998–1016.

Koh, J., Kim, Y., Butler, B., Bock, G., & Woo, G. (2007). Encouraging participation in virtual communities. *Communications of the ACM*, *50*(2), 69–73.

Kohli, A. K., & Jaworski, B. J. (1990). Market orientations: The construct, research proposations, and managerial implications. *Journal of Marketing*, *54*, 1–18.

Kotler, P. (2003). *Marketing Management – Analysis, Planning, Implementation and Control, 11th edition*. New York: Prentice Hall.

Kotler, P. & Lee, N. (2008). *Social marketing: Influencing behaviours for good (3rd Ed.)*. Thousand Oaks, CA: Sage Publications.

Kotler, P., & Keller, K. L. (2012). *Marketing Management, 14th Edition*. Pearson Education.

Kotler, P., & Pföertsch, W. (2006). *B2B Brand Management*. Hoboken, NY: Springer.

Kotler, P., & Zaltman, G. (1971). Social Marketing: An Approach to Planned Social Change. *Journal of Marketing*, *35*, 8–12.

Kotler, P., Burton, S., Deans, K. R., Brown, L., & Armstrong, G. (2013). *Marketing (9th ed)*. Frenchs Forest NSW: Pearson.

Kotler, P., Pfoertsc, P., & Sponholz, U. (2020). *H2H Marketing: The Genesis of Juman-to-Human Marketing*. Springer Nature.

Kouly, M. (2018). *beyondleadershipmichaelkouly.com*.

Kozinets, R. V., De Valck, K., & Wojnicki, A. C. (2010). Networked Narratives: Understanding Word-of-Mouth Marketing in Online Communities. *Journal of Marketing*, *74*(2), 71–89.

Kraaijenbrink, J., Spender, J-C., & Groen, A. J. (2010). The Resource-Based View: A Review and Assessment of Its Critiques. *Journal of Management, 36*, 349–372.

Krake, F. (2005). Successful brand management in SMEs: a new theory and practical hints. *Journal of Product & Brand Management, 14*(4/5), 228–239.

Kramer, M. (2017). Brand purpose: The navigational code for growth. *Journal of Brand Strategy, 6*(1), 1–9.

Kramer, M., & Husein-zadeh, T. (2017). *The Guiding Purpose Strategy: A Navigational Code for Growth*. Clink Street Publishing.

Krishnan, V., Balsaubramanian, S., & Sawhney, M. (2004). Creating Growth with Services. *MIT Sloan Management Review, 45*, 34–43.

Kriss, J. (2014). The Value of Customer Experience, Quantified. *Harvard Business Review*.

Kucuk, S. U., & Krishnamurthy, S. (2007). An analysis of consumer power on the Internet. *Technovation, 27*(1), 47–56.

Kuehnl, C., Jozic, D., & Homburg, C. (2019). Effective customer journey design: consumers' conception, measurement, and consequences. *Journal of the Academy of Marketing Science, 47*, 551–568.

Kumar, V., & Shah, D. (2015). *Handbook of Research on Customer Equity in Marketing*. Cheltenham, UK: Elgar.

Kumar, V., Aksoy, L., Donkers, B., Venkatesan, R., Wiesel, T., & Tillmans, S. (2010). Undervalued or overvalued customers: Capturing total customer engagement value. *Journal of Social Research, 13*(3), 297–310.

Kurtz, D. (2010). *Contemporary Marketing*. Mason, OH: South-Western Cengage Learning.

Kwon, S. H., Cha, M. K., & Lee, S. Y. (2015). Hierarchical Value Maps of Smart Phones, Portal Sites, and Social Network Services Based on User Involvement. *Advances in Journalism and Communication, 3*(3).

La Placa, P., & da Silva, R. V. (2016). B2B: A Paradigm Shift from Economic Exchange to Behavioural Theory: A Quest for Better Explanations and Predictions. *Psychology and Marketing, 33*(4), 232–249.

Lam, C. F., & Mayer, D. M. (2014). When Do Employees Speak up for Their Customers? A Model of Voice in a Customer Service Context. *Personnal Psychology, 67*(3), 637–666.

Lamore, P. R., Berkowitz, D., & Farrington, P. A. (2013). Proactive/responsive market orientation and marketing – research and development integration. *Journal of Product Innovation Management, 30*(4), 695–711.

Lanning, M. J. (1998). *Delivering Profitable Value*. Perseus Publishing.

Lanning, M. J. (2019). Interview with Michael J. Lanning on Value Proposition (& Value Delivery). *Journal of Creating Value, 5*(2), 237–241.

Lash, S. M. (2002). *Critique of Information*. London: SAGE Publications.

Lawton, M. P., Nahemow, L., & Eisdorfer, C. (1973). Ecology and the aging process: The psychology of adult development and aging. *DC American Psychological Association*, 619–674.

Le Guin, U. K. (2021). *The Carrier Bag Theory of Fiction*. London: Ignota.

LeCornu, M. R., McMahon, R. G., Forsaith, D. M., & Stanger, D. (1996). The Small Enterprise Financial Objective Function: An Exploratory Study. *Journal of Small Business Management, 34*(1), 1–14.

Lee, W., O'Cass, A., & Sok, P. (2016). Why doesn't our branding payoff: optimizing the effects of branding through innovation. *European Journal of Marketing, 50*(3/4), 509–529.

Lee, W., O'Cass, A., & Sok, P. (2017). Unpacking brand management superiority. *European Journal of Marketing, 51*(1), 177–199.

Legal & General – Principles. (2020). *10 guidelines for inclusive capitalism: What makes capitalism inclusive and how is Legal & General practising what it preaches?*: retrieved from https://brand.legalandgeneral.com/building-infrastructure/10-guidelines-for-inclusive-capitalism/

Legal & General – Purpose. (2021). *Inclusive Capitalism – Purpose*, retrieved from: https://www.legalandgeneralgroup.com/inclusive-capitalism/

Legal & General – Inclusive Future. (2021). *Inclusive Future; Pioneering an Inclusive Future: Inclusive Capitalism Delivers Positive Change Through Long-Term Investing, press release*, retrieved: https://www.csrwire.com/reports/724741/pioneering-inclusive-future-inclusive-capitalism-delivers-positive-change-through

Legal & General – COVID. (2021). *Our Response to COVID*, retrieved from https://www.legalandgeneralgroup.com/media-centre/press-releases/our-response-to-covid-19-the-coronavirus/

Legal & General. (2021). *Sustainability and Inclusive Capitalism*. retrieved from: https://group.legalandgeneral.com/en/sustainability/sustainability-reporting-centre/sustainability-and-inclusive-capitalism-report-2020

Lemke, F., Clark, M., & Wilson, H. (2011). Customer experience quality: An exploration in business and consumer contexts using repertory grid technique. *Journal of Academy of Marketing Science, 39*, 846–869.

Lemon, K. N., & Verhoef, P. C. (2016). Understanding Customer Experience Throughout the Customer Journey. *Journal of Marketing, 80*(6), 69–96.

L'Etang, J., & Pieczka, M. (2006). *Public Relations: Critical Debates and Contemporary Practice*. United Kingdom: Lawrence Erlbaum Associates.

Lévi-Strauss, J.-P. (1962). *The Savage Mind*. Chicago, Il.: The University of Chicago Press Maldonado.

Levitt, T. (1975). Marketing Myopia. *Harvard Business Review*.

Levitt, T. (1981). Marketing intangible products and product intangibles. *Harvard Business Review, 59*, 94–102.

Levy, S. J. (2003). Roots of Marketing and Consumer Research at the University of Chicago. *Consumption Markets & Culture, 6*(2), 99–110.

Lim, D., Condon, P., & DeSteno, D. (2015). Mindfulness and Compassion: An Examination of Mechanism and Scalability. *PLoS ONE, 10*(2).

Lim, M. (2009). Postmodern paradigms and brand management. *International Journal of Internet Marketing and Advertising, 5*(1/2), 4–16.

Lin, F., Ansell, J., Marshall, A., & Ojiako, U. (2019). Managing and building B2B SME brands: an emerging market perspective. *PSU Research Review, 3*(3), 191–214.

Lindgreen, A., Beverland, M. B., & Farrelly, F. (2010). From strategy to tactics: building, implementing, and managing brand equity in business markets. *Industrial Marketing Management, 39*(8), 1223–1225.

Lingqvist, O., Plotkin, C. L., & Stanley, J. (2013). Follow the customer decision journey if you want B2B sales to grow. *McKinsey Report*.

Lings, I. N., & Greenley, G. E. (2005). Measuring internal market orientation. *Journal of Service Research, 7*(3), 290–305.

Linton, I., & Morley, K. (1995). *Integrated Marketing Communications (Marketing Series: Practitioner)*. London: Butterworth:Heinemann.

Liu, Y.-l., & Picard, R. G. (2014). *Policy and Marketing Strategy for Digital Media*. New York: Routledge.

Löhndorf, B., & Diamantopoulos, A. (2014). Internal branding: social identity and social exchange perspectives on turning employees into brand champions. *Journal of Service, 17*, 310–325.

Long, B. S., & Helms-Mills, J. (2010). Workplace spirituality, contested meaning, and the culture of organisation: A critical sensemaking account. *Journal of Organisational Change Management, 23*(3), 325–341.

López, M., Sicilia, M., & Moyeda-Carabaza, A. A. (2017). Creating identification with brand communities on Twitter: The balance between need for affiliation and need for uniqueness. *Internet Research, 27*(1), 21–51.

Lorek, S., & Vergragt, P. J. (2016). Sustainable consumption as a systemic challenge inter- and transdisciplinary research and research questions. In L. A. Reisch, & J. Thøgersen, *Handbook of Research on Sustainable Consumption*. London: Edward Elgar Publishing.

Louro, M. J., & Cunha, P. V. (2001). Brand management paradigms. *Journal of Marketing Management, 17*, 849–875.

Lovelock, C., & Wirtz, J. (2011). *Service Marketing: People, Technology, Strategy, 7th Ed.* Upper Saddle, NJ: Pearson.

Luck, E., & Moffatt, J. (2009). IMC: Has anything really changed? A new perspective on an old definition. *Journal of Marketing Communications, 15*(5), 311–325.

Lundqvist, A., Liljander, V., Gummerus, J., & Van, J. (2013). The impact of storytelling on the consumer brand experience: The case of a firm-originated story. *Journal of Brand Management, 20*(4), 283–297.

Luo, X., & Homburg, C. (2007). Neglected Outcomes of Customer Satisfaction. *Journal of Marketing, 71*, 133–149.

Lurie, I. (2006). *Conversation marketing: Internet marketing strategies*. Victoria: Trafford Publishing.

Lusch, R. F., & Vargo, S. L. (2004). Evolving to a New Dominant Logic for Marketing. *Journal of Marketing, 68*, 1–17.

Lyer, D., & Srivastava, P. (2020). Market orientation, brand management processes and brand performance. *Journal of Product & Brand Management, 30*(2), 197–214.

Lynch, J., & de Chernatony, L. (2004). The power of emotion; Brand communications in business-to-business markets. *Journal of Brand Management, 11*, 403–419.

Lyons, D. (2001). Gestalt Approaches to the Virtual Gesamtkunstwerk. *Composition Unit, University of Sydney*.

MacDonald, E. K., Wilson, H. N., Martinez, V., & Toosi, A. (2009). Assessing the value-in-use of integrated product-service offerings: A repertory grid approach. *Frontiers in Service Conference*. Hawaii.

Mackey, J., & Sisodia, R. (2014). *Conscious Capitalism: Liberating the Heroic Spirit of Capitalism*. Harvard Business Review Press Publications.

Malnight, W., Buche, I., & Dhanaraj, C. (2019). Put Purpose at the Core of Your Strategy: It's how successful companies redefine their businesses. *Harvard Business Review*.

Maltz, A. C., Shenhar, A. J., & Reilly, R. R. (2003). Beyond the Balanced Scorecard: Refining the Search for Organisational Success Measures. *Long Range Planning, 36*, 187–204.

Marist, A. I., Yuliati, L. N., & Najib, M. (2014). The Role of Event in Building Brand Satisfaction, Trust and Loyalty of Isotonic Drinks. *International Journal of Marketing, 6*(6), 57–66.

Massaro, M., Handley, K., Bagnoli, C., & Dumay, J. (2016). Knowledge management in small and medium enterprises: a structured literature review. *Journal of Knowledge Management, 20*(2), 258–91.

Mayer, C., & Roche, B. (2021). *Putting Purpose Into Practice: The Economics of Mutuality*. Oxford, UK: Oxford University Press.

Mayer, P. (2018). *Prosperity: Better Business Makes the Greater Good*. Oxford: Oxford University Press.

Mayer-Schonberger, V., & Cukier, K. (2013). *Big Data: A Revolution That Will Transform How We Live, Work, and Think*. New York: Houghton Mifflin Harcourt Publishing.

Mazzarol, T. (2004). Strategic Management of Small Firms: A Proposed Framework for Entrepreneurial Venture. *Paper presented at the 17th Annual SEAANZ Conference – 'Entrepreneurship as the Way of the Future'*. Brisbane, Queensland.

McAlexander, J. H., Schouten, J. W., & Koenigg, H. F. (2002). Building brand community. *Journal of Marketing*, *66*, 38–54.

McAlister, D. T., & Ferrell, L. (2002). The role of strategic philanthropy in marketing strategy. *European Journal of Marketing*, *36*(5/6), 689–708.

McCartan-Quinn, D., & Carson, D. (2003). Issues which impact upon marketing in the small firm. *Small Business Economics*, *21*(2), 201–14.

McCracken, G. D. (1988). *Culture and Consumption: New Approaches to the Symbolic Character of Consumer Goods and Activities*. Bloomington, IN: Indiana University Press.

McCracken, G. D. (2005). *Culture and Consumption: Markets, Meaning and Brand Management*. Bloomington, IN: Indiana University Press.

McCracken, G. D. (1989). Who is the Celebrity Endorser? Cultural Foundations of the Endorsement Process. *Journal of Consumer Research*, *16*(3), 310–321.

McCracken, G. D. (1986). Culture and Consumption: A Theoretical Account of the Structure and Movement of the Cultural Meaning of Consumer Goods. *Journal of Consumer Research*, *13*(2), 71–84.

McKinsey. (2020).

McMahan, D. L. (2008). *The making of Buddhist modernism*. Oxford: University Press.

McWilliams, A., & Siegel, D. S. (2001). Corporate social responsibility: A theory of the firm perspective. *Academy of Management Review*, *26*, 117–127.

Medberg, G., & Grönroos, C. (2020). Value-in-use and service quality; Do customers see a difference? *Journal of Service Theory and Practice*, *30*(4/5), 507–529.

Meijer, A., & Thaens, M. (2010). Alignment 2.0: strategic use of new internet technologies in government. *Government Information Quarterly*, *27*(2), 113–121.

Meire, M., Hewett, & Ballings, M. (2019). The Role of Marketer-Generated Content in Customer Engagmenet Marketing. *Journal of Marketing*, *83*(6), 21–42.

Melewar, T. C., & Akel, S. (2005). The role of corporate identity in the higher education sector. *Corporate Communications: An International Journal*, *10*(1), 41–57.

Melewar, T. C., & Karaosmanoglu, E. (2006). Corporate branding, identity and communications: A contemporary perspective. *Journal of Brand Management*, *14*(1/2), 1–4.

Melewar, T. C., & Storrie, T. (2001). Corporate identity in the service sector. *Public Relations Quarterly*, *46*(2), 20–26.

Melo, M., & Garrido-Morgado, A. (2012). Corporate reputation: A combination of social responsibility and industry. *Corporate Social Responsibility and Environmental Management*, *19*, 11–31.

Merz, M., He, Y., & Vargo, S. L. (2009). The evolving brand logic: a service-dominant logic for branding. *Academy of Marketing Science*.

Meyer, C., & Schwager, A. (2007). Understanding Customer Experience. *Harvard Business Review*, *85*(2), pp. 116–126.

Mikulincer, M., & Shaver, P. R. (2007). *Attachment in adulthood: Structure, dynamics, and change*. New York: Guildford Press.

Miles, I. (2008). Patterns of Innovation in Service Industries. *IBM Systems Journal*, *47*(1), pp. 115–128.

Miller, G. (2007). *Spent: Sex, Evolution and Consumer Behaviour*. New York: Viking.

Miller, K. D., Fabian, F., & Lin, S. J. (2009). Strategies for online communities. *Strategic Management Journal, 30*(3), 305–322.

Miller, L. (2015). Marketing Strategy for Democratising Value Creation. *Research Journal of Economics, 10*(1).

Mirvis, P., Googins, B., & Kinnicutt, S. (2010). Vision, mission, values: Guideposts to sustainability. *Organisational Dynamics, 39*, 316–324.

Mitchell, C., & Imrie, B. C. (2011). Consumer tribes: membership, consumption and building loyalty. *Asis Pacifc Journal of Marketing and Logistics, 23*(1), 39–56.

Mitchell, R. K., Agle, B. R., & Wood, D. J. (n.d.). Toward a theory of stakeholder identification and salience: Defining the principle of who and what really counts. *Academy of Management Review, 20*(4), 853–886.

Mohr, H. (2006). Material Religion/Religious Aesthetics a Research Program. *Material Religion, 6*(2), 240–248.

Mohr, J., & Sarin, S. (2009). Drucker's insights on market orientation and innovation: Implications for emerging areas in high-technology marketing. *Journal of the Academy of Marketing Science, 37*(1), 85–96.

Möller, K. (2006). Role of competences in creating customer value: A value-creation logic approach. *Industrial Marketing Management, 35*(8), 913–924.

Moor, L. (2007). *The Rise of Brands*. Oxford: Berg.

Moore, J. F. (2003). *Digital Business Ecosystems in Developing Countries: An Introduction*. Berkman Center for Internet, Harvard Business School Publishing.

Morgan, N., Pritchard, A., & Pride, R. (2011). *Destination brands: Managing place reputation*, New York: Butterworth-Heinemann.

Morgan, N. A., & Rego, L. (2006). The value of different customer satisfaction and loyalty metrics in predicting business performance. *Marketing Science, 25*(9), 426–439.

Morgan, W. T. (2009). *Eating The Big Fish, (2nd ed.)*. Hoboken: John Wiley & Sons.

Morgan-Thomas, A., Dessart, L., & Veloutsou, C. (2020). Digital ecosystem and consumer engagement: A socio-technical perspective. *Journal of Business Research, 121*, 713–723.

Morhart, F., Malär, L., Guèvremont, A., Girardin, F., & Grohman, B. (2015). Brand Authenticity. *Journal of Consumer Psychology, 25*(2), 200–218.

Morrison Wylde, C., Mahrer, N., Meyer, R. M., & Gold, J. (2017). Mindfulness for Novice Pediatric Nurses: Smartphone Application Versus Traditional Intervention. *Journal of Pediatric Nurse, 3*(36), 205–212.

Mosley, R. W. (2007). Customer experience, organisational culture and the employer brand. *Journal of Brand Management, 15*(2), 123–134.

Mosquera, A., Olarte Pascual, C., & Juaneda Ayensa, E. (2017). Understanding the customer experience in the age of omni-channel shopping. *Dialnet, 15*(2).

Mudambi, S. (2002). Branding importance in business-to-business markets: Three buyer clusters. *Industrial Marketing Management, 31*(6), 525–533.

Mudie, P., and Pirrie, P. (2006). *Services Marketing Management*, London: Routledge.

Muñiz, A. M., & O'Guinn, T. C. (2001). Brand Community. *Journal of Consumer Research, 27*, 412–32.

Muzellec, L., & Lambkin, M. C. (2009). Corporate branding and brand architecture: a conceptual framework. *Marketing Theory, 9*(1), 39–54.

Muzellec, L., Doogan, M., & Lambkin, M. (2003). Corporate Rebranding – an Exploratory Review. *The Irish Marketing Review, 16*(2), 30–40.

Nachira, F. and Dini, P. (2007). *A Network of Digital Business Ecosystems for Europe: Roots, Processes and Perspectives*, www.digital-ecosystems.org/book/DBE-2007.pdf.

Nair, M. (2004). *Essentials of Balanced Scorecard*. Holboken, NY: Wiley.

Narver, J. C., & Slater, S. F. (1990). The effect of a market orientation on business profitability. *Journal of Marketing*, *54*, 20–35.

Narver, J. C., Slater, S. F., & MacLachlan, D. L. (2004). Responsive and proactive market orientation and new product success. *Journal of Product Innovation Management*, *21*(5), 334–347.

Nason, R. (2017). *It's Not Complicated: The Art and Science of Complexity in Business*. Toronto: Rotman- University of Toronto Press.

National Social Marketing Centre. (2006). *Its Our Health! Realsing the Potential of Effective Social Marketing*. London: National Social Marketing Centre.

Nelson, R., & Winter, S. (1982). *An Evolutionary Theory of Economic Change*. Cambridge: MA: Belknap Press of Harvard University.

Newell, S., & Marabelli, M. (2015). Strategic opportunities (and challenges) of algorithmic decision-making: A call. *Journal of Strategic Information Systems*, 1–12.

Newman, G. E., & Dhar, R. (2014). Authenticty is contagious: Brand essence and the original source of production. *Journal of Marketing Research*, *51*(3), 271–386.

Nguyen, B., Melewar, T. C., & Hemsley-Brown, J. (2017). *Strategic Brand Management in Higher education*. London: Routledge.

Nguyen, B., Yu, X., Melewar, T. C., & Hemsley-Brown, J. (2016). Brand ambidexterity and commitment in higher education: An exploratory study. *Journal of Business Research*, *69*(8), 3105–3112.

Normann, R. (1984). *Service Management*. New York: Wiley.

Normann, R. (2001). *Reframing Business: When the Map Changes the Landscape*. Chichester: Wiley.

Normann, R., & Ramirez, R. (1993). From Value chain to Value Constellation: Designing Interactive Strategy. *Harvard Business Review*, 65–77.

Norton, D. W., & Pine, B. J. (2013). Using the customer journey to road test and refine the business model. *Stratgey and Leadership*, *41*(2), 12–17.

Nyadzayo, M. W., Matanda, M. J., & Ewing, M. T. (2011). Brand relationships and brand equity in franchising. *Industrial Marketing Management*, *40*(7), 1103–1115.

O'Cass, A., & Viet Ngo, L. (2007). Market orientation versus innovative culture: two routes to superior brand performance. *European Journal of Marketing*, *41*(7/8), 868–887.

O'Shaughnessy, J., & O'Shaughnessy, N. J. (2008). Marketing, Society and Hedonism. In M. Taderjewski, & D. Brownlie, *Critical Marketing Issues in Contemporary Marketing*. Chichester: John Wiley & Sons.

O'Brien, D., Main, A., Kounkel, S., & Stephan, A. R. (2019). Purpose is everything: How brands that authentically lead with purpose are changing the nature of business today. *Deloitte Insights*.

Oh, H., Labianca, G., & Chung, M-H. (2006). A Multilevel Model of Group Social Capital. *Academy of Management Review, 31*(3).

Olsen, R. (2002). The type–role–purpose brand taxonomy. *Brand Management*, *14*(6), 430–441.

Olutayo, B., & Melewar, T. C. (2007). Understanding the Meaning of Corporate Identity: A Conceptual and Semiological Approach. *Corporate Communications: An International Journal*, *12*, 414–432.

Oosterwijk, L., & Loeffen, A. (2005). How to use Buzz marketing effectively Märlardalen International Master Academy. In A. Kimmel, *Connecting with consumers*. New York: John Wiley & Sons.

Orazi, D. C., Spry, A., Theilacker, M. N., & Vredenburg, J. (2017). A multi-stakeholder IMC framework for networked brand identity. *European Journal of Marketing*, *53*(3), 551–571.

Orlikowski, W. J. (2007). Sociomaterial Practices: Exploring Technology at Work". *Organisation Studies*, *28*(9), 1435–1448.

Orr, L. M., Bush, V. D., & Vorhies, D. W. (2011). Leveraging firm-level marketing capabilities with marketing employee development. *Journal of Business Research, 64*(10), 1074–1081.

O'Shaughnessy, J., & O'Shaughnessy, N. (2009). The service-dominant perspective: a backward step? *European Journal of Marketing, 43*(5/6), 784–793.

Osler, R. (2007). The type-role-purpose brand taxonomy. *Journal of Brand Management, 14*, 430–440.

Ospina, J. (2021). Contribution of Millennials in the Development of Companies With Global Purposes. In R. Perez-Uribe, C. Largacha-Martinez, & D. Ocamp, *Handbook of Research on International Business and Models for Global Purpose-Driven Companies*.

Osterwalder, A., & Pigneur, Y. (2010). *Business model generation: A handbook for visionaries, game changers, and challengers*. Hoboken, NJ: John Wiley.

O'Sullivan, S. R., Richardson, B., & Collins, A. (2011). How brand communities emerge: The Beamish conversion experience. *Journal of Marketing Management, 27*(9/10), 891–912.

Ozdemir, S., Gupta, S., Foroudi, P., & Wright, L. (2020). Corporate branding and value creation for initiating and managing relationships in B2B markets. *Qualitative Market Research, 23*(4), 627–661.

Palmer, A., & Koenig-Lewis, N. (2009). An experiential, social network-based approach to direct marketing. *Direct Marketing: An International Journal, 3*(3), 162–176.

Parasuraman, A., Zeithaml, V., & Berry, L. L. (1985). A Conceptual Model of Service Quality and Its Implications for Future Rsearch. *The Journal of Marketing, 49*(4), 41–50.

Park, C. W., Macinnis, D. J., & Priester, J. (2010). Brand Attachment and Brand Attitude Strength: Conceptual and Empirical Differentiation of Two Critical Brand Equity Drivers. *Journal of Marketing, 74*(6), 1–17.

Parmar, B. L., Freeman, R., & Harrison, J. (2010). Stakeholder Theory: The State of the Art. *Management Faculty Publications, 9*.

Parolini, C. (1999). *The Value Net: A Tool for Competitive Strategy*. UK: John Wiley & Sons.

Pavlik, J. V., & Salmon, C. T. (1984). Theoretic Approaches in Public Relations Research. *Public Relations Research and Education, 1*, 39–49.

Payne, A., Ballantyne, D., & Christopher, M. (2005). A stakeholder approach to relationship marketing strategy: The development and use of the "six markets" model. *European Journal of Marketing, 39*(7/8), 855–871.

Payne, A., Storbacka, K., Frow, P., & Know, S. (2009). Co-creating brands: Diagnosing and designing the relationship experience. *Journal of Business Research, 62*(3), 379–389.

Peirce, A. A. (2013). A. A. "Peirce's Theory of Signs", The Stanford Encyclopedia of Philosophy (Summer 2013 Edition), Edward N. Zalta (ed.).

Peñaloza, L., & Venkatesh, A. (2006). Further evolving the new dominant logic of marketing: from services to the social construction of markets. *Marketing Theory, 6*(3), 299–316.

Peppers, D., & Rogers, M. (2004). *Managing customer relationships: A strategic framework*. New York: John Wiley & Sons.

Perrigot, R., Basset, G., & Cliquet, G. (2011). Multi-channel communication: the case of Subway attracting new franchisees in France. *International Journal of Retail & Distribution Management, 39*(6), 434–455.

Pettigrew, J. E., & Reber, B. H. (2010). The new dynamic in corporate media relations: how Fortune 500 Companies are using virtual press rooms to engage the Press. *Journal of Public Relations Research, 22*(4), 404–428.

Piercy, N. (2015). The theory/practice divide: thoughts for the Editors and the Senior Board of EJM. *European Journal of Marketing*, pp. 5–20.

Piff, S. (2020). Head of IDC Asia Pacific.

Pine, B. J., & Gilmore, J. H. (1998). *The Experience Economy: Competing for Customer Time, Attention, and Money*. Harvard Business Review Press.

Pitt, L., Napoli, J., & Van Der Merwe, R. (2003). Managing the franchised brand: The franchisees' perspective. *Journal of Brand Management, 10*(6), 411–420.

Pivato, S., Misani, N., & Tencati, A. (2008). The impact of corporate social responsibility on consumer trust: The case of organic food. *Business Ethics: A European Review, 17*, 3–12.

Pixton, P., Nickolaisen, N., Little, T., & McDonald, K. (2009). *Stand Back and Deliver: Accelerating Business Agility.* Boston: Addisn-Wesley.

Podsakoff, P. M., MacKenzie, S. B., & Podsakoff, N. P. (2016). Recommendations for creating better concept definitions in the organisational, behavioural, and social sciences. *Organisational Research Methods, 19*, 159–203.

Polonksy, M. J., Carlson, L., & Fry, M.-L. (2003). The harm chain: a public developmenet and stakeholder perspective. *Marketing Theory, 3*(3), 345–364.

Polonsky, M. J., & Jevons, D. (2009). Global branding and strategic CSR: an overview of three types of complexity. *International Marketing Review, 26*(3), 327–347.

Ponsignon, F., Smart, A., & Philips, L. (2018). A customer journey perspective on service delivery system design: insights form healthcare. *International Journal of Quality & Reliability Management, 10*, 2328–2347.

Porter, M.E, (1985). *Competitive Advantage.* New York, NY: The Free Press.

Porter, M. E. (2001). The Value Chain and Competitive Advantage. *Understanding Business Processes,* 50–66.

Porter, M. E., & Kramer, M. R. (2011). Creating Shared Value. *Harvard Business Review, 89*(1/2), pp. 62–77.

Porter, M. E., & Kramer, M. R. (2006). Strategy and Society: The link between competitive advantage and corporate social responsibility. *Harvard Business Review, 84*(12), 78–92.

Porter, M., & Kramer, M. (2011). The Big Idea: Creating Shared Value. *Harvard Business Review, 89* (1/2), 62–77.

Prahalad, C. K., & Bettis, R. A. (1986). The Dominant Logic: A New Linkage between Diversity and Performance. *Strategic Management Journal, 7*, 484–501.

Prahalad, C. K., & Hamel, G. (1990). The Core Competence of the Corporation. *Harvard Business Review.*

Prahalad, C. K., & Ramaswamy, V. (2004). Co-creation experiences; The next practice in value creation. *Journal of Interactive Marketing, 18*(3), 5–14.

Prassl, J. (2008). Work on Demand. In J. Prassl, *Humans as a Service: The Perils of Working in the Gig Economy.* Oxford, UK: Oxford University Press.

Prassl, J. (2018). *Humans as a Service: The Promise and Perils of Work in the Gig Economy.* Oxford University Press.

Pratt, M. G., & Ashforth, B. E. (2003). Fostering meaningfulness in working and in work. In K. S. Cameron, J. E. Dutton, & R. E. Quinn, *Positive organisational scholarship: Foundations of a new discipline* (pp. 309–327). San Francisco: Barrett-Koehler.

Prebensen, N. K. (2014). Facilitating for enhanced experience value. In G. A. Alsos, D. Eide, & E. L. Masden, *Handbook of research on innovation in tourism industries* (pp. 154–177). Edward Elgar Publishing.

Principals-Synovate. (2008). *2008 Authentic Brands Index Study.* Melbourne.

Pringle, H., & Field, P. (2008). *Brand Immortality: How brands can live long and prosper.* London: Kogan Page.

Priola, D. (2009). *Six Crucial Behaviors for Customer-Facing Employees, Profiles International Report.* Expert Insight, Profiles International, Inc.

Proshanksy, H., Ittelson, W. H., & Rivlin, L. G. (1974). *Envornmental Psychology.* New York: Holt, Rienhart & Winston.

Quinn, L., Hines, T., & Bennison, D. (2007). Making sense of market segmentation: a fashion retailing case. *European Journal of Marketing, 41*(5/6), 439–65.

Quinton, S. (2013). The community brand paradigm: A response to brand management's dilemma in the digital era. *Journal of Marketing Management, 29*(7/8), 912–923.

Rácz, P. (2013). *Salience in Sociolinguistics: A Quantitative Approach*. Berlin/Bostonr: Walter de Gruyte.

Ramakrishna Velamuri, S., Venkataraman, S., & Harvey, W. S. (2017). Seizing the Ethical High Ground: Ethical Reputation Building in Corrupt Environments. *Journal of Management Studies, 54*(5), 647–675.

Ramaseshan, B., Rabbanee, F. K., & Tan Hsin Hui, L. (2013). Effects of customer equity drivers on customer loyalty in B2B contexts. *Journal of Business and Industrial Marketing, 28*(4), 335–346.

Rathmell, J. (1966). What Is Meant By Services? *Journal of Marketing, 30*, 32–36.

Rauch, M., Wenzel, M., & Wagner, H.-T. (2016). The digital disruption of strategic paths: an experimental study. *International conference on information systems*. Dublin.

Rayport, J. F., & Jaworski, B. J. (2004). Best face Forward. *Harvard Business Review, 82*, 47–58.

Rayport, J., & Jaworski, B. (2000). *E-Commerce*. London: McGraw-Hill.

Rees Jones, I., Hyde, M., Victor, C. A., Wiggins, R. D., Gilleard, C., & Higgs, P. (2008). Consuming health in later life. In I. Rees Jones, *Ageing in a consumer society: From passive to active consumption in Britain*. Oxford University Presss.

Reeves, M. 'The State of the Ecosystem', at the 'Shape The Debate', *Global Peter Drucker Forum*, Vienna, 21–22 November 2019.

Reichheld, F. F., & Sasser Jr, W. E. (1990). Zero defections: quality comes to services. *Harvard Business Review, 68*(5), 105–111.

Remy, S., Kolokotsa, J., Ondrus, J., El Ouarzazi, Y., & Glady, N. (2021). Purposeful Ecosystem Orchestartion. In C. Mayer, & B. Roche, *Putting Purpsoe into Practice The Economics of Mutuality*. Oxford: Oxford University Press.

Renshaw, B. (2019). *Purpose – The extraordinary benefits of focusing on what matters most*. LID Publishing.

Ries, A., & Trout, J. (2000). *Positioning: The Battle for Your Mind, 20th Anniversary Edition*. Palgrave.

Ries, A. (2008). *Differentiate or Die: Survival in Our Era of Killer Competition*. Hoboken, NY: John Wiley & Sons.

Ries, A., & Ries, L. (1998). 22 Immutable laws of Branding. In D. E. Shultz, S. I. Tannenbaum, & R. F. Lauterborn, *The New marketing Paragigm: Integarted Marketing Communications*. Chicago,: NTC Business Books, Harper Business.

Rindell, A. (2007). Image Heritage: The Temporal Dimensions in Consumers' Corporate Image Constructions. *Hanken School of Economics, Finland*.

Ritson, M. (2021). The Long and the Short of It maps exactly onto the challenges of global marketing. *Marketing Week*.

Roberts, J., Kayande, U., & Stremersch, S. (2014). From academic research to marketing practice: exploringthe marketing science value chain. *International Journal of Research & Marketing, 31*, 127–140.

Robson, K. (2013). *Service-Ability: Create a Customer-Centric Culture and Achieve Competitive Advantage*. Chichester: John Wiley & Sons.

Rodgers, S., & Thorson, E. (2017). *Digital Advertising: Theory and Research, 3rd edition*. New York: Routledge, Taylor and Francis Group.

Rogers, E. (1962). *Diffusion of Innovations*. New York: Simon & Schuster.

Romano, B., Sands, S., & Pallant, J. I. (2020). Augmented reality and the customer journey: An exploratory study. *Australasian Marketing Journal*.

Roper, J. (2005). Symmetric communication: excellent public relations or a strategy for hegemony? *Journal of Public Relations Research*, *17*(1), 69–86.

Rosenbaum, M. S., & Massiah, C. A. (2007). When Customers Receive Support From Other Customers: Exploring the Influence of Intercustomer Social Support on Customer Voluntary Performance. *Journal of Service Research*, *9*(3), 257–270.

Rossiter, J. R., & Percy, L. (1997). *Advertising Communications & Promotion Management*. London: McGraw-Hill.

Rowley, J. (2005). The four Cs of customer loyalty. *Marketing Intelligence and Planning*, *23*(6), 574–581.

Russell, R. H. (2015). Balance Scorecard. In C. L. Cooper, J. McGee, C. L. Cooper, & T. Sammut-Bonnici, *Wiley Encyclopedia of Management, vol 12*. Hoboken, NJ: Wiley.

Rust, R. T., Lemon, K. N., & Zeithaml, V. A. (2004). Return on Marketing: Using Customer Equity to Focus Marketing Strategy. *Journal of Marketing*, *68*(1), 109–127.

Rust, R. T., Ziethaml, V. A., & Lemon, K. N. (2000). *Driving Customer Equity: How Customer Lifetime Value Is Reshaping Corporate Strategy*. New York: The Free Press.

Ryan, D., & Jones, C. (2008). *Understanding Digital Marketing: Marketing Strategies for Engaging the Digital Generation*. London: Kogan Page.

Saini, A., & Johnson, J. L. (2005). Organizational capabilities in e-commerce: an empirical investigation of e-brokerage service providers. *Journal of the Academy of Marketing Science*, *33*(3), 360–375.

Saint-Onge, H. (1996). Tacit knowledge: the key to strategic alignment of intellectual capital. *Strategy and Leadership*, *2*, 10–14.

Salim, A. (2016). *Vodaphone's sustainability head on employee values and women's empowerment*. The Drum.

Salinas, G. (2009). *The International Brand Valuation Manual: A complete overview and analysis of brand evaluation techniques, methodologies and applications*. Hoboken, NJ: John Wiley & Sons.

Salter, M. S. (2019). Rehabilitating Corporate Purpose: How the Evolution of Corporate Purpose Has Contributed to a Widening Breach Between Capitalism and Justice . . . and What to Do about It. *Harvard Business Review*, 1–50.

Salzer-Morling, M., & Strannegård, L. (2002). Silence of the Brands. *European Journal of Marketing*, *38* (1/2), 224–238.

Samli, A. C., & Frohlich, C. J. (1993). Consumer-friendly financial services: Combining effciency and effectiveness. *Journal of Business and Psychology*, 145–162.

Santos-Vijande, M. L., del Rio-Lanza, A. B., & Diaz-Martin, A.-M. (2013). The brand management system and service firm competitiveness. *Journal of Business Research*, *66*(2), 148–157.

Saren, M., & Brownlie, D. (2004). The limits of language: marketing praxis and discourse beyond words. *Proceedings of the Academy of Marketing Conference*. University of Gloucester, UK 6–9 July.

Sargeant, A. (2009). *Marketing Management for Non-profit Organizations, 3rd Edition*. Oxford.

Sashi, C. (2012). Customer engagement, buyer-seller relationships and social media. *Journal of Management History*, *50*(2), 253–272.

Sataøen, H. L., & W ras, A. (2013). Branding without unique brands: managing similarity and difference in a pubkic sector context. *Public Management Review*, 443–461.

Schau, H. J., Muñíz, A. M., & Arnould, E. J. (2009). How brand community practices create value. *Journal of Marketing*, *73*(5), 30–51.

Schein, E. H. (2010). *Organisational Culture and Leadership (4th ed.)*. San Francisco: CA: Jossey-Bass.

Schein, E. H. (2017). *Organisational Culture and Leadership*. New Jersey: John Wiley & Sons.

Schembri, S. (2006). Rationalising service logic, or understanding services as experience? *Marketing Theory, 6*, 381–392.

Schembri, S., & Latimer, L. (2016). Online brand communities: constructing and co-constructing brand culture. *Journal of Marketing Management, 32*(7/8), 628–651.

Schlegelmilch, B. B., & Pollach, I. (2005). The perils and opportunities of communicating corporate ethics. *Journal of Marketing Management, 21*(3/4), 267–90.

Schmitt, B. H. (1999). *Experiential Marketing*. New York: The Free Press.

Schmitt, B. H. (1999). Experiential Marketing. *Journal of Marketing Management, 15*(1), 53–67.

Schmitt, B. H. (2003). *Customer Experience Management: A revolutionary approach to connecting with your customers*. Hoboken, NY: John Wiley.

Schneider, B., Ehrhart, M. G., & Macey, W. (2013). Organisational Climate and Culture. *Annual Review of Psychology, 64*, 361–388.

Schroeder, J. E. (2009). The cultural codes of branding. *Marketing Theory, 9*(1), 123–126.

Schroeder, J. E. (2015). Brand and Branding. In D. Cook, & M. J. Ryan, *Wiley-Blackwell Concise Encyclopedia of Consumption and Consumption Studies*. New York: Wiley and Sons.

Schroeder, J. E., & Salzer-Mörling, M. (2006). *Brand Culture*. London: Routledge.

Schultz, D. E. (2003). The next geneartion of integrated marketing communication. *Interactive Marketing. VOL. 4 N O. 4. PP* 318–319 *APRIL/JUNE 2003, 4*(4), 318–319.

Schultz, D. E. (2004). IMC. In D. W. Pickton, & A. J. Broderick, *Integrated Marketing Communications, 2nd edition*. London: Financial Times Prentice Hall.

Schultz, D. E. (2004). A Clean Brand Slate. *Marketing Management, 13*, 10–11.

Schultz, D. E., & Kitchen, P. J. (2000). *Communicating Globally: An Integrated Marketing Approach*. Basingstoke: Palgrave Macmillan.

Schultz, D. E., & Patti, C. (2009). The evolution of IMC: IMC in a customer-driven marketplace. *Journal of Marketing Communications, 15*(2/3), 75–84.

Schwartz, S. H. (1992). "Universals in the content and structure of values: Theoretical advances and empirical tests in 20 countries.". (M. Zanna, Ed.) *Advances in Experimental Social Psychology, 25*, 1–65.

Schmitt, J., Brakus, J., & Zarantonello, L. (2015). From Experiential Psychology to Consumer Experience. *Journal of Consumer Psychology, 25*, 166–171.

Scott, D. M. (2009). *The New Rules of Marketing and PR*. Hoboken, NJ: John Wiley & Sons.

Serafim, G. (2018). Public Sentiment and the Price of Corporate Sustainability. *Financial Analysts Journal, 76*(2), 26–46. Retrieved from Available at SSRN: https://ssrn.com/abstract= 3265502orhttp://dx.doi.org/10.2139/ssrn.3265502

Serrat, O. (2010). Marketing in the public sector. *Washington, DC: Asian Development Bank*.

Seybold, P. B. (2002). *The Customer Revolution*. Hoboken, NY: Wiley.

Shankar, A., Cherrier, H., & Canniford, R. (2005). Consumer empowerment: a Foucauldian interpretation. *European Journal of Marketing, 40*(9/10), 1013–1030.

Shankar, A., Elliott, R., & Goulding, C. (2001). Understanding Consumption: Contributions from a Narrative Perspective. *Journal of Marketing Management, 17*, 429–453.

Shaw, C., & Ivens, J. (2002). *Building Great Customer Experiences*. Basingstoke Hampshire:: Palgrave Macmillan.

Shaw, G., & Williams, A. (2009). Knowledge transfer and management in tourism organisations: An emerging research agenda. *Tourism Management, 30*(3), 325–225.

Sheldon, A. F. (1929). *Service and Conservation: A Manual Devoted to the Principle of Service and the Law of Conservation*. Rochester, NY: Du Bois Press.

Shenhar, A. J., & Dvir, D. (1996). Long term success dimensions in technology-based organizations. In *Handbook of Technology Management*. New York: McGraw Hill.

Sherry Jr., J. F. (1986). The Cultural Perspective in Consumer Research. *Advances in Consumer Research, 13*, 573–575.

Sherry Jr., J. F. (2005). Brand Meaning. In A. M. Tybout, & T. Calkins, *Kellogg on Branding*. Hoboken, NJ: The Kellogg School of Management, John Wiley & Sons.

Sherry Jr., J. F. (1987). Paper delivered to XIV Annual Conference, *Association for Consumer Research in Advances in Consumer Research*. Toronto.

Sheth, J. N., & Parvatiyar, A. (1995). The evolution of relationship marketing. *International Business Review, 4*(4), 397–418.

Sheth, J. N., & Parvatiyar, A. (1995). The exchange versus the relationship perspective in the marketing process. *The evolution of relationship marketing, 4*(4), 397–418.

Shostack, G. L. (1977). Breaking Free from Product Marketing. *Journal of Marketing, 41*(2), 73–80.

Shostack, G. L. (1992). Understanding Services through Blueprinting. In T. Schwartz, & et al, eds., *Advances in Services Marketing and Management* (pp. 75–90). Greenwich, CT: JAI Press.

Shultz, E. S., Tannebaum, R. F., & Lauterborn, H. (1993). *Integrated Marketing Communications: Putting it together and making it work*. NTC Business Books.

Siano, A., Vollero, A., & Palazzo, M. (2011). Role of online consumer empowerment in reputation building. *Journal of Brand Mangement, 19*(1), 57–71.

Sim, S., van Loom, B., & Appignanessi, R. (2004). *Introducing Critical Theory*. New York: Totem Books.

Simeon, R. (2006). A conceptual model linking brand building strategies and Japanese popular culture. *Marketing Intelligence & Planning, 24*(5), 463–76.

Simpson, F. (2021). *Branding For Franchise Success: How To Achieve And Maintain Brand Consistency Across A Franchise Network*. Retrieved from Forbes Media: Retrieved 15th April 2021 (online): https://www.forbes.com/sites/fionasimpson1/2020/02/09/branding-for-franchise-success-how-t

Sinek, S. (2009). *Start With Why: How great leaders inspire everyone to take action*. New York, NY: Penguin.

Singh, J., Nambisan, S., & Bridge, R. G. (2021). One Voice Strategy for Customer Engagement. *Journal of Service Research, 24*(1), 42–65.

Sirmon, D. G., Hitt, M. A., & Ireland, R. D. (2007). Managing firm resources in dynamic environments to create value: Looking inside the black box. *Academy of Management Review, 32*, 273–292.

Skålén, P., Gummerus, J., von Koskull, C., & Magnusson, P. (2012). Exploring value proposition and service innovation: a service dominat logic study. *Academy of Marketing Science*.

Skog, D. A., Wimelius., H., & Sandberg, J. (2018). Digital Disruption. *Business Information Systems Engineering*, 431–437.

Slater, S. F., & Narver, N. L. (1998). Customer-led and market-oriented: let's not confuse the two. *Strategic Management Journal, 19*(10), 1001–1006.

Smith, A., McCarthy, B., & Aaker, J. (2013). The Dragonfly Effect Workbook: The Power of Stories.

Smith, G. (1956). Product Differentiation and Market Segmentation as Alternative Strategies. *Journal of Marketing, 21*(1), 2–8.

Smith, T. D. (2007). The existential consumption paradox: an exploration of meaning in marketing. *The Marketing Review, 7* (4), 325–341.

Smith, T. D. (2011). Brand salience not brand science: a brand narrative approach to sustaining brand longevity. *The Marketing Review, 11* (1), 25–40.

Smith, T. D. (2013). Marketing in situ; marketing in aspic: the relevance of marketing theory to marketing practice. *Academy of Marketing 'Marketing Relevance' Conference, University of Glamorgan, Cardiff*.

Smith, T. D. (2020). *The roots and uses of marketing knowledge: A critical inquiry into the theory and practice of marketing*. Berlin: De Gruyter.

Smith, T., Williams, T., Lowe, S., Rod, M., & Hwang, K. (2015). Context to text to context: marketing practice into theory; maarketing theory into practice. *Marketing Intelligence and Planning*, *33* (7), 1027–1046.

Solis, B. (2011). *Engage: The Complete Guide for Brands and Businesses to Build, Cultivate, and Measure Success in the New Web*. Hoboken, New Jersey: John Wiley & Sons.

Sørensen, F., & Jensen, J. F. (2015). value creation and knowledge development in tourism experience encounters. *Tourism Management*, *46*, 336–346.

Spence, M., & Hamzaoui-Essoussi, H. (2010). SME Brand Building and Management: An Exploratory Study. *European Journal of Marketing*.

Spender, J. C. (1996). Making knowledge the basis of a dynamic theory of the firm", Strategic Management Journal. *17*(52), 45–62.

Spohrer, J., Anderson, L., Pass, N., & Ager, T. (2008). Science Service and Service-Dominant Logic. *Otttago Forum 2*.

Spohrer, J., Maglio, P. P., Bailey, J., & Gruhl, D. (2007). Steps Toward a Science of Service Systems. *IEEE Computer*, *40*, 71–77.

Spohrer, J., Vargo, S. L., Caswell, N., & Magl, P. P. (2008). The Service System Is the Basic Abstraction of Service Science. *Proceedings of the 41st Annual Hawaii International Conference on System Sciences (HICSS 2008)*, (pp. 104–110). Waikoloa, HI, USA.

Srivastava, R. K. (2001). The resource-based view and marketing: The role of market-based assets in gaining competitive advantage. *Journal of Management*, *27*, 777–802.

Srivastava, R., & Shocker, A. D. (1991). *Brand equity: a perspective on its meaning and measurement*. Working Paper Series, Report Number 91–124. Cambridge, MA: Marketing Science Institute.

Stead, M., & Gordon, R. (2009). Proving evidence for social marketing's effectiveness. In J. French, C. Blair-Stevens, D. McVey, & R. Merritt, *Social Marketing and Public Health: Theory and Practice* (pp. 81–96). Oxford: Oxford University Press.

Stearns, P. N. (2006). *Consumerism in world history: The global transformation of desire*. New York: Routledge.

Stein, A., & Ramaseshan, B. (2016). Towards the identification of customer experience touchpoint elements. *Journal of Retailing and Consumer Service*, *30*, 8–19.

Stengel, J. (2011). *Grow. How Ideals Power Growth and Profit at the World's 50 Greatest Companies*. New York: Crown Publishing Company.

Steyn, B. (2004). From strategy to corporate communication strategy: a conceptualisation. *Journal of Communications Management*, *8*(2), 168–83.

Stratton, G., & Northcote, J. (2016). When totem begets clans: The brand symbol as the defining marker of brand communities. *Journal of Consumer Culture*, *16*(2), 493–509.

Stride, H. (2006). An investigation into the values dimensions of branding: implications for the charity sector. *Journal of Philanthropy and Marketing*.

Stuart, H. (2003). Employee Identification with the Corporate Identity. *International Studies of Management and Organisations*, *32*, 28–44.

Sun, K-A., & Kim, D. Y. (2013). Does customer satisfaction increase firm performance? An application of American Customer Satisfaction Index (ACSI). *International Journal of Hospitality Management*.

Surowiecki, J. (2005). *The Wisdom of Crowds: Why the Many Are Smarter Than the Few and How Collective Wisdom Shapes Business, Economies, Societies, and Nations*. New York: Double Day.

Sutton, R. I., & Straw, B. M. (1995). 'What Theory is Not'. *Administrative Science Quarterly*, *40*(3), 371–384.

Sveiby, K. E. (1997). *The New Organisational Wealth: Managing and Measuring Knowledge Based Assets*. San Francisco, CA: Berrett Koehler.

Svensson, P. (2007). Producing marketing towards a social-phenomenology of marketing work. *Marketing Theory*, *7*, 271–290.

Szablewska, N., & Kubacki, K. (2019). A human rights-based approach to the social good in social marketing. *Journal of Business Ethics*, *155* (3), 871–888.

Szreter, S., & Woolcock, M. (2004). Health by association? Social capital, social theory, and the political economy of public health. *International Journal of Epidemiology*, *33*, 650–667.

Tadajewski, M., & Wagner-Tsukamoto, L. (2006). Anthropology and consumer research: Qualitative insights into green behaviour. *Qualitative Market Research: An International Journal*, *9* (1), 8–25.

Tadajewski, M., & Jones, D. B. (2021). From goods-dominant logic service-dominant logic? Service, service capitalism and service socialism. *Marketing Theory*, *2*, 113–131.

Tadajewski, M., & Saren, M. (2009). Rethinking the emergence of relationship marketing. *Journal of Macromarketing*, *29*(2), 193–206.

Tapp, A. (2004). Media neutral planning – A strategic perspective. *Database Marketing & Customer Strategy Management*, *12*(2), 133–141.

Tavassoli, N. T., Sorescu, A., & Chandy, R. (2014). Employee-based brand equity: why firms with strong brands pay their executives less. *Journal of Marketing Research*, *51*(6), 676–690.

Thompson, M. (2002). Marketing Virtue. *Business Ethics: A European Review, 11*(4).

Thorpe, E. R., & Morgan, R. E. (2007). In pursuit of the "ideal approach" to successful marketing strategy implementation. *European Journal of Marketing*, *41*(4/5), 659–677.

Tombs, A. G., & McColl-Kennedy, J. R. (2004). The importance of physical, social, and contextual elements of the social-servicescape on customer affect and repurchase intentions. *ANZMAC 2004: Australian and New Zealand Marketing Academy Conference*. Wellington, New Zealand.

Tonks, D. G. (2002). Marketing as Cooking: The Return of the Sophists. *Journal of Marketing*, *18*(78), 803–22.

Tosti, D. T., & Stotz, R. D. (2001). Brand: Building your brand from the inside out. *Marketing Management*, *10*(2), 28–33.

Trueman, M., Klemm, M., & Giroud, A. (2004). Can a city communicate? Bradford as a corporate brand. *Corporate Comunications: An International Journal*, *9*(4), 317–330.

Tuominem, P. (2007). Energing metaphors in brand management: Towards a relational approach. *Journal of Communications Management*, *11*(2), 182–191.

Twitchell, J. B. (2004). An english teacher looks at branding. *Journal of Consumer Research*, *32*(2), 484–489.

Tybout, A. M., & Sternthal, B. (2005). Brand Positioning. In A. M. Tybout, & T. Calkins, *Kellogg On Branding*. Hoboken, NJ: John Wiley & Sons.

Tynan, C., McKechnie, S., & Chhuon, C. (2010). Co-creating value for luxury brands. *Journal of Business Research*, *63*, 1156–1163.

Unilever. (2017). *How to boost business growth through brands with purpose.*

Vallaster, C., & de Chernatony, L. (2006). Internal branding and structuration: The role of leadership. *European Journal of Marketing*, *40*(7/8), 761–784.

Vallaster, C., & Lindgreen, A. (2011). Corporate brand strategy formation: Brand actors and the situational context for a business-to-business brand. *Industrial Marketing Management*, *40*(7), 1133–1143.

Van Doorn, J., Lemon, K. N., Mittal, V., Nass, S., Pick, D., Pirner, P., & Verhoef, P. C. (2010). Customer Engagement Behaviour: Theoretical Foundations and Research Directions. *Journal of Service Research*, *13*(3), 253–266.

Van Lange, P. A., Kruglanski, A. W., & Higgins, E. T. (2012). *Handbook of Theories of Social Psychology*. London: SAGE Publications.

Vandermerwe, S. (1993). Jumping Into the Customer's Activity Cycle: A New Role for Customer Services in the 1990s. *Columbia Journal of World Business, 28*, 46–66.

Vandermerwe, S. (1996). New Competitive Spaces: Jointly Investing in New Customer Logic. *Columbia Journal of World Business, 31*, 80–102.

Varey, R. J. (2002). *Marketing Communication: Principles and Practice*. London: Routledge.

Vargo, S. L., & Lusch, R. F. (2004). Evolving to a new dominant logic for marketing. *Journal of Marketing, 68* (1), 1–17.

Vargo, S. L., & Lusch, R. F. (2006). Institutions and axioms: An extension and update of service-dominant logic. *Journal of the Academy of Marketing Science*, 44(1), 5–23.

Vargo, S. L., & Lusch, R. F. (2008). Why service? *Journal of the Academy of Marketing Science, 36* (1), 25–38.

Vargo, S. L., & Lusch, R. F. (2011). It's All B2B and Beyond. . . .. Toward a Systems Perspective of the Market. *Idustrial Marketing Management, 40*(2), 181–187.

Veloutsou, C. (2009). Brands as relationship facilitators in consumer markets. *Marketing Theory, 9*(1), 127–130.

Veloutsou, C., & Moutinho, L. (2011). Brand relationships through brand reputation and brand tribalism. *Journal of Brand Research, 62*(3), 314–322.

Venkatesan, V., Rajkumar, A., & Kumar, V. (2004). A customer lifetime value framework for customer selection and optimal resource allocation strategy. *Journal of Marketing, 68*(4), 106–125.

Venter, P., Wright, A., & Dibb, S. (2015). Performing market segmentation: A performative perspective. *Journal of Marketing Management, 31*(1/2), 62–83.

Ventkatesh, P. (1999). Postmodern Perspectives for Macromarketing: An Inquiry into the Global Information and Sign Economy. *Journal of Macromarketing, 19*(12), 2–28.

Verhoef, P., Lemon, K. N., Parasuraman, A., Roggeveen, A., Tsiros, M., & Schlesinger, L. A. (2009). Customer experience creation: determinants, dynamics, and management strategies. *Journal of Retailing, 85*, 31–41.

Vernuccio, M., Pagani, M., Barbarossa, C., & Pastore, A. (2015). Antecedents of brand love in online network -based communities. A social identity perspective. *Journal of Product & Brand Management, 24*(7), 706–719.

Viglia, G., Pera, R., & Bigne, E. (2018). The determinants of stakeholder engagement in digital platforms. *Journal of Business Research, 89*, 404–410.

Voorhees, C. M., Fombelle, P. W., Gregoire, Y., Bone, S., Gustafsson, A., Sousa, R., & Walkowiak, T. (2017). Service encounters, experiences and the customer journey: Defining the field and a call to expand our lens. *Journal of Business Research, 79*, 269–280.

Vorhies, D. W., Orr, L. M., & Bush, V. D. (2011). Improving customer-focused marketing capabilities and firm financial performance via marketing exploration and exploitation. *Journal of the Academy of Marketing Science, 39*(5), 736–756.

Voss, C., Roth, A. V., & Chase, R. B. (2008). Experience, service operations strategy, and services as destinations: foundations and exploratory investigation. *Production and Operations Management, 17*, 247–266.

Wang, C., Walker, E. A., & Redmond, J. (2007). Explaining the lack of strategic planning in SMEs: The importance of owner motivation. *International Journal of Organisational Behaviour, 12*(1), 1–16.

Webb, J., Shirato, T., & Danaher, G. (2002). *Understanding Bourdieu*. London: SAGE Publications.

Weber, L. (2007). *Marketing to the Social Web: How Digital Customer Communities Build Your Business*. Hoboken, NY: John Wiley & Sons.

Weiland, H., Polese, F., Vargo, S. L., & Lusch, R. F. (2012). Toward a service eco system perspective on value creation. *International Journal of Service Management, Engineering and Technology*, *3*(3), 2–25.

Weinstein, A. (2004). *Handbook of Market Segmentation: Strategic Targeting for Business and Technology Firms*. London: The Haworth Press.

Welch, J. (1999). The Financial Times.

Welsch, W. (1997). *Undoing Aesthetics*. London: SAGE.

Wensley, R. (2002). A Bridge Over Troubled Water. *European Journal of Marketing*, *36*(3), 391–400.

Wernefelt, B. (1984). A resource-based view of the firm. *Strategic Management Journal*, *5*(2), 171–180.

Whittington, R. (1996). Strategy as Practice. *Long Range Planning*, *29*, 731–735.

Wiedmann, K. P., & Lang, S. (2010). Spreading the Word of Fashion: Identifying Social Influencers in Fashion Marketing. *Journal of Global Fashion Marketing*, *1*(3), 142–153.

Wieland, H., Hartmann, N. H., & Vargo, S. (2017). Business models as service strategy. *Journal of the Academy of Marketing Science, 45*, 925–943.

Wiesel, T., Skiera, B., & Villaneuva, J. (2008). Customer Equity: An Integral Part of Financial Reporting. *Journal of Marketing*, *72*(2), pp. 1–14.

Wilkinson, I., & Gray, D. M. (2007). The production and consumption of marketing theory. *Australasian Marketing Journal*, *15*(1), 39–52.

Williams, P., & Soutar, G. N. (2009). Value, satisfaction, and behavioural intentions in an adventure tourism context. *Annals of Tourism Research*, *36*(3), 413–438.

Williams, R. (2002). Memetics: a new paradigm for understanding customer behaviour? *Marketing Intelligence & Planning*, *20*(3), 162–167.

Williams, T. (2014) Marketing Chester Cathedral: Developing a Sacred Brand, PhD Thesis, *Lancaster University*.

Wilson, N. (2019, March). Inclusive Capitalism. *Forbes Magazine*.

Wilson, R. M., & Gilligan, C. (2005). *Strategic Marketing Management*. Oxford: Elsevier-Butterworth Heinemann.

Wilson, R., Malik, M., & Kanioura, A. (2018). *Pulse Survey – Real-Time Analytics: The Key to Unlocking Customer Insights & Driving the Customer Experience*. Harvard Business Review Analytics Services, Harvard Business School Publishing.

Wilson-Nash, C., Goode, A., & Currie, A. (2020). Introducing the socialbot: a novel touchpoint along the young adult customer journey. *European Journal of Marketing*, *54*(10), 2621–2643.

Wirtz, J., den Ambtman, A., Bloemer, J., Horváth, C., Ramasehan, B., & Kandampully, J. (2013). Managing brands and customer engagement in online brand communities. *Journal of Service Management*, *24*(3), 223–244.

Witell, L., Kowalkowski, C., Perks, H., Raddats, C., & Schwabe, M. (2020). Characterising customer experience in business markets. *Journal of Business Research*, *116*, 420–430.

Wong, H. Y., & Merrilees, B. (2005). A brand orientation typology for SMEs: a case research approach. *Journal of Product & Brand Management*, *14*(2/3), 155–62.

Wood, L. & Pierson, B. (2006). The brand description of Sainsbury's and Aldi: price and quality positioning, *Business International Journal of Retail & Distribution Management*, 34, 904–917.

Woodhead, L., Heelas, P., & Davie, G. (2003). Introduction'. In G. Davie, P. Heelas, and Woodhead, L. (Eds.), *in Predicting Religion: Christian, Secular and Alternative Futures: 1*. Aldershot: Ashgate.

Woodruff, R. B., & Gardial, S. F. (1996). *Know Your Customer: New Approaches to Understanding Customer Value and Satisfaction*. Cambridge, MA: Blackwell.

Woolcock, M. (2001). The place of social capital in understanding social and economic outcomes. *Canadian Journal of Policy Research*, *2*(1), 1–17.

Yachin, J. M. (2018). The 'customer journey': Learning from customers in tourism exerience encounters. *Tourism Management Perspectives, 28*, 201–210.

Yeshin, T. (1998). *Integrated Marketing Communications*. Butterworth: Heinemann.

Yeshin, T. (2007). Integrated Marketing Communications. In M. J. Baker, & S. J. Hart, *The Marketing Book*.

Yohn, D. L. (2014). *What Great Brands Do: The Seven Brand-Building Principles That Separate he Best From The Rest*. San Francisco: Jossey-Bass, A Wiley Company.

York, J. M. (2018). A Digital Strategy for Enhancing the Customer Journey via a Customer-Centric Website. *Archives of Business Administration, 2018*(4).

Zaltman, G. (2003). How Customers Think: Essential Insights into the Mind of the Market. *Harvard Business School Press*.

Zein, S. A., Consolacion-Segura, C., & Huertas-Garcia, R. (2020). The role of sustainability in brand equity value in financial sector. *Sustainability, 12*(254), 1–19.

Zeithaml, V. A., & Bitner, M. J. (2003). *Services marketing: Integrating Customer Focus Across the Firm 3rd Edition*. New York: Irwin McGraw-hill.

Zeithaml, V. A., Berry, L. L., & Parasuraman, A. (1993). The nature and determinants of customer expectations of service. *Academy of Marketing Science. Journal, 21*(1), 1–12.

Zeithaml, V. A., Rust, R. T., & Lemon, K. N. (2001). The Customer Pyramid: Creating and Serving Profitable Customers. *The California Management Review, 43*(4), 118–142.

Zomerdijk, L. J., & Voss, C. A. (2010). Service design for experience-centric services. *Journal of Service, 13*(1), 67–82.

Zwick, D., & Denegri Knott, J. (2009). Manufcturing customers: The database as a new means of production. *Journal of Consumer Cutlure, 9*(2), 221–246.

Acronyms and Abbreviations

A2A	Actor-to-Actor
ACX	Automated Customer Experience
ADMA	Association for Data-Driven Marketing & Advertising
AI	Artificial Intelligence
AMA	American Marketing Association
ANA	Association of National Advertisers
AoM	Academy of Marketing
AR	Augmented Reality
B2B	Business-to-Business and Business-to-Business Communications
B2C	Business-to-Consumer Communications
BCB	Brand Citizenship Behaviour
BEO	Business Ecosystem Orchestration
BIA	Beneficial Impact Assessment
BMR	Business Marketing Relationships
BSC	Balanced Scorecard
BYOD	Bring Your Own Device
C Suite	Executive level managers such as Chief Executive Officer (CEO), Chief Operating Officer (COO),Chief Marketing Officer (CMO), Chief Financial Officer (CFO), and Chief Information Officer (CIO).
C2B	Consumer-to-Business communications
C2C	Consumer to Consumer communications
CAQDAS	Computer-assisted qualitative data analysis software
CB	Corporate Branding
CBBE	Customer-Based Brand Equity
CBE	Corporate Brand Equity
CBM	Customer Buying Map
CCI	Customer-Company Interface
CEM	Customer Experience Management
CES	Customer Effort Score
CIC	Community Interest Company
CIM	Chartered Institute of Marketing
CIT	Critical Incident Technique
CJA	Customer Journey Analysis
CJD	Customer Journey Design
CLV	Customer Lifetime Value
CMI	Chartered Institute of Management
CMI	Chartered Management Institute
CMO	Chief Marketing Officer
CRM	Customer Relationship Management
CSAT	Customer Satisfaction
CSC	Corporate Social Capital
CSF	Critical Success Factors
CSI	Corporate Social innovation
CSR	Corporate Social Responsibility
CTO	Configure-To-Order
CX	Customer Experience
CXM	Customer Experience Map

https://doi.org/10.1515/9783110718638-024

DFID	The Department for International Development
DMP	Decision-Making Process
DTI	*Dell Technologies'* Digital Transformation Index
EBC	Embedded Brand Communities
EDI	Electronic Data Interchange
EoM	Economics of Mutuality
ERP	Enterprise Resource Planning
ESRC	Economic and Social Research Council
EVA	Economic Added Value
FBBE	Firm-based Brand Equity
FRBBE	Franchisee-based Brand Equity
FoT	Festival of Thrift
FPL	Fantasy Premier League
FSB	Federation of Small Businesses
HE	Higher Education
HEI	Higher Education Institutions
HVM	Hierarchical Value Maps
ICR	Interpersonal Commercial Relationships
ICS	Institute of Customer Service
IDO	Insight Driven Organisation
IMC	Integrated Marketing Communications
IMP	International Marketing and Purchasing Group
IoD	Institute of Directors
Industry 4.0	Fourth Industrial Revolution
IoT	Internet of Things
IP	Intellectual Property
IPO	Initial Public Offering
IRM	Image and Reputation Management
ISMA	International Social Marketing Association
IT	Information Technology
JIT	Just-In-Time
KDD	Knowledge Discovery in Databases
KM	Knowledge Management
KPI	Key Performance Indicator
KPI	Key Performance Indicators
KT	Knowledge Transfer
KTP	Knowledge Transfer Partnership
M1K	Theoretical knowledge
M2K	Knowledge in use
M2M	Machine-to-Machine Communications
MCN	Multi Channel Networks
MIS	Management Information System
MkIS	Marketing Information System
MNP	Media Neutral Planning
More Act	Marijuana Opportunity, Reinvestment, and Expungement
MoT	Moment of Truth
MSI	Marketing Science Institute
NFP	Not-for-profit
NPS	Net Promoter Score

NSD	New Service Development
OBC	Online Brand Community
OCB	Organisational Citizenship Behaviour
OECD	Organisation for Economic Co-operation and Development
OEM	Other Equipment Manufacturers
OTS	Opportunities To See
PBS	Practice Based Studies
PE	Post-Experience
PR	Public Relations
QFD	Quality Function Deployment
QUANGO	Quasi-Non-Governmental Organisation
RBP	Resource-based perspectives
RBT	Resource-based theory
RBV	Resource-based view
REF	Research Excellence Framework
RFM	Recency, Frequency, and Monetary Value
RM	Relationship Marketing
RMO	Responsive market orientation
RXM	Reputation Experience Management
SAP	Systems Applications and Products in Data Processing
SBU	Strategic Business Unit
SCA	Sustainable Competitive Advantage
SCB	Societal Corporate Branding
SDP	Smart Domestic Products
SDS	Service Delivery System
SECI model	Socialisation Externalisation Combination and Internalisation
SEO	Search Engine Optimisation
SM	Stakeholder Management
SME	Small and Medium Enterprise
SNS	Social Network Sites or Social Network Services
SR	Speech Recognition
STP	Segmentation Targeting Positioning
TBL	Triple Bottom Line
TQM	Total Quality Management
UGC	User Generated Content
UX	User Experience
VAL	Values, Attitudes, and Lifestyle
VOC	Voice of the Customer
VR	Virtual Reality
VS	Voice Search
VUCA	Volatile, Uncertain, Chaotic, Ambiguous
WBCSD	World Business Council for Sustainable Development
WEF	World Economic Forum *The World Business Council for Sustainable Development* (WBCSD)
WOM	Word of Mouth
ZMOT	Zero Moment of Truth

List of Figures

https://doi.org/10.1515/9783110718638-025

List of Tables

https://doi.org/10.1515/9783110718638-026

Index

https://doi.org/10.1515/9783110718638-027